AF515952

AMBEDKAR

AWAKENING INDIA'S SOCIAL CONSCIENCE

AMBEDKAR

AWAKENING INDIA'S SOCIAL CONSCIENCE

NARENDRA JADHAV

Konark Publishers Pvt Ltd
New Delhi • Seattle

Konark Publishers Pvt. Ltd
206, First Floor,
Peacock Lane, Shahpur Jat,
New Delhi-110 049.
Phone: +91-11-41055065, 65254972
e-mail: india@konarkpublishers.com
Website: www.konarkpublishers.com

Konark Publishers International
1507 Western Avenue, #605,
Seattle, WA 98101
Phone: (415) 409-9988
e-mail: us@konarkpublishers.com

Cataloging in Publication Data--DK
Courtesy: D.K. Agencies (P) Ltd. <docinfo@dkagencies.com>

Jadhav, Narendra, 1953-
Ambedkar : awakening India's social conscience / Narendra Jadhav.
p. cm.
Includes bibliographical references (p.) and index.
ISBN 9789322008352
ISBN 9789322008369 (pbk.)

1. Ambedkar, B. R. (Bhimrao Ramji), 1891-1956. 2. Social reformers--India--Biography. 3. Statesmen--India--Biography. 4. India--Politics and government--1919-1947. 5. Dalits--India 6. Social reforms--India. I. Title.

DDC 954.04092 23

Copy editor: Rina Tripathi

Typeset by Digigrafics, New Delhi

Printed and bound at Thomson Press (India) Ltd.

Dedicated to
the innumerable known and unknown
"Songsters from the Mudhouse"
who inspite of all odds
kept the memory and legacy of Dr Ambedkar
Alive

Contents

PART VII
POLITICAL UPHEAVALS (1946-47)

PART VIII
NATION BUILDING POST- INDEPENDENCE

PART IX
SEARCH FOR IDENTITY OF DEPRESSED CLASSES

PART X
NATION-BUILDING FROM THE OPPOSITION SIDE

PART XI
EMBRACING BUDDHISM AND NIRVANA

Preface

BHARAT RATNA DR Bhimrao Ramji Ambedkar, affectionately known as Babasaheb Ambedkar, was undoubtedly one of the most illustrious sons of India. He appeared on the Indian socio-political scene in the early 1920s and remained at the forefront of the social, cultural, economic and political transformation of India during the closing decades of the British Rule. After India became Independent from the British Rule in 1947, Dr Ambedkar played a uniquely significant role in laying the foundation of modern India till his death in 1956. Dr Ambedkar was a great social reformer, a valiant champion of human rights and an emancipator of the downtrodden masses of India, who dedicated all his life to awaken the social conscience of modern India.

Dr Ambedkar's life is an incredible saga: an Untouchable boy, humiliated every step of the way from childhood to youth, beats all odds securing the highest and most reputable degrees from world class universities—MA and PhD in Economics from Columbia University, USA and DSc in Economics from London School of Economics besides Bar-at-Law degree from London. He then returns to India and devotes his life to the destruction of the caste-ridden old order, characterized by injustice and denial of human rights. Without being favoured either by family fortune or political lineage, but by the sheer grit of his determination and back-breaking hard work, supreme courage and self-less sacrifice, he overcomes bitter political opposition and perils of caste-discrimination to become the Principal Architect of the Constitution of the Independent India. He then proceeds to build the safeguards of affirmative action for establishing a more equitable society that is capable of delivering social justice to millions of downtrodden, thus heralding in India a new age of social equality and rationalism. In this process, Dr Ambedkar comes to the forefront not only as a valiant upholder of the Indian Republic, but also emerges as the conscience keeper of modern India. (Salient features of Dr Ambedkar's momentous life are presented in Annexure I).

No wonder there are more statues of Dr Ambedkar in India than any other leader in the history of our nation. These statues depict a stocky man, invariably dressed in a blue suit and red tie, holding a book under his arm which, of course, represents the Constitution of India. Such statues can be found everywhere in India, in villages and in cities, usually at cross-roads. It is hardly surprising that every year, on December 6 (the death anniversary of Dr Ambedkar), around 2 million Ambedkarites throng to *Chaitya Bhoomi* in Mumbai to pay homage to the hero they worship as their saviour. It is also not surprising that Dr Ambedkar was voted recently (August 2012) as the "Greatest Indian after Gandhi" in an e-poll initiated by some TV channels (History TV18 and CNN-IBN) with an overwhelming majority of votes.

Against this background, clearly it is grossly unfair to characterize Dr Ambedkar simply as a leader of a leader of Untouchables or Dalits, as is often done even in otherwise responsible quarters. Dr Ambedkar was not simply a leader of Untouchables, not even only a leader of the oppressed people of India. He was a national leader, period. Dr Ambedkar's erudition, his mass movements, his role in the Government and outside clearly shows that he was a patriot of a sterling order. His brand of nationalism was quite different from others in India's freedom struggle. Dr Ambedkar's nationalism was not merely confined to the transfer of political power to the Indians from the British Colonial Rule. It was focused on a much broader notion of sustainable national re-construction that is, building a democratic Republic through creation of social equality and cultural integration in the age-old caste-ridden, inherently unjust and discriminating society.

In the course of his most eventful life, Dr Ambedkar made outstanding contribution as an economist, sociologist, anthropologist, educationist, journalist, as an authority on Comparative Religion, as a policy-maker and administrator, and as a parliamentarian, besides being a jurist who became the Principal Architect of the Indian Constitution.

In spite of being a statesman and a mass leader, Dr Ambedkar always remained a reflective thinker and erudite scholar. Even while being fully engrossed in mass movement and political upheavals, he wrote remarkable treatises on Economics, Sociology, Anthropology, Politics, Law, Religion and Culture which is clearly the mark of a true intellectual.

Dr Ambedkar was a prolific writer. Perhaps no other mass leader in India has produced anywhere even close to the voluminous writings that Dr Ambedkar did. The sheer volume is astonishing: 22 books and monographs completed and published plus 10 books left behind incomplete at various stages, 10 major Memoranda and Statements submitted to various authorities, 10 research papers, articles and book-reviews besides hundreds of articles in Marathi in his various fortnightly newspapers! The analytical rigour and lucidity, insights and passion that exude his writings are truly phenomenal. (A complete listing of Dr Ambedkar's writings is placed at Annexure II).

The range in Dr Ambedkar's works is also equally amazing. On Politics: 11 Books and Monographs including treatises such as *Pakistan or the Partition of India (*1940), *What Congress and Gandhi Have Done to Untouchables* (1945), and the classics such as

Federation versus Freedom (1939), *Ranade, Gandhi and Jinnah* (1943), *States and Minorities(1947)* and *Thoughts on Linguistic States* (1955); on Economics, two path breaking treatises: *The Evolution of Provincial Finance in British India* (1917) and *The Problem of the Rupee: Its Origin and Its Solution* (1925); on Sociology: a timeless contribution such as *Annihilation of Caste* (1936) besides a remarkable essay on "Castes in India: Their Genesis, Mechanism and Development" (1918); on Anthropology, two provocatively original treatises: *Who Were the Shudras* (1946) and *The Untouchables: Who Were They and Why They Became Untouchables* (1948) and finally on Religion: his *magnum opus*: *Buddha and His Dhamma.*

Even if a first-rate scholar devotes himself or herself only to writing alone, it would still be exceedingly difficult to match these contributions. What is simply unbelievable is that Dr Ambedkar produced these magnificent books while being fully engaged in politics and in drafting the Constitution of India!

Dr Ambedkar also delivered a very large number of speeches—537 speeches, to be precise, on a wide range of subjects and in diverse regional, national and international forums. Among the subjects, the speeches ranged from social, economic and religious issues to those relating to law and Constitution, besides politics. In terms of the fora, it included the Bombay Province Legislative Council, (and later) Bombay Legislative Assembly, Round Table Conferences hosted by the British Government in London, in the role as a Labour Member of Viceroy's Executive Council, Central Legislative Assembly (as the First Law Minister of Independent India), Constituent Assembly (as the Chairman, Drafting Committee for the Constitution of India) and the Parliament (Opposition Member, Rajya Sabha). In addition, Dr Ambedkar delivered a large number of public addresses as the most prominent leader of the social and political movement inspired by him.

This book is the first ever intellectual biography of Dr Ambedkar. While a fair amount of writings of Dr Ambedkar is available, there is only one English biography—the one by Dhananjay Keer, first published in 1954. Two other notable biographies of Dr Ambedkar are in Marathi and were written in 1960s by C.B. Khairmode and B.C. Kamble. All the three biographers were close associates of Dr Ambedkar and had great advantage of being able to interact with him in person. On the other hand, these biographers did not have the benefit of accessing all writings and speeches of Dr Ambedkar, which became available only in the subsequent period.

This intellectual biography incorporates all of Dr Ambedkar's writings and most important speeches that he delivered. Deviating from the conventional style of biography writing, this book focuses primarily on Dr Ambedkar's intellectual making, evolution of his thinking and thought processes and the strategic stance that he took from time to time, over his momentous public life.

Responding to the long standing demand, this intellectual biography of Dr Ambedkar has been written in the belief that understanding Dr Ambedkar, in his true spirit, is indeed a need of the hour. It is hoped that this intellectual biography will help people understand the thought processes of this intellectual colossus and will give them an opportunity to correct their misguided impression confining Dr Ambedkar only as a leader of Untouchables.

I have no doubt that this intellectual biography, the first of its kind on the subject, would be welcomed by scholars, researchers, students, political activists, civil society members and lay readers alike.

Narendra Jadhav

Prologue

The Meeting that Shaped Modern India

Place: Mani Bhavan, Mumbai Date: August 14, 1931

IT WAS GOING to be a very special day. The ongoing Mumbai monsoon was going to be unusually stormy with a meeting of two great minds. That very day two of the most influential individuals in Indian history were to meet face to face for the first time.

The contrast between their personas could not have been sharper. One was a lean figure, half clad in traditional Indian garb while the other one was a stocky figure, impeccably dressed in a tailored Western suit. One was determined, yet soft-spoken while the other was a proven firebrand. One was born in a well-to-do family—the son of the *Diwan* of Porbunder state in Gujarat, while the other was born in a poor family—son of a school teacher in the British army. One was brought up in an upper caste conservative Hindu family whereas the other was raised in a family whose forefathers were Untouchables—their mere touch would cause pollution and even whose shadow was a sacrilege. Both divergent upbringings had played an important role in their public personalities: while one had absorbed the essential influences of the *Vaishnavite* tradition, including vegetarianism, fasting from self-purification and compassion for all living beings; the other had come up against all odds, suffering from caste-based discrimination and humiliation which made him defiant to the point of being belligerent. One was already called *Mahatma* (Great Soul) while the other was going to be called *Mahamanav* (Great Human Being). The two great minds meeting that fateful day were Mohandas Karamchand Gandhi (i.e., Mahatma Gandhi) and Dr Bhimrao Ramji Ambedkar (i.e., Dr Babasaheb Ambedkar).

Gandhiji was 22 years older than Dr Ambedkar. In fact, Gandhiji had already become a barrister in the United Kingdom around the same time that Dr Ambedkar was born (1891). Incidentally, when Dr Ambedkar became a barrister himself in 1922, Gandhiji had already emerged as a national leader in India's struggle for political independence.

Much has been written about the interaction between the two, but not much is known about the inner workings of their relationship. What did each of these great minds think, if at all, about the other?

Dr Ambedkar had known of Gandhiji for quite some time, but had not had the opportunity for actual interaction. He knew about Gandhiji's accomplishments: his return to India in 1915 after successfully leading the non-violent movement for civil rights of the Indian community in South Africa, and his efforts to organize peasants, farmers and labourers at Champaran (Bihar) and Kheda (Gujarat) in 1918. After the traumatic Jallianwala Bagh massacre in 1919, Gandhiji had criticized both the actions of the British administration, as well as the retaliatory violence by Indians. Condemning the riots, Gandhiji had made a passionate appeal for peace, advocating the principle that all violence was evil and could not be justified. By December 1921, Gandhiji had become a national leader. Dr Ambedkar was well aware that under Gandhiji's leadership, the Indian National Congress was reorganized to become a mass movement aimed at winning *Swaraj* (i.e., Home Rule). During the Calcutta Congress in December 1928, Gandhiji had pushed through a resolution calling on the British *Raj* to grant India a Dominion Status with the goal of complete Independence for the country or face a renewed campaign of Non-co-operation. Dr Ambedkar referred to Gandhiji as a "Great Man" and, in fact, had acknowledged once; "Before Mahatma Gandhi, no politician in this country maintained that it was necessary to remove social injustices in order to do away with tensions and conflicts."[1]

On the other hand, Gandhiji, at least until that point of time, did not seem to know Dr Ambedkar. Whatever little he did know of Dr Ambedkar was grossly inadequate and even incorrect. Gandhiji, it appears, did not know that Dr Ambedkar was not only a foreign-trained barrister but also had a Ph.D in Economics from Columbia University, USA in addition to a DSc degree in Economics from the London School of Economics. What is even worse, Gandhiji did not know that Dr Ambedkar was an Untouchable. As Gandhiji once confessed to his Secretary Mahadevbhai Desai, "I did not know he [Ambedkar] was a *Harijan*.[2] I thought he was some benevolent Brahmin who took a deep interest in *Harijans* and, therefore, talked intemperately."[3]

Gandhiji and Dr Ambedkar had socio-economic visions which were poles apart. In fact, they had deeply divergent conceptions of the Indian nation itself. While Gandhiji was essentially a traditionalist leader of the Congress, one who sought to identify with India's poor, he was also a social reformer who tried in his own way

---

1. Lelyveld Joseph (2011), p.212
2. A term coined by Gandhiji to refer to Untouchables. Literally, it meant "Children of God". It is resented by modern Dalits.
3. *The Diary of Mahadev Desai*, Vol I, p. 52 quoted in (Keer Dhananjay, 1954, 1997 Reprint, p.169). Many scholars, notably Gail Omvedt, calls this reaction "revelatory of the stereotypes about Dalits that Gandhiji held". (Omvedt, 2004, p. 43).

to overcome the division between social reform and political reform that had prevailed till then. However, Dr Ambedkar believed that Gandhiji's reformism did not go far enough. Gandhiji's *Vaishnavism* was of the mild orthodox form which lacked the burning call for equality that had characterized the more radical saints such as Kabir, Ravidas and Tukaram. This meant that Gandhiji did not find it necessary to denounce the most extreme expressions of caste-based inequality found in the Hindu scriptures. In fact, Gandhiji wrote in *Young India* in December 1920:

> I believe that Caste has saved Hinduism from disintegration [....]. I consider the four divisions [*Chaturvarna*] alone to be fundamental. [The caste system] has suffered from excrescences [....]. I am certainly against any attempt at destroying the fundamental divisions [of *Chaturvarna*]. The caste system is not based on inequality, there is no question of inferiority.[4]

Gandhiji staunchly believed in, and affirmed, the notion of "*Swadharma*"—that is, children following the professions of their fathers. He sought to qualify this notion with the condition that all occupations should be equally respected. Coming from the *Vaishnavaite* tradition, Gandhiji tended to romanticize the village life in India where people had limited needs and happily worked in their traditional occupations. This was symbolized in terms of the notion of *Ram Rajya*, making it easy to understand, through imagery and folk knowledge, for even the illiterate.[5] Gandhiji looked upon the traditional *Chaturvarna* as an ideal model of organization which assigns to each individual a social and occupational vocation, thereby insuring that the collectivity functions harmoniously. Within this framework of a "conflict-free" society, Gandhiji believed that the prevalence of various castes contributed towards social harmony and economic stability.[6]

Ambedkar could not have disagreed more. He looked at the Caste system as a "system of graded inequality". It had an ascending scale of hatred and descending scale of contempt which had done an irreparable damage to the Indian Society. Unlike Gandhiji, he did not accept the theory of karma and was strongly opposed to the four-fold stratification of the varna which, he argued, had turned Indian society into a multi-storey building with no movement allowed from one floor to another; one must die on the floor on which one was born.

Ambedkar also did not have any faith in Gandhiji's romanticization of villages. He called villages "cesspools" that harboured caste-based oppression and socio-economic backwardness. Moreover, what Gandhiji called *Ram Rajya* reminded Dr Ambedkar of Untouchables like Eklavya and Shambuka who were penalized severely for stepping out of their place in the *Chaturvarna*. He, therefore, believed in a "complete overhauling" of Hindu society. His freedom struggle was aimed not

---

4. C. Jaffrelot (2000)
5. Gail Omvedt (2004)
6. As quoted in C. Jaffrelot (2000)

merely at the transfer of power to Indians, but also at building the nation as a socio-economic democracy embodied in the trinity of liberty, equality and fraternity.

It was against this backdrop that the historic meeting between Gandhiji and Ambedkar was going to take place. Somewhat surprisingly, the initiative came from Mahatma Gandhi. On August 9, 1931 Gandhiji had sent a note to Dr Ambedkar inviting him for a personal meeting on the same day at 8 pm. With his characteristic modesty, Gandhiji had even offered to call on Ambedkar at his residence. Ambedkar agreed to meet Gandhiji at Mani Bhavan (where he was staying) but not on the same day since he was running a high fever. The meeting actually took place only on August 14, 1931, just the day before Dr Ambedkar was scheduled to leave for London to participate in the Second Session of the Round Table Conference convened by the British Government.

Given the sharp differences in their views, the meeting was going to be uncomfortable and stormy, and it lived up to its expectations..

★ ★ ★

Dr Ambedkar arrived at Mani Bhavan at 2.00 pm along with few colleagues. They were shown in to the third floor where Gandhiji was busy talking with his partymen and visiting newspaper reporters. Dr Ambedkar and colleagues bowed to Gandhiji and sat on a blanket. For some time, Gandhiji ignored Ambedkar and kept chatting with the foreign journalists. Ambedkar was getting impatient and just when his colleagues feared that he would explode any moment, Gandhiji finally turned to Ambedkar and asked:

"Well, Doctor, what do you have to say in the matter?"

"You have called me to hear your views. Please tell me what you have to say. Or you may please ask me some questions and I shall answer," said Dr Ambedkar.

With a long look at Dr Ambedkar, Gandhiji said:

> I understand that you have got some grievances against me and the Congress. I may tell you that I have been thinking over the problem of Untouchables ever since my school days—when you were not even born. You may perhaps know what enormous amount of effort I had put in to incorporate this problem in the programme of the Congress and make it a plank of the Congress platform. The Congress leaders opposed it on the plea that it was a religious and social question and as such it should not be mixed with political ones. This is not all. The Congress has spent not less than Rupees Twenty Lakhs on the upliftment of the Untouchables. And it is really surprising that men like you should offer opposition to me and to the Congress. If you have to say anything to justify your stand, you are free to do so.

To the complete disbelief of Gandhiji, retorted Dr Ambedkar:

"It is true, Mahatmaji, that you started to think about the problem of Untouchables before I was born. All old and elderly persons always like to emphasize the point of age."

Gandhiji had met many Untouchables before. But he had never come across an Untouchable intellectual. As a matter of fact, till that point of time, nobody had.

Ambedkar continued:

> It is also true that because of you the Congress Party gave recognition to the problem. But let me tell you frankly that the Congress did nothing beyond giving formal recognition to this problem. You say the Congress spent more than Rupees Twenty lakhs on the upliftment of the Untouchables. I say it was all waste. With such a backing I could have effected an astounding change in the outlook and economic conditions of my people. And in that event it would have been imperative for you to see me long before. But I tell you that the Congress is not sincere about its professions. Had it been sincere, it would have surely made the removal of Untouchability a condition, like the wearing of *khaddar,* for becoming a member of the Congress. No person who did not employ Untouchable women or men in his house, or rear up an Untouchable student or eat food at home with an Untouchable student at least once a week should have been allowed to be a member of the Congress. Had there been such a condition, you could have avoided the ridiculous sight where the President of the District Congress Committee was seen opposing the temple entry of the Untouchables.
>
> You might say that the Congress wanted strength and, therefore, it was unwise to lay down such a condition. Then my point is that the Congress cares more for strength than for principles. This is my charge against you and the Congress. You say the British Government does not show a change of heart. I also say that the Hindus have not shown a change of heart in regard to our problem, and so long as they remain adamant we would believe neither the Congress nor the Hindus. We believe in self-help and self-respect. We are not prepared to have faith in great leaders and *Mahatmas*. Let me be brutally frank about it. History tells that *Mahatmas*, like fleeting phantoms, raise dust, but raise no level. Why should the Congressmen oppose our movement and dub me as a traitor?

Dr Ambedkar now grew animated. His face flushed and eyes glowed. He paused for a moment and then continued in a bitter, indignant tone.

"Gandhiji, I have no homeland."

Taken aback, again, Gandhiji cut him short and said:

"You have got a homeland and from the reports that have reached me of your work at the Round Table Conference, I know you are a patriot of sterling worth."

Ambedkar persisted, saying:

> How can I call this land my own homeland and this religion my own where we are treated worse than cats and dogs, where we cannot get water to drink? No self-respecting Untouchable worth his name will be proud of this land. The injustice and sufferings inflicted upon us by this land are so enormous that if knowingly or unknowingly we fall a prey to disloyalty to this country, the responsibility for that act would be solely hers. I do not feel sorry for being branded as a traitor; for the responsibilities of our action lie with the land that dubs me a traitor. If at all I have rendered any national service as you say, helpful or beneficial, to the patriotic cause of this country, it is due to my unsullied conscience and not due to any patriotic feelings in me. If in my endeavor to secure human rights for my people, who have been

trampled upon in this country for ages, I do any disservice to this country, it would not be a sin; and if any harm does not come to this country through my action, it may be due to my conscience. It is owing to the promptings of my conscience that I have been striving to win human rights for my people without meaning or doing any harm to this country.

The atmosphere was charged. Gandhiji was getting increasingly restless. Ambedkar then raised the most pertinent issue, which indeed was the main purpose for the meeting. He asked:

Everybody knows that the Muslims and the Sikhs are socially, politically and economically more advanced than the Untouchables. The first Session of the Round Table Conference has given political recognition to Muslim's demands and has recommended political safeguards for them. The Congress has agreed to their demands. The First Session has also given recognition to the political rights of the Depressed Classes and has recommended for them political safeguards and adequate representation. According to us, that is beneficial to the Depressed Classes. What is your opinion?

By then the veteran leader had recovered from the initial shock. Having regained his composure, Gandhiji's reply was firm and frank. He said,

"I am against the political separation of the Untouchables from the Hindus. That would be absolutely suicidal."

Angry and agitated, Ambedkar rose from where he was seated and curtly said:

"I thank you for your frank opinion. It is good that I know where we stand as regards this vital problem. I take leave of you."[7]

The meeting ended on a grim note, not entirely unexpected. Both Gandhiji and Ambedkar must have surprised each other. Gandhiji was the Supreme leader of the Indian masses. Given his age and authority, nobody could have dared to hit back at Gandhiji as brazenly as Ambedkar had. To talk back to Gandhiji was sure to invite permanent displeasure and bitterness. Understanding it fully well, Ambedkar still did it because of his fiery resolve to fight out the human rights for the down-trodden masses. On his own part, Ambedkar himself must have also been surprised to see Gandhiji not being any less adamant on his own position than he himself was on his point of view.

The die was cast. The spark of confrontation was ignited. It was only the beginning of a series of direct and indirect confrontations. It is in the repeated confrontations between these two great leaders that one can witness the unique conflict between (political) "independence" and (socio-economic) "freedom" and through these public debates unfolds the story of the emergence modern India as a sovereign democratic Republic.

---

7. This account draws from Keer Dhananjay (op cit), p.165-8.

PART I

MAKING OF DR AMBEDKAR

CHAPTER ONE

Early Days

DR BHIMRAO AMBEDKAR was born on April 14, 1891 in Mhow (Military Headquarter of War), a small garrison town in Central India (in the State of Madhya Pradesh as it is called today) to an Untouchable family with a military service background. The family hailed from the coastal region of Konkan in Maharashtra and belonged to the *Mahar* Caste—numerically, the largest Untouchable Caste in the State.[8]

Bhimrao's grandfather Maloji had been in the British army, as had his father Ramji. His father had served in the British Army since 1866 and was promoted to the rank of Subedar. He was later appointed as Headmaster of an army school in Mhow. Bhimrao's mother also came from a *Mahar* family with significant military tradition: her father and six uncles were Subedar-Majors. Since education was compulsory for children of army personnel, even women in the family were literate, which was highly unusual at that time. Ramji and his wife Bhimabai had fourteen children of which only five survived. It was the fourteenth child named Bhima (also called Bhiva) who was to later emerge as Dr Babasaheb Ambedkar.

Initially, living in a military cantonment as he did, Bhima had little contact with the outside world and for the initial years he was protected from the discrimination generally faced by Untouchables. This, however, did not last long. While Bhima was still very young, the family moved to Dapoli in Ratnagiri district and then to Satara (both in today's Maharashtra State) where Ramji took up a job as storekeeper in the Public Works Department.

It was in Satara, in 1900, that young Bhima entered the first standard of the English-medium Government High School, as Bhimrao Ramji Ambavadekar. Originally, the family name was Sankpal and they came from village Ambavade (Taluka: Mandangad, District Ratnagiri). Since the family surname was indicative of a lowly Caste, Bhima's father decided to use the name of their native village

8. According to the 1931 Census, *Mahars* constituted nearly 69 per cent of Untouchables in the Bombay Presidency compared with 16.2 per cent *Chamars* and 14.9 per cent *Mangs*, the other two major Untouchable Castes.

Ambavade instead, and hence the family name was changed to Ambavadekar. Incidentally, one of Bhima's teachers in Satara was a Brahmin named Ambedkar, which sounded like Ambavadekar. The young and bright Bhima became a favourite student of this teacher. In order to shelter Bhima from walking the long distance back to his house, the kind teacher provided him a daily lunch. It was in his honour that Bhima's family name was later re-registered as Ambedkar, instead of Ambavadekar.

Once outside the protected life of the cantonment, in Satara, Bhima was soon exposed to the stark realities of Untouchable life. Dr Ambedkar himself narrated several incidents in his writings and speeches. These incidents, no doubt, sowed the seeds of rebellion and defiance which became a hallmark in the later life of Dr Ambedkar.

In his own words:

> The first incident[9] which I am recording as well as I can remember occurred in about 1901 when we were at Satara. My mother was then dead. My father was away on service as a cashier at a place called Goregaon in Khatav Taluka in the Satara District, where the Government of Bombay had started the work of excavating a Tank for giving employment to famine-stricken people who were dying by thousands. When my father went to Goregaon, he left me, my brother who was older than myself and two sons of my eldest sister who was dead, in charge of my aunt and some kind neighbours. My aunt was the kindest soul I know, but she was of no help to us. She was somewhat of a dwarf and had some trouble with her legs, which made it very difficult for her to move about without the aid of somebody. Often times she had to be lifted. I had sisters. They were married and were away living with their families. Cooking our food became a problem with us especially as our aunty could not, on account of her helplessness, manage the job. We four children went to school, and we also cooked our food. We could not prepare bread. So we lived on pulav which we found to be the easiest dish to prepare, requiring nothing more than mixing rice and mutton.
>
> Being a cashier, my father could not leave his station to come to Satara to see us, therefore, he wrote to us to come to Goregaon and spend our summer vacation with him. We children were thoroughly excited over the prospect especially as none of us had up to that time seen a railway train.
>
> Great preparations were made. New shirts of English make, bright bejewelled caps, new shoes, new silk-bordered *dhotis* were ordered for the journey. My father had given us all particulars regarding our journey and had told us to inform him on which day we were starting so that he would send his peon to the Railway Station to meet us and to take us to Goregaon. According to this arrangement myself, my brother and one of my sister's sons left Satara, our aunt remaining in charge of our neighbours who promised to look after her. The Railway Station was 10 miles distant from our place and a *tonga* (a one-horse carriage) was engaged to take us to the Station. We were dressed in the new clothing specially made for the occasion and we left our home full

9. Waiting for a Visa, BAWS, Vol. 12, p.665.

of joy but amidst the cries of my aunt who was almost prostrate with grief at our parting.

When we reached the station my brother bought tickets and gave me and my sister's son two annas each as pocket money to be spent at our pleasure. We at once began our career of riotous living and each ordered a bottle of lemonade at the start. After a short while the train whistled in and we boarded it as quickly as we could for fear of being left behind. We were told to detrain at Masur, the nearest railway station for Goregaon.

The train arrived at Masur at about five in the evening, and we got down with our luggage. In a few minutes all the passengers who had got down from the train had gone away to their destinations. We four children remained on the platform looking out for my father or his servant whom he had promised to send. Long did we wait but no one turned up. An hour elapsed and the station master came to enquire. He asked us for our tickets. We showed them to him. He asked us why we tarried. We told him that we were bound for Goregaon and that we were waiting for father or his servant to come but that neither had turned up and that we did not know how to reach Goregaon. We were well dressed children. From our dress or talk no one could make out that we were children of the Untouchables. Indeed, the Station Master was quite sure we were Brahmin children and was extremely touched at the plight in which he found us. As is usual among the Hindus the Station Master asked us who we were. Without a moment's thought I blurted out that we were *Mahars*. (*Mahar* is one of the communities which are treated as Untouchables in the Bombay Presidency). He was stunned. His face underwent a sudden change. We could see that he was overpowered by a strange feeling of repulsion. As soon as he heard my reply he went away to his room and we stood where we were. Fifteen to twenty minutes elapsed; the sun was almost setting. The father had not turned up nor had he sent his servant, and now the station-master had also left us. We were quite bewildered and the joy and happiness which we felt at the beginning of the journey gave way to the feeling of extreme sadness.

After half an hour the Station Master returned and asked us what we proposed to do. We said that if we could get a bullock-cart on hire we would go to Goregaon and if it was not very far we would like to start straightaway. There were many bullock-carts plying for hire. But my reply to the station master that we were *Mahars* had gone round among the cartmen, and not one of them was prepared to suffer being polluted and to demean himself carrying passengers of the Untouchable Classes. We were prepared to pay double the fare but we found that money did not work. The station master who was negotiating on our behalf stood silent not knowing what to do. Suddenly a thought seemed to have entered his head and he asked us, 'Can you drive the cart?' Feeling that he was finding out a solution of our difficulty we shouted, 'Yes, we can.' With that answer he went and proposed on our behalf that we were to pay the cartman double the fare and drive the cart and that he should walk on foot along with the cart on our journey. One cartman agreed as it gave him an opportunity to earn his fare and also saved him from being polluted.

It was about 6.30 PM when we were ready to start. But we were anxious not to leave the station until we were assured that we would reach Goregaon before it was dark. We, therefore, questioned the cartman as to the distance and the time he would take to reach Goregaon. He assured us that it would be not more than three hours. Believing his word, we put our luggage in the cart, thanked the station master and got into the cart. One of us took the reins and the cart started with the man walking by our side.

Not very far from the station there flowed a river. It was quite dry except at places where there were small pools of water. The owner of the cart proposed that we should halt there and have our meal as we might not get water on our way. We agreed. He asked us to give a part of his fare to enable him to go to the village and have his meal. My brother gave him some money and he left promising to return soon.

We were very hungry and were glad to have had an opportunity to have a bite. My aunty had pressed our neighbour's women folk into service and had got some nice preparation for us to take on our way. We opened the tiffin basket and started eating. We needed water to wash things down. One of us went to the pool of water in the river basin nearby. But the water really was no water. It was thick with mud and urine and excreta of the cows and buffaloes and other cattle who went to the pool for drinking. In fact, that water was not intended for human use. At any rate the stink of the water was so strong we could not drink it. We had, therefore, to close our meal before we were satisfied and wait for the arrival of the cartman. He did not come for a long time and all that we could do was to look for him in all directions. Ultimately he came and we started on our journey.

For some four or five miles we drove the cart and he walked on foot. Then he suddenly jumped into the cart and took the reins from our hand. We thought this to be rather a strange conduct on the part of a man who had refused to let the cart on hire for fear of pollution to have set aside all his religious scruples and to have consented to sit with us in the same cart but we dared not ask him any questions on the point. We were anxious to reach Goregaon our destination as quickly as possible. And for sometime we were interested in the movement of the cart only. But soon there was darkness all around us. There were no street lights to relieve the darkness. There were no men or women or even cattle passing by to make us feel that we were in their midst. We became fearful of the loneliness which surrounded us. Our anxiety was growing. We mustered all the courage we possessed. We had travelled far from Masur. It was more than three hours. But there was no sign of Goregaon.

There arose a strange thought within us. We suspected that the cartman intended treachery and that he was taking us to some lonely spot to kill us. We had lot of gold ornaments on us and that helped to strengthen our suspicion. We started asking him how far Goregaon was, why we were so late in reaching it. He kept on saying, 'It is not very far, we shall soon reach it.' It was about 10.00 at night when finding that there was no trace of Goregaon we children started crying and abusing the cartman. Our lamentations and wailings continued for long. The cartman made no reply. Suddenly we saw a light burning at some distance. The cartman said, 'Do you see that light? That is a light of the toll-collector. We will rest there for the night.' We felt some relief and stopped crying. The light was distant, but we could never seem to reach it. It took us two hours to reach the toll-collector's hut. The interval increased our anxiety and we kept on asking the cartman all sorts of questions, as to why there was delay in reaching the place, whether we were going on the same road, etc.

Ultimately by mid-night the cart reached the toll-collector's hut. It was situated at the foot of a hill but on the other side of the hill. When we arrived we saw a large number of bullock-carts there all resting for the night. We were extremely hungry and wanted very much to eat. But again there was the question of water. So we asked our driver whether it was possible to get water. He warned us that the toll-collector was a Hindu and that there was no possibility of our getting water if we spoke the truth and said that we were *Mahars*. He said, 'Say you are Mohammedans and try your luck.' On his advice I went to the toll-collector's hut and asked him if he would give us some water. 'Who are you?' He inquired. I replied that we were *Musalmans*. I conversed with him in Urdu which I knew very well so as to leave no doubt that I was a real *Musalman*. But the trick did not work and his reply was very curt. 'Who has kept water for you? There is water on the hill, if you want to go and get it, I have none.' With this he dismissed me. I returned to the cart and conveyed to my brother his reply I don't know what my brother felt. All that he did was to tell us to lie down.

The bullocks had been unyoked and the cart was placed sloping down on the ground. We spread our beds on the bottom planks inside the cart, and laid down our bodies to rest. Now that we had come to a place of safety we did not mind what happened. But our minds could not help turning to the latest event. There was plenty of food with us. There was hunger burning within us; with all this we were to sleep without food; that was because we could get no water and we could get no water because we were Untouchables. Such was the last thought that entered our mind. I said, 'we had come to a place of safety.' Evidently my elder brother had his misgivings. He said it was not wise for all four of us to go to sleep. Anything might happen. He suggested that at one time two should sleep and two should keep watch. So we spent the night at the foot of that hill.

Early at five in the morning our cartman came and suggested that we should start for Goregaon. We flatly refused. We told him that we would not move until 8 O'clock. We did not want to take any chance. He said nothing. So we left at eight and reached Goregaon at eleven. My father was surprised to see us and said that he had received no intimation of our coming. We protested that we had given intimation. He denied the fact. Subsequently, it was discovered that the fault was of my father's servant. He had received our letter but failed to give it to my father.

This incident has a very important place in my life. I was a boy of nine when it happened. But it has left an indelible impression on my mind. Before this incident occurred, I knew that I was an Untouchable and that Untouchables were subjected to certain indignities and discriminations. For instance, I knew that in the school I could not sit in the midst of my class students according to my rank but that I was to sit in a corner by myself. I knew that in the school I was to have a separate piece of gunny cloth for me to squat on in the classroom and the servant employed to clean the school would not touch the gunny cloth used by me. I was required to carry the gunny cloth home in the evening and bring it back the next day. While in the school I knew that children of the Touchable Classes, when they felt thirsty, could go out to the water tap, open it and quench their thirst. All that was necessary was the permission of the teacher. But my position was separate. I could not touch the tap and unless it was opened for it by a Touchable person, it was not possible for me to quench my thirst. In my case the permission of the teacher was not enough. The presence of the school peon was necessary, for he was the only person whom the class teacher could use for such a purpose. If the peon was not available I had to go without water. The situation can be summed up in the statement—no peon, no water. At home I knew that the

> work of washing clothes was done by my sisters. Not that there were no washermen in Satara. Not that we could not afford to pay the washermen. Washing was done by my sisters because we were Untouchables and no washerman would wash the clothes of an Untouchable. The work of cutting the hair or shaving the boys including myself was done by our elder sister who had become quite an expert barber by practising the art on us, not that there were no barbers in Satara, not that we could not afford to pay the barber. The work of shaving and hair cutting was done by my sister because we were Untouchables and no barber would consent to shave an Untouchable. All this I knew. But this incident gave me a shock such as I never received before, and it made me think about Untouchability which, before this incident happened, was with me a matter of course as it is with many Touchables as well as the Untouchables.

★ ★ ★

When Bhima was barely five years old his mother passed away (December 1896). When the family moved to Satara his father married a second time. He resented the idea of another woman taking his mother's place. Bhima then decided to run away to Mumbai and find a job for himself in the textile mills. But he needed cash to be able to travel to Mumbai. He then planned to steal the money from the purse of his aunt in whose company he used to sleep. But it ended up in a fiasco. As Dr Ambedkar himself described later:

> For three successive nights I tried to remove the purse tucked up at the waist of my aunt, but without success. On the fourth night, I did get hold of the purse, but to my disappointment, I found only half an anna in it. And in half an anna, of course, I could not go to Mumbai.[10]

This, however, turned out to be a blessing in disguise and a critical turning point in the life of Bhima. This little boy, who till then had little or no interest in studies, suddenly grew up overnight. As he himself put it later,

> the three nights' experience was so nerve-racking that I gave up the idea of collecting money in this shameful manner and I came to another decision—a decision that gave an entirely different turn to my life. I decided that I must give up my truant habits, that I must study hard and get through my examinations as fast as possible, so that I might earn my own livelihood and be independent of my father.[11]

The result? The little boy who had dreamt of becoming a mill worker in Mumbai rose to become the Labour Minister of India in the Viceroy's Executive Council (1942-1945).

★ ★ ★

10. As quoted in Keer, Dhananjay (*op cit*), p.75.
11. Keer, Dhananjay, *op cit* p.76.

In 1904, Ramji lost his job and hence shifted to Mumbai with his family and lived in a small room in Dabok Chawl, in Parel which, at the time, was populated mainly by textile mill workers. It was Bhima's father who was responsible for his early education. Ramji was deeply attached to the devotional *Varkari* sect and a follower of the Kabir Panth. As such, devotional singing (i.e., *Bhajans*) and recitation of holy texts took place in the family frequently. Ramji was also an admirer of Jyotiba Phule who had pioneered major reforms among the non-Brahmins in the later part of the 19th Century. Not surprisingly, many years later, Dr Ambedkar referred to Buddha, Kabir and Phule as his three Gurus.

Father Ramji was also responsible for Bhima's love for books. His father's strong desire was that his son should not only clear his examinations, but rather pass them with distinction. Dr Ambedkar once recalled, "My father felt great turmoil that I should pass my BA. Before dawn was a good time for study since the mind could be quiet and disciplined. At the time of examinations he used to wake me at 2 AM."[12] Earlier, Bhima ignored his studies and was careless about examinations. However, once the family moved to Mumbai, and he enrolled at Elphinstone High School, that he became interested in studies. Ramji encouraged him and even used his pension to buy almost any book that Bhima demanded. When that small amount was over, Ramji would persuade his sister to give him her jewellery and pawn it to buy more books until the next installment of his pension arrived and he could redeem it. With a meagre income, the family found keeping both sons in school impossible. So the elder son, Balaram, took up a job in a factory while Bhima continued his studies at Elphinstone High School.

While at the Elphinstone High School, Bhima was, one day, called by the teacher to come to the blackboard to solve some arithmetic problem. There was an uproar in the class, as the Caste Hindu children rushed to remove their tiffin-boxes placed behind the blackboard for fear of "pollution". When Bhima wanted to study Sanskrit, he was told that it being the sacred language of the *Vedas,* it was banned to Untouchables; he could only choose between English and Persian. These reminders of Untouchability, no doubt, left deep imprints on young Bhima's mind.

As a young lad, Bhima did not have many friends, and had a reputation for frequent fights with his schoolmates. He spent much of his time reading in a garden near his school. It was during this period that he was noticed by a social activist Krishnaji Arjun Keluskar, the then Principal of Wilson High School. Principal Keluskar took a liking for this hardworking studious boy; he introduced himself, and for long thereafter remained an important well-wisher and supporter of Bhima.

In 1905, Bhima married Ramabai, who was nine years old. It was an arranged marriage. Bhima himself was only 14 when he got married. The venue for the marriage ceremony was also rather unusual. It was the open market shed of the Byculla Market in Mumbai where the ceremony took place after the business hours.

---

12. Khairmode, CB (1968).

Bhimrao became a father seven years later when Yashwant was born. This first son was the only one who survived, though four more children were born subsequently.

In 1907, Bhima passed his Matriculation examination from Elphinstone High School. This was surely an unusual accomplishment for an Untouchable and called for celebrations in his community. After the public ceremony, Bhima was presented by Krishnaji Arjun Keluskar with a biography of the Buddha titled *Life of Gautam Buddha*. There was no way either of them could imagine that in the later years Dr Ambedkar was going to be a great champion of Buddhism and would lead millions of his followers to Buddhism.

Encouraged by his father, Bhimrao joined Elphinstone College in Mumbai. For an Untouchable, it was a whole new world out there. Bhimrao could not escape the pangs of Untouchability—the Brahmin canteen-owner at the college would not give him tea or water. Here again, however, some teachers lent him a helping hand. A European teacher—Professor Muller—lent him books and gave him clothes.

Bhimrao began his studies in right earnest; but, due to ill-health, lost one year. When Bhimrao passed the Intermediate Examination, his father ran out of money and turned to Principal Keluskar for help. Principal Keluskar stepped forward to help. He arranged a scholarship for Bhima from the State of Baroda—a Princely State, then ruled by a progressive Maratha King, Sayajirao Gaikwad. With this opportunity, Bhimrao joined Elphinstone College on a scholarship of Rs 25 a month.

Bhimrao resumed his college education and started working very hard. Around that time, the family moved their residence to another place in Parel—Bombay Improvement Trust (BIT) Chawl No.1 The family occupied two rooms on the second floor, opposite each other. Room No. 50 was used as a study-cum-sitting room, while Room No. 51 opposite was used for household purposes. Dr Ambedkar mentioned many years later, that in those two rooms lived ten family members (parents, brothers and sisters' children) and one she-goat. He studied, sometimes upto 21 hours of the day, under a dim light of kerosene lamp at night.[13] In 1912 he obtained his BA degree from Bombay University in Economics and Political Science. Thus, overcoming innumerable social and financial obstacles, Bhimrao thus became one of the first Untouchables in India to obtain a College degree.

Young Bhimrao, a college graduate at 22, decided to take up a job as a Probationer in the Accountant General Office of the State of Baroda thus honouring the Scholarship Agreement; his monthly salary was Rs 75. His decision caused a disagreement with his father, who wanted Bhimrao to stay in the liberal and cosmopolitan atmosphere of Mumbai. Ramji tried to persuade him against the idea, but Bhimrao persisted and joined the Baroda State on January 15, 1913.

---

13. Marathi Speech at Pune Untouchables Students' Conference, Pune (September 11, 1928).
For the full text of the speech, see *Ambedkar Speaks* (Ed. Jadhav, 2013) Vol.1, pp.443-8.

On reaching Baroda, however, Bhimrao was subjected to Caste-discrimination yet again. He could not find any residence except for sleeping quarters in the Arya Samaj office. He was forced to dine in the distant Untouchable neighborhood of the city. Nor did Bhimrao find any useful assignment in the State. He was tossed across departments without being given any meaningful work. Finally, on hearing of his father's illness, Bhimrao returned to Mumbai to see his ailing father, who died on February 2, 1913.

Thanks again to Principal Keluskar, subsequently, Bhimrao had an opportunity to argue his case before the Maharaja in Mumbai. The kind-hearted Maharaja responded with an offer of scholarship (£11.50 a month for two years) for him to study at Columbia University in New York. As per the Agreement signed (June 4, 1913), Bhimrao was required to serve the State of Baroda for ten years on completion of his education abroad.

Going to the land of Abraham Lincon and Booker T Washington was going to transform the young, bright and hardworking Untouchable Bhimrao's life forever.

CHAPTER TWO

MA-Ph.D at Columbia University, USA

ON JULY 20, 1913, Bhimrao was admitted for Post-Graduate Studies at the Columbia University, New York, and there began a new and exciting phase in the life of Dr Babasaheb Ambedkar.

Bhimrao was among the first group of Indians who went to the USA in the first quarter of the 20th Century to receive advanced training in Economics. These foreign-trained professional economists included CN Vakil, DR Gadgil and John Mathai, among others. Unlike others, however, Bhiramo had come up fighting against the odds of poverty and Caste-based discrimination. He had left a family of some ten-twelve people, barely managing to survive on the earnings of only one person—his brother Balaram, who worked as a common labourer.

Life in the USA was Bhimrao's first exposure to a "free world". On his arrival in New York, initially he stayed at the Hartley Hall—a University dormitory. The dormitory food did not agree with his tastes. A little later, Bhimrao shifted to Cosmopolitan Club at 554 West, 114 Street where a large number of Indian students lived. Later on, Bhimrao shifted to Livingstone Hall where his room-mate was Naval Bhathema, a Parsi student with whom he had a lifelong friendship thereafter.

For Bhimrao, with his Untouchable background, life in New York and at the University Campus was entirely a new world, a new existence indeed. For the first time in his life, Bhimrao could breathe the freedom. With his fellow students and colleagues, Bhimrao could move freely and could mingle with all others with a status of equality, something that he had never experienced before. His day-to-day existence gleamed with a new purpose, a new meaning and it rekindled in him an unsatiated quest for knowledge which was going to be a hallmark for the rest of his life.

Apparently, for the first time Bhimrao realized the importance of education—for both male and female—as the only panacea for the upliftment of the Untouchables. Interestingly in a letter to a family friend in the very first month of his stay at the Columbia University, Bhimrao quoted Shakespeare:

There is a tide in the affairs of men
Which if taken at the flood leads on to Fortune
Omitted the Voyage of their life is
Bound in shallows and miseries

and expressed a view that "our (i.e., that of Untouchables) progress will be greatly accelerated if male education is pursued side by side with female education...." Bhimrao, the young man of 22, advised the elderly family friend: "Let your mission, therefore, be to educate and preach the idea of education to those at least who are near to, and in close contact with, you."[14]

At the Columbia University, Bhimrao came under the influence of several great thinkers including philosopher John Dewey, anthropologist AA Goldenweiser and economist Edwin Seligman who were his teachers at the University. But it was under the guidance of Professor Seligman—a leading authority in public finance and history of economic thought at that time—that Bhimrao was awarded his MA in 1915 (June 2, 1915). His thesis for the MA degree was titled, "Administration of Finances of the East India Company".

The thesis deals with administration and finance of the East India Company. The East India Company got a foothold in India in the name of trading and then, over a period of time, gradually extended its rule over the entire country and finally established by law the so-called Company Government which was subsequently taken over by the British Government of India. In this thesis, Bhimrao provides a historical review of changes in administration and finance of the East India Company during the period, 1792 through 1858, and demonstrates how those changes led to suffering of the Indian people at the hands of the British Rulers.

The thesis recounts:

> Initially, the East India Company carried on its administration and commercial functions jointly. In other words, the revenue returns from administration and commercial returns from trade were merged together without any attempt at their separation. As a result of this combined activity, the Company Government's finances became unduly complicated. In the course of time, by an Act of the British Parliament in 1815, the East India Company was compelled to keep separate accounts of finance and commerce.

For quite some time, the East India Company had monopoly of the Indian trade. The thesis categorically states:

> The British were determined to derive as large a gain as possible for allowing her that privilege. Every weakness in the administration was made an excuse for extortion and interference and renewal of the charter was often an occasion to disgorge her (i.e., the

14. Khairmode, CB, op.cit. pp.77-8.

> Company) of her wealth accumulated by the monopoly of Indian trade....Up to 1833 the Company, by means fair or foul managed to win over the English statesmen to continue her monopoly. But in that year the cry against her monopoly has gone so loud that both the Company and the Ministers had to give in and the East India trade was thrown open to all the English public.

The Thesis recounts further:

> By the British Parliament's Act of 1834, the East India Company ceased to be a commercial corporation but continued her existence as a political sovereign of her territories in India. Her days, however, were 'fast being numbered'; the Company was finally abolished in 1858 and the Company Government was taken over by the British Government.

The Thesis argues that it is an error to attribute this take-over to the "Mutiny" of 1857. The discussion on the takeover of the Company Government of India by the British Government was set afloat well before the "Mutiny". According to him, "....mutiny or no mutiny, the British statesmen were impatient to have direct control over the 'leaves and the fishes' that came but indirectly from their rule in India by a process of disgorging a corporation which directly fed them on beef fat."

The Thesis presents a vivid account of the political process which led to the abolition of the East India Company. A Bill to that effect was introduced first by Lord Palmerstone in 1857. Interestingly, it was the well-known economist John Stuart Mill who drafted the petition on behalf of the East India Company demonstrating fallacy in the arguments in favour of the Bill. However, before the said Bill was passed, Palmerstone's Government was thrown out (for other reasons). Under the new government, Benjamin Disraeli (who was the Chancellor i.e. Finance Minister in the new government), introduced a fresh Bill which could not be passed in the British Parliament. Eventually, a new Bill was introduced in August 1858 designated as an "Act for Better Government of India" which was passed and accordingly the direct rule of the British Government was established in India.

★ ★ ★

A year later, at the age of 26, Bhimrao submitted his Dissertation for Ph.D which was accepted for the Doctorate in 1917. His Ph.D Dissertation was titled, "National Dividend: A Historical and Analytical Study". Several years later in 1925, the dissertation was published in book form with the title: *The Evolution of Provincial Finance in British India*, whereupon Bhimrao was formally awarded his Ph.D degree by Columbia University (June 8, 1927).[15] Interestingly, the book has been dedicated

---

15. According to the then prevailing University rules, the students were required to publish their dissertations in the book form and to submit the copies to the University for a formal award of the Ph.D degree.

to His Highness Shri Sayajirao Gaikwad, Maharaja of Baroda. The dedication reads: "As a token of gratitude for his help in the matter of my education."

The book has Foreword from Professor Edwin RA Seligman, his teacher at Columbia University, from whom Dr Ambedkar learnt his "first lessons in the theory of Public Finance". Professor Seligman says in his Foreword:

> The value of Mr Ambedkar's contribution…lies in the objective recitation of the facts and the impartial analysis of the interesting development that has taken place in his native country. The lessons are applicable to other countries as well; nowhere to my knowledge has such a detailed study of the underlying principles been made.

This book represents Dr Ambedkar's pioneering contribution to the field of Public Finance. In this book, he deals with the Centre-State financial relationship in British India during the period 1833 to 1921. In a sense, this book represents a more detailed and worthy sequel to his earlier work on Finances of the East India Company as Thesis for MA degree.

The setting of the problem is a familiar one. The expanded role of government calls for larger revenue collection from taxation; yet in a poor country like India there are obvious limits to taxation. As a result, the problem of equitable distribution of burden among various forms of government such as the Central Government, Provinces and Local Governments assumes significance. Dr Ambedkar provides a detailed and insightful perspective on the financial relationship between the Central Government and the Provincial Governments in British India during the period 1833 through 1921. In doing so, he presents a pioneering study of the origin, development and mechanism of Provincial finance in India.

According to Dr Ambedkar, the Imperial system of government was established in India in 1833. It was accompanied by the Imperial system of government finance. This centralization of government finances was a failure on account of the faulty fiscal system marked by injurious taxes and extravagant expenditure. As a result, after nearly four decades of its operation, it was abandoned in 1871 and the regime of Provincial Budgets came into force.

For the next five decades, as Dr Ambedkar explains, various alternative fiscal arrangements, such as "Budget by Assignment", "Budget by Assigned Revenues" and "Budget by Shared Revenues" were operational. These schemes were in vogue until 1921 when a "progressive realization of responsible government" was finally accepted as an integral part of the British rule. Accordingly, major fiscal reforms were introduced in 1921 leading to a complete transformation of Provincial finance in India.

Dr Ambedkar presents a perceptive account of all these developments buttressed by painstakingly collected facts and figures. The analytical insights provided by him in the Centre-Provincial financial relationship are as relevant today as they were when this pioneering work was first brought out.

★ ★ ★

During his doctoral studies at Columbia University, Dr Ambedkar also took an Anthrapology Seminar under Professor Goldenweizer. The theme of the Seminar was "Primitive versus Modern Society". As a participant in the Seminar, Dr Ambedkar presented a Research Paper to the fellow-students on May 9, 1916. The title of the paper was: "Castes in India, Their Mechanism, Genesis and Development". It was published later in the Journal: *India Antiquary*, May 1917.

While explaining the genesis and mechanism of Castes in India, Dr Ambedkar said:

> Caste is a parcelling of an already homogeneous unit, and the explanation of the genesis of Caste is the explanation of this process of parceling." Analyzing the work by the then leading scholars—Senart, Nesfield and Ketkar, Dr Ambedkar argues: "Prohibition, or rather the absence of intermarriage—endogamy, to be concise—is the only one that can be called the essence of Caste. Caste in India means an artificial chopping off the population into fixed and definite units, each one prevented from fusing into another through the custom of endogamy. Endogamy is the only characteristic that is peculiar to Caste, and if we succeed in showing how endogamy is maintained, we shall practically have proved the genesis and also the mechanism of Caste.

According to Dr Ambedkar:

> Endogamy is foreign to the people of India. With the people of India exogamy is a creed and none dare infringe it. Exogamy is strictly observed and that there are more rigorous penalties for violating exogamy than there are for violating endogamy. With exogamy as the rule, there could be no Caste, for exogamy means fusion. But we have Castes; consequently in the final analysis creation of Castes, so far as India is concerned, means the superposition of endogamy on exogamy. It is in the consideration of the means utilized for the preservation of endogamy against exogamy that we may hope to find the solution of the problem of the mechanism of Caste.
>
> The group that is desirous of making itself into a Caste the maintenance of equality between the sexes becomes the ultimate goal, for without it endogamy can no longer subsist. If endogamy is to be preserved conjugal rights from within have to be provided, for otherwise members of the group will be driven out of the circle to take care of themselves in any way they can. But in order that the conjugal rights be provided for from within, it is absolutely necessary to maintain a numerical equality between the marriageable units of the two sexes within the group. The problem of Caste, then, ultimately resolves itself into one of repairing the disparity between the marriageable units of the two sexes within it....
>
> It will now be seen that the four means by which numerical disparity between the two sexes is conveniently maintained are: (1) burning the widow with her deceased husband; (2) compulsory widowhood—a milder form of burning; (3) imposing celibacy on the widower; and (4) wedding him to a girl not yet marriageable. These means create and perpetuate endogamy, while Caste and endogamy are one and the same thing. Thus the existence of these means is identical with Caste and Caste involves

these means. This, in my opinion, is the general mechanism of a Caste in a system of Castes.

Our task will be amply rewarded if we scrutinize the solution the Hindus arrived at to meet the problems of the surplus man and surplus woman. They have three singular uxorial customs: (1) Sati or the burning of the widow on the funeral pyre of her deceased husband. (2) Enforced widowhood, by which a widow is not allowed to remarry. (3) Girl marriage. These customs were so highly eulogized proves that they needed eulogy for their prevalence. They were needed to create the structure of Caste and the philosophies in honour of them were intended to popularize them, for they must have been so abominable and shocking to the moral sense of the unsophisticated that they needed a great deal of sweetening. Strict endogamy could not be preserved without these customs, while endogamy is the only characteristic of Caste and when I say Origin of Caste I mean the Origin of the Mechanism for endogamy.

Our study of the genesis of Caste would be very much facilitated, for we have only to determine what was the Class that first made itself into a Caste, for Class and Caste, so to say, are next-door neighbours, and it is only a span that separates the two. A Caste is an Enclosed Class. The study of the origin of Caste must furnish us with an answer to the question—what is the Class that raised this "enclosure" around itself? An answer to this will serve us to elucidate the mystery of the growth and development of Castes all over India.

While explaining the "Development of Castes", Dr Ambedkar said:

These customs in all their strictness are obtainable only in one Caste, namely the Brahmins, who occupy the highest place in the social hierarchy of the Hindu society. The strict observance of these customs and the social superiority arrogated by the priestly Class in all ancient civilizations are sufficient to prove that they were the originators of this 'unnatural institution' founded and maintained through these unnatural means.

There is a strong belief in the mind of orthodox Hindus that the Hindu Society was somehow moulded into the framework of the Caste System and that it is an organization consciously created by the *Shastras*. Not only does this belief exist, but it is being justified on the ground that it cannot but be good, because it is ordained by the *Shastras* cannot be wrong.

The Hindu society in common with other societies was composed of Classes and the earliest known are the (1) Brahmins or the priestly Class; (2) the *Kshatriya*, or the military Class; (3) the *Vaishya*, or the merchant Class, and (4) the *Shudra*, or the artisan and menial Class. Particular attention has to be paid to the fact that this was essentially a Class System. At some time in the history of the Hindus, the priestly Class socially detached itself from the rest of the body of people and through a closed-door policy became a Caste by itself. The sub-division of a society is quite natural. But the unnatural thing about these sub-divisions is that they have lost the open-door character of the Class System and have become self-enclosed units called Castes. The question is: were they compelled to close their doors and become endogamous, or did they close them on their own accord? I submit that there is a double line of answer: some closed the door: Others found it closed against them.

> Endogamy or the closed-door system was a fashion in the Hindu society, and as it had originated from the Brahmin Caste, it was whole-heartedly imitated by all the non-Brahmin sub-divisions or Classes, who, in their turn, became endogamous Castes. Brahmins idolized by scriptures and venerated by the priest-ridden multitude were believed to be the very end of creation. Such a creature is worthy of more than mere imitation. In a way, but only in a way, the status of a Caste in the Hindu Society varies directly with the extent of the observance of the customs of Sati, enforced widowhood, and girl marriage. But observance of these customs varies directly with the distance... that separates the Caste. Those Castes that are nearest to the Brahmins have imitated all the three customs and insist on the strict observance thereof. Those that are less near have imitated enforced widowhood and girl marriage; others, a little further off, have only girl marriage and those furthest off have imitated only the belief in the Caste principle. This leaves no doubt that the whole process of Caste-formation in India is a process of imitation of the higher by the lower.... Some unfortunate groups find themselves enclosed, because others in enclosing themselves have closed them out, with the result that new groups by a mechanical law are constantly being converted into Castes to a bewildering multiplicity.

★ ★ ★

Bhimrao Ambedkar was only 25 when he wrote this brilliant research paper. As noted, "still in his mid-twenties, the prodigious Ambedkar writes of being troubled by the ghost of Manu, that mystical jurist of Hindu tradition, whose classic work *Manusmriti* he will publicly burn in 1927".[16]

16. Aishwary Kumar, "The Lies of Manu", *Outlook,* (August 20, 2012)

CHAPTER THREE

Advanced Studies in London: Discontinuity and Return to India

DR AMBEDKAR WAS keen on getting a Doctorate from the London School of Economics and also on becoming a Barrister, so that after serving the Baroda Government as per the Scholarship Agreement, he could earn his livelihood as a practising lawyer and devote himself to social work and writing books.

However, there was an administrative hitch. His scholarship was expiring in June 1916 and as such, he needed a two-year extension to the scholarship for completing his studies. Accordingly, Dr Ambedkar sent a request letter to the Maharaja of Baroda for a two-year extension (February, 1916), which was turned down. Disappointed and desperate, Dr Ambedkar consulted his Ph.D Guide Professor Saligman, who advised him to re-apply for extension along with his own strong letter of recommendation. This time, it worked and the Maharaja gave an extension, but only for a year for the time being.

In the meantime, "unstoppable" Dr Ambedkar set out for London in May 1916 without waiting for the approval of the request for extension of the scholarships from the Maharaja of Baroda. He carried with him a letter of recommendation from Professor Saligman to Professor Sydney Webb, who was himself a great economist and thinker holding a key-position in the London School of Economics.

As the story goes, Dr Ambedkar left for London without any money in his pocket. On reaching Liverpool by ship (June 1916), his person, clothes, shoes and luggage were meticulously searched by the British Police authorities on the suspicion that he may be connected with the Indian Revolutionary Army. He was released with great reluctance on verification of his recommendation letters. Dr Ambedkar then travelled to London by train without ticket. On arrival in London railway station, he managed to escape without being caught and took a cab to India House where he somehow managed to persuade the Secretary even to pay for the carriage that brought his luggage. Fortunately, two days later, a letter from the Government of Baroda arrived awarding Dr Ambedkar a one-year extension for his scholarship.

Dr Ambedkar was admitted to the London School of Economics and Political Science in October 1918 and also for Bar-at Law at the Grey's Inn in November 1916. Because of the Ph.D earned by him at the Columbia University, USA, and in view of the letter of recommendation from Professor Saligman certifying that he was "an excellent student and a nice fellow, moderate, broad and able", Dr Ambedkar was granted a special permission (December 18, 1916) to appear directly for the M.Sc examination without having to undertake the B.Sc degree from the London University.

Dr Ambedkar was all set now working very hard in the right earnest. Few months later, Dr Ambedkar appealed to the Government of Baroda State to grant him a further extension of two years from June 1917. This was strongly endorsed by his Professors at the London University. This time, however, Dr Ambedkar's request was firmly declined by the Maharaja of Baroda and he was instructed to return to India to serve the Baroda State as per the Scholarship Agreement.

Dr Ambedkar was left with no choice. Utterly disturbed Dr Ambedkar applied to the London School of Economics (June 12, 1917) for condoning his unanticipated discontinuity in studies and allowing him some time. On July 17, 1917 the University of London "excused the interruption of his course of study for a period not exceeding four years from October 1917". Similar permission was also obtained from the Grey's Inn.

The World War I was still not over. Dr Ambedkar, disappointed but determined as ever, insured his 200-300 books and personal effects for Rs 600 and sailed off for India, reaching Mumbai on August 21, 1917.

★ ★ ★

Immediately on Dr Ambedkar's arrival in Mumbai, a felicitating function was organized in Mumbai under the Chairmanship of Rao Bahadur Cunilal Setalwad, the then Chief Presidency Magistrate of Bombay. Depressed and dejected Dr Ambedkar, however, did not attend the meeting.

Dr Ambedkar and family were in a financial crisis. He did not even have to go to Baroda to serve the State. As the luck would have it, the ship carrying his books and baggage was torpedoed and sunk in the Atlantic Ocean. Mercifully, Dr Ambedkar received the compensation of Rs 600, for which it was insured and that sum came in handy to help the family in distress and also to pay for his travel to Baroda.

MILITARY SECRETARY OF BARODA STATE AND RETURN TO MUMBAI

As a part of the scholarship agreement with the Baroda State, Bhimrao had signed a bond for serving the Princely State for 10 years in return for the scholarship to study abroad. Apparently, the Maharaja wanted to appoint Dr Ambedkar as the

Finance Minister of the Baroda State. To begin with, on August 31, 1917, the Maharaja appointed Bhimrao as his Military Secretary on his return to Baroda (Salary Rs 150 per month). Despite his advanced degree and senior rank in the Service, however, Dr Ambedkar was once again subjected to Caste-based discrimination.

Dr Ambedkar managed to find quarters in a Parsi boarding house but only under an assumed Parsi name. There was no comfort at the work place either; Brahmin clerks and subordinates were rude, and kept a distance, literally throwing papers on his desk to avoid any physical contact with him. When he tried to join the club where officers met in their leisure time, he was seated in a corner away from everyone and was told not to take part in any games. Although designated Military Secretary to the Maharaja, Dr Ambedkar had no clear role to play. In the hostile atmosphere of Baroda, he could find no friends and was forced to withdraw himself into solitude. The inhuman treatment reached its climax when on discovering his identity, a group of angry Parsis besieged the boarding house, determined to beat him up. This fiasco was described later byDr Ambedkar himself, as follows:

> After returning from England, in accordance with the terms of the agreement, I came to serve under the Baroda Durbar. I could not get a house to live in at Baroda. Neither a Hindu nor any Muslim was prepared to rent out a house to me in the city of Baroda. Failing to get a house in any locality, I decided to get accommodation in a Parsi *Dharamsala*. After having stayed in America and England, I had developed a fair complexion and an impressive personality. Giving myself a Parsi name, 'Adalji Sorabji', I began to live in the Parsi *Dharamsala*. The Parsi manager agreed to accommodate me at Rs 2 per diem. But, soon the people got the wind of the fact that His Highness the Maharaja Gaikwad of Baroda had appointed a *Mahar* boy as an officer in his Durbar. My living in the Parsi *Dharamsala* under an assumed name gave rise to suspicion, and my secret was soon out.
>
> On the second day of my stay, when I was just leaving for my office after taking breakfast, a mob of some fifteen or twenty Parsis, armed with *lathis* accosted me, threatening to kill me and demanded who I was. I replied, 'I am a Hindu'. But they were not to be satisfied with this answer. Exasperated, they began to shower abuses on me, and made me vacate the room immediately. My presence of mind and knowledge gave me the strength to face the situation boldly. Politely, I asked for permission to stay for eight hours more. Throughout the day, I searched for a house to live in, but miserably failed to get any place to hide my head. I approached my friends, but all turned me down on some pretext or the other, expressing their inability to accommodate me. I was utterly disappointed and exhausted. What to do next? I just could not decide. Frustrated and exhausted, I quietly sat down at one place, tears flowing out of my eyes. Seeing no hope of getting a house, and no alternative but to quit, I tendered my resignation, and left for Bombay by the night train.

Utterly disappointed, humiliated and frustrated Dr Ambedkar left the State for good and returned to Mumbai (August 31, 1917).

★ ★ ★

Back in Mumbai, Bhimrao tried to find ways to make a living for his growing family. His elder brother Anandrao who had supported his family died in November, 1917. Dr Ambedkar was desperate. With help from his Parsi friend Bhathena, he picked up some odd jobs; worked as a private tutor and as an accountant for a Parsee businessman (earning Rs 50 per month). He even set up a small firm for stock-broking and worked as an investment consultant, which failed when his clients found out that he was an Untouchable.

After a lot of struggle and frustrating efforts, Dr Ambedkar got a one-year position as Professor of Political Economy at Sydenham College, Mumbai (salary Rs 450 per month) which he held from November 11, 1918 to March 11, 1920. Even there, while he was popular with the students, colleague teachers objected to his drinking water from the pot reserved for the professional staff!

Not being able to get any Government job, Dr Ambedkar started teaching Economics, Banking and Mercantile Law at Davar's College of Commerce (earning Rs 50 per month). With his monthly earning of Rs 150, it was barely possible to make the two ends meet. There was no scope for saving for financing his incomplete education abroad. As was described by Blake Clarke later, "except for odd jobs,... one of India's best educated man lived in Bombay for the next year and half unemployed, poverty-stricken and miserable."

In spite of the financial distress, Dr Ambedkar continued to read and write. It was during this period that Dr Ambedkar published his famous paper titled, "Small-Holdings in India and their Remedies" in the *Journal of the Indian Economic Society* (1918). Dr Ambedkar also published a Review Article on Bertrand Russell's book titled: *Reconstruction* in the *Journal of the Indian Economic Society* (1918).

★ ★ ★

SMALL HOLDINGS IN INDIA AND THEIR REMEDIES

The Research Paper: "Small Holdings in India and their Remedies" deals with the problem of the size of holdings and its effect on the productivity of agriculture. According to Dr Ambedkar, the holdings of land in India are not only small but they are also scattered. The problems of these holdings are two-fold—(1) How to consolidate the holdings; and (2) after consolidation, how to perpetuate the said consolidation. The heirs of deceased in India, he argued, desire to secure share from each survey number of the deceased rather than distributing complete holdings amongst themselves. This has resulted into rendering the farming most inefficient and causing several problems. Dr Ambedkar discusses methods for consolidation e.g., restriping, restricted sale of the occupancy of the fragmented land to the contagious holder and the right of pre-emption. In this connection, Dr Ambedkar also examined the report of the Baroda Committee and the proposals of Professor Jevons and Mr Keatinge, and pointed out that the consolidation may obviate the evils of scattered holdings, but it will not obviate the evils of small holdings unless the consolidated holding becomes an "economic holding".

While discussing the terms of "economic holding". Dr Ambedkar observes, "Mere size of land is empty of all economic connotation.... It is the right or wrong proportion of other factors of production to a suit of land that renders the latter economic or uneconomic." Thus a small farm may be economic as well as a large farm. Supporting his thoughts by relevant statistics at length, he concludes, "Existing holdings are uneconomic, not, however, in the sense that they are too small but they are too large as against the inadequacy of other factors of production." He, therefore, suggests that the remedy lies in not enlarging the holding, but in the matter of increasing capital and capital goods.

According to Dr Ambedkar, the evil of small holding is the product of mal-adjustment of the Indian social economy. A large part of population of superfluous and idle labour exerts high pressure on agriculture. He tries to analyse how to remedy the ills of agriculture and suggests that industrialization of India is the soundest remedy for the agricultural problems of India.

Dr Ambedkar argued that the cumulative effects of industrialization, namely, a lessening pressure and an increasing amount of capital and capital goods will forcibly create the economic necessity of enlarging the holding. Not only this, but industrialization by destroying the premium on land will give rise to few occasions for its sub-division and fragmentation. Industrialization is a natural and powerful remedy and is to be preferred to such ill-conceived projects as we have considered above. By legislation we will get a sham economic holding at the cost of many social ills. But by industrialization a large economic holding will force itself upon us as a pure gain.

Dr Ambedkar concluded:

> While other countries like the USA starting as agricultural ones are progressively becoming industrial, India has been gradually undergoing the woeful process of de-urbanization and swelling the volume of her rural population beyond all needs. The earlier we stem this ominous tide, the better.

REVIEW OF BERTRAND RUSSEL'S BOOK

Well-known British Philosopher and Thinker Bertrand Russell (1872-1970) wrote a book titled, *The Principles of Social Reconstruction*, published in 1917 when the World War I was going on. Dr Ambedkar wrote a Review of this book which was published in the *Journal of the Indian Economic Society* (Vol.I, 1918). It turned out to be an important Review of a noteworthy contribution by Bertrand Russell.

According to Dr Ambedkar, *Principles of Social Reconstruction* by Mr Bertrand Russell is a war book. Bellicose literature, on the whole, he argued, is either propagandist or preventive. Mr Russell's book, though it falls under the latter, must be distinguished from the rest of the same class, wherein Russell adopts the standpoint of the behaviouristic psychology.

To begin with Dr Ambedkar discusses how the philosophy of war is related to the principles of growth as expounded by Mr Russell. According to him, although Mr Russell is anxious for the abolition of war, he explicitly states, "in spite of all the destruction which is wrought by the impulses that lead to war, there is more hope for a nation which has these impulses than for a nation in which all impulse is dead." According to Russell, a great many of the impulses which now lead nations to go to war are themselves essential to any vigorous or progressive life. Without imagination and love of adventure a society becomes stagnant and begins to decay. Conflict, provided it is not destructive and brutal, is necessary in order to stimulate men's activities and to secure the victory of what is living over what is dead. In other words, activity is the condition for growth. According to Dr Ambedkar, Mr Russell emphatically is against war, but is not for quietism; for, activity leads to growth and quietism is but another name for death.

While critically reviewing Russell's outlook towards the philosophy of war, Dr Ambedkar points out the following difficulties:

> We do not sufficiently control the operations of the means once employed for the achieving of some end. For a means, once employed, liberates many ends—fact scarcely recognized—and not the one only we wish it to produce.

What is advocated to take the place of philosophy of force is essentially an Eastern philosophy or to be specific, Indian philosophy. Of the many reasons urged in support of the Indian view of life, the main one is that under its influence that India alone has survived of all the oldest countries. Actually, there are many modes of survival and not all are equally commendable. For instance, mobility to beat a timely retreat may allow weaker varieties of people to survive. Therefore, it cannot be granted that because people have survived through ages that they have been growing and improving. Thus it is not survival; but the quality, the plane of survival, that is important.

Turning then to Russell's analysis of effects of property, Dr Ambedkar brings out several "misconceptions":

The first misconception is embodied in his statement about the "love of money" in which Russell says, "It leads men to mutilate their own nature from a mistaken theory of what constitutes success and to give admiration to enterprises which add nothing to human welfare." According to Dr Ambedkar, the re-statement of the evils of "love of money" by Mr Russell does not add any philosophic weight to its historic value. Russell criticizes the love of money without inquiring into the purpose of it. In a healthy mind, it may be urged, there is no such thing as a love of money in the abstract. Love of money is always for something and it is the purpose embodied in that "for something" that will endow it with credit or cover it with shame. Having regard to this, there can be no "dead uniformity of character" among the individuals. Thus, Mr Russell's thesis is shaky when looked at from the production side of our life. Moreover, it entirely falls to the ground when looked at from the consumption side, because human nature is fortunately provided by its very make-up against a one-sided development leaving no doubt as to its promise for an all-round development in a congenial environment. Whether it will be able to obtain the miscellaneous food material, intellectual or spiritual it craves for, is a matter beyond its control. If it is mutilated by the lack of variety of food, it will be through social default and not its own.

Another allegation by Mr Russell is that property as the embodiment of the possessive instinct leads to war. According to Dr Ambedkar, one may agree with Mr Russell and yet say that Fredric Nietzsche understood the effects of property better than Mr Russell. The trouble, one might say, is not with property but with the unequal distribution of it: for those who have none of it are prone to perpetrate more destruction for its possession than those who have.

A most fundamental notion that pervades the whole outlook of Mr Russell is:

> Men's impulses and desires may be divided into those that are creative and those that are possessive. Some of our activities are directed to creating that would not otherwise exist, others towards acquiring or retaining what exists already. The best life is that in which creative impulses play the largest part and possessive impulses the smallest.

Dr Ambedkar asks: "Is it possible to divide the impulses? Is there such a thing as an impulse to appropriate? Every impulse, if uninhibited, will lead to some creative act. Whether the product will be appropriate or not is a matter wholly different from any act of impulse or instinct." According to Dr Ambedkar, it depends upon the method of its production, i.e., whether individualistic or otherwise, and upon the nature of its use i.e., whether communal or otherwise. No one sets up a right of appropriation to anything that is produced by common efforts nor to anything that is of joint use. Thus, it is just a question of production and use and not of impulse that a thing is appropriated. In other words, the creative and the possessive impulses at different levels are bound to be different. The more of one will not ensure the less of the latter.

In sum, Dr Ambedkar concludes:

> Mr Russell deserves full credit for having emphasized the psychic basis of social life. Social reconstruction depends upon the right understanding of the relation of individual to society—a problem which has eluded the grasp of many sociologists. I have confined myself to putting Mr Russell in his right place where I thought he was likely to be misunderstood.

CHAPTER FOUR

First Foray in Public Sphere

DR AMBEDKAR WAS initiated into the public sphere, albeit briefly, in 1919; the occasion was the Southborough Committee. In order to fully appreciate Dr Ambedkar's contribution, one must understand the political backdrop to this event.

Just a day before Dr Ambedkar returned to India, the British Government had made a significant announcement on August 20, 1917 adopting "A policy of increasing association of Indians in every branch of the administration and gradual development of self-governing institutions, with a view to the progressive realization of responsible government in India as an integral part of the British Empire". The new policy involved far-reaching changes in the administrative, legislative and financial framework of governance. In the annual session of the Indian National Congress held at Calcutta in December, 1917, the Congress passed the following resolution:

> This Congress urges upon the people of India the necessity, justice and righteousness of removing all disabilities imposed by custom upon the Depressed Classes, the disabilities being of a most vexatious and oppressive character, subjecting those Classes to considerable hardship and inconvenience.

Dr Ambedkar was not impressed at all by this Resolution. Many years later, describing it as a "strange event", he said that the Congress had never done such a thing before, although it had functioned for 32 years.... "No Congress President has referred to the question of Social Reform in his Presidential Address since 1898.... It was even contrary to its declared policy..."[17]

Dr Ambedkar explained the reasons for this "strange event"' as follows:

> Before 1895, the answer is that before 1895 there were two schools among Congressmen on the issue of social reform versus political reform. The viewpoint of one school did

17. See, *What Congress and Gandhi Have Done to Untouchables*, Dr Ambedkar (1945).

recognize the need of social reform, but thought that the Congress Session was not the proper platform for it. The latter denied that there was need for social reform and challenged the view that there cannot be political reform without social reform. Though the two schools within the Congress were fundamentally opposed to each other, they had not upto 1895 developed a spirit of antagonism and intolerance towards each other....

The former school was in a dominant position, and the result was that the Indian National Congress and the Social Conference functioned as two parallel organizations each devoting itself to its own particular aims and objects. So great was the spirit of co-operation and goodwill between the two that the annual sessions of the National Congress and Social Conference were held in immediate succession in the same *pandal* and a large majority of those who came to attend the Congress Session also attended the Social Conference. The Social Conference was, however, an eyesore to the Congressmen who belonged to the Anti-Social Reform section. This section was evidently getting restive at the kindly disposition and the accommodating spirit which the dominant section in the Congress was showing to the Social Conference particularly in the matter of allowing it to use the Congress *pandal* for holding its session.

In 1895 when the Congress met in Poona, this Anti-Social Reform section rebelled and threatened to burn the Congress *pandal* if the Congress allowed it to be used by the Social Conference. This opposition to the Social Conference was headed by no other person than the late Mr Tilak, one of those social Tories and political radicals.... This rebellion had one effect. It settled that the Congress was not to entertain any question of social reform no matter how urgent. This is the explanation why no Congress President after 1895 has referred to the question of social reform in his Presidential Address. The Congress by its action in 1895 had become a purely political body with no interest and no concern in the removal or mitigation of social wrongs.

Against this background the resolution passed by the Congress about the Depressed Classes in 1917 is obviously a strange event.... Why did the Congress think it necessary to pass such a resolution in the year 1917? What made it take cognizance of the Untouchables? Was it because of a change in its angle of vision or was it because of some ulterior motive?

For an answer to these questions one must turn to the following resolutions passed by the Depressed Classes in the year 1917 at two separate meetings held in the City of Bombay under two different Presidents. The first of these meetings was held on the November 11, 1917, under the Chairmanship of the late Sir Narayan Chandavarkar. The second meeting was also held in November 1917 a week or so after the first meeting.

There is a close inter-connection between the resolution passed by the Depressed Classes at their meeting in Bombay under the Chairmanship of Sir Narayan Chandavarkar and the Congress resolution of 1917 on the elevation of the Depressed Classes....

Among others, the first meeting, unanimously resolved:

As the population of the Depressed Classes in India—considered Untouchables and treated as such, is very large, as their condition is very degraded owing to that treatment,

> and as they are behind the rest of the people in point of education being unable to secure fair opportunities for their improvement, thus public meeting of the Depressed Classes strongly feels that in the scheme of reform and reconstitution of the Legislative Councils which Government may be pleased to adopt, due regard be paid to the interest of the Classes. The meeting, therefore, prays the British Government to be so gracious as to protect those interests by granting to those Classes the right to elect their own representatives to the said Councils in proportion to their members.

When the British Government's announcement regarding "progressive realization of responsible Government in India" was made, leading Indian politicians were expecting some such declaration of policy on the part of His Majesty's Government and were preparing schemes for changes in the Constitutional structure of India in anticipation of such a policy. Of the many schemes that were formulated, there were two around which public attention was centered. One was called "The Scheme of the Nineteen". The second was called "The Congress-League Scheme". The second was an agreed scheme of political reforms supported by the Congress and the Muslim League otherwise known as the Lucknow Pact. Both these schemes had come into existence in 1916, a year before the announcement made by Mr Montagu.

Of the two schemes, the Congress was interested in seeing that its own scheme was accepted by His Majesty's Government. The Congress... was keen on giving the Congress-League scheme the status and character of a National Demand. This could happen only if the scheme had the backing of all communities in India. Inasmuch as the Muslim League had accepted the scheme, the problem of securing the backing of the Muslim Community did not arise. Next in numbers came the Depressed Classes. Though not as well organized as the Muslims, they were politically very conscious as their Resolutions show. Moreover, they were all along anti-Congress.

The Congress, while anxious to get the support of the Depressed Classes to the Congress-League Scheme of Reforms knew very well that it had no chance of getting it..., enlisted the services of the late Sir Narayan Chandavarkar, (who) as the President of the Congress. As the President of the Depressed Classes Mission Society... exercised considerable influence over the Depressed Classes, it was as a result of his influence and out of respect for him that a section of the Depressed Classes agreed to give support to the Congress-League Scheme.

The resolutions (in the Depressed Classes meetings)... did not give unconditional support to the Congress-League scheme. It agreed to give support on the condition that the Congress passed a resolution for the removal of the social disabilities of the Untouchables. The Congress resolution was a fulfilment of its part of the contract with the Depressed Classes which was negotiated through Sir Narayan Chandavarkar.

This explains the genesis of the Congress Resolution of 1917 on the Depressed Classes and its inter-connection with the Resolutions of the Depressed Classes passed under the Chairmanship of Sir Narayan Chandavarkar. This explanation proves that there was an ulterior motive behind the Congress Resolution. That motive was not a spiritual motive. It was a political motive.

Three months after the Calcutta Resolution, there was another important meeting of the Untouchables. Under the auspices of the Depressed Classes Mission Society of India, Karmaveer Vithal Ramji Shinde organized its First All-India Depressed Classes Conference (Mumbai, March 28-34, 1918). Sir Narayan Chandavarkar, as the Chairman of the Reception Committee, appealed to the conscience of the country, awakening its reason, its heart and asking the whole of India to remove the blot of Untouchability. While speaking at the Conference, Lokmanya Tilak said, "Untouchability is a disease and it must be removed." Reportedly, he also said, "If God were to tolerate Untouchability, he would not recognize him as God at all." At the conclusion of the Conference on All-India Anti-Untouchability, a Manifesto was issued to the effect that they would not observe Untouchability in their everyday affairs. While all prominent leaders signed the declaration, Lokmanya Tilak refrained from signing it,[18] thus confirming Dr Ambedkar calling him a political radical but a social Tory.

In 1918, Viceroy Lord Chelmsford and Secretary of State for India Edwin Montagu were entrusted the responsibility for a constitutional reform of British India. Montagu-Chelmsford reforms put in place "a responsible government of a limited character" in the Provinces by the Reform Act of 1919. In the context of these reforms, the Southborough Committee was assigned the task of redefining the electoral franchise within the framework of constitutional reform. There were a series of consultations with representatives of different interests and communities, including organizations of (or those working for) the Untouchables.

In this regard, for the Untouchables the main issue was the choice between "Reserved Seats" (in Joint Constituencies) or "Separate Constituencies". In the "Reserved Seats" option, a candidate could only be an Untouchable but a coalition of high and intermediate Castes could elect an Untouchable of their own choice, irrespective of the voting of the local Untouchables—who were typically in a minority. On the other hand, in the "Separate (Community based) Constituencies" option, only Untouchables could vote for Untouchable candidates. Thus, the system of separate electorates would endow Untouchables with their own representatives, whereas the system of reserved seats could allow, in principle, the possibility of Upper Caste-dominated parties co-opting their own "preferred" Untouchables.

Dr Ambedkar's academic credentials had come to the attention of the British who invited him to testify before the Southborough Committee along with the then leaders of Untouchables, especially those from the Depressed Classes Mission.

In his testimony before the Southborough Committee (January 27,1919), Dr Ambedkar focused on two issues:

---

18. Keer, Dhananjay, op cit. p.37.

(1) The definition of the franchise was unfavourable to Untouchables; it did not allow them to vote in large numbers thereby preventing them from becoming a notable political force. He, therefore, suggested lowering the bar for greater participation of Untouchables in the political process.
(2) As to the choice between the electoral systems, Dr Ambedkar recommended, "either to reserve seats [...] for those minorities that cannot otherwise secure personal representation or grant communal electorates.

Around the same time, Dr Ambedkar wrote a letter to *The Times of India* (January 16, 1919) under a pseudonym (since he was working then as a Professor in a Government college). In the letter, Dr Ambedkar argued that Home Rule was as much the birthright of a Brahmin as that of a *Mahar*. Accordingly, the first duty of the advanced Classes was to educate, enlighten and elevate the Depressed Classes.[19]

In the Supplementary Written Statement subsequently submitted to the Southborough Committee, however, Dr Ambedkar came out unambiguously in favour of "Community Electorates" instead of the Reserved Seats formula.

Dr Ambedkar's arguments may be briefly summarized as under:

> Any Scheme of franchise and constituency that fails to bring about representation of opinions as well as representation of persons falls short of creating a popular Government. Both factors are very relevant in the context of the Indian society which is ridden into Castes and religious communities. Social divisions in Europe and the USA do not come in the way of representative Government, but in India, social division matters in politics. They constitute an obstacle in the path of realizing an harmonious political life. Each Caste group tends to create its own distinctive type of like-mindedness, which depends upon the extent of communication, participation or endosmosis. Absence of this endosmosis is most pronounced between Touchable and Untouchable Hindus more than between the religious communities such as Hindus, Muslims, Parsees, etc.

One crux of popular Government is the representation of interests and opinions. The other crux is personal representation.

Territorial constituencies will be sufficient for only one-half the definition of popular Government. They fail to secure personal representation to members of minor groups. The Touchable Hindus, Muslims, Parsees, etc., have on secular plane common material interests. There will be in such groups landlords, labourers and capitalists. The Untouchables are, however, isolated by the Hindus from any kind of social participation. They have been dehumanized by socio-religious disabilities almost to the status of slaves. They are denied the universally accepted rights of citizenship. Their interests are distinctively their own interests and none else can truly voice them.

19. As quoted in Keer, Dhananjay, op cit, p. 40.

On the population basis, Dr Ambedkar demanded for the Untouchables of the Presidency of Bombay eight to nine representatives in the Bombay Legislative Council with franchise pitched as low for them as to muster a sizable electorate. While reviewing the various schemes proposed by different organizations Dr Ambedkar criticized the Congress Scheme which offered communal representation only to the Muslims and left Untouchables to seek representation in general electorate as typical of the ideology of its leaders who are political radicals and social conservatives.

Dr Ambedkar did not agree with the proposals of moderates to reserve only one or two seats for the Untouchables in plural constituencies as this would not give them effective representation. He also brushed aside the proposal of the Depressed Class Mission for nomination by co-option by the elected members of the Council as an attempt to dictate to the Untouchables what their good shall be, instead of an endeavour to agree with them so that they may seek to find the good of their own choice.

According to Dr Ambedkar, the communal representation with reserved seats for the Untouchables will not perpetuate social divisions, but will in fact act as a potent solvent for dissolving them by providing opportunities for contact, co-operation and re-socialization of fossilized attitudes. Dr Ambedkar argued that if the advance Classes are clamouring for application of the principle of self-determination to India as a whole, it would be a patent disharmony if the same principle were not applied to the Untouchables. Accordingly, Dr Ambedkar argued that communal representation cannot be withheld from the Untouchables because communal representation and self-determination are nothing but two different phrases which express the same notion.

Nobody could have realized at that time that this issue was going to bring Dr Ambedkar into a direct conflict with Mahatma Gandhi 13 years later with Dr Ambedkar becoming the only politician whom Mahatma Gandhi contested by resorting to a fast unto death!

★ ★ ★

Another important social initiative by Dr Ambedkar was to begin, in 1920, the publication of a fortnightly titled, *Mook Nayak* (Leader of the Silent) in Mumbai with the help of another great visionary: Maharaja Shahu Maharaj of Kolhapur. Dr Ambedkar was not the official editor of the *Mook Nayak* (since he was working as a Professor in a Government College) but the fortnightly became his mouthpiece. He used this journal to criticize the Indian political community for their reluctance to fight Caste-based discrimination.

In the first issue of *Mook Nayak* (January 31, 1920), Dr Ambedkar advocated the need for a forum, "to deliberate on the injustices let loose or likely to be imposed on us and other depressed people and to think of their future development and appropriate strategies towards it critically". Comparing Hindu Society to a tower which has several storeys but no ladder or an entrance, he said, one must die in the storey in which one was born. In order to save the Depressed Classes from perpetual slavery, poverty and ignorance, herculean efforts must be made, he argued, to awaken them to their disabilities.

In another article of the *Mook Nayak*, Dr Ambedkar asserted that it was not enough for India to be an independent country. India must arise as a good nation guaranteeing equal status in matters of social, economic, religion and politics, to all Classes, offering everyone an opportunity to rise in the scale of life and creating favourable conditions for self-advancement. According to Dr Ambedkar, if the Brahmins were justified in their attack upon and opposition to the unjust power of the British Government, the Depressed Classes were justified a hundred times more so in their opposition to the ruling of the Brahmins in case the transfer of power took place. In a similar vein, Dr Ambedkar argued in yet another article of the *Mook Nayak* that the *Swaraj* (Home Rule) where there were no Fundamental Rights guaranteed for the Depressed Classes, would not be a *Swaraj* for them. It would be a new slavery for them.

In the *Mook Nayak* (Leader of the Silent), the "Silent" had finally found a "leader"!

★ ★ ★

Around this time, Dr Ambedkar also started participating in public meetings and conferences. It was in one such conference of Untouchables at Mangaon near Kolhapur held on March 21, 1920, which Dr Ambedkar presided over.

Dr Ambedkar said:

> This Conference is unique in many ways. Intellectual thought process that started among the Depressed Classes is simply unprecedented. Till today, our people felt that our ill fate has been the sole reason for our misery, and that because there is no way to counter this ill fate, we must quietly bear this state as it is. But the new generation has started realizing that our condition today has not been the result of any divine punishment but because of misdeeds by others.
>
> The Hindu religion, to which we all belong, segregates people into two different Classes, based on two principles. The first is capability and the second one is purity both by virtue of birth. People who are considered lower and impure by virtue of birth are known as Depressed Classes. This kind of segregation, based on such iniquitous principles of purity and superiority determined solely by birth, has deeply affected the Depressed Classes. Entirely because of the accident of birth, the state of our Depressed Classes has become deplorable.
>
> By considering ourselves to be incapable and impure for so many generations, we have lost our inner strength and self-esteem, which are the two pillars of upliftment. According to the Hindu religion, we are not entitled to any rights in social life. We cannot go to schools. We cannot draw water from the common wells. We cannot walk on roads. We cannot use vehicles. Thus, we are prohibited from exercising our human

rights. On account of the incapacity and impurity by birth, we have faced tremendous losses economically. Business, services and agriculture, which are three prime sources of earning are not open to us. The curse of Untouchability takes away all the customers and thus running a business is almost impossible. Being Untouchables, we do not get jobs and sometimes, in spite of being highly talented, people do not work under us because of our Caste. Such feelings have resulted in a decrease in our numbers in the military service. Same goes with agriculture. We simply do not possess pieces of fertile land. A society with such defects would never progress. Natural abilities and favourable environment are the two primary reasons for progress.

There is indeed no shortage of talent in the Depressed Classes. The sole reason causing a hindrance in their progress is the unhealthy social environment. Numerous solutions for improving our state are offered time and again. But in order to progress, we must empower ourselves politically and for that we need a political representation based on Caste. The principle 'Truth Alone Prevails' is hollow one. For the truth to win, we must continue to agitate.

Shahu Maharaj of Kolhapur State who attended the Conference was so impressed by Dr Ambedkar that he made a prophetic announcement:

> You have found your saviour in Ambedkar. I am confident that he will break your shackles. Not only that, a time will come when, so whispers my conscience, Ambedkar will shine as a front-rank leader of all-India fame and appeal.[20]

★ ★ ★

In fact, a beginning in that direction was made by Dr Ambedkar barely within three months thereafter. In the Conference of Indian Depressed Classes held in Nagpur (May 30-31 and June 2, 1920), Dr Ambedkar said:

> We all have gathered over here with the aim to find the ways and means of achieving the progress of the Depressed Classes. Therefore, if a person comes in the path of our development, whether he belong to Depressed Classes or a high-Caste Hindu, or belonging to an organization which works against our well-being presently or has been doing so in the past, then should we not express our deepest protest towards it?

All the delegates unanimously proclaimed that any person or organization hindering their progress should be strongly condemned.

"Is this acceptable to you, then?" Saying this, Dr Ambedkar read out aloud a newspaper report indicating that the Depressed Classes Mission headed by Karmaveer Vithal Ramji Shinde had submitted a Statement to the Government of Bombay Province requesting that representatives of the Depressed Classes proposed

20. Shivtarkar, SN, *The Janata*, Special Number (April 1933).

to be nominated to the Bombay Legislative Council should not be chosen from among the Depressed Classes.

By demonstrating the "treachery", Dr Ambedkar succeeded in dramatically snatching away the leadership of the Depressed Classes towards himself.

★ ★ ★

The affection and admiration of the Maharaja Shahu Maharaj of Kolhapur for Dr Ambedkar grew. It was with the financial help from this visionary ruler a personal loan of Rs 5000 from his old friend Naval Bhathena and his own savings of Rs 7000 that Dr Ambedkar could finally return to London to complete his advanced studies (July 5, 1920).

CHAPTER FIVE

Back to London: Return to India with D.Sc and as a Barrister

ON HIS RETURN to London in August 1920, Dr Ambedkar resumed his studies from September 1920 both at the London School of Economics and Political Science as well as for the Bar at the Grey's Inn.

With the meagre amount of money at his disposal it was a life of extreme abstinence and hardship for the young scholar. Staying at a boarding house, he would rise at 6 am. With a frugal breakfast consisting of a cup of tea, a piece of bread with little bit of jam and a piece of fish, he would rush to the library and would always be the first one to enter. Then he would commence his intense reading and making copious notes for hours together without any break even for lunch. He would be fully engrossed in his readings till the closing of the library, and would always be the last person to leave, which he did only after a friendly reminder by the security guards. The second session of his study would begin soon, after a brief walk and an early dinner at the boarding house which typically comprised a cup of Bovrit with some biscuits and a bit of butter. He had a healthy appetite. So by 10 pm he would feel very hungry. Fortunately, some Indian friends had given him some *papads* (crispy wafers). He had managed to get a thin tin plate to fry those *papads.* A cup of tea and four *papads* would at least partly appease his hunger. After the short break, the reading would start again till the early morning hours. When his room-mate pleaded him to get some rest, he would say: No money, no food; and no time, no sleep!

Days rolled by, Dr Ambedkar's back-breaking research was coming to a fruition. He was awarded the degree of Master of Sciences (M.Sc) for his Thesis: "Provincial Decentralization of Imperial Finance in British India" in June 1921. It was a pre-requisite for the degree of Doctor of Science (D.Sc). In early 1922, he submitted his Dissertation entitled "The Problem of the Rupee" for his D.Sc degree. His supervisor this time was another eminent economist, Professor Edwin Cannon. It was expected that the approval of the submitted Dissertation would take four or five months. On June 28, 1922, Bhimrao was called to the Bar i.e., to become a Barrister.

In the meanwhile, Dr Ambedkar decided to pursue further studies in Germany. He began to study both German and French. On getting the necessary clearance from Bonn University, he left for Germany. Subsequently, however, his supervisor in London informed Dr Ambedkar that his London examiners had refused to approve his Doctoral Dissertation. He agreed to rewrite his dissertation without changing his conclusions. Since Bhimrao was running out of financial resources, there was no choice for him but to return to Mumbai, which he did on April 3, 1923. In the following 5 months, Dr Ambedkar revised his Dissertation and forwarded it to London (August 1923). In November 1923, he was informed by telegram that he was awarded the degree of Doctor of Science (D.Sc) in Economics. This Dissertation was published in the form of a book in the same year with a title: *The Problem of the Rupee: Its Origin and Its Solution.*

The book represents a highly significant contribution by Dr Ambedkar to the field of Monetary Economics. The book has been dedicated to the memory of his Father and Mother, as a token of his abiding gratitude for the sacrifices they made and the enlightenment they showed in the matter of (his) education.

Professor Edwin Cannon, Dr Ambedkar's Guide at the University of London (School of Economics) wrote the Foreword to the Book in which he says:

> I disagree with a good deal of his criticism.... I do not share Dr Ambedkar's hostility to the system, nor accept most of his arguments against it and its advocates. But he hits some nails very squarely on the head, and even when I have thought him quote wrong, I have found a stimulating freshness in his views and reasons.... In his practical conclusion, I am inclined to think, he is right.

The book was reprinted in 1947. In the Preface to the Second Edition, Dr Ambedkar wrote:

> I could not bring out a second edition of the book for the reason that my changeover from economics to politics left me no time to undertake such a task. I have, therefore, devised another plan: it is to bring out an up-to-date edition of the History of Indian Currency and Banking in two volumes, of which *The Problem of the Rupee* forms Volume one. Volume two will contain the History of Indian Currency and Banking from 1923 onwards.

Unfortunately, Dr Ambedkar could not find time to complete the second volume.

The Problem of the Rupee is truly a magnum opus. In this book Dr Ambedkar offers an excellent exposition of the evolution of the Indian currency in terms of its form as a medium of exchange and its equivalence in terms of precious metals, such as gold and silver. Unlike the treatises then available, Dr Ambedkar goes into the most neglected period extending from 1800 to 1893. With this historical perspective brought up to the early 1920s, Dr Ambedkar then focuses on one of the most perplexing problem at that time, viz., the choice of an appropriate currency system for India. It was in respect of the currency crisis of the 1920s that he crossed swords with influential economic thinkers like John Maynard Keynes.

Dr Ambedkar vehemently criticized Keynes and other supporters of the Gold Exchange Standard and argued in favour of the Gold Standard in a modified form. Dr Ambedkar proposed that all further coinage of the Rupee should be permanently prohibited; a suitable gold coin be minted; the ratio between the gold coin and the Rupee may be fixed by law and the Rupee and the gold coin should not be mutually convertible. In course of time, India would thus have Rupee as well as gold coins as unlimited legal tender, since the ratio between the gold coin and the rupee is fixed under law and the supply of gold is stable. He further argued that issue of currency would be regulated leading to stable prices and hence a stable currency standard.

I. THE EVOLUTION OF THE INDIAN RUPEE

Dr Ambedkar presents a lucid account of various stages in the evolution of the Indian Rupee:

> Since the time of Akbar, the founder of the economic system of the Moghul Empire in India, the money in India consisted primarily of gold and silver—the gold *mohur* and the silver *Rupee,* identical in weight, i.e., 175 grs. troy. The two bore a fixed ratio to the *dam* (the copper coin of the Moghul Empire) and hence circulated at a fixed ratio of exchange between them. In Southern India, to which part the influence of the Moghuls had not extended, silver, as a part of the currency, was quite unknown. Under the Hindu emperors, emphasis was laid on gold. The *pagoda,* the coin of the ancient Hindu kings, was the standard of value and also the medium of exchange.

In the general scramble for independence following the disintegration of the Moghul empire, the right to coinage was most wantonly abused. The country was filled with diverse coins presenting bewildering media of exchange. Different kingdoms proceeded to debase their coinage at will; as a consequence, the currency lost its primary quality of general and ready acceptability. With the fall of the Moghul empire, there ceased to be such a thing as an Imperial legal tender currency all through India. In its place there grew up local tenders currency only within the different Principalities into which the Empire was broken up. As a result, the bullion value of each coin had to be ascertained before it could be accepted as a final discharge of obligations, which gave rise to a Class of money-changers called *shroffs,* who specialized in the business of evaluating the coins at their proper discount from the standard purity by means of the dates and other characteristics engraved upon them.

Economic consequences of this plurality were obvious. Although the denomination of the coins was the same, their metallic contents differed significantly. Owing to this, one coin bore a discount or a premium in relation to another of the same name. In the absence of knowledge as to the amount of premium or discount, everyone preferred to receive a coin of the species known to him and current in his territory. As a result, the society sunk into a state of barter (i.e., direct exchange of commodities) which impeded trade and commerce. The task of evolving good money out of bad money, therefore, fell upon the shoulders of the East India Company which in the meanwhile had succeeded to the Moghul Empire in India.

British Consolidation of the Currency System

- The Directors of the East India Company in their famous Despatch, dated April 25, 1806 declared themselves in favour of mono-metallism as the ideal for the Indian currency and prescribed a rupee weighing 180 grs. troy and containing 165 grs. pure silver as the unit of the future currency.

The choice of a rupee weighing 180 grs. emanated from the desire to make it as little of a departure as possible from the rupee coin originally issued from the Moghul mints. "If the weight of the principal coin to be established was to be different from 180 grs. troy, it was believed, there would be an unhappy deviation from the ancient practice which made the weight of the coin the basis of other weights and measures." The choice had also in its favour the added convenience of assimilating the Indian with the English units of weight.

By the year 1833, the uniformity of coinage in India was an accomplished fact. Nothing more remained to carry it to completion than to discontinue the *Sicca* rupee (which weighed 192 grs. troy with silver content of 175.927 grs.) and to demonetize gold. At this point, however, arose a conflict between the Court of Directors and the three Presidency Governments in India (viz., Bombay, Bengal and Madras). Considerable reluctance was shown to the demonetization of gold. The Government of Madras, in fact, insisted upon continuing the coinage of gold along with that of the rupee and stoutly refused to deviate from the system of double legal tender at a fixed ratio prevalent in its territories....

In 1833, however, by an Act of British Parliament, an Imperial administrative system was set up with centralization of all Legislative and Executive authority over the whole of India. The Imperial Government, thus established, was anxious to issue an Imperial coinage in its own name. Accordingly, an early opportunity was taken and, by the Act of 1835, India was placed on a Silver Mono-metallic basis, with a Rupee weighing 180 grs. troy and containing 165 grs. fine silver as the common currency and the legal tender throughout the country.

Supplementing the Silver by Paper Currency

The adoption of silver mono-metallism, though well supported in 1835, proved to be a measure quite inadequate for the needs of the country soon after. According to Dr Ambedkar, this was on account of some structural changes in the economy, such as transition from a "kind economy" to "cash economy" and a rapid increase in external trade.

Under the native rulers, payments to Government employees (including the military) were made in kind which the British replaced by the currency. The Government, having undertaken to pay in cash, was compelled to collect all its taxes in cash. Each citizen being bound to pay in cash, in turn, stipulated to receive nothing but cash, so that there was a very significant transformation of a barter economy into a cash economy. Moreover, India's external trade which was restrained earlier on account of discriminatory tariffs and unjust navigation laws by the British, received a boost with the tariff reforms of 1842 and the repeal of the navigation laws. As a result, there was an increased demand for currency.

Unfortunately, it so happened that after 1850, although the total production of the precious metals had increased, that of silver had not kept pace with the needs of the world, a greater part of which was then on a silver basis. Moreover, India has long been notoriously the sink of the precious metals. A large part of the coined silver must have been abstracted from monetary to non-monetary purposes. This naturally exacerbated the monetary stringency.

The contraction of currency might not have been felt as severely as it did had there been credit money worth the name. Unfortunately, the banking system was not sufficiently developed. The main hindrance to the growth of banking system was the attitude of the East India Company; being itself a commercial body largely dealing in exchange, the company was averse to the development of banking institutions lest they should prove rivals.

The insufficiency of silver, and the want of credit money caused so much inconvenience to trade that there grew up a change in the attitude towards the Currency Act of 1835, and people, for once, began to ask whether... it would not have been better to have preferred Gold Mono-metallism to Silver Mono-metallism. As more and more of gold was imported and coined the stronger grew the demand for giving it a legal status in the existing system of Indian currency. According to Dr Ambedkar, it was unfortunate that this first attempt against the Silver Standard resulted not in the establishment of a Gold Standard, but in the introduction of a Government Paper Currency to supplement the existing Silver Standard.

As a matter of fact, every bank was at liberty earlier to issue its Notes. Notes of the three Presidency banks[21] enjoyed a status slightly superior to that enjoyed by the Notes of other banks in that they were accepted by the Government to some extent in payment of revenue—a privilege for which the Presidency banks had to submit to a stringent legislative control from which the other banks were immune. This freedom of issue however, was not exercised on a large scale, not even by the Presidency banks. It was this freedom that was taken away in 1861, and the power

21. The three Presidency banks were Bank of Bengal, Bank of Bombay and Bank of Madras. The three were amalgamated in 1921 to form the Imperial Bank of India which was later (in 1955) converted into the State Bank of India.

of Note issue was entrusted to the management of a Government department for the whole of India called the Department of Paper Currency.

The Department of Paper Currency, however, had no more discretion in the matter of Paper Currency than the Mint Master had in the matter of metallic currency. The Paper Currency was backed mainly by silver up to the extent of 51 to 63 per cent of the total during 1862 to 1891, and by Government Securities for much of the remainder, the interest thereon being the only source of profit to the Government.

The Paper Currency did not assume a large proportion of the total. Dr Ambedkar attributed it to the following two reasons:

> (1) The lowest denomination (i.e., Rs 10) was too large to displace the metallic currency. In a country where the average range of transactions did not exceed Re 1 and were as low as one *anna* or even lower, it is possible to expect that Paper Currency could not, to any great extent, figure on the dealings of the people. Even Rs 5 Notes, the issue of which was first sanctioned in the year 1871, were not low enough to penetrate into the economic life of the people. (2) The other impediment to the increase of Paper Currency was the difficulty of encashing Notes. For the purposes of the Paper Currency, the country was divided into a number of Circles of issue. Notes issued in a Circle were not a legal tender outside the issuing Circle nor were they encashable outside the Circle. This want of universal encashability proved to be a great hindrance to the popularity of the Notes.

According to Dr Ambedkar, the currency system based on the Silver Standard augmented by paper currency was a failure for it did not lead to stability of value of the currency. He points out that the Indian money market was subject to "convulsions and sudden transitions". Indeed, the rate of discount exhibited abnormal fluctuations.[22] In order that money may be had at a uniform price, its supply should be regulated according to the variations in the demand for it. The explanation for the abnormal fluctuations in the discount rate, according to him, is to be sought in the irregularity of the money supply.

In respect of the demand for money, Dr Ambedkar argues,

> A distinction needs to be made between the changes induced therein by the growth of population, trade, etc., and fluctuations which occur within the course of a year owing to seasonal influences.[23] India is pre-eminently a country subject to seasonal swings. Mid-summer is naturally a period of diminished activity, while autumn brings

22. For example, the rate of discount of the Bank of Bengal for private paper (30 days) was revised 13 times per year on average during the period, 1876 to 1883 and ranged between 5.5 per cent and 14.5 per cent.
23. A modern-day analyst would categorize these changes as secular and seasonal respectively.

> renewed vigour in all activities of social and economic life. Production, consumption and, to an extent, even distribution is seasonal in character. All these generate a kind of rhythm in the social demand for money, rising at certain periods of the year and falling at others.

Money supply accordingly must be regulated in tandem with seasonal variations in demand for money. The Indian currency system prevailing then, however, made no provision for such elasticity.

According to Dr Ambedkar, year-to-year variations (i.e., secular changes) in money demand call for "steadiness and expansibility" of the currency which could be readily furnished by a metallic currency. On the other hand, seasonal variations in money demand call for elasticity of currency which could be provided by the Paper Money. Unfortunately, the Paper Currency Act placed a rigid limit upon the volume of its issue regardless of any changes in the volume of the demand, which, according to Dr Ambedkar, restrained the elasticity of the currency, thereby, leading to abnormal fluctuations in the discount rate. Dr Ambedkar points out that a similar limit on issue of currency Notes was also placed in England and yet there were no abnormal fluctuations in the discount rate there. He attributed it to the fact that whereas English banks have succeeded in implanting the cheque system of using credit in place of the Note system, Indian banks have unfortunately failed, owing to illiteracy and the lack of a banking system conducting its banking business in the vernacular of the people.

Dr Ambedkar succinctly observes:

> In an economy in which almost every businessman must rely, at certain seasons, if not all the year around, on borrowed capital, the margin of profit may be wiped out by a sudden rise, or augmented by a sudden fall in the rate of discount leading to under-trading or over-trading. Such fluctuations increase business risks, lead to higher business expenses and a greater cost to the consumer. They bring about swings in prices, promote speculation, and prepare for panics.

Curiously, however, no serious attempts were made in India to alleviate the sufferings inflicted on the trading community.

Dislocation of Rupee-Sterling Parity

Prior to 1870, England and Portugal were exclusively on a Gold Standard, whereas India and countries of western Europe were exclusively on a Silver Standard. Notwithstanding the differences in their metallic standards, the exchange rate between the Rupee and Sterling was stable prior to 1873, at Re 1 = 1 shilling and 10½ pence. This, of course, was merely a reflection of the gold-silver exchange ratio being stable prior to 1873 at 1 to 15½. After 1873, the Rupee-Sterling exchange rate parity was dislocated as the gold-silver exchange ratio lost its old moorings. In fact, the value of the Rupee steadily depreciated reaching as low as Re 1 = 1 shilling and 3 pence in 1892-93.

Two explanations were offered for this phenomenon. First, demonetization of silver as a medium of exchange by the principal countries of the world,[24] and secondly, the increase in the production of silver as compared to gold. In the former case, contraction of demand for silver was said to be responsible for decline in its value whereas in the latter case, it was the excess supply of silver that was said to be the culprit. Dr Ambedkar carefully weighed evidence in favour of these hypotheses. With a detailed statistics of relative production of gold and silver, he concluded that the decline in the value of the Rupee was not brought about by the excess supply of silver and accepted the view that had there been no demonetization of silver after 1873, the ratio between gold and silver would have probably been preserved as it was during the monetary disturbances of the earlier period.

This rupture of the exchange parity had far-reaching economic consequences for India. India was "a silver-standard country intimately bound to a Gold Standard country, so that her economic and financial values of gold and silver…governed the rupee-sterling exchange." Dr Ambedkar presents a detailed discussion of consequences of the dislocation of the exchange parity:

> The fall in the value of the rupee increased the burden on the Government of India. England being a Gold Standard country, Government of India's payments to England on account of maintenance of European troops, interest on debt and the like had to be made in gold. But the revenues of the Government of India out of which these payments were met were received in silver. As such, the burden on the Government of India increased *pari passu* with the fall in the gold value of silver. The situation was exacerbated further by even growing gold payments. As a result, the rupee cost of the gold payments grew both by reason of the growth in their magnitude, and also by reason of the contraction of the medium, i.e., the appreciation of gold, in which they were payable.

This led to a fiscal policy of high taxation and rigid economy in the finances of the Government. Especially regrettable was the inability of the Government, owing to its financial difficulties, to find money for useful public works.

> Like all governments of poor peoples, the Government of India had therefore, to turn to wealthier countries that had surplus capital to lend. All these countries unfortunately happened to be on the Gold Standard. As long as it was possible to say that so much gold was equal to so much silver, the English investor was indifferent whether the

24. The free coinage of silver was suspended by Germany (1871), USA, Sweden and Denmark (1873), Norway, and Holland (1875), the Latin Union Countries i.e., France, Belgium, Italy, Switzerland and Greece (1878), and Russia and Austria (1878-79). The demonetization of silver, strangely, grew out of a movement towards achieving uniformity in weights and measures of silver coins across the countries.

securities of the Government of India were rupee securities or sterling securities. But the fall in the gold value of silver was also a fall on the gold value of the rupee securities, and what was once a secure investment ceased to be so any more. This placed the Government on a difficult position in the matter of financing its public work.

Consequently, the common people had to suffer.
According to Dr Ambedkar,

> One avenue of escape from the ravages of recurring famines, to which India so pitifully succumbed at such frequent intervals, was the diversification of her industries. To be of any permanent benefit, such diversified industrial life could be based on a capitalistic basis alone. But that depended upon the flow of capital into the country as freely as the needs of the country required. As matters then stood, the English investor, the largest purveyor of capital, looked upon the investment of capital in India as a risky proposition. It was feared that once the capital was spread out in a silver country every fall in the price of silver should not only make the return uncertain when drawn in gold, but would also reduce the capital value of his investment in terms of gold, which was naturally the unit in which he measured all his returns and his outlays. This check to the free inflow of capital was undoubtedly the most serious evil arising out of the rupture of the par of exchange.

Dr Ambedkar also points out,

> Far more disturbing than the fall (in the value of rupee) were the fluctuations which accompanied the fall. Owing to such fluctuations, no (exchange) rate could be assumed in the Budget which was likely to turn out to be the true market rate. As matters stood, the rate realized on an average during a particular year differed so widely from the Budget rate that the finances of the Government became a veritable gamble.

The fall in the value of the rupee had quite a different effect on the trade and industry in India. The foreign trade showed a significant buoyancy after 1870. Indeed, during the period, 1870-71 through 1891-92, exports rose from Rs 5.7 Crore to 11.1 Crore whereas imports increased from Rs. 4.0 Crore to 8.4 Crore. The industrial composition was also greatly altered. Reversing the earlier trend, "India once again began to assume the role of a manufacturing country" (p. 428), rather than an agricultural and a raw material-producing country. Cotton and jute manufactures received a significant fillip. During this period, India's trade to the Far East expanded substantially.

These developments were widely attributed to two factors: First, the depreciation of the rupee stimulated exports from and hindered imports into the silver-using countries and, secondly, it exposed English producers more than others to competition from their rivals in silver-using countries (on account of the over-valued sterling). Dr Ambedkar did not accept this reasoning in its entirety. He argued that the fall in the gold price of silver was a reflection of the more sweeping changes in the general price levels of the two countries, i.e. the fall of the English prices which were measured in gold and the rise of the Indian prices which were measured in silver. "The conclusion, therefore, is that the falling exchange (rate) could not have disturbed established trade relations or displaced the commodities that entered into international trade. The utmost that could be attributed to it is its incidence in economic incentive." Such economic incentive to Indians was said to be provided by bringing about changes in the social distribution of wealth. In the case of England, where prices were falling, it was the employer who suffered; in the case of India, where prices were rising, it was the wage-earner who suffered. In both cases, there was an injustice done to a part of the community, and an easy case for the reform of currency was made out. Dr Ambedkar points out,

> The need for a currency reform was recognized in England; but in India many people seemed averse to it. To some, the stability of the Silver Standard had made a powerful appeal, for they failed to find any evidence of Indian prices having risen above the level of 1873. To others, the bounty of the falling exchange was too great a boon to be easily given away by stabilizing the exchange. The falsity of both the views is patent.

According to Dr Ambedkar,

> Prices in India did rise and that too considerably. Bountry perhaps there was, but it was a penalty on the wage earner. Thus viewed, the need for the reform of Indian currency was far more urgent than could have been said of the English currency... from the point of (its) incidence on the distribution of wealth, very little can be said in favour of a standard which changes its value and which becomes the *via media* of transferring wealth from the relatively poor to the relatively rich.

Besides, private trade became more or less a matter of speculation.

> Fluctuations in exchange are, of course, a common incidence of international trade. But if they are not to produce discontinuity in trade and industry, there must be definite limits to such fluctuation. If the limits are ascertainable, trade would be reasonably certain in its calculation, and speculation in exchange would be limited within the known limits of deviations from an established par. Whereas, on the other hand, the limits are known, all calculations of trade are frustrated and speculation in exchange takes the place of legitimate trading.

According to Dr Ambedkar, with the rupture of the fixed par of exchange and the resultant fluctuations in the value of the standard measure, "Trade advanced by rushes and pauses and speculation became feverishly active."

II. GOLD STANDARD VERSUS GOLD EXCHANGE STANDARD

The establishment of stable monetary conditions was dependent upon the restoration of a common standard of value. Since all important countries of the world had gone over to the Gold Standard, according to Dr Ambedkar, it would have been appropriate to abandon Silver Standard in favour of the Gold Standard. But by an unkind turn of events, the currency system which grew up in place of the Gold Standard was actually the so-called "Gold Exchange Standard".

Dr Ambedkar provides a detailed and critical account of various proposals submitted for the reform of the Indian currency system, the Temple Plan (1872), the Smith Plan (1876), the Government of India Scheme (1886), Herschell Committee (1892), Fowler Committee (1898) and so on. According to him, "The Government did not start to establish a Gold Exchange Standard. Rather, it was contemplating the establishment of a true Gold Standard," but it ended up establishing the Gold Exchange Standard at the hands of men who "inadequately understood" the true Gold Standard.

Dr Ambedkar then goes on to provide an insightful discussion of the relative merits and demerits of the Gold Standard vis-à-vis the Gold Exchange Standard:

> The pure Gold Standard comprises use of gold in some form, especially coins, as a medium of exchange. In its variant called Gold-Convertible Standard, Paper Money is also issued in addition to gold coins and is pledged to be redeemable in gold. In contrast, under the Gold Exchange Standard, the medium of exchange comprises only paper money which is kept exchangeable at fixed rates with gold and authorities back it up with foreign currency reserves of such countries as are on the Gold Standard.

★ ★ ★

In the controversy regarding the relative effectiveness of these currency standards in the Indian context, Dr Ambedkar crossed swords with Keynes. In his treatise Indian Currency and Finance (1909), Keynes had favoured the Gold Exchange Standard and maintained that the Gold Exchange Standard contains an essential element as the ideal standard of the future Dr Ambedkar vehemently criticized Keynes and other supporters of the Gold Exchange Standard and argued in favour of the Gold Standard in a modified form.

Dr Ambedkar argues that the Gold Exchange Standard does not have the stability of the Gold Standard. Under the Gold Standard, additions to the supply of currency are so small that stability is not affected. On the other hand, under the Gold Exchange Standard, additions are dependent upon the will of the issuer and can be augmented to such an extent that stability could be jeopardized. He provided statistical evidence to show that in the Indian context, prices varied much less under the Gold Standard than under the Gold Exchange Standard. The supporters of the Gold Exchange Standard, like Keynes, had argued that the Gold Standard is a hard standard as it ties mankind to the wheel of nature, and that the Gold Exchange Standard allows an escape from this frigidity. Dr Ambedkar's counter-argument was that there must be some regulator by which the discretion left to the issuer is regulated. Under the Gold Exchange Standard, the discretion left to the issuer is unregulated and is, therefore, undesirable. To the argument that the Gold Exchange Standard economizes on gold, Dr Ambedkar reasoned that economizing of gold raises its supply, thereby lowering its value and, as a depreciating commodity, it becomes unfit to that extent to function as a standard of value.

He proposed that all further coinage of the rupee should be permanently prohibited; a suitable gold coin be minted; the ratio between the gold coin and the rupee may be fixed by law and the rupee and the gold coin should not be mutually convertible. In course of time, India would thus have rupee as well as gold coins as unlimited legal tender, since the ratio between the gold coin and the rupee is fixed under law and the supply of gold is stable. He further argued that issue of currency would be regulated leading to stable prices and hence a stable currency standard.

★ ★ ★

Dr Ambedkar was now a Barrister with two Doctoral Degrees in Economics—Ph.D from Columbia University in the USA, and D.Sc from London School of Economics—a feat that was exceedingly difficult for anybody, and simply incredible for an Untouchable!

What Bhimrao acquired in the United States went way beyond the formal advanced education culminating into a Doctorate. His thought process widened immensely. The egalitarian individualism of Thomas Paine made a deep impression on his mind. Abraham Lincoln made a great impact on him. He was very impressed with the 14th Amendment to the Constitution of US which declared the freedom for the Blacks in America. He was also moved by Booker T Washington's approach of promoting education as a means of African-American emancipation. It is, therefore, fair to say that Dr Ambedkar acquired in the United States "a strong, unwavering belief in the power of democratic institutions to bring about social equality."[25]

25. Zelliot, Eleanor, (1992).

PART II

SCHOLAR IN MASS MOVEMENT (1924-30)

CHAPTER SIX

Initiating a Mass Movement

BACK HOME IN India, Dr Babasaheb Ambedkar faced the problems of setting up a household, with his wife and child, as well as his sister-in-law and his nephew as dependants. To start his law practice, he had registered at the Mumbai High Court (on the Appellate side) in June 1923. Unable to afford an office near the High Court in South Mumbai, Dr Ambedkar set up an office at Damodar Hall in Parel with the help of contributions from friends. It took months to get his first case. The so-called high-Caste Hindus were reluctant to give him cases. Much later, in June 1925, he managed to get a part-time job teaching Mercantile Law at the Botliboi Accountancy Institute (where he served till end-March 1928; salary: Rs 200 per month) and also earned some supplementary income as an examiner for Bombay University.

BAHISHKRIT HITAKARINI SABHA

On March 9, 1924 Dr Ambedkar took the first step towards initiating a mass movement by forming a social organization for the Depressed Classes which he called the *Bahishkrit Hitakarini Sabha,* with himself as the Chairman of its Managing Committee.[26] The motto of the organization: "Educate, Organize and Agitate" was going to resonate in India for decades. The stated objectives of this organization were to promote the spread of education, *inter alia,* by opening hostels; to promote the spread of culture by opening libraries, social centres or study circles; to improve economic conditions by starting Industrial and Agricultural Schools; and to represent the grievances of the Depressed Classes. The *Sabha* initially started a small library in Parel and a hostel for Depressed Class students in Solapur (January, 1925). It also began to holding rallies and meetings throughout the Bombay Presidency.

26. A number of highly distinguished Touchables were office-bearers, namely, Sir Chamanlal Setalvad (President) and Dr RP Paranjpye as well as BG Kher as Vice Presidents (Fifteen years later Shri BG Kher became the Prime Minister for the Bombay Province).

In his early speeches, Dr Ambedkar clearly set out his mission and explicitly carved out a role for himself. In the speech (March 9, 1924) before a group of social workers in the meeting that founded *Bahishkrit Hitakarini Sabha,* Dr Ambedkar announced:

> I am going to work hard with complete honesty to ensure an all-round development of the Depressed Classes. It is for this purpose that I have acquired so much knowledge. I would certainly not limit the use of the power of my intellect only to my family and my Caste. I will render them to the benefit of entire Depressed Classes, to help them build their social movement and struggle.
>
> The challenges lying before the Untouchables are formidable. I am aware that I may not be able to solve all their problems. But I am confident that I can pose these challenges before the world and bring our agony to their notice. The challenges before the Untouchables are like the mighty Himalayas. I am going to bang my head against these Himalayas. So please remember that even if I am not able to bring down the Himalayas, seven crore Untouchables, on witnessing my bloodied head, would be ready to sacrifice their lives to bring the Himalayas down. However, if you continue to encourage hostile feelings among yourselves, then not only I, but even God, will not be able to help you.

Likewise, while addressing a Conference of the Depressed Classes [27] Dr Ambedkar said:

> I consider it to be my duty to bring out publicly the intellectual trickery of this (i.e. Brahmin) Class to keep the Untouchables away from them, because I am a stick in the hands of my blind masses.

Another set of Dr Ambedkar's early speeches was focussed on awakening self-respect among the Depressed Classes. "Lack of collective willpower is holding us back," he said. On January 1, 1927, Dr Ambedkar addressed a meeting at Koregaon War Memorial,[28] near Pune and reminded his Untouchable *Mahar* followers how

---

27. Satara District *Mahar* Conference, Rahimatpur (District: Satara) (May, 1926). For details, see *Ambedkar Speaks* (Ed. Jadhav Narendra) Vol.I. p.36.
28. Marathi Speech; Meeting at the Koregaon War Memorial, Koregaon near Pune, (January 1, 1927).
    English Report: Keer, BAWS Vol.17 (3), pp.3-7.
    Koregaon War Memorial is an obelisk—65 feet high, standing on a stone platform of about 32 sq. feet. The War Memorial was erected by the British to commemorate mostly *Mahar* soldiers who "fought tenaciously and with magnificent courage" in a great fight on January 1, 1818 between the British forces—very small in number, led by Capt Stawton and the Army of Peshwa Bajirao II led by General Gokhale, which was several times larger in size. The British forces, comprising mostly of *Mahar* soldiers "fought without rest or respite, food or water, continuously for twelve hours." This action of "heroic valour and enduring fortitude" displaying "disciplined intrepidity" and "devoted

their forefathers had fought tenaciously and with magnificent courage. Dr Ambedkar later reminded them: "We are no slaves, we are a warrior clan. Nothing is more disgraceful for a brave man than to live a life devoid of self-respect and without the love for the country."

Yet another set of Dr Ambedkar's early speeches were aimed at creating political awareness among the Depressed Classes. In his Nipani Speech (April 11, 1925) Dr Ambedkar informed his followers about the *Satyagraha* launched by Untouchables at Vaikom, Kerala and the efforts that Gandhiji was making personally to arrive at a compromise.[29] In one of these rare occasions when Dr Ambedkar spoke positively about Mahatma Gandhi, his comments were:

> Mahatma Gandhi is only statesman in our country to have said that ending this type (i.e., Touchable – Untouchable) of segregation and division is of utmost importance and we must fight against the social injustice in our country. Every Indian should strive towards this end as a fundamental duty.

Gandhiji maintained, Dr Ambedkar said, that social and political issues are one and the same speech, almost apologetically. Dr Ambedkar adds: "When everyone is shunning us, the sympathy shown by Mahatma Gandhi is no less."

Most importantly, Dr Ambedkar, for the first time, fully spelt out his vision for Untouchables in the context of *Swaraj* early on (May 24, 1924) stating, "If *Swaraj* is coming, we must get equal political rights in it."

Explaining that Untouchability is worse than slavery, he said:[30]

> It is our good fortune that we Untouchables were not deemed to be slaves. Otherwise, we would have been traded like grocery, commodities, or farm animals.... Untouchability is in fact worse than slavery. History is replete with examples wherein slaves were liberated and then became independent citizens of the State. But there is not a single example in India, where Untouchables became Touchable. Roman slavery was time bound and there were many ways to get liberated from it. On the contrary, Untouchability (in India) is eternal and there is no way to get liberated from it. Because of the strict rule that an Untouchable is Untouchable by birth, centuries have passed and yet the situation has not changed at all. In several other respects, Untouchability in India is worse than slavery in ancient Rome. Untouchability is several times a greater hurdle in the path of progress of the Untouchables in India, than slavery was for Romans....

---

courage and admirable constancy" won great renown for the *Mahar* soldiers. The names of the *Mahar* soldiers killed and wounded have been inscribed on the Monument.

29. For fuller summary, see *Ambedkar Speaks* (Ed. Jadhav Narendra), Vol 1, pp.79-82.
30. Marathi Speech, Conference of Depressed Classes from Bombay Province, Barshi, District Solapur (May 24, 1924). For English translation, see *Ambedkar Speaks* (Ed. Jadhav, Narendra, 2013) Vol. III, pp.49-53.

In the same speech, Dr Ambedkar discussed various options for the Depressed Classes to come out of Untouchability, including mass conversion to another religion. He said:

> Such is a travesty of Untouchability that all people have heeded their attention to the task of eradicating Untouchability. Many ways are being suggested. Sometimes, we are told that Untouchables should migrate to another country altogether.... But it is not possible for all our people to migrate. Very few people would be able to do it. Therefore, we must search for ways of eradication of Untouchability, by staying in the confines of this Country. The second option is that of Conversion. We should look at any religion with rationality and pragmatism. In the context of philosophy, the Hindu religion is as good as any other religion, even better. 'There is the same soul in all human beings'—is the fundamental principle of Hindu philosophy. If our social constitution was in reality, actually a reflection of this noble thought, then Hindus would have definitely treated all citizens with equal respect. However, this has not happened.... Where is the convergence between thought and action? We worship and uphold the same Vedic philosophy and yet, they hate us. Not only that, they treat us lower than even animals. Why respect a religion which does not respect human beings? Why stick to religion which keeps us away from material prosperity and pushes us in to despair and despondency?
>
> Besides conversion and migration, there is yet another alternative being talked about, that is, change of names. Recently, it has been suggested that the Untouchables should call themselves Adi-Hindus.... I do not understand the insistence.... If the purpose behind this is to unite all Untouchable Castes, then isn't the term 'Excluded' well suited for that purpose? If you feel that Untouchability will vanish by such tricks, then that is only an illusion.... In my view, Untouchability and Caste-distinctions are embedded in names and, therefore, we must get rid of our names. But it would not be enough if this phenomenon is confined only to Untouchable Hindus. All people should leave their Caste indicating names and adopt a common name.... That way no one will treat each other lowly; sympathy among the people will not be based on Caste affiliation but will be free from discrimination.

In the same speech, Dr Ambedkar heartily welcomed the possibility of attaining the Independence. He said:

> That will be the historic day when all these transformations will really take place. But the big question is how to make this transition actually happen. Sometimes amelioration of social injustice takes place only under the initiative of the Governments. British Government had decided not to interfere in the Caste System and Customs. In this context, a welcome development is the possibility to attaining Independence for our country.
>
> Our people are somehow afraid of the Independence, and they feel Peshwa rule will return after the Independence. It must be remembered that there is a big difference. Peshwa did not rule with consent of people, they rule by hereditary regimes. It wasn't peoples' rule. In future, no State will rule without the consent of the people. *Swaraj* with the consent of people at large is the best possible political system. I am rather

surprised that our people are apprehensive about such a rule. We must clearly understand what *Swaraj,* that is, Independence, portends.

We must pursue this issue. If Independence is attained, then we must get equal rights as everyone else, and to achieve that we must secure the right to vote. Today right to vote is so limited that only about two per cent people are qualified to vote. Securing the right to vote will help us in two ways. One the Legislative Council will no longer ignore our plight. Those people who get elected because of our votes, will not be able to overlook our interests. Moreover, it will no longer be possible to maintain the *Varnashram Dharma*. If a Brahmin has to beg for votes from Untouchables, what would remain of the *Varnashram Dharma*? It will also be a great assault on the Caste System. We must accept this course to begin with.

Dr Ambedkar underscored the need for an organization of Untouchables. He said:

It is not enough to enunciate sound principles underlying the broad objectives that we set before ourselves. What is more important is to create an institutional framework that will pursue implementation of those principles. All this leads me to think that we must create a wide-ranging organization of Untouchables. Two purposes could be served by this organization. First, we will be able to collect funds for the public purpose. Some people doubt our ability to lead this movement because we are poor. Yes, our people are poor. But if only two lakh people out of the 24 lakh population give eight *annas (*roughly 50 paisa), then annual fund will be around one lakh rupees. Our community is poor but it is strong in terms of number. If we could collect rupees one lakh every year, then the progress of our community will not take much time. But this calls for creation of one centralized institution which will not only deal with fund collection, but will also help in attracting attention of people. This organization should start collecting funds and use it for development of Untouchables. It is not enough to keep complaining about thus we should make conscious efforts aimed at increasing capability of our people. If there is equality in virtues then the Caste-based discrimination and Untouchability will disappear over time.

From the viewpoint of our country, these are extra-ordinary times. The process of laying of the foundation of *Swaraj* began in 1917. Since then this country has witnessed formation of three groups: (1) European, (2) *Musalman*, (3) Hindu. Before 1917, Muslims had a volatile relationship with Hindus but that has been reversed. Together, both have taken their own share from British in the form of independence. But now there are tensions between the two groups. Issue that has been agitating their minds is which community gets a larger share of the incipient *Swaraj*. Obviously, the group with a larger population would get proportionately larger share. In this struggle the spotlight is increasingly coming to Untouchables. Both groups have realized the importance of number that we have. If we continue to remain Hindus, then alone this country will be able to perpetuate the Aryan culture, on the other hand, if we convert ourselves to Islam, this country will have dominance of Islamic culture.

Both Hindus and Muslims seem to recognize this fully well. If it were not the case, Brahmins would not have come forward to undertake *Satyagraha* for Untouchables at Vaikom nor would have the Muslims been willing to spend crores of rupees to welcome us in their religion. Although we are at the rock bottom of the Indian society, in this conflict of cultures (that is, Aryan v/s Islamic), our numbers are critical and, therefore, if we create organizational strength, we certainly would have a great bargaining power.

While concluding, Dr Ambedkar made an earnest appeal to his followers. He said:

Our community is backward in all respects. Financially it is weak; it is lacking in confidence. It is very difficult to say what would be the future of our people who are suffering from political, social, and religious inequality and injustice; who are lost in ignorance, and who are at complete loss of direction in their lives. That is precisely why those who do understand this grave situation and those who have a sense of duty must come forward and selflessly devote themselves to the betterment of Untouchable masses.

My educated Brothers, if you want your future generations to remember you with respect and regards, if you want the condition of your children and grandchildren to be better than the situation that you have been in, please do come forward. It is your solemn duty to do our very best so as to rectify the situation.

★ ★ ★

Interestingly, while being fully devoted to the cause of upliftment of the Untouchables, Dr Ambedkar remained highly active as a Professional Economist.

CONTRIBUTION AS A PROFESSIONAL ECONOMIST

In April 1925, Dr Ambedkar published an exceedingly important research paper on a subject of great contemporary relevance. This two-part paper was titled:[31] "The Present Problem in Indian Currency: 2 Shilling Versus 1s. 4d. Ratio".

According to Dr Ambedkar, the then controversy about the Indian Rupee involved two distinct questions: (a) Should we stabilize our exchange; and (b) What should be the ratio at which we should stabilize? As to the first question, Dr Ambedkar argued:

If Rupees in India rise in purchasing power or remain stationary or rise less rapidly while pounds in England fall in purchasing power (i.e. if the Indian price level falls relatively to the English price level) fewer Rupees would be worth as much as a pound. In other words, when Rupee price in India will fall the exchange value of the Rupee in terms of the pound will rise. Contrariwise, if Rupees in India fall in purchasing power while pounds in England rise in purchasing power or remain stationary or fall

31. For fuller summary of the paper, see Jadhav Narendra (ed.), *Ambedkar Writes* (2013) Vol II, pp. 348–57.

less rapidly (i.e. if the Indian price level rises relatively to the English price level) fewer pounds would be worth as much a Rupee. In other words, when Rupee prices in India will rise, the exchange value of the Rupee will fall… as a general proposition the exchange ratio of two units of account is on a par with the exchange ratio of their purchasing powers. This is in short the doctrine of Purchasing Power Parity as an explanation of a particular exchange ratio between two currencies or units of account.

According to Dr Ambedkar:

Grossly absurd and foolish is the view that the exchange ratio of a unit of account is determined not by its purchasing power but by the balance of trade. This view is a pure inversion of cause and effect.

If you want to stabilize exchange, you must control the purchasing powers of the two currencies concerned, so that their movements will be alike in depth as well as in direction. To stabilize exchange we must have therefore some controlling instrument which would act as a common regulator bringing about proportionate changes in the two currencies in the same direction. Hitherto one such good instrument had been found and that was a common Gold Standard. That standard has now been destroyed all over the world except in the United States. Consequently, an automatic stable exchange on the basis of a Gold Standard is impossible for the present, except with the United States.

There is no doubt that stabilization will promote… the revival of international credit and the movement of capital to where it is most required. But there is no doubt that the benefit to be derived will not be worth the cost involved. Our external transactions are infinitesimal as compared to our internal transactions. To dislocate our internal arrangements by constant changes in our price level to preserve external parity is too big a price for a gain which is after all paltry…. By consenting to move our price level in sympathy with theirs we would be committing our welfare to the care of bankrupt governments and their desperate ministers. A currency which is managed on a basis approved by science would no doubt do the best.

As to the second question, regarding the rate at which to stabilize the currency, Dr Ambedkar argued:

I would choose 1s. 6d. as the ratio at which we should stabilize if we can and for the following reasons. It would indeed be better if we can stabilize our prices as well as our exchange. But because other countries cannot stabilize their price levels there is no reason why we should not adopt measures that will give us stable prices at home which is really the most that is to be got out of a currency medium. In my opinion we should stabilize our prices forthwith by linking the Rupee to gold at 1s. 6d. sterling. European countries will soon realize that it is insane to reach back to pre-War parities with gold and will learn that in matters of currency the real at any given time is the natural and normal…. How can we most nearly maintain stability after we have attained it is more worthy of our consideration than the question of attaining stability.

Dr Ambedkar also published that year a "no non-sense" hard hitting review of a book titled, *Indian Currency and Exchange* which is clearly indicative of the exacting standards that he expected from academicians and researchers. The real moment of professional glory came with the arrival in India of the Royal Commission on Currency and Finance.

Royal Commission on Indian Currency and Finance—also known as the Hilton Young Commission—came to India and submitted its Report in 1926. It was on the recommendations of this Report that the Reserve Bank of India was founded on April 1, 1935. Dr Ambedkar submitted a Statement of Evidence to the Commission, in response to the Questionnaire issued by them. Dr Ambedkar's authority and expertise in Monetary Economics is fully reflected in this Statement of Evidence.[32]

According to Dr Ambedkar:

> Gold Exchange Standard cannot be continued with any advantage to India and for the following reasons: The Gold Exchange Standard does not have the native stability of the Gold. The Gold Exchange Standard is economical. But for that very reason it is insecure. It will certainly not do if it is not secure. You cannot both economize gold, and also use it as a standard. If you want to economize gold, then you must abandon gold as a standard of value. In other words, the economy of the Exchange Standard is incompatible with its security. The choice, therefore, can never be between a Gold Standard and an Exchange Standard. I think the Gold Standard must be accepted as the only system of currency which is 'knave proof' and 'fool proof'.

Regarding the next important question of the Gold Reserve, Dr Ambedkar pointed out:

> I do want to say that there are many people who are under the impression that the introduction of a Gold Standard means merely the starting of a mint and the issuing of a gold coin. Nothing can be more erroneous than this. Gold Standard means not the starting of a gold mint but making provision whereby gold will become current. For currency is the standard. Now in order that gold may be current, it is necessary that other forms of currency must be limited in their volume. There are two ways by which currency may be limited. One way is to make it convertible and the other is to fix a positive limit on its issue.
>
> I prefer the fixity of issue system. My reasons are two: One of the evils of the Exchange Standard is that it is subject to management. Now a convertible system is also a managed system. Therefore, by adopting the convertible system we do not get rid of the evil of management which is really the bane of the present system. A fixed issue system besides eliminating management will make provision for a larger use of gold in currency. Besides at the present time there is no necessity to economise gold, because there is all over the world such a great plethora of money that the less we economise gold the better. The Exchange Standard, once a boon, is now a curse. It

32. For fuller summary of the Statement, see Jadhav Narendra: *Ambedkar Writes,* Vol. II, pp. 360-67.

> served a useful purpose for some time. From 1873 the production of gold had fallen off and the economy affected by the Exchange Standard was indeed very welcome. But after 1910 conditions changed and the production of gold increased with the result that the continuance of the Exchange Standard thereafter not only did not help the countries to check the rise of prices but became a direct cause of the rise of prices.

The following then were the requirements of Dr Ambedkar's plan for the reform of the Indian currency:

(a) Stop the coinage of Rupees by absolutely closing the mints to the Government as they are to the public.
(b) Open a gold mint for the coinage of a suitable gold coin.
(c) Fix a ratio between the gold coin and the rupee.
(d) Rupee not to be convertible in gold, and gold not to be convertible in rupees, but both to circulate as unlimited legal tender at the ratio fixed by law.

Turning to the question next in importance, namely, "The ratio between Gold and Rupee", Dr Ambedkar reasoned:

> There is but this difference between India and the other countries. The other countries have yet to reach the pre-War parity. India, on the other hand, has in fact overreached the pre-War parity. In European countries the problem is one of deflating the currency, i.e., appreciating it; in other words of bringing about a fall in prices. In India the problem becomes one of inflating the currency, i.e., depreciating it; in other words of bringing about a rise in prices. For a change from 1s. 6d. gold to 1s. 4d. gold means this and nothing else.
>
> There are some people who are under the impression that the restoration of pre-War parity would give justice and would also give us the old price level to which we were so long accustomed. Both these views are fallacious. First: the restoration of pre-War parity is not a restoration of the pre-War price level. For it is to be remembered that 1s. 4d. gold in 1925 is not the same thing as 1s. 4d. gold in 1914, if measured in terms of purchasing power. The same ratio of exchange does not necessarily mean the same level of purchasing power. The ratio between two currencies may remain the same though their respective volumes have undergone enormous changes, provided the variations in volumes are equal and in the same sense. This is exactly the result of a mere nominal restoration of the pre-War parity. If by restoring pre-War parity is meant the restoration of the pre-War level of prices then the ratio instead of being lowered from 1s.6d. in the direction of 1s. 4d. must be raised in the direction of 2s. gold. In other words, instead of an inflation there must be a further deflation of the currency. Second: the restoration of pre-War parity even nominally would be unjust. As a standard of deferred payment a currency should not disturb monetary contracts.
>
> Given these two facts the best solution would be to strike an average between 1s. 4d. and 1s. 6d., and to see that it is nearer 1s. 6d. and away from 1s. 4d. If it is realized that low exchange means high internal prices, it will at once become clear that this gain is not a gain to the nation coming from outside, but is a gain from one Class at the cost of another Class in the country. Now the Class that suffers is the poor

labouring Class, which pays the bounty to the richer or the business Class. Such a transference of wealth from the poor to the rich can never be in the general interest of the country. I am, therefore, strongly opposed to high prices and low exchange, and no righteous Government should be party to such clandestine picking of the pockets of the poorer Classes in the country.

CHAPTER SEVEN

In the Bombay Provincial Legislative Council (1)

BY THE YEAR 1926, while the mass movement initiated by Dr Ambedkar was beginning to gain momentum, on the family front the difficulties were unending. In July 1926, there was yet another rude shock to the family when the newly born child, named Rajratna, died. In a letter to a friend, Dr Ambedkar wrote:

> There is no use pretending that I and my wife have recovered from the shock of our son's death and I do not think that we ever shall. We have in all buried four precious children, three sons and a daughter, all sprightly, auspicious and handsome children.... My last boy was a wonderful boy the like of whom I have seldom seen. With his passing away, life to me is a garden full of weeds.

★ ★ ★

Times started changing favourably when in December 1926, Dr Ambedkar was nominated as a Member of Bombay Legislative Council (BLC). Under the Government of India Act, 1919, there was a provision for one Nominated Member to the Council representing the Depressed Classes. On behalf of the *Bahishkrit Hitakarini Sabha* Dr Ambedkar was trying to persuade the British Government to increase the number of Nominated Members representing the Depressed Classes in the Province. In the second week of December, 1926, the Government raised the number for the Bombay Provincial Council to two and appointed Dr Ambedkar and Dr PG Solanki to those positions. For Dr Ambedkar, this was going to be the beginning of a long and distinguished career as a Legislator.

As a nominated Member of the BLC Dr Ambedkar quickly earned himself a reputation for his studious, analytical and comprehensive interventions.

(A) ON PROVINCIAL BUDGETS

In his maiden speech in the BLC (February 24, 1927) Dr Ambedkar dealt with the Budget 1927-28 of the Province. He criticized the prevailing revenue system for not being reliable. From the standpoint of tax-payers, he argued that the revenue system was iniquitous—for example, the land tax must be paid in proportion to land holding irrespective of the yield, whereas the income tax recognized the capacity of the tax-payer to pay. Dr Ambedkar also lamented that the House had very limited degrees of freedom confined to only 40 per cent of revenue and 64 per cent of expenditure. Finally, he criticized the Government for sharp increase in unproductive expenditure leading to large budget deficit.

While participating in the discussion on Budget: 1928-29, the following year (February 21, 1928), Dr Ambedkar called the Budget not "merely satisfactory", but a "deplorable" one. He argued that the spirit of the Montague-Chelmsford reforms has been defeated in the Bombay Province. According to those reforms it was expected that the "Transferred Subjects" would receive greater consideration in the Provincial Budgets than the "Reserve Subjects". Analysing in detail, the data from 1921 to 1926, Dr Ambedkar showed that percentage increase in expenditure on the "Transferred Subjects" was the lowest in Bombay *vis-à-vis* all other regions. Dr Ambedkar demonstrated that the finances of the Province were "badly managed" and that the financial position of the Presidency was "indeed very serious".

(B) ON EDUCATION

In the Council, Dr Ambedkar consistently emphasized the importance of education—both school education and higher education.

While speaking on school education in the BLC (March 12, 1927). Dr Ambedkar argued:

- Per capita expenditure on education must be raised at least to the level of per capita revenue from excise duty on liquor;
- The wastage in expenditure on education is immense;
- There is great disparity in the comparative advancement in education of the different Classes i.e., Advanced Hindus, Mohammedans, Intermediate Class and Backward Class. There is a need for establishing an inspecting agency so as to ensure that the Depressed Classes are not neglected by the educational bodies such as School Boards etc.
- The method of giving scholarship is really a waste of public money. Instead, the public money should be spent on promoting hostels for students from the Depressed Classes.

In a similar vein, Dr Ambedkar participated extensively in the debate on the Bombay University Act (Amendment) Bill (July 23, 1927 and October 1,3 and 5, 1927) Dr Ambedkar pointed out: "One of the greatest defects from which this (i.e. Bombay) University has suffered ever since it was established was that it was primarily constituted as an examining body." Dr Ambedkar critically analyzed the proposals before the BLC and made suggestions so as to organize the University of

Bombay into a better teaching University, promoting higher education and research. In that regard, he dealt with several issues including the relations of the Syndicate, the Senate and the Academic Council, relation of colleges to the University, appointment of Rector in the University, etc.

(C) ON PROHIBITION

Participating in the debate on "Prohibition" (March 10, 1927) Dr Ambedkar said:

The Minister for Excise gave us certain figures to show that the people of Bombay were not drinking as much as the people of the other Provinces in India. While people are drinking less of licit liquor, the manufacture of illicit liquor in this Presidency has been on the increase. So, if we take into consideration the fact that although the drinking of licit liquor is decreasing, the drinking of illicit liquor is on the increase; the result that we get is that the consumption is not less. On the whole, we are not gainers, because the only result is that people are drinking less of licit liquor and more of illicit liquor.

I think... the increase in the manufacture of illicit liquor in this Presidency is entirely due to the high tariff on country liquor. Now, it is an admitted principle of political economy—that when the price of a certain commodity rises, then, there is always a tendency on the part of the people to substitute another commodity in its place which is equally serviceable and which costs less. Applying the same principle to this case, I submit... that the increase of illicit drink in this Presidency is entirely due to the high tariff on country liquor. My Honourable friend the Minister for Excise will, therefore, pay a little more attention to this aspect of the question. If he is really a believer in prohibition, he must regulate his tariff. If he does not regulate the tariff, I submit that although he may succeed in controlling the consumption of licit liquor, he will give a direct incentive to the increase in illicit liquor.

The other point that I wish to speak of is regarding the policy of prohibition. I was glad to hear from my Honourable friend the Leader of the House that prohibition is now the accepted policy of the Government, and that the Government under no circumstances would go back on the policy resolved upon by the Legislative Council. He told us that the issue before the House was what methods we should adopt in bringing about prohibition: whether we should adopt the method of rationing or whether we should adopt the method of local option. Sir, in my view, the two methods are more or less equally efficient. Whether you adopt the policy of rationing or whether you adopt the policy of local option makes no difference in the situation whatsoever, because the effect of either is to control the supply of liquor that will be put on the market. Sir, the question is how far we can go on in advancing the policy of prohibition, and that question, I think my Honourable friend the Leader of the House has not taken into account.

I feel, ... that the problem of prohibition, and whether you will be able to carry it out to a successful issue or not, entirely depends upon the financial solution of the question, upon how we will manage to make good the losses we are bound to incur as a result of our new excise policy. We at least on this side feel that we are not opposed to the additional taxation, provided, of course, the Government will use the taxes for nation-building proposes. We are certainly opposed to additional taxation if the Government is going to use the taxes merely to maintain the Government, merely to govern. But if they are going to make life happy, and not merely try to make life possible, then, I think we on this side are certainly willing to support any tax.

Sir, I think no Government ought to make any promise as regards carrying out a policy of prohibition unless it has made up its mind as to how it will make good the loss of revenue. Unless, therefore, my Honourable friend has got the courage—that is far more important than mere conviction—unless he has the courage to tax the people who have not been taxed so far, people who have better capacity to bear the burden, it is no use... trying to incur the odium of making a promise and not carrying it out. The best thing for the Honourable the leader of the House would have been to bring forward a proposal for taxation, and to test the sincerity of this House as regards the policy which it has been asking him to pursue. I think the House understands as well as anybody that this policy is going to cost money, and it was the duty and interest of my Honourable friend the Leader of the House to have obtained from the House an assurance that it was willing to meet the cost of the policy it was so strenuously enforcing upon him.

CHAPTER EIGHT

Launching a Mass Movement

DR AMBEDKAR'S STRATEGY for launching a mass movement for upliftment of Untouchables was now taking a concrete shape. Clearly, in that initial phase, which was going to last for nearly a decade, Dr Ambedkar was going to fight for social justice, while remaining within the fold of the Hindu religion. He was going to orient his mass movement as a struggle for civic rights for the Untouchables.

It all began with the simple demand to drink water from a public reservoir. The issue was one of asserting the elementary right to water for Untouchables and the setting was a small town of Mahad in Konkan.

For hundreds of years, Untouchables were prevented from collecting or drinking water from any of the points where the Upper Castes did. In 1926, the Government of Bombay Province adopted a resolution abolishing such discrimination. In its wake, the Mahad Municipality had passed a resolution to allow Untouchables full access to all waterfronts, including its largest reservoir, the so-called Chavdar Lake. However, this resolution had remained only on paper, and the Hindu Untouchables were not allowed to draw any water from the lake, even while Muslim and Christian Untouchables could do so. Others could even take their cattle to Chavdar Lake, but the so-called Untouchable human beings could not. It was around this cause that Dr Ambedkar chose to launch a mass movement of the downtrodden.

CHAVDAR LAKE STRUGGLE

Dr Ambedkar decided to hold a meeting at Mahad, where the Untouchables would exercise their right en masse. On March 19, 1927, the *Bahishkrit Hitakarini Sabha* sponsored a Conference of Depressed Classes in Mahad. The response was simply unprecedented. Thousands of people of all ages, mostly wearing rags and carrying *bhakris* wrapped in cloth bags, assembled from different parts of Maharashtra in response to Dr Ambedkar's call. In that historic meeting, Dr Ambedkar first explained how the British had let the Untouchables down and urged them to keep alive the (new) fire of awareness. He said:

> I am very happy. But at the same time I cannot help saying that it also pains me. There was a time when this place was quite forward in respect of Untouchables. This place was full of officers from the Untouchable communities. And these communities had also progressed in education as compared to most other communities.
>
> One of the important reasons for that progress was military profession. We cannot say with certainty how much scope for progress was available to Untouchables prior to the commencement of British rule. The sentiments about Untouchability were so strong that an Untouchable had to move aside while walking on roads to avoid his shadow from falling upon Caste Hindus; he was required to put a pot around his neck lest his spit would pollute the ground. He was required to tie a black thread on his wrist so that he could be easily identified. Under those circumstances there could be hardly any scope for their progress.
>
> When the British rule began, Untouchables got some scope to raise their heads. And taking full advantage of the opportunity, they could prove how brave they are! They could prove what high level of intelligence they possess! If you want a proof of this just have a look at the old records of army. Several of Untouchables from this area had become Subhedars, *Jamadars* and Hawaldars in the British Army. Many from ordinary schools rose to responsible positions of Headmaster, Adjutant Clerks, Quarter Master Clerk, etc.... It will be enough to say that Untouchables who were living as village servants and beggars had become masters of their destiny only because of the service of the Army.
>
> Army service had certainly brought about a great revolution in the structure of Hindu Society. The same Maratha and other people who would not allow even a touch of *Mahar* and *Chamar* persons in the village had to respectfully salute the *Mahar* or *Chamar* Subhedar in the army. They would feel insulted if the *Mahar* or *Chamar* person did not salute with 'Johar' or 'Ram-Ram' in the village. But in army the same people would not raise their head even if *Mahar* or *Chamar* uttered abuses for their laxity. The Untouchables never ever had such an authority anywhere in this country. The Untouchables of this area had raised their living standards and had also progressed in education very substantially.... And not only men but women also were quite ahead in education. The Untouchable women also were so progressed that they would explain the *Puranas* in the meetings predominated by males. Of course, military profession was largely helpful for such a progress in education.
>
> Many people are now saying that even after 150 years of the British rule primary education is not compulsory and free. They probably are not aware that at least for the military department of East India Company, the primary education was compulsory and free. It was equally applicable to the males as well as females. In respect of boys, the secondary education was also compulsory. And this compulsion was very strict. Nobody could get away just by paying the fine for non-attendance. The new army recruits also were required to attend night schools. This practice continued even after the British Government took over the rule of India from East India Company. But after the mutiny of 1857 when British Government constituted an Enquiry Commission for Indian Army, some witnesses complained that spread of education in the army will invite further troubles. As a result, British Government first neglected compulsory education and later completely stopped it.

Nevertheless, so long as that education was available, it helped a lot to improve the conditions for Untouchables. The Untouchables used their education so well that you cannot but feel proud about it. They collected a kaleidoscope of literature which was disproportionately larger than their number and resources. Many Untouchables had collection of rare manuscripts of many old saints and social reformers. Such a passion for knowledge by those for whom all doors of education were once closed by the society is unparalleled....

Research shows that the '*Anarya Dosh Pariharak Mandali*' was the first institution which pioneered the works for upliftment of Untouchables in Bombay Province. They wrote a long petition with the help of Shri Mahadev Govind Ranade to the British Government in 1893 against stoppage of recruitment of Untouchables in the army. The same institution had also written to the Indian National Congress in 1897 questioning their right to ask for political independence without social reforms. It shows the spirit of this institution. And this society was established at Dapoli in Ratnagiri District. Therefore, it is very clear that the first movement for upliftment of Untouchables had started from this area, and by this society called '*Anarya Dosh Pariharak Mandali*'. They not only had tried to mitigate the problems of Untouchables but had also created wide-spread awakening through literature.... And look at the wretched condition of Untouchables in this area now. They have become so poor, so illiterate, absolute destitute. It is impossible to find such a low level even amongst Untouchables in any other areas. What could be the reason for such a reversal of fortunes; it's a big question. I have no doubt this has happened because of stoppage of army recruitment for Untouchables.

It is greatly unjust to ban any member of public from getting government job. It is unjust politically, morally and also economically. Banning Untouchables from army recruitments is not only discriminatory, it is also a breach of trust and unfriendly. The British could not have entered India without the help of Untouchables.... British would not have won any war in India without army of local people. And British should ask themselves who were those local people. None other than Untouchables! Without the brave army of Untouchables, British would not have been able to capture this country. Driving away those very people who helped them capture new territories is a typical way of the British, one may say.

Another example of selfish and erratic ways of working of the British Government is relatively recent—i.e., that of 1917. When the World War broke out, the Government again remembered Untouchables and started army recruitment for them. They wanted just one Battalion, but ever willing Untouchables thronged in large numbers, enough to create two Battalions. Government recruited only one Battalion. We felt happy thinking that at last fortunes of Untouchables have started looking up. Alas! Once the War was over, Government disbanded the Battalion in the name of austerity. What to say about such irrational working of the Government?

Dr Ambedkar then elaborated the essentials for the progress of Untouchables. He said:

Gentlemen, it is my opinion that Government always neglects us because we are cooperative. We accept whatever Government offers; we do whatever we are told to do; we live in whatever conditions we are kept. This very nature of servitude is a cause of our neglect by the Government. We meekly tolerate all kinds of injustice. If somebody slaps us on one cheek, we offer another instead of raising our hand in defence. We blame our fate for all kinds of problems. Sooner we discard this suicidal attitude, the better. We must try to the best of our ability to remove the ban on our recruitment in the army.

In my opinion two things are essential for the progress of Untouchables. First, the rust of retrograde thoughts of inferiority accumulated in their minds must be cleaned up. Unless the attitude, thoughts and speech are cleaned, the seeds of awakening and progress cannot take roots in the minds of Untouchables. In the present circumstances nothing can grow on the hard rocks of their mind.... If we want that we should make government to take favourable decisions, we should enter government jobs to make it happen. Otherwise, we will be always neglected.

Gentlemen, I want to remind you of one very unhappy thing. I told you that this area was full of Subhedars and *Jamadars* of army. They had done many good things, except one. They did not educate their children.... Gentlemen, they were not poor. They were getting good pension. They could have easily provided education up to graduation, even post-graduation. These educated children would have become Collectors, Judges and Officers which would have helped the Untouchables now. They would have provided us the much-needed protection. Today we are lying in open, unprotected, burning under the hot sun.... I strongly advise you that you should give special attention to the best quality education. What one BA pass boy can do will not be possible to achieve with even one thousand 4th standard pass boys. I am not suggesting that we should neglect primary education. But it is necessary to take as many students as possible to higher levels of education. For this purpose, I feel we should have suitable hostel and boarding arrangement for our students. I propose to open one at Panvel which will be convenient for the students from Colaba and Thane Districts.

Another profession that I have suggested to you is farming. The reason is we Untouchables should make arrangements for economically independent life. Today, amongst Untouchables, *Mahars* are like a herd of useless people. They have developed a habit of living on State food begged from house to house. They do it as if it is their great right; begging door to door for State food. As a result, nobody respects them. They have lost their self respect and dignity. They have lost their independence and cannot take a path of progress. If they think of entering temple, or attempt to draw water from public place, or decide not to carry dead animals, the next day they lose their State food. It is most shameful to sell your humanity for a few State crumbs. Will it not be good if you stop begging for crumbs and start farming like all other people to do?

You may not be able to buy land. But forest department has lots of fallow land which you can try to get from officials. It is not impossible. But how will it happen? I think there will not be any change so long as we get free crumbs to eat. Nobody treads a new path as long as old path is available. We have lost our humanity by adopting the traditional path. How long to follow this path, you decide. Whenever, any progressive steps are discussed, 'our elder's custom is better' is the kind of approach of people in this area. Their attitude is that the old custom may be highly detrimental but

> must be followed. But don't you think that every parent wants that his children should live better than him at least, a little better? If they do not think so then what is the difference between them and animals?

Having urged the Untouchables assembled to rebel against the humiliating and enslaving tradition of village duties, Dr Ambedkar then made a passionate appeal. He said:

> Gentlemen, if not for you, at least for the sake of your children please listen to what I say. You may ask, 'why do all these difficult things when you are comfortable, maybe on half a bread.' You may ask me, 'why leave assured half bread for an imaginary full bread.' But I must warn you, if you do not do what I tell, you will not get even this half bread in times to come.
>
> I want to emphasize that we all have to undertake this work of social awareness very enthusiastically. The people in this area have gone into a deep slumber ever since their military past has come to an end. There is hardly any movement. After several Conferences in other areas, now after a long time this Conference is taking place. You must not let this fire of awakening douse.

THE MAHAD MARCH

The Day One of the Conference was a great success. The historic gathering of more than 10,000 Untouchables was visible moved by the inspiring speech of Dr Ambedkar. The Day One also witnessed the passage of several resolutions, including notably, that Touchables should bury their dead cattle themselves and not expect the Untouchables to do so any more and that the Resolution allowing all Untouchables access to all water fronts should be made operational. The same day evening, Dr Ambedkar had a strategy meeting with his key advisors both Touchable as well as Untouchables.

The next day, the deliberations of the Conference continued. In the afternoon, just as the Conference was about to be announced closed, a local Touchable Hindu leader Shri Anantrao Chitre stood up (as decided in the strategy meeting) and suddenly announced:

"Let's go to Chavdar Lake and implement the Mahad Municipality Resolution."

And there began a historic march!

The congregation of more than 10,000 people marched to Chavdar Lake with Dr Babasaheb Ambedkar leading the procession. The crowd marched in a disciplined manner, in rows of four, shouting slogans: "Educate, Unite, and Agitate!" The reservoir was surrounded by the houses of the so-called Upper Castes on all sides. Every door, window, and terrace of every house was full of shocked people, who looked on at the huge, determined crowd gathered around their tank, "polluting" its sanctity. After reaching Chavdar Tank, Dr Ambedkar walked down the half-dozen steps with firm resolve and looking at the thousands of expectant followers, calmly bent down, cupped some water in his hands, and drank. The crowd roared and let loose cheers of "Jai Bhim" (Glory to Bhim) as everyone took a symbolic sip of water. A social rebellion had begun.

While addressing the excited crowd, Dr Ambedkar proclaimed that the Untouchables were asserting their rights as human beings. They were making history. Indeed they had defied the arrogance of the tyrants who boasted that their religion treated even animals with forbearance, while in reality treated Untouchables worse than cats and dogs.

A couple of hours later, a large crowd of Upper-Castes armed with bamboo sticks gathered at the street corners, catching the delegates unawares. A rumour was afloat that the Untouchables were planning to forcibly enter the local Temple. The passive yet conservative town was in ferment. The Upper-Castes declared that their religion was being threatened, and that their God was being polluted. The rowdies charged at the delegates who fled. They spared no one—men, women nor children—knocking their food into the dirt and pounding their utensils. The protestors were screaming with rage, itching for retaliation. A word or signal from Dr Ambedkar and Mahad would have turned into a battlefield. Dr Ambedkar, however, appealed for peace and discipline. He said that their struggle was to enforce the law, not to break it.

★ ★ ★

The "Mahad March" was a momentous event. For the first time, historically, the Depressed Classes had made a collective public attempt to assert the civic rights denied to them for generations, under the leadership of Dr Ambedkar was opened in the annals of India.

While Dr Ambedkar emerged as the savior of the downtrodden, enkindling among them the flame of self-respect and self-elevation. Directly as result of the Mahad Conference, several of the Untouchables gave up eating carrion, skinning carcasses and many stopped begging for crumbs. In the meantime, Dr Ambedkar felt an acute need for a mouthpiece. Therefore, he started a fortnightly Marathi paper from Mumbai, on April 3, 1927, titled: *Bahishkrut Bharat*, and began to respond to critics of his mass movement and to explain his points of view to the public.

★ ★ ★

Bahishkrit Hitakarini Sabha convened a public meeting in Mumbai (July 3, 1927) to protest against the oppression in Mahad. In the meeting, Dr Ambedkar announced his intention to do a *Satyagraha* in Mahad and he said, "We need bold and self-respecting people for *Mahad Satyagraha*." More specifically, he said:

> *Satyagraha* means a battle. But this battle is not to be fought with weapons such as sword, guns, cannon and bombs. This is a weapon-less battle. On the lines of the

Satyagraha done by people of Patullakhali, and Vaikom, we are going to do a *Satyagraha* in Mahad. While doing this *Satyagraha* the Government might arrest us under some clause for disturbing the peace. You should be ready to go to prison. To those who want to look after families, I say do not participate in this *Satyagraha*. For *Satyagraha* we need people of courageous heart and self-respect and only those brave-hearts who believe that Untouchability is a black spot on this country and are determined to abolish it, only those people should take up part in the *Satyagraha*. I am sure I will find enough such brave-hearts among Depressed Classes.

This was widely publicized in *Bahishkrut Bharat* (July 15, 1927).

Dr Ambedkar tried to enlist support from all other Untouchable communities, something that he had to do repetitively throughout his public life, but with somewhat limited success at least in his lifetime. In a public meeting in Mangwada (in Pune, July 20, 1927), Dr Ambedkar emphasized that he was striving for all Depressed Classes. He said:

I belong to the *Mahar* Caste as you all know. My critics say that *Mahar* Caste is selfish. I question the non-*Mahar* Untouchable leaders whether they have worked any time for *Mahars* selflessly? As a matter of fact, those belonging to the Caste other than *Mahar* among Untouchables have had good education and are rich. In Mumbai, some persons from *Chamar* and Dhor Caste are able to pay income tax. Despite this, they do not seem to have not done anything for the empowerment of the *Mahars*. On the other hand, we have started several institutions for the empowerment of not just *Mahars* but for all the Castes from the Untouchable community. We have established '*Bahishkrit Hitkarini Sabha*' for the same purpose. We have started hostels for Untouchables in Solapur. *Chamars* have not given any help for this. Still, we have allowed the students from *Mahar*, *Mang*, *Chamar* etc. in that hostel. We are also striving hard to empower the Untouchables by opening hostels in Nasik and Jalgaon. I, therefore, cannot understand why the *Mahar* Caste is being criticized.

The critics also say that all the benefits of the government schemes are being grabbed by *Mahars*. Mr Nikalje of *Mahar* Caste was nominated for Mumbai Corporation. But when I found that he is unable to perform to my satisfaction, I did not hesitate to nominate Mr P Balu, who is a famous cricketer belonging to *Chamar* Community. In Satara City, *Mahars* are larger in number, yet in the Municipality the Government-appointed members are from *Chamar* Caste. It is through these instances that one can see how the charges being made are totally baseless.

There was a big public meeting at Elphinstone Road, Mumbai (September 17, 1927) where Dr Ambedkar said: "We must demonstrate our rights through *Satyagraha*." His words were:

The speakers before me have already told you why we need to go for a *Satyagraha*. Untouchability is not our stigma but it is a stigma on our mothers and sisters. Those who consider themselves 'Touchable' feel that their mothers are superior than the

> mothers who give birth to Untouchables. But truth is that every woman delivers a baby after nine months. As such, no woman is superior than any other. To those who think that we are lesser mortals, we must demonstrate that we are no less than anybody else. From religion's point of view, the rights of all human beings are the same. That is why we must establish this fact through our *Satyagraha*. I request those who want to participate in the protest to come forward and those who are unable to participate should help financially as much as they can.

While the momentum was building up for the Mahad *Satyagraha*, some Untouchable activists initiated a Temple-Entry *Satyagraha* in Ambadevi Temple at Amravati (in Vidarbha region of Maharashtra). While the Temple-Entry agitation was going on, a Conference of Untouchables from Berar (i.e. Vidarbha) was organized in Amravati.

In his Presidential Address[33](November 13, 1927), Dr Ambedkar expressed, in some details, his philosophy behind the *Satyagraha* movement.

Philosophy Behind the Mahad Satyagraha

Dr Ambedkar said:

> The Untouchables and Touchables both agree that they both belong to the same religion. The Touchables never tell Untouchables that they are not Hindus. During 1910 Census when some Muslims suggested that the Untouchables should not be counted as Hindus, not only the reformist Hinds but also the most orthodox Touchables insisted that the Untouchables should be counted as Hindus only. And Untouchables also wanted it that way. Both the parties since ancient times feel that they belong to the same religion. However, today there is great change in the outlook of Untouchables, as is clearly visible. They are wondering if they are also Hindus why they do not have the same rights like the other Hindus? Why cannot they draw water from the same well or lake which is used by other Hindus? Why can't they enter the temple where Hindus worship their Gods? They are asking these questions of equality. They are insisting on getting these equal rights. We never went to any temple before this! We never went to any public lake or well before this! Now if we insist on this, will it be right? Will it be considered a *Satyagraha*? These are but natural doubts in the minds of Untouchables. Because, success or failure of any action depends on its being moral as much as on the resources available. Therefore, each one of us Untouchables should try to understand the moral nature of the action we are taking.
>
> To understand this, let us consider whether our demand for temple entry is a demand for truthful right or a false pretext. We must first determine what is 'True' and what is 'Untrue' if we want to start a *Satyagraha*. The success of the *Satyagraha* depends upon the self-confidence of the person doing it, and this self-confidence comes from the knowledge and belief that what he is doing is moral and pure truth. In my opinion, whatever is for fraternity and brotherhood is truth. If you are having selfish motives,

---

33. For full English summary, see Jadhav, Narendra, *Ambedkar Speaks* (2013), Vol I, pp.83-92.

then you cannot think of fraternity, rather you will think of dividing the people. But if you have faith in equality, you will never attempt to divide the people, you will try to bind them together instead. Therefore, based on these principles, where there is equality, there is fraternity and where there is fraternity there is truth. And any action to establish these principles is *Satyagraha*!

Now, this is not my own thinking. I have taken it from Gita. Some people will be surprised that I am taking support of Gita for our *Satyagraha*. Many people believe that *Satyagraha* is not a subject-matter of Gita; but that is not a correct understanding. In fact, *Satyagraha* is the basic tenet of Gita. If you carefully consider why Gita was preached by Shri Krishna you will easily find that what I say is correct. When Arjuna climbed down the chariot, and sat crestfallen seeing his elders and teachers in front of him in war, what Shri Krishna advised him? Shri Krishna said, 'Do not be sad. Be determined to fight for your rights with those who have taken away your Kingdom.' Upon this Arjuna asked, 'Tell me, how what you tell is truth, and how my demand is *Satyagraha*?' And the entire Gita is an answer by Shri Krishna to this one question by Arjuna.... And that is why I have taken the Gita as a basis for our demand for equal rights from the Touchables.

There is another reason why I have taken the Gita as a basis for our *Satyagraha*. It is because Gita is acceptable to both the parties, Touchables as well as Untouchables. Had we taken any other religious text as a basis, the Touchables who are always on look-out for excuses, they would have simply rejected it saying that it is not acceptable to them. If the *Satyagraha* started by the Untouchables passes through the test of Gita, then they will have absolutely no excuse to oppose it, because it will amount to rejecting the Gita itself!

Now let us see whether our *Satyagraha* really stands the test of Gita. Firstly, whether our movement is an action for fraternity? Some people think that our movement is limited only to make us Touchables by removing the stigma of Untouchability. It is not that Untouchability has caused loss only to the Untouchables; it has caused loss to the Touchables as well and has done immense damage to the nation. It has blotted not only Untouchables but also blemished the Touchables. Those who are looked down upon get, no doubt, insulted, but those who insult others also lower themselves down in morality. If Untouchables come out of that stigma and participate in nation-building, they will only contribute to the progress of the nation. Therefore, this movement for removal of Untouchability is in true sense a movement for nation-building and fraternity. If Untouchables have a selfish motive limited to removing their Untouchability only, then they don't have to adopt a difficult way of *Satyagraha*. Because they can achieve the purpose of equal and human treatment, just by conversion to another religion.

The behaviour of Hindus is rather very amusing; that is so long as somebody is a part of Hindu society, the barbarous rule of Untouchability, sin and virtue, significance-insignificance are applied to them. If he leaves the Hindu religion then these rules cease to operate; he is treated with equality. That is the reason why Hindus do not consider Muslims as Untouchables. They do not consider even animals such as cats and goats to be Untouchables. Untouchables are part of Hindu religion and that is why their barbarous rules are applied to them. Untouchables know it well that if any Untouchable gets converted to another religion like Islam or Christianity he is treated with humanity, with equality. Still Untouchables do not want to follow this simple path. Instead of abandoning the Hindu religion and causing its decline, they want to remain within the Hindu religion and use all their energy to fight for the rights of humanity. They are not demanding any special rights and status; they are demanding only equal treatment. The Untouchables are not demanding that whatever rights available to Hindus should be available to only themselves but not to others. Their demand is only for equal rights with the Touchables. Now, if you apply the principles of Gita, you will find that this movement of Untouchables is a movement for *Satyagraha*.

There are some mischievous elements who argue that it is not correct that God's worship is complete only when you go into the temple because in Hinduism worshipping the idol in the temple is not the only form of worship. In Hinduism there are several ways to offer prayers to the God. He can be worshipped in the form of idol; He can be worshiped in meditation; and He can also be worshipped by chanting his name. They argue that there is no ban on Untouchables to adopt any of those methods of God worship. Any one of these methods is good enough for observance of the Hindu religion.... My reply to these arguments is this: Agreed there are several methods of worship and any one of them is good enough; but if anybody wants to offer his prayers to an idol in the temple, why should that not be allowed to him? Why this method should be open to some and banned for others?

Another argument these Touchables give that even if they do not allow the Untouchables into their temples, all are free to build a temple for themselves. I would like to ask those so-called learned ones that why do they object to Railways for having separate coaches for Whites and Indians? Although Railways have kept separate coaches for Whites, you have all the freedom to travel in other coaches. Still why do you claim your right to travel in the same coaches which are reserved for Whites? There is only one answer to this and that is: it is not a matter of travel only, it is a matter of equality!

The Untouchables have the same reason for demanding the right to worship God in the same temple. They want to prove that the temple is not defiled by their entry; neither sanctity of God's idol is lost by their touch. That cannot be proven by building a separate temple. We say God's sanctity is lost only by the touch of sinners, not by our touch; we are not sinners. The principle of our movement is that nobody is pious or blemished in worshiping the God and that is the reason why we demand to worship the same God's idol which is worshiped by the Touchables. Should anybody still have a doubt that this is not a *Satyagraha*?

These are not the only objections. They are raising some other objections as well. They say the custom of Untouchability, for good or bad, is age-old. We have built our temples only after that and we are maintaining them for all these years from time immemorial. Now suddenly why should the Untouchables claim their right on those temples? Is that justifiable? They claim that this is not a question of Touchability or Untouchability, but of legal justice. Here in Amravati itself, the trustees of Ambadevi temple have shown dustbin to the request of the Untouchables because even a single trustee can invoke the law of customary usage to prevent entry of the Untouchables.

The Untouchables fully agree that the Touchables have built up the temples and they have maintained these temples. But that cannot be the reason for denial of their entry. Because whoever is Hindu, he has a right to go into that temple. The

Untouchables are entitled to Hinduism as much as the Touchables are. If the Brahmins like Vashishta, the *Kshatriyas* like Krishna, the *Vaishyas* like Harsh and the *Shudras* like Tukaram have re-established Hinduism; the Untouchables like Valmiki, Chokhamela and Rohidas have also equally contributed to re-establish it. Thousands of Untouchables have laid their lives to protect Hinduism; they are countless from the times of Gita to the Sidnak *Mahar* of the battle of Kharda. The Touchables and Untouchables together have built up this Hindu religion and protected it with their lives. Therefore, temples built in the name of Hinduism belong to the Untouchables as much as they belong to others. They have the same rights. There cannot be the case that one becomes a master and others remain only servant. The Untouchables are not servants. They are Hindus. On the basis of this alone they should accept the rights of the Untouchables. And when there are rights there is no question of custom of usage.

Legally, the right to public property is not required to be established by any deed; it is available automatically to everybody. Even if he has no usage or it was not continuous, it does not deprive him of that right. Suppose, somebody did not walk on a particular road, does that mean he can never use that road? Therefore, it would be quite idiotic to say that since Untouchables never went to the temple or never drew water from the public wells, so now they cannot do that. Thus legally also our position is strong. The Untouchables need not carry any doubt. Their movement is genuinely a *Satyagraha*....

Now let us discuss how the Untouchables should carry on this movement. We should first decide what should be our model of *Satyagraha*. Mahatma Gandhi is the proponent of *Satyagraha* movement of the modern times. And everybody presumes that there cannot be any other model of *Satyagraha* other than the one prescribed by Mahatma Gandhi. He has kept no scope for violence in his model for *Satyagraha*. He says if there is violence there is no *Satyagraha*. I am of the opinion that there cannot be agreement on the logic of this approach to *Satyagraha*. The validity of *Satyagraha* shall depend upon the morality of its purpose. If the purpose of movement is virtuous, then it must be treated as *Satyagraha*? The violence-non-violence is only a means to reach the destination. If somebody adopts non-violence for absolutely immoral purpose, will you call it *Satyagraha*! And if somebody is forced to use non-violence for a rightful objective, will you call it *non-Satyagraha*? If that is so, what would you say of Shri Krishna who forced Ajuna to adopt the means of violence to achieve his rightful demand? Was he a devil? I don't think any Hindu will accept it.

It is true that violence is not proper and cannot be acceptable but if it is unavoidable in self-defence, it has to be excused. We will have to apply the same principle for success of *Satyagraha*. Accordingly, Gandhi's non-violent *Satyagraha* is rather impractical; to call it non-violent is also pretense, pure deception. Violence means only killing is a very narrow approach to distinguish between violence and non-violence. The meaning of violence includes hurt to body or feelings of another person. Therefore, non-violence means not to cause pain of any nature to any living being. If we apply this broader definition of non-violence, then Mahatma Gandhi's non-violence also is violence in a way. Because, according to his methods even though nobody is physically hurt, it hurts the sentiments of opposite parties. Even then Mahatma Gandhi says there is no violence in his movement. In our opinion that is not a correct stand. In fact, *Satyagraha* should adopt non-violence as far as possible and may have to resort to violence in case of need; that should be the approach and that would be a practical approach.

Now we must discuss against whom is our *Satyagraha.* Our demand for equal rights is before the Touchables and they are the ones who are refusing to grant us our legitimate rights. Obviously, Untouchables would think that their fight is against the Touchables. But that is not an entirely correct view. We must visualize the sequence of possible events to come to know against whom we are fighting.

If the public peace is disturbed because of obstinate opposition by the Touchables, the Government steps in because it is Government's prime duty to maintain peace and order in the society. If it happens, we do not know what position Government will take. If Government extends support of its vast powers to grant rightful demand to the Untouchables, then our problem is instantly solved. But if Government takes a stand that the Untouchables are asking every time for something new which is causing disturbances and orders that they should stop all this. If this happens our fight turns against the Government. The Untouchables must fully understand repercussions of their struggle. The Untouchables may be required to disobey Government orders to obtain their rights for the temple entry or for drawing water from public wells. As a result Government may put them in jail. So the Untouchables should jump into this struggle with the full knowledge that they may also have to go to jail.

Frankly speaking, Untouchability is such an inhuman practice that some of us can sacrifice even our lives to remove it. Touchables believe that the things defiled by our touch are purified by spraying cow urine. Things become impure by the touch of human beings of your own religion and can be purified by the urine of an animal! It is such a shameful thinking. In the view of Touchables, animal's dung and urine are more pious than the human touch of the Untouchable. Is such a life worth living?

In my opinion, time has come when every Untouchable mother should tell her… son that go and show your bravery even for a moment without fearing of death. It is better to die in battle than living decomposing in bed for hundred years. We are not demanding life from the Untouchables. We are only demanding that you should be ready to go to jail for the sake of your struggle. If Untouchables cannot do even this much then they are not men but the eunuchs….

I am sure some of you are ready for sacrificing your life and many of you are ready to go to jail for the success of your *Satyagraha.* And there is no doubt about success of our movement. After all for how long and how many people Government will put into jail and how long the Touchables will depend upon the government support. Some day or the other Government will have to be concerned about public shame. If Government does not feel it, the Untouchables will have to make it feel, it is in their hands. If Government prevents us from exercising our just rights for equality in the name of public peace, we can take up the matter to the court of civilized nations i.e. United Nations and call Government's bluff in the United Nations. And the Touchables also will have to explain for whose obstinacy the government is punishing the Untouchables.

The Touchables do not have any love lost for Untouchables but they are certainly worried about themselves. Now it is in our hands to make them feel the heat of these worries through our *Satyagraha.* If the Touchables really get determined to test our patience, what will happen? Our movement might fail; but still who would be at loss? The Touchables! When the Untouchables will realize that despite struggle, the

Touchables are not ready to yield equal rights to them, they will be compelled to think of leaving the Hindu religion. They will tell the Touchables, keep your religion which is dead like stones. We are going to adopt another religion. I don't think the Touchables will let things to come to such a *passe.* But we must organize our *Satyagraha* on such a large scale that all jails should be full and there should be no space left in any jail....

Our *Satyagraha* is for regaining our human rights. But it is also a *Yajna* for our self-introspection and purification. All Untouchables, whether women or children, should jump into this *Satyagraha* and get themselves purified in this *Yajna*. It is true that the Touchables treat the Untouchables as impure and inauspicious. But the Untouchables also consider themselves as impure and inauspicious, and behave like that. It has become their habit. The Untouchability has survived for so many years because of Untouchables only. They think that the Touchables are superior to them, the Touchables are their masters and they are servants. The Untouchables have become habituated to behave the way they are told to behave by the Touchables, because the Touchables have been successful in establishing their superiority over the Untouchables. Unless this inferiority complex is completely removed from the minds of the Untouchables, they will not understand the value of dignity and self-respect. It is, therefore, necessary that each and every Untouchable should actively participate in this struggle. Secondly, unless a large number of people participate in this movement there will be no impact on those who do not accept our rightful demands. People should participate in such a large number that the Touchables should feel harassed and compelled to accede to our demands. Since many people may not be able to participate because of family compulsions, I advise that we should create a battalion of 5,000 Untouchable youth to undertake *Satyagraha* wherever it will be arranged. If we can create such a battalion then there is no doubt that our movement shall be successful. But to organize and manage such a large battalion of youth for *Satyagraha* at various places, we will require funds. It will also take some time. In the meantime Untouchables should start the *Satyagraha* in whatever small numbers.

I am aware that some Touchables are suggesting that the matter of equal rights for the Untouchables should be allowed to be resolved by the Touchables amongst themselves. It cannot be resolved by the movement of the Untouchables. The Untouchables should wait till the Touchables willingly allow them such equal rights. How can it be trusted that they will willingly grant such rights to the Untouchables? It will be sheer stupidity to wait for such a miracle to happen.

Another section of the Touchables tells us that even if we launch our movement, we will not succeed. If we launch struggle, whatever few Touchables who have sympathy with our cause will feel offended and we will lose their sympathy. The progressive Touchables will then join the orthodox Hindus against us. I want to tell them that if they have sympathy for us, if they feel anguished about the injustice caused to us, then they should support us wholeheartedly like the Whites supported the Blacks in America to end slavery. Otherwise, it does not matter whether you have sympathy or hatred towards us.

Yet another section of Touchables tells us that *Satyagraha* is done against the outsiders, not against our own people. They tell us, after all, we are part of the same society. When there are attacks on Hinduism from foreigners already, we should not have feuds within our own family. Very sweet advice! But why should the Untouchables

> listen to this when they have no place in the religion? The Touchables have all the rights to Hindu religion, they should protect it. The Untouchables are repenting that they have protected the Hindu religion so far. What right Touchables have to advise Untouchables that they should not fight within family? What does their 'Gita' say? We are following the same advice as Shri Krishna gave to Arjuna on the battlefield of Kurukshetra. Krishna knew fully well that thousands of people will die in this war but he did not bother. All this for what? For getting the Kingdom of Pandavas back from Kauravas who had wrongfully taken it. The purpose of *Satyagraha* of Arjuna is worth pennies as compared to the cause of the Untouchables. Pandavas would not have died without Kingdom. They at least had dignity and respect. The Untouchables are fighting for their dignity and self-respect. Krishna justifies killing of elders, teachers, Gurus, brothers and a whole clan merely for the sake of a Kingdom. Then why the Untouchables should not do at least a peaceful *Satyagraha* for much nobler cause—the cause of humanity?
>
> In any struggle, there are negotiations first and then war. I think we have had enough negotiations and consultations. Several great persons, from time to time, tried to convince the Touchables to remove the curse of Untouchability. But they are so prejudiced that they are not prepared to budge even slightly. There is no reason to believe that the Touchables will grant any rights to us by their own volition. We should, therefore, wake up at least now and fight for our rights. Our earlier generations were not educated enough and they could not do much. But we have the benefit of education. And still if we do not strive for removal of the curse of Untouchability then we cannot be called worthy heirs.

★ ★ ★

The symbolic march to the Chavdar Lake had kindled in Untouchables the flame of their awakening. On August 4, 1927 the Mahad Municipality revoked its earlier resolution granting Untouchables access to the water tank. Dr Ambedkar took this as a challenge and announced that he would intensify the struggle by holding another protest meeting in Mahad.

The Mahad Satyagraha

December 1927 saw an even bigger meeting in Mahad where Dr Ambedkar explained, at length, that the Mahad *Satyagraha* was for laying the foundation of equality. He said:[34]

> Many of you would recollect that we had together gone to the Mahad Chawdar Lake on the March 19. Although, the Touchables had not objected to our going there, they

---

34. Presidential Speech in Marathi, Mahad Satyagraha Conference (December 25-27, 1927).
For full English summary, see *Ambedkar Speaks* (Ed. Jadhav Narendra 2013), Vol.I, pp.93-101.

registered their objection by assaulting the Untouchables later on. They faced the legal consequences as well; they have been punished with four months' rigorous imprisonment and they are now in jail. If there were no opposition to us on March 19, it would have established that our right to draw water from the lake is acceptable to the Touchables. And this today's Conference would not have been necessary. Unfortunately, it did not happen that way and we are forced to convene this Conference.

This water lake of Mahad is a public property. The Touchables of Mahad are so generous that they allow to draw water by all the people; even the Muslims and persons of other religions also are free to draw water from there. Not only that, they do not have objection to even animals to drink water from this lake. They allow all animals even those belonging to the Untouchables. The Touchable Hindus are so kind and peace-loving people that they never do any violence and never harm anybody. That is the result of so many saints being born in this religion. Obliging others is their virtue and causing pain is a sin, such is their attitude. They worship and protect the harmless animals like cow and also harmful serpents, etc with equal respect. 'One soul pervades all creatures' is their principle! But this same noble Touchable Hindus prevent people of their own religion from drawing water from this Mahad Lake.

Naturally, the question arises as to what is the reason for such a behavior on the part of the Touchables. We must clearly understand the answer to this question.... There are four *Varna* (Class) of Hindus as per religious texts, but they are five by custom; i.e. Brahmin, *Kshatriya*, *Vaishya*, *Shudra* and Untouchables. This system of *Varna* is first of the devil rules of Hindu religion. One *Varna* below the other is its second devilish rule.

There is a ban on inter-Caste marriages, inter-Caste dining, inter-Caste communion and inter-Caste meetings. There is a misunderstanding that these limitations are limited just for social living. But actually these limitations are to demarcate the social status of each Caste; these are not only for the sake of living. These limitations are the symbols of inequality amongst these Castes. The higher Castes are striving to retain these limitations to retain their supremacy. If these symbols of demarcation are abolished, there will be equality and they will lose their supremacy over the others.

The Touchables of Mahad are opposing Untouchables to draw water from Mahad Lake not because its water will get polluted or it will vanish in the thin air. They oppose it because they do not want to accept that the Untouchables are equal to them. Gentlemen, you will understand the significance of the movement of *Satyagraha* we have launched. Please do not be under the impression that the *Satyagraha* Committee has invited you for drinking of water of this Mahad Lake. You have never used its water in the past. It is not that if we do not use it we are going to die. Our objective is to prove that we are human beings just like others. Therefore, this Conference is arranged to lay a foundation for establishing the social equality. And, therefore, this Conference is unique and historical. There is no parallel to this event in the entire history of India.

If at all, we may find a parallel in the history of Europe. About 138 years ago on May 5, 1789 there was similar French National Conference at Versailles. Many historians blame this French National Conference for initiating violent revolution that occurred in France and entire Europe for the next 15 years. But these historians miss out on the real issue. They forget that it is only because of this French Revolution of

1789 that not only France but all the countries in whole of the Europe today are enjoying prosperity and peace.

We need to understand the social condition prevailing in France in 1789. We all know our Hindu religion is based on *Varnashram*, four different Classes strictly divided in a hierarchical way, one above the other. Similar kind of social system was there in France around 1789, the only difference being there were three Classes. There were higher Classes like Brahmins and *Kshatriyas* but remaining *Vaishya*, *Shudra* (and *Ati-Shudra*-Untouchables) were clubbed together to form one Class. It is important to note that the social system was similar, based on inequality in France just like in our country. The French Revolutionary National Conference was held in May 1789 to remove this inequality. It is called as Versailles Conference.

Today, we have assembled here with the same objective to remove inequality from our Hindu Society and to unify it. Therefore, there is great similarity in the French Revolutionary Conference of 1789 held at Versailles and this Mahad *Satyagraha* Conference we are having here today on December 25, 1927.

Let us understand what were the governing principles of French Revolutionary Conference. Certainly, it covered a wide spectrum of issues ranging from political, social, religious and various others. But we are right now concerned only with unifying our society socially and religiously. We are not concerned right now about political unity. What were the principles of Versailles Conference in respect of social and religious issues? These are found in three important Declarations issued by the Versailles Conference.

The First Declaration was issued on June 17, 1789. It was about the religious *Varnashram*. The declaration abolished the three Classes and made all of them into one. It also abolished the arrangement of reservation of separate seats for different Classes in the political assembly of the country. Their Second Declaration was about appointments of religious priests. There it was a custom that the priests were appointed not by the country but by the Pope who was not from the same country. The Pope in his capacity as a sole guardian of the religion was empowered to appoint anybody as a priest irrespective of his ability. The Versailles Declaration abolished this custom of authority to one individual and empowered the national government to appoint and decide the honorarium of the priests at various churches and other religious bodies. The Third Declaration was of general nature related to various aspects of the social structure. This was the most important declaration; rather a King of all Declarations. It was later known as Declaration of the Fundamental Rights throughout the world. It created revolutionary changes in France and in all the countries in Europe and also elsewhere. It has 17 Articles of which the following are important:

(a) All persons are born equal and remain of equal status till death. The distinction, if any, could be only in the public interest.
(b) The polity of the nation must always ensure that these human rights are protected.
(c) People are the supreme authority to grant any authority or powers. No authority of any community or person shall be valid unless it is granted by people. There shall be no other basis, whether political or religious, for getting such authority.

(d) Every person has complete freedom of behavior as per his Fundamental Rights. If there are to be any restrictions on him those will be to ensure that other's Fundamental Rights are not violated and such restrictions shall be imposed only by law. These restrictions shall not be imposed on the basis of religion or any other consideration.
(e) The law will impose only such restrictions as may be necessary for social harmony.
(f) Law does not mean restrictions imposed by any particular community. Law shall be made by the People or their duly elected representatives. All laws whether these are protective or punitive shall be equally applicable to every citizen. All people shall be equally eligible for respect, honour, human rights or profession. There shall be no restrictions on the basis of birth, sex, Caste or creed.

We should remember these principles of Versailles Conference for this Mahad Conference of ours. This Conference should follow the same path and same programmes to dismantle the frames of *Varnashram* in Hinduism; we should adopt the programmes for unifying all the five *Varnas* and to form only one solid Class of all the Hindus. Unless it is done the Untouchability will not vanish and there will be no equality and fraternity in our society.

Some of you think that it is enough for us if Untouchability is removed. Let there be *Varnas* in Hindu religion, how does that matter? It is absolutely wrong. It does matter. Our aim should not be small and narrow. It should be high and mighty. We should not be ashamed of big dreams. If at all, we should be ashamed of having low aim.

If the Untouchability is removed, what happens? The *Ati-Shudras* will become *Shudras*! But could we say that the Untouchability, discrimination, inequality has vanished completely? If you have to kill a serpent, you must hit it on the head, not on the tail! If you want to remove any harmful thing you must remove it from the roots; else it will crop up again.

You all know by your personal experience that the doctor needs to ascertain the cause of ailment, without which his treatment will not be effective. There are several examples how the best intended steps for removing social ailments have failed in the history. I can explain one such event which is very eye opening.

In ancient Rome, there were two Classes called Patricians and Plebeians. The Patricians were considered superior and the Plebeians as inferiors. The Patricians enjoyed all the privileges and the Plebeians were treated very badly and were discriminated against. The Plebeians eventually rallied together and demanded that there should be some written law for the conduct of society instead of just customs. The Patricians readily agreed and prepared a written law of 12 articles. But this eventually, proved to be of no use for the Plebeians because the implementation of these laws was completely in the hands of officers belonging to Patricians. Even the head of the Tribunal was a Patrician! Therefore, discrimination against the Plebeians in actual implementation of laws was common place. The Plebeians then demanded that the Tribunal should be of two persons one from each community. It was decided that two representatives on the Tribunal shall be elected by the respective communities. This demand too was accepted by the Patricians. The Plebeians thought that they have achieved their objective of equality. But they did not realize that there was a custom in Rome that anything to be done shall be acceptable to their Goddess called Delphi. So whenever a member on Tribunal was elected if the Delphi rejected him, another person was required to be elected. Do you know, who was to decide what the Goddess Delphi likes or dislikes? It was a priest who used to decide on behalf of goddess Delphi. And this priest was necessarily from the Patricians because of another strange custom prevailing in Rome. The said priest would reject any Plebeian elected member if he was not favourable to the Patricians. The priest (in the name of Goddess Delphi) would approve only such Plebeian member who was pliable. So what was it that the Plebeians had achieved? Nothing! Why? Because when they demanded a Tribunal of two persons, they should have also demanded their right to appoint the priest for the Goddess Delphi. The solution to their problem lay not in making the laws only but also to capture the position to effectively implement them. If we do not understand this situation then our efforts also will be futile.

Do not be under wrong impression that the Untouchability will be removed only by removal of ban on personal meetings and drawing of water from common wells. It will remove at the most Untouchability in the outer world but not from inside the house. For that, the ban on inter-Caste marriages will have to be removed. Once this happens, Untouchability will vanish from inside the house. And when the major reason is removed the minor ones get automatically resolved. Therefore, our aim should be higher, to remove ban on inter-Caste marriages. That is the only way the Untouchability can be removed forever.

Who can do this? Obviously, it cannot be done by the Brahmins. The Brahmins will retain their superiority so long as this social system based on *Varnashram* continues. Nobody would like to easily relinquish their higher social status. The Brahmins have ruled over the other Classes for the last several centuries and I don't think they will easily agree to accept the equal status with all others. Therefore, it is futile to expect that Brahmins or even the non-Brahmin higher Castes will take upon themselves to remove the inequalities in our society. These communities cannot contribute anything for the social revolution. Therefore, this mighty work of elimination of Untouchability and social inequality undertaken by us will have to be completed by ourselves only. We should presume that we are born only for this purpose.

This work for our self-emancipation is going to remove all the difficulties in the path of our progress. You are fully aware how the Untouchability has spoiled our economic progress. Once upon a time, many of our people used to get recruited in the military. In fact, we had monopoly in military jobs which was a great solace to our people. But now our entry in military and also in the police and other government offices is stopped not because it is banned by the law, but because the Government has meekly accepted the objections from the higher Castes to our recruitment in Government services. This curse of Untouchability does not allow us to do government jobs and also any business because we do not have money required for that. And even if we do any business, doubt remains, who will buy our goods? Thus, you will realize that this social system of discrimination is not as plain as it looks. It is the root cause of our poverty, wretchedness and humiliating status. If we have to rise above this position we must take up this difficult task of social reform.

This work of social reforms is not only in our self-interest but is in the interest of the nation. The Hindu society cannot survive unless the discrimination based on *Chaturvarna* is eliminated. The social value is an important ingredient for a cohesive society, the society without frictions. However, in Hindu society such values which create social discrimination are considered as virtuous, whereas those which bring about unity in the society are treated with contempt. This needs to be changed. We will have to completely eliminate this discriminatory, dehumanizing structure of the society to make our nation strong.

Some people laugh at the concept of equality. They argue that every person has different physical and mental capabilities. How can they be treated equal? But these people have not fully understood the meaning of equality. They do not realize that the power to control others cannot be granted on the basis of birth, it should be granted only on the basis of qualities. But all should be treated equal till they are trained and educated to become capable for the grant of powers.

As per the principles of Social Science, the social system is largely responsible for development of natural qualities obtaining in any individual. If anybody always gets discriminative treatment then the only quality that will develop in him will be that of servitude and the person will never be capable of any position of authority. Similarly, if a bad person is always discarded by the good persons, he will never try to improve himself. Therefore, it is clear that without non-discriminatory, equal treatment there cannot be development of any individual. The social discrimination in Hinduism hinders the personal development of its members on one hand and also it denies their contribution in the nation building. Therefore, I say that our purpose of this Mahad Conference is not only for our self-development but it is also for the benefit of the nation.

We have initiated this movement for social revolution. Nobody should be under impression that this is something for the amusement of slothful. We have our heart in this movement which gives us strength to carry on. Nobody can now stop us. I pray His Almighty to bless us that this social revolution which is started here by us achieves its objective peacefully. But it is equally true that it will largely depend upon our opponents whether this revolution remains peaceful. If the higher Caste people do not oppose our movement, if they do not try to suppress it with the help of foreigners or the people of other religions and if they discard their atrocious religious texts, behave in accordance with the ethical laws, we assure them that we will complete our movement peacefully.

Dr Ambedkar's response to the criticism of the "Mahad March" can be seen from his Presidential Address (November 27, 1927).[35] He said:

We had a Conference of Untouchables on March 18, to establish our civil rights on the public water source at Mahad. I have no doubt that this Conference will be written in golden letters in the history. The Touchables had prevented the Untouchables to draw water from the lake. As a result the organizers of the Conference had to declare that now Mahad is our Panipat. Not only that, they had taken a pledge to do *Satyagraha* to achieve their objective.

35. Presidential Speech in Marathi at the Solapur District *Vatandar Mahar Parishad*, Solapur, (November 27, 1927). For full summary in English, see, *Ambedkar Speaks,* (Jadhav Narendra, Vol. I, pp.93-101.)

The Touchables have started advising the Untouchables now. Mr Chitrav Shastri, who is said to be 'know all', started telling, rather seriously: 'The difference between the population of Touchables and Untouchables should not be forgotten in this movement. In our Marathi-speaking areas at least ¾th are the Touchables and only ¼th are Untouchables. Whatever might be the differences amongst Touchables, they are about the custom of Untouchability. This can be seen in Mahad and other areas and the livelihood of Untouchables is entirely in the hands of Touchables. When the Untouchables will have their own independent arrangement for their livelihood then they may like to sacrifice their lives for their human rights. That will be a historical day, not only for the Hindus, but for the whole of Hindustan.' Similarly, an editor of a weekly published by a Hindu Organization from Mumbai, who in the garb of social work, actually wants to establish superiority of their own Caste, has started a similar smear campaign. This honourable editor says, '*Satyagraha* no doubt is very sweet word but we should not forget that it is a double edged sword. Dr Ambedkar may test the water of Mahad Lake along with his followers on the strength of his *Satyagraha*. But when its repercussions start in each and every village what will be the fate of the Untouchables? It will be like coming out of steam to get caught in a fire. Who will be responsible for this? Does the Doctor Saheb think that Untouchability will vanish from the whole of Hindustan if their *Satyagraha* becomes successful at one or two places? We strongly believe that this *Satyagraha* of Doctor Saheb will result into severe social conflict, maybe, even bloodshed.'

This is the way Touchables of Mahad area are giving warnings to the Untouchables. Similar warnings are also being voiced in the Berar area. The Untouchables of Amravati who are trying to enter a temple of Amba goddess are receiving such threats as reported in the *Swarajya* daily published from Poona. Last month there was a Conference of the Touchables on the grounds of Shri Hanuman Vyayam Mandir. In this Conference, the Untouchables have been reminded that they are destitutes and dependants; hence they should not hurt the sentiments of Touchable Hindus. If you do it and try to resolve your problem by threats and coercion, then the Touchables will completely stop giving shelter and support to you to bring you to your knees by starving you!

Wealth is an effective tool for the progress of any nation. For this, it is essential that it should be accumulated. But if the same wealth is used to enslave the poor population or to dwarf their growth and when the wealthy people use their wealth to show off their status and superiority then such wealth becomes devil's wealth as per our religious texts. Such wealth is sham! Those who are giving us advice should also be aware about this religious teaching. In Bombay, when the labours go on strike against the mill-owners these same Touchables do not advise them that the livelihood of these labourers is in the hands of mill-owners. Rather they encourage labourers to struggle against the mill owners. They also suggest the mill-owners that they should not try to exploit the poor labourers, on the strength of their wealth.

We don't feel bad about this; instead, we appreciate their sympathy for the labourers. But we want to ask one question to them. If misuse of wealth against the people fighting for economic equality is unethical then is it ethical to do it against the people fighting for social equality? And if that is not ethical, and is against the religion as well, then those who are taking trouble of advising the Untouchables, why are they not advising the Touchables that social boycott of the Untouchables is a sin? Had they done this, we could have understood their piousness. But since they have not done it, we do not believe that their advice is just a caution to the Untouchables. We see that it is full of poison of threats. Because some people feel ashamed of openly condemning, they resort to such kind of advice. But, it is neither an advice nor a condemnation; it is much beyond that. We feel that it is to remind the Untouchables of the kind of weapon that Touchables have in their hands to teach them a lesson.

Those who sympathize with this cause, advise Untouchables to refrain from the *Satyagraha* because they know that the livelihood of Untouchables is in the hands of Touchables. They should also have advised the Touchables not to misuse their power of wealth to defeat the *Satyagraha*. But, this did not occur to them! In fact, there is no reason why the Untouchables should be told that they will be boycotted if they go on the *Satyagraha*. The Untouchables are fully aware of this from the very beginning. Who should be afraid of the boycott? The one who has no purpose in life will fear! They will never fear who have a clear vision of the purpose of their life. They know fully well that rigorous efforts are required to achieve any objective, howsoever small it may be. And when the objective is high and noble, even more rigorous work is necessary. There is no example in history of anybody reaching to his goal without perseverance. It is not that just luxury and health are the purpose of any living being. If that be so, so many amazing things befitting the humanity would not have happened in this world. Only animals will be satisfied with eating and playing.

The food, rest, fear and other physical attributes may be common amongst human beings and animals but God has given wisdom only to the human beings. If that wisdom is not awakened then a human being is no different than an animal. He may remain happy with his good health. But the person whose wisdom is awakened has to decide whether he needs only good health or he wants to achieve the objective of his life. The Untouchables are now awakened and the time has come for them to decide whether they want just a peaceful existence or equality in social status. They have decided to achieve the social equality and I am sure these awakened Untouchables will sacrifice everything that is required to remove the difficulties in their path. Not only that they may even sacrifice their lives!

Why the boycott should bother them who are almost at the nadir? And what is the reason to caution those people who have willingly chosen this path of *Satyagraha*? There is no reason to get unnecessarily scared by the threats from the opponents of our movement. Because nobody is going to use the self-defeating weapon of boycott, and even if someone does, it won't last for long.

We all are aware that similar action of boycott of foreign goods was adopted against the British Government. It was there for quite a few years but everybody knows that it hardly had any effect on the British Government. The reason is simple. The boycott may become successful where the mutual economic relationship is that of owner and beggar. If the owner boycotts the beggar, there is no loss to the owner. But if the economic relationship is that in the nature of exchange or contract then the boycott does not work. Under these conditions boycott will result into loss of trade. Since everybody has a self-interest in trade, business and exchange; nobody is going to be willing to sacrifice that interest. If that were not so, then the mill-owners would have boycotted the ever-demanding labourers; and the boycott against British also would have been successful. This did not happen. But this weapon of boycott is a strange one, in that it harms both, the enemy as well as the one who uses it. Those who threaten of using this weapon of boyçott probably have not realized this typical nature of the boycott. Or probably they thought the Untouchables are the beggars who survive at the mercy of the Touchables.

Burning of Manu Smriti

Dr Ambedkar challenged the authority of all Hindu Scriptures. He said:

"If you say your religion is our religion, your rights and ours must be equal. Is this the case? If not, on what grounds do you say that we must remain in the Hindu fold?"

Dr Ambedkar denounced the *Manu Smruti*. This book, compiled around 1500 years ago, had traditionally governed the laws and lives of Hindus. Revered by the so-called Upper-Caste Hindus, it was reviled by the Untouchables, as it directed that molten lead be poured into the ears of Untouchables if they heard or read the sacred Vedas. Dr Ambedkar felt that the Manu Smruti was a charter of rights for the so-called Upper-Caste Hindus but a Bible of slavery for the Untouchables. He condemned it as a symbol of tyranny among the Hindus. He then gave a call to publicly burn copies of the Holy Book. That evening, the *Manu Smruti* was placed on a special pyre and ceremoniously burned amid cheers from the Untouchables. This bold gesture was enacted to essentially demonstrate that Untouchables were no longer willing to abide by the religious and ritual confinements propagated by the Caste Hindus.

★ ★ ★

[*The Next day i.e., December 26, 1927, the conference was converted into a Committee so as to pass resolutions about the movement. Accordingly, Dr Ambedkar advised the volunteers not to allow any outsider in the hall. Then Dr Ambedkar put up the following proposal.*]

Dr Ambedkar said,

> Yesterday I was called by the Collector for a meeting. He explained to me that the administration is not against the *Satyagraha*, per se. But since the Touchable Hindus have appealed to the court and obtained Prohibitory Orders against our action of going to the Mahad lake, he has to step in. I replied that I have myself come determined to do *Satyagraha*. I am not going to change my decision about *Satyagraha*. And I will advise the same thing to my people. Only thing, I will not force them for it. But I am not going to discourage them because of Prohibitory Orders. Then the Collector desired that if majority of our people decide to do the *Satyagraha* then he would like to speak a few words to them. I promised him that he would get that opportunity. Beyond that I have not committed anything more. But I still leave it to you to take whatever decision you like. We have to remember one thing that if we want to achieve

anything of sustainable benefit we must be ready to suffer great difficulties. There is no instance anywhere in the history of success without strong perseverance. Therefore, we should not be afraid if we are required to go to jail on account of violating the Prohibitory Orders. The Prohibitory Orders are obtained on the grounds of usage. It needs to be decided whether the said usage is just or unjust. Otherwise we will end up in accepting the injustice, while trying to follow the court orders. *Satyagraha* is a difficult test of persistence. You will have to observe very strong restraint on yourself while suffering the difficulty in *Satyagraha*. We are willingly offering our lives to others. You will not be allowed to carry sticks to the *Satyagraha* place. You will not be allowed to disobey any order of the Government officers. None of you should ask for pardon if arrested during the *Satyagraha*. You must keep saying till the end that whatever you have done is right. In sum (1) No sticks to be carried; (2) Follow Government orders; (3) Be ready to go to the jail; and (4) Do not seek pardon for doing *Satyagraha*.

You must strictly follow these rules. Then only you can participate in the *Satyagraha*. Do not join the movement because I am telling you. Our fight is for the justice. If you are convinced and you are ready for facing the troubles and difficulties then only join the *Satyagraha*.

[After his speech Dr Ambedkar requested others to speak "For" and "Against" the proposal and accordingly take a decision. After such speeches were over Dr Ambedkar said….]

Considering all the speeches it appears that this Committee is in favour of doing the *Satyagraha*. I am really happy about it. But I do not want blind followers. I do not want those who might repent about going to the jail by participating in the *Satyagraha* for my sake. Therefore, before we decide to do the *Satyagraha* we should ascertain how many of you are ready for this difficult work. It cannot be ascertained by raising the hands. We will have to count those who are willing to go to the jail. If I find that majority of you are ready for *Satyagraha* then I will inform the Collector and invite him to address you in the evening. If you are firm on your resolve for *Satyagraha* even after listening the Collector then we will proceed with our movement.

Accordingly, considering that majority of people were in favour of doing the *Satyagraha* the Collector was invited to address the gathering. The Collector spoke about Prohibitory Orders of the court and advised the people to desist from the *Satyagraha*. He also cautioned that if they still go on *Satyagraha* they will invite ire of the Government who is otherwise favourable to their demands for equality.

After the Collector left, people again spoke in favour of *Satyagraha* but Dr Ambedkar announced that there will be further discussions later in the evening and decision will be taken next day morning. After discussions amongst few selected leaders, it was decided that the *Satyagraha* be deferred for the time being. Instead a rally be taken in the village around the lake. Accordingly, the Collector was informed in the late evening. But who should pilot the proposal for deferment of *Satyagraha* before the Committee? Again, it was decided that it should be done by Dr Ambedkar only because people would not listen to any other leader.

Next day, i.e., December 27, 1927, the resolution was moved for deferment of *Satyagraha* till the court decision on the Civil suit filed by the Touchables. While moving this, Dr Ambedkar said,

> Yesterday I had moved a resolution in favour of *Satyagraha* and today I am moving a resolution to defer it. You might think I am wavering kind of a person. But it is not correct. I have done both the things after due consideration. Yesterday, I wanted to see what is the depth of your resolve. I have seen that your resolve is firm. Nobody can have any doubt about it. I am satisfied about it. Firm resolve was one thing that was missing amongst us and that was great weakness. That weakness is now removed. You have become strong.
>
> Now my advice about deferring the *Satyagraha* is after due consideration: it is not proper to use your strength immediately simply because you have regained it. We should use our strength sparingly and at an appropriate time only. After much thought, I feel we should not use our strength today. If we do this *Satyagraha* today it will be against the Government. If the Government is not favourable we will do our *Satyagraha* against the Government as well; there is no harm in that. But is the Government unfavourable? No, it is in fact favourable to our cause. Then why unnecessarily embarrass the Government? Secondly, the Touchables are not at all favourable to us. They are totally non-cooperative. The markets are closed for us, lands are withdrawn for us, our cattle are not allowed for grazing. We are going through all these harassments, Government support is necessary to come out of these harassments. In such a situation, we should not waste the sympathy of the Government by resorting to *Satyagraha* against it. Therefore, I request you to pass this resolution.
>
> Nobody can laugh at you. The Collector himself has requested you. Nobody can say that you are cowards and hence you have deferred this *Satyagraha*. Nobody can say that. At best people may say that your leaders have backed out. But you need not worry about it. I am not worried. I am happy, nay proud, that my followers have gone a step further ahead of me.
>
> We are deferring this *Satyagraha* but remember that our objective is to capture this Mahad Lake and we shall not sit quiet till we achieve our objective.

[*Later all the assembled people took out a huge rally on the roads of Mahad and passed it encircling the Lake. It was so huge a rally that it took more than two hours at such a small place. It was very disciplined. The Touchable Hindus had literally confined themselves inside their houses and all the shops were closed. Although Satyagraha did not actually enter the Mahad lake, they had literally captured it by surrounding it by a rally on all sides.*]

Ironically, following the Chavdar Lake stuggle earlier, the orthodox high born of Mahad had the Brahmin priests "purify" the "desecrated" reservoir by pouring into it 108 pots of curd, milk, cow dung and cow urine amid loud religious chants. By burning the Hindu scriptures at the same place only a few months later, Dr Ambedkar had succeeded in converting the fight for the right to drinking water into a socio-cultural struggle of the downtrodden masses.

It was around this time that Dr Ambedkar formed the *Samaj Samata Sangh* (September 1927) and the *Samata Sainik Dal* (December 1927) with a view to aggressively pursuing the agenda of social equality.

CHAPTER NINE

Interaction with the Indian Statutory Commission (Simon Commission)

THE GOVERNMENT OF India Act, 1919 had introduced a system of diarchy for governing the Provinces of British India. The Act had stated that a Commission would be appointed after ten years to review the progress of the Governance Scheme and to suggest further steps for reform. Accordingly, a Commission of seven British MPs was appointed in 1927 to look into the state of Indian Constitutional Reforms. This Commission titled the Indian Statutory Commission was chaired by Sir John Simon and hence also called the Simon Commission.

The Indian Statutory Commission (the Simon Commission) commenced its work in Mumbai on February 3, 1928. The Simon Commission which was entrusted the responsibility of consultations with representatives of political and social groups, however, did not have any Indian members. In protest against this exclusion, the Indian National Congress decided to boycott the proceedings of the Simon Commission altogether. On the other hand, several minority and Depressed Class Associations did take part in the deliberations.

What was Dr Ambedkar doing at this time? While being in the whirlwind of the mass movement—Mahad *Satyagraha* and public burning of *Manu Smriti*, Dr Ambedkar was appointed as Acting Professor, at the Government Law College, Mumbai (June 1928). When the Simon Commission came to India, Dr Ambedkar submitted a Statement (May 1928) on behalf of his *Bahishkrit Hitakarini Sabha,* entitled: "Protection of the Interests of the Depressed Classes".

Dr Ambedkar's Statement to the Simon Commission presents in detail the safeguards for the Protection of the Interests of the Depressed Classes as a minority in the Bombay Presidency and suggests changes in the composition of, and guarantees from, the Bombay Legislative Assembly so as to ensure them under Provincial Autonomy. This Statement was submitted by Dr Ambedkar on May 29,

1928 on behalf of the social organization that he had founded, *Bahishkrita Hitakarini Sabha*.

The Statement deals with two aspects of protection of the interests of the Depressed Classes:

(a) Protection through Adequate Representation, and
(b) Protection through Guarantees

The Statement notes that the promises made under the Montague-Chelmsford Reforms were thrown to the wind by the Southborough Franchise Committee and demands 22 representatives of the Depressed Classes in a Council composed of 140 members.

The Southborough Committee had given a grossly under-estimated figure as to the population of the Depressed Classes in the Bombay Presidency, leading to their just two representatives in the Assembly. The Census of 1921 conservatively placed the population of the Depressed Classes in India at about 53 million, whereas that in the Bombay Presidency was estimated to be 25 lakh people at the minimum. On the basis of population alone, the Depressed Classes, it was argued, were entitled to 15 seats out of a total of 140. Additional demand of seven representatives (over and above the 15 on population basis) was defended on the grounds of two principles:

(a) The lower the standing of a community the greater is the electoral advantage it must get over the rest;
(b) If a minority is to be protected then there must be enough representatives of the minority to save it from being entirely submerged.

Treatment of all minority communities in respect of application of these principles must be impartial. The Statement demonstrated that the Muslims had been allocated seats disproportionately larger than their share in the population. But the same principles were not extended to the Depressed Classes. The Statement protested against this grading of the citizens on the basis of their political importance.

The Statement opposed the principle of nomination and insisted instead upon the extension of the principle of election to the Depressed Classes. Selection rather than nomination, it was argued, would be important from the standpoint of political education of the Depressed Classes as also for them to be eligible to find place in the Cabinet of the country.

Two objections are put forth against the application of the principle of election to the Depressed Classes:

(a) Difficulty in forming constituencies, and
(b) Difficulty in getting a sufficiently large electorate

In respect of the first objection, the Statement points out that Moslems and Europeans are no less scattered than the Depressed Classes and yet, the principle of election was extended to them. In respect of the second objection, the Statement concedes the difficulty in getting a sufficiently large electorate. But it could be easily overcome by lowering the pitch of the franchise. In any case, the existing pitch of the franchise is unjustifiable on every ground. It means a Government of the whole Presidency of two crore people by a minority of only seven lakh voters, which is a mockery of responsible Governments. While alleging the Congress politics for giving only a subordinate place to the question of franchise, the Statement emphatically states that the fear that a lowering of the franchise will bring in a large part of unintelligent people is without foundation.[36]

The Statement does not ask for communal electorates, and opines that it would be sufficient if the Depressed Classes are provided with reserved seats in general constituencies.

The Statement demands that three members from the Depressed Classes of the Bombay Presidency should be elected to the Legislative Assembly by their representatives in the Local Legislative Council.

In addition, the Statement demands guarantees for civil rights of the Depressed Classes as a minority in the Bombay Presidency. Specifically, the Statement demands inclusion of clauses in the Constitution of the country and as a fundamental part thereof, guaranteeing for the Depressed Classes education, unrestricted recruitment in the army, navy and the police, priority in recruitments to all posts in all Civil Services for a period of thirty years, appointment of a special inspector of police from among Depressed Classes for every district, effective representation on the Local Boards and the right for appeal to the Government of India in cases of violation of these rights.

As to the need for guarantees in addition to adequate representation in the Council, the Statement demurs to this much faith in the efficacy of a representative form of Government to effectively protect a minority from the tyranny of the majority. Pointing out that there is an enormous dread of the Reforms prevalent amongst the Depressed Classes, the Statement argues that nothing can allay such fears as the system of guarantees can do.

★ ★ ★

In all, as many as 18 Depressed Class Associations submitted their Memoranda to the Commission. Interestingly, 16 out of 18 such associations pleaded for separate electorates for the Depressed Classes. The only two exceptions were the Madras Central Adi-Dravida Mahajana Sabha (which favoured nomination for the Depressed Classes) and the *Bahishkrut Hitakarini Sabha* which demanded joint electorates with reservation of seats for the Depressed Classes (22 out of 140 seats in the Bombay Legislative Council). Dr Ambedkar called for adult suffrage but rejected separate

36. Dr Ambedkar was advocating universal adult franchise at a time when Europe was still considering female franchise and the USA the vote for Blacks. See Raja Sekhar Vundru, "The Other Father", *Outlook* (Special Independence Day Issue : August 20, 2012).

Caste-based electorates. While Dr Ambedkar's Untouchable supporters hailed the Memorandum as a Manifesto of Untouchables' Rights, many others dubbed him as a British stooge and a traitors.[37]

Around the time, a major strike of textile mill workers in Mumbai (numbering around 1,50,000) was on. In that context, in response to questions by a member of the Simon Commission, Major Attlee (who later became the Prime Minister of Britain), Dr Ambedkar clarified that a large number of mill workers who were from the Depressed Classes do not cease to be thus upon finding employment. They face discrimination based on Untouchability, being entirely left out of the most well paying departments. It is important to note that Dr Ambedkar did not favour the strike because the then prevailing labour unions fought for workers' economic rights but did not care for the human rights of the Untouchable workers. It was this consideration which was going to prompt Dr Ambedkar eight years later to set up a political party called the Independent Labour Party.

★ ★ ★

After an all party-meeting in February and May, 1928 the Congress Party appointed a Committee under the Chairmanship of Motilal Nehru to draft a *Swaraj* Constitution of India—which was perhaps the first Indian attempt at Constitution-making. While preparing the counter-proposals on the Constitution, the Motilal Nehru Committee consulted all minorities, but did not consult the Depressed Class Groups. In fact, the Motilal Nehru Committee Report stated:

> We have not made any special provision for the representation of the Depressed Classes in the legislatures. This could only be done by way of special electorates or by nomination.

However, both these methods were considered harmful and unsound. The Nehru Committee stated that they would not extend either principle.

It is clear that Dr Ambedkar was strongly opposed to the Motilal Nehru Committee Report. The Nehru Committee Report was inspired by Western Liberal Values based on the notion of a nation as a collection of individuals, not very different from Dr Ambedkar's own line of thinking. However, despite the yearning for the emergence of an individualist society, free from Caste cleavages, Dr Ambedkar recognized that in the hierarchical Indian Society, social equality could be promoted only by relying upon the logic of groups: Untouchables needed to be helped collectively for an unspecified period of transition. [38]

The Simon Commission submitted its report on May 7, 1929 which recommended 10 reserved seats for the Depressed Classes in joint electorates (and 33 per cent of

---

37. Keer, Dhanajnay, op cit, p.116.

38. See Jaffrelot, op cit, and Vidhu Verma (1999) for this argument.

elected seats out of 140 seats to the Muslims with separate electorates). In the absence of participation by the Indian National Congress, however, the Report remained a dead letter. In order to break the impasse, the British Government had to resort to another set of consultations, which came to be known as the Round Table Conference.

★ ★ ★

PROVINCIAL COMMITTEE TO CO-OPERATE WITH THE SIMON COMMISSION

When the Simon Commission came to India in 1928 to look into the State of Indian Constitutional Reforms, the people all over the country were outraged. This is because the Simon Commission, which was to determine the future of India, did not include even a single Indian member. The Indian National Congress as well as the Muslim League resolved to boycott the Government.

Lord Irwin, the Viceroy of India, responded by establishing an All-India Committee for co-operation with the Simon Commission. Government of Bombay Presidency also established a similar Committee for co-operation with the Simon Commission choosing members from the Provincial Legislative Council. Dr Ambedkar who was then a Nominated member of the Bombay Legislative Council was elected to serve as a Member of the Bombay Province Committee for co-operation with the Simon Commission (August 3, 1928). Dr Ambedkar testified before the Bombay Provincial Committee (in Pune) on October 23, 1928.

When the Bombay Province Committee for co-operation with the Simon Commission submitted its "Report on the Constitution of the Government of Bombay Presidency", Dr Ambedkar did not agree in the tenor of the Report..., and was not able to accept the more important of the conclusions..... Accordingly, Dr Ambedkar submitted a separate report containing his own views and recommendations, which turned out to be bulkier that the report submitted by the Bombay Province Committee.

The sum and substance of Dr Ambedkar's "separate" report may be summarized as follows:

Summary of Recommendations of Dr Ambedkar's Separate Report

There should be no separation of Karnatak or Sind from the Bombay Presidency.

(a) There should be complete responsibility in the Provincial Executive.
(b) Under no circumstances should the Executive be made irremovable. There shall be no communal representation in the Executive. Ministers should be amenable to courts of law for illegal acts. The Constitution should provide for the impeachment of Ministers. There should be joint responsibility in the

Executive. The Executive should be presided over by a Prime Minister and not by the Governor.

(c) The Governor should have the position of a Constitutional head. He should have no emergency powers.

(d) There should be adult franchise.

(e) The Legislature should be wholly elective. All Class and communal electorates should be abolished except for Europeans. Reserved seats should be provided for Mohammedans, Depressed Classes and Anglo-Indians and to the Non-Brahmins only if the franchise continues to be a restricted one.

(f) The Legislature should consist of 140 members. Of these Mohammedans should have 33 and the Depressed Classes 15. The under-representation of certain districts and the over-representation of others should be rectified on the basis of population. There should be a Committee to adjust seats between different Classes and interests. The requirement of a residential qualification for a candidate should be removed.

(g) Lucknow Pact is not a permanent settlement, and cannot prevent consideration of the question arising out of it afresh and on their own merits.

(h) There should be no second chamber in the Province.

(i) The Legislature should have the power of appointing and removing the President, of defining its privileges and regulating its procedure.... The Legislature should have the power to move "A motion of non-confidence". The Legislature should have the power to alter the Constitution subject to certain conditions.

(j) There should be complete Provincial autonomy. The division of functions between Central and Provincial should be reconsidered with a view to doing away with the control of Central Government now operating through the system of previous sanction and subsequent veto.

(k) Within the limits fixed by the functions assigned to the Provincial Government the relations between that Government and the Home Government should be direct and not through the medium of the Central Government.

(l) There should be a distinct Provincial Civil Service, and the Secretary of State should cease altogether to perform the function of a recruiting agency. His functions regarding the Services may be performed by a Provincial Civil Service Commission. Indianisation of Services should be more rapid. Its pace should vary with the nature of the different departments of State. Indianisation should be accompanied by a different scale of salary and allowances. In the course of Indianisation of the Services, arrangement should be made for the fulfilment of claims of the Backward Classes.

CHAPTER TEN

In the Bombay Provincial Legislative Council (2)

SMALL HOLDERS' RELIEF BILL

This Bill which was introduced in the Provincial Legislative Council in the second half of 1927 had aimed at addressing the two problems which affected the agriculturists in Bombay Presidency, viz., the problem of scattered farms and the problem of small farms.

This was the problem that Dr Ambedkar had extensively dealt with in his Research Paper published in 1918. Dr Ambedkar, therefore, participated in the Council debate and when he disagreed with the thinking of the House, he submitted a Minute of Dissent (July 10, 1928). Dr Ambedkar's contention may be summarized as under:

(a) Part I of this Bill starts with the assumption that for the purposes of profitable cultivation it is necessary to have bigger farms than what we have now. I am not at all satisfied that this assumption is correct.

(b) The mechanism employed by the Bill to maintain the standard unit once it is laid down in two-fold. First it severely penalizes the owners of farms smaller than the standard so that ownership of a small farm shall to him become a burden instead of a benefit. Secondly, it prohibits the ownership of small farms in that it provides that in future small farms shall not come into existence at all.

(c) I object to this mechanism on three grounds. Firstly, because it affects the rights of property.

(d) The second ground of my objection to the mechanism of the Bill is that it will be infructuous, and will largely leave things as they are.

(e) Apart from all this, I think that the mechanism of Part-I of the Bill overshoots the purpose which the Bill has in view. The purpose of the Bill is to have larger farms under single cultivation than is the case now. Now I feel that if we can combine small farms owned by different owners for cultivation we ought to stop there and not attempt to bring them under the ownership of a single individual unless it was proved that single ownership was necessary for combine cultivation. I am certain that the establishment of co-operative farms of standard size will give us all that we want under the Bill and will save from destruction the small farm-owners. The co-operative farm will be like a shareholders' company in which the company remains even though the shareholders change. The scheme is simple in its operation and avoids the evils of the present Bill.

(f) I do not see what objection there can be to such a plan. As a matter of fact such a system is actually working in many European countries and particularly in Italy.

(g) For the reasons given above, I cannot support Part I of the Bill although I am not opposed to its aims and objects. Regarding Part II, I have no objection to raise, now that it is confined purely to consolidation. I may however say this that under my scheme separate provision for consolidation would be unnecessary. A co-operative farm would be both a large and a consolidated holding.

ON MATERNITY BENEFIT BILL

Around the same time, while supporting the first reading of the Bill on Maternity Benefits, Dr Ambedkar said (July 1928):

> I rise to support the first reading of this Bill. The pre-natal conditions which affect the mother are an important factor in the Bill and the subsequent bringing up of the child. I do not think anybody will controvert that proposition. And I believe, therefore, Sir, that it is in the interests of the nation that the mother ought to get a certain amount of rest during the pre-natal period and also subsequently, and the principle of the Bill is based entirely on that principle. That being so, Sir, I am bound to admit that the burden of this ought to be largely borne by the Government. I am prepared to admit this fact because the conservation of the people's welfare is primarily the concern of the Government. But that being so Sir, I am not prepared to admit that the employer who employs a woman, under such circumstances, is altogether free from the liability of such benefit in the interests of the woman and the reason for this, is this: There is no doubt that an employer employs women in certain industries because he finds that there is a greater profit to be gained by him by the employment of women than he would gain by the employment of men. He is able to get pro rata larger benefits out of women than he would get by employing men. That being so, it is absolutely reasonable to say that to a certain extent at least the employer will be liable for this kind of benefit when he gets a special benefit by employing women instead of men. I, therefore, say that although there ought to have been some liability imposed on the Government in the matter of maternity benefit, I think the Bill is not altogether wrong if it seeks to impose the liability under the present circumstances on the employer. I, therefore, support the Bill on that account.
>
> I think, therefore, the benefits contemplated by this Bill ought to be given by this Legislature to the poor women who toil in our factories in this Presidency.

BILL ABOUT *MAHAR VATAN*

Dr Ambedkar, on his own initiative, moved a very important Bill titled: The Hereditary Offices Act (Amendment) Bill in August 1928. (*The Bill was approved nine years later, on September 17, 1937*).

While moving this Bill, Dr Ambedkar said:

I rise to move that Bill to amend the Bombay Hereditary Offices Act, 1874. The hereditary officers referred to in this Bill are known under the Hereditary Offices Act as the inferior officers. At the present moment, such inferior hereditary officers cover the *Mahars* in the Deccan, the Vethias or the Varthanias in Gujarat, the Ramoshis or the Juglias and the Holiyas in Karnatak. A large part of these inferior holders are *Mahars*, and in the course of the remarks that I propose to offer this House. I shall largely speak of the *Mahars* as representative of the inferior officers.

Sir, the House should know the wrongs and the grievances which have led me to bring forth this Bill. Now the wrongs are very many; First, Sir, it will be remembered that these inferior holders of *vatan* are Government servants according to the *Vatan* Act. But, Sir, the duties of these Government servants are not defined anywhere. It is not known, in fact nobody as a matter of fact can say, to what particular department these *vatandar Mahars* belong. As a matter of fact, every department claims their services. That I submit is an extraordinary system.

Every Government servant knows to which department he belongs and the services that are expected of him. No department I understand employs any individual as servant who can be called upon as the maid of all work but *Mahars* for all practical purposes are and are treated as maid of all work of all the Government departments.

Further, he may be called upon to render service at any hour of day or night. Every other Government servant, however humble his position between particular hours; But that is never the case with these *Mahars*. They can be called upon to render service not only during the day not even between sunset and sunrise but they can be called upon to render service at night. If an officer calls upon the *Mahar* to render service during night, whether it is raining or there is lightning or any other difficulty, he dare not refuse to do so.

The third grievance is this. In the case of *Mahars* the officiator is the person whose name is entered in what is called the service register and he is not the only one person who is liable to render service to Government, but his whole family is liable to render service to Government. Not only the male member but, I submit that in their absence the female members also are impressed into Government service. Sir, there is no escape out of the system as it exists today. Under the system as it operates, not only the officiator is obliged to render service but the whole family is obliged to render the service. I submit that this is a most oppressive system not obtainable in any other department of Government services.

What is the remuneration that these poor people for their hard and arduous labour that they do for all the 24 hours get? This House will be surprised if I tell them that the Government practically pays nothing from their treasury directly for the services it exacts from these people. I have before me the figures given by the Government themselves. In Thana district, the amount paid by Government directly to the *Mahar* officiator comes to Rs1.5 per month. There is practically no remuneration whatsoever which Government gives to these poor *Mahars* for the services it exacts from them.

The sources of income for these people, the *vatandar Mahars*, are two. The first source is the *inam* land, and the second source is what is called the *Baluta* or the collection of grain made by the *vatandar Mahars* from the villagers. These *inam* lands were not given by British Government, but they were given to these *Mahars* by the ancient Emperors of this country. The *Maharvatan* is the most ancient *vatan* that we have in this country and all the lands have been given to them in ancient times. But the British Government has never paid a moment's attention to the remuneration of these people. They have left these poor people with such land as the ancient Rajas were pleased to give them. The *Mahar* population has increased enormously and the land assigned to the *Mahars* is divided and sub-divided to such an extent that the income these people get from the *inam* lands is absolutely not worthy of being taken into consideration.

The main part of the remuneration which these people get comes largely from the second source, namely, the *Baluta*. Now, Sir, the peculiarity of this mode of payment is really worthy of notice by this Honourable House. Again I will repeat that the *Mahars* are Government servants; but the Government does not take upon itself the responsibility of paying the remuneration to the person whom the Government employs. In every other case Government takes upon itself the responsibility of paying the peon, the clerk, the officer and employers but in the case of *Mahars*, so far as *Baluta* is concerned, there is no way by which Government takes upon itself the responsibility that the remuneration shall be paid to them. The reason is that under the *Vatan* Act with regard to the payment of the *Baluta*, the *Mahar* is left entirely to the sweet will of the ryots. If the ryots are pleased to pay a *Mahar*, he can get it. If the ryots are not pleased to pay the *Mahar* at the end of 12 months after exacting service from him, the *Mahar* will find that he has rendered service for nothing.

That, I submit, Sir, is an atrocious system. A system which has no justice in it whatsoever. If the Government desires that these people should work for them, it is absolutely necessary that the Government should take upon its shoulders the responsibility of paying these *Mahars*: they ought not vicariously to throw off this burden in a most careless way upon a third party, namely the *ryot*; but that is exactly what is happening under the present system.

Then, Sir, is there any security that the *vatan* will be continued? Is there any security that the *Maharvatan* will not be suspended or resumed? Sir, there is no guarantee whatsoever. There is no security that the 'Patil' or the 'Kulkarni' will not make a report that the *Mahar* is not discharging his duty—an absolutely false and concocted report. There have been innumerable cases where such reports have been made by 'Patils' and 'Kulkarnis' and acted upon by the mamlatdar, and the *Mahars* have had their *vatans* suspended or resumed. In my own experience, which I admit does not extend over a very large number of years, I have come across innumerable cases where *Maharvatans* have been suspended or resumed. Grounded in that feeling of security there is no limit to the oppression or tyranny these people exercise over these unfortunate Class of people. That, I submit, is another evil which is inherent in this system.

Sir, the House will not probably believe it when I say that as a result of the *Vatan* system it is not open to the *Mahar* population in villages to claim the benefit of Dr Paranjpye's circular that their children should be made to sit along with children of the other Classes; although this Council has passed a resolution that the Depressed Classes should be allowed the use of *Dharamshalas* and all public places, it is not open to the Depressed Classes to ask for these privileges that this Council has been pleased to give them.

Whenever, for instance, any *Mahar* community in any particular village desires to make progress in any particular direction and that direction is not liked by the *ryot*, the one immediate step that the *ryot* takes is to stop the *Baluta* and to proclaim a social boycott

Sir, such a system which enslaves the whole population, which smothers the spirit of progress, which blocks the way for furtherance, is a system which, I think, no right-minded person, no man with any feelings, will sustain or will justify. Sir, no wonder that the whole of the *Mahar* population is absolutely tired of this *Vatan* system and is desirous of getting rid of it as soon as possibly can. With these few preliminary remarks I will now proceed to explain the provisions of the Bill which is before this House today.

I propose to make two divisions of the *vatandar Mahar* population. The first division is one which is absolutely tired of and would have nothing to do with the *vatan* at all, a Class which would like to be immediately relieved of the obligation to serve. Their only condition is that if they choose to give up their *vatan*, that is to say, their right to serve hereditary, they should not be deprived of the lands which they have in their possession. I propose that if a representative body of *vatandar Mahars* or a majority of them represent to the Collector in writing that they do not want to serve, and that they are willing to pay the full rate of assessment on their lands, the Collector should relieve them of their obligation to serve. That is the meaning of the proviso.

I now come, Sir, to the other Class of *vatandar Mahars*, those who care to carry on with the *vatan*, those who are prepared to render services provided their grievances are remedied. These *Mahars* I have provided for in Clause 6 of my Bill. The provision in this Section mainly consist in the re-organization of the *Baluta* System. If Honourable members will go through the Clauses which are enacted therein, they will find that there is, first of all, a provision made for the conversion of the *Baluta* into a money cess. Secondly, provision is made for the recovery of the money cess along with the land revenue. Thirdly, provision is made for the division of that cess into two parts, one for services rendered to the ryot and another for services rendered to the Government; so that that part of the cess which will be apportioned for services to the Government will be obligatory, while that part of the cess which will be apportioned for private services to the ryot will be optional. Those ryots who care to employ the services of the *Mahars* for their private service will be obliged to pay only that part of the cess which will have been assigned for private. The *Mahars*, on the other hand, if they do not want to render service to the ryot but want to render service only to the Government shall forfeit that part of the money cess which will have been assigned for private services.

What my Bill aims at is freedom of contract; if the ryots do not want to employ the *Mahars*, they ought to have perfect liberty not to employ them, and if the *Mahars* do not want to serve, the *Mahars* should have perfect liberty not to serve. But under the present system, under the system of joint remunerations, this liberty of contract is negative and is not obtainable. My scheme provides for that freedom of contract, and

I think at least in this century when every society has advanced from status to contract we ought not for instance block the progress of Indian society by refusing the *Mahars* and the ryots the liberty of contract.

I am an enemy of the *Vatan* System. I have striven all along to destroy the Maharaki *Vatan* System, although I know that in the immediate future the *Mahars* will suffer a great loss. But I am convinced that these shackles of the *Vatan* System are the principal causes which are keeping them backward. I am taking a long view of the matter and it is this that leads me to be indifferent to the immediate benefits to the *Mahars* from their *vatans*. I cannot, therefore, be particularly striving to steal an advantage over the ryots, not particularly striving for benefitting the *Mahars* at the cost of the ryot.

Before I bring my remarks to a close I think I ought to make it very clear to the Honourable the Revenue Member that this Bill has the support of the entire *Mahar* population. There is no division of opinion on that point at all. In fact, there cannot be a division of opinion on this Bill and for very good reason. The Bill is not an obligatory Bill. It is purely a discretionary Bill. Unless the *vatandar Mahars* desire that the provisions of this Bill should be brought into operation, they will not be brought into operation. Things will continue as they are now. A change will come only when the *Mahars* will feel the necessity for it. It will not be forced upon them against their will.

I say there cannot be any opposition to this Bill on the part of the *Mahars* themselves because the Bill is not an obligatory one and it does not compel them to take advantage of it. It only makes certain provisions in their interest if they want to avail themselves of them. The *Mahars* have not, therefore, objected to this Bill. Indeed, there cannot be any objection on their part. Not only have they not opposed the Bill, but they have whole-heartedly welcomed it.

Since the time I have been at this Bill I have never kept anything secret from the *Mahar* population. I have placed the principles and the provisions of this Bill before the whole *Mahar* population at several meetings to enable them to express their opinion on this Bill, and I am glad to say that the whole of the Bill and the principles embodied in it have been unanimously accepted by them. In order that the Government may not have any occasion to say that these meetings were engineered by me for the purpose of obtaining support for the Bill. I have, for the most part, abstained myself from attending these meetings, which have been held under the Chairmanship of members of other communities. My Honourable friend Mr Bole, sitting just by my side, will corroborate me when I say that in the city of Bombay a meeting of over 5,000 *vatandar Mahars* was held under his Presidentship. Of course, some people tried to fool the *Mahars* that the Bill is going to do them harm, but I think that the Honourable member will corroborate me whether or not the *Mahars* supported the Bill unanimously without a single dissenting voice. In the same manner, I would refer to my Honourable friend Mr Rajma Lakhichand. A meeting was held of the *vatandar Mahars* of Khandesh at Jalgoan under his Presidentship where I addressed them on the provisions and the principles of this Bill. Conservatively estimated, that meeting again was attended by something like 3,000 *Mahars*; the theatre was full to its capacity, and when the resolution was moved, there was not a single *Mahar* who opposed it. I think my Honourable friend Mr Thorat will corroborate me that a similar meeting was held in the Ahmadnagar district, where also the Bill was unanimously supported. I need not, of course, refer to the minor meetings held at different places. I can assure the House that the *Mahar* people are absolutely determined to have the Bill, and I may tell my Honourable friends that if the Government refuses to liberate these people on grounds of finance, on grounds of convenience, or on any other ground, that it will be a war between the Revenue Department and the *Mahars*.

It this Bill does not pass, I for myself am not going to be in the Council; I am going to spend the rest of my time in seeing that the *Mahars* organize a general strike, and bring the Honourable the Revenue Member to feel that the principles of this Bill are absolutely essential for the welfare of the *Mahar* people. I am speaking from the bottom of my heart; I do not want to keep anything behind. I want to say in all seriousness that that is our aim. Sir, I have been laboring in the cause of the Depressed Classes for the last three years as far as I possibly can. I have come across many difficulties in my way, and I have come definitely to know that the *vatan* is probably the greatest difficulty that I have to face in order to carry the *Mahar* population further. I am happy to find that the *Mahars* as well are convinced that these *vatans* stand in the way of their advancement. I, therefore, hope that this Council will unanimously pass this Bill. With these words, I move the first reading of the Bill.

CHAPTER ELEVEN

Deepening the Mass Movement

ON JUNE 14, 1928, the *Bahishkrit Hitakarini Sabha* was dissolved and a new organization was created, namely, the Depressed Classes Education Society for spreading education among these strata of the society. Dr Ambedkar appealed to the Government for financial assistance, which responded positively by granting a scheme for five hostels for the secondary school students belonging to the Depressed Classes.

Another important initiative by Dr Ambedkar around that time was formation of a social organization called *Samata Samaj Sangh* (Social Equality League). The Social Equality League believed and asserted that the principle of social equality is the corner-stone of a stable society. The principle of equality applied to all fields—social, economic, political and religious.

During the years 1928 and 1929, Dr Ambedkar, in the aftermath of the Mahad *Satyagraha* delivered some very important speeches.

In a Ganesh Festival in Mumbai (September 25, 1928), Dr Ambedkar delivered a Marathi speech in which he refuted all the major objectives raised against the movement initiated by him and argued that "Untouchability streams directly from the Caste System".[39] He said:

> Primarily there are three objections raised against our movement. First, one is that we run a separate movement and don't co-operate with Caste Hindus. Second objection is that our stance is aggressive. Third objection is that we unnecessary complicate two entirely different issues: Untouchability and Casteism, and treat them as one. This is unnecessarily delaying the eradication of Untouchability, it is said.
>
> Let me take up the first objection. If the objection means that we don't co-operate or wish to take help from a single Touchable fellow, then the objection is not valid. We are always ready to co-operate with 'our people' (about whom we are pretty sure) irrespective of whether he is Brahmin or non-Brahmin. Our 'Samaj Samata Sangh' has been trying hard to break Casteism and eradicate Untouchability from the Hindu

39. For full English Summary, see *Ambedkar Speaks* (Ed. Jadhav, Narendra), Vol. I, pp.119-21.

Society. This organization involves people from all Castes and everybody is allowed an entry, irrespective of their Caste. Untouchables have taken the reins of their movement in their own hands. Nothing strange in that.

When a society or Class lives in an extremely deprived state, few people from progressive society do come forward to lend a helping hand. Illustratively, it was some English men who had taken initiative to establish the Indian National Congress. Few people from the Liberal Party in England were responsible to create Labour Party in England. But such help from progressive Class can be received only to a limited extent. Such upholders can later become competitors, opponents and even enemies. The Liberal Party, which was supporter of Labour Party once, is today the enemy and competitor of the same. But no intellectual can say that the Labour Party is ungrateful, or it should not run a separate movement.

Untouchability eradication movement has a similar history. Initially, some progressive and liberal people from white-collar Brahmin Class helped Untouchables. Social reformers like Ranade used to say that there is no harm to touch Untouchables. They used to participate in their meetings and convey sympathetic words to Untouchables. For this, they in fact had to tolerate slander from their own high Castes. However, these social reformers wanted to make progress only in the Castes to which they belonged. They dealt with white collar issues such as whether tonsure of widows is permitted by religion or not, re-marriage of Brahmin women, whether men should keep long hair or not, whether women should be given education or not and the like. These discussions had no bearing whatsoever on the situation of Untouchables. Whether Brahmin women got re-married or not, or tonsure of women was discontinued or not, these issues could hardly be construed as an attack on the custom of Untouchability.

This was the general direction and limitation of efforts towards Untouchability eradication during the times of Maharashtrian Brahmin revolutioners like Ranade and Agarkar. Nowadays, Maharashtra is fired with the efforts of Hindu Sabha. However, the fervor that was visible in the times of Ranade and Agarkar is certainly not seen among the people of these Hindu associations in Maharashtra. They are more interested in purification of members of other religions rather than self-purification, and in mere numbers instead of organization. Hindus have large numbers, but it is useless because they don't have unity within them. Not that they are not aware of this fact, but most of those leaders are fair-weather friends. If Untouchables feel that there is no point in relying on them to free themselves from Untouchability, they cannot be blamed.

The only example in the world history where one human race has fought to free another human race from slavery is that of Whites in America. During the Civil War in the USA even father and sons, brothers and friends fought with each other. Gautam Buddha was the one and the only warrior in our country who fought relentlessly to eradicate the sin of Untouchability, thus attempting inherently to destroy the casteism. But such revolutionary incidents are very rare. Hence, we can't rely on the hope that this will happen yet again.

The second objection against us is that we have an aggressive stance and that we are not modest in our demands. As such, even those who sympathize with the cause of eradication of Untouchability are turning against us. Those who have this objection should be ashamed of themselves. There is no other community in the world as modest as Untouchables. We have remained modest for hundreds of years. Haven't we remained meek under the most humiliating and inhuman circumstances for ages? At least now, please don't teach us the lessons of modesty. Teach them to upper Caste Hindus. If the requests, applications and delegations would have helped to reclaim the lost freedom and suppressed rights, the moderates would have by now ruled India, and religious power of Hindus would have by now been surrendered to the Untouchables. We are not used to arrogance or aggression. We are fully pre-occupied by hand-to-mouth living through enormous hard work. We are into this movement because humanity is dearer to us than food. Doors are not opened unless you knock them, and our basic rights of humanity are not being released by you people unless we grab them.

Before answering to the third objection, I want to tell you that our movement for Untouchability eradication is not limited to only Untouchable Class but aspires to destroy the hereditary Untouchability in the Hindu Society. Achieving this is not going to be easy. We are aware of it. But if anyone has the real intention to overcome this disease, then those are only us—the Untouchables. All Castes except Brahmins have experienced or are experiencing at least some amount of social and religious Untouchability. Even within Brahmins there is caste-specific feeling of inferiority-superiority and Untouchability. *Chitpavan* Brahmin gets polluted from a Palshikar Brahmin during *puja*. A *Brahmin* lady keeps *kumkum* down so as to avoid the pollution from a *Kayastha* lady. The only difference is that it has reached its extreme in the case of Untouchables. That's why, even if we become Touchables like members of other religions, say, Muslims, the feeling of Untouchability will not die. The practice of inter-caste dining and marriage needs to be encouraged so as to kill that feeling. Otherwise, the disease of Untouchability will not be destroyed completely. But it must be destroyed completely. That is precisely why we are struggling. If we just wanted to become 'Touchable', we would have changed our religion and done so long back. Then there would have been any need for such strenuous effort.

Few months later, Dr Ambedkar delivered a speech in Marathi at Social Conference of the Belgaum District Depressed Classes wherein he maintained that the Depressed Classes must adopt an aggressive stance to establish their rights.

In his hard-hitting speech, Dr Ambedkar said:[40]

It is already quite late and it is about to rain also. Secondly, my mother-tongue is different from yours. I have my own doubts whether you will understand my speech because of different language. Still I would like to speak at least briefly.

We organize so many conferences, make speeches and pass resolutions. Many a time, great speakers are invited. But I don't think the Untouchability can be eliminated by these methods. We may pass resolutions about the harassment and exploitation caused to our people; and submit those resolutions to the Government. Presuming that the Government makes laws to remove ban on our entry to the temples and hotels, drawing water from the public wells and ponds, etc., the question is who will implement those laws? Unless we are capable to get the laws implemented, they will not be of any use.

We will have to eliminate the Untouchability ourselves. The Untouchability will vanish only if we become strong and fearless. We will have to do a severe hard work and, if necessary, also fight with the Touchables. We will have to become strong and

40. For fuller English Summary, see *Ambedkar Speaks* (Ed. Jadhav, Narendra), Vol.III, p. 64-5.

brave. It is true that our community is dependent on the others. It is difficult for us to survive if we do not cooperate with them. Therefore, many of you would wonder as to how our purpose will be served if we do not cooperate with the Touchables. But, you should not forget that any method, other than the self-reliance, will be absolutely useless to achieve our purpose of social equality.

Your worth is not recognized only because you are born in a particular Untouchable Caste; even though you might be well qualified, very intelligent and efficient. Therefore, we will have to adopt aggressive methods to establish our rights. Unless we do it, our efforts would be futile. Another method to remove the injustice caused to us is to capture the power. We need to have the political power to dismantle this frame of *Chaturvarna* and get an entry into politics. Why you think there is predomination of Maharashtrian Brahmins? Whatever might be the reason, one thing is true that it is because the political power is in their hands.

I can tell you a historical story about the reason for predomination of the Brahmins in Maharashtra. The Brahmins were in a bad shape before the rule of Peshwas. But, once they assumed political powers during the period of Peshwas, they have become all important and powerful in the State. But supposing all the Brahmins are removed from the Government jobs, will they be still powerful? In other Provinces, Brahmins have no value. In Gujarat, they are not much above the watermen and cooks. The Brahmins in Punjab and United Provinces, in fact, beg for cooked food just like the *Mahars* and Mangs.

Evidently, there are only two methods by which we can remove our Untouchability and establish our equality. These methods are one, an aggressive and insistent approach, and the second one is to capture the political power!

In another important speech,[41] Dr Ambedkar maintained that the Depressed Classes will not get human rights unless they declare war against the oppression. He said:

It is imperative that the movement for protection of our dignity should be vigorously implemented. A strong movement alone will create proper understanding about the discrimination between the Untouchables and other communities. There is no time to debate about the emancipation of Untouchability. The time has come for the awakening about the self-respect. The overall situation of the Untouchables is extremely pitiable and wretched. Simply because of a birth in the Untouchable family, even the most efficient amongst us cannot do anything despite having better qualities than most of the Touchables.

This social system which is entirely created by the higher Caste Hindus is inimical to our dignified progress and respectful survival. The Untouchables are harassed and banned from entry into the temples, from drawing water from public wells and ponds and such other social and human freedoms. The Untouchables should awaken their self-respect and launch a sustained movement for their human rights.

★ ★ ★

41. Presidential Speech (Marathi) in *the Conference of Swabhimaan Samrakshak Parishad* (Chittegaon District Nashik (June 21, 1929).

In the year 1929, Dr Ambedkar was appointed by the Government of Bombay as a Member of the Starte Committee to inquire into the educational, economic and social conditions of the Depressed Classes and Aboriginal Tribes of the Bombay Presidency, and to recommend measures for their uplift. As a Member of the Starte Committee, Dr Ambedkar travelled all over the Bombay Presidency. During these travels, two incidents have been reported:[42]

(a) Incident One: Even in the exalted position of Dr Ambedkar, one Headmaster of a Primary Local Board School did not allow him to enter the classroom!
(b) Incident Two: At Chalisgaon (District Dhule), Dr Ambedkar's followers gave him a grand reception and wished to take him to their locality. However, all *tonga*-drivers refused to drive the Untouchable Leader! As a compromise, an Untouchable was allowed to ride the *tonga*. Not being accustomed to the task, he could not handle it. The horse bolted and Dr Ambedkar was thrown off, hitting the stone pavement and was severely injured. A month later, Dr Ambedkar said in a letter: "The *tonga* in which I was travelling on October 23, 1929 overturned and I was thrown out.... One of the bones of my right foot was fractured. As a result..., I was confined to bed till the last week of December (1929), and though I am in a position to move about, I cannot do so without the help of a stick."

While being bed-ridden, Dr Ambedkar came across an article in the Bombay Chronicle (October 1929) by a Parsee gentleman against Parsee priests advocating abolition of priesthood as a Caste. Dr Ambedkar wrote a rejoinder to the article in the same newspaper which was titled: "Wanted an Anti-Priest Craft Association". While supporting the Parsee gentleman's article, Dr Ambedkar argued that the Hindu priestly Class stood in no way superior—ethically, educationally or otherwise. He pointed out that the hereditary Hindu priests are 'a clog on the wheel of civilization'. Dr Ambedkar described the officiating Brahmin as a miserable specimen of humanity. "He practises the sham of being a middleman between the unseen powers and the helpless man and makes a living by it.... Be it an occasion of job like a wedding or of sorrow like death, it is equally availed of by the priests, many of whom pray... in order to be able to prey in their victims."

⋆ ⋆ ⋆

In the meantime, inspired by the *Mahad Satyagraha* there were two Temple-entry *Satyagraha* efforts in 1929—one in Kali Temple, Kapilmuni, Khulana in Bengal (July 9, 1929) and another one in the Parvati Temple, Pune.

---

42. Keer, Dhananjay, op.cit, p.133.

PARVATI TEMPLE SATYAGRAHA

A public meeting was organized in Mumbai to extend support to "Parvati *Satyagraha* in Poona" (October 16, 1929). In that meeting to begin with Dr Ambedkar explained in brief a history of *Satyagraha* in Poona and emphasized that it is the pious duty of every person from the Depressed Classes to support this *Satyagraha* in every possible way. He asked the gathering whether they are ready to go to Poona for the *Satyagraha* if need arises which was responded by the public with huge "Yea"!

Dr Ambedkar said:

> There are people who are advising the Depressed Classes to wait and watch for the change in the attitude of the Upper Castes. What a deplorable advice! On one hand, the Congress has given an ultimatum to British that if the Dominion Status is not granted by December 31, (1929), they will severe all relations with the British Government. And on the other hand, these people are advising the Depressed Classes to wait and watch for getting human rights and social freedom. I wonder if this is not a deception! Clearly it is the meanness of the Upper Castes that they have not granted social freedom to the Depressed Classes despite a wait of thousands of years. And now, again they are advising us to 'wait'. This is nothing but their sweetened deception. But the Depressed Classes are no longer so ignorant that they will become a prey to such cunning of the Upper Castes. The Untouchables have become now dignified and awakened and the 'Poona *Satyagraha*' is the proof of it. In Mumbai also the Untouchables have firmly resolved to start the *Satyagraha* for temple entry.

Dr Ambedkar advised the Depressed Classes that they have right to protest against any kind of exploitation. However, since he had opposed the strike of Mill Workers' Union against the mill owners, one person from the audience had asked him, what is the reason for his opposition to which Dr Ambedkar had promised to reply before concluding this meeting; accordingly Dr Ambedkar replied thus:

> It seems that many people do not know the reasons for the strike of mill workers and my opposition to the Mill Workers' Union. First of all, this strike is not a general one, none of the Muslim labourers have joined the strike, and all mills having majority of Muslim labourers are functioning normally. Secondly, the President and Secretary of the Union along with two more persons had come to meet me just one day before the strike. After a long discussion I had clearly told them that it is sheer stupidity to go on strike without sufficient reasons and enough capital support. I had also told them that if there are valid reasons for the strike and also there is some welfare of the Depressed Classes then I will happily support the strike and also participate in it.
>
> Later, when I myself enquired about the reasons for the strike, I found that some leaders are bent upon for going on strike purely for their personal ego. The situation is such that the Union Leaders themselves do not keep their promises and, therefore, they do not command any respect. Everybody should know that those very Union Leaders had unashamedly deposed before the Strike Enquiry Committee that they had

to go on strike to prevent their Union from disintegration. The said Committee was appointed by the Bombay Government to enquire about the strike.

Thirdly, there has been no benefit or justice to the Depressed Classes by whatever strikes have taken place so far. They are still not allowed in the cotton mills because the Hindu are not ready to accept the Untouchables in the cotton mills. We had brought 130 persons from the Berar area to teach cotton weaving to the Untouchables, but the Touchable Hindus refused to work with them and they even went on strike. As a result, the Untouchable labourers and persons who had come from the Berar had to go back. If the focus of labour movement is only on committing atrocities against the Untouchables, then the leaders of the higher Castes who claim that labourers do not have Caste should explain this situation.

The Depressed Classes and the Untouchables should get justice if their cooperation is expected. I am always ready to cooperate and work with such people who would work wholeheartedly in the movement to give justice to the Depressed Classes and to free them from the social bondage. If the basic principle of every movement is justice and equitable treatment to the Untouchables, only then that movement will be just and appropriate. I have nothing to do with the movement which is for the benefit of only selfish Touchables.

KALA RAM TEMPLE SATYAGRAHA

In the meantime, the next stage of Dr Ambedkar's mass movement came in the form of a temple entry agitation at the Kala Ram Temple at Nashik.[43] A call was issued to Untouchables all over Maharashtra to come to Nashik on March 1, 1930 and assert their right to worship Lord Ram in the Kala Ram Temple. Thousands of Untouchables had flocked to Nashik in response to Dr Ambedkar's call. The mass movement initiated by Dr Ambedkar had gathered further momentum.

In the public meeting, Dr Ambedkar explained the purpose of the struggle and recounted his efforts towards peaceful negotiations.

"We will not die if we are not allowed in the Temple, nor are we going to be immortalized by gaining entry. We are fighting for equal rights as human beings, and we are not going to accept anything less," he said to thunderous applause.

Soon after the public meeting, Dr Ambedkar, once again led a procession towards the disputed place. This time, he was followed by a band playing martial tunes, which was in turn followed by the volunteers. Next in line were about five hundred women. This was a revolution in itself, as it was for the first time that Untouchable women were participating in a mass movement. They were followed by thousands of orderly protesters, walking with discipline and determination. When the procession reached the Temple, the gates were closed and barricaded. A contingent

43. See Jaffrelot, op cit and Vidhu Verma (1999) for this argument. The Kala Ram Temple in Nashik, Maharashtra, was constructed in 1782 at the site believed to have been inhabited by Ram, Sita and Laxman during their exile.

of armed police was guarding the main entrance. Dr Ambedkar spoke to the Police Superintendent and then directed the procession to the Godavari River where another rally was held.

A peaceful agitation in front of the Temple gates began the next day. There were four gates with hundreds of armed policeman at each gate. The Police Superintendent had set up office in a tent pitched right in front of the Temple, and had camped there expecting the agitators to strike in the dead of night. With thousands of protestors taking turns and forming a human barricade, the Temple was sealed and nobody was allowed to enter. The agitation continued for several days.

Towards the end of March in 1930, Ram Navami, Lord Ram's birth anniversary, was drawing close. The trustees opened the Temple almost a month after it was sealed. The protestors were waiting for this, and they sprang into action. They formed a human barricade at the entrance, insisting that worship ought to be allowed on a first-come, first-served basis. The gates were hurriedly closed again. Thousands courted arrest for crossing picket lines and acting as barricades. With baton blows raining, they were packed into police vans. The local jails were overflowing with protestors. They were driven outside the city and dumped there, with no food, water, or shelter. However, they remained unfazed. They marched right back, singing and chanting, and within four to five hours were back at the Temple.

Two days after Ram Navami, tradition called for a procession of Lord Ram's chariot, through the Nashik city. Although, the Untouchables were not admitted to the Temple, traditionally they were allowed to pull the chariot. In view of the disturbance, a hurried compromise was reached—the Upper Castes would pull the chariot up to the Temple's main gate, and from there it would be carried by the Untouchables. The priests had announced a specific time for the procession to start, but then quietly the Caste Hindus gathered much earlier. They hastily led the chariot, cheered on by the priests, and went well past the main gate. The protestors were caught unawares, but they quickly got into action and collectively forced the chariot to a halt midway. The chariot was sidetracked as fights ensued. The police beat the protestors back with strikes, pushing them into alleys. Their batons flew freely and they spared no one, not even women and children. There was rioting and a few agitators set some shops on fire. The fire spread rapidly, damaging a lot of property, bicycles, and cars. Many protestors, including Dr Ambedkar, were injured. Most among those who were hurt were Untouchables. They were furious and wanted revenge, but Dr Ambedkar, injured though he was, addressed and calmed them. All gatherings near the Temple were now forbidden and would warrant arrest. The matter went to court, and pending the court decision the agitation was temporarily suspended.

Around that time, it was announced that Mahatma Gandhi had defied the salt laws imposed by the British in a town called Dandi in today's Gujarat. Gandhiji had also announced a nationwide Civil Disobedience Movement against the British rule on behalf of the Indian National Congress.[44]

★ ★ ★

The All-India Depressed Classes Congress was held in Nagpur (August 8-9, 1930) under the Presidentship of Dr Ambedkar. The main objective of the Conference was "to settle the formation of an All-India Body to voice the sentiments of the Depressed Classes on all problems arising in the country from time to time". The context was the Report of the Simon Commission (which had submitted its Report in May 1930) and then forthcoming Round Table Conference, organized by the British Government at London (which Dr Ambedkar was invited to attend as one of the two representatives of the Depressed Classes).

Dr Ambedkar prepared his Presidential Address for the said Conference in English and published it as a booklet and had them distributed at the Congress. This historic speech is really Dr Ambedkar's Vision Document which forms the intellectual basis of the subsequent struggles led by him.

This all-important speech "demanding a transfer of power which will result in a real social change" may be summarized as under:

> The one question that is looming large on the horizon today is: 'Is it possible for the people of India to become one united self-governing community?' The question is asked: How can a heterogeneous mass of humanity function as a self-governing community? To insist that the divergent elements in a country shall be one united whole before it can have the blessings of self-government is sometimes to reverse the order of things, and to ignore the unifying effects of the great process of self-government. Indeed, if the ideal is that India should be a united nation, self-government would be the most potent instrument for the realization of that ideal.
>
> The diversity of conditions and peoples prevalent in India must be taken into account in framing the Constitution for a self-governing India.[45] In a self-governing India which did not recognize the hard facts of Indian society, the strings of political power will be in the hands of the ambitious members of the upper strata of Indian society drawn from the high-placed, well-educated, and opulent Castes, i.e. in the hands of the aristocracy of wealth, education, and social standing.
>
> No country is good enough to rule over another. But the proposition does not end there. It is equally true that no Class is good enough to rule over another Class. The talents of the aristocracy are a great asset to the country. But these talents by themselves cannot give it any title to manage the affairs of the country. In India 50-60 million of people are suffering from the curse of Untouchability. Huge population of aboriginals

44. The parallel between the movements led by Mahatma Gandhi and Dr Ambedkar, respectively, becomes apparent here. Indeed, Dr Ambedkar's declaration of social independence for Untouchables coincided with Mahatma Gandhi's declaration of political Independence for India.
45. For full text of the Presidential Address, see Jadhav, Narendra (ed.), *Ambedkar Writes* (2013), Vol. I, pp. 59-81.

and hill tribes are left to roam about in a nomadic and barbarous state. These things bear an eloquent testimony to the spirit of service and the sense of responsibility which the aristocracy has shown in the past.

We are told that the settlement of the social problem should wait till the political freedom of the country is achieved. You cannot hope the effectuation of the settlement of the social problem if you allow power to slip into the hands of those who stand to lose by the settlement unless you are prepared to have another revolution to dethrone those whom you have helped to capture power. The best guarantee for the settlement of social problems is the adjustment of the political machine itself, and not the will of those who are contriving to be left in unfettered control of that machine.

The scheme for the protection of minorities which exists in some European States consists of the enactment of Clauses in the Constitution recognizing what are called the Fundamental Rights of the minorities. No declaration of rights—howsoever comprehensive in its scope and howsoever clear in its terms and tenor—can ensure the enjoyment of those rights. The guarantee of a right consists not in its declaration but in the provision of a remedy for its enforcement in case it is violated.

The Motilal Nehru Committee's Report does not even have an appeal Clause against the infringement of the Fundamental Rights. The guarantee in the Nehru Constitution is, therefore, quite illusory.

The safest remedy for the protection of own interests lies in securing control over the future executive in self-governing India in your own hands, and that you can have only by means of adequate representation in the Legislatures of the country.

There is prevalent in the Congress circles, a theory according to which adequate representation is tantamount to representation according to population. This arithmetical theory of the representation of minorities is a crude and absurd doctrine, and forms the best reflex of the prevailing ungenerous attitude of the majority towards the minorities in India. From the standpoint of the protection of the minority interest, any reform in order to be a real reform, must involve a change in the balance of power in favour of the minorities, and this can be secured only by allowing, over and above its population ratio, some weightage in the allotment of its representation. This weightage cannot be uniform for all the minorities, and it must vary with their social standing: to be high, if the standing of the minority is low; and to be low if the standing of the minority is high.

Regarding the formation of the electorates, there are two alternatives open to us. One is the scheme of separate electorates, and the other is that of joint electorates, with reserved seats. If we can get adult suffrage, we ought to have no objection to the scheme of joint electorates, with reserved seats being applied to the Depressed Classes.

Every Minority in formulating the safeguards it needs must take care that they will not be incompatible with the realization of our ideal that is a united India. From this point of view, the scheme of joint electorates and reserved seats must be pronounced to be superior to that of separate electorates. It meets the realities of the present, and also helps the ideal of the future.

We should demand a certain percentage in the public service to be preserved for the Depressed Classes, and there will be no difficulty in guaranteeing this safeguard by a Clause in the Constitution. As regards the manner of our representation and the strength of our representation, the recommendations of the Simon Commission are very disappointing.

The Nomination principle deprives our people of their liberty to choose their best men to represent them, and it leaves our nominated representatives no freedom of action. It is regrettable that the Simon Commission does not discard that vicious system. The Simon Commission makes a most undesirable proposal by recommending that the Governor may authorize persons who are themselves not members of the Depressed Classes to represent them in the Legislatures.

Direct election should be the basis of the Legislative Assembly, and indirect elections from Provincial Legislatures with the system of proportional representation would be the most appropriate device for the Constitution of the Council of States. The Simon Commission has attempted to make some provision for the representation of the Depressed Classes in the Central Legislature. But its provision covers only the Legislative Assembly, and does not reach the Council of States. I have also to complain about the niggardly treatment that the Commission has meted out to us. Surely a community so much sinned against must, in all honesty, receive the most generous treatment.

The British choose to advertise our unfortunate conditions not with the object of removing them but only because such a course serves well as an excuse for retarding the political progress of India.

The demand for Independence we may dismiss from our consideration. It is impracticable and, in my opinion, it will be disastrous in the present state of the country. It is only people cemented by the feeling of one country, one Constitution, and one destiny who may take the risk of being independent. No one can deny that this country is miles distant from this position. The ideal of Dominion Status seems to me superior, for it has in it the substance of Independence without the attendant risks involved in complete Independence.

There can be no doubt that the advent of the British in India has been a great boon to the country. But the question is, at what cost? There is no doubt that a kind of dwarfing or stunting of the Indian race is going on under the British rule. The aim of the British Government all along has been to disgorge the growth of trade and industry in this country. It is an admitted principle of British administration that India be so governed that she will always remain an open market for British goods. It is this policy which has made India the land of chronic poverty.

You cannot keep on singing the praise of a bureaucracy because it has given improved roads, constructed canals on more scientific principles. We must not forget the people, including the Depressed Classes, do not live on law and order; what they live on is bread and butter. This inexorable law of life must make even the Depressed Classes demand a Government that will help the economic prosperity of the country, and thereby effect a betterment in their material life. The reason why the British Government does not intervene is because it is afraid that its intervention to amend the existing code of social and economic life will give rise to resistance. Of what good is such a Government to anybody? We must have a Government in which the men in power will give their undivided allegiance to the best interest of the country. This role the British Government will never be able to play. It is only a Government which is of the people, for the people, and by the people—in other words, it is only the *Swaraj* Government—that will make this possible.

Your wrongs have remained as open sores, and they have not been righted. Nobody can remove your grievances as well as you can, and you cannot remove them unless you get political power in your own hands. No share of this political power can come to you so long as the British Government remains as it is. It is only in a *Swaraj* Constitution that you stand any chance of getting political power into your own hands, without which you cannot bring salvation to your people.

The conclusion is to introduce responsibility in every sphere except where its introduction is not for the present feasible. I know of no reason why the Provincial Executive should not be made fully responsible. Nor does it seem to me difficult to introduce responsibility in the Central Government, except in matters pertaining to the Military and Foreign affairs. The welfare of the country, including that of the Depressed Classes, is more intimately and more extensively bound up with the Central Government than it is with the Provincial Government.

A Provincial Executive responsible to the Provincial Legislature cannot possibly take its order from a Central Government which is subject not to the Central Legislature but to the Secretary of State. And in this conflict, the administration of the country may be completely paralysed in times of emergency. You cannot, therefore, introduce responsibility in the Provincial Executive without, at the same time, introducing some degree of responsibility in the Central Executive.

Even if we support the ideal of Dominion Status with safeguards, does it necessarily follow that we must join the Civil Disobedience Movement started in this country by Mahatma Gandhi in March last? The question is not whether the movement of Civil Disobedience is right or wrong. The question is whether it is opportune and consistent with the safety and security of our interests. I am opposed to the Civil Disobedience Movement because I am convinced that it is extremely inopportune.

The fight for undertaking and understanding of one sort or another with the Viceroy or the British Cabinet seems to me needless. At any rate, nothing could have been lost if the Congress had accepted the Round Table Conference. Its failure would entail nothing but the postponement of Civil Disobedience by a year, and would be of positive value to the Congress. The Congress has committed a great blunder in starting the Civil Disobedience Movement at this juncture, and in rejecting the method of peaceful negotiations provided by the Round Table Conference.

Another reason why I cannot support the Civil Disobedience Movement is that I do not think it is compatible with the safety and security of our interests. What we want is a transfer of power accompanied by such a distribution of that power that the result will be a real social change in the relative strength of the forces operating in society.

I cannot oppose Dominion Status for India because I feel convinced that the British Government will never be able to solve our problem. But I cannot understand how, by joining the Congress, we can be any nearer to its solution. It is said that the Congress does not recognize Untouchability, and that it is the only organization which stands for the masses.

If one were to judge the colour of the Congress by its resolutions, one will be slow to accept that the Congress stands for the masses. Its economic resolutions reflect the interests of the higher and the middle Classes. Its commercial resolutions concern only the trader and the manufacturer, and the working man is severely left out.

> I agree that for the Depressed Classes to be independent and yet be without the power to make themselves a force to be reckoned with, is not a happy situation. But, what I like to ask is: what is the advantage in being dependent either upon the Government or the Congress? Merely to make yourselves agreeable to any party that happens to be powerful, without caring whether you are reckoned with or not, is the way of the beggar and amounts to an ignominious surrender which no respectable people ought to tolerate.
>
> The Depressed Classes movement seems to me to suffer from two grave lacunae. First of all, there is no such thing as a public opinion of the Depressed Classes; and, secondly, there is no means for a concerted action by the Depressed Classes as a whole. You must have an organization which will be a live institution, which will express the true sentiments of the Depressed Classes, and will gather in its fold the true workers of the community, with its network spread over the whole of the country.
>
> That political power cannot be a panacea for the ills of the Depressed Classes. Their salvation lies in their social elevation. These results will not follow the advent of political power in our hands. We must recognize that that is only a means to an end.

This historic speech was severely criticized. *The Evening News of India* (August 10, 1930) headlines were: "Depressed Classes Not for Independence". *The Bombay Chronicle* had published a summary of the speech prominently. Even *Kesari*—the newspaper started by Lokmanya Tilak—wrote an editorial "Et Tu Brute!" As a result, Dr Ambedkar was termed as a traitor, a stooge of the British Government.

Of course, the Litmus test of Dr Ambedkar's nationalism was going to come in the form of the Round Table Conference, shortly to be organized in London by the British Government. This would also be the first opportunity for Dr Ambedkar to take up the issues of the Depressed Classes to the global level, for the first time.

PART III

AMBEDKAR–GANDHI CONFLICT (1930-36)

CHAPTER TWELVE

Round Table Conference: Session One

THE REPORT OF the Simon Commission was published in May 1930. It proposed the abolition of diarchy and recommended establishment of representative Government in the Provinces. It also recommended that separate communal electorates be retained, but only until tensions between Hindus and Muslims had died down. In the meantime, Shri Motilal Nehru presented his report (called Nehru Report) in September 1928 which refuted the charges that Indians could not find a Constitutional consensus among themselves. The Nehru Report also advocated that India be given a Dominion Status of complete internal self-Government.

Since the educated Indians were opposed to the Simon Commission, and also that communal tensions between Hindus and Muslims had increased rather than decreased, the British Government opted for another method of dealing with the Constitutional Reforms in India which involved taking into account the Indian public opinion.

Accordingly, three Round Table Conferences (RTCs) were organized by the British Government at London during the period 1930-32. The first RTC was inaugurated on November 12, 1930 by the King George V and chaired by the British Prime Minister Ramsay MacDonald. The three British political parties were represented by 16 delegates while the Indian delegation consisted of 89 delegates (including 57 political leaders from British India, and 16 delegates from the Princely states). The Indian National Congress boycotted the first and the third RTC. Dr Ambedkar, along with Rao Bahadur Srinivasan, represented the Depressed Classes of India. Dr Ambedkar participated in all three RTCs.

The Round Table Conference (RTC) was essentially focused on two principal problems in respect of proposed Constitutional Reform:

(a) Should India have a responsible Government and, if so, when and to whom that Government should be responsible?
(b) Issues relating to the form of the proposed representative Government.

Dr Ambedkar participated extensively in the Plenary sessions, as well as in the Sub-Committee on Provincial Constitution, Sub-Committee on Franchise, Sub-Committee on Minorities and Sub-Committee on Defence.

(A) OPENING PLENARY SESSION

In the Opening Plenary Session (November 20, 1930), Dr Ambedkar announced that he himself and his colleague Rao Bahadur Srinivasan were honoured to place before the Conference the point of view of the Depressed Classes numbering 43 million people, or one-fifth of the total population of British India and forcefully argued the need for political power for the Depressed Classes.

In his opening remarks, Dr Ambedkar said:[46]

> The Depressed Classes form a group by themselves which is distinct and separate from the Mohammedans and, although they are included among the Hindus, they in no sense form an integral part of that community....
>
> The position assigned to the Depressed Classes is totally different. It is one which is midway between that of the serf and the slave, and which may, for convenience, be called servile—with this difference that the serf and the slave were permitted to have physical contact, from which the Depressed Classes are debarred.... Due to their *Untouchability, involves*, not merely the possibility of discrimination in public life, but actually works out as a positive denial of all equality of opportunity and the denial of those most elementary of civic rights on which all human existence depends.... Such a community, as large as the population of England or of France, and so heavily handicapped in the struggle for existence, cannot but have some bearing on the right sort of solution of the political problem.
>
> The point of view I will try to put as briefly as I can. It is this that the bureaucratic form of Government in India should be replaced by a Government, which will be a Government of the people, by the people, and for the people. This statement of the view of the Depressed Classes, I am sure, will be received with some surprise in certain quarters.... We have not taken this decision simply because we wish to throw in our lot with the majority. Indeed, as you know, there is not much love lost between the majority and the particular minority I represent.
>
> We have judged of the existing administration solely in the light of our own circumstances and we have found it wanting in some of the most essential elements of a good Government. When we compare our present position with the one, which it was our lot to bear in Indian society of the pre-British days, we find that, instead of marching on, we are only marking time. Before the British, we were in the loathsome condition due to our Untouchability. Has the British Government done anything to remove it?
>
> The British Government has accepted the social arrangements as it found them, and has preserved them faithfully in the manner of the Chinese tailor. Our wrongs have remained as open sores and they have not been righted, although 150 years of British

---

46. For full text of the Speech, see *Ambedkar Speaks*, op cit, Vol.III, pp.101-07.

rule have rolled away.... It is not merely a case of indifference, rather it is a case of sheer incompetence to undertake the task.... It is not because they cannot help us in these things but because it is against their character, motives and interests to do so.

The Government of India does realize the necessity of removing the social evils which are eating into the vitals of Indian society, and which have blighted the lives of the downtrodden Classes for so many years. Yet it is a most painful thing that it has not dared to touch any of these evils. Why? Is it because it has no legal powers to remove them? No. The reason why it does not intervene is because it is afraid that its intervention to amend the existing code of social and economic life will give rise to resistance. Of what good is such a Government to anybody?

We must have a Government in which the men in power will give their undivided allegiance to the best interests of the country. We must have a Government in which men in power, knowing where obedience will end and resistance will begin, will not be afraid to amend the social and economic code of life which the dictates of justice and expediency so urgently call for. This role the British Government will never be able to play. It is only a Government which is of the people, for the people and by the people that will make this possible....

The bureaucratic Government of India, with the best of motives, will remain powerless to effect any change so far as our particular grievances are concerned. We feel that nobody can remove our grievances as well as we can, and we cannot remove them unless we get political power in our own hands. No share of this political power can evidently come to us so long as the British Government remains as it is. It is only in a *Swaraj* constitution that we stand any chance of getting the political power into our own hands, without which we cannot bring salvation to our people....

The Depressed Classes, while they stand for Dominion Status with safeguards, wish to lay all the emphasis they can on one question, and one question alone. And that question is: how will Dominion India function? Where will be centre of political power be? Who will have it? Will the Depressed Classes be heirs to it? These are the questions that form their chief concern....

It must be recognized that Indian Society is a gradation of Castes forming an ascending scale of reverence and a descending scale of contempt—a system which gives no scope for the growth of that sentiment of equality and fraternity so essential for a democratic form of Government. It must also be recognised that while the intelligentsia is a very important part of Indian society, it is drawn from its upper strata and although it speaks in the name of the country and leads the political movement, it has not shed the narrow particularism of the Class from which it is drawn. In other words, what the Depressed Classes wish to urge is that the political mechanism must take account of and must have a definite relation to the psychology of the society for which it is devised. Otherwise, you are likely to produce a constitution which, however symmetrical, will be truncated one and a total misfit to the society for which it is designed....

We are often reminded that the problem of the Depressed Classes is a social problem and that its solution lies elsewhere than in politics.... Then the problem of Depressed Classes is, I submit, eminently a political problem and must be treated as such....

We know that political power is passing from the British into the hands of those who wield such tremendous economic, social and religious sway over our existence. We are willing that it may happen, though the idea of *Swaraj* recalls to the mind of many of us the tyrannies, oppressions and injustices practised upon us in the past, and fear of their recurrence under *Swaraj*. We are prepared to take the inevitable risk of the situation in the hope that we shall be installed, in adequate proportion, as the political sovereigns of the country along with our fellow countrymen. But we will consent to that on one condition and that is that the settlement of our problems is not left to time. I am afraid the Depressed Classes have waited too long for time to work its miracle. At every successive step taken by the British Government to widen the scope of representative Government, the Depressed Classes have been systematically left out. No thought has been given to their claim for political power. I protest with all the emphasis I can that we will not stand this any longer. The settlement of our problem must be a part of the general political settlement and must not be left over to the shifting sands of the sympathy and goodwill of the rulers of the future....

We cannot, therefore, hope for the effectuation of the settlement of our social problem. If we allow power to slip into the hands of those who stand to lose by settlement unless we are to have another revolution to dethrone those, whom we today help to ascend the throne of power and prestige. We prefer being despised for too anxious apprehensions, rather than ruined by too confident a security, and I think it would be just and proper for us to insist that the best guarantee for the settlement of our problem is the adjustment of the political machine itself so as to give us a hold on it, and not the will of those who are contriving to be left in unfettered control of that machine....

Although, we want responsible Government, we do not want a Government that will only mean a change of masters. Let the Legislature be fully and really representative if your Executive is going to be fully responsible....

Depressed by the Government, suppressed by the Hindu and disregarded by the Muslim, we are left in a most intolerable position of utter helplessness to which I am sure there is no parallel and to which I was bound to call attention....

As members of a minority, we look to the Central Government to act as a powerful curb on the Provincial majority to save the minorities from the misrule of the majority. As an Indian, interested in the growth of Indian nationalism, I must make it plain that I am a strong believer in the Unitary form of Government. This Unitary Government has been the most potent influence in the building up of the Indian nation.... I should be loathed to withdraw this most powerful stimulus in the formative period and before it has worked out its end.... I shall be prepared to consider a Federal form, if it can be shown that in it local autonomy is not inconsistent with Central unity.

What that solution should be rests entirely upon the view that British delegates choose to take. Addressing myself to them I will say whether you will meet the situation by conciliation or by applying the iron heel must be a matter for your judgement for the responsibility is entirely yours. To such of you as are particular to the use of force and believe that a regime of *letters de cachet* and the Bastille will ease the situation, let me recall the memorable words of the greatest teacher of political philosophy, Edmund Burke. This is what he said to the British nation when it was faced with the problem of dealing with the American colonies:

'The use of force alone is but temporary. It may endure for a moment, but it does not remove the necessity of subduing again;

Terror is not always the effect of force, and an armament is not a victory. If you do not succeed, you are without resource; for conciliation failing, force remains, but force failing, no further hope of reconciliation is left. A further objection to force is that you impair the object by your very endeavours to preserve it.'

The worth and efficacy of this advice you all knew. You did not listen to it and you lost the great Continent of America. You followed it to the lasting good of yourself and the rest of the Dominions that are with you.

I am afraid it is not sufficiently realized that, in the present temper of the country, no Constitution will be workable which is not acceptable to the majority of the people. The time when you were to choose and India was to accept is gone, never to return. Let the consent of the people and not the accident of logic be the touchstone of your new Constitution, if you desire that it should work.

★ ★ ★

Dr Ambedkar's speech was very well received. The clarity and lucidity of his exposition, and fearless manner of his delivery won Dr Ambedkar many admirers. The *Indian Daily Mail* described the speech as one of the finest bits of oratory during the whole Conference.

Coincidentally, Maharaja of Baroda His Highness Sayajirao Gaikwad who was also participating in the Conference, was so moved by the speech of Dr Ambedkar that he later arranged a special dinner for him and ended the years of estrangement over the scholarship issue.

(B) ON PROVINCIAL CONSTITUTION[47]

While addressing the Sub-Committee on Provincial Constitution (December 4, 1930), Dr Ambedkar organized his "general" remarks expressing the point of the Depressed Classes under three heads:

(i) Provincial Autonomy
(ii) Responsibility in the Provinces, and
(iii) Provincial Services

Dr Ambedkar said:[48]

Viewing the problem of Provincial autonomy from the standpoint of the particular Class I represent in this Conference and of the interests of India as a whole and the working Classes in particular, I think that in any future Constitution that we propose to devise for endowing the Provinces with Provincial autonomy we must take into consideration certain facts which are bound to limit the character of that autonomy....

47. Dr Ambedkar was not the member of this Sub-Committee. He was, however, included as member of the Federal Structure Committee in the 2nd R.T.C.

48. For full text of the Speech, see *Ambedkar Speaks* op cit, Vol.III, pp.108-12.

The first limiting factor in the Provincial autonomy is that it must be made subject to such questions of a Provincial character which are, although Provincial in nature, also of an all-India character. The Provinces may have their say with regard to these subjects, and yet the Central Government should not be excluded from its jurisdiction with regard to them. For instance, I would like to draw an illustration from labour legislation, legislation affecting tenants and affecting agriculture....

They cannot be regarded as entirely Provincial and without an all-India character, the Central Government must have some jurisdiction over subjects of this character, notwithstanding that it cuts across Provincial autonomy....

Secondly, I should state that in dividing the powers of Government between the Central and the Provincial Governments in the future Constitution of India with a view to giving the Provinces as complete an autonomy as possible, it will also be necessary that such powers as remain undefined must be left with the Central Government....

In the present situation in India, where the separatist tendency exists to such an extent as we all know it, where Provincial and local parochialism is more dominant than national feeling. While we are building up a Federated India with complete autonomy of the units, we still have the problem of making India as a whole a strong and united country.... I do not think that the reservation of powers in the Central Government is likely to affect the autonomy of the Provinces....The second is that that autonomy must be limited by affording of protection for the interests of the minorities and of the Depressed Classes....

In all the Provinces the Depressed Classes, whom I represent, will be in a minority. They will be in a minority in every Province. I cannot understand how we can at this stage permit the Provincial majorities to have a complete uninterrupted and undiluted sway over the destinies of these poor people, without any right of appeal being given to the latter in regard to mal-administration or neglect of their interests. There must be some authority somewhere, over and above the Provincial Government, which will be in a position to intervene and rescue them from any adverse position in which they may be placed by the Provincial majorities...

Coming to the question of the character of responsibility in the Provincial Governments, my first observation is that the whole question of responsibility in the Provincial Legislature is entirely dependent upon the kind of Legislature that you are going to get in the Provinces. If the Legislature that you are going to get in the Provinces is a Legislature which is going to be a mirror of the whole population of the Province, if it is going to be thoroughly representative....

I think in a Legislature of that sort there will be no harm in conceding the principle that Provincial responsibility may be introduced to the fullest extent. That is my first observation....

Making that a condition that the Legislatures shall be fully and adequately representative of all the Classes, I see no objection to the subjects which are now reserved being transferred to popular control....

Coming to the question of whether the responsibility in the Provinces should be joint or should be individual I have not the slightest hesitation in saying that the responsibility not only should be joint but must be joint....

Ministries have been working as a kind of loose confederation, without having any complete or unanimous view on a particular policy which they adopted....That in no instance have we had any considered policy put forward by the Cabinet as a whole, worked out in detail and placed before the Legislative Council. Things have been done by fits and starts, and I do not think we want our responsibility in future to be bungled in that fashion....

My submission is that there is a better way of dealing with that sort of evil, and it seems to me that if the minorities could get Constitutional and Statutory guarantees laid down in the Constitutional Act itself against anything likely to injure their interests being done or left undone by the Cabinet, the danger which most of us apprehend from the fact that the Cabinets may be communally dominated, will vanish, and we shall not have much cause to insist on communal representation in the Cabinet....

A Cabinet Minister has not merely to look after the interests of the minorities; he has to see to the safety and interest of the Province as a whole. That demands ability and competence; it does not merely demand a communal outlook, and it is from that point of view that I look at the matter. I should like to have the interests of the minorities and the Depressed Classes safeguarded in such a manner that Constitutionally it would be impossible for Ministers drawn from the majority communities to do anything prejudicial to the minorities or to neglect their interests....

Coming to the question of the relations between the Governor and his Ministry. No Constitution, if it is really to embody full responsible Government and collective responsibility, can permit the Governor the power to interfere in the day-to-day administration of the country.... The Ministry must be allowed to carry on the day-to-day administration on the basis of joint responsibility.

When we come to the question of the emergency powers which it is suggested should be left with the Governor.... I do not understand exactly what is meant. Is it meant that when an emergency arises the Governor should simply dismiss the Ministry and have nothing to do with it, and should promulgate whatever laws, ordinances or measures he thinks are necessary to meet the situation, notwithstanding the fact that they are opposed by the Ministry? I can quite understand the Governor should have the absolute, undoubted and unrestricted power of dismissing a Ministry which he thinks is not acting in the best interests of the country, but I cannot understand how there can be responsible Government in a Province in which the Governor is allowed to do a thing without a Ministry.... I think this point will have to be worked out in some deal, for, as I say, I do not quite understand it.

Coming to the question of the Services, there is one observation I am bound to make.... I quite agree in principle that with Provincial autonomy the power of regulating the Services in a Province should belong to that Province, and that the Provinces should have full liberty to Indianize the Services as they desire and according to their means and circumstances.

However, I cannot forget that Indians are communal minded. We do hope it is only a hope that a time will come when all Indians will cease to look at problems from a communal point of view in administrating matters which are left to their charge, but that is only a hope; it is not a fact. The fact is that Indians do discriminate between Class and Class, community and community, in administering such discretion as is left to them in their administration of the law....

My fear with regard to the future Constitution of India is that having regard to the present position of the Depressed Classes, having regard to the fact that education is not widely spread amongst them, and having regard to the fact that there is hardly a single individual holding a Gazetted post in the Bombay Presidency for instance....

I very much fear that this Indianisation may work out as a tyranny, and therefore, from my particular point of view, I should like to emphasize that at any rate for some time it will be necessary to maintain a British element in the Services. I do not say there should be no Indianisation, but I do say that, having regard to our interests, it should be rather slower than some people desire it to be.

★ ★ ★

(C) ON FRANCHISE

While participating in the Sub-Committee on Franchise (December 22, 1930), Dr Ambedkar made out a strong case for adult franchise and also discussed the "thorny" question of joint electorates versus separate electorates. Dr Ambedkar's arguments could be summarized as under:

In the Plenary sessions we all joined in one chorus in demanding that India should have a responsible form of Government, and I, for one, speaking on behalf of the Depressed Classes in that Plenary session, joined with my friends sitting opposite in demanding responsible Government for India. I was under the impression that the Indian people were also united in the view as to whom that Government should be responsible.

I am sorry to say, Sir, that I have been deluded. I find now that although some of our people would desire me and others to join them in their demand for Dominion Status....They do not join with us in demanding that the Government which will be set up under that Dominion Status shall be responsible to the people of India as a whole.

Now, Sir, speaking on behalf of the Depressed Classes I cannot honestly consent to responsible Government or to Dominion status unless I can be sure that the people for whom I speak are to have a place in that Constitution....

As an objection has been raised to the proposal for adult suffrage by some of my friends, I propose to deal with the arguments brought forward against it....

It is suggested that we should follow the stages adopted in this country from 1832 to 1918. Those who take their stand on the political history of enfranchisement in this country seem to think that there was some philosophical course of action thought out by the English people in devising the steps that were taken by them in enfranchising the people from 1832 onwards, that they had decided before-hand that they must enfranchise only a limited number of people in 1832, that otherwise it would be philosophically wrong; that they should take the next step only in 1867, and not in 1866; that they should take the next step in 1884 and not in 1867....The question of franchise was treated in this country as a mere matter of party politics; that each party tried to extend the franchise because it thought that as a political catch-word it would influence and augment that party....

The second thing I should like to point out to my friend is this. Does he really mean to tell us that because the franchise in this country was limited, that, therefore, the Government produced under that franchise was a good Government? That because the franchise was limited, that, therefore, there was not trouble, and that everybody was satisfied in this country? Surely that is not the case....

Thirdly, I should like to point out to my friend, if he really is serious and if he really believes what he says, that the people of India ought not be given adult suffrage, because they are not fit for it, then the only alternative for him is to go back to India and not to demand Dominion Status or responsible Government, for surely, if it is the view of the gentleman who puts forward this case that the Indian people are not fit to exercise the franchise, are not fit to take upon themselves the responsibilities of Government, then I do not understand in whose name he asks for responsible Government. Is it for this Class? Is it for himself? For whom is it? The only argument, as I understand in favour of responsible Government and in favour of Dominion Status, is the assumption which must constitute the basis of any such argument, that the people of India are fit to undertake the responsibility of Government. If my friend does not believe that the Indian people are capable of exercising that responsibility, then the only conclusion is that the Indian people cannot have Dominion Status and cannot have responsibility....

Now, Sir, as I understand it, to me the suffrage and the franchise are nothing else but the right of self-defence; it means that you will create a legislature which will have the amplest power of passing laws which will affect the life, liberty and property of the people. Surely, if that is going to be the position, if your legislature is going to have that power of affecting your life in these most vital matters, then surely every individual who is going to be subject to that legislation ought to have the power to defend himself against laws which will probably in the circumstances invade his liberty, invade his life and his property. It is not a mere question of the ballot box; it is not a mere question of polling booths....

If I understand the franchise, I understand it to be the right to regulate the terms of what one might call associated life in society; that is the essence of the franchise. When you give a man the franchise, what you mean is that you give him power to regulate the terms on which he will live in relationship with other individuals in society. Now, if that is the meaning of the suffrage, surely you cannot give the higher Classes, the intellectuals as they are called, or the propertied Classes, the power to regulate the terms of associated life, and leave the lower Classes at their mercy. They, too, must have the power to regulate the terms of associated life....

It cannot be a one-sided bargain; it must not be a one-sided bargain.

It seems to me the franchise is something which must be regarded as the inherent right of every individual in the State....Then surely you cannot make an inherent right of a people dependent upon the convenience of your administration ....

If the franchise is an inherent right, and if there are administrative difficulties in the effectuation of that franchise, then the remedy is not to curtail the franchise, but the remedy is to provide the necessary machinery, so that every man or woman capable of enjoying that franchise shall be in a position to give effect to it.

We are told that the constituencies in India are very vast; and, surely, as we see from the Report of the Simon Commission, they are of a most fabulous character. It is said that if you increase the number of electors in the existing constituencies, as they exist today, the whole machinery will break down. My submission to this Conference is this: Surely this difficulty can easily be met. It seems to me this difficulty can be met in this way. It seems to me that the difficulty arises largely because of the composition and strength of your Legislative Councils today; that composition is so very limited that you cannot help having the large constituencies that you have today. It seems to me that from the standpoint of numbers the existing strength of the legislatures in the Provinces is ridiculous.

Now, surely if you are going to cramp these vast aggregations of people into Legislative Councils which do not exceed 140 in membership, you are bound, as a result, to have very large constituencies. Why are you afraid of increasing the numbers in the Legislature? I cannot understand it. If you are not afraid, and if you follow the parallels in other countries, then surely you can very easily reduce the size of the electorates, and thereby remove one of the difficulties that is said to exist in the matter of adult suffrage....

Then another difficulty which was pointed out was that we do not have a sufficient number of polling officers. Now that difficulty to my mind also does not seem to be of a very serious character. It seems to me that if all the college students in India could be drafted into the service of the electoral departments, this difficulty could be very easily solved....

It seems to me, therefore, that the difficulties of the situation are not insuperable. Let me point this out to my friends opposite who object to adult suffrage on this ground. It seems to me their position is of a somewhat curious character. Where a member of the British Delegation raises a difficulty, and says there are heaps of difficulties in the way of India, and, therefore, India must not have Dominion Status or responsible Government, the gentlemen sitting opposite would not allow the English gentlemen to take advantage of the difficulties; they would tell him at once; 'Why, you bolster up difficulties to put down our claims. These are difficulties which surely can be met....We say that if there are difficulties in the way of getting the power in our hands, those difficulties ought to be solved. We are not going to let you have the advantage of the situation....'

Now let me put one or two arguments which I think are in favour of adult suffrage, and which, in my opinion, are more or less decisive. The first argument that I will put is this, that you cannot have in India any system of suffrage short of adult suffrage which will give equality of representation to all the Castes and communities in India; there is no other system you can devise for India which will give that result....

Take, for instance, again Bengal and the Punjab; there again the Mohammedans pre-dominate in population, and yet in the voting list they are in the minority. Take again the Depressed Classes; under the existing franchise they are nowhere at all in the electorate. I think it is a most disgraceful thing to have a franchise of this sort....

Now surely you do not want to create a system of political Government in which only some Castes and some communities will predominate. Surely you do not want to create in India a South Africa where only some people will have the vote and the rest will not. I say, if you are interested in giving every man a vote, in giving every man the political franchise, so that he may work out his destiny, then you cannot have any other system of franchise in India than that of adult suffrage....

I am not opposed to female suffrage.... It is suggested that there should be a franchise of literacy. I do not propose to call it a fancy franchise, but let me tell you what will be the effect of it. The effect of it would be this: that some communities would have their voting strength almost doubled, while other communities would stand where they are. Literacy in India is so unevenly distributed, that some communities would have all the increase of the franchise added to their stock, while other communities would remain where they are. Surely you do not want to create that sort of situation....

Therefore my submission is, that if this Conference believe that India must have responsible Government, and that Government must be responsible to the people, then I submit there is no alternative to adult suffrage....

We all of us know that the question of joint versus separate electorate is a most thorny question; it seems to me to be a very crucial question...The question of joint versus separate electorates is inextricably bound up with the question of franchise. You will not ask any minority in India, you will not compel any minority in India, and you will not get the consent of any minority in India, to agree to joint electorates unless that minority has adult suffrage....

I am not going to place myself under the thumb and authority of any majority Government, unless I am certain that I can exercise in the elections electoral power which is commensurate with my social power. Unless I know that every man and every woman in the Depressed Class community will be able to exercise the vote and to determine the destiny of the candidate who is going to represent the mass of people in the country, I certainly am not going to consent to joint electorates: certainly not. I am not going to place myself in a minority position: I am not going to allow the majority to select my candidate. No, under no-circumstances...The decisiveness of this fact was acknowledged by the Motilal Nehru Committee and by three members of the Indian Central Committee....

My friend and I are only two in a Conference of 80 or 90, we represent 43 millions of people.

In the afternoon session, Dr Ambedkar said:

I take it that this Committee is agreed that the ideal is adult suffrage. Some of us think that it ought to be realized immediately; the rest of our friends think that it ought to be evolved by stages. We have, therefore, put before us two concrete suggestions. One suggestion is that we should adopt the system of instalment and increase the suffrage by a graduated scheme of 25 per cent addition to the existing voting list, say at an interval of a certain number of years. We have on the other hand the suggestion of our noble friend the Marquess of Zetland in which also effect is sought to be given to some realization of this ideal of adult suffrage....

My concrete suggestion, therefore, is that this Committee should appoint a small Sub-Committee in order to consider this system and to report upon it, so that we may be better able, with full knowledge and information, to recommend this to a Franchise Committee that may hereafter be left to work out the system.

★ ★ ★

(D) ON THE ISSUE OF MINORITY REPRESENTATION

While participating in the Sub-Committee on Minorities (December 31, 1930), Dr Ambedkar appreciated,

> It is for the first time that the case of the Depressed Classes from the political point of view has come to be considered....In view of that and in view of other matters, namely, that in a Committee consisting of so many members we are only two to voice the grievances of 43 millions of people, and grievances which...are unparalleled by the case of any other community that exists in India,...the task is really an enormous one, and I should have expected more latitude in the matter of time allowed to me for presenting this case.

Lamenting however, that it would not be possible, "...in anticipation of that, I and my colleague Rao Bahadur Srnivasan, thought it advisable to submit... a written Memorandum giving in clear-cut language what the Depressed Classes desire by way of political safeguards in the future Constitution of India."

The Memorandum titled "A Scheme of Political Safeguards for the Protection of the Depressed Classes in the Future Constitution of a Self-Governing India" was circulated among the Members of the Sub-Committee on Minorities and during the deliberation of the Sub-Committee, Dr Ambedkar presented only the highlights of the Memorandum.[49]

The Memorandum presents the following terms and conditions on which the Depressed Classes would agree to place themselves under a majority rule in a self-governing India:

(i) The Depressed Classes must be made free citizens entitled to all the rights of citizenship in common with other citizens.

(ii) An appropriate "Fundamental Right" must be introduced in the Constitution aimed at securing the abolition of Untouchability and for creating the equality of citizenship.

(iii) Declaration of rights for the Depressed Classes must not be mere pious pronouncements but they should be realities of everyday life. For that purpose, the rights must be protected by adequate pains and penalties from interference in the enjoyment of those declared rights.

(iv) Social boycott is often a menace to the rights and liberties of the Depressed Classes. As such social boycott must be made an offence punishable by law.

(v) It must be rendered impossible in law for the Legislature or the Executive to make any invidious discrimination against the Depressed Classes.

(vi) The Electoral Law must have the following provisions.

(aa) Right to adequate representation in the Legislatures, both Provincial and Central

(ab) Right to elect their own men as their representatives, by (1) adult suffrage, and (2) by separate electorates for the first ten years and thereafter by joint electorates and reserved seats.

---

49. For full text of the speech, see *Ambedkar Speaks*, op cit, Vol.III, pp.122-8. For full text of the Memorandum, see *Ambedkar Writes* op cit, Vol.I, pp. 84-92.

(vii) The monopoly of Caste Hindus in the Public Service must be destroyed and the recruitment should be regulated in such a manner that all communities including the Depressed Classes will have an adequate share in them.

(viii) The Depressed Classes should have the means of redress given to them in the Constitution so that prejudice to their interest and neglect of their vital needs cannot be overlooked.

(ix) The Constitutional Law should impose upon the Government of India a statutory obligation to maintain at all times a department to deal with their problems.

(x) In common with other minorities, the Depressed Classes claim their moral rights to be represented in the Cabinet should be recognized.

Later that year (on November 4, 1931) a Supplementary Memorandum was submitted. While the original Memorandum had demanded special representation for the Depressed Classes as one of political safeguards in the Constitution for a self-governing India, the details of the special representation claimed were not explicitly defined. The reason was that the proceedings of the Minorities Sub-Committee came to an end before the question was reached. The Supplementary Memorandum aimed at making good the omission so that the Minorities Sub-Committee would have the requisite details before it considers the question.

(E) IN SUB COMMITTEE ON DEFENCE

While participating in the deliberations of the Sub-Committee on Defence, Dr Ambedkar moved an amendment to the effect that immediate steps be taken to see that recruitment to the Indian Army is thrown open to all subjects...including the Depressed Classes, consistently with consideration of efficiency and the possession of the necessary qualifications.

Dr Ambedkar said:

> My amendment is very simple one; it seeks to remove all discriminations between the different Classes of His Majesty's subjects to enter Military Service.... I am not asking the Committee to confer any favour. I am asking the Committee to see us realize in practice the principle recognized in the Government of India Act that no subject of His Majesty shall be debarred from entering any Public Service by reason of his Caste, creed or colour....
>
> The Report of Service Committee appointed by this Committee, you will find that the Service Committee did make a serious effort to see that all subjects of His Majesty had a fair and adequate chance in Pubic Services of the country....They went out of their way to make special recommendations, mentioning certain specific communities, such as the Anglo-Indians and the Depressed Classes....
>
> But, Sir, this amendment is not merely in the interests of the Depressed Classes. I submit it is also in the interests of all communities....

Sir, that it is a great public danger that any community in India should be allowed to monopolise any services in the country. I say it is a great public danger, because it not only excites a sense of superiority in these particular communities which have been placed in the position of advantage, but it also jeopardises the welfare of the people by making them dependent upon the protection afforded to them by certain specific communities. I, therefore, submit that as we are enunciating a new Constitution for India, we ought to begin with a system which will permit every member of His Majesty's community to play such part as he is capable of by reason of his fitness in any Public Service of the country.... The defence of India should be to an increasing extent the concern of all Indian people, it must be the concern of Indian people and not the concern of any particular community.

★ ★ ★

(F) CLOSING PLENARY SESSION

Dr Ambedkar's remarks in the Plenary session (General Review) were remarkably sharp, analytically cogent and yet passionate in their appeal. Here are some excerpts from Dr Ambedkar's remarks:

On the question of responsible government in the Provinces I have very little to say. I accept the report of the Committee and subject to my dissents, I stand by it. But regarding the question of responsible government in the Centre, I am afraid I take a different view. It would be dishonest to say that the report of the Federal Structure Sub-Committee does not contemplate change in the bureaucratic form of Government as we know it today. But it would be equally dishonest for me to conceal from you my opinion that this change is shadowy and not substantial, and the responsibility is bogus and not real....

The Lord Chancellor told us that he had sown the seed, and it was for us to tend the plant....Grateful as I am to him, I am not sanguine that the plant he promises will grow. I fear the grain he has chosen for his seed is sterile and the soil in which he has cast it is not congenial to its growth.

But, Sir, if the Constitution for the Central Government contained in the Report of the Committee satisfies Sir TB Sapru if it is agreeable to Mr Jayakar, who proclaimed himself the representative of the Youth of India, and if it pleases Sir AP Patro, who speaks, as he says, in the name of the non-Brahmins of India, it is not for me to oppose. My attitude, therefore, is that of one who does not approve but who also does not obstruct. I will leave it to those who bless it to carry it through....

But I do have a mandate and that is, while not opposing responsible government, to see that no responsible government was established unless it was at the same time accompanied by a truly representative government. It is when I look at the achievement of the Conference to find out how it has dealt with the question of representative government that I feel most disappointed....

The franchise and the representation of the Different Classes in the Legislatures are the two pillars of which a truly representative government can rest. Everybody knows that the (Motilal) Nehru Committee had adopted adult suffrage....

When I came to this Conference I had thought that so far as the question of franchise was concerned the battle had already been won. But in the Franchise Committee I was completely disillusioned. I found to my great surprise that it was difficult to persuade even the Indian Liberals to consent to enfranchise 25 per cent of the population for Provincial Legislatures. The franchise for the Central Legislature is no doubt an unknown quantity. But I have no hope that it will be such as to make the Central Legislature more representative of the people than the Provincial Legislatures are going to be. A franchise so limited must necessarily make the future government of India a government of the masses by the Classes.

Regarding the question of the distribution of seats among the majority and the various minority communities we all know that there is a deadlock. The deadlock is largely due, in my opinion, to the mischief done in the past. I am sure that if the authorities in India had acted in the past on the principle of justice to all and favour to none, the problem would not have become so difficult of solution. The British Government set different values on different communities according to the political use they made of them and gave to many communities an extraordinary share of political power by denying it to the Depressed Classes in a measure which was their rightful due.

In this matter the most aggrieved community is the Depressed Classes, and I was hoping that this Conference would proceed on the principle that what is wrongly settled is never settled, and give to the Depressed Classes their rightful quota of seats by a revaluation of the old values. But this has not happened. The claims of the other minorities have already been acknowledged and defined....

The case of the Depressed Classes is totally different. Their claims have just been heard. They have not even been adjudged and I do not know how many of them will be admitted. To my mind it is not improbable that having regard to the helplessness of their position, the claims of the Depressed Classes for representations may be whittled down to satisfy the ever-increasing scramble by other communities who are manoeuvring not so much for protection as for power....

As the rights of the Depressed Classes in the future Constitution are not defined, any announcement that might be made on behalf of His Majesty's Government regarding the introduction of responsibility in the Centre as well as in the Provinces should make it clear that any advance in that direction must be on condition and subject to an agreement between the communities which would provide effective safeguards for the rights and interests of the Depressed Classes....

I must emphasize the gravity of the situation, and bring to your notice that no announcement will be acceptable to us unless the position is made perfectly clear in this behalf, and that failing this I and my colleague will be unable to accept the responsibility of participating in the further work of the Conference, and will be compelled to dissociate ourselves from it.

Sir, in asking you to do so, I am not asking you to do more than give effect to your pledged word. The British Parliament and those who speak for it have always stated that they are trustees for the Depressed Classes and I am sure that what they have been saying is not one of those conventional lies of civilization which we are all led to utter to keep human relations as pleasant as possible. In my opinion it is, therefore, the bounden duty of any Government to see that that trust is not betrayed and let me tell you, Mr Prime Minister, that the Depressed Classes would regard it as the greatest betrayal on the part of His Majesty's Government if it were to leave us to the mercy of those who have taken no interest in our welfare and whose prosperity and greatness are founded on our ruination and degradation.

For saying so I will be called a communalist by the nationalists and patriots on India. I am not afraid of that. India is a peculiar country and her nationalists and patriots are a peculiar people. A patriot and a nationalist in India is one who sees with open eyes his fellowmen treated as being less than men. But his humanity does not rise in protest. He knows that men and women for no cause are denied their human rights. But it does not prick his civic sense to helpful action. He finds whole Class of people shut out from public employment. But it does not rouse his sense of justice and fairplay. Hundreds of evil practices that injure man and society are perceived by him. But they do not sicken him with disgust. The patriot's one cry is power and more power for him and for his Class. I am glad I do not belong to that Class of patriots. I belong to that Class which takes its stand on democracy and which seeks to destroy monopoly in every shape and form.

Our aim is to realize in practice our ideal of one man one value in all walks of life, political, economic and social. It is because representative Government is one means to that end that the Depressed Classes attach to it as great a value and it is because of its value to us that I have urged upon you the necessity of making your declaration subject to its fulfilment. You may tell me that the Depressed Classes have your sympathy. My reply is, for a stricken people what is wanted is something more concrete, something more defined. You may despise me for being unduly apprehensive. My reply is it is better to be despised for too anxious apprehensions rather than be ruined by too confident a security.

★ ★ ★

At the First Round Table Conference, Dr Ambedkar emerged as a staunch nationalist. He forcefully argued that Independence from the British rule was a precondition for creating an egalitarian, Caste-free society. This vision of nationalism, like that of Mahatma Phule, Periyar and other leaders of the anti-Caste movement, focused on building the nation as a democracy, not merely a transfer of power to Indians. Dr Ambedkar gave that vision a fully modernist thrust—the society he envisioned was democratic and rational, embodying the Enlightenment values, encapsulated in the trinity of liberty, equality and fraternity.[50]

Dr Ambedkar participated in several Committee and Sub-Committee meetings during the first RTC, always presenting well-thought out arguments. He gave special attention to the need for a strong Central Government, noting that the government had welfare functions to undertake especially for oppressed groups such as the Untouchables. He reasoned that political power was needed by the Untouchables and that could only be won in the framework of an Independent India.

Outside the formal proceedings of the Round Table Conference, Dr Ambedkar gave interviews to the foreign press, contributed articles to foreign journals and

50. See, Omvedt, Gail (2004), op cit, p.39.

addressed several small gatherings including those of Members of the British Parliament. Dr Ambedkar made the fullest use of the opportunity to bring the abominable plight of the Depressed Classes in India to the notice of the thought-leaders in the Western world. The world opinion became quite supportive. Some British newspapers, however, were hostile to Dr Ambedkar because he did not oppose the move for Dominion Status. At a later date, *Sunday Chronicle* paid a glowing tribute to Dr Ambedkar for his contribution to the Round Table Conference, saying,

"At heart a true nationalist, he had to put up a stern fight against the persuasive coquetry of the British diehards who are anxious to win him over to their side…."

What did Dr Ambedkar think of the Conference? In a letter from London to his colleague in Mumbai, Dr Ambedkar indicated that he was in two minds as to the outcome of the Conference. He felt that the Conference had laid the foundation of the self-government of India. Viewed in this light, the Conference was a success. Yet viewed from another angle, the foundation (of the self-government in India) had more of sand than mortar and hence was not strong enough. Dr Ambedkar also informed in the latter that so far as the rights of the Depressed Classes were concerned, it was a tremendous success.

The Round Table Conference was adjourned on January 19, 1931 and Dr Ambedkar left for India by ship boarding to Marseilles on February 13, 1931.

Dr Ambedkar's role in the First Round Table Conference and his brilliant presentations at the Conference gave him wide publicity in Europe and in America. In the meantime, the Indian National Congress called off its Civil Disobedience movement, and a pact was reached between Mahatma Gandhi and Lord Irwin, the then Viceroy of British India. Gandhiji agreed to participate in the Second Round Table Conference scheduled for September 1931, and the stage was set for a historic Ambedkar-Gandhi conflict.

CHAPTER THIRTEEN

Round Table Conference: Session Two

ON HIS RETURN to India from the Round Table Conference (RTC) first Session (February 27, 1931) Dr Ambedkar was given a rousing felicitation (March 1, 1931). Responding to the welcome Dr Ambedkar explained the proceedings at the RTC to his followers. He said:

> I am happy to meet you after a gap of about five months.... I am also aware that it is entirely my responsibility to find a way for coming out of the wretchedness of our society. The representatives of Muslims, Sikhs and other communities were clearly briefed about their role in the Round Table Conference (RTC). But, while bidding farewell for the RTC, you had put the entire responsibility to find the solution to your problems on my shoulders. But I am happy that whatever solutions I could find out after great efforts are acceptable to you, and I would like to briefly explain them to you.
>
> I, along with Shri R B Srinivasan, have put up a scheme before the RTC in which there were eight demands. Those were about equal citizenship and human rights. Whether India should get *Swaraj*? What should be the form of that *Swaraj*? Whatever may be the kind of *Swaraj* it must give equal rights and status to the Untouchables. It will be meaningless *Swaraj* for us, howsoever good it may be, if it does not grant us equality and respect. We are afraid that the political power is going to be passed on into the hands of higher Castes. Unless a legal provision to ban the Untouchability is made before the *Swaraj* is granted, the said *Swaraj* will not be acceptable to us.
>
> It was necessary to decide that all the people will enjoy similar rights even after legal provision for banning the Untouchability was made. The exploitation or torment of the Untouchables, should be considered as crime against the State. In this regard Mr Ramsey McDonald has assured us. The issue will be further discussed and decided upon in the next RTC.
>
> The Untouchables are rightly afraid that despite all the political rights, they will be discriminated against by the law or an executive order in the future scheme of things. Therefore, unless we ensure that any Legislative Body or the Executive will not be in a position to make any discriminatory law or rule, we cannot accept to be ruled by the majority community of India. The Untouchables are going to remain in minority

in the Legislative Bodies forever in future. There will be hardly 10 to 15 per cent of them which is very minuscule. Therefore, there should be no provision for the Legislative Bodies to make any law based on the castes. The RTC has accepted our demand that the principal element of the *Swaraj* shall be of equal human rights to all the people.

The present position as regards the franchise is not at all satisfactory. Only the rich and middle Class can presently exercise their franchise. The poor and manual labour cannot elect their proper and suitable representatives. The percentage of poor in India is almost 90. They have to look at the Government for solution to their problems, and they are totally dependent on others. Therefore, I have demanded the system of adult franchise for all the sections of the society in the future *Swaraj* so as to improve upon the present demeaning conditions of the poor. There was lot of hot argument on this issue. Only we four representatives emphasized forcefully on this matter but without much of the success. A question was raised whether the Untouchables should get the separate electorates or there should be joint electorates. I suggested there should be the adult franchise with arrangement for separate electorates for first 10 years followed by the joint electorates and it should be based on reserved constituencies for the Untouchables.

The decision about appointments in the Government jobs will be in the hands of a separate Commission and not in the hands of any individual officer. But the most beneficial arrangement which is agreed is about proportionate representation for the minorities and the Untouchables in the Government jobs. In this regard all the power will be vested in the hands of the Governor.

What would we do if the majority people neglect us in the Legislative Bodies, or do not consider our requirements in the budget? In this regard, we have been granted power to make an appeal before the Governor. And if the Governor also neglects us then we can appeal to the Viceroy. Besides, the problem of Untouchables is pan-Indian. Therefore, we demanded that with a view to have a common approach to the problems of Untouchables, there should be a Tribunal under the Central Legislature to decide upon their grievances. However, no consensus could be reached on this issue.

A complete freedom has been granted for recruitment of Untouchables in the police and military. There will be no discrimination on the basis of caste or religion to get entry into these departments. All the members in the RTC supported this demand.

The ultimate purpose of all these efforts is to ensure the right of adult franchise to each person of each community so that the rule for the welfare of all the people including the minorities and Untouchables is established in the future *Swaraj*. The society based on '*Bahujan Hitaya, Bahujan Sukhaya*!' The question of franchise or the right to vote is very important and it is my earnest belief that without it the life of poor is not secure in any *Swaraj*.

While Dr Ambedkar was away, there were three important developments back home:

(a) Dr Ambedkar's lieutenants, as directed by him, started a new fortnightly paper, called the *Janata* (November 24, 1930);

(b) Dr Ambedkar was re-nominated to the Bombay Legislative Council; and
(c) The court-case regarding Mahad *Satyagraha* was decided in favour of the Depressed Classes by the Mahad Sub-Judge Court.

* * *

The political situation in India was changing rapidly. On January 26, 1931, the Viceroy Lord Irwin released all Congress leaders including Gandhiji from jail. There were detailed negotiations between Gandhiji and Viceroy Irwin. On March 5, 1931, a pact was reached between the two according to which Gandhiji withdraw the Civil Disobedience Movement and promised to participate in the Second Session of the Round Table Conference, scheduled to commence on September 7, 1931.

In the third week of July, 1931, the names of the delegates to the Second Session of the Round Table Conference were announced. Dr Ambedkar not only was selected for the Second RTC but he was also placed on the Federal Structure Committee, which was going to play a critical role in drafting the new Constitution for India.

Within a fortnight thereafter, Gandhiji wrote to Dr Ambedkar and sought a meeting with him in person. The historic meeting actually took place on August 14, 1931 at Mani Bhavan in Mumbai. The next day Dr Ambedkar left for London by a steamer, amid a farewell by 2000 volunteers shouting "Long Live Dr Ambedkar" and reached London on August 29, 1931.

When Dr Ambedkar was sailing for London on board the ship he ran into Sir Prabhashankar Pattani. Sir Pattani asked about the outcome of Dr Ambedkar's meeting with Gandhiji; he had been present at the meeting but had abruptly left in the middle. Naturally, Dr Ambedkar asked as to why Sir Pattani had had to suddenly excuse himself from that meeting. The response was rather unexpected. Sir Pattani explained that according to Hindu scriptures a gentleman should leave the place where a detractor reviles a good man, if he was not in a position to cut out the tongue of the detractor on the spot. Upon hearing this, thus came Dr Ambedkar's curt response: "What is the punishment prescribed by your Hindu scriptures for a rank hypocrite and an abject flatterer?" Others on board had to intervene to control the situation.

Gandhiji along with Pandit Malaviya, Sarojini Naidu and others sailed for England on August 29, 1931 and reached London on September 12, 1931. The Second Session of the RTC was scheduled to commence on September 7, 1931 and it was in this Session that Dr Ambedkar was going to come to a head-on collision with Gandhiji.

* * *

When the Second Session of the Round Table Conference began on September 7, 1931 nobody could have imagined a major and bitter debate between Mahatma

Gandhi (who was attending the Conference for the first time as the representative of the Indian National Congress) and Dr Ambedkar.

To begin with, participating in the deliberations of the Federal Structure Committee, Dr Ambedkar extensively dealt with the issues such as composition of Federal Legislature, representation of native (Princely) States and representation of other "Special Interests" such as Landholders, Trade, Commerce, Labour and the like.

Among other things, Dr Ambedkar said:

> The first thing that I propose to deal with is the subject of the composition of the Federal Legislature; and before I proceed with that subject let me make my position clear with respect to the question as to whether the Federal Legislature of future India shall be unicameral or bicameral. Now, I confess at the very outset that I have never been a believer in a bicameral system. I have never accepted that the Second Chamber has any utility at all… but I do not wish to raise any objection to a bicameral system being introduced in India.
>
> Having said that, let me turn to the question of the representation of the British Indian Provinces in the Federal Legislature of India. In doing that, the first question with which we are concerned and confronted is whether the representation shall be direct or whether the representation shall be indirect. It seems to me that so far as the Lower Chamber of the Federal Assembly is concerned, there can be no two opinions. It must be constituted by direct election. I am quite conscious of the fact that the Simon Commission, in dealing with this question, recommended that the Lower Chamber, instead of being constituted by direct election, should be constituted by indirect election; and in support of that they observed that, as a matter of fact, there was no distinction between direct election and indirect election, and that indirect election was only direct election one step removed.
>
> Now, logically, perhaps that position is correct; but I submit that psychologically there is a great difference between direct election and indirect election. In my opinion, what is of the utmost importance is that the people of India should be impregnated with the sense that, in the last resort, they are responsible for the good government of the country. And I venture to suggest that unless the Indian citizen is made to feel that it is he who can make or unmake the government, we shall never be able to succeed in establishing the true foundations of a responsible government in India….
>
> It follows that we must have some system of election whereby a direct contact will be established between the government and the citizens of the country; and, therefore, I submit that the blind of an indirect election between the Central Government and the citizens must be removed, and they must be allowed to see the effect of their election upon the government of the country and upon their welfare. I can, under no circumstances, consent to a system which will not provide for direct election to the Lower Chamber of the Federal Assembly.
>
> Coming to the constitution of the Upper Chamber, I approve of the method suggested by the Federal Structure Sub-Committee—namely, that it should be constituted by the method of indirect election in which the Provincial Legislative Councils will form the constituencies. I approve of the system because the election, instead of being carried out by the watertight methods of separate or communal

electorates, will be carried out on the basis of proportional representation. Now, I think it is a great advantage in a country like India, where, unfortunately, owing to various circumstances, we cannot avoid the separate representation of distinct communities—where we cannot ignore safeguarding the interests of various groups—to have in the constitution a Chamber which will be non-communal, a Chamber the members of which will have a mandate which will not be drawn exclusively from one particular community, but a mandate which will be broad-based....

The minorities in India are not only anxious to have their interests and their communities represented in the various Legislatures, but they are also insistent upon the fact that they shall get a certain minimum quantum of representation. Now, my fear is that although proportional representation may give them some representation in the Upper Chamber, we do not know that the various communities will succeed in getting the quantum of representation which they want. I would, therefore, like to suggest that, to this recommendation of the Federal Structure Sub-Committee, a proviso something on the lines of Article 35 of the Austrian Constitution should be added. That proviso, of course, does not speak of the representation of the communities; it speaks of the representation of political parties. But it can be easily made applicable to the representation of the communities....

I do not say that this could be taken bodily and adopted in the Indian Constitution; but that the principle enunciated there that along with the institution of proportional representation shall be a proviso which will guarantee a quantum of representation, maybe adopted in the Constitution....

I come now to the other part of the subject, namely, the representation of the Native States in the Federal Legislature. This subject raises two issues for consideration. One is whether each and every State shall be represented individually or whether they shall be grouped for the purposes of representation; and the second issue which arises out of it is how they shall be represented, whether by election or by nomination.

I take issue No. 1: The Federal Structure Sub-Committee has recommended that this is a matter that can be left to the (Native) States themselves. With all respect to the Sub-Committee, I beg to differ from their position.... In India, on the assumption I am making that every State is to be represented, we shall have a Federation which will have something like 570 units.... The thing that disturbs me is this: are we going to recognize every Indian State as an independent unit of the future Federation of India, irrespective of the question whether the units so recognised are capable of bearing the burdens of modern civilisation; or are we going to admit into our Federation units which are going to be units of the utmost lowest possible vitality? We are not quite aware of the multiplicity and variety of the circumstances which will be found in the different States....

I propose to read a small passage from a book called, *The States and their People in the Indian Constitution* by DV Gundappa:

'374 States have a revenue of less than Rs1 lakh. As many as 15 States have territories, which in no case reach a square mile; while 27 others possess just 1 square mile. Fourteen States exist in Surat district, not one of which realized a revenue of more than Rs 3,000 in the previous financial year. Three of these States could not boast of a population of 100 souls, and 5 of a revenue of Rs. 100....'

Once you accept the proposition that every State, whatever the attributes of the State may be, is entitled to become a member of the Indian Federation, then you give that State an independent right of existence for ever.... No unit in these modern days can exist on a scale such as modern civilisation demands unless it has sufficient resources at its command; and it is no use trying to please the fancy of an Indian Prince simply because he delights to call himself a Prince by letting his State be a separate entity, irrespective of the consideration whether his people can benefit by it.... I submit that at any rate this Committee should lay down certain qualifications which a State must fulfil before it can be admitted into the Indian Federation....

I would prescribe a certain area and a certain revenue as the tests.... If the Ruler of a State wants his State to exist as an independent State and to become a part of the Indian Federation, he should be able to prove that his country has the necessary resources and capacity to give to its citizens a civilized life. That is the stand I take.

Coming to the second part of the question, namely, the representation of the Indian State in the Federal Legislature, the Indian States have made it clear that they will come into the Indian Federation only if they are permitted to nominate their representatives to the Federal Legislature. Now, with all respect to the Indian Princes, I am afraid I cannot agree with them, and I must insist that their representation shall be by election....

I, for one, can never forget that is the principal objective and the principal task of this Committee. It follows from this that no concession can be made, no scheme can be adopted, if ultimately it is found that concession or that scheme is going to compromise the system of responsibility or is going to whittle down the system of responsibility at which we are all aiming.... Now, applying that test, it follows that you cannot consent to the claim of the Princes for nomination of their representatives.

Not only do the Princes want to come into the Legislature, but they also want to be represented in the Central Executive of the country; and it is only right that the Princes should have that objective, because they would gain nothing by merely coming into the Legislature—their real gain consists in having a hand in the Executive of the Country.

You have in the Federal Structure Sub-Committee laid down that the system of responsibility in the Central Legislature will be a system of collective responsibility. If the representatives of British India are going to come into the Federal Legislature by election, and if the representatives of the Indian States are coming into the Federal Legislature by nomination with definite instructions from those who will nominate them, I, for one, fail to understand how the system of collective responsibility—with divided mandates, with different instructions—is going to work in the future Constitution of the country.

We all know that the Princes carry on the administration of their States under what is called the system of paramountcy, and I think we all know that one of the incidents of the doctrine of paramountcy is that the Paramount Power claims the right of advising the Princes on the matter of important appointments. (Interruption)... Add to this the fact the paramountcy in the new Constitution is contemplated to remain a reserved subject. Now, supposing the Political Department, which will be exercising the powers of paramountcy, claims the right to advise the Princes in the matter of nomination to the Federal Legislature, what is the effect? The only result will be that Princes' nomination will in fact be nothing less, and nothing else than the official bloc replaced in another form.

We were all agreed on the fact that the thing that is best administered is responsible government. Therefore, although I am willing to make any concession possible in order to bring this Federation into existence, I cannot be a party to any concession or any compromise, as I said, which will only give us the skeleton of Federation without the soul, namely, responsible Government. In any case I must make it plain, so far as I am concerned, that I shall not be a party to any system which permits the representation of the States by nomination.

Now, My Lord Chancellor, I will take up the other head of discussion, namely, representation of special interests.... The first thing I would like to make clear is this I do not want the Depressed Classes to be treated as a special interest. I want the Depressed Classes to be treated as a separate community for political purposes in the same way as the Mohammedans or the Christians are treated. They must have the same right of representation, not only in the Provincial Legislative Councils, but also in both Houses of the Central Legislature. (*Interruption*)....

Now I come to the other interests which have so far been recognized: namely, Trade, Commerce, Landholders and Universities....I am afraid I cannot give my consent to the representation of these special interests. First of all, I do not quite understand why, for instance, a landholder needs any special representation. I do not know what are the difficulties and disabilities from which he would suffer if he were to stand out in a general constituency and seek the suffrages of his people. There is nothing to prevent him from doing that....

My further objection to making any special provision for the representation of these interests is this: first of all, these interests get themselves represented by a very, very narrow constituency; it is almost by a clique. Now, if their voting power were confined to matters which concern them, the evil would be comparatively small. But they do not only come on the basis of this restricted constituency into the Legislative Council; they vote upon all and sundry matters that come before the Legislative Council.

Now Trade and Commerce in the Bombay Presidency have been the monopoly of a special community which I am sorry to say is the most orthodox community known to me....Now, such members get these easy pocket constituencies in order to get themselves into the Legislative Council. Then, if any progressive measure is brought forward, they come and side with the orthodox and thereby defeat the ends of freedom and progress. I, therefore, object to it....

With regard to Labour I would say this.... If the system of adult suffrage comes into operation—and I hope that, with the help and support of Mahatma Gandhi we shall be able to carry it through in this Conference—then there may perhaps be no necessity for the special representation of Labour; but if we adopt a system of representation which keeps out a large body of the working Classes from the Constitution, so that they cannot control the Government and influence it for bringing about their welfare and their prosperity, then there would certainly be a necessity for making special provision for the representation of Labour, and I think that could be done by recognising the various unions as the electoral colleges for the purposes of such representation.

The next topic to which I propose to refer is the question of nominated members. I suppose—I am not sure—that the object of having a bloc of nominated members in the Federal Legislature is principally to give support to what are called Crown subjects, or what in the Provinces, under the Dyarchical System, were called reserved subjects. First of all I should like to make it plain that I have a great horror of this nominated bloc of officials. If there is any institution which, in my opinion, has absolutely destroyed the system of responsibility in the Provincial Governments, which was sought to be introduced by the Montagu-Chelmsford Reforms, it is this institution of the nominated official bloc. It is this which has perverted the whole system. It is this group which has made possible, in the Provinces, Government by a minority against a majority. It is this group which has made alliances with all sorts of people and groups—not necessarily groups which needed its help or support, but groups which were ready to sell themselves for petty gains. I have, as I say, the strongest objection to a nominated official bloc....

There is one last subject to which I should like to refer, namely, the question of the Oath. This question, in my opinion, is a very big one.... I hold the view that there can be no real Federation unless there is common citizenship. It would be a misnomer to call a Constitution a Federal Constitution if it did not provide for a common citizenship....

★ ★ ★

Mahatma Gandhi made his first speech in the Federal Structure Committee of the RTC on September 15, 1931. In his address, Gandhiji argued that the Congress represents all Indian interests and Classes, including the Muslims and Depressed Classes; the latter because removal of Untouchability was a plank on the political platform of the Congress. And, since he was the sole representative of the Congress, it followed that he was the sole representative of the Indian nation as well.

Speaking in the same Committee the next day, Gandhiji again made a reference to the problem of special representation for different communities and said:

> The Congress had reconciled itself to special treatment of the Hindu-Muslim-Sikh tangle. There are sound historical reasons for it, but the Congress will not extend that doctrine in any shape or form... so far as the Untouchables are concerned. I have not yet quite grasped what Dr Ambedkar has to say, but of course, the Congress will share the onus with Dr Ambedkar of representing the interests of the Untouchables. The interests of Untouchables are as dear to the Congress as the interests of any other body or of any other individual throughout the length and breadth of India. Therefore, I would most strongly resist any further special representation.

Dr Ambedkar did not take on Gandhiji on this subject because it was going to come up before the Minorities Committee scheduled to meet on September 28. Before that meeting, Gandhiji's son Devdas arranged a second meeting between Dr Ambedkar and Gandhiji on September 26, 1931. The second meeting between Gandhiji and Dr Ambedkar was also equally awkward.

In spite of the skepticism about the outcome, Dr Ambedkar elaborated his position for three hours, while Gandhiji listened quietly, spinning. Gandhiji's unwillingness to respond, in contrast to his discussions with Muslim leaders like Jinnah, disturbed Dr Ambedkar very much. He saw Gandhiji's behaviour as *Chanakya Niti*—an attempt simply to gauge the position of an irreconcilable opponent.

★ ★ ★

Speaking to the Minorities Committee on October 1, 1931, Gandhiji called for its adjournment on the grounds that no compromise could be reached in his meetings with Muslim leaders of various groups. Gandhi suggested that informal consultations would solve the "Communal Problem", for which he needed more time. It was in the Minorities Committee Meeting after a week (October 8, 1931) that Gandhiji and Dr Ambedkar faced each other and all hell broke loose. Here are excerpts from the Gandhi-Ambedkar debate, in full:

Chairman: When we met last Thursday, by common consent we adjourned for a week in order to enable informal and unofficial consultations to take place, with a view of coming to an agreement. Perhaps our first business is to receive a report from those who conducted the negotiations. May I ask Mr Gandhi to speak first?

Mr Gandhi: Prime Minister and friends, it is with deep sorrow and deeper humiliation that I have to announce utter failure on my part to secure an agreed solution of the communal question through informal conversations among and with the representatives of different groups. I apologize to you, Mr Prime Minister, and the other colleagues for the waste of a precious week. My only consolation lies in the fact that when I accepted the burden of carrying on these talks I knew that there was not much hope of success, and still more in the fact that I am not aware of having spared any effort to reach a solution.

But to say that the conversations have to our utter shame failed is not to say the whole truth. Causes of failure were inherent in the composition of the Indian Delegation. We are almost all not elected representatives of the parties or groups whom we are presumed to represent; we are here by nomination of the Government. Nor are those whose presence was absolutely necessary for an agreed solution to be found here. Further, you will allow me to say that this was hardly the time to summon the Minorities Committee. It lacks the sense of reality in that we do not know what it is that we are going to get. If we knew in a definite manner that we were going to get the thing we want, we should hesitate fifty times before we threw it away in a sinful wrangle, as it would be if we are told that the getting of it would depend upon the ability of the present Delegation to produce an agreed solution of the communal tangle. The solution can be the crown of the *Swaraj* Constitution, not its foundation— if only because our differences have hardened, if they have not arisen, by reason of the foreign domination. I have not a shadow of a doubt that the iceberg of communal differences will melt under the warmth of the sun of freedom.

I, therefore, venture to suggest that the Minorities Committee be adjourned sine die and that the fundamentals of the Constitution be hammered into shape as quickly as may be. Meanwhile, the informal work of discovering a true solution of the communal problem will and must continue; only it must not baulk or be allowed to block the progress of Constitution-building. Attention must be diverted from it and concentrated on the main part of the structure.

Lastly, inasmuch as the only reason for my appearance at these deliberations is that I represent the Indian National Congress, I must clearly set forth its position. In spite of appearances to the contrary, especially in England, the Congress claims to represent the whole nation, and most decidedly the dumb millions, among whom are included the numberless Untouchables, who are more suppressed than depressed, as also in a way the more unfortunate and neglected Classes known as Backward Races.

It seems to have been represented that I am opposed to any representation of the Untouchables on the Legislature. This is a travesty of the truth. What I have said, and what I must repeat, is that I am opposed to their special representation. I am convinced that it can do them no good, and may do much harm; but the Congress is wedded to adult franchise. Therefore, millions of them can be placed on the Voters' Roll. It is impossible to conceive that, with Untouchability fast disappearing, nominees of these voters can be boycotted by the others; but what these people need more than election to the Legislatures is protection from social and religious persecution. Custom, which is often more powerful than law, has brought them to a degradation of which every thinking Hindu has need to feel ashamed and to do penance. I should, therefore, have the most drastic legislation rendering criminal all the special persecution to which these fellow-countrymen of mine are subjected by the so-called superior Classes. Thank God, the conscience of Hindus has been stirred, and Untouchability will soon be a relic of our sinful past.

Dr Ambedkar: Mr Prime Minister, last night when we parted at the conclusion of the meeting of the informal Committee, we parted although with a sense of failure, at least with one common understanding, and that was that when we met here today none of us should make any speech or any comment that would cause exasperation. I am sorry to see that Mr Gandhi should have been guilty of a breach of this understanding. Excuse me, I must have the opportunity to speak. He started by giving what were, according to him, the causes of the failure of the informal Committee. Now, I have my own causes which I think were responsible for the failure of the informal Committee to reach an agreement, but I do not propose to discuss them now. What disturbs me after hearing Mr Gandhi is that instead of confining himself to his proposition, namely, that the Minorities Committee should adjourn sine die, he started casting certain reflections upon the representatives of the different communities who are sitting round this table. He said that the Delegates were nominees of the Government, and that they did not represent the views of their respective communities for whom they stood. We cannot deny the allegation that we are nominees of the Government, but, speaking for myself, I have not the slightest doubt that even if the Depressed Classes of India were given the chance of electing their representatives to this Conference, I would, all the same, find a place here. I say, therefore, that, whether I am a nominee or not, I fully represent the claims of my community. Let no man be under any mistaken impression as regards that.

The Mahatma has been always claiming that the Congress stands for the Depressed Classes, and that the Congress represents the Depressed Classes more than I or my colleague can do. To that claim I can only say that it is one of the many false claims which irresponsible people keep on making, although the persons concerned with regard to those claims have been invariably denying them.

I have here a telegram which I have just received from a place which I have never visited, and from a man whom I have never seen; from the President of the Depressed Classes Union, Kumaun, Almora, which I believe is in the United Provinces, and which contains the following resolution:

'This Meeting declares its no-confidence in the Congress movement which has been carried on in and outside the country, and condemns the methods adopted by the Congress workers.'

I do not care to read further, but I can say this (and I think if Mr Gandhi will examine his position he will find out the truth), that although there may be people in the Congress who may be showing sympathy towards the Depressed Classes, the Depressed Classes are not in the Congress. That is a proposition which I propose to substantiate. I do not wish to enter into these points of controversy. They seem to be somewhat outside the main proposition. The main proposition which Mr Gandhi has made is that this Committee should be adjourned sine die. With regard to that proposition, I entirely agree with the attitude taken up by Sir Muhammad Shafi. I, for one, cannot consent to this proposition. It seems to me that there are only two alternatives—either that this Minorities Committee should go on tackling the problem and trying to arrive at some satisfactory solution, if that is possible, and then, if that is not possible, the British Government should undertake the solution of that problem. We cannot consent to leave this to the arbitration of third parties whose sense of responsibility may not be the same as must be the sense of responsibility of the British Government.

Prime Minister, permit me to make one thing clear. The Depressed Classes are not anxious, they are not clamorous, they have not started any movement for claiming that there shall be an immediate transfer of power from the British to the Indian people. They have their particular grievances against the British people, and I think I have voiced them sufficiently to make it clear that we feel those grievances most genuinely. But, to be true to facts, the position is that the Depressed Classes are not clamouring for transfer of political power. Their position, to put it plainly, is that we are not anxious for the transfer of power; but if the British Government is unable to resist the forces that have been set up in the country which do clamour for transference of political power—and we know the Depressed Classes in their present circumstances are not in a position to resist that—then our submission is that if you make that transfer, that transfer will be accompanied by such conditions and by such provisions that the power shall not fall into the hands of a clique, into the hands of an oligarchy, or into the hands of a group of people, whether Mohammedans or Hindus; but that solution shall be such that the power shall be shared by all communities in their respective proportions. Taking that view, I do not see how I, for one, can take any serious part in the deliberations of the Federal Structure Committee unless I know where I and my community stand.

Mr Gandhi: One word more as to the so-called Untouchables.I can understand the claims advanced by other minorities, but the claims advanced on behalf of the Untouchables that to me is the 'unkindest cut of all'. It means the perpetual bar-sinister. I would not seal the vital interests of the Untouchables even for the sake of winning the freedom of India. I claim myself in my own person to represent the vast mass of the Untouchables. Here I speak not merely on behalf of the Congress, but I speak on my own behalf, and I claim that I would get, if there was a referendum of the Untouchables, their vote, and that I would top the poll. And I would work from one end of India to the other to tell the Untouchables that separate electorates and separate reservation is not the way to remove this bar-sinister, which is the shame not of them but of orthodox Hinduism.

Let this Committee and let the whole world know that today there is a body of Hindu reformers who are pledged to remove this blot of Untouchability. We do not want on our register and on our census Untouchables classified as separate Class. Sikhs may remain as such in perpetuity, so may Mohammedans, so may Europeans. Will Untouchables remains Untouchables in perpetuity? I would fear rather that Hinduism died than that Untouchability lived. Therefore, with all my regard for Dr Ambedkar, and for his desire to see the Untouchables uplifted, with all my regard for his ability, I must say in all humility that here the great wrong under which he has laboured and perhaps the bitter experiences that he has undergone have for the moment warped his judgment.

It hurts me to have to say this, but I would be untrue to the cause of the Untouchables, which is as dear to me as life itself, if I did not say it. I will not bargain away their rights for the kingdom of the whole world. I am speaking with a due sense of responsibility, and I say that it is not a proper claim which is registered by Dr Ambedkar when he seeks to speak for the whole of the Untouchables of India. It will create a division in Hinduism which I cannot possibly look forward to with any satisfaction whatsoever. I do not mind Untouchables, if they so desire, being converted to Islam or Christianity. I should tolerate that, but I cannot possibly tolerate what is in store for Hinduism if there are two divisions set forth in the villages. Those who speak of the political rights of Untouchables do not know their India, do not know how Indian society is today constructed, and, therefore, I want to say with all emphasis that I can command that if I was the only person to resist this thing I would resist it with my life.

★ ★ ★

In the meeting of the Minorities Committee, Gandhiji announced with profound regret his inability in forging a consensus through informal consultations. In the same breath, he blamed the lack of agreement on the composition of the Committee, indicating that the British had stacked the Conference with non-elected political lightweights and non-entities as a way of getting around the national movement. To this, Dr Ambedkar immediately took an exception.

Dr Ambedkar took everyone by surprise when he said that the Depressed Classes were not anxious about the transfer of power under the present circumstances. But if the Government wanted to transfer power, it should be accompanied by such conditions that power does not find itself concentrated into the hands of the oligarchy; the solution should be such that power is share by all communities in their respective proportions.

Proceeding further in his direct attack on Gandhiji, Dr Ambedkar said:

To say in public that I will agree if all others agreed and then set out to work in private to prevent others from so agreeing by buying off those who are willing to agree, is, in our opinion, a piece of conduct unbecoming a Mahatma and to be expected only from an inveterate opponent of the Depressed Classes. Mr Gandhi is not only not playing the part of a friend of the Depressed Classes, but he is not even playing the part of an honest foe.

★ ★ ★

For the last meeting of the Minorities Committee, leading representatives of the Muslims, Depressed Classes, Christians and Anglo-Indians jointly submitted a Memorandum which advocated a general principle:

No person shall, by reason of his origin, religion, Caste or creed, be prejudiced in any way in regard to public employment, office of power or honour or with regard to enjoyment of civic rights and the exercise of any trade or calling.

Dr Ambedkar submitted a supplementary Memorandum asking for special representations for the Depressed Classes in all Provincial Legislatures and in the Central Assembly in proportion to their population in India. The Memorandum also demanded separate electorates, although if the system of joint electorates with reserved seats was to exist, it should take place only after a referendum, and not for atleast the next twenty years. Interestingly, a demand was also made for a change of nomenclature viz., they should now be called 'non-Caste Hindus, Protestant Hindus' or 'non-conformist Hindus' instead of Depressed Classes.

Gandhiji, nonplussed by Dr Ambedkar who was much younger, but full of irreverent audacity, and who spoke with a cultivated ferocity and the fervour of an iconoclast, was bound to react sharply and personally.

At one point Gandhiji had reportedly said of Dr Ambedkar: "Dr Ambedkar commands my sympathies in all he says. He needs the gentlest treatment." On another occasion, Gandhiji said: "He has a right to spit upon me, as every Untouchable has, and I would keep on smiling if he did so." This resolutely smiling face was not a mask. It was a measure of the man. But when Gandhiji confronted Dr Ambedkar at the Second Round Table Conference, Gandhiji's smile faded.[51]

Gandhiji and Dr Ambedkar both went away with hurt feelings. Gandhiji called it "the most humiliating day of my life," while Dr Ambedkar reportedly, said later acidly:

Unfortunately, the Congress chose Mr Gandhi as its representative. A worse person could not have been chosen to guide India's destiny. As a unifying force he was a failure. Mr Gandhi presents himself as a man full of humility. But his behavior at the Round

51. Lelyweld, Joseph, *Great Soul* (2011), p.214-5.

Table Conference showed that in the flush of victory Mr Gandhi could be very petty-minded.[52]

The Second Round Table Conference ended in a stalemate. It created a lot of bitterness between Gandhiji and Dr Ambedkar. When Dr Ambedkar was leaving for the First Round Table Conference (which Gandhiji had boycotted), Gandhiji's followers had protested against him with black flags. In turn, when Gandhiji returned from London after attending the Second Round Table Conference, hundreds of Dr Ambedkar's followers assembled at the Mole Station—the marine terminal in Mumbai—to protest against the "uncharitable" stance taken by him. The cheers from Gandhiji's followers were drowned in the slogans of Dalits. In fact, the battles of slogans soon turned physical. Stones, sticks and bottles started flying. The police had difficulty controlling the mobs, and several people were injured.

52. Ambedkar B R, *What Congress And Gandhi Have Done to the Untouchables*, p. 35.

CHAPTER FOURTEEN

Direct Confrontation with Gandhiji

DR AMBEDKAR RETURNED to Mumbai reaching on January 29, 1932. On his arrival, he was given a hero's welcome. Along with the Muslim leader Maulana Shaukat Ali, he addressed the huge crowd of Depressed Classes and Muslims gathered at the Mole Station, Mumbai where Maulana Shaukat Ali commended Dr Ambedkar for the extraordinary courage shown by him fighting for his cause.

In the farewell function on the eve of his departure to attend the Second Round Table Conference (August 14, 1931), Dr Ambedkar had addressed his men and women followers when he had said:

> In a Conference of one hundred and twenty-five members, we are two, but rest assured that we will move heaven and earth for the sake of your welfare. I had a talk with Mr Gandhi this afternoon. At present he must do anything to promote your interests. We must stand on our own feet and fight as best as we can for our rights. So carry on your agitation and organize your forces. Power and prestige will come to you through struggle.

Interestingly, while addressing the large gathering of his women followers, Dr Ambedkar had said:

> If you stand by your resolve to extirpate your slavery root and branch, and undergo all trials and tribulations for it, the credit and success of my being able to discharge the onerous task will be yours.

When Dr Ambedkar returned to Mumbai having shouldered the onerous task with distinction, in the public meeting the same day evening (January 29, 1932), he was given an Address of Welcome which said:

> You have, indeed, proved to the hilt our claim for equality of status and treatment, and, but for the valiant fight you put on our behalf, our claims would have been ignored. You have done all that is humanly possible in safeguarding our rights and we are sure

> to stand as a result of your endeavor in London, on an equal footing with all other major communities in India in the near future. The Address concluded: The sense of responsibility and the present outlook of our community, which is now out to assert its rights all over the country is—it will not be an exaggeration to say—but the fruit of your exclusive efforts and guidance.

Dr Ambedkar, visibly moved by the abiding love and gratitude of his followers, declared to the vast audience that whatever services he could render were the summation of the co-operation of all the workers and the unflinching backing of his people. He said that no leader was by himself responsible for the fulfilment or failure of a mission; so he asked them to continue the struggle. He said:

> I am described as a traitor by Congressmen, he observed, because I opposed Gandhi. I am not at all perturbed by this charge. It is baseless, false and malicious. But it was a great shock to the world that Gandhi himself should have sponsored violent opposition to the breaking of your shackles. I am confident that the future generations of Hindus will appreciate my services when they study the history of the Round Table Conference.

Dr Ambedkar also disclosed how he happened to see Gandhi four or five times in London, how Gandhi went secretly to the Aga Khan with a copy of the Holy Koran in his hand and asked the Muslim leader to withdraw his support to the Depressed Classes, and how the Aga Khan had refused to do so. Lastly, he appealed to his people not to deify him as he hated deification.[53]

While thanking the audience, Dr Ambedkar said that he would not have been able to place before the RTC the case of the Depressed Classes had he not been supported by the solidarity of the seven crore of the Untouchables. He referred to the difference of opinion that existed between himself and a certain section of the Depressed Classes, and assured them that he did not stand for any particular section of the Depressed Classes but was prepared to accept any scheme safeguarding the interests of the whole community.

Dr Ambedkar criticized the attitude of Mr Gandhi in dealing with the minorities problem and said that he, while negotiating with the Depressed Classes, was at the same time secretly confabulating with the Mohammedans. He asked the audience not to place reliance on a leader but always depend on their own strength. At the conclusion of the meeting, Dr Ambedkar congratulated the Nasik temple entry *Satyagrahis*.[54]

---

53. After the direct confrontation in the RTC, Dr Ambedkar never addressed Gandhiji as Mahatma, not even Gandhiji; he addressed Gandhiji only as Mr Gandhi.
54. Around the same time, the temple entry *Satyagraha* at *Kala Ram* Temple in Nasik was gathering momentum.

LOTHIAN COMMITTEE ON FRANCHISE

Following the recommendations by the Franchise Sub-committee of the Round Table Conference, the Indian Franchise Committee was constituted in December, 1931. The Committee was chaired by Mr Lothian, British Parliamentary Under Secretary of State for India, and had 18 Members including Dr Ambedkar. The main term of reference for the Committee was to devise a system of franchise whereby:

> The Legislatures to which responsibility was entrusted should be representative of the general mass of the population and that no important section of the community may lack the means of expressing its needs and its opinions.

Dr Ambedkar made a submission before the Lothian Committee on May 1, 1932. His submission covered the all-important issues of franchise and tests of Untouchability. The main points of the Submission may be summarized in his own words as follows:

> I have agreed to confine the term Depressed Classes to Untouchables only. In fact, I have myself sought to exclude from the Untouchables all those in whom there cannot be the same consciousness of kind as is shared by those who suffer from the social discrimination that is inherent in the system of Untouchability... and who are, therefore, likely to exploit the Untouchables for their own purposes....
>
> In the first place it is urged in some quarters that whatever tests are applied for ascertaining the Untouchable Classes they must be applied uniformly all over India. In this connection,... it would hardly be appropriate to apply the same test or tests all over India. India is not a single homogeneous country. It is a continent. The various Provinces are marked by extreme diversity of conditions and there is no tie of race or language. Owing to absence of communication each Province has evolved along its own lines with its own peculiar manners and modes of social life. In such circumstances the degree of uniformity with which most of the tests of Untouchability are found to apply all over India is indeed remarkable. For instance, bar against temple entry exists everywhere in India. Even the tests of well-water and pollution by touch apply in every Province, although not with the same rigidity everywhere. But to insist on absolute uniformity in a system like that of Untouchability which after all is a matter of social behaviour and which must therefore vary with the circumstances of each Province and also of each individual is simply to trifle with the problem. The Statutory Commission was quite alive to this possible line of argument and after careful consideration rejected it by recognizing the principle of diversity in the application of tests of Untouchability....
>
> Another point which I wish to emphasize is the futility of insisting upon the application of uniform tests of Untouchability all over India. It is a fundamental mistake to suppose that differences in tests of Untouchability indicate differences in the conditions of the Untouchables. On a correct analysis of the mental attitude they indicate, it will be found that whether the test is causing pollution by touch or refusal to use common well, the notion underlying both is one and the same. Both are outward registers of the same inward feeling of defilement, odium, aversion and

contempt. Why will not a Hindu touch an Untouchable? Why will not a Hindu allow an Untouchable to enter the temple or use the village well? Why will not a Hindu admit an Untouchable in the inn? The answer to each one of these questions is the same. It is that the Untouchable is an unclean person not fit for social intercourse. Again, why will not a Brahmin priest officiate at religious ceremonies performed by an Untouchable? Why will not a barber serve an Untouchable? In these cases also the answer is the same. It is that it is below dignity to do so. If our aim is to demarcate the Class of people who suffer from social odium then it matters very little which test we apply. For as I have pointed out, each of these tests is indicative of the same social attitude on the part of the Touchables towards the Untouchables....

In the second place the view is put forth that in applying the test of 'causing pollution by touch' for ascertaining the Untouchable Classes, effect must be given to it in its literal sense—and not in its notional sense. In the literal sense Untouchables are only those persons whose touch not only causes pollution and is, therefore, avoided, or if not avoided is washed off by purification. In the notional sense an Untouchable is a person who is deemed to belong to a Class which is commonly held to cause pollution by touch, although contact with such a person may for local circumstances not be avoided or may not necessitate ceremonial purification. According to those who seek to apply the test in its literal sense the conclusion would be the so-called Untouchables should cease to be reckoned as Untouchables wherever conditions have so changed that people do not avoid the touch of an Untouchable, or do not trouble to purify themselves of the pollution caused by their touch. I cannot accept this view which, in my opinion, is based on a misconception. An individual may not be treated as an Untouchable in the literal sense of the term on account of various circumstances. Nonetheless outside the scope of such compelling circumstances he does continue to be regarded as an impure person by reason of his belonging to the Untouchable Class. The difference between Untouchability in its literal and notional sense is a distinction which makes no difference to the ultimate situation; for as the extract shows Untouchability in its notional sense persists even where Untouchability in its literal sense has ceased to obtain. This is why I insist that the test of Untouchability must be applied in its notional sense....

In the third place the idea is broadcast that Untouchability is rapidly vanishing. I wish to utter a word of caution against the acceptance of this view, and to point out the necessity of distinguishing facts from propaganda. In my opinion what is important to be borne in mind in drawing inference from instances showing the occasional commingling of Brahmins and non-Brahmins, Touchables and Untouchables is that the system of Caste and the system of Untouchability form really the steelframe of Hindu society. This division cannot easily be wiped out for the simple reason that it is not based upon rational, economic or racial grounds. On the other hand, the chances are that Untouchability will endure far longer into the future than the optimist reformer is likely to admit on account of the fact that it is based on religious dogma. What makes it so difficult, to break the system of Untouchability is the religious sanction which it has behind it. At any rate the ordinary Hindu looks upon it as part of his religion and there is no doubt that in adopting towards Untouchables in what is deemed to be an inhuman way of behaviour he does so more from the sense of observing his religion than from any motive of deliberate cruelty. Based on religion the ordinary Hindu only relaxes the rules of Untouchability where he cannot observe them. He never abandons them. For abandonment of Untouchability to him involves a total abandonment of the basic religious tenets of Hinduism as understood by him and the mass of Hindus. Based on religion Untouchability will persist as all religious notions have done. Indian history records the attempts of many a Mahatma to uproot Untouchability from the Indian soil. They include such great men as Buddha, Ramanuja and the Vaishnava saints of modern times. It would be hazardous to assume that a system which has withstood all this onslaught will collapse. The Hindu looks upon the observance of Untouchability as an act of religious merit, and non-observance of it as sin. My view, therefore, is that so long as this notion prevails Untouchability will prevail....

Nomenclature

The revision of the electoral rolls consequent upon the proposed changes in the Constitution is a very good occasion for considering the question of having a proper and appropriate nomenclature for the Depressed Classes. I, therefore, propose to express my opinion on this question. There is considerable objection on the part of the communities which are now called 'Depressed Classes' to the use of that term in describing them. Several witnesses who have appeared before the Committee have given expression to this sentiment. Besides the term 'Depressed Classes' has led to a great deal of confusion in the Census because it includes others who are not strictly Untouchables. Secondly, it gives the impression that the Depressed Classes are a low and helpless community when as a matter of fact in every Province numbers of them are both well-to-do and well-educated, and the whole community is acquiring consciousness of its needs, is charged with ambition for securing a respectable status in Indian society and is making stupendous efforts to achieve it. On all these grounds the term 'Depressed Classes' is inappropriate and unsuitable....

Mr Mullan, the Census Superintendent of Assam, has brought into use a new term called 'Exterior Castes' to cover the Untouchables. This designation has many advantages. It defines exactly the position of the Untouchables who are within the Hindu religion but outside the Hindu society and distinguishes it from Hindus who are economically and educationally depressed but who are both within the pale of Hindu religion and Hindu society. The term has two other advantages. It avoids all the confusion that is now caused by use of the vague term Depressed Classes and at the same time is not offensive. Our Committee did not feel competent to make recommendation in this behalf. But as a representative of the Depressed Classes I have no hesitation in saying that until better nomenclature is found the Untouchable Classes should hereafter be described by the more expressive term 'Exterior Castes' or 'Excluded Castes' and not as Depressed Classes....

Reservations

Before concluding this note I would like on my part to make the same reservation which my Muslim colleagues on the Committee have made namely that the allocation of seats to labour women, and other special interests must not affect the proportion of seats which the Depressed Classes have claimed in the Minorities Pact submitted to the Round Table Conference.

* * *

Several years later, in his treatise titled: *What Congress and the Gandhi Have Done to Untouchables*[55] (first published in 1945), Dr Ambedkar records his observations regarding working of the Lodhian Committee as follows:

> The Committee started its work early in January 1932. For doing its work the Committee took the help of the Provincial Governments and of the Provincial Franchise Committees consisting of non-officials specially constituted for that purpose Province by Province. The Committee issued questionnaires. They were replied to by the Provincial Governments, by the Provincial Franchise Committees and by individuals. Witnesses were examined by the Committee sitting with each Provincial Franchise Committee. The Provincial Governments and the Provincial Committees submitted their reports separately to the Committee. They were discussed by the Committee with the Provincial Government and the Provincial Committee before it came to its own conclusion. Besides the general tasks assigned to the Lothian Committee, it had a special task with which it was charged by the Prime Minister. It had relation, to the political demands of the Untouchables.
>
> Following upon these instructions, it became the task of the Committee to come to some conclusion as to the total population of the Untouchables in British India.
>
> To the question what is the population of the Untouchables the replies received were enough to stagger anybody. Witness after witness came forward to say that the Untouchables in his Province were infinitesimally small. There were not wanting witnesses who said that there were no Untouchables at all!! It was a most extraordinary sight to see Hindu witnesses perjuring themselves regardless of truth by denying the existence of the Untouchables, or by reducing their number to a negligible figure. The members of the Provincial Franchise Committee were also a party to this plan. Strange to say that some of the Hindu members of the Lothian Committee were in the game.
>
> This move of denying the very existence of the Untouchables or reducing their number almost to nil was particularly rampant in certain Provinces. How the Hindus were prepared to economize truth, even to a vanishing point, will be evident from the following figures. In the United Provinces, the Census Commissioner in 1931 had estimated the total population of the Untouchables at 12.6 millions, the Provincial Government at 6.8 millions but the Provincial Franchise Committee at 0.6 millions only!! In Bengal, the Census gave the figures of 10.3 millions, Provincial Government fixed it as 11.2 millions but the Provincial Franchise Committee at 0.07 millions only!

---

55. For full summary of the book, see *Ambedkar Writes*, op cit, Vol.I, pp. 259-380.

Before the Round Table Conference no Hindu bothered about the exact population of the Untouchables and were quite satisfied with the accuracy of the Census figures which gave the total of the Untouchables at about 70 to 80 millions. Why did then the Hindus start suddenly to challenge this figure when the question was taken up by the Lothian Committee? The answer is very clear.

Before the time of the Lothian Committee the population of the Untouchables had no value. But after the Round Table Conference the Hindus had come to know that the Untouchables were demanding separate allotment of their share of representation; that such share must come out of the lump which the Hindus had been enjoying in the past and that the measure of the share must depend upon the population of the Untouchables. The Hindus had realized that to admit the existence of the Untouchables was detrimental to their interest. They did not mind sacrificing truth and decency and decided to adopt the safest course, namely, to deny that there are any Untouchables in India at all, and thereby knock out the bottom of the political demands of the Untouchables and leave no room for argument. This shows how the Hindus can, conspire in a cold, calculated manner against the Untouchables out of pure selfishness and do indirectly what they cannot do directly.

⋆ ⋆ ⋆

About the confrontation with Mahatma Gandhi in the Second Round Table Conference, Dr Ambedkar in *What Congress and Gandhi Have Done to Untouchables*, Dr Ambedkar wrote:

Those, who were friends of Mr Gandhi, could not understand Mr Gandhi's attitude to the demands of the Untouchables. To give recognition to the Muslims and the Sikhs and to refuse it to the Untouchables came to them as a surprise and a puzzle. Whenever they asked for an explanation, Mr Gandhi did nothing except to get angry. Mr Gandhi himself could not give a logical and consistent defence of his opposition to the Untouchables. Inside the Round Table Conference his defence was that the Hindus had seriously taken up the cause of the Untouchables and that, therefore, there was no reason to give them political safeguards. Outside the Round Table Conference he gave totally different reasons. In a speech in defence of his position Mr Gandhi said:

'Muslims and Sikhs are all well organized. The 'Untouchables' are not. There is very little political consciousness among them and they are so horribly treated that I want to save them against themselves. If they had separate electorates their lives would be miserable in villages which are the strongholds of Hindu orthodoxy. It is the superior Class of Hindus who have to do penance for having neglected the 'Untouchables' for ages. That penance can be done by active social reform and by making the lot of the 'Untouchables' more bearable by acts of service, but not by asking for separate electorates for them. By giving them separate electorates you will throw the apple of discord between the 'Untouchables' and the orthodox. You must understand I can tolerate the proposal for special representation of the *Musalmans* and the Sikhs only as a. necessary evil. It would be a positive danger for the 'Untouchables'. I am certain that the question of separate electorates for the 'Untouchables' is a modern manufacture of Government. The only thing needed is to put them on the voters' list, and provide for fundamental rights for them in the Constitution. In cases they are unjustly treated and their representative is deliberately excluded they would have the right to special election tribunal which would give them complete protection. It should be open to these tribunals to order the unseating of an elected candidate and the election of the excluded men.

Separate electorates to the 'Untouchables' will ensure them bondage in perpetuity. The *Musalmans* will never cease to be *Musalmans* by having separate electorates. Do you want the 'Untouchables' to remain 'Untouchables' forever? Well, the separate electorates would perpetuate the stigma. What is needed is destruction of Untouchability, and when you have done it, the bar-sinister which has been imposed by an insolent 'superior' Class upon an 'inferior' Class will be destroyed. When you have destroyed the bar-sinister, to whom will you give the separate electorates? Look at the history of Europe. Have you got separate electorates for the working Classes or women? With adult franchise, you give the 'Untouchables' complete security. Even the orthodox would have to approach them for votes.

Now then you ask, does Dr Ambedkar, their representative, insist on separate electorates for them? I have the highest regard for Dr Ambedkar. He has every right to be bitter. That he does not break our heads is an act of self-restraint on his part. He is today so much saturated with suspicion that he cannot see anything else. He sees in every Hindu a determined opponent of the 'Untouchables' and it is quite natural. The same thing happened to me in my early days in South Africa, where I was bounded out by Europeans wherever I went. It is quite natural for him to vent his wrath. But the separate electorates that he seeks will not give him social reform. He may himself mount to power and position but nothing good will accrue to the 'Untouchables'. I can say all this with authority, having lived with the 'Untouchables' and having shared their joys and sorrows all these years.'

According to Dr Ambedkar, Mr Gandhi at the Round Table Conference was not satisfied with mere propaganda. When he found that the propaganda was not succeeding as well as he expected he resorted to intrigue. When Mr Gandhi heard that at the suggestion of the Prime Minister, the minorities were about to produce a settlement and that this settlement would have the effect of the Untouchables getting the support of the other minorities and particularly of the Muslims, Mr Gandhi felt considerably disturbed. He devised a scheme to isolate the Untouchables. For this Mr Gandhi planned to buy out the *Musalmans* by giving to the *Musalmans* their fourteen demands, which Mr Gandhi was not in the beginning prepared to agree. When he found the *Musalmans* were lending their support to the Untouchables, Mr Gandhi agreed to them their fourteen points on condition that they withdrew their support from the Untouchables. The agreement was actually drafted.

Dr Ambedkar provided a copy of the draft agreement and wrote:

It is true that the Untouchables are not mentioned in the draft agreement. But that the *Musalmans* are bound not to support any other minority except the Sikhs makes it quite clear that they were not to support the Untouchables. In this intrigue, Mr

> Gandhi failed as he was bound to. The *Musalmans* who were out to demand safeguards for themselves could not stand up and oppose the demands of the Untouchables. Mr Gandhi in his passion for suppressing the Untouchables had lost his sense of discrimination to such extent as not to be able to distinguish between means which are fair and means which are foul. Mr Gandhi did not care to honour his word.
>
> In the Minorities Committee, Mr Gandhi had said that if the Committee agreed to accept the claim of the Untouchables for separate recognition it was free to do so, which meant that he would abide by the decision of the majority. But when he came to know that the other minorities had agreed to support the Untouchables, he did not hesitate to approach the *Musalmans* and turn them against the Untouchables by accepting their fourteen points which the Congress, the Hindu *Maha Sabha* and even the Simon Commission had rejected. Even if Mr Gandhi was prepared to flout public opinion, and public morality this diabolical plot of Mr Gandhi fell through because the *Musalmans* refused to disgrace themselves by joining in it.
>
> When the Second Session of the Round Table Conference was dissolved, the delegates to the Minorities Committee accepted the proposal of the Prime Minister to put in a signed requisition authorizing him to arbitrate and give his decision on the communal issue. Many delegates did it including Mr Gandhi. There was nothing left for the delegates but to return to India and await the decision of the Prime Minister and having made him the sole arbitrator to accept it with good cheer....

★ ★ ★

Gandhiji was in the Yeravada jail when the Communal Award was announced by the British Prime Minister. Apparently, on account of a Statement that Gandhiji made in an interview to a newspaper in Rome to the effect of 'threatening to review his campaign of Civil Disobedience' that he was arrested on arrival in India and put in Jail (January 4, 1932).

Well before the announcement of the Communal Award, Gandhiji wrote a letter to Sir Samuel Hoare, the then Secretary of State for India, which *inter alia* stated:

> You will perhaps recollect that at the end of my speech at the Round Table Conference when the Minorities' claim was presented, I had said that I should resist with my life the grant of separate electorates to the Depressed Classes. This was not said in the heat of the moment nor by way of rhetoric. It was meant to be a serious statement. In pursuance of that statement, I had hoped on my return to India to mobilize public opinion against separate electorates, at any rate, for the Depressed Classes. But it was not to be.
>
> From the newspapers, I am permitted to read, I observe that any moment His Majesty's Government may declare their decision. At first I had thought, if the decision was found to create separate electorates for the Depressed Classes, I should take such steps as I might then consider necessary to give effect to my vow. But I feel it would be unfair to the British Government for me to act without giving previous notice.
>
> I need hardly reiterate all the objections I have to the creation of separate electorates for the Depressed Classes.... I hold that separate electorate is harmful for them and for

> Hinduism, whatever it may be from the purely political standpoint. To appreciate the harm that separate electorate would do them, one has to know how they are distributed amongst the so-called Caste Hindus and how dependent they are on the latter. So far as Hinduism is concerned, separate electorates would simply vivisect and disrupt it.
>
> For me the question of these Classes is predominantly moral and religious. The political aspect, important though it is, dwindles into insignificance compared to the moral and religious issue.
>
> I feel that no penance that the Hindus may do can in any way compensate for the calculated degradation to which they have consigned the Depressed Classes for centuries.
>
> But I know that separate electorate is neither a penance nor any remedy for the crushing degradation they have groaned under. I, therefore, respectfully inform His Majesty's Government that in the event of their decision creating separate electorate for the Depressed Classes, I must fast unto death.
>
> All I can urge in defence is that for me the contemplated step is not a method, it is part of my being. It is the call of conscience which I dare not disobey. I am hoping, however, all my fears are wholly unjustified and the British Government have no intention whatever of creating separate electorate for the Depressed Classes.

In his reply dated April 13, 1932 to Mahatma Gandhi the Secretary of State wrote:

> I write this in answer to your letter of March 11, and I say at once I realize fully the strength of your feeling upon the question of separate electorates for the Depressed Classes. I can only say that we intend to give any decision that may be necessary solely and only upon the merits of the case. As you are aware, Lord Lothian's Committee has not yet completed its tour and it must be some weeks before we can receive any conclusions at which it may have arrived. When we receive that report we shall have to give most careful consideration to its recommendations, and we shall not give a decision until we have taken into account, in addition to the view expressed by the Committee, the views that you and those who think with you have so forcibly expressed. I feel sure if you were in our position you would be taking exactly the same action we intend to take. You would admit the Committees report, you would then give it your fullest consideration, and before arriving at a final decision you would take into account the views that have been expressed on both sides of the controversy. More than this I cannot say. Indeed I do not imagine you would expect me to say more.

After giving a warning to Sir Samuel Hoare, Gandhiji was under impression that his threat to fast unto death was sufficient to scare the British Government, and persuade them into accepting the claim of the Untouchables for separate electoral representation.

In the meantime, Dr Ambedkar made yet another trip to London at end of May 1932 lobbying with Members of the British Cabinet in favour of his position. While Gandhiji was complacent, these manoeuverings apparently had some positive effect to swing the British support towards Dr Ambedkar's viewpoint.

No wonder, when the British Prime Minister Ramsey MacDonald announced the Communal Award (August 16, 1932) granting separate electorates for Untouchables and giving them 78 seats in the Legislature, it came to Gandhiji as a bombshell.

Earlier, when the Communal Deadlock was found to be difficult to resolve at the Round Table Conference, Gandhiji had committed in writing that the final decision given by Ramsey MacDonald would be acceptable to him. Yet, when the Communal Award provided for separate electorates for Untouchables, Gandhiji refused to accept it and announced an indefinite fast unto death if separate electorates for the Depressed Classes were not abolished. Gandhiji commenced his "fast unto death" on September 20, 1932.

CHAPTER FIFTEEN

Truce with Gandhiji: The Poona Pact

GANDHIJI'S ANNOUNCEMENT OF "fast unto death" threw the country into a state of consternation. As soon as he announced that he was beginning his fast to the death in response to the Communal Award, Gandhiji received messages of support from all over India. The Mahatma by then embodied a form of holiness which allowed him to reconcile the Great and the little Traditions of Hinduism; he transcended Caste and his discourse was, therefore, acceptable by the majority including Untouchables. Public appeals were made to Gandhiji and the Government, statements were issued to the Press and prayers were offered. Leaders like Dr Rajendra Prasad said that Hinduism was on its trial. There was confusion and nervousness among the Hindus because the life of Mahatma was at stake.

Pandit Malviya declared his intention to hold a Conference of Hindu leaders in Mumbai, on September 19, 1932, to resolve the deadlock and save the life of the Mahatma, and informed Dr Ambedkar about it by wire. (The title of the meeting, "Conference of Hindu and Untouchable Leaders", was paradoxical but revealing: even when Gandhiji refused to consider the Untouchables as being outside Hinduism, the qualification of "Hindus" was reserved for the Upper Caste Congressmen participating in the Conference). In order to save the life of the Mahatma it was necessary to alter the British Premier's Award, and to amend the Award, it was necessary to get the approval of Dr Ambedkar who had wrested these rights for the Depressed Classes. Naturally, all eyes turned to Dr Ambedkar as a man of the moment. Ironically the leaders and the Press that had refused till then to recognize Dr Ambedkar as the leader of the Depressed Classes were now compelled to recognize his leadership as well as spokesmanship for the Depressed Classes. He now became the cynosure of the whole country.[56]

Dr Ambedkar knew the significance and magnitude of the crisis arisen out of Gandhiji's "fast unto death". Gandhiji had hurled a most dangerous weapon at him.

56. The detailed account here has drawn upon Keer Dhananjay, op.cit, p.205 onwards, as well as Jaffrelot C, op cit, p.65.

On the eve of the Conference of the Hindu leaders, Dr Ambedkar issued a statement to the Press in which he said: "So far as I am concerned, I am willing to consider everything, though I am not willing to allow the rights of the Depressed Classes to be curtailed in any way. It is no use holding a Conference in a vacuum or discussing things without any specific data." He indicated this to the Indian multi-millionaire, Seth Walchand Hirachand. He indicated that Gandhiji could have discussed his proposal with the British Premier; since he was not putting forth any proposal, Gandhiji alone was to blame.

Visitors, leaders and friends began to call upon Dr Ambedkar. A furious campaign was launched against Dr Ambedkar. He was again called a monster, a traitor and a hireling. BG Horniman wrote a furious article in the *Bombay Chronicle* on the eve of the Mumbai Conference, saying that Dr Ambedkar could not talk as if he had the Depressed Classes in the hollow of his hand.

Dr Ambedkar was calm and collected. He issued another statement, on the eve of the Conference: "It would have been justifiable," he observed, "If Mr Gandhi had resorted to this extreme step for obtaining Independence for the country, on which he was so insistent all through the Round Table Conference debates." "It is also a painful surprise," he went on, "that Mr Gandhi should have singled out special representation for the Depressed Classes in the Communal Award as an excuse for his self-immolation.... Separate electorates are granted not only to the Depressed Classes but to the Indian Christians, Anglo-Indians and Europeans as well as to the Mohammedans and the Sikhs." Dr Ambedkar further said that if separate electorates to the Mohammedans and Sikhs did not split up the nation, Hindu society could not be sad to be split up if the Depressed Classes were given separate electorates. Concluding his Statement, Dr Ambedkar said in his vitriolic vein:

> The Mahatma is not an immortal person, nor the Congress,... it is not a malevolent force and is not to have an abiding existence.... There have been many Mahatmas in India whose sole object was to remove Untouchability and to elevate and absorb the Depressed Classes, but every one of them has failed in his mission. Mahatmas have come and Mahatmas have gone. But the Untouchables have remained as Untouchables.

* * *

As declared, the Conference of the Hindu leaders was held amidst this tense situation at the "Hall of the Indian Merchants" Chamber on September 19, 1932, under the Presidentship of Pandit Madan Mohan Malaviya. Dr Ambedkar and Dr Solanki were seated just near the President's Chair. Among those present were Sir Chimanlal Setalvad, Walchand Hirachand, Dr Rajendra Prasad, Kamala Nehru, Sapru, AV Thakkar, P Baloo and others. Seth Walchand Hirachand suggested to Malaviya that he should call upon Dr Ambedkar to speak first.

Dr Ambedkar said:

> Looking at the agenda for today's Conference it seems to me that there is no need to have this Conference. Mahatma Gandhi has strong opposition to our demands, so much so that he has put his life at the stake. Obviously, everybody must think of saving the life of Mr Gandhi. However, Mr Gandhi should have proposed some alternative scheme before going on the fast-unto-death. Considering the present stalemate, unless Mr Gandhi puts forward some new scheme, any efforts for settlement are not going to be fruitful; there is nothing that remains to be decided.
>
> This Conference may go on discussing but unless we know what Mr Gandhi has to say, no new way out can be found out. And I want to make it absolutely clear that I am not bound by any scheme of any of your Leaders or the organizers of this Conference; I will only consider what the Mahatma Gandhi has to say. What reply can I give unless I know what he wants to say?
>
> You first let me know what he wants to say then only I will put forward my views. And I will consider it only when you, the Touchable Leaders, come up with Mr Gandhi's views in the legitimate capacity as his representatives. And I want to make it clear that I will not consider any of his views if these are brought forward through any leader from the Untouchable community. It has to be through you only.
>
> I do not want to be responsible to betray the just and basic rights of my brethren to save the life of Mahatma Gandhi!

The Hindu Leaders' Conference then adjourned and met at noon the next day, September 20, in order to hear the Deputation that had called on Gandhiji at Yeravada Jail. Sir Chunilal, the Leader of the Deputation, told the Conference that Gandhiji had no personal objection to the reservation of seats for the Depressed Classes. Dr Ambedkar was then requested to say something on the point at issue. Indicating to the Conference that he was placed on the horns of a dilemma, he said:

> It has fallen to my lot to be the villain of the piece. But I tell you I shall not deter from my pious duty, and betray the just and legitimate interests of my people even if you hang me on the nearest lamp post in the street. You better appeal to Gandhi to postpone his fast about a week and then seek for the solution of the problem.

This was again a great shock to the Conference. The Conference then adjourned till two in the afternoon, (next day, September 21). But immediately the leading Members of the Conference went to Birla House and there Sir Tej Bahadur Sapru evolved a Scheme of Primary and Secondary elections for the reserved seats. According to it, the Depressed Classes themselves were to select for every seat a panel of not less than three candidates and then out of those three chosen candidates one was to be selected by the joint electorate of the Caste Hindus and the Depressed Classes. When informed of the Scheme, Dr Ambedkar said that he would consult his colleagues and come back within two hours with his proposal. Dr Ambedkar returned late evening and told them that he would accept the proposal but demanded a much large number of seats than the British Prime Minister's Award had given them. The leaders accepted his suggestion; and Jayakar, Sapru, Birla, Rajagopalachari and Dr Rajendra Prasad left for Pune by the midnight train.

On the early morning of Wednesday, September 21, they saw Gandhiji in the office room of Yeravda Jail at seven o'clock. Gandhiji said he would consider the proposal and let them know. At noon Sapru telephoned to Dr Ambedkar from Pune requesting him to come to Pune immediately. Dr Ambedkar left by the midnight train. On the same day Rajah and Malaviya, too, left Mumbai for Pune.

On Thursday morning (September 22) Gandhiji had a talk with Dr Rajendra Prasad and Rajagopalachari and said he did not like that election to some of the reserved seats should be both by primary and secondary election system, and to some only by joint electorates. He said the primary and secondary election system should be applied to all seats alike. This was communicated to Dr Ambedkar, who said he wanted "concrete" proposals, and that he was not a man to run after a mirage.

Late in the evening Dr Ambedkar, accompanied by Jayakar, Birla, Chunilal Mehta and Rajagopalachari, went to meet Gandhiji in the jail. It was a grave political crisis. When the party entered the prison court, Gandhiji was lying on a white iron-cot with a jail mattress on it, under the thick shade of a low mango tree. Sardar Patel and Sarojini Naidu sat near Gandhiji.

When Dr Ambedkar approached the cot, there was an echoless silence and a breathless eagerness. Would it move Dr Ambedkar? Jayakar had foretold that Dr Ambedkar's intransigence would collapse when he saw Gandhiji. Dr Ambedkar was now once again in the presence of the Mahatma. Gandhiji was weak. He lay in his bed. The talk began. Sapru related to Gandhiji the whole story. Malaviya put the Hindu point of view. Then in a soft, slow flow Dr Ambedkar said,

"Mahatmaji, you have been very unfair to us."

"It is always my lot to appear to be unfair," replied Gandhiji.

"I cannot help it."

Then Dr Ambedkar explained the whole situation and his viewpoints. The sober Biblical language had its visible effect upon Gandhiji. He was convinced of the justice of Dr Ambedkar's demands. At length Gandhiji replied:

"You have my fullest sympathy. I am with you, Doctor, in most of the things you say. But you say you are interested in my life."

"Yes, Mahatmaji, in the hope that if you would devote solely to the cause of my people, you would become our hero too," said Dr Ambedkar in reply.

"Well, then, if it is so, then you know what you have got to do to save it. Do it and save my life. I know you do not want to forgo what your people have been granted by the Award. I accept your panel system, but you should remove one anomaly from it. You should apply the panel system to all the seats. You are Untouchable by birth, and I am by adoption. We must be one and indivisible. I am prepared to give myself to avert the disruption of the Hindu community."

Dr Ambedkar accepted Gandhiji's suggestion. The interview ended, and the leaders started to settle other details regarding the number of men in the panel, number of total seats in the Provincial assemblies, duration of the Primary System, duration of the reserved seats and distribution of posts.

Friday, September 23, dawned. For hours hot discussions raged over the number of candidates required to make the panel. Then there was the question of seats. Dr Ambedkar demanded 197 seats in the Provincial Assemblies and the leaders reduced the number to 126. Negotiations dragged on. Hours rushed by. After ten hours of discussion, some points were referred to Gandhiji and he upheld Dr Ambedkar's points. But still the negotiations seemed to break down on the question of duration of Primary election and referendum to decide the duration of reserved seats.

Dr Ambedkar said that the system of primary election should terminate at the end of ten years; but he insisted that the question of reserved seats should be settled by referendum of Depressed Classes at the end of further fifteen years. The leader's opinion was that the evil of reserved seats and separation would be perpetuated by making its removal dependent upon the will of the Depressed Classes. Dr Ambedkar's insistent demand for a referendum at the end of twenty-five years created a furore among the Caste Hindu circles. Dr Ambedkar frankly told them that he refused to believe that Untouchability would be no more in the next twenty years or so, and, therefore, he said that faced with the sword of Damocles, the Caste Hindus would be compelled to change their inhuman attitude to the Untouchables.

It was now four in the evening. News came in that Gandhiji's health had taken a serious turn, and he was fast losing strength. Gandhi's son, Devdas Gandhi, with tears in his eyes, described the condition of his father to Dr Ambedkar and entreated him not to hold over the agreement by pressing for a referendum.

It was decided to refer this matter to Gandhiji. Dr Ambedkar with selected leaders saw Gandhiji in the jail at nine o'clock that night. Gandhiji approved of the idea of referendum, but said it should take place after five years. Gandhiji's voice had now sunk to a whisper. The jail Doctors intervened and stopped further conversation. There was a breathless silence. Dr Ambedkar was not prepared to give up his point. His willpower was on the strain. Letters threatening his life came in showers. Murderous looks were cast at him in the street, and some of the leaders insanely reviled him behind his back.

On the sixth day [of the fast] Devdas Gandhi [one the Mahatma's sons] came to the conference from the jail. [...] He said, "Father is sinking". The agony of the whole conference was something only you can imagine. Ambedkar had come to Poona, but was staying in a hotel and was speaking somewhat cynically. His point was that he [Ambedkar] was the sole representative of the Untouchables, and not the Mahatma, that the Mahatma had no business to presume that he was the leader of the Untouchable as against himself. And he said somewhat cynically and somewhat cruelly also: "Who was the Mahatma to fast? Let him come and have dinner with me." And these statements outraged people who were all suffering agonies. At that stage, Mr MC Rajah, another leader of the Untouchables from Madras, who was in the conference [...] said to Ambedkar,

> For thousands of years we had been treated as Untouchables, downtrodden, insulted, despised. The Mahatma is staking his life for our sake, and if he dies, for the next thousands of years we shall be where we have been, if not worse. There will be such a strong feeling against us that we brought about his death, that the mind of the whole Hindu community and the whole civilized community will kick us downstairs further still. I am not going to stand by you any longer. I will join the conference, and find a solution and I will part company from you.

That brought Dr Ambedkar round. He said, "I am willing to compromise."

Friday night grimly witnessed all this in suspense. On Saturday morning discussions were resumed. The question of the total number of seats was decided by granting 148 seats to the Depressed Classes in the Provincial Assemblies, and it was also decided that 10 per cent of the seats of the Hindus from British India in the Central Assembly should be given to the Depressed Classes. And then discussion was held for hours on the question of referendum which had baffled the solution as before. As nobody would agree to Dr Ambedkar's demand, he thought it proper to see Gandhiji once again in the matter. So, accompanied by Dr Solanki and Rajagopalachari, he went to Gandhiji. Gandhiji told Dr Ambedkar that his logic was irrefutable; but he said mere statutory guarantee would not root out the disease. He, therefore, entreated Ambedkar to give a last chance to Hinduism to make a voluntary expiation for its sinful past and added that there should be a referendum but not at the end of any period longer than five years. "Five years or my life," said Gandhiji with a tone of finality.

Returning to the place of discussion, Dr Ambedkar said that he was not prepared to yield on the point of the period of referendum which should be, he averred, not less than ten years. After an hour or so they decided to make the agreement without the condition of referendum attached to it! Rajagopalachari explained it to Gandhiji in the jail at three in the afternoon. Gandhiji said it was excellent and gave his consent. Rajagopalachari returned post-haste to 1, Ramakrishna Bhandarkar Road, Shivlal Motilal's Bungalow, and amidst rejoicings announced that Gandhiji had blessed the agreement.

It took them no time to draft the agreement amidst an atmosphere of joviality. The agreement was signed at five in the evening on Saturday, September 24, 1932 and it went down the history as the "Poona Pact". On behalf of the Depressed Classes, Dr Ambedkar signed it; and on behalf of the Caste Hindus, Pandit Madan Mohan Malaviya signed it. The other signatories were Jayakar, Sapru, GD Birla, Rajagopalachari, Dr Rajendra Prasad, Rao Bahadur Srinivasan, MC Rajah, Devdas Gandhi, Rajbhoj, P Baloo, Gavai, Thakkar, Solanki etc. Rajagopalachari was so much overjoyed that he exchanged his fountain-pen with Dr Ambedkar.

Text of Poona Pact

The following is the text of the agreement:

(1) There shall be seats reserved for the Depressed Classes out of the general electorate seats in the Provincial Legislatures as follows:

Madras 30; Bombay with Sind 15; Punjab 8, Bihar and Orissa 18; Central Provinces 20; Assam 7; Bengal 30; United Provinces 20; Total 148.

These figures are based on the total strength of the Provincial Councils, announced in the Prime Minister's decision.

(2) Election to these seats shall be by joint electorates, subject, however, to the following procedure:

All the members of the Depressed Classes registered in the general electoral roll in a constituency will form an electoral college, which will elect a panel of four candidates belonging to the Depressed Classes for each of such reserved seats, by the method of the single vote; the four getting the highest number of votes in such Primary election, shall be candidates for election by the general electorate.

(3) Representation of the Depressed Classes in the Central Legislature shall likewise be on the principle of joint electorates and reserved seats by the method of Primary election in the manner provided for in Clause (2) above, for their representation in the Provincial Legislatures.

(4) In the Central Legislature, eighteen per cent of seats allotted to the general electorate for British India in the said Legislature shall be reserved for the Depressed Classes.

(5) The system of Primary election to a panel of Candidates for election to the Central and Provincial Legislature, as hereinbefore mentioned, shall come to an end after the first ten years, unless terminated sooner by mutual agreement under the provision of Clause (6) below.

(6) The system of representation of the Depressed Classes by reserved seats in the Provincial and Central Legislatures as provided for in Clauses (1) and (4) shall continue until determined by mutual agreement between the communities concerned in the settlement.

(7) Franchise for the Central and Provincial Legislatures for the Depressed Classes shall be as indicated in the Lothian Committee Report.

(8) There shall be no disabilities attaching to anyone on the ground of his being a member of the Depressed Class in regard to any elections to local bodies or appointment to the Public Services. Every endeavour shall be made to secure fair representation of the Depressed Classes in these respects, subject to such educational qualifications as may be laid down for appointment to the Public Services.

(9) In every Province out of the educational grant an adequate sum shall be earmarked for providing educational facilities to the Members of the Depressed Classes.

★ ★ ★

The contents of the Pact were cabled to the British Cabinet, wired to Viceroy, and also handed over to the Secretary of the Bombay Governor by each party separately, and next morning the leaders returned to Bombay to ratify the pact.

At 2 PM the leaders held a meeting at the Indian Merchant's Chamber Hall. Presiding over the meeting, Malaviya declared that no one should be regarded as Untouchable by reason of his birth, and appealed to Hindus to make the idea of Untouchability disappear from the land. Mathuradas Vasanji moved the resolution ratifying the Pact and Sapru supported it. With a full throated tribute to Dr Ambedkar, Sapru congratulated him on his valiant fight for cause which he represented and added that Dr Ambedkar promised to be a good fighter in the future life of the country.

When Dr Ambedkar rose to support the resolution, a thunderous applause greeted him. Dr Ambedkar said that what had happened the previous day was beyond his dream. After a tremendous struggle and confusion, they had found the solution, he said. No man was ever placed in such a dilemma as he was. There was the life of the greatest man of India to be saved, and on the other side the interests of the downtrodden community were to be safeguarded. But at last, he said, with the cooperation of Gandhi, Sapru and Rajagopalachari they could arrive at the solution.

"My only regret is," he added, "why did not Mahatmaji take this attitude at the Round Table Conference? If he had shown the same consideration to my point of view then, it would not have been necessary for him to go through this ordeal."

Concluding his speech, he earnestly appealed to the Caste Hindus to abide by the Pact and trusted that they would look upon the document as sacrosanct and work in an honourable spirit.

The British Government announced on September 26, that it would recommend to Parliament the endorsement of the Poona Pact. In the evening prayers were said in the Prison yard. Kasturba then handed Gandhiji orange juice, and he broke his fast about half-past five amidst a gathering of some two hundred disciples and admirers, poet Rabindranath Tagore, Sarojini Naidu, Sardar Patel and Swarup Rani Nehru being conspicuous.

The Poona Pact thus resonated throughout the country and had repercussions throughout the world. It proved once more that Dr Ambedkar whom in pre-Poona Pact days the Congress leaders and the press refused to recognize as the leader of the Depressed Classes, came out as the accredited leader of the Depressed Classes all over India.

In the new arrangement both the sides had to lose something. The Caste Hindu had to grant 148 seats instead of 71. The Depressed Classes lost their chance of bending the Caste Hindu leaders to their will as the Depressed Classes were under the Award entitled to elect their own representatives to the Assemblies separately, and besides they were to vote in general constituencies with the Caste Hindus in electing the Caste Hindu representatives. Now the Caste Hindus got the power to elect the representatives of the Depressed Classes.

Dr Ambedkar was the only Indian politician whom Gandhiji contested by resorting to a fast. He did this precisely because he knew that Dr Ambedkar would not respond by resorting to violence. Dr Ambedkar was a lawyer who never turned the law to his advantage and he even adopted the *Satyagraha* as his modus operandi in *Mahad* in 1927. Upendra Baxi points out that in 1932 Gandhi 'gambled' on Dr Ambedkar's self-restraint and won.

* * *

Here's the story of the "Poona Pact" as recounted by Dr Ambedkar in his book: *What Congress and Gandhi Have Done to Untouchables* (1945):

> The story of this fast has been told by Mr Pyarelal in a volume which bears the picturesque and flamboyant title of 'The Epic Fast'. There is another side to it, but there is neither time nor space to present it here. All I can do is to invite attention to the statement I issued to the Press on the eve of Mr Gandhi's fast exposing his tactics. Suffice it is to say that although Mr Gandhi declared a fast unto death, he did not want to die. He wanted very much to live.
>
> The fast nonetheless created a problem, and that problem was how to save Mr Gandhi's life. The only way to save his life was to alter the Communal Award which Mr Gandhi said hurt his conscience so much. The Prime Minister had made it quite clear that the British Cabinet would not withdraw it or alter it of its own, but that they were ready to substitute for it a formula that may be agreed upon by the Caste Hindus and the Untouchables. As I had the privilege of representing the Untouchables at the Round Table Conference, it was assumed that the assent of the Untouchables would not be valid unless I was a party to it. The surprising fact is that my position as the leader of the Untouchables of India was not only, not questioned by Congressmen, but it was accepted as a fact. All eyes naturally turned to me as the man of the moment or rather as the villain of the peace.
>
> As to myself it is no exaggeration to say that no man was placed in a greater and graver dilemma than I was then. It was a baffling situation. I had to make a choice between two different alternatives. There was before me the duty, which I owed as a part of common humanity, to save Gandhi from sure death. There was before me the problem of saving for the Untouchables the political rights which the (British) Prime Minister had given them. I responded to the call of humanity and saved the life of Mr Gandhi by agreeing to alter the Communal Award in a manner satisfactory to Mr Gandhi. This agreement is known as the Poona Pact.

The terms of the Pact were accepted by Mr Gandhi and given effect to by Government by embodying them in the Government of India Act. The Poona Pact had produced different reactions. The Untouchables were sad. They had every reason to be. There are, however, people who do not accept this. They never fail to point out that the Poona Pact gave the Untouchables larger number of seats than what was given to them by the Prime Minister in his Communal Award. It is true that the Poona Pact gave the Untouchables 148 seats, while the Award had only given them 78. But to conclude from this that the Poona Pact gave them more than what was given by the Award is to ignore what the Award had in fact given to the Untouchables.

The Communal Award gave the Untouchables two benefits: (a) a fixed quota of seats to be elected by separate electorate of Untouchables and to be filled by persons belonging to the Untouchables; (b) double vote, one to be used through separate electorates and the other to be used in the general electorates.

Now, if the Poona Pact increased the fixed quota of seats, it also took away the right to the double vote. This increase in seats can never be deemed to be a compensation, for the loss of the double vote. The second vote given by the Communal Award was a priceless privilege. Its value as a political weapon was beyond reckoning. The voting strength of the Untouchables in each constituency is one to ten. With this voting strength free to be used in the election of Caste Hindu candidates, the Untouchables would have been in a position to determine, if not to dictate, the issue of the General Election. No Caste Hindu candidate could have dared to neglect the Untouchable in his constituency or be hostile to their interest if he was made dependent upon the votes of the Untouchables. Today, the Untouchables have a few more seats than were given to them by the Communal Award. But this is all that they have. The increase in the number of seats for the Untouchables is no increase at all and was no recompense for the loss of separate electorate and the double vote.

The Hindus, although they did not celebrate the Poona Pact, did not like it. Throughout their commotion to save Mr Gandhi's life there was a definite current of conscious feeling that the cost of saving his life may be great. Therefore, when they saw the terms of the Pact they very definitely disliked it, although they did not have the courage to reject it. Disliked by the Hindus and disfavoured by the Untouchables, the Poona Pact was given recognition by both parties and was embodied in the Government of India Act.

The signing of the Poona Pact was followed by the appointment of the Hammond Committee to demarcate constituencies, to fix the number of seats for each constituency and settle the system of voting for the legislatures to be set up under the new Constitution.

In carrying out its functions, the Hammond Committee had to take into account the terms of the Poona Pact and the special sort of electoral plan, agreed upon to meet the needs of the Untouchables. Unfortunately, the Poona Pact having been concluded in a hurry had left many things undefined.

Of the things that were left undefined the most important were two namely: (a) Does the 'panel of four' to be elected at the primary election imply four as a maximum or a minimum? (b) What was intended to be the method of voting in the final election? It was contended on behalf of the Hindus that the 'panel of four' was intended to be a minimum. If four candidates are not forthcoming there could be no primary election and, therefore, there can be no election for the reserved seat, which they said must remain vacant and the Untouchables should go without representation.

On behalf of the Untouchables, I was called to state my interpretation of the disputed points. I contended that four in the Poona Pact meant 'not more than four'. It did not mean 'not less than four'. On the question of voting, the Hindus contended that the compulsory distributive vote was the most appropriate. On behalf of the Untouchables I contended that the cumulative system of voting was the proper system to be introduced. Fortunately for the Untouchables, the Hammond Committee accepted the views propounded by me and rejected those of the Hindus.

It is interesting to know why the Caste Hindus put forth their contentions. One may well stop here for a moment and ask why did the Hindus raise their particular contentions before the Hammond Committee? Was there any particular motive behind the stand they took? So far as I am able to see the object which the Hindus had in demanding four candidates as the minimum for a valid primary election was to place the Hindus in a position to capture the seat for an election of such a representative of the Untouchable candidate, who would be their nominee and who would be most willing to be the tool of the Hindus.

The object of insisting upon the system of compulsory distributive vote was the same, namely, to enable the Hindus to capture the seats reserved for the Untouchables. Under the cumulative vote the elector has as many votes as there are seats. He may give them all to one candidate or he may distribute them over two or more candidates as he may desire. Under the distributive system of voting the elector has also as many votes as there are seats, but he can give only one vote to any one candidate. Although the two look different yet in effect there may be no difference, because even under the cumulative vote a voter is not prevented from distributing his votes. He is free to give one vote to one candidate. But the Hindus did not want to take any chance. Their main object was to flood the election to the seat reserved for the Untouchables in the joint electorate by using the surplus votes of the Hindus in favour of the Untouchable candidate, who happens to be their nominee.

In the light of these considerations, it cannot but appear that the Poona Pact was only the first blow inflicted upon the Untouchables and that the Hindus who disliked it were bent on inflicting on it other blows as and when circumstances gave them an occasion to do so. The two contentions, which the Hindus raised before the Hammond Committee, furnish the best evidence of the existence of a conspiracy by the Hindus, the object of which was to make the Poona Pact as it could not be repudiated, of no benefit to the Untouchables.

★ ★ ★

The Poona Pact shaped India's electoral system and the electoral method by which reserved constituencies were defined. It has been argued that Gandhiji "skewed the electoral method, which made the election of a reserved candidate dependent upon the dominant caste vote. This rendered them subservient to the interests of dominant social forces, defeating the very purpose for which such representation was secured."[57]

Consequently, the Poona Pact laid the foundation for Dr Ambedkar's defeats and he lost heavily in Assembly elections from 1942 onwards and could not win the two Lok Sabha elections that he contested.

57. Raja Sekhar Vundru, *Outlook* (August 20, 2012)

CHAPTER SIXTEEN

Failure of Gandhi-Ambedkar Joint Efforts

THE POONA PACT was signed on September 24, 1932. The very next day (i.e., September 25, 1932), in a public meeting of Hindus held in Mumbai, a resolution was passed which, going beyond the support to the Poona Pact, explicitly stated:

> This Conference resolves that henceforth, amongst Hindus, no one shall be regarded as an Untouchable by reason of his birth, and that those who have been so regarded hitherto will have the same right as other Hindus in regard to the use of public wells, public schools, public roads, and all other public institutions. This right shall have statutory recognition at the first opportunity and shall be one of the earliest Acts of the *Swaraj* Parliament, if it shall not have received such recognition before that time.
>
> It is further agreed that it shall be the duty of all Hindu leaders to secure, by every legitimate and peaceful means, an early removal of all social disabilities now imposed by custom upon the so-called Untouchable Classes, including the bar in respect of admission to temples.

In the following week, on September 30, 1932, another public meeting of Hindus was held under the Chairmanship of Pandit Madan Mohan Malaviya, to form an All-India Anti-Untouchability League with headquarters in Delhi and branches in different Provinces. Shri G D Birla, the wealthy industrialist who had already financed many of Gandhiji's favourite projects, was chosen as the President while Shri Amritlal Thakkar (alias Thakkar Bappa) was chosen as the General Secretary. This project was also inspired by Gandhiji who renamed the League as the "Harijan Sevak Sangh" (i.e., a Society of those engaged in the service of the Untouchables).

On the 3rd November 1932, Mr Birla and Mr Thakkar issued a statement to the Press in which they set out the programme of this organization and the set-up of the machinery to carry out the programme. As to the programme the statement said:

> The League believes that reasonable persons among the *Sanatanists* are not much against the removal of Untouchability as such, as they are against inter-Caste dinners

> and marriages. Since it is not the ambition of the League to undertake reforms beyond its own scope, it is desirable to make it clear that while the League will work by persuasion among the Caste Hindus to remove every vestige of Untouchability, the main line of work will be constructive, such as the uplift of Depressed Classes educationally, economically and socially, which itself will go a great way to remove Untouchability. With such a work, even a staunch *Sanatanist* can have nothing but sympathy. And it is for such work mainly that the League has been established. Social reforms like the abolition of the Caste System and inter-dining are kept outside the scope of the League.

For facilitating the implementation of the programme, it was proposed that each Province should be divided into a number of units and each unit to be in charge of paid workers. A unit may or may not be coterminous with a district. It may be formed by grouping together two districts or two States.

The statement also set out a normal Budget for the year. It was to be of the following dimensions:

> A sum of six lakhs of Rupees is intended to be collected and spent per year in the whole country for the removal of Untouchability and ameliorative work of *Harijans*. This programme, particularly if the ameliorative work is to be effective, should continue at least for 5 years. When spread out over 22 Provinces, including States and 4 crores or 400 lakhs of Harijans in the country, this is a small budget indeed.

To provide funds for the work of the *Sangh,* Gandhiji undertook an All-India tour which began on November 7,1933 and ended on July 29, 1934. Total collection was Rupees eight lakhs. As the object of the tour was to arouse enthusiasm among the Hindus for the cause of the Untouchables as also to collect funds, Gandhiji did most of the tour on foot and collected Rs. 8 lakhs. With this amount and the annual donation of Gandhiji's wealthy friends the *Sangh* started its work.

In addition, in February 1933 Gandhiji started a new weekly newspaper titled, *Harijan* (which literally meant "Children of God"). Agitations on behalf of Untouchables became one of Gandhiji's main concern. "Untouchability Abolition Week" was launched by Gandhiji in September-October, 1932. To top it all, Gandhiji launched a country-wide campaign during November 1933 to August 1934, promoting the interests of Untouchables.

To begin with, these developments mollified Dr Ambedkar's hostility towards Gandhiji. In November, 1932, heading for England to take part in the Third Round Table Conference, Dr Ambedkar began to appreciate Gandhiji's public declarations concerning Untouchables. He wrote to his colleagues that he had noticed a gradual convergence with his own position on certain issues, even though he regretted that Gandhiji still refused to endorse inter-Caste marriage and inter-Caste eating. In one of these letters, Dr Ambedkar indicated, in a very Gandhian manner: "The Touchables and Untouchables cannot be held together by law, certainly not by any electoral law substituting joint electorate for separate electorates. The only thing that can hold together is love." In another letter he even quoted Tolstoy, one of Gandhiji's main sources of inspiration, "Only those who love can serve."[58]

Over the following year, however, the viewpoints and agendas of Gandhiji and Dr Ambedkar turned out to be increasingly irreconcilable as can be seen from the critical assessment offered by Dr Ambedkar many years later in 1945 in his book: *What Congress and Gandhi Have Done to Untouchables*.[59]

Dr Ambedkar's critique may be discussed under three sub-heads:

(a) The Temple Entry Movement;
(b) Legislation for Temple Entry; and
(c) Activities of the Harijan Sevak Sangh

A. THE TEMPLE ENTRY MOVEMENT

According to Dr Ambedkar,

> The resolution was followed by a feverish activity on the part of the Hindus to throw open Temples to the Untouchables. No week passed in which the *Harijan*, a weekly paper started by Mr Gandhi, which did not publish a long list of temples thrown open, wells thrown open and schools thrown open to the Untouchables set out under special column headed 'Week to Week' on the first page.
>
> When the owners or trustees of temples were not prepared to throw open their temples to the Untouchables, the Hindus actually started *Satyagraha* against them to compel them to fall in line. The *Satyagraha* by Mr Kelappan for securing entry to the Untouchables in the temple at Guruvayur was a part of this agitation. To force the hands of the trustees of the temples who had the courage to stand against the current, many Hindu legislators came forward, tumbling over one another, with Bills requiring the trustees to throw open temples to the Untouchables if a referendum showed that the majority of the Hindu worshippers voted in favour. There was a spate of such Bills and a race among legislators to take the first place. There was a Temple Entry Bill by Dr Subbaroyan of the Madras Legislative Council....
>
> In this agitation Mr Gandhi also joined. Before 1932, Mr Gandhi was opposed to allow Untouchables to enter Hindu Temples. To quote his own, words Mr Gandhi said:
>
> 'How is it possible that the *Antyajas* (Untouchables) should have the right to enter all the existing temples? As long as the law of Caste and ashram has the chief place in Hindu Religion, to say that every Hindu can enter every temple is a thing that is not possible today.'
>
> His joining the movement for Temple entry must, therefore, remain a matter of great surprise. Why Mr Gandhi took this somersault it is difficult to imagine. Was it an honest act of change of heart, due to a conviction that he was in error in opposing the entry of the Untouchables in Hindu temples? Was it due to a realisation that the political

58. See Jaffrelot, C, op cit, p.68.
59. For full summary, see *Ambedkar Writes*, Vol.I, pp. 293-309.

separation between the Hindus and the Untouchables brought about by the Poona Pact might lead to a complete severance of the cultural and religious ties and that it was necessary to counteract the tendency by some such measure as Temple Entry as will bind the two together? Or was his object in joining the Temple Entry movement to destroy the basis of the claim of the Untouchables for political rights by destroying the barrier between them and the Hindus which makes them separate from the Hindus? Or was it because Mr Gandhi saw before him looming large a possibility of adding to his name and fame and rushed to make the most of it, as is his habit to do? The second or the third explanation may be nearer the truth....

What was the attitude of the Untouchables to this movement for Temple entry? I was asked by Mr Gandhi to lend my support to the movement for Temple entry. I declined to do so and issued a statement on the subject to the Press. As it will help the reader to know the grounds for my attitude to this question I have thought it well to set it in full. Here it is!

Dr Ambedkar's Statement on Temple Entry Bill (February 14, 1933)

Although, the controversy regarding the question of Temple Entry is confined to the Sanatanists and Mahatma Gandhi, the Depressed Classes have undoubtedly a very important part to play in it, in so far as their position is bound to weigh the scales one way or the other when the issue comes up for a final settlement. It is, therefore, necessary that their viewpoint should be defined and stated so as to leave no ambiguity about it.

To the Temple-Entry Bill of Mr Ranga Iyer as now drafted, the Depressed Classes cannot possibly give their support. The principle of the Bill is that if a majority of Municipal and Local Board voters in the vicinity of any particular temple on a referendum decide by a majority that the Depressed Classes shall be allowed to enter the temple, the Trustees or the Manager of that temple shall give effect to that decision. The principle is an ordinary principle of Majority rule, and there is nothing radical or revolutionary about the Bill, and if the Sanatanists were a wise lot, they would accept it without demur.

The reasons why the Depressed Classes cannot support a Bill based upon this principle are two: One reason is that the Bill cannot hasten the day of temple-entry for the Depressed Classes any nearer than would otherwise be the case. It is true that under the Bill, the minority will not have the right to obtain an injunction against the Trustee, or the Manager who throws open the temple to the Depressed Classes in accordance with the decision of the majority. But before one can draw any satisfaction from this clause and congratulate the author of the Bill, one must first of all feel assured that when the question is put to the vote there will be a majority in favour of Temple Entry. If one is not suffering from illusions of any kind one must accept that the hope of a majority voting in favour of Temple Entry will be very rarely realized, if at all. Without doubt, the majority is definitely opposed today—a fact which is conceded by the author of the Bill himself in his correspondence with the Shankracharya.

What is there in the situation as created after the passing of the Bill, which can lead one to hope that the majority will act differently? I find nothing. I shall, no doubt, be reminded of the results of the referendum with regard to the Guruvayur Temple. But I refuse to accept a referendum so overweighted as it was by the life of Mahatma Gandhi as the normal result. In any such calculations, the life of the Mahatma must necessarily be deducted.

Secondly, the Bill does not regard Untouchability in temples as a sinful custom. It regards Untouchability merely as a social evil not necessarily worse than social evils of other sorts. For, it does not declare Untouchability as such to be illegal. Its binding force is taken away, only if a majority decides to do so. Sin and immorality cannot become tolerable because a majority is addicted to them or because the majority chooses to practise them. If Untouchability is a sinful and an immoral custom, then in the view of the Depressed Classes it must be destroyed without any hesitation even if it was acceptable to the majority. This is the way in which all customs are dealt with by Courts of Law, if they find them to be immoral and against public policy.

I really cannot understand how the Bill satisfies Mahatma Gandhi, who has been insisting that Untouchability is a sin! It certainly does not satisfy the Depressed Classes. The question whether this particular Bill is good or bad, sufficient or insufficient, is a subsidiary question.

The main question is: Do the Depressed Classes desire Temple Entry or do they not? This main question is being viewed by the Depressed Classes by two points of view. One is the materialistic point of view. Starting from it, the Depressed Classes think that the surest way for their elevation lies in higher education, higher employment and better ways of earning a living. Once they become well placed in the scale of social life, they would become respectable and once they become respectable the religious outlook of the orthodox towards them is sure to undergo change, and even if this did not happen, it can do no injury to their material interest. Proceeding on these lines the Depressed Classes say that they will not spend their resources on such an empty thing as Temple Entry. There is also another reason why they do not care to fight for it. That argument is the argument of self-respect.

Not very long ago there used to be boards on club doors and other social resorts maintained by Europeans in India, which said, 'Dogs and Indians' not allowed. The temples of Hindus carry similar boards today, the only difference is that the boards on the Hindu temples practically say: 'All Hindus and all animals including dogs are admitted, only Untouchables not admitted'. The situation in both cases is on a parity. But Hindus never begged for admission in those places from which the Europeans in their arrogance had excluded them. Why should an Untouchable beg for admission in a place from which he has been excluded by the arrogance of the Hindus? This is the reason of the Depressed Class man who is interested in his material welfare. He is prepared to say to the Hindus, 'to open or not to open your temples is a question for you to consider and not for me to agitate. If you think, it is bad manners not to respect the sacredness of human personality, open your temples and be a gentleman. If you rather be a Hindu than be gentleman, then shut the doors and damn yourself for I don't care to come.'

I found it necessary to put the argument in this form, because I want to disabuse the minds of men like Pandit Madan Mohan Malaviya of their belief that the Depressed Classes are looking forward expectantly for their patronage.

The second point of view is the spiritual one. As religiously minded people, do the Depressed Classes desire temple entry or do they not? That is the question. From the spiritual point of view, they are not indifferent to temple entry as they would be, if the material point of view alone were to prevail. But their final answer must depend upon the reply which Mahatma Gandhi and the Hindus give to the question, namely: What is the drive behind this offer of temple entry? Is temple entry to be the final goal of the advancement in the social status of the Depressed Classes in the Hindu fold? Or is it only the first step and if it is the first step, what is the ultimate goal? Temple Entry as a final goal, the Depressed Classes can never support. Indeed they will not only reject it, but they would then regard themselves as rejected by Hindu Society and free to find their own destiny elsewhere. On the other hand, if it is only to be a first step in the direction, they may be inclined to support it.

The position would then be analogous to what is happening in the politics of India today. All Indians have claimed Dominion Status for India. The actual Constitution will fall short of Dominion Status and many Indians will accept it. Why? The answer is that as the goal is defined, it does not matter much if it is to be reached by steps and not in one jump. But if the British had not accepted the goal of Dominion Status, no one would have accepted the partial reforms which many are now prepared to accept. In the same way, if Mahatma Gandhi and the reformers were to proclaim what the goal which they have set before themselves is for the advancement of the Social Status of the Depressed Classes in the Hindu fold, it would be easier for the Depressed Classes to define their attitude towards Temple Entry.

The goal of the Depressed Classes might as well be stated here for the information and consideration of all concerned. What the Depressed Classes want is a religion, which will give them equality of social status. To prevent any misunderstanding, I would like to elaborate the point by drawing a distinction between social evils which are the results of secular causes and social evils which are founded upon the doctrine of religion. Social evils can have no justification whatsoever in a civilised society. But nothing can be more odious and vile than that admitted social evils should be sought to be justified on the ground of religion. The Depressed Classes may not be able to overthrow inequities to which they are being subjected. But they have made up their mind not to tolerate a religion that will lend its support to the continuance of these inequities.

If the Hindu religion is to be their religion, then it must become a religion of Social Equality. The mere amendment of Hindu religious code by the mere inclusion in it of a provision to permit temple entry for all cannot make it a religion of equality of social status. All that it can do is to recognise them as nationals and not aliens, if I may use in this connection terms which have become so familiar in politics. But that cannot mean that they would thereby reach a position where they would be free and equal, without being above or below anyone else, for the simple reason that the Hindu religion does not recognise the principle of equality of social status; on the other hand, it fosters inequality by insisting upon grading people as Brahmins, *Kshatriyas*, *Vaishyas* and *Shudras*, which now stand towards one another in an ascending scale of hatred and descending scale of contempt. If the Hindu religion is to be a religion of social equality then an amendment of its code to provide temple-entry is not enough. What is required is to purge it of the doctrine of *Chaturvarna*. That is the root cause of all in equality and also the parent of the Caste System and Untouchability, which are merely forms of inequality. Unless it is done not only will the Depressed Classes reject Temple Entry, they will also reject the Hindu faith.

Chaturvarna and the Caste System are incompatible with the self-respect of the Depressed Classes. So long as they stand to be its cardinal doctrine the Depressed Classes must continue to be looked upon as low. The Depressed Classes can say that they are Hindus only when the theory of *Chaturvarna* and Caste System is abandoned and expunged from the Hindu *Shastras*.

Do the Mahatma and the Hindu reformers accept this as their goal and will they show the courage to work for it? I shall look forward to their pronouncements on this issue before I decide upon my final attitude. But whether Mahatma Gandhi and the Hindus are prepared for this or not, let it be known once for all that nothing short of this will satisfy the Depressed Classes and make them accept Temple Entry. To accept temple entry and be content with it is to temporize with evil and barter away the sacredness of human personality that dwells in them.

There is, however, one argument which Mahatma Gandhi and the reforming Hindus may advance against the position I have taken. They may say: 'Acceptance by the Depressed Classes of Temple Entry now will not prevent them from agitating hereafter for the abolition of *Chaturvarna* and Caste'. If that is their view, I like to meet the argument right at this stage so as to clinch the issue and clear the road for future developments. My reply is that it is true that my right to agitate for the abolition of *Chaturvarna* and Caste System will not be lost, if I accept Temple Entry now. But the question is on what side will Mahatma Gandhi be at the time when the question is put. If he will be in the camp of my opponents, I must tell him that I cannot be in his camp now. If he will be in my camp he ought to be in it now.

Mr Gandhi did not mind any opposition and was indifferent as to whether it came from the orthodox Hindus or from the Untouchables. He went on in mad pursuit of his object. It is interesting to ask, what happened to this movement?

To put it briefly, after a short spurt of activity in the direction of removing Untouchability by throwing open temples and wells the Hindu mind returned to its original state. The reports appearing in the 'Week to Week' columns of the *Harijan* subsided, became few and far between and ultimately vanished. For myself I was not surprised to find that the Hindu heart was so soon stricken with palsy. For I never believed that there was so much milk of human kindness locked up in the Hindu breast as the 'Week to Week' column in the *Harijan* would have the world believe. As a matter of fact a large part of the news that appeared in the 'Week to Week' was faked and was nothing but a lying propaganda engineered by Congressmen to deceive the world that the Hindus were determined to fight Untouchability. Few temples if any were really opened and those that were reported to have been opened most of them were dilapidated and deserted temples which were used by none but dogs and donkeys. The same fate overtook the Guruvayur Temple *Satyagraha* and the legislation for securing Temple Entry for the Untouchables. As these are matters which were pursued by Mr Gandhi and Congressmen their history might be told in some detail inasmuch as it reveals the true mentality of Mr Gandhi and the Congress towards the Untouchables....

To begin with the Guruvayur Temple *Satyagraha*. A temple of Krishna is situated at Guruvayur in the Ponnani *taluk* in Malabar. The Zamorin of Calicut is the trustee of the temple. One Mr Kelappan, a Hindu who was working for the cause of the Untouchables of Malabar, began an agitation for securing the Untouchables entry into the temple. The Zamorin of Calicut as the trustee of the temple refused to throw open the temple to the Untouchables. On September 20, 1932, Mr Kelappan commenced a fast in protest lying in front of the temple in the sun till the Zamorin revised his views in favour of the Untouchables. To get rid of this annoyance and embarrassment the Zamorin appealed to Mr Gandhi to request Mr Kelappan to suspend his fast for a time. After a fast for ten days Mr Kelappan at the request of Mr Gandhi suspended the fast on October 1, 1932 for three months. The Zamorin did nothing. Mr Gandhi sent him a wire telling him that he must move in the matter and get over all difficulties legal or otherwise. Mr Gandhi also told the Zamorin that as Mr Kelappan had suspended his fast on his advice he had become responsible for securing to the Untouchable entry into the temple to the extent of sharing the fast with Mr Kelappan....

The Zamorin refused to yield and issued a counter-statement to the press. In these circumstances a fast by Mr Gandhi became inevitable, and obligatory. But Mr Gandhi did not go on fast. He modified his position and said that he would refrain from fasting if a referendum was taken in Ponnani taluk in which the temple was situated and if the referendum showed that the majority was against the throwing open of the temple to the Untouchables. Accordingly, a referendum was taken. Voting was confined to those who were actual temple goers. Those who were not entitled to enter the temple and those who would not enter it were excluded from the voters' list. It was reported that 73 per cent of eligible voters voted. The result of the poll was 56 per cent were in favour of temple entry, 9 per cent against, 8 per cent were neutral and 27 per cent abstained from recording their votes....

On this result of the referendum, Mr Gandhi was bound to start the fast. But he did not. Instead, on December 29, 1932 Mr Gandhi issued a statement to the press which he concluded by saying:

'In view of the official announcement that the Viceregal decision as to sanction for the introduction in the Madras Legislative Council of Dr Subbaroyan's permissive Bill with reference to the temple-entry could not possibly be announced before January 15, the fast contemplated to take place on the second day of the New Year will be indefinitely postponed and in any case up to the date of the announcement of the Viceregal decision. Mr Kelappan concurs in this postponement.'

The Viceregal pronouncement mentioned by Mr Gandhi had reference to the Viceroy's granting permission or refusing permission to the moving of the Temple Entry Bills in the Legislature. That permission was given by the Viceroy. Yet, Mr Gandhi did not fast. Not only did he not fast, he completely forgot the matter as though it was of no moment! Since then nothing has been heard about Guruvayur Temple *Satyagraha* though the Temple remains closed to the Untouchables even to-day....

B. LEGISLATION FOR TEMPLE ENTRY

Let me now turn to the other project, namely, legislation for Temple Entry. Of the many Bills the one in the name of Mr Ranga Iyer in the Central Legislature was pursued. The rest were dropped. There was a storm at the very birth of the Bill. Under the Government of India Act as it then stood no legislative measure which affected religion and customs and usages based on religion could be introduced in the Assembly unless it had the previous sanction of the Governor-General. When the Bill was sent for such sanction another commotion was created by the reports that were circulated that the Governor-General was going to refuse his sanction. Mr Gandhi was considerably excited over these reports....

The decision of the Government was announced on January 23, 1933. Lord Willingdon refused sanction to Dr Subbaroyan's Temple Entry Bill in the Madras Council, but His Excellency permitted the introduction in the Legislative Assembly, of Mr Ranga Iyer's Untouchability Abolition Bill. The announcement further stated that the Governor-General and the Government of India desired to make it plain that it was essential that consideration of any such measure should not proceed unless the proposals were subjected to the fullest examination in all their aspects, not merely in the Legislature but also outside it, by all who would be affected by them. This condition can only be satisfied if the Bill is circulated in the widest manner for the purpose of eliciting public opinion. It must also be understood that the grant of sanction to the introduction in the Central Legislature, Bills relating to temple entry do not commit the Government in any way to the acceptance or support of the principles contained therein....

On the next day, Mr Gandhi issued a statement in which he said:

I must try to trace the hand of God in it. He wants to try me through and through. The sanction given to the All-India Bill was an unintentional challenge to Hinduism and the reformer. Hinduism will take care of itself if the reformer will be true to himself. Thus considered the Government of India's decision must be regarded as God-send. It clears the issue. It makes it for India and the world to understand the tremendous importance of the moral struggle now going on in India. But whatever the Sanatanists may decide the movement for Temple Entry now broadens from Guruvayur in the extreme south to Hardwar in the north and my fast, though it remains further postponed, depends not now upon Guruvayur only but extends automatically to temples in general.

One can well realize under what fanfare the Bill began its legislative career. On March 24, 1933, Mr Ranga Iyer formally introduced the Bill in the Assembly. As it was a Bill for Mr Gandhi the Congress members of the Assembly were, of course, ready to give it their support. Mr Gandhi had appointed Mr Rajagopalachari and Mr GD Birla to canvass support for the Bill among the non-Congress members with a view to ensuring safe passage for the Bill. He said they were better lobbyists than he was. The motion for introduction was opposed by the Rajah of Kollengode and Mr Thampan raised a preliminary objection that the Bill was ultra vires of the legislature. The latter objection was overruled by the President and the House allowed the Bill to be introduced. Mr Ranga Iyer next moved that the Temple Entry Bill be circulated to elicit public opinion by July 30.

The discussion of the Bill was resumed on August 24, 1933 during the Autumn session of the Central Legislature. Sir Harry Haig on behalf of the Government explained that their support to the motion for circulation of the Bill should in no way be construed as implying support to its provisions....

Opinions were duly received. They fill a whole volume of over a thousand foolscap pages. The Bill was ready for the next stage, namely, to move for the appointment of a Select Committee. Mr Ranga Iyer had even given notice for such a motion. A strange thing happened. The Government of India decided to dissolve the Assembly and order new election. The result of this announcement was a sudden change in the attitude of the Congress members in the Central Legislature towards Mr Ranga's Bill. One and all stood out against it and refused to give any further support to the Bill. They were terrified of the electorates....

Here was a case of retreat from glory! And what an inglorious retreat? How did Mr Gandhi react to it? In a statement issued on, November 4, 1932, Mr Gandhi said:

> Untouchables in the villages should be made to feel that their shackles have been broken, that they are in no way inferior to their fellow villagers, that they are worshippers of the same God as the other villagers and entitled to the same rights and privileges that the latter enjoy.
>
> But if these vital conditions of the Pact are not carried out by Caste-Hindus, could I possibly live to face God and man? I ventured even to tell Dr Ambedkar, Rao Bahadur MC Raja and other friends belonging to the suppressed group that they should regard me as a hostage for the due fulfilment by Caste-Hindus of the conditions of the Pact. The fast, if it is to come, will not be for coercion of those who are opponents of reform, but it will be intended to sting into action those who have been my comrades or who have taken pledges for the removal of Untouchability. If they belie their pledges or if they never meant to abide by them and their Hinduism was a mere camouflage, I should have no interest left in life.

He (Gandhiji) was never tired of repeating this. Exclusion of the Untouchables from the Hindu Temples, he described, as the agony of his soul. What did Mr Gandhi do in this connection? Did he resent this betrayal by Mr Rajagopalachari of this project without which he said he had no interest left in life? One would naturally expect Mr Gandhi to denounce this betrayal by the Congress Party to achieve success at the polls? Quite the contrary.

Instead of blaming Mr Rajagopalachari, he blamed Mr Ranga Iyer for his violent denunciation of the Congress Party for withdrawing its support to the Bill. This is what Mr Gandhi said in the issue of the *Harijan* dated August, 1934:

The ill-fated Temple Entry Bill deserved a more decent burial, if it deserved it at all, than it received at the hands of the mover of the Bill. It was not a Bill promoted by, and on behalf of, the reformers. The mover should, therefore, have consulted reformers and acted under instructions from them. So far as I am aware, there was hardly any occasion for the anger into which he allowed himself to be betrayed or the displeasure which he expressed towards Congressmen. On the face of it, it was, and was designed to be, a measure pertaining to religion, framed in pursuance of the solemn declaration publicly made in Bombay at a meeting of representative Hindus, who met under the chairmanship of Pandit Malaviyaji on September 25, 1932. The curious may read the declaration printed almost every week on the front page of Harijan. Therefore, every Hindu, Caste or Harijan, was interested in the measure. It was not a measure in which Congress Hindus were more interested than the other Hindus. To have, therefore, dragged the Congress name into the discussion was unfortunate. The Bill deserved a gentler handling.

The Temple Entry, what one is to say of, except to describe it a strange game of political acrobatics! Mr Gandhi begins as an opponent of Temple Entry. When the Untouchables put forth a demand for political rights, he changes his position and becomes a supporter of Temple Entry. When the Hindus threaten to defeat the Congress in the election, if it pursues the matter to a conclusion, Mr Gandhi, in order to preserve political power in the hands of the Congress, gives up Temple Entry! Is this sincerity? Does this show conviction? Was the 'agony of soul' which Mr Gandhi spoke of more than a phrase?

C. ACTIVITIES OF THE HARIJAN SEVAK SANGH

Wrote Dr Ambedkar:

The *Harijan Sevak Sangh* has been going on, since September 1932. It has been held out as a glorious testimony to the agony of Mr Gandhi's soul for the condition of the Untouchables, and to the passion he feels for their elevation. The General Secretary of the Sangh has invited many Americans to the Home of the Sangh in Delhi and shown them round as an unrivalled piece of social work that is being done by Mr Gandhi for the welfare of the Untouchables....

Any welfare work for a down-trodden people must be welcomed by all. But this does not mean that it must never be criticised. That can hardly be accepted. It would be legitimate to inquire what work the Sangh is doing since so much is made of it. Anyone who has read the Annual Reports of the Sangh will see that it follows certain well defined and stereotyped lines. In the field of education, the Sangh has sought to encourage higher education among the Untouchables by instituting scholarships for the Arts, technical and professional courses. The Sangh also gives scholarships to High School students. The Sangh also maintains Hostels for Untouchable students attending colleges and high schools. The great part of the educational activities of the Sangh is taken up in maintaining separate schools for primary stage children, where there were no common schools in the vicinity or where common schools were closed to them....

Next comes the welfare activities of the Sangh. The medical aid which the Sangh undertakes to render to the Untouchables falls under this head. This is done by itinerant workers of the Sangh who go in Harijan quarters to give medical aid to the sick and ailing among the Untouchables. The Sangh also maintains a few dispensaries for the use of the Untouchables. This is a very small activity of the Sangh....

The more important part of the welfare activity of the Sangh relates to water supply. The Sangh does this by (1) sinking new wells or installing tube wells and pumps for the use of the Untouchables; (2) repairing old ones; and (3) persuading Local Governments and Bodies to sink and repair wells for the Untouchables....

The third line of activity undertaken by the Sangh is economic. The Sangh seems to run a few industrial schools and it is claimed that the industrial schools run by the Sangh produced a number of trained artisans who have taken to independent living. But according to the reports, more successful and substantial work was done by way of organising and supervising co-operative societies among the Untouchables....

From this summary of its activities, an impression may be created that the Sangh must be spending quite a lot of money on the welfare of the Untouchables. What are the facts? It will be recalled that the normal amount of money which the Sangh expected to be able to spend on the uplift work among the Untouchables was to be about Rs. 6,00,000 per year. How much has the Sangh been actually spending?

On this basis the Sangh's expenditure comes to about Rs. 3,43,888 per year, which is 50 per cent less than what the Sangh hoped to collect. It will be seen that the Sangh is not as big as it is made out to be by its friends. The Sangh has been carrying on a very poor existence. A Budget of three lakhs per year for a population of 50 millions of Untouchables is not a matter on which the Untouchables need be very jubilant. Even this much show the Sangh would not have been able to put up if during the two years that they were in office, the Congress Governments in different Provinces had not given large grants to the Sangh....

The Sangh cannot be blamed for its poor finances. The blame lies with the Hindus. The stagnant, if not the deteriorating, condition of the Sangh shows how little the Hindus care for the welfare of the Untouchables. For political purposes they contributed one crore of Rupees which went to make up the Tilak *Swaraj* Fund. For General Welfare work they have very recently contributed one crore and 15 lakhs which will make up the Kasturba Memorial Fund. Compared with these the contributions made by the Hindus to the Harijan Sevak Sangh are paltry....

One may differ with the Sangh on the nature of the welfare work it does. Much of the work the Sangh does is obviously the work which any civilized Government is bound to undertake out of public revenues. It may well be asked: why should the Sangh ask Government to undertake this work and use its funds on projects which Government does not do and yet is urgently required to be done?

This, however, cannot give rise to feelings of animosity on the part of the Untouchables towards the Sangh. It may be admitted that such animosity does exist. The writer in the Indian Social Reformer pleads that Untouchables should be associated with the management of the Sangh. His statement might lead people to believe that Untouchables were never represented on the Central Board of the Sangh. That would be a mistake. The correct position is that when the Sangh was started prominent Untouchables in substantial numbers were on the Central Board of the

Sangh. The statement issued by Mr Birla and Mr Thakkar on November 3, 1932 gives the names of those who were constituting the Central Board. Out of 8 members, 3 were drawn from the Untouchables. After my retirement from the Board, the other two, namely, Rao Bahadur MC Rajah and Rao Bahadur Srinivasan also retired....

It is right and proper that I should state the reasons why I severed my connection with the Sangh. After the Poona Pact I proceeded in a spirit of forget and forgive. I accepted the bona fides of Mr Gandhi, as I was asked to do by many of his friends. It was in that spirit that I accepted a place on the Central Board of the Sangh, and was looking forward to play my part in its activities. In fact, I wanted to discuss with Mr Gandhi the programme of work which I felt the Sangh should undertake. Before I could do that, I was called to go to London to attend the third Round Table Conference. The next best thing I could do was to communicate my views to Mr AV Thakkar, the Secretary of the Sangh. Accordingly I wrote (a letter, which stated):

'In my opinion there can be two distinct methods of approaching the task of uplifting the Depressed Classes. There is a school which proceeds on the assumption that the fact of the individual belonging to the Depressed Classes is bound up with his personal conduct. If he is suffering from want and misery it is because he must be vicious and sinful. Starting from this hypothesis this school of social workers concentrates all its efforts and its resources on fostering personal virtue by adopting a programme which includes items such as temperance, gymnasium, co-operation, libraries, schools, etc., which are calculated to make the individual a better and virtuous individual.

In my opinion, there is also another method of approach to this problem. It starts with the hypothesis that the fate of the individual is governed by his environment and the circumstances he is obliged to live under, and if an individual is suffering from want and misery it is because his environment is not propitious. I have no doubt that of the two views the latter is the more correct, the former may raise a few stray individuals above the level of the Class to which they belong. It cannot lift the Class as a whole.

My view of the aim of the Anti-Untouchability League is that it has come into existence not for helping a few individuals at random or a few selected boys belonging to the Depressed Classes but for raising the whole Class to a higher level. Consequently, I would not like the League to dissipate its energies on a programme calculated to foster private virtue. I would like the Board to concentrate all its energies on a programme that will effect a change in the social environment of the Depressed Classes. Having stated in general terms my views, I venture to place some concrete proposals for work to be undertaken by the League:

(1) A Campaign to Secure Civil Rights

I think the first thing that the League should undertake is a campaign all over India to secure to the Depressed Classes the enjoyment of their civic rights such as taking water from the village wells, entry in village schools, admission to village *chawdi*, use of public conveyance, etc. Such a programme if carried into villages will bring about the necessary social revolution in the Hindu Society, without which it will never be possible for the Depressed Classes to get equal social status.

(2) Equality of Opportunity

The second thing I would like the Anti-Untouchability League to work for is to bring about equality of opportunity for the Depressed Classes. Much of the misery and poverty of the Depressed Classes is due to the absence of equality of opportunity which in its turn is due to Untouchability. I am sure you are aware that the Depressed Classes in villages and even in towns cannot sell vegetables, milk or butter—ways of earning a living which are open to all and sundry. A Caste Hindu will buy these things from a non-Hindu, but he will not buy them from the Depressed Classes. In the matter of enjoyment, his condition is the worst. In Government Departments the bar-sinister operates and he is denied the place of a constable or even a messenger. In industries he fares no better.

(3) Social Intercourse

Lastly, I think the League should attempt to dissolve that nausea, which the Touchables feel towards the Untouchables, and which is the reason why the two sections have remained so much apart as to constitute separate and distinct entities. In my opinion the best way of achieving it is to establish closer contact between the two. Only a common cycle of participation can help people to overcome the strangeness of feeling which one has when brought into contact with the other. Nothing can do this more effectively in my opinion than the admission of the Depressed Classes to the houses of the Caste Hindus as guests or servants. The live contact thus established will familiarize both to a common and associated life and will pave the way for that unity which we are all striving after.

(4) Agency to be Employed

The League will have to employ a very large army of workers to carry out its programme. I attach very great importance to the selection of a proper agency to be employed in this behalf. As Tolstoy said, 'Only those who love can serve.' In my opinion that test is more likely to be fulfilled by workers drawn from the Depressed Classes. I should, therefore, like the League to bear this aspect of the question in mind in deciding upon whom to appoint and when not to appoint.

Before closing this I wish to say just this. It was Balfour, I think, who said that what could hold the British Empire together was love and not law. I think that observation applies equally to the Hindu Society. The Touchables and the Untouchables cannot be held together by law certainly not by any electoral law substituting joint electorates for separate electorates. The only thing that can hold them together is love. Outside the family justice alone, in my opinion, can open the possibility of love, and it should be the duty of the Anti-Untouchability League to see that the Touchable does, or failing that is made to do, justice to the Untouchable. Nothing else in my opinion can justify the project or the existence of the League.

I am releasing this to the Press so that the general public may know my views and have an opportunity to consider them.

★ ★ ★

To my great surprise, I found that no attention was paid to my proposals. Indeed, my letter was not even acknowledged! I felt that there was no use in my remaining in the Sangh. I dissociated myself from it. I found that in my absence the aims and objects had undergone a complete change. At the meeting held in Cowasjee Jehangir Hall in Bombay on September 8, 1932 the aims of the organization were stated to be:

> Carrying propaganda against Untouchability and taking immediate steps 'to secure as early as practicable that all public wells, *dharamshalas*, roads, schools, crematoriums, burning ghats and all public temples be declared open to the Depressed Classes, provided that no compulsion or force shall be used and that only peaceful persuasion shall be adopted towards this end.

But in the statement issued by Mr GD Birla and Mr AV Thakkar on November 3, two months after its inauguration it was stated:

> The League believes that reasonable persons among the Sanatanists are not much against the removal of Untouchability as such, as they are against inter-Caste dinners and marriages. Since it is not the ambition of the League to undertake reforms beyond its own scope, it is desirable to make it clear that while the League will work by persuasion among the Caste Hindus to remove every vestige of Untouchability, the main line of work will be constructive, such as the uplift of Depressed Classes educationally, economically and socially, which itself will go a great way to remove Untouchability. With such a work even a staunch Sanatanist can have nothing but sympathy. And it is for such work mainly that the League has been established. Social reforms like the abolition of the Caste System and inter-dining are kept outside the scope of the League.

Here there was a complete departure from the original aims of the organization. Removal of Untouchability had only a nominal place in the programme. Constructive work became the main part of the work of the Sangh. It is pertinent to ask why this change in the aims and objects was made. This change in the aims and objects could not have been brought about without the knowledge and consent of Mr Gandhi. The only reason one can see is that the original programme was most inconvenient to Mr Gandhi. Removal of Untouchability as a platform was very good, but as a programme of action it was bound to have made Mr Gandhi very unpopular with the Hindus. He was not prepared to court such unpopularity. He, therefore, preferred the programme of constructive work which had all advantages and no disadvantages. The Hindus did not mind it. Mr Gandhi could pursue it without incurring the displeasure of the Hindus. The programme of constructive work had no such disadvantage. On the other hand, it had a positive advantage to recommend it. It had the possibility of destroying the independent movement which the Untouchables had built up and which had forced Mr Gandhi in 1932 to yield to its demands by agreeing to the Poona Pact by dangling well before them the benefits of the constructive work, a consummation which all Congressmen so devoutly wish. It could make Untouchables Congressmen and most gracefully too. The programme of constructive work had the possibility of being converted into a plan to kill Untouchables by kindness. This as a matter of fact has happened. The Harijan Sevak Sangh is intolerant of any movement on the part of the Untouchables which is independent and opposed to the Hindus and the Congress and is out to destroy it. Anticipating that such would be the consequences of the change in the aims and objects, I retired from the Sangh.

Since the first batch of the Untouchables left the Sangh no attempt was made by Mr Gandhi to appoint other Untouchables in their places. Instead, the management of the Sangh has been allowed to pass entirely into the hands of the Hindus of the Congress persuasion. Indeed, it is now the policy of the Sangh to exclude Untouchables from the management and higher direction of the Sangh. As will be seen from the refusal of Mr Gandhi to agree to the suggestion made by deputation of Untouchables, requesting him to appoint Untouchables to the managing body. Mr Gandhi has propounded a new doctrine to console the deputations. He says:

> The welfare work for the Untouchables is a penance which the Hindus have to do for the sin of Untouchability. The money that has been collected has been contributed by the Hindus. From both points of view the Hindus alone must run the Sangh. Neither ethics nor right would justify Untouchables in claiming a seat on the Board of the Sangh.

Mr Gandhi does not realize how greatly he has insulted the Untouchables by his doctrine, the ingenuity of which has not succeeded in concealing its gross and coarse character. If Mr Gandhi's point is that the money is collected by the Hindus and the Untouchables have, therefore, no right to say how it shall be spent, no self-respecting Untouchable will bother him.…It is pertinent to ask: "Why at one time he was anxious to have Untouchables on the Governing Body of the Sangh, and why is he determined now to exclude them?"

⋆ ⋆ ⋆

The fate of the Harijan Sevak Sangh and Gandhiji's soft-pedalling the issue of Untouchables have to be seen in relations to the growing hostility of orthodox Hindus to Gandhiji's policy.[60] According to B Ray, British officials thought that Gandhiji's campaigning tour had prompted him to re-think his position: "Mr Gandhi apparently is getting more and more chory of giving offence to orthodox opposition, the strength of which, it is suggested, he had not fully

60. See Jaffrelot C, op cit, for this argument.

appreciated, at any rate with regard to temple entry. Congress, as a party, has gained little, if anything, by this tour."[61]

According to Jaffrelot:

> Ultimately the struggle between Gandhi and Ambedkar ended with the former's victory: while the social status quo was not totally preserved, the politicization of Untouchables by means of a separate electorate had been defused. Gandhi's signal success was the Poona Pact, which was to have serious consequences....
>
> First the reserved seats scheme did not allow Untouchables to benefit from political representation proportional to their demographic weight. The Government of India of 1935 granted them only 7 seats out of 156 seats in the Council of States (the Upper House of the Parliament at New Delhi), 19 out of 250 in the Central Assembly (in the Lower House of Parliament) and 151 out of 1585 in the various legislative assemblies of the provinces. Above all, reserved seats thwarted Ambedkar's desire to transform Untouchable into a political force. Given that they never found themselves in a majority in a constituency, an alliance (explicit or tacit) of the upper and intermediate Castes could even elect an Untouchable of their choice for whom Untouchables themselves would not have voted. Ultimately, Congress was to become a pastmaster in this kind of co-option.
>
> The debates 1932-33 eroded the little hope which Ambedkar still had in Gandhi, though be continued to be praised by him. In 1934 he addressed students in Karachi as follows:
>
> 'The magnitude of (Dr Ambedkar's) sacrifice is great. He is absorbed in his own work. He leads a simple life. He is capable of earning one to two thousand rupees a month. He is also in a position to settle down in Europe if he so desires. But he doesn't want to stay there. He is only concerned about the welfare of the *Harijans*.'
>
> To be fair to Gandhi, he was the first and only Indian politician to make the abolition of Untouchability central to *Swaraj*, and to act so single-mindedly in order to challenge it. As a result, he was detested by the orthodox Hindus who figure so largely in Congress. Gandhi had to make compromises with these people, who thought he was going too fast. For Ambedkar, the Mahatma was going too slowly. He was deeply disappointed and dismayed by Gandhi's actions.

★ ★ ★

While Dr Ambedkar had succeeded in awakening the downtrodden masses and uniting them, there was a brief period in the aftermath of the Poona Pact of 1932 when the movement was seemingly losing some of its momentum. To be sure, there were a few agitations and occasional public meetings, but the earlier fervor was somehow missing. Both of Dr Ambedkar's mass movement initiatives—the one at

---

61. B Ray (Ed 1996) *Gandhi's Campaign Against Untouchability*, 1933-34, p.243.

the Chavdar Lake at Mahad[62] and at the Kala Ram Temple in Nashik—were stuck in litigations. Dr Ambedkar was fighting the legal suits but the cases were dragging on.

While returning from Mahad to Mumbai after one of the Court hearings, Dr Ambedkar's car apparently broke down on the way. It was raining heavily. No one in the village nearby would offer food or shelter to an Untouchable. After spending the night under a tree, wet and hungry, Dr Ambedkar was so agitated that on his return to Mumbai he locked himself in a room.

There was some of the possibility of Dr Ambedkar being appointed a Judge in the Mumbai High Court. So depressed was Dr Ambedkar that he even started discussing the idea of quitting politics. In August 1933 Dr Ambedkar wrote to one of his trusted friends: "I am going to withdraw myself from politics and devote myself entirely to my profession as soon as the work of this Round Table Conference will be finished."

To the great relief of millions of his followers, however, this was not going to be. Dr Ambedkar was soon to make a dramatic come back with even greater passion, eloquence and commitment.

62. Much later, in March 1937, the Mumbai High Court settled the long-drawn Mahad case, allowing Untouchables to draw water from the *Chavdar* Lake.

CHAPTER SEVENTEEN

"I Will Not Die a Hindu!"

BY 1935, THE struggle for Independence led by Mahatma Gandhi had cooled down considerably. The Indian National Congress had withdrawn the Civil Disobedience Movement. The British Parliament had passed the Government of India Act of 1935, which provided for Legislatures at the Federal and Provincial level. The Act provided for a Constitutional relationship between the Indian States and British India on a Federal basis. Accession of the States to the Federation was also provided for. Gandhiji had given his consent to work within the framework of the Government of India Act of 1935.

In the aftermath of the tumultuous events of 1932, Dr Ambedkar underwent a major tragedy in his personal life. The health of his wife, Ramabai, had been failing, while his only surviving son, Yashwant, was suffering from rheumatism. Dr Ambedkar often said that one day he would earn enough money to send his wife and son for specialized treatment in London. Unfortunately, before he could do that, Ramabai passed away on May 26, 1935. Ramabai (Rama *Mata* as she is now referred to) had gone through all the ups and downs of life together with Dr Ambedkar during the early part of his struggle. Her early death at the age of only 40 years was a big blow to Babasaheb. He was in despair. After the death of Ramabai, Dr Ambedkar who was in his mid-forties became very lonely. His own health was also failing. After repeated bouts of ill-health, he was advised to seek a change of climate. Towards the end of 1936, he finally managed to find some time to go to Europe.

★ ★ ★

On Sunday October 13, 1935, Dr Ambedkar went to Vinchur and thereon to Yeola in Nashik District. Yeola Municipality presented an Address to him in the morning. While replying to the Address, Dr Ambedkar indicated that he had lost all hopes of reforming Hinduism from within. He said:

> Now we come to the conclusion that there is no change in attitude of the Touchables and they are not ready to behave with us with affection, despite our continuous

> struggle. As such we have decided to remain separate from Hindus, to live with self-help and struggle to attain self-elevation.

Dr Ambedkar then moved on to Yeola where he was going to make a historic announcement.

★ ★ ★

Dr Ambedkar presided over the Yeola Conference[63] the same day (October 13, 1935) which was attended by about 10,000 Untouchables of all shades of opinion including representatives from the Hyderabad State and the Central Provinces. In his hard-hitting speech lasting over an hour and a half, Dr Ambedkar recounted the plight of the Depressed Classes in all spheres—economic, social, educational and political—and pointed out the immense sacrifices made by them to secure the barest human rights as members of the same community under the aegis of Hinduism. He especially referred to the Kalaram Temple Entry Movement wherein inhuman treatment was meted out to them during the past five years, and told them how their struggle to secure elementary rights and equal status in the Hindu Society had come to naught. He said that it gave him a very painful realization that the time and money spent on and efforts made to achieve those objectives had proved utterly fruitless.

Dr Ambedkar, therefore, expressed his opinion that the time for making a final decision to settle the matter had arrived. The disabilities they were labouring under and the indignities they had to put up with, he added, were the result of their being members of the Hindu Community.

Dr Ambedkar described to the huge gathering of his followers how the struggle over the past decade to secure basic human rights and equal human status within the Hindu society had failed. For the first decade or so of his public life, he had chosen to reform the Hindu religion by fighting it from within. He had tried to create a legitimate place for the Depressed Classes in the Hindu society, but the Upper Castes had not budged. Out of sheer frustration, he said he was contemplating a change of religion.

"Would it not be better to give up Hinduism and embrace another faith that would unreservedly give us an equal status?" he asked.

There was an audible hush in the crowd. A moment later, he came out with his famous assertion:

> Unfortunately, I was born a Hindu Untouchable—there was nothing I could do to prevent it. However, it is well within my power to refuse to live under ignoble and humiliating conditions. I solemnly assure you that I will not die a Hindu.

---

63. Marathi Speech, For English Summary, see *Ambedkar Speaks*, op cit, Vol. II pp.274–77.

Dr Ambedkar then announced a change of strategy. He exhorted them to sever their connections with Hinduism and seek solace and self-respect in another religion, but warned them to be very careful in choosing the new faith, and to see that equality of treatment, status and opportunities was guaranteed to them unreservedly.

Dr Ambedkar asked his people to stop the Kalaram Temple *Satyagraha* as the past five years had demonstrated the futility of such agitation against the tyrannical Caste Hindus, who had thwarted their attempts and showed impenitent hearts. He exhorted them to conduct themselves in such a way in future as would leave no doubt to the outside world of their decision to be and to remain a separate community outside the Hindu fold, carving out for themselves a future worthy of free citizens.

Accordingly, after a full discussion, the Conference passed, in view of the callous and criminal indifference shown by the Caste Hindus to their demand for social equality, a Resolution instructing the Depressed Classes to stop the struggle which they had carried on for the past ten years for raising the Untouchables to a status equal with that of the Caste Hindus and in the hope of consolidating and strengthening both sections into a great and powerful society. It further exhorted the Untouchable to stop frittering away their energies over fruitless attempts and to devote themselves to securing an honourable status, and an independent position on the basis of equality with the other societies in Hindustan.

Dr Ambedkar's announcement to renounce the Hindu religion and to embrace some other religion got wide publicity on a global scale. It was like tornado hurled at the impenitent Hindu Society. The announcement sent shock waves throughout the country. Some called it a bluff and a political stunt. Others, who knew the strength of Dr Ambedkar's character, could not doubt his determination. Some called him a messiah; others felt it was a suicidal step.

All eyes were on Gandhiji for his reaction, which was not long in coming:

> Religion is not like a house or a clock which can be changed at will. It is an integral part of one's own self, rather than of the body. I am convinced that a change of faith will not serve the cause which they have at heart.

Interviewed by the Associated Press representative regarding Dr Ambedkar's Speech, Gandhiji said,

> The speech attributed to Dr Ambedkar seems unbelievable. If, however, he has made such a speech and the Conference had adopted the resolution of complete severance from Hinduism and acceptance of any faith that would guarantee equality, I regard both as unfortunate events, especially when one notices, despite isolated events to the contrary, Untouchability on its last legs.
>
> I can understand the anger of a high-souled and highly educated person like Dr Ambedkar over atrocities such as were committed in Kavitha and other villages. But religion is not like house or cloak which can be changed at will. It is more an integral

part of one's self than of one's body. Religion is the tie that binds one to one's creator and whilst the body perishes and it is the religion that persists even after death.

If Dr Ambedkar has any faith in God, I would urge him to assuage his wrath and reconsider his position and examine his ancestral religion on its own merits and not through the weakness of its unfaithful followers.

Lastly, I am convinced, change of faith by him, and those who passed the resolution would not serve the cause which they have at heart; for millions of unsophisticated illiterate Harijans would not listen to him especially when it is remembered that their lives for good or evil are intertwined with those of Caste Hindus.

Dr Ambedkar's Rebuttal to Gandhiji

When Gandhiji's comment on Dr Ambedkar's announcement of conversion was shown to him, he responded:

"What religion we shall belong is not decided: what ways and means we shall adopt, we have not thought out; but we have decided one thing, and that after due deliberations and with deep conviction, that Hindu religion is not good for us."

"Inequality," Dr Ambedkar said

> is the very basis of it, and its ethics is such that the Depressed Classes can never acquire their full manhood. Let no one think I have done this in a huff, or as a matter of wrath against the treatment meted out to the Depressed Classes at Kavitha village or any other place. It is a deeply deliberated decision. I agree with Gandhiji that religion is necessary, but I do not agree that man should have his ancestral religion if he finds that that religion is repugnant to his notions of the sort of religion he needs as a standard for the regulation of his own conduct and as a source of inspiration for his advancement and well-being.

Asked when he proposed to get himself converted and whether it would be an individual action or mass action, Dr Ambedkar said:

> I have made up my mind to change my religion. I do not care if the masses do not come. It is for them to decide. If they feel it is good they will follow me; but on the contrary, if they feel it is not they will not follow my example. My own advice is that Gandhiji should allow the Depressed Classes to chalk out their own line of action. Kavitha does not represent an isolated incident but it is the very basis of the system found in the ancestral religion of the Hindus.

Gandhiji had predicted that millions of illiterate and unsophisticated Untouchables would not renounce their faith, for they were concerned with day-to-day survival rather than Dr Ambedkar's "attention-seeking stunts". Gandhiji's pronouncements however, did not convince other religious minorities such as the Muslims, Christians, and Sikhs. They saw this as a great opportunity to convert the Untouchables *en masse* and gain strength for their own faiths. Dr Ambedkar's house was flooded with letters and telegrams. While most of them waxed eloquent about the reasons as to why their religion was superior, some offered tangible rewards. On the other hand, a few letters sent by Hindu fanatics were reportedly written in blood. The social movement had taken on a new and exciting dimension. There was no turning back.

★ ★ ★

Time reported an interesting incident at around this time (March 16, 1936): "Dr Ambedkar is probably the only man alive who ever walked out in a huff from a private audience with the Pope of Rome, His Holiness Pius XI, having heard from Dr Ambedkar about the miseries of Indian outcastes, replied: 'My son, it may take three or four centuries to remedy these abuses, be patient.'"[64]

★ ★ ★

From time to time, Dr Ambedkar reviewed the progress of the mass movement led by him. The first of such reviews was after ten years in social life. In a public meeting in Nagpur (May 4, 1936), Dr Ambedkar explained to his followers that "what could not happen over hundreds of years has finally occurred in the last ten years". He said:[65]

> We have done so much good work during the past ten years. This could not have been achieved if we had waited even for hundreds of years. This divine work could not have happened without our struggle for self-respect and self-reliance. We do not have huge funds like the Congress. We also do not have manpower or other support for our social work. In spite of all the difficulties and deprivations we have covered a wide spectrum by our movement for justice. All this was possible only because of your love and enthusiasm!
>
> This divine achievement of the past ten years because of which all the people including a mighty party like the Congress is scared of you could be possible only because of your unity. Barring few exceptions, there is unity amongst us which has increased our esteem and political importance in the eyes of all people. And ever since we declared our intention of conversion to another religion, the Muslims, Christians and Sikhs, all are after us begging to join their religion. We should retain this unity so that we could reach our goal of leaving the Hinduism for elevation in our social status.
>
> Recently, horrible atrocities have been committed on the Untouchables by the Touchable Hindus in Jodhpur and Gujarat. This atrocious slavery will come to an end only if we leave this religion; there is no other way. If Hindus are not ready to remain under the British rule despite a Dominion Status that is being offered then why should we remain under the rule of Hindus?

64. As quoted in *Outlook* (August 20, 2012).
65. Marathi Speech, for English Summary, see *Ambedkar Speaks*, op cit, Vol. I, p.38.

> Another tree does not grow under any tree. It needs independent sun rays for its growth. Likewise, there cannot be our growth under this decaying tree of Hinduism. We must, therefore, change our religion.

Dr Ambedkar presented his detailed rebuttal to Gandhiji in his essay:*Mukti Kaun Pathe?* (*Which Way to Emancipation*). In that essay, Dr Ambedkar extensively dealt with reasons why Dalits could no longer remain within the fold of Hinduism. In October 1935, Dr Ambedkar made an historic announcement of his intention to leave the Hindu religion. About eight months thereafter, All-India Mumbai Area *Mahar* Conference was held in Mumbai on May 31, 1936 which was attended by around 35,000 people. Dr Ambedkar delivered his Presidential Address to the Conference which was essentially aimed at assessing the support of Untouchables for conversion (from Hinduism into some other religion). This Address in Marathi, with a title: *Mukti Kaun Pathe* has been translated into English[66] and may be summarized as follows:

- The matter of Conversion should be viewed in terms of two dimensions: Social as well as Religious; Material as well as Spiritual.
  It is necessary to understand, at the outset, the nature of Untouchability, and how it is practised in our country. In order to have a clear understanding of Untouchability and its practise in real life,.... recall the stories of the atrocities perpetrated against you....What is at the root of their tyranny?
- These instances of atrocities have nothing to do with the virtues or vices of an individual. This is not a feud between two rival men. The problem of Untouchability is a matter of Class struggle. It is a struggle between Caste Hindus and the Untouchables....This is a matter of injustice being done by one Class against another. This Class struggle has a relation with the social status.
- This conflict begins as soon as you start claiming equal treatment with others. Your behaving on par with them insults them.Your status in their eyes is low; you are impure; you must remain at the lowest rung; then alone will they allow you to live happily.The moment you cross your level, the conflict arises.
- Untouchability is not a short or temporary phenomenon. It is a permanent one.... It is eternal because the religion which has placed you at the lowest level of the society is itself eternal, according to the belief of the high-Caste people. No change, according to time and circumstance, is possible.You are at the lowest rung of the ladder today.You shall remain lowest forever.This means the conflict between the Hindus and the Untouchables shall continue forever.
- How will you survive through this struggle is the main question. And unless you think it over, there is no way out. The question which you must now consider is: do you have enough power to survive through this struggle?

66. For full English summary, see *Ambedkar Speaks*, op cit,Vol I, p.177.

- Three types of strength are known to man: (a) Manpower; (b) Wealth; and (c) Mental strength. Which of these do you think you possess? So far as manpower is concerned, it is clear that you are in a minority. Your meagre population is of no use as a fighting force for the Untouchables. Financial strength is also the same. It is an undisputed fact that you at least have a little bit of manpower; but finances, you have none. Thousands of Untouchables tolerate insult, tyranny, and oppression at the hands of the Hindus without a sigh or complaint because they have no capacity to bear the expenses of the Courts. And, as regards mental strength, the condition is worse. For centuries, you have not only served the higher Caste but have also tolerated their insults and tyranny without grudge and complaint. This has killed the sense to retort and revolt. Confidence, vigour, and ambition have completely vanished from you. All of you have become helpless, unenergetic, and pale. Everywhere, there is an atmosphere of defeatism and pessimism; even the slightest idea that you can do something does not arise in anybody's mind.
- The conclusion is: If you depend only upon your own strength, you will never be able to face oppression. Two facts are established: Firstly, you cannot face tyranny without strength. And secondly, you do not possess enough strength to face tyranny. Having established these two facts, the third automatically follows. That is, the strength required to face this tyranny needs to be secured from outside. How you are going to gain this strength is really an important question.
- In this country, nobody seems to be pained by the poverty and sufferings of people. People do come to the help of those in poverty, sorrow, and suffering, but only amongst one's own Caste or religion. Though this is a perverted sense of morality, it cannot be forgotten that it is prevalent in this country. If you ask them, they reply that it is not their business to interfere, and that had you been members of their religion, they would have helped you.... Conversion is much needed also for a sense of spiritual well-being. What is religion for? Why is it necessary? One definition is most meaningful and agreeable to all—that which holds people is religion. Religion means the rules imposed for the maintenance of society.... Although this definition, realistically or logically, appears to be correct, it does not disclose or clarify the nature of the rules which govern a society. The question 'what is religion?' and 'what is not religion?' does not depend on its definition, but on the motive and nature of the rules that bind and govern a society.
- What should be the nature of real religion? Modern social philosophers have postulated three answers to this question. Some have said that the ultimate goal of society is to achieve happiness for the individual. Some say that society exists for the development of the inherent qualities and energies of man, and to help him develop himself. Still others claim that the chief object of social organization is not the development or happiness of the individual but the creation of an ideal society.

- The ideas of the Hindu religion, however, are very different from all these concepts. There is no place for an individual in the Hindu religion. The Hindu religion is constituted on the basis of Class. The Hindu religion does not teach how one individual should behave with another individual.
- Individual welfare and progress (individual development) should be the real aim of religion. A man's life is independent. He is born not for the service of society but for his self development. I do not accept a religion in which one Class alone has the right to gain knowledge; another has a right to use arms; the third one to trade; and the fourth, only to serve. Everyone needs knowledge. Everybody needs arms. Everyone wants money. The religion which forgets this and has the intention to educate only a few and keep the rest in darkness is not a religion but a conspiracy to keep people in mental slavery. A religion which permits one person to bear arms, and prohibits another from doing the same is not religion but a craftiness to keep the latter in perpetual slavery. A religion which opens the path to acquisition of property for some, and compels others to depend on these few even for the daily necessities of life is not a religion but sheer self-aggrandizement. This is what is called the *Chaturvarna* in Hinduism.
- The basic idea underlying a religion is to create an atmosphere conducive to the spiritual development of an individual. It is clear that you cannot develop yourself at all in Hinduism. Three factors are required for the uplift of an individual. They are: Sympathy, Equality, and Liberty. Can you say that any of these factors exists for you within Hinduism?
- So far as sympathy is concerned, it does not exist for you in Hinduism.... Hindus have no sense of brotherhood towards you. You are treated worse than foreigners.
- Untouchability is nothing but concrete inequality. Such a living example of inequality is to be found nowhere. Nowhere, at no point of time in the history of the world can we find such inequality, which is more intense than Untouchability....
- Some people say that Untouchability is a stigma on the Hindu religion. This statement, however, does not convey any sense at all. No Hindu believes that the Hindu religion is a stigma. The majority of Hindus, however, believe that you are a stigma; that you are impure. How have you been brought to this condition? I think you have been thrust into this condition because you have continued to be Hindus. Those of you who have become Muslims are treated by the Hindus neither as the Untouchables nor as unequals. The same can be said of those of you who have become Christians. They are treated by the Hindus neither as the Untouchables nor as unequals.
- The principle of equality as taught in Christianity and Islam has no concern whatsoever with knowledge, wealth, or dress which are outward aspects of one's self. Both these religions consider a sense of humanity as the main feature of their religion. They preach that humanity should be respected by all, and none should disrespect the other; none should treat others as unequals. These

teachings are completely wanting in the Hindu religion. What is the use of such a religion in which the man's sense of humanity is not respected? And what is the good of clinging to it?

- Some Hindus cite the Upanishadas, and proudly say that God is all-pervading according to the principle enunciated in the Upanishdas. If the Hindus insist on saying that the omnipresence of God is not the principle of Philosophy but the basic principle of their religion, I would simply say that nowhere in the world is such meanness found as it exists amongst the Hindus. The Hindus can be ranked among those cruel people whose utterances and acts are poles apart. They have Ram on their tongue and a knife under their armpits. They speak like saints and act as butchers. They keep company with those who believe that God is omnipresent, but treat men worse than animals; they are hypocrites. Do not keep contact with those who feed ants with sugar, but kill men by prohibiting them from drinking water; they are hypocrites.
- The Hindus consider you as lowest of the low, so the Muslims and the Christians also consider you likewise. They fear that if they treat you as equals, the Hindus will also treat them as low. Hence, Muslims and Christians also follow Untouchability like the Hindus.
- If you have to get rid of these shameful conditions, if you have to cleanse this stigma and make this precious life graceful, there is only one way, and that is to discard Hindu religion and Hindu Society.
- Are you free in the Hindu region? Do you have any freedom to carve out your own aims? In my opinion, not only have you no freedom but you are worse than slaves. Your slavery has no parallel. In the Hindu religion, none can have freedom of speech. In Hinduism, conscience, reason, and thoughts have neither any importance nor any scope. A Hindu must necessarily be a slave of either the Vedas or the *Smritis* or must imitate the great men; he is not supposed to use his reasoning. Hence, so long as you are a part of the Hindu religion, you cannot expect to have freedom of thought.
- Everyone in the Hindu religion is not equally affected by the adverse effects that this mental slavery has produced. It is an undisputed fact that the whole of the Hindu religion is the creation of high-Caste Hindus for the welfare and prosperity of the high Castes. It is what they call a religion that has assigned you the role of the slave. Every arrangement is made in the religion itself, so that you may not be able to escape from this slavery. Therefore, for you there is a greater need of breaking the bondage of mental slavery of the Hindu religion. In view of this, Hinduism has marred your progress from two sides. It has sucked your mental freedom and made you slaves. In the outer world also, it has doomed you to the conditions of a slave. If you want freedom, you must change your religion.
- The responsibility for this tradition of Casteism and Untouchability falls on the Caste Hindus, and not on the Untouchables. Castes cannot be abolished by inter-Caste dinners or stray instances of inter-Caste marriages. Caste is a state of mind. It is a disease of the mind. The teachings of the Hindu religion are

the root cause of this disease. We practise Casteism and we observe Untouchability because we are asked to do so by the Hindu religion in which we live. To talk of annihilating Castes while living within Hinduism is like talking of changing poison into *Amrit*.

- In short, so long as we remain in the religion which teaches a man to treat another man as filthy, the sense of discrimination on account of Caste—which is deeply rooted in our minds—cannot be abolished. For annihilating the Castes and Untouchability from among the Untouchables, a change of religion is the only antidote.
- To reform Hindu Society is neither our aim nor our field of action. Our aim is to gain freedom for ourselves. If we can gain our freedom by Conversion, why should we shoulder the responsibility of reforming Hindu Society? And why should we sacrifice our vitality, strength, and wealth for that? You must understand that the main object of our movement is not the reform of the Hindu religion. The principal object of our movement is to achieve social freedom for the Untouchables; it is equally true that this freedom cannot be secured without Conversion. I do accept that the Untouchables need equality as well, and to secure equality is also one of the objectives of our movement. But nobody can say that this equality can be achieved only by remaining in the Hindu religion.
- To my mind, there are two ways of achieving equality. Equality can be achieved either by remaining in the Hindu fold, or by Conversion. If equality is to be achieved by remaining within the Hindu fold, the mere removal of the polluting contact will not serve the purpose. Equality can be achieved only when inter-Caste dinners and marriages take place. This means that the *Chaturvarna* must be abolished and the Brahminic religion must be uprooted. Is this possible? And if not, will it be wise to expect the treatment of equality by remaining within the Hindu religion? And can you be successful in your efforts? On the other hand, the path of Conversion is much easier. Hindu Society gives equal treatment to the Muslims; Hindu Society gives equal treatment to the Christians. Obviously, social equality is easily achieved by Conversion. If this is true, then why should you not adopt this simpler path of Conversion?
- By Conversion, the roots of all quarrels will vanish. Then you will have no right to claim their temples and, in fact, there will be no need for the same. There will be no reason for you to struggle for social rights such as inter-Caste dining, inter-Caste marriages etc; and if these quarrels cease to exist, mutual love and affection will develop among you.
- Conversion is the only right path of freedom which ultimately leads to equality. Thus, Conversion is not the path of escapism; it is not the path of cowardice; it is the path of wisdom.
- Conversion is as necessary for the Untouchables as Self-Government is necessary for India. Conversion is as important to the Untouchables as Self-

Government is for India. The ultimate object of both Conversion and Self-Government is the same. There is not the slightest difference in their ultimate goal. This ultimate aim is to attain freedom. And if the freedom is necessary for the life of mankind, the Conversion of the Untouchable which brings them complete freedom cannot be called worthless by any stretch of imagination.

- What should be initiated first: Economic progress or Conversion?
- I fail to understand how you can achieve economic progress so long as you have the stigma of being an Untouchable. Untouchability is a permanent obstacle in your path of progress. And, unless you remove it, your path cannot be smooth. Without Conversion, this hurdle cannot be removed.
- Untouchability is a kind of curse. You have been completely ruined, and all your virtues have turned useless. Under these circumstances, what more qualifications can you acquire? And even if you acquire them, what will be their use? If you sincerely desire that your qualifications should be valued, your education should be of some use to you, the doors of your financial progress should be opened for you, then you must throw away the shackles of Untouchability.
- Conversion is the only way to eternal bliss. Nobody should hesitate, even if the political rights are required to be sacrificed for this purpose. Conversion brings no harm to political safeguards. In short, our political rights will accompany us. So nobody should be afraid of the loss.
- So long as you remain within the Hindu religion and in Hindu society, you cannot take the stand that you are entitled to political safeguards because your society is different. But you will be able to take this stand on the day on which you liberate yourselves from the serfdom of Hindu society by virtue of Conversion, and not otherwise. Unless you take such an independent stand and claim political safeguards, your political rights and safeguards cannot be deemed to be permanent and free from danger. Looking through this perspective, it can be said that Conversion is not a hindrance but a path for strengthening our political safeguards. If you remain in the Hindu religion, you will lose your political safeguards. If you do not want to lose your political safeguards, go for Conversion; your political rights will be permanent only by Conversion.
- For myself, I have already taken a decision. My Conversion is for sure. My Conversion is not for any material gain. Nothing but spirituality is at the core of my Conversion. The Hindu religion does not appeal to my reason. The Hindu religion does not appeal to my self-respect. However, for you, Conversion is a must for spiritual as well as for material gain.
- That man is not for religion; religion is for man. To become human, convert yourselves. To get organized, convert yourselves. To achieve strength, convert yourselves. To secure equality, convert yourselves. To get liberty, convert yourselves. To make domestic life happy, convert yourselves.
- Why do you remain in that religion which does not treat you as human beings? Why do you remain in that religion which does not allow you to be educated?

Why do you remain in that religion which prohibits you from entering a temple? Why do you remain in that religion which prohibits you from taking water? Why do you remain in that religion which obstructs you from getting a job? Why do you remain in that religion which insults you at every step?

- A religion which prohibits righteous relations between man and man is not a religion but a display of force. A religion which does not recognise a man as a human being is not a religion but a disease. A religion which allows the touch of animals but prohibits the touch of human beings is not a religion but a mockery. A religion which precludes one Class from education, and forbids it to accumulate wealth or to bear arms is not a religion but a mockery of the life of human being. A religion that compels the illiterate to be illiterate, and the poor to be poor is not a religion but a punishment.
- What message I should give you on this occasion, I take refuge in the words of Gautam Buddha: "Be your own guide. Take refuge in your own reason. Do not listen to the advice of others. Do not succumb to others. Be truthful. Take refuge in truth. Never surrender to anything."

After Dr Ambedkar's enlightening speech, the Conference adopted a Resolution that they were prepared to change their religion *en masse*, and as a preliminary step towards the change of religion, urged the *Mahar* community to refrain thereafter from worshipping Hindu deities, to put a stop to the observance of Hindu festivals and to stop visiting Hindu places of worship.[67]

* * *

While making the historic announcement of conversion, and in the public pronouncements thereafter, Dr Ambedkar had shrewdly refrained from indicating the name of the religion which he had chosen.

Dr Ambedkar while concluding his "Which Way to Emancipation" Speech (May 31, 1936) had quoted Gautam Buddha asking his followers to seek refuge in reason. This had the effect of some people believing that Dr Ambedkar was leaning towards Buddhism. While the heads of different faiths were trying hard to persuade Dr Ambedkar to embrace their own religion, in an expected and possibly strategic gesture, Dr Ambedkar sent his son and nephew to the Gurudwara in Amritsar. On September 18, 1936, Dr Ambedkar deputed 13 of his followers to the Sikh Mission in Amritsar to study the Sikh religion. Dr Ambedkar had encouraged them but had not asked them to embrace Sikhism. The over-enthusiastic 13 followers, however, went over to Sikhism on their own. When they returned to Mumbai, they were received coldly and "sank into oblivion".[68]

---

67. Keer, Dhananjay, op cit, p. 275.

68 Keer, Dhananjay, op cit, p. 284.

CHAPTER EIGHTEEN

War Against the Caste System

DR AMBEDKAR'S WAR against the Caste System began with publication of his brilliant book: *Annihilation of Castes*. This, one of the finest books written by Dr Ambedkar, has a very interesting genesis. Actually, the book is based on a speech prepared for the 1936 Annual Conference of the *Jat-Pat-Todak Mandal* of Lahore, but not delivered owing to the cancellation of the Conference by the Reception Committee on the ground that the views expressed in the speech would be unbearable to the Conference.

The *Jat-Pat-Todak Mandal* was an organization of "Caste Hindu Social Reformers, with the one and only aim, namely, to eradicate the Caste System from amongst the Hindus". The *Mandal* invited Dr Ambedkar around November 1935 to preside over their Annual Conference. Dr Ambedkar declined the invitation initially, but later accepted it. From the beginning there were several logistical issues discussed in long correspondence relating to the date of the Conference and printing of the Presidential Address. The dialogue finally broke down when the *Mandal* objected to certain passages in the Presidential Address, saying, "In case you still insist upon the printing of the Address in toto (i.e., including the objectionable passages) we would very much regret it would not be possible—rather advisable—for us to hold the Conference, and would prefer to postpone it *sine die*...."

Here are some excerpts from Dr Ambedkar's profound essay:

A. ANNIHILATION OF CASTES

The path of social reform in India is strewn with many difficulties. Social reform in India has few friends and many critics. The critics fall into two distinct Classes. One Class consists of political reformers and the other of the Socialists. It was at one time recognized that without social efficiency no permanent progress in the other fields of activity was possible.

It was due to the recognition of this fact that the birth of the National Congress was accompanied by the foundation of the Social Conference. While the Congress was concerned with defining the weak points in the political organization of the country, the Social Conference was engaged in removing the weak points in the social organization of the Hindu Society. But soon the two wings developed into two parties between whom there raged a fierce controversy. In course of time, the party in favour of political reform won and the Social Conference vanished and was forgotten.

Does it prove that the victory went to those who were in the right? Does it prove conclusively that social reform has no bearing on political reform? It will help us to understand the matter if I state the other side of the case. I will draw upon the treatment of the Untouchables for my facts.

Under the rule of the Peshwas in the Maratha country, the Untouchable was not allowed to use the public streets if a Hindu was coming along, lest he should pollute the Hindu by his shadow. The Untouchable was required to have a black thread either on his wrist or in his neck as a sign or a mark to prevent the Hindus from getting themselves polluted by his touch through mistake. In Poona, the capital of the Peshwa, the Untouchable was required to carry, strung from his waist, a broom to sweep away from behind the dust he trod on, lest a Hindu walking on the same should be polluted. In Poona, the Untouchable was required to carry an earthen pot hung around his neck wherever he went, for holding his spit lest his spit falling on the earth should pollute a Hindu who might unknowingly happen to tread on it.

Having stated the facts, let me now state the case for social reform. In doing this, I ask the political-minded Hindus, 'Are you fit for political power even though you do not allow a large Class of your own countrymen like the Untouchables to use public schools? Are you fit for political power even though you do not allow them the use of public wells? Are you fit for political power even though you do not allow them the use of public streets? Are you fit for political power even though you do not allow them to eat any food they like?' I can ask a string of such questions. But these will suffice. I am sure no sensible man will have the courage to give an affirmative power.

How is it then that the Social Reform Party lost the battle? It is necessary to make a distinction between social reform in the sense of the reform of the Hindu Family and social reform in the sense of the reorganization and reconstruction of the Hindu Society. The former has a relation to widow remarriage, child marriage etc., while the latter relates to the abolition of the Caste System. The battle that was fought centered round the question of the reform of the family. It did not relate to the social reform in the sense of the break-up of the Caste System. The break-up of the Caste System was never put in as an issue by the reformers.

What is the significance of the Communal Award with its allocation of political power in defined proportions to diverse Classes and communities? It shows that the politicians who denied that the social problem in India had any bearing on the political problem were forced to reckon with the social problem in devising the Constitution.

Let political reformers turn in any direction they like, they will find that in the making of a Constitution, they cannot ignore the problem arising out of the prevailing social order. History bears out the proposition that political revolutions have always been preceded by social and religious revolutions. The political revolution led by Chandragupta was preceded by the religious and social revolution of Buddha. The political revolution led by Shivaji was preceded by the religious and social reform brought about by the saints of Maharashtra. The political revolution of the Sikhs was preceded by the religious and social revolution led by Guru Nanak. These will suffice to show that the emancipation of the mind and the soul is a necessary preliminary for the political expansion of the people.

Let me now turn to the Socialists. The Socialists of India following their fellows in Europe are seeking to apply the economic interpretation of history to the facts of India. They propound that man is an economic creature, that his activities and aspirations are bound by economic facts, that property is the only source of power. They, therefore, preach that political and social reforms are but gigantic illusions and that economic reform by equalization of property must have precedence over every other kind of reform.

The economic power is the only kind of power, no student of human society can accept. Religion, social status and property are all sources of power and authority, which one man has to control the liberty of another. One is predominant at one stage; the other is predominant at another stage. If the source of power and dominion is social and religious then social reform and religious reform must be accepted as the necessary sort of reform.

It is a pity that Caste even today has its defenders. It is defended on the ground that the Caste System is but another name for division of labour, and if division of labour is a necessary feature of every civilized society then it is argued that there is nothing wrong in the Caste System. Now the first thing to be urged against this view is that Caste System is not merely division of labour. It is also a division of labourers. Civilized society undoubtedly needs division of labour. But in no civilized society is division of labour accompanied by this unnatural division of labourers into watertight compartments. The Caste System is not merely a division of labourers, it is an hierarchy in which the divisions of labourers are graded one above the other. In no other country is the division of labour accompanied by this gradation of labourers. This division of labour is not spontaneous; it is not based on natural aptitudes. Social and individual efficiency requires us to develop the capacity of an individual to the point of competency to choose and to make his own career. This principle is violated in the Caste System insofar as it involves an attempt to appoint tasks to individuals in advance—selected not on the basis of trained original capacities, but on that of the social status of the parents. If a Hindu is seen to starve rather than take to new occupations not assigned to his Caste, the reason is to be found in the Caste System. The division of labour brought about the Caste System is not a division based on choice. Individual sentiment, individual preference has no place in it. It is based on the dogma of predestination. As an economic organization Caste is, therefore, a harmful institution, inasmuch as it involves the subordination of man's natural powers and inclinations to the exigencies of social rules.

Some have dug a biological trench in defence of the Caste System. It is said that the object of Caste was to preserve purity of race and purity of blood. The Caste System cannot be said to have grown as a means of preventing the admixture of races or as a means of maintaining purity of blood. As a matter of fact (the) Caste System came into being long after the different races of India had commingled in blood and culture. The Caste System does not demarcate racial division. Caste System is a social division of people of the same race.

Caste does not result in economic efficiency. Caste cannot improve, and has not improved the race. Caste has, however, done one thing. It has completely disorganized and demoralized the Hindus. The first and foremost thing that must be recognized is that Hindu Society is a myth. The name Hindu is itself a foreign name. It does not occur in any Sanskrit work prior to the Mohammedan invasion. Hindu society as such does not exist. It is only a collection of Castes. Each Caste is conscious of its existence. Its survival is the be-all and end-all of its existence. Castes do not even form a federation. A case has no feeling that it is affiliated to other Castes, except when there is a Hindu-Muslim riot. On all other occasions each Caste endeavours to segregate itself and to distinguish itself from other Castes. There is an utter lack among the Hindus of what the sociologists call 'consciousness of kind'. In every Hindu the consciousness that exists is the 'consciousness of his Caste'. That is the reason why the Hindus cannot be said to form a society or a nation. The Caste prevents common activity; and by preventing common activity it has prevented the Hindus from becoming a society with a unified life and a consciousness of its own being.

The literature of the Hindus is full of Caste genealogies in which an attempt is made to give a noble origin to one Caste and an ignoble origin to other Castes. The anti-social spirit, this spirit of protecting its own interests, is as much a marked feature of the different Castes in their isolation from one another as it is of nations in the isolation. The Brahmin's primary concern is to protect 'his interest' against those of the Brahmins. The Hindus, therefore, are not merely an assortment of Castes, but are so many warring groups, each living for itself and for its selfish ideal. The existence of Caste and Caste Consciousness has served to keep the memory of past feuds between Castes green, and has prevented solidarity.

The recent [Constitutional] discussion about the excluded and partially included areas has served to draw attention to the position of what are called the aboriginal tribes in India. They number about 13 millions, if not more. Thirteen millions of people living in the midst of civilization are still in a savage state, and are leading the life of hereditary criminals!! But the Hindus have never felt ashamed of it. These aborigines have remained in their primitive uncivilized state in a land which boasts of a civilisation thousands of years old.

Not that a Hindu could not be taught the sense of duty to fallen humanity, but the trouble is that no amount of sense of duty can enable him to overcome his duty to preserve his Caste. Caste is, therefore, the real explanation as to why the Hindu has let the savage remain a savage in the midst of his civilisation without blushing, or without feeling any sense of remorse or repentance. The higher-Caste Hindus have deliberately prevented the lower Castes who are within the pale of Hinduism from rising to the cultural level of the higher Castes.

The Hindu religion was once a missionary religion must be admitted. It could not have spread over the face of India, if it was not a missionary religion. That today it is not a missionary religion is also a fact which must be accepted. The real question is why did the Hindu religion cease to be a missionary religion? Hindu religion ceased to be a missionary religion when the Caste System grew up among the Hindus. Caste is inconsistent with conversion. Inculcation of beliefs and dogmas is not the only problem that is involved in conversion. To find a place for the convert in the social life of the community is another and a much more important problem that arises in connection with conversion. Hindu Society being a collection of Castes and each Caste being a close corporation there is no place for a convert. Thus it is the Caste which has prevented the Hindus from expanding and from absorbing other religious communities. So long as Caste remains, there will be no *Sanghatan*; and so long as there is no *Sanghatan* the Hindu will remain weak and meek....

Why is the Hindu indifferent? In my opinion, this indifferentism is the result of the Caste System, which has made *Sanghatan* and co-operation even for a good cause impossible. A Caste has an unquestioned right to excommunicate any man who is guilty of breaking the rules of the Caste; and when it is realized that excommunication involves a complete cessation of social intercourse, it will be agreed that as a form of punishment there is really little to choose between excommunication and death. No wonder individual Hindus have not had the courage to assert their independence by breaking the barriers of Caste. A Caste is ever ready to take advantage of the helplessness of a man, and to insist upon complete conformity to its code in letter and in spirit. Caste in the hands of the orthodox has been a powerful weapon for persecuting the reformers and for killing all reform.

The effect of Caste on the ethics of the Hindus is simply deplorable. Caste has killed public spirit. Caste has destroyed the sense of public charity. Caste has made public opinion impossible. A Hindu's public is his Caste. His responsibility is only to his Caste. His loyalty is restricted only to his Caste. Virtue has become Caste-ridden, and morality has become Caste-bound. There is no sympathy for the deserving. There is sympathy, but not for men of other Castes. There is charity to the needy. There is charity, but it begins with the Caste and ends with the Caste.

The reasons which have made *shudhi* impossible for Hindus are also responsible for making *Sanghatan* impossible. The idea underlying *Sanghatan* is to remove from the mind of the Hindu that timidity and cowardice which so painfully make him off from the Mohammedan and the Sikh, and which have led him to adopt the low ways of treachery and cunning for protecting himself. The question naturally arises: From where does the Sikh or the Mohammedan derive his strength which makes him brave and fearless? I am sure it is not due to relative superiority of physical strength, diet or drill. It is due to the strength arising out of the feeling that all Sikhs will come to the rescue of a Sikh when he is in danger and that all Mohammedans will rush to save a Muslim if he is attacked. The Hindu can derive no such strength. He cannot feel assured that his fellows will come to his help. Being one and fated to be alone he remains powerless, develops timidity and cowardice and in a fight surrenders or runs away. The Sikh as well as the Muslim stands fearless and gives battle because he knows that though one he will not be alone. The presence of this belief in the one helps him to hold out and the absence of it in the other makes him to give way.

If you pursue this matter further and ask what is it that enables the Sikh and the Mohammedan to feel so assured, and why is the Hindu filled with such despair in the matter of help and assistance you will find that the reasons for this difference lie in the difference in their associated mode of living. The associated mode of life practised by the Sikhs and the Mohammedans produces fellow-feeling. The associated mode of life of the Hindus does not. Among Sikhs and Muslims there is a social cement which makes them *Bhais*. Among Hindus there is no such cement, and one Hindu does not regard another Hindu as his *Bhai*. This explains why a Sikh says and feels that one Sikh, or one Khalsa is equal to *Sava Lakh* men. This explains why one Mohammedan is equal to a crowd of Hindus. This difference is undoubtedly a difference due to Caste. So long as Caste remains, there will be no *Sanghatan* and so long as there is no *Sanghatan* the Hindu will remain weak and meek.

Why is the Hindu so indifferent? In my opinion this indifferentism is the result of Caste System which has made *Sanghatan* and co-operation even for a good cause impossible. A Caste has an unquestioned right to excommunicate any man who is guilty of breaking the rules of the Caste; and when it is realized that excommunication involves a complete cessation of social intercourse it will be agreed that as a form of punishment there is really little to choose between excommunication and death. No wonder individual Hindus have not had the courage to assert their independence by breaking the barriers of Caste....A Caste is ever ready to take advantage of the helplessness of a man, and to insist upon complete conformity to its code in letter and in spirit. Caste in the hands of the orthodox has been a powerful weapon for persecuting the reforms and for killing all reform.

The effect of Caste on the ethics of the Hindus is simply deplorable. Caste has killed public spirit. Caste has destroyed the sense of public charity. Caste has made public opinion impossible. A Hindu's public is his Caste. His responsibility is only to his Caste. His loyalty is restricted only to his Caste. Virtue has become Caste-ridden and morality has become Caste-bound. There is no sympathy to the deserving. There is sympathy but not for men of other Caste. There is no charity to the needy. There is charity but it begins with the Caste and ends with the Caste. The capacity to appreciate merits in a man apart from his Caste does not exist in a Hindu. My Caste-man, right or wrong, my Caste-man, good or bad. It is not a case of standing by virtue and not standing by vice. It is a case of standing or not standing by the Caste. What is your ideal society if you do not want Caste is a question that is bound to be asked. If you ask me, my ideal would be a society based on Liberty, Equality and Fraternity. And why not?

What objection can there be to Fraternity? In an ideal society there should be many interests consciously communicated and shared. There should be varied and free points of contact with other modes of association. In other words there must be social endosmosis. This is fraternity, which is only another name for democracy. Democracy is not merely a form of Government. It is essentially an attitude of respect and reverence towards fellowmen.

Any objection to Liberty? Why not allow a person the liberty to benefit from an effective and competent use of a person's powers? The supporters of Caste who would allow liberty in the sense of a right to life, limb, and property, would not readily consent to liberty in this sense, inasmuch as it involves liberty to choose one's profession. But to object to this kind of liberty is to perpetuate slavery. It is found where, as in the Caste System, some persons are compelled to carry on certain prescribed callings which are not of their choice.

Any objection to equality? This has obviously been the most contentious part of the slogan of the French Revolution. Equality may be a fiction, but nonetheless one must accept it as the governing principle. A man's power is dependent upon (1) physical heredity; (2) social inheritance or endowment in the form of parental care, education, accumulation of scientific knowledge, and finally; (3) on his own efforts. In all these three respects men are undoubtedly unequal. But the question is, shall we treat them as unequal because they are unequal?

But what would happen if men were treated as unequally in the first two respects? It is obvious that selection under such circumstances would not be a selection of the able. It would be the selection of the privileged. The reason, therefore, requires that in the third respect we should treat men unequally and that in the first two respects we should treat men as equally as possible. The Statesman, therefore, must follow some rough and ready rule, and treat all men alike, not because they are alike but because classification and assortment is impossible.

The three Classes, Brahmins, *Kshatriyas* and *Vaishyas*, although not very happy in their mutual relationship, managed to work by compromise. The Brahmin flattered the *Kshatriya*, and both let the *Vaishya* live in order to be able to live upon him. But the three agreed to beat down the *Shudra*. He was not allowed to acquire wealth, lest he should be independent of the three [higher] *Varnas*. He was prohibited from acquiring knowledge, lest he should keep a steady vigil regarding his interests. He was prohibited from bearing arms, lest he should have the means to rebel against their authority. That this is how the *Shudras* were treated by the *Tryavarnikas* is evidenced by the laws of Manu.

Why have the mass of people tolerated the social evils to which they have been subjected? There have been social revolutions in other countries of the world. Why have there not been social revolutions in India? There is only one answer and it is that the lower Classes of Hindus have been completely disabled for direct action on account of this wretched Caste System. They could not bear arms, and without arms they could not rebel. On account of the Caste System, they could receive no education. They could not think out or know the way to their salvation.

Social war has been raging between the strong and the weak far more violently in Europe than it has even been in India. Yet the weak in Europe has had in his freedom of military service, his physical weapon; in suffering, his political weapon; and in education, his moral weapon. These three weapons for emancipation were never withheld by the strong from the weak in Europe. All these weapons were, however, denied to the masses in India by the Caste System.

There is only one period in Indian history which is a period of freedom, greatness and glory. That is the period of the Mourya Empire. At all other times the country suffered from defeat and darkness. But the Mourya period was a period when the Caste System was completely annihilated—when the *Shudras*, who constituted the mass of the people, came into their own and became the rulers of the country. The period of defeat and darkness is the period when the Caste System flourished.

The strength of a society depends upon the presence of points of contact, possibilities of interaction between different groups which exist in it. These are what Carlyle calls "organic filaments"—i.e., the elastic threads which help to bring the disintegrating elements together and to reunite them. There is no integrating force among the Hindus to counteract the disintegration caused by Caste, whereas among the Non-Hindus there are plenty of these organic filaments which bind them together.

The Caste does not have the same social significance for non-Hindus as it has for Hindus. Ask a Mohammedan or a Sikh who he is. He tells you that he is a Mohammedan or a Sikh, as the case may be. He does not tell you his Caste, although he has one; and you are satisfied with his answer. But you are not satisfied if a person tells you that he is a Hindu. You feel bound to inquire into his Caste. Why? Because so essential is Caste in the case of a Hindu that without knowing if you do not feel sure what sort of a being his is. Secondly, if you take into consideration the consequences which follow breach of the Caste, the difference becomes amply clear: a Hindu is sure to be outcasted if he broke Caste. There is also a third and a more important difference. Caste among the non-Hindus has no religious consecration; but among the Hindus most decidedly it has. Religion compels the Hindus to treat isolation and segregation of Castes as a virtue. Religion does not compel the non-Hindus to take the same attitude towards Caste. It is, therefore, a dangerous delusion to take comfort in the mere existence of Caste among non-Hindus, without caring to know what place Caste occupies in their life, and whether there are other 'organic filaments' which subordinate the feeling of caste to the feeling of community.

Some Hindus deny that Caste presents any problem at all for the Hindus to consider. Such Hindus seek comfort in the view that the Hindus have survived. This point of view is well expressed by Professor S Radhakrishnan in his 'Hindu View of Life'. It seems to me that the question is not whether a community lives or dies; the question is on what plane it lives. There are different modes of survival. But not all are equally honourable. For an individual as well as for a society, there is a gulf between merely living and living worthily. To fight in a battle and to live in glory is one mode. To beat a retreat, to surrender, and to live the life of captive is also a mode of survival. What he must consider is what the quality of their survival is.

There is no doubt that unless you change your social order you can achieve little by way of progress. You cannot mobilize the community either for defence or for offence. You cannot build anything on the foundations of Caste. You cannot build up a nation, you cannot build up a morality. Anything that you will build on the foundations of Caste will crack, and will never be a whole.

The only question that remains to be considered is—How to bring about the reform of the Hindu social order? How to abolish Caste? This is a question of supreme importance. There is a view that in the reform of Caste, the first step to take is to abolish sub-Castes. This view is based upon the supposition that there is a greater similarity in manners and status between sub-Castes. I think this is an erroneous supposition. Assuming that the fusion of sub-Castes is possible, what guarantee is there that the abolition of sub-Castes will necessarily lead to the abolition of Castes? Another plan of action for the abolition of Caste is to begin with inter-Caste dinners. This also, in my opinion, is an inadequate remedy. I am convinced that the real remedy is inter-marriage. Fusion of blood can alone create the feeling of being kith and kin, and unless this feeling of kinship, of being kindred, becomes paramount, the separatist feeling—the feeling of being aliens—created by Caste will not vanish. The real remedy for breaking Caste is inter-marriage. Nothing else will serve as the solvent of Caste.

Inter-dining and inter-marriage are repugnant to the beliefs and dogmas which the Hindus regard as sacred. Caste may be bad. Caste may lead to conduct so gross as to be called man's inhumanity to man. All the same, it must be recognized that the Hindus observe Caste not because they are inhuman or wrong-headed. They observe Caste because they are deeply religious. What is wrong is their religion, which has inculcated this notion of Caste. Obviously, the enemy to grapple with is not the people who observe Caste, but the *Shastras* which teach them this religion of Caste. Occasionally holding inter-Caste dinners and celebrating inter-Caste marriages is a futile method of achieving the desired end. The real remedy is to destroy the belief in the sanctity of the *Shastras*.

Not to question the authority of the *Shastras*—to permit the people to believe in their sanctity and their sanctions, and then to blame the people and to criticize them for their acts as being irrational and inhuman—is an incongruous way of carrying on social reform. Reformers working for the removal of Untouchability, including Mahatma Gandhi, do not seem to realize that the acts of the people are merely the results of their beliefs inculcated in their minds by the *Shastras*, and that people will not change their conduct until they cease to believe in sanctity of the *Shastras* on which their conduct is founded. To agitate for and to organize inter-Caste dinners and inter-Caste marriages is like forced feeding brought about by artificial means. Make every man and woman free from the thralldom of the *Shastras*, cleanse their minds of the pernicious notions founded on the *Shastras*, and he or she will inter-dine and inter-marry, without your telling him or her to do so.

You must take the stand that Buddha took. You must take the stand which Guru Nanak took. You must not only discard the *Shastras*, you must deny their authority, as did Buddha and Nanak. You must have courage to tell the Hindus that what is wrong with them is their religion – the religion which has produced in them this notion of the sacredness of Caste. Will you show that courage?

Social reforms fall into different species. The most difficult one among them is the reform which not only touches the religious principles but is diametrically opposed to those principles, and invites people to depart from and to discard their authority, and to act contrary to those principles. Caste is the natural outcome of certain religious beliefs which have the sanction of the *Shastras*. The destruction of Caste is a reform which falls under this category.

This is a stupendous task, well-nigh impossible. The Hindus hold to the sacredness of the social order. Caste has a divine basis. You must, therefore, destroy the sacredness and divinity with which Caste has become invested. In the last analysis, this means you must destroy the authority of the *Shastras* and the Vedas.

This task is herculean. Out of the many reasons which have led me to take this view, I will mention some which I regard as most important.

The first reason is the attitude of hostility which the Brahmins have shown towards this question. The Brahmins from the vanguard of the movement for political reform, and in some cases also of economic reform. But they are not to be found even as camp-followers in the army raised to break. The break-up of the Caste System is bound to adversely affect the Brahmin Caste. Is it reasonable to expect that the Brahmins will ever consent to lead a movement, the ultimate result of which is to destroy the power and prestige of the Brahmin Caste?

The Brahmins form the intellectual Class of the Hindus. It is not only an intellectual Class, but it is a Class which is held in great reverence by the rest of the Hindus. When such an intellectual Class, which holds the rest of the community in its grip, is opposed to the reform of Caste, the chances of success in a movement for the break-up of the Caste System appear to me very, very remote.

The second reason why I say the task is impossible will be clear, if you will bear in mind that the Caste System has two aspects. In one of its aspects, it divides men into separate communities. In its second aspect, it places these communities in a graded order one above the other in social status. Each Caste takes its pride and its consolation in the fact that in the scale of Castes it is above some other Caste. As an outward mark of this gradation, there is also a gradation of social and religious rights, technically spoken of as *Ashtadhikaras* and *Sanskaras*. The higher the grade of a Caste, the greater the number of these rights; and the lower the grade, the lesser their number. All are slaves of the Caste System. But all the slaves are not equal in status.

Castes from a graded system of sovereignties, high and low, which are jealous of their status and which know that if a general dissolution came, some of them stand to lose more of their prestige and power than others do. You cannot, therefore, have a general mobilization of the Hindus for an attack on the Caste System. Can you appeal to reason, and ask the Hindus to discard Caste as being contrary to reason? That raises the question: Is a Hindu free to follow his reason?

So far as Caste and *Varna* are concerned, not only the *Shastras* do not permit the Hindu to use his reason in the decision of the question, but they have taken care to see that no occasion is left to examine in a rational way the foundations of his belief in Caste and *Varna*.

It is true that Manu has included *Sadachar* as one of the sanctions along with *Shruti* and *Smriti*. As though to warn people against the view *Sadachar* means good acts or acts of good men, and fearing that people might understand it that way and follow the acts of good men, the *Smritis* have commended the Hindus in unmistakable terms not to follow even Gods in their good deeds, if they are contrary to *Shruti*, *Smriti* and *Sadachar*. This may sound to be most extraordinary, most perverse, but the fact remains that it is an injection issued to the Hindus by their *Shastras*.

Reason and morality are the two most powerful weapons in the armoury of a reformer. To deprive him of the use of these weapons is to disable him for action. How are you going to break up Caste if people are not free to consider whether it accords with reason? How are you going to break up Caste if people are not free to consider whether it accords with morality? The wall built around Caste is impregnable, and the material of which it is built contains none of the combustible stuff of reason and morality. Add to this the fact that inside this wall stands the army of Brahmins who form the intellectual Class, Brahmins who are the natural leaders of the Hindus, Brahmins who are there not as mere mercenary soldiers but as an army fighting for its homeland, and you will get an idea why I think that the breaking up of Caste among the Hindus is well-nigh impossible. At any rate, it would take ages before a breach is made.

But whether the doing of the deed takes time or whether it can be done quickly, you must not forget that if you wish to bring about a breach in the system, then you have got to apply the dynamite to the Vedas and the *Shastras*, which deny any part to reason; to the Vedas and *Shastras*, which deny any part to morality. You must destroy the religion of the *Shrutis* and the *Smritis*. Nothing else will avail. This is my considered view of the matter.[69]

Some may not understand what I mean by destruction of Religion; some may find the idea revolting to them, and some may find it revolutionary. Let me, therefore, explain my position. I draw a distinction between principles and rules. Rules are practical; they are habitual ways of doing things according to prescription. But principles are intellectual; they are useful methods of judging things. Rules seek to tell an agent just what course of action to pursue. Principles do not prescribe a specific course of action. Rules, like cooking recipes, do tell just what to do and how to do it.

69. This thought of applying dynamite to the Vedas and *Shastras* became the most contentious leading to the cancellation of the Conference organized by the Jat-Pat Todak Mandal of Lahore.

What is this Hindu Religion? Is it a set of principles, or is it a code of rules? Now the Hindu Religion, as contained in the Vedas and the *Smritis*, is nothing but a mass of sacrificial, social, political and sanitary rules and regulations, all mixed up.

What is called Religion by the Hindus is nothing but a multitude of commands and prohibitions. Religion, in the sense of spiritual principles, truly universal applicable to all races, to all countries to all times, is not to be found in them; and if it is it does not form the governing part of a Hindu's life. That for a Hindu, *Dharma* means commands and prohibitions. To put it in plain language, what the Hindus call Religion is really Law, or at best legalized Class-ethics.

The first evil of such a code of ordinances is that it tends to deprive moral life of freedom and spontaneity, and to reduce it to a more or less anxious and servile conformity to externally imposed rules. Under it, there is not loyalty to ideals; there is only conformity to commands. But the worst evil of this code of ordinances is that the laws it contains must be the same yesterday, today, and forever. They are iniquitous in that they are not the same for one class as for another. But this iniquity is made perpetual in that they are prescribed to be the same for all generations. I have, therefore, no hesitation in saying that such a religion must be destroyed, and I say there is nothing irreligious in working for the destruction of such a religion.

Indeed, I hold that it is your bounden duty to tear off the mask, to remove the misrepresentation that is caused by misnaming this Law as Religion. This is an essential step for you. Once you clear the minds of the people of this misconception, and enable them to realize that what they are told is Religion is not Religion, but that it is really Law, you will be in a position to urge its amendment or abolition. So long as people look upon it as Religion they will not be ready for a change, because the idea of Religion is, generally speaking, not associated with the idea of change. But the idea of law is associated with the idea of change, and when people come to know that what is called Religions is really Law, old and archaic, they will be ready for a change, for people know and accept that law can be changed.

While I condemn a Religion of Rules, I must not be understood to hold the opinion that there is no necessity for a religion. On the contrary, I agree with Burke when he says, "True religion is the foundation of society, the basis on which all true Civil Government rests and both their sanction." Consequently, when I urge that these ancient rules of life be annulled, I am anxious that their place shall be taken by a religion of Principles, which alone can lay claim to being a true Religion. The following, in my opinion, should be the cardinal items in this reform:

(1) There should be one and only one standard book of Hindu Religion, acceptable to all Hindus and recognized by all Hindus. All other books of Hindu religion such as Vedas, *Shastras* and Puranas, which are treated as sacred and authoritative, must by law cease to be so, and the preaching of any doctrine, religious or social, contained in these books should be penalized.

(2) The priesthood must cease to be hereditary. Every person who professes to be a Hindu must be eligible for being a priest. The priestly Class must be brought under control by some legislation. This will prevent it from doing mischief, and from misguiding people. It will democratize it by throwing it open to everyone. It will certainly help to kill the Brahminism and will also help to kill Caste, which is nothing but Brahminism incarnate. Brahminism is the poison which

has spoiled Hinduism. You will succeed in saving Hinduism if you will kill Brahminism.

You must give a new doctrinal basis to your Religion—a basis that will be in consonance with Liberty, Equality and Fraternity; in short, with Democracy. This means a complete change in the fundamental notions of life. It means a complete change in the values of life. It means a complete change in outlook and in attitude towards men and things.

It means new life. But a new life cannot enter a body that is dead. New life can enter only into a new body. The old body must die before a new body can come into existence and a new life can enter into it. To put it simply: the old must cease to be operative before the new can begin to enliven and to pulsate. This is what I meant when I said you must discard the authority of the *Shastras*, and destroy the religion of the *Shastras*.

I would like, before I close, to place before the Hindus, if they will allow me some questions which I regard as vital, and invite them seriously to consider the same.

In the first place, the Hindus must consider whether it is not necessary to make an attempt to find out what kind of morality, beliefs, habits, and outlook have worked best and have enabled those who possessed them to flourish, to grow strong, to people the earth and to have dominion over it.

Secondly, the Hindus must consider whether they should conserve the whole of their social heritage, or select what is helpful and transmit to future generations only that must and no more.

Thirdly, the Hindus must consider whether they must not cease to worship the past as supplying their ideals.

Fourthly, the Hindus must consider whether the time has not come for them to recognize that there is nothing fixed, nothing eternal, nothing sanatan; that everything is changing, that change is the law of life for individuals as well as for society. In a changing society, there must be a constant revolution of old values; and the Hindus must realize that if there must be standards to measure the acts of men, there must also be readiness to revise those standards.

These views are the views of a man who has been no tool of power, no flatterer of greatness. They come from one, almost the whole of whose public exertion has been one continuous struggle for liberty for the poor and for the oppressed, and whose only reward has been continuous shower of calumny and abuse from national journals and national leaders, for no other reason except that I refuse to join with them in performing the miracle—I will not say trick—of liberating the oppressed with the gold of the tyrant, and raising the poor with the cash of the rich.

Yours is more difficult than the other national cause, namely, *Swaraj*. In the fight for *Swaraj* you fight with the whole nation on your side. In this, you have to fight against the whole nation and that too, your own. But it is more important than *Swaraj*. There is no use having *Swaraj*, if you cannot defend it. More important than the question of defending *Swaraj* is the question of defending the Hindus under the *Swaraj*. In my opinion, it is only when Hindu Society becomes a Casteless society that it can hope to have strength enough to defend itself. Without such internal strength, *Swaraj* for Hindus may turn out to be only a step towards slavery.

★ ★ ★

B. GANDHIJI'S CRITIQUE

Soon after the publication of *Annihilation of Castes*, Mahatma Gandhi responded by way of two articles:[70]

(i) "Dr Ambedkar's Indictment" (*Harijan*, July 18, 1936); and
(ii) "*Varna* Versus Caste" (*Harijan*, August 15, 1936)

The second article also contains a letter from Shri Sant Ram of the *Jat-Pat-Todak Mandal*, Lahore.

Dr Ambedkar reprinted the two articles in the Second Edition of his book (1937) as Appendix I and also presented his own views in reply to Gandhiji's two articles, as (Appendix II) titled: "A Reply to the Mahatma".

Dr Ambedkar's motivation in writing this Article has been articulated in the Preface to the Second Edition. He said:

> Besides Mr Gandhi, many others have adversely criticized my views as expressed in my speech. But I have felt that in taking notice of such adverse comments I should limit myself to Mr Gandhi. This I have done not because what he has said is so weighty as to deserve a reply, but because to many a Hindu he is an oracle, so great that when he opens his lips it is expected that the argument must close and no dog must bark. But the world owes much to rebels who would dare to argue in the face of the pontiff and insist that he is not infallible. I do not care for the credit which every progressive society must give to its rebels. I shall be satisfied, if I make the Hindus realize that they are the sick men of India and that their sickness is causing danger to the health and happiness of other Indians.

C. DR AMBEDKAR'S "REPLY TO THE MAHATMA"

The full text of Dr Ambedkar's response is as follows:

> I appreciate greatly the honour done me by the Mahatma in taking notice in his *Harijan* of the speech on Caste which I had prepared for the *Jat Pat Todak Mandal*. From a perusal of his review of my speech it is clear that the Mahatma completely dissents from the views I have expressed on the subject of Caste. I am not in the habit of entering into controversy with my opponents unless there are special reasons which compel me to act otherwise. Had my opponent been some mean and obscure person I would not have pursued him. But my opponent being the Mahatma himself I feel I must attempt to meet the case to the contrary which he has sought to put forth.
>
> I must confess to a sense of surprise on finding that of all the persons, the Mahatma should accuse me of a desire to seek publicity, as he seems to do when he suggests that in publishing the undelivered speech my object was to see that I was not 'forgotten'. Whatever the Mahatma may choose to say, my object in publishing the speech was to provoke the Hindus to think and take stock of their position. I have never hankered for publicity and, if I may say so, I have more of it than I wish or need. But supposing

70. For the two Articles by Gandhiji, see *Ambedkar Speaks*, op cit. Vol. I, pp. 165-68.

it was out of the motive of gaining publicity that I printed the speech who could cast a stone at me? Surely not those, who like the Mahatma live in glass houses.

Motive apart, what has the Mahatma to say on the question raised by me in the speech? First of all anyone who reads my speech will realize that the Mahatma has entirely missed the issues raised by me and that the issues he has raised are not the issues that arise out of what he is pleased to call my indictment of the Hindus.

The principal points which I have tried to make out in my speech may be catalogued as follows:

(1) That Caste has ruined the Hindus;

(2) That the reorganization of the Hindu society on the basis of *Chaturvarnya* is impossible because the *Varnavyavastha* is like a leaky pot or like a man running at the nose. It is incapable of sustaining itself by its own virtue and has an inherent tendency to degenerate into a Caste System unless there is a legal sanction behind it which can be enforced against every one transgressing his *Varna*;

(3) That the reorganization of the Hindu Society on the basis of *Chaturvarnya* is harmful, because the effect of the *Varnavyavastha* is to degrade the masses by denying them opportunity to acquire knowledge and to emasculate them by denying them the right to be armed ;

(4) That the Hindu society must be reorganized on a religious basis which would recognize the principles of Liberty, Equality and Fraternity;

(5) That in order to achieve this object the sense of religious sanctity behind Caste and *Varna* must be destroyed;

(6) That the sanctity of Caste and *Varna* can be destroyed only by discarding the divine authority of the *Shastras*.

It will be noticed that the questions raised by the Mahatma are absolutely beside the point and show that the main argument of the speech was lost upon him.

Let me examine the substance of the points made by the Mahatma. The first point made by the Mahatma is that the texts cited by me are not authentic. I confess I am no authority on this matter. But I should like to state that the texts cited by me are all taken from the writings of the late Mr Tilak who was a recognised authority on the Sanskrit language and on the Hindu *Shastras*. His second point is that these *Shastras* should be interpreted not by the learned but the saints and that, as the saints have understood them, the *Shastras* do not support Caste and Untouchability.

As regards the first point, what I like to ask the Mahatma is what does it avail to any one if the texts are interpolations and if they have been differently interpreted by the saints? The masses do not make any distinction between texts which are genuine and texts which are interpolations. The masses do not know what the texts are. They are too illiterate to know the contents of the *Shastras*. They have believed what they have been told and what they have been told is that the *Shastras* do enjoin as a religious duty the observance of Caste and Untouchability. With regard to the saints, one must admit that howsoever different and elevating their teachings may have been as compared to those of the merely learned, they have been lamentably ineffective. They have been ineffective for two reasons. Firstly, none of the saints ever attacked the Caste System. On the contrary, they were staunch believers in the System of Castes. Most of them lived and died as members of the Castes which they respectively belonged. So passionately attached was Jnyandeo to his status as a Brahmin that when the Brahmins of Paithan would not admit him to their fold, he moved heaven and earth to get his status as a Brahmin recognized by the Brahmin fraternity.

And even the saint Eknath who now figures in the film, *Dharmatma*, as a hero for having shown courage to touch the Untouchables and dine with them did so not because he was opposed to Caste and Untouchability but because he felt that the pollution caused thereby could be washed away by a bath in the sacred waters of the river Ganges. The saints have never, according to my study, carried on a campaign against Caste and Untouchability. They were not concerned with the struggle between men. They were concerned with the relation between man and God.

They did not preach that all men were equal. They preached that all men were equal, in the eyes of God a very different and a very innocuous proposition which nobody can find difficult to preach or dangerous to believe in.

The second reason why the teachings of the saints proved ineffective was because the masses have been taught that a saint might break Caste but the common man must not. A saint, therefore, never became an example to follow. He always remained a pious man to be honoured. That the masses have remained staunch believers in Caste and Untouchability shows that the pious lives and noble sermons of the saints have had no effect on their life and conduct as against the teachings of the *Shastras*. Thus it can be a matter of no consolation that there were saints or that there is a Mahatma who understands the *Shastras* differently from the learned few or ignorant many.

That the masses hold different view of the *Shastras* is fact which should and must be reckoned with. How is that to be dealt with except by denouncing the authority of the *Shastras*, which continue to govern their conduct, is a question which the Mahatma has not considered.

The third point made by the Mahatma is that a religion professed by Chaitanya, Jnyandeo, Tukaram, Tiruvalluvar, RamkrishnaParamahansa etc., cannot be devoid of merit as is made out by me and that a religion has to be judged not by its worst specimens but by the best it might have produced. I agree with every word of this statement. But I do not quite understand what the Mahatma wishes to prove thereby. That religion should be judged not by its worst specimens but by its best is true enough but does it dispose of the matter? I say it does not.

The question still remains—why the worst number so many and the best so few? To my mind there are two conceivable answers to this question: (1) That the worst by reason of some original perversity of theirs are morally uneducable and are, therefore, incapable of making the remotest approach to the religious ideal; or (2) That the religious ideal is a wholly wrong ideal which has given a wrong moral twist to the lives of the many and that the best have become best in spite of the wrong ideal—in fact by giving to the wrong twist a turn in the right direction.

Of these two explanations I am not prepared to accept the first and I am sure that even the Mahatma will not insist upon the contrary. To my mind the second is the only logical and reasonable explanation unless the Mahatma has a third alternative to explain why the worst are so many and the best so few. If the second is the only explanation then obviously the argument of the Mahatma that a religion should be judged by its best followers carries us nowhere except to pity the lot of the many who have gone wrong because they have been made to worship wrong ideals.

The argument of the Mahatma that Hinduism would be tolerable if only many were to follow the example of the saints is fallacious for another reason.[71] By citing the names of such illustrious persons as Chaitanya etc. What the Mahatma seems to me to suggest in its broadest and simplest form is that Hindu society can be made tolerable and even happy without any fundamental change in its structure, if all the high-Caste Hindus can be persuaded to follow a high standard of morality in their dealings with the low Caste Hindus. I am totally opposed to this kind of ideology.

I can respect those of the Caste Hindus who try to realize a high social ideal in their life. Without such men India would be an uglier and a less happy place to live in than it is. But nonetheless anyone who relies on an attempt to turn the members of the Caste Hindus into better men by improving their personal character is in my judgment wasting his energy and bugging an illusion. Can personal character make the maker of armaments a good man, i.e. a man who will sell shells that will not burst and gas that will not poison? If it cannot, how can you accept personal character to make a man loaded with the consciousness of Caste a good man, i.e. a man who would treat his fellows as his friends and equals? To be true to himself he must deal with his fellows either as a superior or inferior according as the case may be; at any rate, differently from his own Caste fellows. He can never be expected to deal with his fellows as his kinsmen and equals.

As a matter of fact, a Hindu does treat all those who are not of his Caste as though they were aliens, who could be discriminated against with impunity and against whom any fraud or trick may be practised without shame.

In fact, what is wrong is the entire basis of his relationship to his fellows. The best of men cannot be moral if the basis of relationship between them and their fellows is fundamentally a wrong relationship. To a slave his master may be better or worse. But there cannot be a good master. A good man cannot be a master and a master cannot be a good man. The same applies to the relationship between high-Caste and low-Caste.

I have argued in my speech that a society based on *Varna* or Caste is a society which is based on a wrong relationship. I had hoped that the Mahatma would attempt to demolish my argument. But instead of doing that he has merely reiterated his belief in *Chaturvarnya* without disclosing the ground on which it is based.

Does the Mahatma practise what he preaches? One does not like to make personal reference in an argument which is general in its application. But when one preaches a decline and holds it as a dogma there is a curiosity to know how far he practises what he preaches. It may be that his failure to practise is due to the ideal being too high. To be attainable; it may be that his failure to practise is due to the innate hypocrisy of the man. In any case, he exposes his conduct to examination, and I must not be blamed if I asked how far has the Mahatma attempted to realize his ideal in his own case.

The Mahatma is a *Bania* by birth. His ancestors had abandoned trading in favour of ministership which is a calling of the Brahmins. In his own life, before he became a Mahatma, when occasion came for him to choose his career he preferred law to scales.

71. In this connection see illuminating article on "Morality and the Social Structure" by Mr HN Brailsford in the *Aryan Path* for April 1936.

On abandoning law he became half saint and half politician. He has never touched trading which is his ancestral calling.

His youngest son—I take one who is a faithful follower of his father—born a *Vaishya* has married a Brahmin's daughter and has chosen to serve a newspaper magnate. The Mahatma is not known to have condemned him for not following his ancestral calling. It may be wrong and uncharitable to judge an ideal by its worst specimens. But surely the Mahatma as a specimen has no better and if he even fails to realize the ideal then the ideal must be an impossible ideal quite opposed to the practical instincts of man.

When can a calling be deemed to have become an ancestral calling so as to make it binding on a man? Must man follow his ancestral calling even if it does not suit his capacities, even when it has ceased to be profitable? Must a man live by his ancestral calling even if he finds it to be immoral? If everyone must pursue his ancestral calling then it must follow that a man must continue to be a pimp because his grandfather was a pimp, and a woman must continue to be a prostitute because her grandmother was a prostitute. Is the Mahatma prepared to accept the logical conclusion of his doctrine? To me his ideal of following one's ancestral calling is not only an impossible and impractical ideal, but it is also morally an indefensible ideal.

The Mahatma sees great virtue in a Brahmin remaining a Brahmin all his life. He is satisfied that these are real Brahmins who are living on alms freely given to them, and giving freely what they have of spiritual treasures. This is how a hereditary Brahmin priest appears to the Mahatma—a carrier of spiritual treasurers.

But another portrait of the hereditary Brahmin can also be drawn. A Brahmin can be a priest to Vishnu—the God of Love. He can be a priest to Shankar—the God of Destruction. He can be a priest at Buddha Gaya worshipping Buddha—the greatest teacher of mankind who taught the noblest doctrine of Love. He also can be a priest to Kali, the Goddess, who must have a daily sacrifice of an animal to satisfy her thirst for blood. He will be a priest of the temple of Rama—the *Kshatriya* God! He will also be a priest of the Temple of Parshuram, the God who took Avatar to destroy the *Kshatriyas*! He can be a priest to Bramha, the Creator of the world. He can be a priest to a Pir whose God Allah will not brook the claim of Bramha to share his spiritual dominion over the world! No one can say that this is a picture which is not true to life.

If this is a true picture, one does not know what to say of this capacity to bear loyalties to Gods and Goddesses whose attributes are so antagonistic that no honest man can be a devotee to all of them. That a man is ready to render homage to many Gods and Goddesses may be cited as evidence of his tolerant spirit.

I am sure that this toleration is merely insincerity. Not only must such a person be deemed to be bankrupt of all spiritual treasures, but for him to practice so elevating a profession as that of a priest simply because it is ancestral, without faith, without belief, merely as a mechanical process handed down from father to son, is not a conservation of virtue; it is really the prostitution of a noble profession which is no other than the service of religion.

Why does the Mahatma cling to the theory of every one following his or her ancestral calling? He gives his reasons nowhere, but there must be some reason although he does not care to avow it. Years ago writing on 'Caste versus Class' in his *Young India* he argued that Caste System was better than Class System on the ground that Caste was the best possible adjustment of social stability. If that be the reason why the Mahatma clings to the theory of every one following his or her ancestral calling, then he is clinging to a false view of social life.

Everybody wants social stability and some adjustment must be made in the relationship between individuals and Classes in order that stability may be had. Stability is wanted but not at the cost of change when change is imperative. The Second thing nobody wants is mere adjustment. Adjustment is wanted but not at the sacrifice of social justice.

Can it be said that the adjustment of social relationship on the basis of Caste i.e. on the basis of each to his hereditary calling avoids these two evils? I am convinced that it does not. Far from being the best possible adjustment I have no doubt that it is of the worst possible kind inasmuch as it offends against both the canons of social adjustment—namely, fluidity and equity.

Some might think that the Mahatma has made much progress inasmuch as he now only believes in *Varna* and does not believe in Caste. It is true that there was a time when he condemned the cry for inter-dining, inter-drinking and inter-marrying, and argued that restraints about inter-dining to a great extent helped the cultivation of willpower and the conservation of certain social virtue.

It is good that he has repudiated this sanctimonious nonsense and admitted that Caste is harmful both to spiritual and national growth, and maybe, his son's marriage outside his Caste has had something to do with this change of view.

But has the Mahatma really progressed? What is the nature of the *Varna* for which the Mahatma stands? Is it the Vedic conception as commonly understood and preached by Swami Dayanand Saraswati and his followers, the Arya Samajists? The essence of the Vedic conception of *Varna* is the pursuit of a calling which is appropriate to one's natural aptitude.

What is the difference between Caste and *Varna* as understood by the Mahatma? I find none. As defined by the Mahatma, *Varna* becomes merely a different name for Caste for the simple reason that it is the same in essence—namely, pursuit of ancestral calling. Far from making progress the Mahatma has suffered retrogression. By putting this interpretation upon the Vedic conception of *Varna* he has really made ridiculous what was sublime.

The Mahatma's view of *Varna* not only makes nonsense of the Vedic *Varna* but it makes it an abominable thing. *Varna* and Caste are two very different concepts. *Varna* is based on the principle of each according to his worth-while; Caste is based on the principle of each according to his birth. The two are as distinct as chalk is from cheese. In fact, there is an antithesis between the two. If the Mahatma believes as he does in every one following his or her ancestral calling, then most certainly he is advocating the Caste System, and that in calling it the *Varna* System he is not only guilty of terminological inexactitude, but he is causing confusion worse confounded.

I am sure that all his confusion is due to the fact that the Mahatma has no definite and clear conception as to what is *Varna* and what is Caste and as to the necessity of either for the conservation of Hinduism.

In his article on 'Dr Ambedkar's Indictment' he says, 'The essence of Hinduism is contained in its enunciation of one and only God as Truth, and its bold acceptance of *Ahimsa* as the law of the human family.'

But in his article in reply to Mr Sant Ram will say, 'Yes.' In that article he says, 'How can a Muslim remain one if he rejects the Quran, or a Christian remain as Christian if he rejects the Bible? If Caste and *Varna* are convertible terms, and if *Varna* is an integral part of the *Shastras* which define Hinduism, I do not know how a person who rejects Caste, i.e. *Varna* can call himself a Hindu?'

Why this prevarication? Why does the Mahatma hedge? Whom does he want to please? Has the saint failed to sense the truth? Or does the politician stand in the way of the Saint?

The source of confusion is the double role which the Mahatma wants to play—of a Mahatma and a Politician. As a Mahatma he may be trying to spiritualize Politics. Whether he has succeeded in it or not Politics have certainly commercialized him. A politician must know that Society cannot bear the whole truth and that he must not speak the whole truth; if he is speaking the whole truth it is bad for his politics. The reason why the Mahatma is always supporting Caste and *Varna* is because he is afraid that if he opposed them he will lose his place in politics. Whatever may be the source of this confusion the Mahatma must be told that he is deceiving himself and also deceiving the people by preaching Caste under the name of *Varna*.

The Mahatma says that the standards I have applied to test Hindus and Hinduism are too severe and that judged by those standards every known living faith will probably fail. But the question is not whether they are high or whether they are low. A People and their Religion must be judged by social standards based on social ethics. No other standard would have any meaning if religion is held to be a necessary good for the well-being of the people.

The conclusion that every known religion would fail if tested by my standards may be true. But this fact should not give the Mahatma as the champion of Hindus and Hinduism a ground for comfort any more than the existence of one madman should give comfort to another madman or the existence of one criminal should give comfort to another criminal.

I like to assure the Mahatma that it is not the mere failure of the Hindus and Hinduism which has produced in me the feelings of disgust and contempt. I am disgusted with Hindus and Hinduism it is because I am convinced that they cherish wrong ideals and live a wrong social life. My quarrel with Hindus and Hinduism is not over the imperfections of their social conduct. It is much more fundamental. It is over their ideals.

Hindu society seems to me to stand in need of a moral regeneration which it is dangerous to postpone. And the question is who can determine and control this moral regeneration? Obviously, only those who have undergone an intellectual regeneration and those who are honest enough to have the courage of their convictions born of intellectual emancipation.

The Hindu masses are, of course, incredibly heedless in the formation of their beliefs. But so are the Hindu leaders. And what is worse is that. These Hindu leaders become filled with an illicit passion for their beliefs when any one proposes to rob them of their companionship.

The Mahatma is no exception. The Mahatma appears not to believe in thinking He prefers to follow the saints. But it is equally true that dependence on saints cannot lead us to know the truth.

Insofar as he [the Mahatma] does think, to me he really appears to be prostituting his intelligence to find reasons for support this archaic social structure of the Hindus. He is the most influential apologist of it and, therefore, the worst enemy of the Hindus.

Unlike the Mahatma there are Hindu leaders who are not content merely to believe and follow. They dare to think and act in accordance with the result of their thinking. But unfortunately they are either a dishonest lot or an indifferent lot when it comes to the question of giving right guidance to the mass of the people. For one honest Brahmin preaching against Caste and *Shastras* because his practical instinct and moral conscience cannot support a conviction in them, there are hundreds who break Caste and trample upon the *Shastras* every day but who are the most fanatic upholders of the theory of Caste and the sanctity of the *Shastras*. Why this duplicity? Because they feel that if the masses are emancipated from the yoke of Caste, they would be a menace to the power and prestige of the Brahmins as a Class. The dishonesty of this intellectual Class, who would deny the masses the fruits of their thinking is a most disgraceful phenomenon.

The Hindus in the words of Mathew Arnold are 'wandering between two worlds, one dead, the other powerless to be born.' What are they to do? The Mahatma to whom they appeal for guidance does not believe in thinking, and can, therefore, give no guidance which can be said to stand the test of experience. The intellectual Classes to whom the masses look for guidance are either too dishonest or too indifferent to educate them in the right direction.

In the face of this tragedy all one can do is to lament and say—such be thy Leaders, O! Hindus.

PART IV

SCHOLAR - POLITICIAN
(1936-42)

CHAPTER NINETEEN

Formal Entry into Politics

IN THE EARLY 1930S, Dr Ambedkar had favoured a political strategy based on the demand for separate electorates for the Untouchables. When Gandhiji succeeded in countering his strategy through the Poona Pact of 1932, after the initial setback, Dr Ambedkar made a comeback through a war on the Caste System and announcement of conversion into some other religion.

Dr Ambedkar's bold declaration of war on Hinduism not only broadened his support base and ensured his continued leadership of the Depressed Classes but also brought about further intellectual transition towards socio-economic radicalism.

Under the Government of India Act, 1935, Provincial Autonomy was going to be inaugurated through election. The Government of India Act, 1935 conferred new responsibilities on the Legislative Councils besides widening the franchise, and granted to Untouchables the quota of reserve seats as per the Poona Pact. Dr Ambedkar quickly re-oriented his strategy to position the Depressed Classes in the new institutional framework. In view of the proposed first ever Provincial elections in August 1936, Dr Ambedkar formed his first political party, called the Independent Labour Party (ILP).

In the 1920s, when the labour movement in India was dominated by the Communist-led trade unions, several calls for strike were given by textile workers in 1924, 1925, 1928 and 1929. Reportedly, the April 1929 strike covered as many as 75,000 workers from textile mills in Mumbai. Yet another major strike was called in April 1934 during the year in which Dr Ambedkar became the President of Bombay Municipal Karmachari Sangh. During this period, Dr Ambedkar, through his mouth-pieces—Bahishkrit Bharat and later Janata, had appealed to the Depressed Class Workers to refrain from joining the strikes on the ground that the strikes were politically motivated and would cause economic distress to them. Not surprisingly, the Communists had branded Dr Ambedkar as an "enemy of labour".

INDEPENDENT LABOUR PARTY: BROAD PROGRAMME

In an interview with a representation of the *Times of India*, Dr Ambedkar declared that having regard to the fact that the present was no time for the parties communally organized, he had broadened the name and also the programme of the party, so as to permit political co-operation between the other Classes and the Depressed Classes. The nucleus of the Party would still be the fifteen members of the Depressed Classes. But members of the other Classes were free to join the party.

Dr Ambedkar added that the Depressed Classes possessed large voting strength in constituencies in which no seat was reserved for them, and it would be possible for them to place that voting strength at the disposal of any candidate, who cared to become a member of the party.

He made it clear that the Party membership was open to persons of all creeds and communities, although the Depressed Classes' votes could by reason of the law be made available to persons belonging to such communities and creeds as were included in the general electorate. Already, some persons from other Classes had expressed their willingness to join the party, and others who cared to take advantage of that opportunity might correspond with the Secretary of the Party.

Questioned what cohesion the Independent Labour Party would have, Dr Ambedkar pointed out that the Party would have its roots in the electorate, and its members would have fought the election as such, would have pledged to the electorate to uphold a common and clearly defined programme, and to be bound by the rules of discipline framed by the party.

Asked what prompted him to select that particular name for the Party, Dr Ambedkar explained that the party would be independent of every other political organization, although it would be ready to co-operate with any other political party where co-operation was possible. The Party was a labour organization in the sense that its programme was mainly to advance the welfare of the labouring Classes. "The Party believes in having a correct ideology suited to the section of the people whose interests it regards as paramount. The word 'Labour' is used instead of the word 'Depressed Classes', because labour includes the 'Depressed Classes' as well."

(A) Working the Constitution Despite Defects

Explaining the programme of the Party, Dr Ambedkar said that it had been formulated after mature consideration and in consultation with all those who were interested in it, so far as the new Constitution was concerned.

> The Party recognizes that the new Constitution is full of defects and falls much short of full responsible Government. The party objects to several features of the Provincial Constitution, particularly the institution of the second Chamber. All the same Party believes in working the Constitution. But while prepared to work the Constitution, the Party will strive to see that the Special Emergency and Reserved Powers vested in

the Governor are not exercised in a manner which altogether nullifies the system of responsible Government.

(B) Economic Questions

As regards the economic questions:

The Party will undertake to establish land mortgage banks, agriculturist producer's co-operative societies and marketing societies with a view to improving the productivity of agriculture.

The Party thinks that 'fragmentation of holdings' is a severe handicap in the way of the application of capital and improved methods of cultivation to agriculture, and is, therefore, a direct cause of the poverty of the agriculturists.

The Party, however, believes that the fragmentation of holding and the consequent poverty of the agriculturists are mainly due to the pressure of population on the land, and unless the pressure is relieved by draining off the excess population subsisting on land, fragmentation will continue, and the condition of the agriculturists will remain as poverty-stricken as it is today. In the opinion of the Party the principal means of helping the agriculturists and making agriculture more productive consists in the industrialization of the Province. The Party will, therefore, endeavour to rehabilitate old industries and promote such new industries as the natural resources of the Provinces will permit.

To raise the efficiency and productive capacity of the people the Party will endeavour to undertake an extensive programme of technical education.

The Party accepts the principle of State management and State ownership of industry, whenever it may become necessary in the interest of the people.

The Party will endeavour to remove all obstacles to free and full life and to alter, amend or abolish any economic system which is unjust to any Class or section of the people.

The Party will undertake legislation to protest agricultural tenants from the exactions and evictions by the landlords in general and in particular the tenants under (i) the *Khoti* System; and (ii) the *Talukdari* system.

The Party will endeavour to provide for the workers, agricultural as well as industrial, a minimum standard of living compatible with civilized life.

For the benefit of the industrial workers the Party will endeavour to introduce legislation to control the employment, dismissal and promotion of employees in factories, to fix maximum hours of work, to make provision for the payment of adequate wages, for leave with pay and as many amenities of life as possible, and provide payment to the workers of bonuses, pensions or other provisions on retirements from active work, on account of old age or other incapacity.

The Party will also introduce a scheme of social insurance which will provide the workers against sickness, unemployment and accident. The Party will endeavour to provide cheap and sanitary dwellings for the workers.

For the benefit of the agricultural workers the party will endeavour to extend to them the same benefits which it proposes to secure for the industrial workers with such modifications as circumstances may require.

The Party accepts the principle that it is the duty of the State to relieve unemployment, and the party will, therefore, endeavour to carry out this obligation by introducing schemes of land settlement and by starting public works to provide for the unemployed and the landless labourers.

The Party will undertake legislation to protect the debtor Class from undue exactions, usurious dealings and fraudulent transactions of the money-lenders and endeavour to tackle the problem of rural indebtedness.

The Party will undertake legislation to afford adequate protection to the lower middle Class in the matter of house rents in industrial centres in big cities and towns.

(C) Taxation Problems

The attitude of the Party towards taxation is:

It believes that for the improvement in the well-being of the people, every government must undertake a large number of nation-building activities and that these activities can be undertaken only when Government has money in its treasury. This money can come mainly from taxation levied on the people. A prosperous government is the best guarantee of good government.

The Party thinks that to preach reduction of taxation as a principle and to tell the people that the reduction of taxation even at the sacrifice of useful nation-building activities is in their interest, is to misguide the people and to deceive the poorer Classes. This does not mean that the Party wishes to keep the system of taxation as it is. On the contrary, the Party definitely recognizes that the present system of taxation is unjust and weighs heavily on the poorer sections of the population. The party will endeavour to rectify this inequity in the general system of taxation. The party has great objections to the present system of levying land revenue and it will undertake legislation to make it more equitable and more elastic.

(D) Social Reforms

With regard to social reform:

The party will undertake legislation for the advancement of all necessary social reforms (i) to prevent social reformers from being outcasted by the orthodox; and (ii) to penalize all forms of organized attempts at direct action such as terrorism and boycott to prevent individuals or Classes from exercising the rights and liberties given to them by law.

The Party will undertake legislation to regulate the administration of all public charities with a view to preventing the mismanagement and misapplication of the charity funds, and to secure the use of any surplus that may be left over to the advancement of such secular purposes as education etc.

The Party will undertake legislation to deal with the Problem of beggars and other destitute persons.

The attitude of the Party towards rural reconstruction is:

(i) The Party will endeavour to make village life cheerful by providing as many amenities of life as may be necessary for the object in view.

(ii) The Party will endeavour to improve village sanitation and housing by introducing a scheme of village planning somewhat on the lines of town-planning.

(iii) The Party will endeavour to establish village libraries, village halls, village radios and rotary cinemas in order to modernize the outlook of the villager and to make him a progressive person.

(E) Education Issues

In matters of education:

The Party will give effect to the scheme of free and compulsory primary education.

The Party will undertake a scheme of adult education so as to make all people literate.

The Party will lay special emphasis on technical education.

The Party will endeavour to provide facilities for higher education in India and abroad by means of State aid to deserving persons from communities which are educationally backward.

The Party will undertake legislation to reorganize the university education in the Presidency by establishing regional universities and to make them teaching universities. The Party believes that this is the only remedy by which the curse of examination which has blasted the intelligence and effort of the student population can be removed.

The attitude of the Party towards the administration is:

The party will endeavour to see that the administration is good, efficient and free from corruption.

To secure the ends of good and efficient administration, the party will endeavour (i) to secure the separation of the Judiciary from the Executive; and (ii) to amend the *Vatan* System in a way suited to modern conditions.

The Party will also endeavour to prevent the administration from becoming the monopoly of any single Caste or community. Consistently with efficiency of administration the Party will endeavour to bring about a fair admixture of all Castes and communities in the administration of the Presidency.

Dr Ambedkar made a trip to London, ostensibly on the health grounds.[72] But before his departure, he explained the rationale behind the formation of the

72. Some analysts have argued that his real motive was to sound the British Statesmen whether the safeguards provided to the Depressed Classes would be available to them if they went over to Sikhism. See Keer Dhananjay, op cit, p. 286.

Independent Labour Party while addressing a meeting of Samata Sainik Dal in Mumbai (November 8, 1936). He said:

> According to the new Constitution fifteen seats have been reserved in the Legislative Assembly for the Depressed Classes. Election to the Legislative Assembly will be held in February next year. We have been allotted these fifteen seats in different districts of the Province. I have nominated candidates from the Independent Labour Party to contest elections against these seats.
>
> Why did my colleagues and I choose to form the Independent Labour Party to contest the coming elections? It has a very simple answer. The main object of the Congress is to achieve the Independence. My colleagues and I also want to attain freedom but to achieve freedom is not so simple or easy task. Even the weapon of '*Satyagraha*' evolved by Mr Gandhi is not likely to be efficacious. Even with Non co-operation and Civil Disobedience, it is not possible to achieve the Independence. This certainly is beyond our capacity. So long as we do not have the strength and capacity to win true freedom, it is wise and profitable to follow the well-tried methods to achieve our objective....
>
> India has not yet become a nation. This country is divided into as many as 4000 Castes. Besides this, there are the evils like Casteism, provincialism, religious differences and numerous other conflicts and quarrels which divide the country. With these divisive forces it is difficult to perceive that India will ever be united. Hindus, Muslims and Christians do not have a common goal. Granted that the British Raj comes to an end in the present situation, will not those who do not believe in one nation, religious fanatics and Caste-conscious people fight against each other to capture the political power? In the absence of real strength to capture real and true freedom, it would be harmful to entertain dreams of freedom....
>
> On the other hand, there is a distinct difference between our stand and that of the Congress. Congress does not like the Constitutional Reforms. It is opposed to the reforms. They may put an end to the reforms after entering the Legislative Assembly. But, notwithstanding the fact that these reforms do not conform with our aspirations and demands, we prefer to work with them and to use the opportunity to secure more rights in the Legislative Assemblies than those which have been given to us....
>
> Today Congress presents the picture of a motley crowd. Starting from the lowly porter, poor-labourer, peasants, petty traders, shopkeepers to landlords, usurers, merchants, middle Class people, capitalists and exploiters are found in the Congress. In short, people with all sort of conflicting interests are found in the Congress. Can those who thrive on the blood of the poor ever be the friends of the exploited? Congress is sitting in the lap of wealthy people. How can they help the poor peasants, farmers and workers? Congress is not the party of the peasants and workers. Congress is the protector of the capitalists. It is difficult for the Congress to protect and safeguard the interests of working Classes and common people. As opposed to this our organization—Independent Labour Party stands for the protection of the weaker sections of the society. It would be easy for our party to safeguard the interest of peasants and working Classes than it would be for the Congress....
>
> The main purpose of our Party is to fight for the interests of the Untouchables, the working Classes, the poor and the deprived people. Without compromising our

declared principles and policies we shall form alliances with other parties to win elections….

Many a time a question is asked as to why, leaving aside the cause of the Untouchables, I have chosen to work along with other people. In this connection I would like to say that in the proposed Legislative Assembly, according to the new Constitution, there will be 175 Members who will be elected. Out of these 175 representatives there will be fifteen from the Untouchables. It is not possible for these fifteen members to work in an effective manner. It is, therefore, very essential to have a larger number of people to help us. They must be friends having similar ideas and principles. Those among the non-Untouchables who have sincerely helped us, sacrificing their own interests and fought side by side with us for our cause must be adopted by us to contest election as our party Independent Labour Party (ILP) candidates. And, therefore, we must not waste our time in polemics at this stage. In order to achieve the objectives of our party, we must leave aside the bickerings, petty quarrels, wasteful activities and discussions. If you follow the spirit and the principles of the Party in right earnest and work sincerely to make it a success, then whatever I have been able to achieve for our people will be strengthened further….

You must clearly understand and remember that there is nobody to help you. I would like to advise you not to become a victim to any conspiracy. At such time you will have to give up selfishness, greed and narrow-mindedness. Some persons, whose inclusion in the list of Party candidates has not been found possible, easily take to the path of disintegration and disruption of the Party out of resentment and frustration. You must bear in mind that the tree, which gives us shelter, cool and refreshing shade, comfort and protection, has to be nurtured and protected. I trust that you will never try to destroy its branches in any manner….

Leaving aside all other activities for the time being I have chalked out this programme with the help and co-operation of our colleagues and I am placing it before you. I hope all of you, members of the Samta Sainik Dal, will endeavour to work for its success in a disciplined and earnest manner….

We have to face very strong and powerful enemies. Therefore, there should be a force of at least two thousand Samta Sainiks in the city of Bombay. Having sufficient manpower with devotion, dedication and unity, it has never been a difficult task for me to find a way out of any situation, no matter how grave it may be. Congress and other organizations hostile to our cause are trying to put many obstructions in my election. I fully trust that all members of our community will cast their valuable votes in my favour and that no member residing in my ward will remain without casting his vote. This can be accomplished only if Samta Sainik Dal takes up this task in their hands….

Dr Ambedkar visited Europe, according to him, purely for reasons of health and spent most of the time in Vienna and Berlin. He was in London only for a week. While he was in London, a representative of the *Vividha Vritta,* a leading Marathi weekly, sent news that Dr Ambedkar had married an English lady and was coming to India with her on January 14, 1937. Looking at the close friendship of the editor with Dr Ambedkar, it could not be said that it was out-and-out stunt in the world of Journalism. There was a rumour that an English lady was captivated by Dr Ambedkar's great personality and was insisting on marriage.

On January 14, 1937, Ambedkar returned to Mumbai. When asked in an interview on landing, if he had married, he flatly denied the rumour and dismissed it as entirely baseless. He added that he had no reason to marry stealthily. He said that he had no interviews of a political nature with anyone in London. As regards the change of religion, he affirmed, he held to his decision although he had not made up his mind as to the faith he would embrace. His immediate concern, he concluded, was the ensuing elections to the Bombay Legislative Assembly.[73]

Elections to the Bombay Legislative Assembly were scheduled for February 1937. On his return from the Europe tour (in mid-January), Dr Ambedkar started his election campaign immediately. He toured all the districts in the Bombay Presidency and delivered election speeches in Nashik, Ahmednagar, Khandesh, Solapur, Satara and Belgaum. As an example of Dr Ambedkar's election speeches, probably the one at Nashik (January 17, 1937) is a typical one. He said:[74]

> We have to think over whom are we going to elect in the forthcoming elections of the Bombay Provincial Legislature.
>
> This country has seen many kings. A hundred and fifty years have passed since the British came to India. These Councils have been functioning for approximately 60 years of these 150 years of British rule and through these Councils, the people's representatives have been putting forth their grievances before the government. But never before in the world's history that a representative of the Untouchables has been placed in the Council to put forth grievances of eight crore Untouchables. This has been achieved only because of our efforts.
>
> The People of Nasik district have now been given the right to send a representative to the Legislature from the coming April 1937. We now have an opportunity to appeal to the Council about our grievances. Although our practice till date has been to address our grievances through government officers, from now on we shall address them through the Legislature. Hence it is extremely important that your representative to this Council should be a most deserving one. These posts are not merely prestigious, but are key-positions. The person entering the Legislature does not go in there for himself, but rather for the whole society. We have to select a person who will be capable of effectively presenting the problems faced by our society and will fight for us. Legislature is an instrument of self-defence.
>
> It is important that the issue of *MaharVatan* is examined through this Legislature. Since you do not possess any land, you wish to acquire fallow lands. Our society has fallen behind in education and hence our children should have access to a decent education. The poor should get government scholarships for education. To put an end to your humiliation, as Untouchables, there should be a law to abolish Untouchability. There should be a provision to ensure that our people are enrolled into government

---

73. Keer, Dhananjay, op cit, p. 288.
74. Marathi Speech. For English Summary, see *Ambedkar Speaks*, op cit, Vol.III, pp.165-6.

> jobs in adequate numbers. Several such things could be acquired by fighting through the Legislature.
>
> In our day-to-day affairs we see that if some person needs a carpenter to build a house then he appoints the person who knows carpentry. For a mason's work we only appoint someone who knows masonry. Like-wise it is vital that you think and decide that who is more capable in carrying out the work in the Legislature. Do not favour your relatives. You should not fall prey to external pressures. You should not be guided by feelings of hatred towards others and should not be swayed away by revenge. Only the one whom you think is capable enough to put forth our grievances to the Legislature and addresses them there should be voted for and elected. Send only that person to the Legislature who deserves to be there.

Dr Ambedkar immediately launched his election campaign.

In the first ever general elections to the Bombay Legislative Assembly, held in February 1937, the Independent Labour Party had fielded 18 candidates in the Bombay Province, 12 on reserved seats and six on general seats. In addition, 14 candidates ran for election in the Central Provinces. The new party had a good showing, 15 candidates were elected in Bombay Province of which 12 were from the Depressed Classes.

The Congress nominee to oppose Dr Ambedkar himself was the famous cricket player P Balu (whose real family name was Palvankar, which he had changed to conceal his Untouchable background).

Dr Ambedkar was elected with a thumping majority and, thus, he started a new inning as an elected Legislator in Bombay Legislative Assembly.

CHAPTER TWENTY

In Bombay Provincial Legislative Assembly

IN THE BOMBAY Legislative Assembly debates as well as outside the Assembly, Dr Ambedkar gave effective expression to the grievances of the rual poor combining them with mass movements. In this regard, the following three areas of contribution are especially noteworthy:

(a) *Khoti* System
(b) *MaharVatan* and
(c) Regulation of Money-lenders

A. ABOLITION OF THE KHOTI SYSTEM

Khoti was a peculiar system of land tenure that prevailed in pockets of the Konkan region of Maharashtra. *Khots* had rights to land which was cultivated by farmers and, in return, *Khots* collected land revenue from them and passed on a part thereof to the Government. It was an oppressive system that had subjected a vast majority of the rural poor in the region to virtual serfdom. All farmers and their families coming under the system were treated by *Khots* as bonded labour for generation and generation. This exploitation had continued in the region for several decades.

On April 14, 1929, Ambedkar presided over an Agricultural Conference in Chiplun (District Ratnagiri).In his Presidential Address, he had fired the first salvo against the *Khoti* System. He said to the farmers:

> I know your grievances. The *Khoti* System is sucking your blood. This system of land tenure must be abolished, its abolition will bring you peace and progress. In order to achieve your goal you must keep the agitation going on.... You must take particular care to send to the Legislatures the right type of men as your representatives who would devoutly struggle for the abolition of this *Khoti* System.

This was going to be the beginning of a long-drawn struggle.

In 1936, when Dr Ambedkar founded the Independent Labour Party (ILP), its manifesto had explicitly accorded a high priority to the abolition of the exploitation of the rural poor by the *Khoti* System.

On September 17, 1937, Dr Ambedkar introduced a historic Bill in the Bombay Legislative Assembly aimed at abolition of the *Khoti* System.[75]

While introducing the Bill, Dr Ambedkar said:

> I rise to move for leave to introduce a Bill to abolish the *Khoti* System. The brief statement which you have directed us to make in support of the motion will, in my case, consist of nothing more than a reference to the statement of objects and reasons. And before I do so, I would point out, Mr Speaker, that this is the shortest statement of objects and reasons ever drafted to a Bill which is so important as the abolition of the *Khoti* System.
>
> The *Khoti* System is one of the minor land tenures in the Bombay Presidency. It is found mostly in the Ratnagiri district and in some parts of the Kolaba and Thana districts. The terms of the *Khoti* tenure and in some cases regulated by law, in some by custom and usage and in the rest by grant. In the Ratnagiri district the terms are regulated by Bombay Act I of 1880, in the Kolaba district the terms are regulated by custom and usage, and in the Thana district by grant. The *Khoti* tenure differs from the ordinary *Rayatwari* tenure inasmuch as in the latter the Government collects revenue directly from those who are in occupation of the land while in the former the Government is required to employ the services of the *Khot* for the purpose of collecting revenue.
>
> The system of *Khoti* tenure, while it binds the *Khot* to pay revenue to the Government, leaves him free to do what he likes to the inferior holders, and this freedom has been so grossly abused by the *Khots* that the inferior holders are not only subjected to all kinds of exactions but they have been reduced to a state of abject slavery. In recent years, the inferior holders have been carrying on a great agitation against the *Khots* and have been demanding the abolition of the *Khoti* System. The relations between the *Khots* and the inferior holders have been so strained that three *Khots* were murdered by them.
>
> While the *Khoti* tenure may have the advantage of facilitating the collection of revenue, its disadvantages are so great that the tenure cannot be allowed to continue hereafter without causing grave disturbance to the peace and tranquillity of the Presidency. It is, therefore, imperative to abolish the system.
>
> The Bill aims: (1) to abolish the *Khoti* System and to establish direct relationship between Government and those who are in possession or occupation of the land which is under the management or beneficial enjoyment of the *Khot*; (2) to make provision for the payment of reasonable compensation to the *Khot* for the loss of his rights; and (3) to give those inferior holders who are in actual occupation of the land the status of occupants within the meaning of the Land Revenue Code, and (4) to provide for other incidental purposes. With these words, Sir, I beg leave of the House to introduce the Bill.

---

75. For fuller summary of the debate, see *Ambedkar Speaks*, op cit, Vol. I, pp. 372-73.

It is noteworthy that Dr Ambedkar was one of the first Legislators in India to introduce a Bill for the abolition of the slavery of agricultural tenants. The Bill aimed at securing occupancy rights to the tenants with a provision for payment of reasonable compensation to the *Khots* for the loss of their rights. The Bill proposed Abolition of the *Khoti* System and substitution of the *Ryotwari* System, with a view to giving the poor farmer who were in actual possession of land the status of occupants under the Land Revenue Code, 1879.

The *Khoti* Abolition Bill caused an unprecedented turmoil in the then Bombay Province. *Khots* in Konkan organized a counter-agitation. A persecution campaign began, depriving the Depressed Classes of drinking water, ostracizing them and often resorting to physical attacks. In those years of turmoil, Dr Ambedkar toured extensively, addressed rallies after rallies and roused awakening among the rural poor of their rights. Inspired by the leadership of Ambedkar, the poor and oppressed refused to give up their struggle.

Dr Ambedkar led a massive procession of farmers on January 10, 1938 to the Bombay Legislative Assembly. Thousands of farmers from the districts of Thane, Kolaba (now Raigad), Ratnagiri, Nasik and Satara joined the procession, clad in torn clothes, the traditional blankets on their shoulders and staffs in their hands. A delegation led by Dr Ambedkar submitted a representation to the Government, which demanded that economically wasteful and socially tyrannous *Khoti* System must be abolished. The delegation also demanded that the minimum standard of wages must be enforced for the benefit of agricultural labourers. Furthermore, a demand was made for reducing the irrigation rates payable by small holders by 50 per cent.

On May 14, 1938, Dr Ambedkar presided over a Conference of the Depressed Classes at Kankavli (District: Ratnagiri) where he declared that he was determined to end their serfdom by abolishing the *Khoti* System. He appealed to them to be prepared to launch a passive resistance if the *Khoti* Abolition Bill failed in the Bombay Legislative Assembly. During the same tour, Dr Ambedkar once lashed out at the socialists who, he said, were all those years shouting for the confiscation of all *Zamindari* lands and the abolition of the capitalist system, but were now inactive when a concrete Bill was brought forward to put an end of the *Khoti* System.

In 1939, the Bombay Legislative Assembly was dissolved in the wake of the collective resignation by the elected government. As such, a debate on the *Khoti* Abolition Bill could not take place in the Bombay Legislative Assembly. The mass awakening created by Dr Ambedkar's devout struggle, however, could not be suppressed. The movement led by Dr Ambedkar had created not only an awareness among the rural poor about their rights, but had also instilled in them the courage to fight for those rights relentlessly. Not surprisingly, this movement of the rural poor which transcended the barriers of Castes and Creeds culminated eventually in the abolition of the *Khoti* System in 1949.

B. *MAHAR VATAN*

Mahar Vatan was yet another form of unbridled exploitation of the rural poor. A section of the rural poor belonging to the *Mahar* Caste were subjected to this mode of oppression.

According to the Bombay Hereditary Offices Act (1874) the *Mahars* holding low level Government jobs were treated as servants for all work of all Government Departments at any hour of the day and night for a pittance. In the absence of a *Mahar* servant, any member of his family was forced into the Government service. The duties of these Government servants were never clearly defined. As such, all sorts of odd jobs were assigned to them, including disposal of carcass of animals, and running alongside the *tonga* of a Government officer from one destination to another. For this arduous and ceaseless work, the *Mahars* were compensated with a piece of land called *Vatan* and what was referred to as *Baluta* (i.e., the collection of grain made by *Vatan* holding *Mahars* from their villages). At times, they were also entitled to cash wages of a meagre amount. Moreover, this paltry flow of income was not steady. In the drought years, the Government readily exempted farmers, in part, from giving the *Baluta* to *Mahars* while in the good years, Government often confiscated parts of these lands under the pretext that they were excessive.

While in actuality the *Mahar Vatan* was a form of unmitigated and inhuman exploitation of *Mahars*, these ignorant masses were led to believe that they were *Vatandars* (i.e., landlords) and it was their right to perform the assigned duties. This belief, widespread as it was, had the unfortunate effect of making *Mahars* complacent. It meant loss of their self-respect with their ambition confined to those trifling menial jobs in total disregard to their actual potential.

Dr Ambedkar took upon himself the task of breaking these shackles of servitude. During September 2, 1927 through December 7, 1928, he published a series of thought-provoking articles of the *Mahar Vatan* in his paper: *Bahishkrit Bharat*. Dr Ambedkar also organized several meetings and conferences to educate people about the ills of *Mahar Vatan*. Especially noteworthy were meetings held at Kamathipura, Mumbai (November 5, 1927), Nasik (November 13, 1927) and Jalgaon, which were attended by thousands of *Mahar Vatandars.*

On March 19, 1928, Dr Ambedkar introduced a Bill in the Bombay Legislative Council to amend the Bombay Hereditary Offices Act, 1874. Moving the Bill on August 3, 1928, Dr Ambedkar brought to the notice of the House that *Vatan* lands were given to those *Mahars* by the ancient emperors of India and the Government had neither increased the land assigned nor the remuneration of those people, in spite of the increase in the cost of living for which other Government servants were duly compensated. He argued that with the increase in population, the land assigned was divided and sub-divided thereby reducing the flow of income from the *Vatan* lands to virtually nothing. He therefore, proposed that the *Vatan* lands should be given to the holders at the full rate of assessment and most of them should be relieved from the obligation to serve. Those who are retained in the Government service should be paid from the revenue derived from the assessment levied on the *Mahar Vatans* and from the *Baluta*, so that there would be no additional burden on the Government Treasury.

In a well-reasoned and yet emotionally charged speech, Dr Ambedkar observed:

> (*Mahar Vatan*) is a atrocious system, a system which has no justice in it whatsoever, if the Government desired that these people should work for it, it is absolutely necessary that the Government should take upon its shoulder the responsibility of paying these *Mahars*. It ought not vicariously throw off this burden in a most careless way upon a third party, the ryot; but that is exactly what is happening under the system.

He observed further

> If the Government has got the nerve, the courage and the sympathy for others (teachers and *talathis*) to bring forward financial measures to remunerate their services, why should not Government have the same nerve, the same courage and the same sympathy in the case of these *Mahars*?

The Bill introduced by Dr Ambedkar was referred to a Select Committee comprising 23 Members of the House. At the hands of the Committee, however, the Bill was transformed beyond recognition, and in despair Dr Ambedkar withdrew the Bill on July 24, 1929.

Eight years later, on September 17, 1937, the same day on which the *Khoti* Abolition Bill was introduced in the Bombay Legislative Assembly, Dr Ambedkar once again submitted a Bill seeking amendments to the Hereditary Offices Act. The Bill was quite similar to the one he had introduced in 1928, except for the fact relinquishing of the *Mahar Vatan* was made voluntary.

In the meantime, under the persuasion of Dr Ambedkar and his Independent Labour Part (ILP), the duties of *Vatan* holding *Mahars* were clearly defined by the Government. Dr Ambedkar reprinted his five articles on the *Mahar Vatan* in a book form entitled, *Mahars and their Vatan or Slavery in the Twentieth Century*. Dr Ambedkar also organized mass support for the Bill through a number of meetings and conferences. Unfortunately, the Bill could not pass even for the second time. The persistent efforts of Dr Ambedkar, however, were not in vain. The *Mahar Vatans* were finally abolished under the Bombay Inferior Village *Vatan*s Abolition Act 1 of 1959.

C. THE BOMBAY MONEYLENDERS BILL

Dr Ambedkar knew the needs and sufferings of the rural poor as well as virtues and vices of the industrial workers. When he realized the extent of exploitation of these poor people at the hands of money-lenders, he prepared a Bill aimed at preventing the malpractices of money-lenders. Indeed, this Bill was the first of its kind in India, recommending specific corrective measures.[76]

The Bombay Moneylenders Bill prepared by Dr Ambedkar way back in 1938 had some very innovative provisions, even by the prudential standards advocated today. These included money lenders being subjected to licenses from the Government renewable every year, compulsion of written records of all lending operations and mandatory issue of pass-books detailing all transactions between borrowers and lenders.

D. ON MEASURES FOR BIRTH CONTROL

While moving a Bill in the Assembly on measures for birth control (November, 1938) (on behalf of Dr Ambedkar), the following arguments were made:

> Very few have an adequate idea of the immense loss sustained by children born of persons who are handicapped either physically, mentally or financially. The parents as well as the society also suffer very much. The prevention of the births of such children would considerably reduce the death-rate among mothers who succumb to child-birth and its concomitant diseases, lower infantile mortality, improve public health by removing the many persons, check the offences perpetrated by persons suffering from intense poverty and would bring about an all-round upliftment of society by affording full scope to its spiritual advancement.
>
> The present keen struggle of life renders timely marriage impossible for many and thus exposes them to various diseases and habits. Many women become invalid for life and some even lose their lives by the birth of children in their diseased condition or in too great numbers or in too rapid succession. Attempts at abortion, resorted to for the prevention of unwanted progeny, exact a heavy toll of female lives. Unwanted children are often neglected by their mother and hence they become nothing but a burden to society which is further deteriorated by the addition of defective progeny from diseased persons. Birth-control is the only sovereign specific that can do away with all these calamities. Whenever a woman is disinclined to bear a child for any reason whatsoever, she must be in position to prevent conception and bringing forth progeny which should be entirely dependent on the choice of woman. Society would in no way profit by the addition of unwanted progeny. Only those children, who are welcomed by their parents, can be of social benefit and hence every woman must be enabled to resort to prevention of conception quite easily.
>
> When we have thus realized that birth control is the *sine qua non* for every progress, we must consider the means to attend that end. To be satisfied with only that much of sexual enjoyment that is necessary for getting the desired number of children and to

76. YD Phadke has pointed that in his Ambedkari Chalwal (1990) Marathi that Dr Babasaheb Ambedkar's Writings and Speeches (BAWS), Volume 2, published by the Government of Maharashtra which deals with Ambedkar's contributions in the Bombay Legislature, has somehow overlooked this historic Bill.

banish sexual thoughts from one's mind when progeny is not required, is one of the ways. The use of modern contraceptives is the other way. As for the first way, it must be remembered that while continence in the unmarried state may be possible, it is nothing but displaying ignorance about human nature to expect from young and healthy married couples, living together and fond of each other, can observe continence for years altogether. The cases of strong-willed persons, whose minds are not affected in the presence of objects of enjoyment apart, there is no doubt that ordinary human beings are bound to fall a prey to the influence of enticement. Is it not strange, therefore, that this fact, which is as clear as daylight, is denied by some.

Self-control has been proved to be absolutely useless for birth control from the experience of several countries and ages. Even the advocates of continence cannot claim that ordinary person will be able to eschew sexual intercourse altogether throughout their lives. The laying aside of continence even for single day every year may lead to an annual conception. Even if we assume that self-control enables certain persons to bring about birth control, we cannot draw the conclusion that others will be able to follow them. It is necessary to remember that just as appetite for food differs in the case of different persons, so sexual appetite also varies from person to person.

If men had to bear the pangs which woman have to undergo during child birth none of them would ever consent to bear more than a single child in his life.

It is wrong to hold that because the ideal of large families is before society up to this time nobody wishes to limit his family. Human beings, who earnestly desire to be saddled with large families, are rare. Ordinary persons do want to limit their families and do not even flinch to have recourse to diabolical methods such as abortion, infanticide, etc. Such attempts are witnessed everywhere. It is bitter and terrible poverty that makes the parents expose their infants. In the light of such instance, it is futile to hope that ordinary persons will be able to avoid progeny merely through self-control. It is, therefore, established that there is no go without recourse to modern contraceptives. To deny the necessity of those remedies is to show one`s preference for abortions, infanticides, etc.

CHAPTER TWENTY ONE

Emergence as a Labour Leader

DR AMBEDKAR'S INVOLVEMENT in the Indian labour movement appears to have passed through several interesting phases. In the 1920s, when the labour movement in India was dominated by the Communist-led Trade Unions, several calls were given for strikes by textile workers in 1924, 1925, 1928 and 1929. The April 1929 strike covered as many as 75,000 workers from 43 textile mills. Yet another major strike was called in April 1934. During these strikes, Dr Ambedkar, through *Bahishkrit Bharat* and later *Janata,* appealed to the Depressed Class workers to refrain from the joining the strikes on the grounds that they were politically motivated and would bring economic distress to them. Not surprisingly, Dr Ambedkar came to be branded by the Communists as an "enemy of the labour".

In 1934, Dr Ambedkar became the President of Bombay Municipal *Karmachari Sangh.* He founded a new political party called Independent Labour Party (ILP) in August, 1936. Subsequently, in 1938, when the first successful strike against a popular Government was launched by the opposition parties, Dr Ambedkar and his Independent Labour Party played a very significant role and, indeed, were the main architects of its success.

To many Dr Ambedkar's initial opposition to strikes in the late 1920s and in the early 1930s and his subsequent participation in the general strike of 1938 with the lion's share in its success had remained a paradox—a contradiction that defies logical explanation. A careful analysis of the situation, however, reveals a completely consistent pattern based on sound reasoning and judgment.

Dr Ambedkar firmly believed in the worker's right to strike, but that weapon, he argued, should be used judiciously and always in the interest of workers, not for political gains. Dr Ambedkar's initial opposition to the Communist-inspired strikes of 1920s and the early 1930s was on account of the underlying political motivations of the Unions. Indeed, Dr Ambedkar initiated extensive counter-campaigns against the Girni Kamgar Union in 1929. In *Bahishkrit Bharat,* Dr Ambedkar argued that he was not in favour of the 1929 strikes because the condition of the Depressed Class workers had already been worsened by the previous strikes, with the result that the grip of the creditors and the money-lenders was more tightened on their neck and honour.[77] Indeed, so concerned Dr Ambedkar was regarding these problems that he subsequently prepared a Bill for the Bombay Legislative Assembly aimed at preventing malpractices of the money-lenders.[78]

Dr Ambedkar's political strategy became discernible in several of his public speeches in 1937 and 1938. Two of these speeches are especially noteworthy. First, while addressing a Public Rally at the culmination of a Peasants' March to the Council in Mumbai (January 10, 1935), Dr Ambedkar exhorted the peasants and workers to think over the causes of their poverty and told them that they lay in the richness of the exploiters. The way out for them was to organize a labour front without any regard to Caste or Creed, and to elect to the Legislatures those who were their real representatives. If they did so, they would have shelter, clothing and they who produced the food and wealth of the nation would not die of hunger.

The philosophical basis of Dr Ambedkar's strategy was fully spelt out in his Presidential Address at the Conference of Untouchable Workers of the Great Indian Peninsula (GIP) Railway, Manmad (February 13, 1938), as can be seen from the following excerpts:[79]

> The Depressed Classes have hitherto agitated principally for the removal of social grievances. They have not taken up the work of the removal of their economic grievances. This is the first time when they are meeting to consider their economic grievances. Hitherto they were meeting as Pariahs. Now you are meeting as workers....
>
> I am not prepared to say that we have been wrong in concentrating our efforts in emphasizing social grievances. Whatever other people may say, there are grievances under the load of which our very manhood is crushed out. Nor can it be said that our agitation has borne no fruit. It is true that we have not succeeded in the removal of Untouchability. It is true that we have not succeeded in securing some of the most elementary rights to which all human beings are entitled. But it is also true that our agitation has succeeded in so far as we have obtained possession of political power....
>
> Power is the only means whereby one can secure liberty and free himself from all obstacles and political power has a potency which if it is not as great as religious or economic power is quite real and effective as far as it goes. I am sorry that the political power which the Depressed Classes have got under the new Constitution has been frittered away by the machinations of our enemies and by the selfishness of needy and profligate adventurers from among ourselves. Power behind which there is no organization, power behind which there is no consciousness is no power. I hope one day, not before very long, the Depressed Classes will become organized, will become conscious of the power they have got and will begin to put it to wise and effective use in order to secure their social emancipation....

77. *Bahishkrit Bharat*, May 31, 1929.
78. Available information about this Bill has been presented in the last chapter.
79. Marathi Speech. For full English Summary, see *Ambedkar Speaks* op cit, Vol. III, pp. 174–86.

I confess that we have too long neglected to lay the same emphasis on the economic problems with which we are faced as we do on social problems and I am, therefore, glad that we have met today more as workers than as Untouchables. It is a new departure....

There are in my view two enemies which the workers of this country have to deal with. The two enemies are *Bramhanism* and *Capitalism*. The accusation by our critics arises partly because the critics fail to reckon *Brahmanism* as an enemy which the workers have to deal with. I do not want to be misunderstood when I say that Brahmanism is an enemy which must be dealt with....

By *Brahmanism* I mean the negation of the spirit of Liberty, Equality and Fraternity. In that sense it is rampant in all Classes and is not confined to the Brahmins alone though they have been the originations of it. It is also an incontrovertible fact that this *Brahmanism* gives certain Classes a privileged position. It denies certain other Classes even equality of opportunity. The effects of *Brahmanism* are not confined to what are *social rights* such as inter-dining or inter-marriage. If that was so, one would not mind it. But it is not so. It extends to *civic rights* as distinguished from *social rights*. Use of public schools, of public wells, of public conveyances, of public restaurants are matters of civic rights. Everything which is intended for the public or maintained out of public fund must be open to every citizen. But there are millions to whom these civic rights are denied. Can anybody doubt that this is the result of *Brahmanism* which has been let loose in this country for thousands of years and which is functioning even now as a livewire?

So omnipresent is *Brahmanism* that it even affects the field of economic opportunities. Take the Depressed Classes worker and compare his opportunities with a worker who does not belong to the Depressed Classes. It is notorious that there are many avocations from which a Depressed Classes worker is shut out by reason of the fact that he is an Untouchable....

In those avocations where he has a chance to obtain work he is employed in the lowest grade. He is excluded from any place of power or authority. He is not only employed in the lowest grade but he is confined to that grade until he retires. There is no rise for him. There is no career for him and often there is no promotion for him. This is what happens to him when there is no slump. In days of slump he is the first to be fired as in the boom he is the last to be employed....

Labour leaders who are accusing us are undoubtedly suffering from certain delusion. They have read in Karl Marx that there can be only two Classes—owners and workers and, on reading Marx they straightaway assume that in India there are only owners and workers and proceed on their mission of demolishing Capitalism....

This would be positively erroneous with regard to India. A clear-cut division does not exist in India. That all labourers are one, form one Class is an ideal to be achieved and it is the greatest error to assume it as a fact. How are we to consolidate the ranks of labour? The real way to bring about unity is to remove the causes which make one worker the antagonist of another worker on the ground of race and religion. The real way to bring about unity is to tell the worker that he is wrong in claiming rights which he is not prepared to give to other workers. The real way to bring about unity is to tell the worker who makes these social distinctions which result in unfair discrimination are wrong in principle and injurious to the solidarity of workers....

In other words, we must uproot *Brahmanism*—this spirit of inequality—from among the workers if the ranks of labour are to be united. I have heard labour leaders speaking vociferously against Capitalism. But I have never heard any labour leader speaking against *Brahmanism* amongst workers. On the other hand, their silence on this point is quite conspicuous....

So long as *Brahmanism* remains a living force and so long as people continue to stick to it because it confers privileges upon one Class and puts handicaps on others, I am afraid, that till then there will be the necessity for those who suffer from these handicaps to organize themselves....

There is no question that you must organize if you want to remove your grievances....

Trade unionism in India is in a sorry state. The chief aim of trade unions is completely lost sight of. The chief aim of trade unionism is to protect the standard of living of the working Class from being reduced. If there is any country where trade unionism was an absolute necessity, in my opinion it was India. But as I said today trade unionism in India is a stagnant and stinking pool. It is entirely due to the fact that the leadership of trade unionism is either timid, selfish or misguided, there are some labour leaders who are only arm-chair philosophers or politicians who have limited their task to issuing statements in the papers. Organizing the workers, educating the workers and helping them to agitate does not form part of their duty....

A second category of labour leaders is of those who are engaged in forming unions for the sole purpose of finding a place for themselves as Secretaries, Presidents or Chairmen....

The third Class of labour leaders is composed principally of the Communists. They may be well meaning, but I have no hesitation saying that they are a misguided body of men, and I go further and say that nobody has brought a greater ruination on the workers than these men. Their aim seems to bring about discontent among the workers as though there was any absence of it, because they believe that with a discontented body of workers they will bring about a revolution and establish the rule of the proletariat. Therefore, to bring about discontent they launched upon a systematic campaign of organizing disorganization....

Whether they have created greater discontent or not they have most certainly destroyed the very trade union organizations which were the source of their strength and their power and now they are practically on the streets seeking to take shelter under all sorts of capitalist organizations....

There is no question that you must organize a union for trade purposes. But that is not enough. You must also organize for political purposes....

Trade Unions must enter politics because without political power they cannot protect purely trade union interests. Even for the purpose of securing such reforms as standard rate, normal day, common rule, minimum living wage, collective bargaining are aims which cannot be secured merely by organizing unions. The power of unions must be strengthened by the force of law. This cannot happen until in addition to organizing yourselves into unions you also begin to play your part in the politics of the country....

The protection of purely trade union interests cannot be the only reason why trade union must enter politics. On the contrary, your aim should be to replace this system of wage-slavery by a system which will recognize the principles of liberty, equality, and fraternity. This means re-building of society and I say that it is the primary concern of the labouring Class to bring about such a reconstruction of society....

To enter politics means the formation of a party. Politics without a party behind it is a futility. The question is what party you should join. I have no hesitation in saying that labour should have a separate organization in politics independent of the Congress. I know that this view is opposed by a section of the labour leaders. There is a section represented by the Congress Socialists who would like to have labour organizing itself for the achievement of Socialism but the organization must be within the Congress. There is another section—calling itself Communist—represented by Mr Roy which is vehemently opposed to any separate organization by labour or by any Class in India either inside or outside the Congress. I am entirely in disagreement with either group....

The only rationale justification that one can give for so queer a view is that Mr Roy looks upon the destruction of Imperialism as the first and foremost aim of Indian politics. This view would be correct if it could be proved that with the disappearance of Imperialism all vestige of Capitalism will also disappear from India. But it does not require much intelligence to realize that even if the British depart from India, the landlords, the mill-owners, the money-lenders will remain in India and continue to bleed the people and that even after Imperialism has gone, labour will have to fight these interests just as much....

The Congress Socialists evidently realize that labour has to fight capitalism as much as Imperialism and, therefore, agree that labour must organize. The aim of the Congress Socialists is to bring about Socialism, so they say. How they hope to bring it about, by converting the right wing of the Congress. That is the explanation they give for not going out of the Congress. A more pathetic case involving utter ignorance of human nature cannot be imagined....

If Socialism is to be the aim then the way to bring it about is to preach it to the masses and organize them for that purpose. Socialism will not come by wooing the Classes....

Indian Politics has become wrapped by its reaction to imperialism. Labour is made to forget its real enemy, namely, the vested interest. Even if Imperialism is to be dealt with as the common enemy, it does not mean that all Classes must forget Class interests and join in one organization. Imperialism could be fought by the different Class organizations making a common front. It is not necessary to dissolve all organization for this purpose. It is not necessary to have a merger. Common front is quite enough. I am sorry that many people do not seen to realize that the Right wing of the Congress is merely using Imperialism as an excuse for preventing separate and independent organization of labour, and I warn you against falling in to this error. Politics must be based upon Class consciousness. Politics which is not Class conscious is hypocrisy....

You must, therefore, join a political party which is based upon Class interests and Class consciousness. Applying this test I find no other party than the Independent Labour Party to which you can join without detriment to your interests. It is the only party which has a clear programme, which gives the interests of the workers a first and foremost place, which has a definite line of action, which proposes to exhaust all Constitutional means for furthering its programme and will not agree to resort to

> unconstitutional means unless forced to do so, which is willing to avoid Class war but is not prepared to give up the principle of Class organization....
>
> And so far as the assured quota of representation to the Depressed Classes is concerned it is an advantage not to the Depressed Classes only but to Labour as a whole. The Depressed Classes being sure of representation can give great support to other labouring Classes in their attempt for political organization if they care to avail themselves of this support. How great can be the support of the Depressed Classes to Labour in general for securing political representation to Labour is proved in the last election. The Depressed Classes were able to elect three representatives of Caste Hindus to the Bombay Legislative Assembly who stood on the ILP ticket and rendered help to several others who did not stand on its ticket but who were approved by the Party....

★ ★ ★

This stand of Dr Ambedkar was not inconsistent with his wholehearted participation in the general strike against the Industrial Disputes Bill in 1938. The Bill had aimed at restricting the right of the labourer to strike and making strike illegal.

In a hard-hitting elaborate speech in the Bombay Legislative Assembly (September 15, 1938), on the Industrial Disputes Bill, Dr Ambedkar said:

> This Bill is intended to replace the Bombay Trade Disputes Conciliation Act of 1934, and the question, therefore, that primarily arises for consideration is whether any case has been made out by the Prime Minister, who is in charge of this measure, for the change which he is now introducing by this Bill. The Act of 1934 was intended to provide a machinery for conciliation. The principle of the Act of 1934 was voluntary conciliation. Now this Bill introduces a change, namely, that the conciliation shall be compulsory, and the question, I submit, that arises for the consideration of the House is whether any case has been made out for altering the voluntary provision of the Act of 1934 and giving it a compulsory character.
>
> What happened between the year 1934 and the year 1938 which compels this House to alter the provisions of that Act, changing voluntary conciliation into compulsory conciliation?
>
> Now, in order to make out a case for compulsion, the Prime Minister started by giving us certain figures of strikes that have taken place in this country, in order to make out that the strikes that have taken place in this country were so frequent and of such a grave character that the necessity had now arisen for changing the voluntary provision into a compulsory one. Now I have examined the figures of the strikes, the number of work-people involved and the number of working days lost. I have no hesitation in saying that I stand unconvinced by what the Honourable Prime Minister seemed to say as a result of the figures relating to strikes....
>
> My first submission, therefore, is this, no case has been made out by the Government, and by the Honourable Prime Minister which would induce, at any rate, this part of the House, at any rate induce me to consent to so radical a change in the provisions of the Act of 1934. So much for the necessity of introducing compulsory conciliation....

Turning to the other provisions of the Bill, the provision to which I wish to advert are the provisions relating to strikes which undoubtedly are the most important, which this part of the House, at any rate the Party I represent, stoutly oppose. Now, the Bill makes strikes under certain circumstances illegal....

Then, in order to make this Clause effective, the Bill prescribes certain penalties for indulging in illegal strikes....

Now, Sir, it has been said that these Clauses are justifiable, because there is no such things as a right to strike, and the Bill, therefore, in penalizing what the labourers call the right to strike is certainly not contravening any rule of ethics or any rules of jurisprudence...

Sir, my first concern in this speech will be to refute that argument and repudiate that position. It is better, I think, to understand the meaning of the term 'strike'. In plain popular language, a strike is nothing more than a breach of contract of service. When a worker strikes, all that it means is that he commits a breach of contract of service. And the next question that I propose to raise is this: How is this breach of contract of service dealt with by the law as it stands today on the Indian Statute Book? Does the Indian law recognize this right to strike? And, if it does, in what way; and, if it punishes, in what way does it punish it? Sir, here again, I will begin with an elementary proposition, and that elementary proposition is this: that an act or an omission may be a civil wrong, or it may be a crime. The first question I propose to raise is: Is breach of contract of service a civil wrong? The answer that the law gives is: Yes, it is a civil wrong. What are the remedies for an aggrieved person who has suffered this civil wrong? There again the answer is that the present law provides two remedies for an aggrieved person whose contract has been broken by a workman, and those are damages and specific relief. Now, although the law does provide these two remedies, namely, damages and specific relief wherever there is a civil wrong, there is one provision which applies particularly to contracts of service. Whenever a man breaks a contract of service all that the aggrieved party is entitled to is damages; he can never seek specific relief, and the court can never give relief whereby it can compel a man to perform the contract of service which he has entered upon. All that the aggrieved party would be entitled to is damages. Sir, that is the position as far as breach of contract of service is concerned as a civil wrong. For this civil wrong the employer can get nothing more than damages....

Looking at this breach of contract of service as a crime, the question is: Is it a crime? What has been the provision of the Indian law so far as breach of contract of service is concerned?

Now, Sir, taking stock of all that I have stated so far relating to the legal position involved as a result of breach of contract of service, what is the position? The position is this. A breach of contract of service is not a crime, and is not punishable under the Indian law except when the case falls under Section 491. That means it is only a civil wrong; it is not a crime. And, further, it is a civil wrong for which the remedy can only be damages and never a specific performance. I want to emphasize that...

Now, the question which I am sure the House would like to consider with all the seriousness that it can command is this: Why is it that the Indian law does not make a breach of contract of service a crime? And why is it that the Indian law does not provide for a specific performance? Whatever answer other Members of the House would choose to give, my answer is very simple. My answer is this, that the Indian Legislature does not make a breach of contract of service a crime because it thinks that to make it a crime is to compel a man to serve against his will; and making him slave....

Now, Sir, it has been said that there is no such things as the 'right to strike'. My reply is that this statement can come from a man who really does not understand what a strike is. If Members are prepared to accept my meaning of the word 'strike' as being nothing more than a breach of contract, then I submit that a strike is simply another name for the right to freedom; it is nothing else than the right to the freedom of one's services on any terms that one wants to obtain. And once you concede the right to freedom, you necessarily concede the right to strike, because, as I have said, the right to strike is simply another name for the right to freedom. If you accept that the right to freedom is a divine right...

I wonder if Members opposite wish to argue from it that there is no right to strike because a strike by a body of workers is a conspiracy. If they do, I would like those gentlemen opposite who rely on Section 120A as a ground for submitting that there is no right to strike for a body of workers, to prove that a strike is a conspiracy. Unless they prove that a strike is a conspiracy Section 120A will not apply, and I contend that a strike is not a conspiracy....

Therefore, my submission is that in order to bring strikes under section 120A what would be necessary for the prosecution to prove is that the purpose of the strike was to cause injury. If injury merely resulted from the strike, that would not make the strike an unlawful combination within the meaning of Section 120A. Therefore, my first contention is this, that this Bill, by penalizing a strike, is reducing the workers to a state of slavery and nothing else....

The Bill really, in my judgment, ought to be called 'The Workers' Civil Liberties Suspension Act'. That would be the proper title for it. Some have got the impression that, after all, the suspension is only for two months—until the conciliation proceedings are terminated—and after that the workers would be at liberty to strike if they wish. Sir, I would like to say that this would be a very wrong impression. My contention is that provisions of this Bill, when they are set in operation, will bring about perpetual slavery and the workers will never be able to strike....

This has always been the view taken that if you want to restrict the right to strike and to make it illegal, then you must do it only in relation to services on which the sustenance of the life of the community depends. Now, it is obvious that this Bill extends to every industry....

What would be the evil if the matter of the organization of labour is left to the will of the worker? Why are you concerned with it? I do not understand. Why is it, and what is it that you will get by bringing all persons working in one industry in one particular Union? I fail to understand. On the other hand, my view is, as I submitted, that if you make these impossible conditions, people will not care to form unions at all. The Mohammedans who prefer, and I think we must all agree to allow them the liberty to choose their politics, that there will be no use in having a trade union, if their trade union is not able to follow the policy laid down by the Muslim League, they may not have any union at all. In the same way if the Untouchables feel that if they are not allowed to make some provision for the education of their children and other amenities pertaining to their Classes, they would rather not have it. What is the situation that you are creating thereby? The situation that you are creating is you are compelling people not to have any union at all and I submit, therefore, that this is a provision which is fraught with great mischief....

Sir, the second point that arises out of the provisions 4 to 20 is this. What is going to be the effect of this Bill on the stability of the trade union movement? Supposing that some kind of trade union which could ultimately aspire to be free from the control of the master does grow up, is there any guarantee under the provisions contained in this Bill that union will remain as a functioning union? So far as I have been able to study the provisions of this Bill that a union once registered will continue to enjoy that registration. Clause 10 is the most dangerous Clause. That Clause will always be hanging like a sword upon a union: Though registered, its life will always be in jeopardy and it can never be certain that while it has a legal existence today, it will not continue to have a legal existence tomorrow, because under the provisions of this Clause its registration may be cancelled at any time provided certain circumstances happen, and once a registration is cancelled, the whole structure which might have been built up with enormous industry, with enormous energy, will simply have been washed away....

Now, Sir, there is a further mischief, if I may say so, which is contained in this Bill. It is this that the cancellation of the registration of a union is left to a rival union or to an employer, which means that there will be mutual rivalry, mutual jealousy and a cut-throat competition, if I may say so, between the different trade union men in order to destroy a rival union. A trade union, therefore, which is once registered under this Bill, in order that it may enjoy a perpetual existence, shall have to show at all times that it had 51 per cent membership of the total number of workers employed?

Sir, if in a country like England, where trade unionism may be said to be like the breath of the nostrils to a workman, the trade union membership fluctuates by 50 per cent within a decade, I cannot understand how any man can expect any body of organizers of trade unions in this country of ours to maintain on its rolls at all times a membership of 51 per cent. If the membership falls by 1 per cent, the union stands to have its registration cancelled. The whole show will have to be wound up. I ask is this a reasonable condition; is this a condition which could ensure the growth of the trade union movement? If every trade union which is registered stands to have its registration cancelled, and stands in fear of it from day-to-day, what prospect is there of trade unionism growing in this country?

Now the question that I would like to ask is this. Why is it that there should be this perpetual disqualification? I can quite agree that there may be a disqualification for a temporary period. It may be possible to argue that persons who have obtained a registration by reason of fraud, by reason of misrepresentation, should be on probation for some time. I can quite understand the reasonableness of a proposal of that sort. But I do not understand the reasonableness of a provision which says that because a man was guilty of fraud or misrepresentation, he should be perpetually debarred from even coming before the Registrar and obtaining the registration of his union....

What is happening today in this industry of ours? I am sorry I have to make a plain breast of what I feel on this occasion. We have Mills in Bombay City managed by Parsis. There are Mills there managed by Gujaratis. There are Mills in Bombay which are managed by Jew or by Europeans. I visited all these Mills in my younger days when some members of my family were working there. I used to carry their bread to the Mills where they were working. Recently also I visited some of the Mills though not often times. The most surprising thing about all these Mills is that they have been made the heaven for the cousins of the Managers. Hundreds of useless people are employed in higher grades simply because they are related to the managing agents in some way. You go to a Parsi mill, you will see hundreds of Parsis employed whether they are wanted or not. Go to a mill managed by Gujaratis. You will see hundreds of Gujaratis employed whether they are wanted or not. Go to a mill managed by Jews. You will see hundreds of Jews employed, whether they are wanted or not. The best part of the earning of the workers are taken away by the managers in order to feed these people who are employed in the Mills, whether they are efficient or not, or whether they are wanted or not. All these people who are controlling the industry float the capital and bloat it up by all sorts of paper transactions. When the worker says that he gets less wages, the man controlling the industry says. 'It is my capital'. All this is bogus capital, stock exchange capital, bolstered up by speculators. A good part of the earning of the industry is swallowed by these people. From the little balance that is left, the workers are asked to eke out their existence....

If the Honourable Prime Minister wants to introduce equity, let him make the workers' wages the first charge on the profits of industry. I do not understand why the Mill owners or, for the matter of that, any owner of any industry, should not be required by law to present his budget annually. Government is required to present is budget every year; annually we get a budget of Government in which Government say how many Ministers are employed, how many *Chaprasis* are allowed to the Ministers, how many Superintendents are there in departments, how many Clerks, this, that and the other. This House is in a position to understand whether the establishment is excessive or not. This House gets to know whether the money is spent properly or not. Why is it that a Mill owner or, for the matter of that, the owner of an industry, who gets his earning, not entirely by his capital but also by the sweat of another man, be not compelled to give the details of his management? This is a very fair demand to make. The advantage would be this. Once a budget of that kind is presented by the owner of an industry, the workers would be in a position to realize and scrutinize whether the balance that is left to be divisible among the labours is fair or whether the employer has taken an undue portion of the total profit. What is the use of having a conciliation board and asking the employers to produce their account books when the employee is not placed in a position to scrutinize what is really the state of affairs?

If the procedure I suggest is adopted, I am sure about it that there will be less labour troubles, the conciliation would be more effective and there will be more industrial peace. If the Honourable Prime Minister wants to treat labour and capital on a footing of equality in the sense in which I have suggested, namely, that there should be equality, then there is no basis for equity in the provisions of this Bill. Secondly, there is no basis for equality between capital and labour because the Government in any dispute is always on the side of employers. This is clear from the use of the police that Government makes in strikes. The police force is maintained out of public fund, out of the taxes we all bear. It is intended for the benefit of all. Surely, no Government is entitled to use this police force merely because strike by the workers results in a breach of peace. What is further necessary is to show that the breach of peace has been caused by one particular section of the industry. If the breach of peace is caused by some unreasonable demand made by labour, you may be justified in using police force against them. If, on the other hand, the beach of peace is broken by something which has been done by the employer which does not stand to reason and which is contrary to justice and equity, then Government have no right to use the police force against the workers.

Real equality between employers and employees can be brought about only by incorporating these two provisions. The employer must be compelled to disclose his budget and the Government must cease to use the police force against the workers merely because there is breach of peace. Without this there can be no equality between capital and labour as to bargaining power. Will you do it? If you do this, you will lose case with the employers. If you don't you cannot be the friend of labour. The Bill, as it is, I am sure about it, should not be passed. It only handicaps labour. Labour may not now know what this Bill does. But when the Bill comes into operation and the labourer stands face to face with the Bill he will say that this Bill is bad, bloody and a brutal Bill, Sir, I cannot be a party to it.

★ ★ ★

In conformity with this cause, Dr Ambedkar joined forces with others, including the Communist-led Unions and brought the strike against the Industrial Disputes Bill to a successful conclusion, thus creating history. There was neither a contradiction nor a paradox.

While addressing a massive rally of workers for condemning the Industrial Disputes Bill in Mumbai (November 1938), Dr Ambedkar said:

All I wish to say is that when the Congress came to power, it passed totally unjustified Bills with the power of brute majority and when people raised their voices against it, the Congress Party has given up its professional values of truth and non-violence, and has been shamelessly accusing these people of wrong-doing….

Let the Congressmen propagate the irate that 'Labour Leaders are cunning and selfish'. Let me ask you a straight question. Who is cunning and selfish? Congress leaders who went back on their avowed policy of protecting the interests of labour and now creating a new law which slices the throats of workers, or the Labour leaders who have tolerated all insults of the Congress intoxicated by power and supported the labour fearlessly in the Assembly? You decide. The entire responsibility of patriotism and protecting the nation's interest lies with Congress, by inheritance, they claim! 'Dr Ambedkar is Casteist' they argue! 'Dr Ambedkar is a traitor' they say, 'as he never went to a prison!' I do not understand that how does a man become patriotic just by going to the prison. It is true that I have never been to a prison. What would have been the use of my going to a prison? If I were imprisoned I would definitely have got an A-class. I am not a hypocrite that I would enjoy the luxuries of A-class and deceitfully lie to my followers. Today's Congressmen have endured the prison life for only the name sake. True jail-term was endured by Lokmanya Tilak and other such leaders of Maharashtra!

The kind of one-sided and foul publicity may mislead some people but a neutral person would definitely recognize the hollowness in it....

When the Congress Guru Mahatma Gandhi went to the Second Round Table Conference, we the nation praised him as the sole representator of India. It is my open challenge to the followers of Mahatma Gandhi that they put together, side by side, in a book all speeches by myself and Gandhiji in the Round Table Conference, which are preserved in the proceedings of the Round Table Conference. They should publish it as follows: Dr Ambedkar Speeches, Part 1, Mahatma Gandhi's Speeches, Part 2 and let people decide who is a real traitor! Any impartial and selfless Judge should give his decision. I am ready to accept it.

Tomorrow's strike is actually not a strike. Our quarrel today is not with the owners. The Bombay Provincial Government has stubbornly passed the Bill which destroys the labour in order to appease the owners. Of course, it was passed in the Assembly. It would not take much time to pass it in the Council. We are going to strike for a day tomorrow to express the disagreement of the entire worker and labourer Class. Through this peaceful one-day strike we are going to make the world realize the massive strength of worker and labourer Class....

It is my wish that you all participate in this strike and make it successful. But I do not feel that you should participate in it on my suggestion alone. What I wish to convey to you is that on thinking about the purpose of this strike which is to reveal the hideous nature of the Bill against which we have protested and on consideration of your duty towards this, strike if you feel that it is appropriate for you to participate.

Please do not think that if you successfully carry out tomorrow's strike, your responsibilities are over. Remember that this is a foundation-stone for the battles that you have to fight in the near future. I thank you for responding in such huge numbers for this meeting.

★ ★ ★

In the chronology of events, Ambedkar's involvement in labour movement began formally in 1934 when he became the President of the Bombay Municipal Karmachari Sangh. The big moment, however, came with the establishment of the Independent Labour Party (August, 1936), the manifesto of which was a document so unique that it has a distinctive place of its own.

The manifesto stated that in the rural sector, the pressure of population and the fragmentation of land holdings were the causes of poverty. It advocated an extensive programme of technical education for improving efficiency and productivity and favoured the principle of State-management and State-ownership wherever necessary. In respect of the Industrial workers, the manifesto favoured legislation to control the employment, dismissal and promotion of employees. It also advocated legislation to fix maximum hours of work, to provide for remunerative wages, leave with pay and to provide inexpensive and sanitary dwellings. The manifesto also proposed village-level planning for housing and sanitation and for modernizing the outlook of the villagers.

The Independent Labour Party was not welcomed by the Communists who viewed it as an unnecessary division of the labourers. In Class struggle, they argued, the interests of Dalits and non-Dalits were the same, and, therefore, there was no need for an 'Independent Labour Party'; the labour movement could be organized under the same manner.

The rationale behind the "Independent Labour Party" was explained by Dr Ambedkar in a Conference of Untouchable Railway Workers convened at Manmad (District: Nasik) on February 12 and 13, 1938. Dr Ambedkar argued that the Communist leaders were fighting for the rights of workers but never for the human rights of Dalit workers. For example, the textile mill unions had never raised their voice against the prohibitive barriers that kept the Dalit workers away from the lucrative departments in the mills on account of Untouchability.

Dr Ambedkar asked the Depressed Class workers to compare the opportunities of their Class with those of other workers. He observed that they had less opportunities in the mill industry and in railways where they were deprived of many appointments on account of being Untouchables. Dr Ambedkar then questioned his Communist critiques how they would consolidate the working Classes when they never made any attempt to remove such glaring shortcomings of their movement which were detrimental to the principle of solidarity.

In a hard-hitting critique of the Communists, Dr Ambedkar had stated that Communism and labour movements were not one and the same thing. He observed that "Trade Unionism in India was in a sorry state. It was a stagnant and stinking pool because its leadership was either timid, selfish or misguided. The Communists, according to him, had exploited labourers for their political ends."[80]

Yet during the general strike of 1938 against the Industrial Disputes Bill, Dr Ambedkar organized a united front with the Communists in the interests of labour welfare. The main challenge then was to oppose, tooth and nail, the Bill which he had described as "bad, bloody and bloodthirsty". Dr, Ambedkar did this while keeping his Independent Labour Party intact from the machinations of the Communists.

There were other struggles that the Independent Labour Party organized on its own. Noteworthy in this regard was the settlement of some problems of the workers of the Bombay Municipal Corporation. The Independent Labour Party also took up the struggle for the rights of workers of the *bidi* industry of the Province, then called the Central Province and Berar.

By end 1938 Dr Ambedkar had emerged as a Labour Leader.

---

80. Presidential Address (in Marathi) at District Conference of the Depressed Classes, Masur, District Satara (September 1937).

CHAPTER TWENTY TWO

Pronouncements Inside and Outside the Assembly

AS AN ELECTED member of the Bombay Legislative Assembly, Dr Ambedkar made a significant contribution from the Opposition side. A glimpse of his numerous and varied interventions in the Assembly, always substantiated with relevant facts and figures, and his pronouncements outside the Assembly in public meeting may be provided here.

(I) ON PROVINCIAL BUDGETS

While participating in the discussion on the Bombay Province Budget: 1938-39 (March 2, 1936) Dr Ambedkar said:

> I have no hesitation in saying that this is not only the most paltriest Budget that I have ever seen, but it is a hollow and insubstantial Budget. It discloses no vision of the future and no recognition of the problems with which this Presidency is faced. This may appear somewhat extravagant, but I am presently going to substantiate what I am saying.
>
> The first thing, Sir, to which I would like to draw the attention of this House is what I regard certain examples of financial impropriety. Now, Sir, when one looks at the Blue Book which has been circulated, one notices an admission on the part of the Government that for none of these items which are included in the financial proposal is there any scheme in existence. All these heads on which this expenditure is intended to be incurred are still in incubation. They themselves do not know what are the purposes on which this money is to be spent. The second thing is that this House has not passed any of the legislative measures on which this expenditure is supposed to follow. Sir, this expenditure which practically asks for a blank cheque from this House with the fullest liberty for the Members of the Government to spend it on anything they like so long as it falls under the main heads such as education, police etc. amounts altogether to 31 lakhs of rupees.
>
> Sir, I cannot help saying that this Government has been constantly encroaching upon the privileges of this House. Time in and time out it encroached upon this

privilege of the House. This lifting of money, this asking for a blank cheque is I regard another inroad and an encroachment upon the privileges of this House.

It has always been accepted that no Minister shall place before the Legislature a demand for any lump sum without specifying the particular services, the particular items which are supposed to be included in that demand. The reason is two-fold. The House must know what are the details on which funds are being spent. Secondly, it is necessary for the Audit and Accounts Department to know how the money granted by the House has been spent. And I say, Sir, that it is something which is quite inexcusable, that this Government should have had the courage—I say, the audacity to come forward before this Legislature and merely say that they want Rs 31 lakhs for spending on certain items, about the propriety of which the House has never decided and as to the details of which the Government itself has not made up its mind. I say it is audacity.

The Government has come forward with as a permanent addition of expenditure for meeting the social services of this Province is not what is alleged to be this big sum of Rs 1,16,00,000 but the sum of Rs 68,56,000. From that you have also to make a further deduction in my judgment, and that further deduction is Rs 31,45,000 due to prohibition. That is merely a negative thing. It adds nothing positively to meeting the needs of the Province. It is merely the forgoing of an amount of revenue which was due to Government. Therefore, ultimately what one finds as the real budget providing for permanent expenditure is nothing more than Rs 37,11,000.

Is this Government to be congratulated when, as a matter of fact, it comes before this House and demands nothing more than this paltry sum of Rs 37,11,000?

Sir, I have no hesitation in asking, having regard to the needs of this Province, having regard to the illiteracy, having regard to the poor health, having regard to malaria, having regard to gonorrhea and syphilis and the other diseases that are prevalent in this Province, whether it connotes a sense of responsibility, whether it connotes a sense of adequacy on the part of this Government to come forward with nothing more than a paltry budget of Rs 37,11,000.

Is there any chance of this expenditure provided for by the Government in this budget becoming permanent? Is there any chance of the Rs 29 lakhs which the Government proposes to spend on education being available for the next year or the year after that? Sir, I cannot give a positive answer. But it will be clear to all of us if we really ask one question, and it is this: how is this expenditure financed by the Government? What are the means adopted by it for the purpose?

Are these sources, these ways and means which have been devised by my Honourable friend the Finance Minister permanent and lasting? Can they be depended upon to return from year to year?

For this additional expenditure of 37 lakhs of rupees, all the revenue we have is 8 lakhs of rupees on which we can depend. Therefore, I feel I am justified in saying even this petty show which has been presented to us in the form of a budget of 37 lakhs may not come again next year.

Now, Sir, it is quite clear that, traditionally taking things they stand in this Province up to this day, Government have undertaken, although they have never fulfilled, their responsibilities and duties which certainly cover such fields as education, public health, medical relief, and one may say, to a certain extent water supply. These are admittedly the functions of Government. The Congress Government have accepted that over and above these, what are called the essential services—education, public health, medical relief, and water supply—there are, by common standards now prevailing in all modern countries, other duties, which Government must undertake. These duties I find, are unemployment benefit, sickness insurance, old-age pensions, maternity benefits and premature death benefits to dependants. Therefore, we have got to start with this position that my Government who claims to have the reins of office in its hand must look upon these duties as part of their functions. And the question, therefore, is what are going to be the total liabilities of Government, if Government were to decide upon discharging these obligations?

We, therefore, find ourselves in this position, that our revenues are not increasing at all; they are practically in a stagnant position. Now add to that two new factors. The first is that this position is now going to be worse off by the prohibition policy which has been adopted by this Government. Secondly, we have to bear in mind that this Government has announced its policy of reducing the land revenue. Now, it is a fact that these two items of revenue together make up something like 7 crores of rupees. These 7 crores of rupees, having regard to the policy laid down by the Government, must now be regarded as the vanishing assets of the Province. Therefore, the net revenue which you can calculate as a permanent basis for building up anything that could be permanent is only 5 cores of rupees. As against this, you have to set up, as I said, an ultimate liability of 24 crores of rupees.

This Budget is a most retrograde budget. It is a Budget which shows that the Government has gone back on its plighted word.

Although taxation in this Province is very high, it is clear to us that most of this taxation is being borne by the poorer people in the Province. The land tax, the excise tax, the stamps and court fees, the taxes on public conveyances, the tax on country grown tobacco—all these are being mostly paid by the poorer Classes. The income-tax is the only tax paid by the rich, and that at present is beyond the reach of the Provincial Government. Between the poorer Classes who pay most of the Provincial taxes and the richer Classes who pay the income-tax to the Central Government, there is a considerable body of people who ought to bear a portion of the financial responsibilities of their Province. The wealthier Classes whose contribution to Provincial Revenues is inadequate must also come forward to take their proper share in them. Pledged in as we are by numerous restrictions, it is no easy task to device taxes which will affect only the taxable untaxed. Though today, I am not in a position to anticipate the decisions of the future, I may state that we are exploring the possibilities of many proposals with a view to submitting to this House proposals which may provide the necessary funds for not only recouping ourselves from the loss which a policy of prohibition may involve but will also enable us to undertake some expansion, though not all the expansion, that we desire in the many fields of social service, social service in the widest sense of the term.

There are many public utility services which are at present being utilized for the benefit of a few at the cost of the community as a whole. There is no reason why the State should not nationalize these activities and appropriate the profits for the good of the community as a whole. Many other potential sources of income which could fairly be taken up by Government remain unutilized or are allowed to be exploited for the benefit of a few. There is a large field which we must explore, to which state activities could be extended, and Government will look forward with confidence to activities of this nature as possible sources of public benefit.

My Honourable friend has been congratulated, I think, on the ground that there has been no new taxation. I for myself have the greatest condemnation for the Government for not coming forward with taxation. This Budget, therefore, I say, is a rich man's budget. It is not a poor man's budget. The poor man wants more and more. The rich man can afford to be independent of the Government. It is the poor who wants Government to come to his succour; it is the poor man that needs more service. No Government worthy of its name, no Government with any sincerity, can tell the poor Classes that it cannot provide these amenities because it has not the courage to levy taxes. The sooner such a Government abdicates the better for all.

The Governments in India, no matter what the Province is, will never do any good if they confine their attention to what in European countries are merely called social services. I do maintain and I state it emphatically, that one of the principal duties of this Government must be to tackle the problem of poverty. The Government must see that they do adopt ways and means whereby the national income of this Province rises to some substantial level, whereby the majority of the people can live in amenities which rightly belong to all modern and civilized men. The system of social services which has so far prevailed in European countries, whereby the Government gives what are called doles or unemployment benefits, maternity benefits, and so on, presupposes one thing: it presupposes that a majority of the people are above want, are above the line of poverty, and that it is only those few who, either by the vagaries of the economic system or by any misfortune befalling them, fall below that line of poverty, that need assistance from the Government. It is, therefore, perfectly possible, perfectly justifiable, for European governments not to bother with problems of general economic uplift of the people as a whole. But the problems with which we are faced in this country are of a totally different character. I have no hesitation in saying and I do not suppose there is anybody in this House who would quarrel with me if I state it, that we are all a nation of beggars and coolies. That is the description which one can give of all this mass of people. Therefore, no Government worthy of its name can sit silent and not take account of this grave problem.

Now, Sir, having regard to the Budget proposals which we have before us, is there anything to indicate that this Government is aware of this problem, that it does take cognizance of it, that, after all, the one supreme aim must be to see that the national income of this country rises, that the national dividend rises? I do not see anything. There seems to be one idea which is prevalent all over and which I really want to examine at this stage. The view is held by all that a large part of the poverty of the agriculturists arises out of what is called the heavy burden of land revenue. Therefore, the view is held—and I have no doubt that that is the view of the Finance Minister—that all that needs to be done in order that the people's income may increase would be to reduce that burden of land revenue.

Now, Sir, I take the liberty of saying that nothing can be more fallacious than this view. That does not mean that I am opposed to the reduction of the land revenue: I am for it; I will insist upon it because I say that this Government has really no right to take what are called the profits of agriculture, as distinguished from mere rent for the use of land.

This Government was generous enough and could afford to remit the whole of the land revenue, namely, 3½ crores, let us distribute this precious sum of 3½ crores over the two crores of the population. Now, on a rough calculation I find that the total addition to the income of one individual, under these circumstances, would be Rupee 1.5. That is the highest. Converting it into a monthly allowance I find that the addition that would be made to the income of each man would be of 2½ annas.[81] Now, I like to ask whether anybody would seriously contend that an addition of 2½ annas, which would be the result of the remission of the whole of the land revenue, would increase our economic welfare in such a way that the problem of poverty would be abolished from our midst.

Sir, the problem needs different remedies—altogether different remedies. But I do want to say that this is something which this Government does not seem to be aware of, and I do say that a Government does not seem to be aware of, and I do say that a Government which is not cognizant of this problem, a Government which has not the ways and the means of solving this problem, can bring no relief, can be a source of no happiness to the people of this Province; and therefore, I will say, in conclusion, that this is a Budget which is a most disappointing budget, a budget which is designed to relieve the rich and to starve the millions.

* * *

The next year, while speaking in the Assembly on the Provincial Budget: 1939-40 (February 1939) Dr Ambedkar, *inter alia,* said:

The first Budget that was submitted by him was, as a matter of fact, not his Budget; it was probably the Budget prepared by the Interim Ministry and undoubtedly the Finance Minister could not be held responsible for whatever blemishes the first Budget contained. The second Budget had the excuse of having been made in a hurry, without Government's having had sufficient time to prepare their plans and to digest the whole thing. But I am sure none of these excuses or extenuations could apply to the present Budget which has been presented to us. It must be said that this is a budget which has been prepared after mature consideration. It undoubtedly embodies in it the full plan which the Ministry has with regard to the taxation and with regard to the proposals of expenditure which, from their point of view, are matters of urgency. I think that this Budget, therefore, needs to be more specifically scrutinized.

Speaking for myself, when I refer to the revenue side of the Budget as well as its expenditure side, my own view is that the proper description of this Budget would be that on the revenue side it is a reckless Budget and on the expenditure side, it is a senseless Budget.

There are six different proposals in the Finance Bill. First of all, the Bill proposes to continue for a year more the additions made to the stamp duties, and the court fees sanctioned by the Bombay Finance Act II of 1932. Secondly, it increases the duty on the consumption of electricity. Thirdly, it increases the stamp duties in certain cities

81. Re one equals 16 annas.

and urban areas on conveyances of immoveable property. Fourthly, it levies a tax on leases of immovable property. Fifthly, it imposes a tax of 10 per cent on the annual letting value of buildings in Bombay, Bombay Suburban District, and Ahmedabad City. And sixthly, it imposes a sales tax not exceeding 6¼ per cent on three items, namely, motor spirit of lubricants, manufactured cloth, and silk yarn.

Now, Sir, in the light of this, compare the figures of our Presidency. The Bombay Presidency has a population of 180 lakhs. The total revenue from excise is 325 lakhs. Can anyone say that this consumption of liquor in the Bombay Presidency can be said to create a problem which the State must undertake immediately to meet? A man who said 'Yes' and gave an affirmative answer would certainly be a man who has lost all his bearings. Sir, with these figures before me, I claim to say that with nobody who is a fair-minded person would be able to say that drink is such a problem in this country that it ought to be tackled forthwith.

Then, Sir, the next question that I want to ask is this. Is this such an urgent problem that we must keep aside everything and deal with it first? In order to answer that question, it is necessary to bear in mind what the different needs are of the people of this Province. Are the other needs fully satisfied? Are they tolerably satisfied, so that because they are tolerably satisfied we ought to keep them aside for the moment and tackle this one and only question?

Let me take a few illustrations. First of all, take the question of education. With regard to adult education, the position in this Province is this. That means that practically 86 per cent of the male population and 98 per cent of the female population needs still to be taught the rudiments of education. We have had a Committee appointed by the Government to report upon this matter. That Committee has made its report. But I do not find any provision made in the present Budget to carry out the proposals made by that Committee.

Take children's education, what is the position in this Province? In this Province, one thing which is absolutely undeniable is this, that this Government have repudiated their responsibility in regard to college education. I think there can be no doubt on the point. This Government do not regard giving higher education to the boys of this Province any business of theirs. That has been left by Government to private agencies. With regard to secondary education, the matter is more or less on the same footing. Government do not take responsibility on their shoulders but they supplement the monies collected by private agencies by small grants from public treasury. Therefore, we are really under a very limited field of activity so far as education is concerned. Then, primary education. What have Government done with regard to primary education? From the figures that I have been able to collect yesterday, I find the present position is this. The Primary Education Act applies to children who are between 6 and 11 years of age. The total number of children between 6 and 11 is 2,479,000. Of these children, I think 754,000 are in schools; and the rest of them are not in schools. This proportion works out in this way. Out of every three children, one is in school and two are still outside school. Examine the question from another point of view, from the point of view of facilities provided by Government for primary education. According to Government figures, there are in the towns of this Province 184 primary schools. This is with regard to towns. What is the position with regard to villages? The total number of villages in this Province is 21,484. Out of these only 8,599 villages have got schools; and 12,885 villages have no schools at all. That is the position. Governments do not even care to provide facilities for them, apart from the question of carrying out the provisions of the Primary Education Act. Now, Sir, one curious thing which strikes me at any rate, and I do not know whether it strikes the Honourable Finance Minister, is what would be cost of making primary education compulsory. According to the figures worked out by the Primary Education Committee, what Bombay Government needs to make primary education compulsory is 1.30 lakhs. Now Sir, that is just the amount the Honourable Finance Minister is raising by his taxation proposals. Apart from the question whether the taxation proposals are good or not, confining my attention to the question as to the best method the proper purpose for which this money ought to be spent, the question that I should like to ask of the Honourable Finance Minister is this. You are raising practically 1.30 lakhs of rupees; is it necessary that you should spend this money on improving the lots of a drunkard or should you spend this money on educating children who do not get education? What is the choice that you make? That is really the whole question. Is the education of children more important? Is the education practically of 17 to 18 lakhs of children less important than the lot of 10 lakhs of city people who choose to drink? Sir, I do not believe in it.

Take another alternative thing. I refer to public health. The total expenditure this Province incurs on public health is a paltry sum of Rs 31,48,000. It works out at the rate of 2½ per cent on our total expenditure. Now, Sir, village water supply is a crying need; there are hundreds of villages which have no water supply at all. Anyone who goes to the villages will mark that every village in this Province is nothing else but a dung heap. It is a misnomer to call it a village, it is a misnomer to call it a place fit for human habitation. The improvement of the insanitary conditions and the abomination that exist in villages is certainly the crying need of our Province. Hundreds of people are dying from malaria, are dying from all sorts of diseases. There are hardly any dispensaries. There is hardly any provision made for distribution of medicine or medical treatment. There is no water supply, as I said. Last year, a provision of 10 lakhs was made. We do not know how that money has been spent. This year, I find there is some provision made, about Rs 8,55,000, what is all this having regard to the enormity of the want? Hundreds of people are dying by reason of the fact that there is no medical aid, no clear water to drink. The Finance Minister has chosen to spend this money in saving the souls, to use a Biblical expression, in curing the souls or in being the curate of 10 lakhs of drunkards in Bombay and Ahmedabad.

Then, Sir, take another point. The same point has been made that we are taxing the city dwellers; we are taxing the urban population. Why are we taxing the urban population? The reason why we are taxing the urban population is because we want to improve the amenities of the village folk. Is there anything of the kind done in this Budget? Personally, I would be very glad indeed; I will withdraw all my opposition to these taxation measures if he spends all this money on wiping out the land revenue. Is he doing that? Why is he not doing that?

Now, Sir, there are just one or two points which I should like to touch upon. In this Budget, the Honourable Finance Minister seems to take credit for two things. One is, that after all he is levying all these taxes from the urban areas. The second is, that taking things by their total, there is no additional burden imposed because what is levied by way of a new tax is remitted by prohibition and, therefore, on the total the sums are equal.

Sir, that being the position, the view I take is—and I say this with full deliberation—that the salvation of this Province and, if I may say so, the salvation of the whole of India lies in greater urbanization: in reviving our towns, in building our industries, in removing as much population as we possibly can from our villages to the towns. What is there in villages? After all, our village folks have no capital to run their agriculture in the best way in which agriculture ought to be run. Population is increasing every decade, and land is being fragmented every time a man and heirs come on the spot. Everywhere, the situation is as bad as one could conceive it. The only way by which you can increase the standard of living of the people in the villages is not to give them an antiquated machine like *charkha* or to force them to weave cloth which they cannot sell in a competitive market. The way to increase the standard of living is not to destroy industries and other revenues of service in the towns and force them to go to villages. The way lies in the other direction, namely, in taking away as many people as you possibly can from the villages and bringing them to the towns, giving them employment in industries and establishing better ways to economic life. That is the way. Sir, I have no hesitation in saying that a man who is bent upon breaking up such little industry, such little urbanization, as we possess is certainly no friend of people; if I may say so, I look upon him as an enemy of the people.

Practically the cost of collection in this Province makes up 15 per cent our revenue; Superannuation is 10 per cent; Interest takes away 10½ per cent; Law and Order including Justice, Police and Jails takes away 18 per cent of our revenue; and what little remains is spent on the other subjects which may be said to be subjects of public welfare. This is the position. In fact, it is a very tight corner; so far as the revenue is concerned, our capacity is less, and so far as our appropriations are concerned, many items are such that they really do not give us anything by way of public welfare. In a situation like this, I think it was but necessary that the Honourable Minister for Finance ought to have been more cautious than he has been. I am sorry to say that he has not.

(II) ON THE INDEPENDENCE OF JUDICIARY

In March 1938, Jamnadas Mehta had moved an adjournment motion seeking to draw public attention to Government interference undermining the authority of the Bombay High Court. The then Home Minister of the Province, Kanhaiyya Lal Munshi had suspended the sentence of two rich prisoners after the High Court had rejected their application.

Dr Ambedkar strongly supported the motion pointing out that "there has never been a precedent, at any rate to my knowledge, of ordinary convicts having their sentences suspended for any reason by any of the Home Ministers...."

Dr Ambedkar also asked a very important question to the Prime Minister.[82]

82. It may be noted that the Chief Ministers of the Province were addressed then as Prime Ministers.

The question is this: Was this order passed with the knowledge of the Prime Minister? Was this order passed with the knowledge of the Cabinet or was it passed only by the Honourable Home Minister? Sir, I ask these questions for a very great reason. We are entitled to suppose, although we have no positive evidence on this point that under the new Act the Congress Cabinet is working as a collective body with a collective responsibility; and, therefore, I am entitled to presume that this matter was placed before the whole of the Cabinet, and if not before the whole of the Cabinet, at any rate, before the Prime Minister who, in the eyes of the people, is the person who is solely responsible for the administration of this Province.

I am particularly bound to make this reference and ask these questions because I treat this as a very grave matter. Suspension of sentence passed upon a convicted person is certainly a violation of the law and I submit that so grave an act involving such serious consequences to the administration of justice, to the welfare of the people of this Province, could not have been carried out without the knowledge of the Prime Minister.

(III) ON NATIONALISM

In April 1938, while participating in the Bombay Assembly Debate on "Creation of a Separate Karnataka Province", Dr Ambedkar opposed the Resolution (Much later, Dr Ambedkar did some detailed thought-provoking work on Linguistic Re-organization of States).

In the Assembly debate, Dr Ambedkar made a very important observation. He said:

That common goal is the building up of a feeling that we are all Indians. I do not like what some people say, that we are Indians first and Hindus afterwards or Muslims afterwards. I am not satisfied with that, I frankly say that I am not satisfied with that. I do not want that our loyalty as Indians should be in the slightest way affected by any competitive loyalty whether loyalty arises out of our religion, out of our culture or out of our language. I want all people to be Indian first, Indian last and nothing else but Indians and, therefore, I say, that this is a resolution which directly runs counter to this ideal.

Sir, this is an ideal which we ought to cherish very zealously. I can quite understand that in a country like America, in a country like Germany, in a country like Europe, where the feeling of oneness is solidified, where there is no need to make anybody feel that he is not a German to tolerate anything that is of a separatist character but where the feeling that we are Indians is still in embryo, is only beginning to ripen, to allow other loyalties feeling of culture, feelings of nationality to grow simultaneously—I say deliberately—is the greatest crime that we can commit and I, for myself, will not be a party to it and I strongly, very strongly, oppose this resolution.

(IV) ON COMMUNAL VIOLENCE

In April, 1938, when a Bill was moved in the Assembly to confer the authority on the Police Commissioner to expel the trouble-makers during communal violence,

Dr Ambedkar strongly supported it with an amendment to safeguard against arbitrary action.

Participating in the debate, Dr Ambedkar said:

> If the House would allow me to say so, I am very familiar with the kind of evil to which he has referred. I have spent a very great part of my life in what I may call the underworld of Bombay City. I have lived from 1911 to 1933 in the Improvement Trust *chawls* among labourers and the lower Classes, and I know perfectly well, more than the Commissioner of Police or the Honourable Home Minister, how these poor people are molested by what are called *mavalis* and *dadas*, how utterly impossible it is for these victims of their to obtain any redress, because they themselves, for fear of further molestation, would not go to court of law and seek to get a conviction. I, therefore, think that the Bill that has been brought forward is thoroughly justified by the circumstances of the case.
>
> I have here some figures relating to the communal riots that have taken place in the City of Bombay. Between the year 1851 and 1938, there have been altogether 9 communal riots in the City of Bombay. The first riot took place on October 17, 1851. That riot was between the Muslims and Parsis. The second riot took place in the year 1874; that was also between the Muslims and Parsis. The third riot took place in 1893 and it was between the Hindus and Muslims. The fourth was in 1929 that was also between the Hindus and Muslims. The fifth took place in 1932; the sixth in 1933; the seventh in 1936: the eighth in 1937; and the ninth on April 17, 1938. All these were riots between the Hindus and *Musalmans*.
>
> In the riot of 1893, there were 80 persons killed, 60 temples were destroyed, 7 mosques were destroyed and 27 durgas were destroyed. I have not got the figures for the others. In the riot of 1929, 51 persons were killed; in the riot of 1932, 300 persons were killed and more than 300 were wounded. In 1936, 61 persons were killed and 550 were wounded. In the year 1938—I don't have exact figure—12 persons were killed and more than 120 were wounded.
>
> The rapidity with which these riots have taken place is also interesting and important which the House should bear in mind. As I told you, the first riot took place in 1852; the second riot took place within 23 years of the first riot; the third took place after 19 years of the second riot; the fourth riot took place 36 years after the third riot; the fifth riot took place within 3 years of the fourth; the sixth riot took place within one year of the fifth; the seventh riot took place within 3 years of the sixth; the eighth riot took place within one year of the seventh; and the ninth riot took place within less than one year of the eighth.

(V) ON POLICE FIRING

In March 1939, Dr Ambedkar spoke in the Assembly at length on the Disturbance Enquiry Committee Report. The Enquiry Committee was appointed to investigate the police firing that had taken place during the workers' agitation against the Industrial Disputes Bill.

While strongly condemning the police brutality, Dr Ambedkar narrated a shocking story:

> At the time when the Round Table Conference met, the civilians who had gone back from here were divided into two groups—one group opposed to Indian Home Rule, and the other supporting Indian Home Rule. Sir Edward Thompson was one of those who led the group in support of the Indian claim. As a member of that group, he came before the Joint Parliamentary Committee to give evidence and to support his point of view, namely, as to why India should be given Home Rule. We were all very pleased that at any rate a section of the Indian civilians should come forward honestly and wholeheartedly to support the Indian cause. But I frankly say that I was horrified by the argument that he advanced. What was the argument that he advanced? The argument that he advanced was this. He said, 'I am an Irishman. I live in Southern Ireland. I have witnessed the rebellion that took place in Southern Ireland during 1916 and onwards.' The one thing that convinced him, he said, in favour of Irish home rule was this: 'So long as the rebellion was going on, no Englishman could shoot an Irishman, however violent his action was, because if an Englishman shot an Irishman, the whole Irish country went up in arms.' He said that as soon as Home Rule was granted, it was possible for Cosgrave to shoot Irishmen, and nobody rose in rebellion against it. He said that one advantage that the Englishman would have from home rule to India would be that the Indian Ministers would be able to shoot Indians without any qualms. This is exactly what is happening.

And then, Dr Ambedkar concluded:

> Disturbances are no doubt very unfortunate, but they could never be otherwise. The only question is this: Whether, in maintaining peace and order, we shall not have regard for freedom and for liberty. And if Home Rule means nothing else—as I am thinking, it can mean nothing else—than that our own Minister can shoot our own people, and the rest of us merely laugh at the whole show or rise to support him because he happens to belong to a particular Party, then I say Home Rule has been a curse and not a benefit to all India.

* * *

Outside the Bombay Legislative Assembly, Dr Ambedkar, during this period remained highly critical of the Indian National Congress.

While addressing a public meeting in Chalisgaon (July 31, 1937), Dr Ambedkar said that the main thing to be borne in mind was that the British rulers, who were indifferent to Untouchables, were now replaced by a set of leaders who belonged to the Party of social oppressors of the Depressed Classes. Those were the days, he continued, of union organization and precaution from the point of view of the Untouchables. He then pointed out how Brahmanism was asserting itself in India through Ministries installed by the Congress. Also the Congress Ministries were, he remarked, led by Brahmins while there were no Depressed Class Ministers.

On January 1, 1988, while replying to a Civic Address by Solapur Municipality, Dr Ambedkar remarked:

In this country we have Democracy, but it is a Democracy which has ceased to exercise its intelligence. It has bound itself hand and foot to one organization and only one. It is not prepared to sit in judgment over the doings or thinking of this organization. I consider it the greatest malaise, a disease and a sickness. It has affected all our people. They are intoxicated.

Unfortunately, the Indian people are by tradition men who have more faith and less wit. Anyone who does anything out of the ordinary does something so eccentric as to be called in other countries an insane person, acquires in this country the status of a Mahatma or Yogi. And people follow him as the sheep follow the shepherd....

I am sure that if this continues, we could reap no benefit from the political advancement which this country has secured under the Act (i.e., Government of India Act, 1935)....

Later that year, delivering a Gujarati-Hindi speech in Ahmedabad (October 22-23, 1938), Dr Ambedkar criticized the policies of the Congress Government of Bombay.

Dr Ambedkar maintained that the Congress Government of Bombay was not reducing the land revenue, nor was it prepared to tax the rich. The former Government had recommended the grant of waste lands to the Depressed Classes for cultivation, recruitment of Depressed Classes in the Police services, and a certain percentage of reservation in Government Departments for the Depressed Classes. But the Congress Government did not care for them.

While being critical of the Congress Government of Bombay, Dr Ambedkar kept trying to imbibe democratic values among his followers. In a public meeting in Nagpur (May 1, 1938), Dr Ambedkar advised his followers to keep watch on their elected representatives. He said:

The persons whom you elect should do their duty of emancipation of our society; and it is your duty to ensure that they do it. It is also your duty to be the watchdog of your Representatives to ascertain that they raise in the Legislatures the issues for your welfare, introduce Resolutions and get them passed in the Assembly for the welfare of our people. They should do their Legislative duties with utmost diligence. You should call the public meetings like the one we are having right now after every Assembly session to take a review of work done by your Representatives. Those who have not functioned to your expectations for the welfare of the society should not be re-elected if they are contesting now. This is your duty. If you keep watch on them then only they will work in the Assembly for your benefits. If you follow this method a lot of good changes will take place for your benefits and progress in future.

In December 25, 1938, Dr Ambedkar gave a reception to Swami Shahjananda, President, All-India Kisan Sabha. Swami Shahjananda in his speech argued that this nation has got to be free from foreign domination first, and all available forces must be united for that purpose, and the Congress with all its past experiences and traditions is best able to do it.

Dr Ambedkar's considered response to the proposal was this:

We are the most down-trodden, poverty-stricken, oppressed people. We suffer from injustices of a type from which no other Class suffers. But we shall set aside our differences with the higher Classes for the moment. We shall postpone insisting on our Class demands and shall join the Congress, if it decided to fight Imperialism.

I can understand the need for a united political organization of all Classes of people of this country in their endeavour to fight their common opponent foreign Imperialism. I shall support the temporary liquidation of all political organizations in the event of a fight against the common foe. I shall be glad to wind up the Independent Labour Party and place my forces at the disposal of the Indian National Congress if it were to launch such a struggle.

What is the position today? The Congress is not engaged in an anti-Imperialist struggle. It is using the Constitutional machinery to advance the interest of Capitalists, and other vested interests; it is engaged in bolstering them up by sacrificing the interests of workers and peasants. Its administrative activities have evoked encomiums not from the masses, but from Imperialism itself which the Congress is supposed to be fighting.

When the Congress is thus busy exploiting even the fragmentary powers that it has secured in advancing its Class interests, it becomes our obvious duty to set up our own Class organization to protect our interests and to resist encroachments on our rights and liberties by Congress or any other Ministries. It would be suicidal for us to join the Congress at such a stage.

CHATPER TWENTY THREE

On the Goal of India's Political Evolution: Federation versus Freedom

THE GOVERNMENT OF India Act, 1935 passed by the British Parliament in August 1935 had several significant parts including:

(i) The grant of a large measure of autonomy to the Provinces of British India (thus ending the system of diarchy introduced by the Government of India Act 1919); and
(ii) Provision for the establishment of a "Federation of India" composed of both British India and some or all of the "Princely States".

Lord Linlithgow was appointed as the new Viceroy with the responsibility of bringing the Act into effect. As per the Act, Provincial elections were held in 1937 and thus commenced the era of Provincial Autonomy in India. Following the 1937 elections Viceroy Linlithgow worked hard to garner support for the Federation part of the Act.

While the debate regarding the Federation of India was at its peak, Dr Ambedkar delivered a public address i.e., Kale Memorial Lecture at the Gokhale Institute of Politics and Economics in Pune on January 29, 1939. The theme was: "What's the Goal of India's Political Evolution?" This lecture was also published as a book in the same year with the title: *Federation Versus Freedom.*

In the book Dr Ambedkar sets out briefly the outline of the Scheme of Federation and examines it in the light of accepted tests of democratic federations in operation elsewhere in the world. Here are some excerpts from the noteworthy treatise

A. THE FEDERAL SYSTEM

The Federal Scheme is a vast thing. Its provisions are contained, first in 321 Sections of the Government of India Act 1935. Secondly, in the nine Schedules which are part of the Act. Thirdly, in 31 Orders-in-Council issued under the Act, and fourthly, the hundreds of Instruments of Accession to be passed by the Indian States.

There are five countries which are known in the modern times to have adopted the federal form of government. They are: USA, Switzerland, Imperial Germany, Canada and Australia. To these it is now proposed to add sixth which is the All-India Federation. The Indian Federation in point of area is 3/5thof USA and of Australia and half of Canada. It is nine times of Germany and 120 times of Switzerland. In point of population, it is three times of USA, five times of Germany, 35 times of Canada, 58 times of Australia and 88 times of Switzerland.... It is really a monster among Federations.

The Authority of the Federation is derived from the Crown. In this respect the Indian Federation differs from the Federation in the USA. In the USA, the powers of the Federation are derived from the people. The people of the United States are the fountain from which the authority is derived.... The Indian Federation (however) resembles the Federations in Australia and Canada. That the Indian Federation should differ in this respect from the American Federation, and agree with the Canadian and Australian Federation is perfectly understandable. The United States is a republic while Canada and India are dominions of the Crown. In the former, the source of all authority are the people. In the latter the source of all authority is the Crown....

The units of this Federation do not form one single whole with a common spring of action. The units are separate. They are just held together. For some purposes the position of the units cannot be altered at all. For some purposes alteration is permissible but such alteration cannot bind all the units alike. Some will be bound by it but some will not be unless they consent to the bound. In other words, in this Federation there is no provision for growth. It is fixed. It cannot move. A change by evolution is not possible and where it is possible it is not binding unless it is accepted.

(I) The Federal Legislature

The Federal Legislature is a bicameral legislature. There is a Lower House which is spoken of as the Legislative Assembly and there is an Upper House which is called the Council of States. The total membership of the Federal Assembly is 375 and of the Council of States 260. These seats are divided in a certain proportion between British India and the Indian States. Of the 375 seats in the Federal Assembly 250 are allotted to British India and 125 to the Indian States. In the Council of States, out of the 260 seats, 156 are allotted to British India and 104 to the Indian States.

It may be noticed that distribution between British India and the Indian States is not based upon an equalitarian principle. It is possible to take the population as the basis of representation. It is also possible to take the revenue as the basis of representation. But neither of these has been taken as the basis of distribution of seats. Whether you take population as the basis or whether you take revenue as the basis, you will find that British India has been under-represented, while the Indian States have been over-represented in the two Chambers.

The method of filling the seats is also noteworthy. The representatives of the British India in both the Chambers will be elected. The representatives of the Indian States, on the other hand, are to be appointed i.e., nominated, by the Rulers of the States. It is open to a Ruler to provide that the representatives of his State, though appointed by him, may be chosen by his subjects but this is a matter which is left to his discretion. He may appoint a person who is chosen by his people or he may, if he pleases, do both, choose and appoint. In the final result a State's representative is to be appointed by the Ruler as distinguished from being elected by the people. In the case of British India, the representatives are to be elected, but here again there is a peculiarity which may be noticed. In the case of all bi-cameral Legislatures the Lower House being a popular house is always elected directly by the people, while the Upper House being a revising Chamber is elected by indirect election. In the case of the Indian Federation this process is reversed. The Upper Chamber will be elected by direct election by the people and it is the Lower Chamber which is going to be elected indirectly by the Provincial Legislatures. The life of the Federal Assembly is fixed for a term of five years, although it may be dissolved sooner. The Council of States on the other hand is a permanent body not liable to dissolution. It is a body which lives by renewal of a third part of its membership every three years.

Now the authority of the two Chambers to pass laws and to sanction expenditure may be noted. With regard to the authority to pass laws some constitutions make a distinction between money Bills and other Bills and provide that with regard to money Bills the Upper Chamber shall not have the power to initiate such a Bill, and also that the Upper Chamber shall not have the authority to reject it. It is given the power only to suspend the passing of the Bill for a stated period. The Indian Constitution makes no such distinction at all. The money Bills and other Bills are treated on the same footing and require the assent of both the Chambers before they can become law.... With regard to the authority to sanction expenditure: here again there is a departure made in the accepted principles of distributing authority between the two Chambers when a Legislature is bi-cameral....

It will thus be seen that the two Chambers are co-equal in authority, both in the matter of their authority to pass laws and in the matter of sanctioning expenditure. A conflict between the two Chambers cannot end by one Chamber yielding to the other if that Chamber does not wish so to yield. The procedure adopted for the resolving of differences between the two Chambers is the method of joint sessions.

The Federal Government has the Right to tax even where it gives the right to collect it and even where it gives the power to levy the tax it does not give the right to collect it. The States are just subjected to pay the surcharge and the Federal Government has no right to collect it. The collection is left to the Ruler of the State.

The Ruler instead of collecting surcharge from his subjects may agree to pay the Federation a lump sum.

(II) Is the Federation a Perpetual Union?

The Indian Federation is not a perpetual Union, and the Indian States have a right to secede, which is in contrast to the Constitution of USA, which says nothing as to the right of secession.... The 1935 Act ordains and establishes a Federal Government for British India only. The Federal Government will become a Government for the States only when a State adopts it by its Instrument of Accession. The Indian Federation is (thus) a compact and not a perpetual Union.

B. RELATIONSHIP OF THE UNITS TO THE FEDERAL GOVERNMENT

(I) In the Matter of Legislation

The Federal List contains 59 and the Concurrent List contains 36 items as subjects of legislation. Both lists are binding on the Provinces. They cannot pick and choose the matters on which they will legislate.... On the contrary, there is no obligation upon the Prince to accept all subjects in the Federal List as a condition precedent for his entry into the Federation. He may accept some or he may accept all. One Ruler may accept one item and another Ruler may accept another item....

(II) In the Matter of the Executive

Again in the matter of the Executive the States and the Provinces do not stand on the same footing. With regard to the States the Federation can have no Executive authority in respect of subjects in the Concurrent List, but also the Federation is not entitled to have exclusive authority with respect to matters included in the Federal Legislative List.

(III) In the Matter of Administration

A State by the Instrument of Accession may stipulate that the administration of Federal Laws in the State shall be carried out by the State agency and not by the agency of the Federation and if it does so stipulate then Federation shall have no administrative power inside the State. The benefit of a law depends upon its administration. The Indian Federation is the only Federation in which some units of the Federation are permitted to say that the Federal Government shall have no administrative power in its territory.

With regard to a Province the Executive Authority of the Federation extends to all matters over which the Federation has legislative authority. With regard to the State the position is different. The mere fact that the Federal Legislature has authority to legislate in respect of a subject does not give the Federation any Executive authority over the State in respect of that subject. Such Executive authority can be conferred only as a result of a law passed by the Federation. Whether it is possible to pass such a law is problematic in view of the large representation which the States have in Federal Legislature. Whatever may be the eventuality, in theory the Executive authority of the Federation does not extend to a Federated State. The position is that while with regard to the Provinces the Federation can legislate as well as execute, in the case of the Federated States, the Federation can legislate, but cannot execute. The execution may be with the State.

(IV) In the Matter of Finance

The disparity between the Provinces and the States is a glaring disparity

Now, while the Provinces are liable to bear taxation under any of these heads.... the same is not true for the States. For instance, the States are not liable in ordinary time to ordinary taxes falling under certain heads. While the Provinces are liable, with regard to extraordinary taxation, the States are not liable to contribute even in times of financial stringency....

Another difference from the financial point of view between States and Provinces is that the field of taxation for the Provincial Governments has been defined by an Act. But there is nothing in the Act which defines the power of a Federated State with regard to its system of taxation.

Every individual stands in a dual relationship, one with the Federal State and the other with the State/Province, in which he may reside. The subject of an Indian State is a foreigner in British India as well as in another Indian State. The subject of a British Indian Province is a foreigner in every Indian State. A British Indian will continue to be a foreigner in every Indian State even though it is a Federal State after the Federation, as he was before the Federation. Similarly, a subject of a Federated Indian State will be a foreigner in every British Indian Province after the Federation as he was before Federation. There is no common nationality.

C. BENEFITS OF THE FEDERAL SCHEME

Following are the three benefits perceived of the Federal system in India:

(I) Federation and the Unity of India

The advantages of common system of government are indeed very real. To have a common system of law, administration and a feeling of oneness are some of the essentials of good life. How much of this Indian India is going to be brought under this Federation? Many will be inclined to say that as this is spoken of as an all-India Federation every inch of this area will be included in the Federation and will be subject to the authority of the Federal Government. Such an impression is no doubt created by the wording of Section 6 (7) which relates to the accession of the States.

This Section speaks of a Ruler declaring his desire to join the Federation and thereby suggesting that every State is entitled to join the Federation. If this is true, then no doubt the Federation can in course of time be an all-India Federation

(II) What is the Total Number of the States which Can Join the Federation?

Schedule I limits it to 147. This means 480 States will remain outside the Federation and can never become a part of Federation, as the total number of States is 627. This shows that the Federation is not an all-India Federation.

(III) What about nation building?

The people in the Indian States remain the subjects of the States. The Federal Government cannot deal with them directly. Everything has to be done through the State. There is no contact between the two, not even for purposes of taxation. How can a feeling that they belong to the national Government grow in the subject of the Indian States if they are excluded from any and every influence and are not even made to feel the existence of the National Government. United States of India will not be more than a mere body of United States. It has no potentiality of forging a nation out of these States and probably the framers of the Scheme have had no such intention.

(IV) Democratization of Autocracies

One of the advantages of the Federal Scheme which is claimed by its protagonists is that it brings beneath the dome of a single political edifice the new democracies of British India and the ancient autocracies of the Indian States and that by bringing the two under one edifice it provides contact between democracy and autocracy and thus enables the democracy in British India to democratize the autocracies in the Indian States. But the Federation has no or very little power to legislate or execute in the Indian States against the will of the Ruler, for example Section 84 prevents any member of a Provincial Legislature from asking any question with regard to the personal conduct of the Ruler of any Indian State or the affairs of a State, but the States can raise any matter in the Federal Legislature.... The representatives of the Federal States have all the powers of the Chamber they are in, they can vote on the budget, legislate for British India but the vice-versa cannot be done except on matters State chooses to surrender.

Thus States are placed by law in a position to control affairs of British India and by the same law British India is disabled from exercising any influence over the States. So this will not result in democratization of the Indian States. On the other hand, it helps the Indian States to destroy democracy in British India.

The Lower and the Upper Chamber have members nominated by the Rulers of the States and these seats may be filled by the advice of the political department of

Government which exercises its power on behalf of the Crown. These representatives will be under the control of the Viceroy, so the Legislature is not independent in all senses.

(V) The Bane of the Federal Scheme

There is no one who does not recognize that the Scheme of All-India Federation is full of defects. There is the attitude of those who think that bad as it is, we should accept the Federation and work it so as to derive whatever good it can yield. On the other hand, there is the attitude of those who think that certain changes must be made in the Constitution of the Federation before it can be accepted and worked.

The Congress is not opposed to the idea of Federation;[83] but a real Federation must, even apart from the question of responsibility consist of free units enjoying more or less the same measure of freedom and civil liberty, and representation by the democratic process of election. The Indian States participating in the Federation should approximate to the Provinces in the establishment of representative institutions and responsible Government, civil liberties and method of election to the Federal Houses. Otherwise the Federation as it is now contemplated, will, instead of building up Indian unity, encourage separatist tendencies and involve the States in internal and external conflicts....

To me the fundamental question is whether this Federal Scheme is capable of so evolving that in the end India will reach her goal. I realize that no Constitution is a perfect Constitution. Imperfections there are bound to be. But I think a distinction must be drawn between imperfections and inherent and congenital deficiencies. Imperfections can be removed....

The greatest deficiency in the Constitution is that it will not lead to Dominion Status.... So, how can India secure Dominion Status? My answer is India will get Dominion Status only if the Princes who join the Federation, consent to its being granted. If the Princes object to the grant of Dominion Status to India, then India cannot get Dominion Status. The destiny of India will be controlled by the Princes.

Under the Government of India Act neither the Federal Legislature nor the Provincial Legislature has any powers of altering or amending the Constitution. The only thing, which the Act by virtue of Section 308 does, is to permit the Federal Legislature and Provincial Legislature to pass a resolution recommending any change in the Constitution, and make it obligatory upon the Secretary of State to place it before both Houses of Parliament.... Even if the Parliament amended any of the

83. According to Dr Ambedkar, Gandhiji was willing to accept the Federation unconditionally in whatever form. See Dr Ambedkar's Presidential Remarks at the Bijapur District Harijan Conference, Bijapur (February 12, 1939).

provisions of the Act, which Schedule II says shall not be amended, the Princes would get the right to secede from the Federation....

D. THE FATALITY OF FEDERATION

What shall we do with the Indian States?

Some people with Republican faith in them desire their total abolition.... The internal administration of the States is a bye-word for mismanagement and mal-administration. Very few States will escape this charge.... The cure for this ill is not a popular government. It is the lack of resources which is the problem.... Out of a total of 627 States, 566 have annual revenue less than Rs 10 lakhs. How can these States provide their subjects all the services which relate to matters falling under law and order such as revenue, executive and judicial and all the services which affect public welfare such as education, sanitation, roads etc....

The only way out is to reorganize the whole area occupied by the Indian States. The proper solution would be to fix an area of a certain size and of certain revenue and to constitute it into a New Province and to pension off the Rulers now holding any territory in that area. The States cannot be reorganized after accession because when they are admitted into the Federation that means their sovereign status of the State are recognized. That means its right to integrity of its territory and to guaranteeing of its powers of internal administration.

The State's problem is one which, I believe, could be solved by the Paramount Power along the lines I have suggested or along any other line consistently with the welfare of the people, if it wishes to do so. Paramount is like the Trimurti of Hindu Theology. It is Brahma because it has created the States. It is Vishnu because it preserves them. It is Shiva because it can destroy them. Paramountcy has played all these parts in different times in relation to the States. At one time, it played the part of Shiva. It has now been playing the part of Vishnu. To play the part of Vishnu with regard to the States is from the point of view of the good of the people the cruellest act. Should British India be a party to it? It is for you to consider.

E. FEDERATION FROM DIFFERENT POINTS OF VIEW

There are different points of views to be discussed:

• The Princes

They had been complaining of the encroachment of the Political Department of the Government of India upon their treaty rights under the Doctrine of Paramountcy. Unfortunately for the Princes they were disappointed, because the Butler Committee reported that the Paramountcy was paramount and that there could be no definition or delimitation of it. Federal solution of their problem offered two advantages to the Princes. The first was that it would secure to the States internal autonomy which they were very anxious to have while the second advantage of the Federation was that Paramountcy would disappear to the extent of the Federal authority.

• The Muslims

The Muslims had an interest which not only coloured their whole vision but made it so limited that they did not care to look at anything else. That interest was their interest as a minority.... The creation of Muslim majority Provinces and to make them strong and powerful was their dominant interest. To accomplish this they demanded the separation of Sindh and the grant of responsible government to the North West Frontier Provinces so that the Muslims could have a command of four Provinces. To make the Provinces strong they insisted on making the Centre weak. As a means to this end the Muslims demanded that residuary powers should be given to the Provinces and the Hindu representation in the Centre should be reduced by giving the Muslims not only 1/3 of seats from the total fixed for British India but also 1/3 from the total assigned to the Princes.

• The Hindus

The Hindus as represented by the Hindu Mahasabha were concerned with only one thing. How to meet what they called the menace of the *Musalmans*? The Hindu Mahasabha felt that the accession of the Princes was an accretion to the Hindu strength. Everything else was to them of no consequence. Its point of view was Federation at any cost.

• The Indian Commercial Community

This Small Community has been behind the Congress. It is this community which has supplied the Congress the sinews of war and it knows that having paid the piper it can call for the tune.... The Indian Commercial Community is out to displace Europeans from Trade and Commerce and take their place. This it claims to do in the name of nationalism. It wants the right to lower the exchange rate and make profit in its foreign trade. This also it claims to do in the name of nationalism.

In his concluding remarks, Dr Ambedkar said:

> We are standing today at the point of time where the old age ends and the new begins. The old age was the age of Ranade, Agarkar, Tilak, Gokhale, Wachha, Sir Pherozeshah Mehta and Surendranath Bannerjee. The new age is the age of Mr Gandhi and this generation is said to be Gandhi generation. As one who knows something of the old age and also something of the new I see some very definite marks of difference between the two....
>
> The type of leadership has undergone a profound change. In the age of Ranade the leaders struggled to modernize India. In the age of Gandhi the leaders are making her

a living specimen of antiquity. In the age of Ranade leaders depended upon experience as a corrective method of their thoughts and their deeds. The leaders of the present age depend upon their inner voice as their guide. Not only is there a difference in their mental makeup, there is a difference even in their viewpoint regarding external appearance. The leaders of the old age took care to be well clad while the leaders of the present age take pride in being half clad...

The leaders of the Gandhi age are, of course, aware of these differences. But far from blushing for their views and their appearance they claim that the India of Gandhi is superior to India of Ranade. They say that the age of Mr Gandhi is an agitated and an expectant age, which the age of Mr Ranade was not....

Those who have lived both in the age of Ranade and the age of Gandhi will admit that there is this difference between the two. At the same time they will be able to insist that if the India of Ranade was less agitated it was more honest and that if it was less expectant it was more enlightened. The age of Ranade was an age in which men and women did engage themselves seriously in studying and examining the facts of their life, and what is more important is that in the face of the opposition of the orthodox mass they tried to mould their lives and their character in accordance with the light they found as a result of their research. In the age of Ranade there was not the same divorce between a politician and a student which one sees in the Gandhi age. In the age of Ranade a politician, who was not a student, was treated as an intolerable nuisance, if not a danger. In the age of Mr Gandhi learning, if it is not despised, is certainly not deemed to be a necessary qualification of a politician....

To my mind, there is no doubt that this Gandhi age is the dark age of India. It is an age in which people instead of looking for their ideals in the future are returning to antiquity. It is an age in which people have ceased to think for themselves and as they have ceased to think they have ceased to read and examine the facts of their lives. The fate of an ignorant democracy which refuses to follow the way shown by learning and experience and chooses to grope in the dark paths of themystics and the megalomaniacs is a sad thing to contemplate....

Such an age I thought needed something more than a mere descriptive sketch of the Federal Scheme. It needed a treatment which was complete though not exhaustive and pointed without being dogmatic in order to make it alive to the dangers arising from the inauguration of the Federal Scheme....

I am not opposed to a Federal Form of Government. I confess I have a partiality for a Unitary form of Government. I think India needs it. But I also realize that a Federal Form of Government is inevitable if there is to be Provincial Autonomy. But I am in dead horror about the Federal Scheme contained in the Government of India Act. I think I have justified my antipathy by giving adequate reasons. I want all to examine them and come to their own conclusions....

Let us, however, realize that the case of Provincial Autonomy is very different from that of the Federal Scheme. To those who think that the Federation should become acceptable, if the Governor-General gave an assurance along the same lines as was supposed to be done by the Governors that he will not exercise his powers under his special responsibilities. I want to say two things. First, I am sure the Governor-General cannot give such an assurance because he is exercising these powers not merely in the interest of the Crown but also in the interest of the States. Secondly, even if he did, that cannot alter the nature of the Federal Scheme....

To those who think that a change in the system of State representation from nomination to election will make the Federation less objectionable, I want to say that they are treating a matter of detail as though it was a matter of fundamental. Let us note what is fundamental and what is not. Let there be no mistake, let there be no fooling as to this. We have had enough of both. The real question is the extension and the growth of responsibility. Is that possible? That is the crux. Let us also realize that there is no use hugging to Provincial Autonomy and leaving responsibility in the Centre hanging in the air. I am convinced that without real responsibility at the Centre, Provincial Autonomy is an empty shell.

★ ★ ★

The debate on the proposed Federation came to an abrupt end in September 1939 when the then Viceroy Lord Linlithgow proclaimed a state of war between India and the Nazi forces. Consequently, on September 11, 1939 the Viceroy announced the British Government's decision to hold the proposed Federation under suspension.

CHAPTER TWENTY FOUR

On Participation in the World War

IN SEPTEMBER 1939, the Viceroy Lord Linlithgow proclaimed a state of war between India and the Nazi forces. This was done without consulting anyone, including even Mahatma Gandhi. In the aftermath of this declaration there was an unprecedented political turmoil in India.

Initially, Gandhiji, by his own admission, "broke down" shedding tears as he pictured the destruction of the Houses of Parliament, Westminster Abbey and the heart of London. But Gandhiji's resolution promising support to the British war efforts by all available non-violent means was rejected by the Congress. Gandhiji himself called it a "conclusive defeat".[84] Instead, the Congress decided to make its promise of support conditional on a British commitment to granting Independence to India, and Gandhiji disassociated himself from the Congress. Several months later, when the Viceroy brushed off the Congress Party's demand, Gandhiji was invited back to take on the leadership of the Congress in order to set out the strategy for the confrontation with the British.

While Gandhiji wavered, Dr Ambedkar had no hesitation in supporting the war efforts. Although Dr Ambedkar believed that Independence would provide the only political framework within which oppressed groups could get real power, he was more concerned with the kind of nation that would come to exist post-Independence than with the 'event' of Independence. He saw the war against fascism as a life-and-death struggle for democracy. For him, an independence gained on the basis of Britain's defeat by fascists could never lead to any true equality in India.

Dr Ambedkar disagreed with those who held that England's difficulty was India's opportunity. In a statement issued, Dr Ambedkar stated that it was the duty of Britain to reassure India of the status the country would occupy in the British Empire after the war was over.

In October 1939, after consulting several Indian leaders including Gandhiji and Dr Ambedkar, Lord Linlithgow, the Viceroy of India, clarified the British Government's

84. Lelyweld, Joseph *Great Soul* (2011), p. 285.

stance as follows: "At the end of the war, the Government of India Act would be revised in consultation with all the leading parties in India, and (importantly) no substantial political advance would be made without the consent of the minorities. A consultative committee would be formed during the war in which all parties would be represented."

The Congress Party declared that the Viceroy's proposal was entirely unsatisfactory because any help to Britain would amount to an endorsement of their imperial policy. Dr Ambedkar lamented this stance of the Congress Party and issued a statement pointing out that patriotism was not a monopoly of Congressmen, and therefore, persons holding views divergent to the Congress had a perfectly legitimate right to exist and be recognized. The Congress Party set up its own War sub-Committee under the chairmanship of Pandit Jawaharlal Nehru, which visited Mumbai, where Pandit Nehru had detailed discussions with Dr Ambedkar (That was their first meeting, which took place in the presence of Mahadev Bhai Desai).

The issue of resignation by the elected Ministry of the Bombay Province en masses was discussed and debated in the Provincial Assembly. On October 25, 1939, the Speaker proposed the following resolution:

> This Assembly regrets that the British Government have made India a participant in the War between Great Britain and Germany without the consent of the people of India. This Assembly recommends to the Government to convey to the Government of India and through them to the British Government that in consonance with the avowed aims of the present war, it is essential in order to secure the co-operation of the Indian people that the principles of democracy be applied to India and her policy be guided by her people; and that India should be regarded as an independent nation entitled to frame her own constitution and that the British Government will agree to give effect to such constitution on being satisfied through the representatives appointed by the minor communities, that the constitution so framed safeguards the life and liberty of these communities, and further that suitable action should be taken insofar as it is possible in the immediate present to give effect to that principle in regard to present governance of India, it being premised that such action shall not be in derogation of the fundamental right of the said communities to have a voice through their accredited representatives in the machinery established for the governance of the country.

Dr Ambedkar's immediate response to the draft resolution was as under:

> No. The question of resignation of the Ministry is a matter for the party. It is not a matter for the House. It is just a matter for the party whether they should stick to office or should not. It would be quite another matter if the Ministry state that the people of this country should not participate in the war. On that point the House can express its opinion. My submission is that the suggestion made by my Honourable friend is not before the House. I do not know whether such an amendment to delete the words 'while recording its fullest confidence in the Ministry' is coming or not. I will make my submission when the other amendment is before the House.

During the next two days Dr Ambedkar actively participated in the debate on the draft resolution suggesting his own amendments and also commenting on the amendments proposed by others. Here are some excerpts from Dr Ambedkar's 90-minute speech:

> Sir, turning to the resolution which the Honorable Prime Minister has moved, I cannot help saying that this resolution, to my mind, seems to be improper and inopportune. This resolution asks the House to demand a certain declaration, and further proceeds to invite the House to sanction a certain procedure in case those demands are not met. First of all, I want to know who made these demands? Obviously, the demands which have been made to his Excellency the Viceroy were not made by this House....
>
> The Honorable Prime Minister did not think this House to be a worthwhile place for him to table the demands in the name of the Country and to have the backing of this House before they were sent to His Excellency the Viceroy....
>
> My submission is that this was the proper place where the demands ought to have been placed. He did not choose to do so. If they were tabled they were passed at the back of this House by somebody unknown to the Constitution and unrecognized by this House and after having done that, he now quietly comes to the House and says: 'Well, the thing has been bungled; come to our rescue'. I submit that this is a most insulting procedure....
>
> The second thing which I have to say about this resolution is that this resolution asks for a declaration in certain terms. Now, Sir, it seems to me that a certain kind if the declaration has been made by His Excellency the Viceroy. That declaration was known to the people of India on the 18th of this month; some seven clear days have now elapsed after that. Now all that the House, in all propriety, could do is to express its opinion that that declaration is not a satisfactory declaration; but the resolution does not do that. Although there is a declaration, the Honorable Prime Minister has worded his resolution without in any way expressing whether that declaration is acceptable or not, or whether some other declaration ought to be made or not. The whole thing seems to sound trivial. Sir, I do not wish to proceed in that strain, because my Honourable friend the Prime Minister has requested the Members of the Opposition to treat this resolution as though it was a non-contentious matter.
>
> Sir, as I am going to make some comments upon the resolution as such, and also upon the amendments, I would like at the outset to show to the House in what respect I agree with the resolution. Insofar as the resolution says that India has been made a participant in the war between Great Britain and Germany without the consent of the people of India, I am in wholehearted agreement with it. In fact, I would have gone a step further because the position is really very anomalous. Here we are tied down to the chariot wheel of the British Cabinet. The British Cabinet controls the foreign policy of the Empire. In the making of the foreign policy this country has no voice. In the Declaration of War this country has no voice. In the settling of peace terms this country has no voice. Probably an invitation might be extended to some members from the public to go to Versailles or to some other place, where the peace is signed, in order to sign their names on the document. Beyond that, this country, I am sure, will not have any place. That is certainly a most anomalous position....
>
> I say that India has a greater right to participate in the foreign policy of Great Britain, a far greater right than the Dominions have. As Honourable Prime Minister

referred in the course of his speech, under the Statute of Westminster it is open to the Dominion to declare herself to be neutral and to exempt herself from the consequences of a war for the outbreak of which she was not responsible. Unfortunately, we have at present no Dominion Status. We have no right to declare ourselves to be neutral. Without our will and without our consent we are dragged in this slaughter; and I say that, if this is the case, we have a far greater right than any Dominion possesses in order to insist that we shall be consulted all along. Therefore, so far as that portion of the resolution is concerned, I give my full support….

There is one other matter also to which I would like to make a brief reference. Although this country has been involved in the war without her consent, as the resolution rightly says, this country from the standpoint of defence is in a most defenceless condition. Supposing the question of defence of this country arose, then where is the army? Where is the navy? Where are the aeroplanes that can protect this country? As a member of the Round Table Conference, I remember we fought for one principle, and that principle was that the defence of India should be recognized as the responsibility of Great Britain and Indians should be taught to defend themselves. I am sorry to say that so far as I have been able to observe, (in formulating) the defence policy of the Government of India, they have not taken any satisfactory measures along that line. I see nothing in their policy so far as the fulfilment of that principle is concerned. Therefore, I think that also is a legitimate part of the complaint which India could make. Now, these are the points on which I agree with the Government; but I am sorry to say that there my agreement ends….

Sir, as you know, I have tabled in all four amendments. I propose to take together the two amendments which deal with the rights of the minorities, and I will take the other amendments separately….

The Honorable Prime Minister ended by drawing the attention of the House to the principle embodied in the Constitution of the United States. He read a passage from the Constitution of the United States which referred to democracy, to life and liberty and to pursuit of happiness. And he commented that those of us who are sitting on the Opposition benches should have a regard for that ancient and very human document which embodied the principles of democracy. Sir, I would on my part, take the liberty to remind the Honorable Prime Minister of the condition of affairs relating to South America….

Sir, the point that I want to emphasize is this, that a Constitution, like a suit, must fit. A Constitution which does not fit is no Constitution—it cannot be a Constitution. For instance, the coat which the Honourable the Home Minister, with his slim body, is wearing could not fit on the corpulent structure that I carry. Therefore, in talking about democracy, we must talk about fitting theories to fact….

Now, the point that I am going to elaborate is this: Would the principle of democracy suit the people of India? My Honourable friend the Prime Minister has not enlightened us by enunciating what he regards as the principles of democracy. But I take of that what he means by democracy is majority rule, because unless we all accept majority rule as the fundamental working principle, there can be no political democracy. Obviously that is the root, that is the basis, that is the line from which we must proceed to discuss this question….

Now, Sir, there is one thing which is unalterable; and that thing which is unalterable is this, that the Hindus will remain in a majority, and the Muslims and the Scheduled

Castes will remain in a minority, that I submit, is an incontrovertible fact I am going to deal with it purely from the standpoint of what are called the Untouchable people of this country....

To begin with, I will ask the House to note the relative position that we shall occupy under this democracy. Under this democracy which the Prime Minister wishes to be established in this country there will be a Hindu majority, and scattered all throughout this land, scattered all throughout every village there will be a small appendix, if I may use that expression, a few cluster of huts, a few mud houses of people who are called Untouchables....

Now, my Honourable friend asks me to submit to democracy. Well, I think he will allow me to say that my answer to this question would depend upon how this majority behaves towards me. Is this majority a tolerant majority? Does this majority recognize equality, liberty and fraternity? Will this majority permit me to live, to breathe, and to grow? (*Interruption*)

What is the attitude of the majority? That is the only question that will have to be considered. Let us look to the facts...

The question I should like to ask is this: Has there been any change since 1928? Now, Sir, so far as evidence is available to me, I have no hesitation in saying that the situation has not only not changed, but has worsened. I will give a few illustrations in order to support my contention....

Sir, I do not wish to repeat *ad infinitum* cases which show how intolerant this Hindu majority is so far as Untouchables are concerned....

Now, the next question I ask is this: What protection do the Scheduled Caste get as against this harassment....

Therefore, Sir, the position with which we must start at the outset is that the Hindus are not only in a majority so far as the population is concerned, but the Hindus are in a majority so far as the administration is concerned. I think I have shown, I trust to his satisfaction, that the Hindu majority must undoubtedly be reckoned as a hostile majority. How do Untouchables fare in the matter of protection against this harassment? I want to take again a few cases to show that the whole of the administration, manned as it is by the Caste Hindus, is certainly hostile to Untouchables; that they do not desire, and they do not care for justice when the parties to the quarrels are the Caste Hindus on the one side and Untouchables on the other....

If any argument was needed in support of the two amendments which I have tabled, namely, that in any Constitution that is going to be framed and not only the Hindus but even the state has not taken sufficient care of these people. If any argument was needed in support of the two amendments which I have tabled, namely, that in any Constitution that is going to be framed, the Untouchables must have adequate safeguards, I think the arguments that I have now submitted to the house would be more than sufficient. I know that there is a certain amount of response on the other side. Two amendments have been tabled by the Honourable Home Minister. I must tell that I am not in a position to accept those amendments and I shall tell the House presently why I cannot accept his amendments in preference to mine....

The first amendment of the Honourable Home Minister is to the effect that the Constitution shall provide adequate safeguards for the protection of the minorities. The position that I take is very simple and it is this: Not only must we have safeguards but these must be to our satisfaction. That is the fundamental point. The Honourable Home Minister evidently supposes that he is a trustee for the Untouchables and that as trustee he could enact certain provisions in the constitution which according to him must suffice for the protection of the rights of the minorities. Now, I at once want to say that I repudiate that position. Nobody is my trustee; I am my own trustee. They may make their constitution, but we shall claim our right. Whatever provisions they may make relating to our safeguards must be certified by the accredited representatives of the Depressed Classes that they are adequate. Their definition of adequacy will not satisfy me, and that is why I am not in a position to accept the first amendment moved by my learned friend....

With regard to the other amendment, no doubt, the Honourable Home Minister is prepared to meet half-way. He is prepared to recognize that the minorities should have a voice in the governance of the country. There again I find that there is certain amount of difference between him and me. My second amendment has been most deliberately worded. I have taken particular care to use the words 'Fundamental Right,' and I want to explain my position to some extent as to why I have used the expression 'Fundamental Right.' The one thing that I have realized in the course of the working of the Constitution is this: Whether we admit it or not, the political system of this country is reflective of what we call the *Chaturvarna*. In that system, the theory was this: That the Kshatriya must rule; that the Brahmin must advise; that the *Vaishya* must trade but the *Shudras* or the *Ati Shudras* must serve. That was the position in olden time. I find in politics the position has changed to some extent. The Vaishya no longer trades. If he trades, he trades in politics only (*Laughter*). One thing has, however, remained unalterable, and it is that the *Shudras* shall have no part in the governance of this country...."

As I observe conditions in this country; as I observe the political Constitution of the different cabinets that have been formed all throughout India, I notice that while we Untouchables are *Shudras* or *Ati Shudras* socially, the Congress Government—if not the Congress Government, the exigencies of the situation – are such that it will ultimately lead us to become political *Shudras*. I will not tolerate it. I will shed the last drop of my blood to uproot that position. (Loud cries of '*hear, hear*'). I will not tolerate it, if to the social dominance, the economic dominance and the religious dominance which the Hindu exercises over me, is added the political dominance also. I will certainly not tolerate it. I repeat again that I will never allow it. We shall fight tooth and nail against politics being perverted for the purpose of establishing an oligarchy of a ruling Class. I will not allow that. I repeat, I cannot allow a Constitution in which I am not free and I am not an equal partner. Never will I allow that....

Sir, I know these are strong words. I know that in this country when a man belonging to a minority community stands up for the rights of his community, the whole crowd comes out against him, dubs him as communal, dubs him an anti-Indian and dubs him as a tool acting in the hands of some bureaucrat working for the destruction of this country. Sir, I want to caution this crowd which is taking this attitude....

I would say one word in the end. I know my position has not been understood properly in the country. It has often been misunderstood. Let me, therefore, take this opportunity to clarify my position. Sir, I say this, that whenever there has been a conflict between my personal interest and the interest of the country as a whole, I have always placed the claim of the country above my personal claims ('*hear, hear*'). I have never pursued the path of private gain. If I had played my cards well, as other do, I might have been in some other place. I do not want to say anything about it, but I did not do it. So far as the demands of the country are concerned, I have never lagged behind. Many European members who were at the Conferences rather felt embarrassed that I was the enfant terrible of the Conferences. But I will also leave no doubt in the minds of the people of this country that I have another loyalty to which I am bound and which I can never forsake. That loyalty is the community of Untouchables, in which I am born, to which I belong, and which I hope I shall never desert. And I say this to this House as strongly as I possibly can, that whenever there is any conflict of interest between the country and Untouchables, so far as I am concerned, Untouchables' interests will take precedence over the interests of the country....

I am not going to support a tyrannizing majority simply because it happens to speak in the name of the country. I am not going to support a party because it happens to speak in the name of the country. I shall not do that. Let everybody here and everywhere understand that is my position. As between the country and the Depressed Class, the Depressed Classes, will have precedence—the country will not have precedence. That is all that I would say with regard to these two amendments of mine....

Now, Sir, before sitting down I would like to say one or two words with regard to the other amendments that are before the House. In doing so, I would advert first to the amendment moved by the honourable Member, the leader of the Opposition. It is true that the leader of the Opposition in his amendment says that democracy has failed. We see now that he is opposed to democracy; but, Sir, he may not be opposed to self-government. After all, democracy, autocracy, republicanism—these are all forms of government; they all come under self-government. So long as the Honourable Member the Leader of the Opposition does not take the view that this country is not entitled to self government, I think too much blame ought not to be attached to the unfortunate language that has been used. After all, he is with us....

And I do not understand my Honourable friend the Prime Minister insisting upon the democracy as the only solution. I remember reading the speeches of the leaders of the Honourable Prime Minister at the Tripuri Congress. I think at the Tripuri Congress the friends of the Honourable Prime Minister, Pandit Govind Vallabh Pant, Mr Rajgopalchari, Pandit Jawaharlal Nehru and all of them were singing the praises of Mussolini and Hitler....(*Interruption*).

All that I am saying is this, that so long as people in India have self-Government, whether the self-Government takes the form of democracy, whether it takes the form of autocracy, or whether it takes some other form, it is a matter of detail, about which there ought to be no quarrel. And, therefore, my submission is this: that in judging of the resolution, which, as I said, is somewhat unfortunately worded, his intention should not be misconstrued....

There is one amendment, however, to which I cannot lend any support, and that is the one which is to the effect that the House approves of the intention of the Ministry resigning—or something like that. Now, Sir, what I should like to say is this. That this is really a matter for their party caucus. It is not a matter for the House to decide.

> Whether the Ministry should go out or should not go out is entirely a matter for their party to decide. Why does he want my sanction for his going out?
>
> Why does he need it? I put to him another conundrum. Suppose I bring an amendment to say that the Ministry shall not come back unless I invite them, will he accept it? I am sure he would not tie himself down in that manner. If you want my sanction for going out, it will be some honour to me if you will also make your re-entry dependent on my sanction. But you will not do that, and I feel bound in consciences to oppose that amendment.

In the same speech, Dr Ambedkar reiterated his position on war policy and declared that the Untouchables would never accept a political status that would make them political *Shudras*. He said: "I am not going to support a tyrannizing majority simply because it happens to speak in the name of the country. I am not going to support a party because it happens to speak in the name of the country."[85]

It is clear that the defense of Untouchables remained Dr Ambedkar's priority and having become disenchanted with Gandhiji and the Congress, he started leaning towards close cooperation with the British Government. In fact, when BG Kher, the Chief Minister of the Bombay Presidency, criticized the separatism of Dr Ambedkar and said: "The part can never be greater than the whole. The whole must contain the part."

Dr Ambedkar retorted by saying: "I am not a part of the whole at all; I am a part apart."[86]

85. Keer, Dhananjay, op. cit, p.329.
86. Jaffrelot, Christophe, op cit, p.187.

CHATER TWENTY FIVE

Pakistan or the Partition of India

ON MARCH 26, 1940, the Muslim League at its Annual Session at Lahore passed a Resolution demanding the creation of an Independent State (i.e., Pakistan), comprising the North-Western and Eastern Parts of India, where Muslims would be in a majority. Dr Ambedkar was probably the first one to come to terms with the implications of the Lahore Resolution. By the end of the year 1940, Dr Ambedkar came up with a full-length treatise titled, "Pakistan or the Partition of India". When the Muslim League passed the resolution at its Lahore Session, making out a case for Pakistan, the whole country was taken by a storm. In the midst of that turmoil, Dr Ambedkar wrote this masterpiece on the subject, the first edition of which was released on December 28, 1940.

According to Dr Ambedkar, the appeal of Pakistan for the Muslim masses emanated from the failure of the Congress to strive for social reforms and democratize society. He argued in the book that once an identity becomes a political force, then the consequences of its formation have to be faced.[87] The book, argued that the Muslims are a nation, and that must be accepted without cavil. Assuring that the creation of Pakistan will not leave Hindustan in a weakened condition, the book argues that it is better to have Muslims whose loyalty to India is doubtful, without and against, rather than within and against.[88]

In the "Introduction" of the first edition, Dr Ambedkar observed:

> Some see the Resolution of the Muslim League on Pakistan as a case of political measles .... Others have taken it as a permanent frame of the Muslim mind and not merely a passing phase and have in consequence been greatly perturbed.... Some argue that this demand for partitioning India into two political entities under separate national states staggers their imagination. Some others are so choked with a sense of righteous indignation at this wanton attempt to break the unity of a country which has stood as one for centuries.... You don't cut a baby into two because two women

87. Rodriques, Valerian (2002), p.13
88. Keer, Dhananjay, op cit, *p.333*

> are engaged in fighting out a claim as to who its mother is....I have no doubt that the only proper attitude to Pakistan is to study it in all its aspects, to understand its implications and to form an intelligent judgement about it.
>
> There is no partisanship in this book. The aim is to expound the scheme of Pakistan in all its aspects and not to advocate it. The aim is to explain and not to convert. It would, however, be pretence to say that I have no views on Pakistan. Two things, however, may well be said about my views. In the first place, wherever they are expressed, they have been reasoned out. Secondly, whatever the views, they have certainly not the fixity of a popular prejudice. They are really thoughts and not views. In other words, I have an open mind, though not an empty mind. A person with an open mind is always the subject of congratulations. My excuse is that I have no intention to hurt. I had only one purpose, that is, to force the attention of the indifferent and casual reader to the issue that is dealt with in the book. I ask the reader to put aside any irritation that he may feel with me and concentrate his thoughts on this tremendous issue which is to be, Pakistan or no Pakistan?

This monumental book, by itself, created an intellectual storm. When the second (enlarged) edition was released on January 1, 1945, Dr Ambedkar wrote in the Preface:

> I cannot help recalling with regret how much of my time it has consumed when so much of my other literary work of great importance to me, than this is held up for want of it....
>
> The Book by its name might appear to deal only with the XYZ of Pakistan. It does more than that. It is an analytical presentation of Indian history and Indian politics in their communal aspects.... The Book is more than a mere treatise on Pakistan. The material relating to Indian history and Indian politics contained in this book is so large and so varied that it might well be called 'Indian Political What Is What'.

About the overwhelming response to the first edition, Dr Ambedkar observed:

> The book appears to have supplied a real want. I have seen how the thoughts, ideas and arguments contained in it have been pillaged by authors, politicians and editors of newspapers to support their sides. I am sorry they did not observe the decency of acknowledging the source even when they lifted not merely the arguments but also the language of the book. But that is a matter I do not mind. I am glad that the book has been of service to Indians who are faced with this knotty problem of Pakistan. The fact that Mr Gandhi and Mr Jinnah in their recent talks cited the book as an authority on the subject which might be consulted with advantage bespeaks the worth of the book....
>
> The book has displeased both Hindus as well as Muslims....That it is disowned by the Hindus and unowned by the Muslims is to me the best evidence that it has the vices of neither and that from the point of view of independence of thought and fearless presentation affects the book is not a party production.

It may be noted that the Second Edition is considerably enlarged (483 pages). Importantly, several parts were added to the book because of the criticism levelled against the First Edition, as Dr Ambedkar observes, "While I wrote about Pakistan, I did not state what views I held on the subject," which he elaborated in the Second Edition.

A. STRUCTURE OF THE BOOK

Part 1: Muslim Case for Pakistan

The Muslim Case for Pakistan is often justified on the following grounds:

(i) Muslims are asking for the creation of administrative areas which are ethnically more homogeneous.
(ii) The Muslims want these areas to be constituted into separate States,
   (a) Because the Muslims by themselves constitute a separate nation and desire to have a national home, and
   (b) Because experience shows that the Hindus want to use their majority to treat the Muslims as though they were second-class citizens in an alien State.

This part is devoted to the explanation of these grounds.

Part 2: Hindu Case against Pakistan

There seem to be three reasons present to the mind of the Hindu who are opposing this Scheme of Pakistan. They object to the Scheme:

(i) Because it involves the breaking-up of the unit of India
(ii) Because it weakness the defence of India
(iii) Because it fails to solve the communal problem

Is there any substance in these objections?

This part is concerned with an examination of the validity of these objections.

Part 3: What if Not Pakistan

Having stated the Muslim case for Pakistan and the Hindu case against it, it is necessary to turn to the alternatives to Pakistan, if there be any. In forming one's judgement on Pakistan, one must take into account the alternatives to it. Either there is no alternative to Pakistan; or there is an alternative to Pakistan, but it is worse than Pakistan. Thirdly, one must also take into consideration what would be the consequences, if neither Pakistan nor its alternative was found acceptable to the parties concerned.

These issues are examined in this part with all the available data.

Part 4: Pakistan and the Malaise

The Hindu-Muslim problem has two aspects to it. In its first aspect, the problem that presents itself is the problem of two separate communities facing each other and seeking adjustment of their respective rights and privileges. In its other aspect, the problem is the problem of the reflex influences which this separation and conflict produce upon each of them. In the course of the foregoing discussion we have looked at the project of Pakistan in relation to the first of the aspects of the Hindu-Muslim problem. We have not examined the project of Pakistan in relation to the second aspect of that problem. Yet, such an examination is necessary because that aspect of the Hindu-Muslim problem is not unimportant. It is a very superficial if not an incomplete view to stop with the problem of the adjustment of their claims. It cannot be overlooked that their lot is cast together as such they have to participate in a course of common activity whether they like it or not. And if in this common activity they face each other as two combatants do, then their actions and reactions are worth study, for they affect both and produce a state of affairs from which if it is a deceased state, the question of escape must be faced. A study of the situation shows that the actions and reactions have produced a malaise which exhibits itself in three ways: (l) Social Stagnation, (2) Communal Aggression, and (3) National Frustration of Political Destiny. This malaise is a grave one. Will Pakistan be a remedy for the malaise? Or, will it aggravate the malaise? This part is devoted to the consideration of these questions.

Part 5: Epilogue

Different people have thought differently on the question of Pakistan. One set of people have alleged that I have only stated the two sides of the issue and the problems arising out of it but have not expressed my personal views on either of them. This is not correct. I have expressed my views in quite positive terms, if not on all, certainly on many questions. In particular I may refer to two of the most important ones in the controversy, namely: Are the Muslims a Nation, and have they a case for Pakistan. There are others whose line of criticism is of a different sort. They do not complain that I have failed to express my personal views. What they complain is that in coming to my conclusions I have relied on propositions as though they were absolute in their application and have admitted no exception. I am told, 'Have you not stated your conclusions in too general terms? Is not a general proposition subject to conditions and limitations? Have you not disposed of certain complicated problems in a brief and cavalier fashion? Have you shown how Pakistan can be brought into existence in a just and peaceful manner?' Even this criticism is not altogether correct. It is not right to say that I have omitted to deal with these points. It may be that my treatment of them is brief and scattered. However, I am prepared to admit that there is much force in this criticism and I am in duty bound to make good the default.

This part is, therefore, intended and is devoted to the consideration of the following subjects:

(i) What are the limiting considerations which affect the Muslim case for Pakistan?

(ii) What are the problems of Pakistan? And what is their solution?
(iii) Who has the authority to decide the issue of Pakistan?

B. SUMMING UP

- Indeed, the issue of Pakistan or to put it plainly of partitioning India is of such a grave character that the Muslims will not only have to discharge this burden of proof but they will have to adduce evidence of such a character as to satisfy the conscience of an international tribunal before they can win their case. Let us see how the case for Pakistan stands in the light of these limitations.
- India is a single geographical unit. Her unit is as ancient as Nature. Within this geographic unit and covering the whole of it there has been a cultural unity from time immemorial. This cultural unity has defied political and racial divisions. And at any rate for the last hundred and fifty years all institutions—cultural, political, economic, legal and administrative—have been working on a single, uniform spring of action. In any discussion of Pakistan the fact cannot be lost sight of, namely, that the starting point, if not the governing factor, is the fundamental unity of India. Why destroy its unity now, simply because some Muslims are dissatisfied?
- Must there be Pakistan because there is communal antagonism between the Hindus and the Muslims? The question, however, is, is the antagonism such that there is no will to live together in one country and under one constitution? Surely, that will to live together was not absent till 1937. The history of India from 1920 up to 1935 has been one long tale of communal conflict in which the loss of life and loss of property had reached a most shameful limit. Never was the communal situation so acute as it was between this period of 15 years preceding the passing of the Government of India Act, 1935, and yet this long tale of antagonism did not prevent the Hindus and the *Musalmans* from agreeing to live in a single country and under a single Constitution. Why make so much of communal antagonism now?
- India is not the only place where there is communal antagonism. If communal antagonism does not come in the way of the French in Canada living in political unity with the English, if it does not come in the way of the English in South Africa living in political unity with the Dutch, if it does not come in the way of the French and the Italians in Switzerland living in political unity with the Germans why then should it be impossible for the Hindus and the Muslims to agree to live together under one Constitution in India?
- Must there be Pakistan because the Muslims have lost faith in the Congress majority? Muslims cite some instances of tyranny and oppression practised by the Hindus and connived at by the Congress Ministries during the two years and three months the Congress was in office. It may be that the Congress during the two years and three months that it was in office did not show statesmanship, did not inspire confidence in the minorities, nay, tried to suppress them. But can it be a reason for partitioning India?

- Must there be Pakistan because the *Musalmans* are a nation? If the *Musalmans* want to be a different nation it is not because they have been but because they want to be. There is much in the *Musalmans* which, if they wish, can roll them into a nation. But isn't there enough that is common to both Hindus and *Musalmans* which, if developed, is capable of moulding them into one people. If the emphasis is laid on things that are common, there need be no two nations in India. If the emphasis is laid on points of difference, it will no doubt give rise to two nations.
- The view that seems to guide Mr Jinnah is that Indians are only a people and that they can never be a nation. Granted Indians are not a nation, that they are only a people. What of that? History records that before the rise of nations as great corporate personalities, there were only peoples. There is nothing to be ashamed if Indians are no more than a people. Nor is there any cause for despair that the people of India—if they wish—will not become one nation.
- The *Musalmans* of India… are not as yet a nation in the *de jure* or *de facto* sense of the term and all that can be said is that they have in them the elements necessary to make them a nation.
- If the Muslims insist on separation, the cynic may well conclude that there is so much that is common between the Hindus and the *Musalmans* that the Muslim leaders are afraid that unless there is partition whatever little distinctive Islamic culture is left with the *Musalmans* will eventually vanish by continued social contact with the Hindus with the result that in the end instead of two nations there will grow up in India one nation. If the Muslim nationalism is so thin then the motive for partition is artificial and the case for Pakistan loses its very basis.
- Must there be Pakistan because otherwise *Swaraj* will be a Hindu Raj? The *Musalmans* are so easily carried away by this cry that it is necessary to expose the fallacies underlying it.
- If Hindu Raj does become a fact, it will, no doubt, be the greatest calamity for this country. No matter what the Hindus say, Hinduism is a menace to liberty, equality and fraternity. On that account it is incompatible with democracy. Hindu Raj must be prevented at any cost. But is Pakistan the true remedy against it?
- What makes communal Raj possible is a marked disproportion in the relative strength of the various communities living in a country. This disproportion is not more marked in India than it is in Canada, South Africa and Switzerland. Nonetheless, there is no British Raj in Canada, no Dutch Raj in South Africa, and no German Raj in Switzerland. How have the French, the English and the Italians succeeded in preventing the Raj of the majority community being established in their country? Surely not by partition: What is their method? Their method is to put a ban on communal parties in politics.
- Have the Muslims thought of this method of avoiding Hindu Raj? Hindu Maha Sabha and Hindu Raj are the inescapable enemies which the *Musalmans* have brought upon themselves by having a Muslim League. It is action and

counter-action. One gives rise to the other. Not partition, but the abolition of the Muslim League and the formation of a mixed party of Hindus and Muslims is the only effective way of burying the ghost of Hindu Raj.

- There are many lower orders in the Hindu society whose economic, political and social needs are the same as those of the majority of the Muslims and they would be far more ready to make a common cause with the Muslims for achieving common ends than they would with the high-Caste of Hindus who have denied and deprived them of ordinary human rights for centuries. To pursue such a course cannot be called an adventure. Herein lay the most fruitful method of achieving communal harmony among Hindus and Muslims and of destroying the danger of a Hindu Raj.
- In 1937 Mr Jinnah made his entry into Muslim politics and strangely enough he regenerated the Muslim League which was dying and decaying and of which only a few years ago he would have been glad to witness the funeral. Everybody felt that with the leadership of Mr Jinnah the League could never become a merely communal party. The resolutions passed by the League during the first two years of its new career indicated that it would develop into a mixed political party of Hindus and Muslims.
- By some early resolutions Mr Jinnah showed that he was for a common front between the Muslims and other non-Muslim minorities. Unfortunately, the catholicity and statesmanship that underlies these resolutions did not last long. In 1939 Mr Jinnah took a somersault and outlined the dangerous and disastrous policy of isolation of the *Musalmans* by passing that notorious resolution in favour of Pakistan.
- One need not quarrel over the question whether the Muslims are a nation or a community. But one finds it extremely difficult to understand how the mere fact that the Muslims are a nation makes political isolation a safe and sound policy? Unfortunately, Muslims do not realize what disservice Mr Jinnah has done to them by this policy.
- Will Pakistan obviate the establishment of Hindu Raj in Provinces in which the *Musalmans* are in a minority? Obviously it cannot. This is what would happen in the Muslim minority Provinces if Pakistan came. Take an all-India view. Can Pakistan prevent the establishment of Hindu Raj at the Centre over Muslim minorities that will remain Hindustan? It is plain that it cannot. What good is Pakistan then? Only to prevent Hindu Raj in Provinces in which the Muslims are in a majority and in which there could never be Hindu Raj!! To put it differently Pakistan is unnecessary to Muslims where they are in a majority because there is no fear of Hindu Raj. It is worse than useless to Muslims where they are in a minority, because Pakistan or no Pakistan they will have to face a Hindu Raj. Can politics be more futile than the politics of the Muslim League? The Muslim League started to help minority Muslims and has ended by espousing the cause of majority Muslims. What a perversion in

the original aim of the Muslim League! What a fall from the sublime to the ridiculous! Partition as a remedy against Hindu Raj is worse than useless.

- What is my position regarding the issue of Pakistan in the light of the objections, which I have set out? I have no doubts as to my position. I hold firmly that, subject to certain conditions… if the *Musalmans* are bent on having Pakistan then it must be conceded to them. I know my critics will at once accuse me of inconsistency and will demand reasons for so extraordinary a conclusion—extraordinary because of the view expressed by me that the Muslim case for Pakistan has nothing in it which can be said to carry the compelling force which the decree of an inexorable fate may be said to have. I withdraw nothing from what I have said as to the weaknesses in the Muslim case for Pakistan. Yet I hold that if the Muslims must have Pakistan there is no escape from conceding it to them. As to the reasons which have led me to that conclusion I shall not hesitate to say that the strength or weakness of the logic of Pakistan is not one of them. In my judgement there are two governing factors which must determine the issue. First is the defence of India and second is the sentiment of the Muslims.
- The army is the ultimate sanction which sustains Government in the exercise of its authority inside the country, when it is challenged by a rebellious or recalcitrant element. Suppose the Government of the day enunciates a policy which is vehemently opposed by a section of the Muslims. Suppose the Government of the day is required to use its army to enforce its policy. Can the Government of the day depend upon the Muslims in the army to obey its orders and shoot down the Muslim rebels? This again depends upon to what extent the Muslims in the army have caught the infection of the two-nation theory. If they have caught it, India cannot have a safe and secure Government.
- Turning to the second governing factor the Hindus do not seem to attach any value to sentiment as a force in politics. The Hindus seem to rely upon two grounds to win against the Muslims. The first is that even if the Hindus and the Muslims are two nations, they can live under one state. The other is that the Muslim case for Pakistan is founded on strong sentiment rather than upon clear argument. I don't know how long the Hindus are going to fool themselves with such arguments. It is true that the first argument is not without precedent. At the same time, it does not call for much intelligence to see that its value is extremely limited. Two nations and one state is a pretty plea. It has the same attraction which a sermon has and may result in the conversion of Muslim leaders. But instead of being uttered as a sermon if it is intended to issue it as an ordinance for the Muslims to obey it will be a mad project to which no sane man will agree. It will, I am sure, defeat the very purpose of *Swaraj*. The second argument is equally silly. That the Muslim case for Pakistan is founded on sentiment is far from being a matter of weakness; it is really its strong point.

It does not need deep understanding of politics to know that the workability of a Constitution is not a matter of theory. It is a matter of sentiment. A Constitution like clothes must suit as well as please. If a Constitution does not please, then, however perfect it may be, it will not work. To have a Constitution which runs counter to the strong sentiments of a determined section is to court disaster if not to invite rebellion.

- Suppose the new Constitution for a United India contained in it all the provisions necessary to safeguard the interests of the Muslims. But suppose the Muslims said 'Thank you for your safeguards, we don't want to be ruled by you'; and suppose they boycott the Legislatures, refuse to obey laws, oppose the payment of taxes; what is to happen? Are the Hindus prepared to extract obedience from Muslims by the use of Hindu bayonets? Is *Swaraj* to be an opportunity to serve the people or is it to be an opportunity for Hindus to conquer the *Musalmans,* and for the *Musalmans* to conquer the Hindus? *Swaraj* must be a Government of the people, by the people and for the people. This is the *raison d'etre* of *Swaraj* and the only justification for *Swaraj*. If *Swaraj* is to usher in an era in which the Hindus and the Muslims will be engaged in scheming against each other, the one planning to conquer its rival, why should we have *Swaraj* and why should the democratic nations allow such a *Swaraj* to come into existence? It will be a snare, a delusion and a perversion.
- The non-Muslims do not seem to be aware that they are presented with a situation in which they are forced to choose between various alternatives. Let me state them. In the first place they have to choose between Freedom of India and the Unity of India. If the non-Muslims will insist on the Unity of India they put the quick realization of India's freedom into jeopardy. The second choice relates to the surest method of defending India, whether they can depend upon Muslims in a free and united India to develop and sustain along with the non-Muslims the necessary will to defend the common liberties of both: or whether it is better to partition India and thereby ensure the safety of Muslim India by leaving its defence to the Muslims and of non-Muslim India by leaving its defence to non-Muslims.
- As to the first, I prefer Freedom of India to the Unity of India. On the second issue I prefer the partitioning of India into Muslim India and non-Muslim India as the surest and safest method of providing for the defence of both. It is certainly the safer of the two alternatives. I know it will be contended that my fears about the loyalty of the Muslims in the army to a Free and United India arising from the infection of the two-nation theory is only an imaginary fear. That is no doubt true. That does not militate against the soundness of the choice I have made. I may be wrong. But I certainly can say without any fear of contradiction that, to use the words of Burke, it is better to be ridiculed for too great a credulity than to be ruined by too confident a sense of security. I don't want to leave things to chance. To leave so important an issue, as the defence of India, to chance is to be guilty of the grossest crime.

- Nobody will consent to the Muslim demand for Pakistan unless he is forced to do so. At the same time, it would be a folly not to face what is inevitable and face it with courage and common sense. Equally would it be a folly to lose the part one can retain in the vain attempt of preserving the whole. These are the reasons why I hold that if the *Musalman* will not yield on the issue of Pakistan then Pakistan must come. So far as I am concerned the only important question is: Are the *Musalmans* determined to have Pakistan? Or is Pakistan a mere cry? Is it only a passing mood? Or does it represent their permanent aspiration? On this there may be difference of opinion. Once it becomes certain that the Muslims want Pakistan there can be no doubt that the wise course would be to concede the principle of it.

PART V

SCHOLAR–POLITICIAN–ADMINISTRATOR (1942-46)

CHAPTER TWENTY SIX

Collaboration and Confrontation with the British

THE DEFENSE OF Untouchables remained as always Dr Ambedkar's priority and having been disenchanted with Gandhiji and disillusioned by the Congress, he started leaning towards close co-operation with the British Government. In fact, when BG Kher, the Chief Minister of the Bombay Presidence, criticized the separatism of Dr Ambedkar and said: "The part can never be greater than the whole. The whole must contain the part." Dr Ambedkar retorted: "I am not a part of the whole at all; I am a part apart."[89]

For Dr Ambedkar the strategy of collaborating with the colonial power for securing concessions for Untouchables was, of course, far more important than his desire to contribute to the British war efforts. In early 1941, he pressed for enlargement of recruitment of Untouchables in the army, which was granted. Notably, Dr Ambedkar also succeeded in reinstatement of the Mahar battalion, for which his father Ramji had made a representation decades earlier. In the same spirit, Dr Ambedkar also agreed to serve as a Member of the Defence Advisory Committee set up by the Viceroy of India. A turning point came on July 2, 1942, when Dr Ambedkar was appointed as the Labour Member (i.e., Minister) in the Viceroy's Executive Council of India[90]

In one of the felicitation meetings following his appointment, Ambedkar declared that he would never surrender in the battle he would have to wage for protecting and advancing the interests of working classes in India. Indeed throughout his tenure as the Labour Member, Ambedkar redoubled his efforts for promoting labour welfare.

89. Jaffrelot, Christophe, Op cit, p.187.

90. This appointment was unique not only because for the first time in history an Untouchable was placed in the Executive Council (as a Minister) but also because he was the first mass leader in India to be so appointed.

Dr Ambedkar came a long way in the Indian labour movement. As a child, he had planned to run away from Satara to Bombay to become a mill worker (a plan which failed as he could not steal money from his aunt's purse for the journey). From there, he emerged a labour leader with a repute of lifetime championing the cause of the underdog and fighting for labour's rights. Then he went on to become the first Untouchable and also the first mass leader in India to be placed as the Labour Member in the Viceroy's Chief Executive Council of the Government of India, where he was instrumental in laying the foundations of industrial relations in Independent India.

CRIPPS MISSION

In March 1942, amidst the growing Japanese threat in Asia, the British Prime Minister Winston Churchill appointed a new Mission headed by Sir Stafford Cripps to bring about a negotiated political settlement in India.

The British Government sent the Cripps Mission to India in March, 1942 essentially to secure India's full co-operation and support to Britain's efforts in World War II. The Mission was headed by Sir Stafford Cripps, a Minister in the War Cabinet of Prime Minister Winston Churchill. The Mission attempted to negotiate an agreement with Mahatma Gandhi and Jinnah that would keep India loyal to the British War effort in exchange for a promise of full self-government after the War.

The Mission proved a failure. The Cripps' proposals were too radical for Churchill and the British Government and too conservative for the Indians; no middle path was found. There was a major trust deficit between the British and the Congress at that time. The talks failed and Mahatma Gandhi demanded immediate self-government in return for war support. Gandhiji described the Cripps' offer of Dominion Status after the War as a "post-dated cheque drawn on a crashing bank". The failure of these negotiations paved the way for the "Quit India" movement on August 9, 1942.

FORMATION OF A NEW POLITICAL PARTY: SCHEDULED CASTE FEDERATION

Politically, the events of the period led to a tumultuous change for the Untouchables. The ILP's broad Class alliance had not borne the expected results. The British began questioning Dr Ambedkar's legitimacy as a representative of the Scheduled Castes when he did not have a specific Scheduled Caste organization behind him. Therefore, Dr Ambedkar held discussions with Scheduled Caste leaders in Delhi and decided to wind up the Independent Labour Party(ILP).

A third session of the Depressed Classes Conference was called in Nagpur in July 1942. The Conference was chaired by N Shivraj of Madras, since being a Member of the Viceroy's Council, Dr Ambedkar's direct political participation was ruled out.

On July 18 1942, 75,000 people gathered in Nagpur. Volunteers from Dr Ambedkar's youth organization, the *Samta Sainik Dal*, were on guard duty. It was with reference to these volunteers that Dr Ambedkar made his famous statement: "Goats and sheep are sacrificed, not tigers." The militant Scheduled Caste youth in the Samta Sainik Dal were determined to be tigers.

A new organization was formed at the Nagpur Conference, named Scheduled Caste Federation (SCF). Whereas the earlier ILP had carried a red flag, now the young volunteers carried the blue flag of the SCF. Unlike the ILP, the SCF took shape as a genuinely national party. It drew on the organizational accomplishments and the emerging leadership of Scheduled Caste movements that had flourished in the major Provinces of India in the 1920s. Important representatives of almost every Province came to Nagpur. It was from this period that Dr Ambedkar's movement widened to the North and North-western India.

The Nagpur Conference took some other important decisions. Its delegates found the proposals of the Cripps Mission unacceptable, and protested against them. They also declared that no Constitution would be acceptable to the Scheduled Castes unless it recognized that they were distinct from the Hindus, and constituted an important element in the national life of India. They called for financial provisions for primary and advanced education, for representation in public services and Government, for separate electorates and for rural restructuring.

"So long as the Scheduled Castes continue to live on the outskirts of the village, with no source of livelihood and in small numbers compared to the Hindus, they will continue to remain Untouchables and subject to tyranny and opposition of the Hindus and will not be able to enjoy free and full life."

Thus it was argued that a radical change in the village system should include the establishment of separate villages on cultivable Government land and a step towards local economic and political autonomy....

The 1942 Nagpur Conference marked the beginning of a new era of organizing. While the Class radicalism of the ILP had been given up, the national scope of the SCF indicated a new stage of the Scheduled Caste movement in India as a whole. Movements that had begun independently in various Provinces were now coming together and asserting their presence to help a consolidated movement to emerge as an autonomous force at the national level, in the face of staunch Congress opposition. Importantly, Dr Ambedkar was their sole acknowledged leader.

* * *

Dr Ambedkar was opposed to the proposals put forth by the Cripps Mission because there was no mention of Depressed Class representation or separate electorates. He issued a Press Statement immediately after the Depressed Classes Conference in Nagpur in July 18-20, 1942. The Press Statement was intended to put across the viewpoint of the Scheduled Castes towards the proposals put out in the Cripps

Mission. The Statement pointed out that the Cripps Proposals show a sudden *volte face* on the part of the British Government, which in the course of War had become panic stricken and was losing its nerve. According to Dr Ambedkar, the proposals now put forth as the best were the very proposals which had been rejected and condemned by the British Government as the worst only a few months earlier. In spite of being in the British Viceroy's Executive Council, Dr Ambedkar had no hesitation in directly attacking the British.

Here are some excerpts from Dr Ambedkar's Statement:

> The War Cabinet's proposals show a sudden *volte face* on the part of His Majesty's Government. The putting forth of these proposals, which were denounced by them as an invasion of minority rights, is an indication of their complete surrender of right to win might. This is Munich mentality, the essence of which is to save oneself by sacrificing others, and it is this mentality which is writ large on these proposals....
>
> It is reported that the American and English people are annoyed at Indians not welcoming the proposals of His Majesty's Government relating to the Constitutional advancement of India and thereby allowing the mission of Sir Stafford Cripps to fail. One can forgive the Americans for their attitude, but surely the English people and Sir Stafford Cripps ought to know better. It does not seem to have been sufficiently realized that the proposals of His Majesty's Government now put forth as the best are the very proposals which have been rejected and condemned by His Majesty's Government as the worst only a few months previously. Those who realize this cannot but help saying that this is the ugliest part of the whole business of Constitutional advance, which His Majesty's Government is now rushing to undertake....
>
> The proposals fall into three parts:
>
> (1) There is to be a Constituent Assembly with a right to frame the Constitution for India. This Assembly is to have the fullest power to frame such Constitution as the majority in the Assembly may choose to decide.
>
> (2) The new Constitution is not to include all the present Provinces of India, but only such Provinces as may be willing to be bound by it. For this the Provinces have been given a right to decide whether they shall join the new Constitution or stay out of it. This is left to be done by a plebiscite in which a bare majority is declared enough to decide the issue.
>
> (3) The Constituent Assembly shall be required to enter into a treaty with the British Government. The treaty is to contain provisions for the safety and security of racial and religious minorities. After such a treaty is signed, the British Government is to withdraw its sovereignty and the Constitution framed by the Constituent Assembly is to come into operation.
>
> Such in brief outline is the scheme of His Majesty's Government.
>
> The proposal regarding Constituent Assembly is not a new proposal. It was put forth by the Congress when the war broke out and what is important is that this proposal of the Congress was rejected by His Majesty's Government...On April 23, 1941, Mr Amery (Secretary of State for India) referred to the demand of the Constituent Assembly and expressed himself in the following terms:
>
> 'India's future Constitution should be devised by Indians for themselves and not by the British Government. India's future Constitution should be essentially an Indian

Constitution, framed in accordance with the Indian conception of Indian conditions and Indian needs. The only essential condition is that the Constitution itself and the body which is to frame it must be the outcome of agreement between principal elements in India's national life.'

Such were the views expressed and pledges given by His Majesty's Government regarding Constituent Assembly which is now conceded.

Regarding the demand for Pakistan it was a demand put forward by the Muslim League. This demand was also rejected by His Majesty's Government....

'It is quite obvious that the proposal for a Constituent Assembly is intended to win over the Congress, while the proposal for Pakistan is designed to win over the Muslim League.' How do the proposals deal with the Depressed Classes? To put it shortly, they are bound hand and foot and handed over to the Caste Hindus. They offer them nothing, stone instead of bread. For the Constituent Assembly is nothing short of a betrayal of the Depressed Classes. There can be no doubt as to what the position of the Depressed Classes will be in the Constituent Assembly nor can there be any doubt regarding the political program of the Constituent Assembly. In the Constituent Assembly there may be no representatives of the Depressed Classes at all because no communal quotas are fixed by these proposals. If they are there they cannot have a free, independent and decisive vote....

In the first place the representatives of the Depressed Classes will be in a hopeless minority. In the second place all decisions of the Constituent Assembly are not required to be by a unanimous vote. A majority vote is enough to decide any question no matter what its Constitutional importance is. It is clear that under this system the voice of the Depressed Classes in the Constituent Assembly cannot count. In the third place the present system of proportional representation by which the members to the Constituent Assembly are to be elected under the terms contained in His Majesty's proposals cannot but result in the Caste Hindus having virtually the right to nominate the representatives of the Depressed Classes to the Constituent Assembly. Such representatives of the Depressed Classes will be the tools of the Caste Hindus. In the fourth place the Constituent Assembly will be filled with the Congresses, who will form the dominant majority party able to carry out its own program. There is no doubt that Mr Gandhi, whatever may be said about his endeavours in the matter of the social uplift of the Depressed Classes, is totally opposed to giving political recognition to the Depressed Classes in the Constitution as a separate and distinct element in the national life of India. That being the case, the program of the majority party in the Constituent Assembly will be to wipe out the political safeguards already granted to the Depressed Classes in the present Constitution....

Anyone who realizes what is implied in the Constituent Assembly will admit that His Majesty's Government, by their proposals have literally thrown the Depressed Classes to the wolves. It may be said that while there is the Constituent Assembly which may deny Constitutional safeguards to the Depressed Classes, His Majesty's Government have been careful to include in their proposals the provisions for a treaty with the Constituent Assembly the object of which is to secure the interests of the Depressed Classes....

This proposal of a treaty is evidently borrowed from the plan adopted by His Majesty's Government for the settlement of the Irish dispute. The proposal regarding the treaty does not say: what are the safeguards, His Majesty's Government will decide to include in the treaty. This is an important point because there may be a difference of opinion between His Majesty's Government and the Depressed Classes on the nature, number and method of the political safeguards that may be necessary to protect the interests of the Depressed Classes under the new Constitution.

The second and equally important question about the treaty is what is going to be the sanction behind the treaty. Will the treaty be a part of the Constitution framed by the Constituent Assembly, so that any provision in the Constitution, which is repugnant with the treaty, will be *null and void*. Or, will the treaty be just a treaty between the two Governments—the Indian National Government and His Majesty's Government, as any trade treaty. If the treaty is to be of the former kind it will be the law of the land and will have legal sanction of the Indian Government behind it. If, on the other hand, the treaty is to be of the latter kind it is obvious, it will not be the law of the land and will have no legal sanction behind it. Its sanction will be a political sanction. Now a treaty cannot override the Constitution framed by the National Government for the obvious reason that such a thing is incompatible with Dominion Status. The only sanction behind such a treaty will be a political sanction. It is obvious that the use of such sanction must depend upon the colour of the Government and the state of public opinion.

Given this fact the questions that arise are two: (a) What are the means which His Majesty's Government will have at its disposal to enforce the treaty obligations; (b) Will His Majesty's Government be prepared to use these means to coerce the Indian National Government to abide by the terms of the treaty.

With regard to the first question it is obvious that the means for enforcing the treaty are two-fold, use of force and trade war. As to the military force, the Indian army will not be available. It will be entirely transferred to the control of the new Indian National Government. His Majesty's Government will have, therefore, lost this means of enforcing the treaty. It is impossible to believe that His Majesty's Government will send its own army to compel the National Government to obey the treaty. A trade war is not possible. It is a suicidal policy....The treaty, therefore, is going to be an empty formula, if not a cruel joke, upon the Depressed Classes.

His Majesty's Government has sent out these proposals to be welcomed by Indians. But neither His Majesty's Government nor Sir Stafford Cripps have offered any explanation as to why they are offering to Indians the very proposals which His Majesty's Government have been condemning in scathing terms only a few months ago. A year ago His Majesty's Government said that they would not grant Constituent Assembly because that would be a coercion of the minorities. His Majesty's Government is now prepared to grant Constituent Assembly and to coerce the minorities. A year ago His Majesty's Government said that they will not allow Pakistan because that is Balkanization of India. Today they are prepared to allow the partition of India.

How the Government of a Great Empire lost all sense of principle? The only explanation is that His Majesty's Government has, as a result of the course of the War, become panic-stricken. The proposals are the result of loss of nerve. How great is the panic that has overtaken His Majesty's Government can be easily seen if one compared the demands made by the Congress and the Muslim League, and the concessions made to them by these proposals. The Congress, while it demanded that the Constitution should be framed by a Constituent Assembly, did not demand that the question of safeguards for the minorities should be decided by the Constituent Assembly by a mere

Dr Ambedkar at the London School of Economics and Political Science (1922)

Dr Ambedkar with the Simon Commission (1928)

Dr Ambedkar at the Second Round Table Conference in London (1931) along with Mahatma Gandhi and other delegates

Dr Ambedkar with his wife, Ramabai, and other family members at their residence—Rajgraha, Mumbai (1934)

Dr Ambedkar with Periar Ramaswami Naicker and Barrister Jinnah (January 8, 1940)

Dr Ambedkar, Labour Minister in Viceroy's Executive Council (1944)

Addressing Annual Conference (3rd) of Scheduled Castes Federation (May 1945)

Dr Ambedkar , Law Minister in the Cabinet of Ministers along with Lord Mountbatten, Pandit Nehru and Others (1947)

Dr Ambedkar and the Drafting Committee for Indian Constitution (August 1947)

Dr Ambedkar with his second wife, Savita (1948)

Dr Ambedkar, the Chairman of the Constitution Drafting Committee, presenting the final draft to President, Dr Rajendra Prasad (November 25, 1949)

Dr Ambedkar leaving for the United States of America (USA) to receive Honorary LLD from Columbia University (1952)

Dr Ambedkar accepting Dhamma Deeksha at the Conversion Ceremony, Nagpur (October 14, 1956)

The Final Journey (December 6, 1956)

majority vote. On the other hand, when the Viceroy announced that the British Government will not be a party to the coercion of the minorities involved in the demand by the Congress, the Working Committee of the Congress at its meeting at Wardha held on August 22, 1940 passed the following resolution:

'The Committee regrets that although the Congress has never thought in terms of coercing any minority, much less of asking the British Government to do so, the demand for a settlement of a Constitution though through a Constituent Assembly of duly elected representatives has been misrepresented as coercion and the issue of minorities has been made into an insuperable barrier to Indians progress....The Congress had proposed that minority rights should be amply protected by agreement with the elected representatives of the minorities concerned.'

This shows that even the Congress did not demand that the decision of minority rights should be included in the purview of the Constituent Assembly. His Majesty's Government has not only given the Congress what it did not ask for but has given them the additional right to decide this minority rights issue by a bare majority vote.

With regard to the question of Pakistan, the same attitude is noticeable. The Muslim League did not demand that Pakistan must be conceded immediately. All that the Muslim League had asked for was that at the next revision of the Constitution the *Musalmans* should not be prevented from raising the question of Pakistan. The present proposals have gone a step beyond and distinctly given to the Muslim League the right to create Pakistan. These are Constitutional proposals. They are intended to lead India to wage a total war in which Hindus, *Musalmans*, Depressed Classes and Sikhs are called upon wholeheartedly to participate. Yet, Sir Stafford Cripps, either with the consent or without the consent of His Majesty's Government, has been making discrimination between major parties and minor parties. The major parties are those whose consent is necessary. Minor parties are those with whom consultation is believed to be enough.

So far as the Depressed Classes are concerned, I am not aware of any pronouncement in which the Depressed Classes were placed on a lower plane than the one given to the *Musalmans*. I quote the following from the speech of Viceroy made in Bombay on January 10, 1941, from which it will be seen that the Depressed Classes were bracketed with the *Musalmans*.

'There are insistent claims of the minorities. I need refer only to two of them; the great Muslim minority and the Scheduled Classes; there are the guarantees that have been given to the minorities in the past, the fact that their position must be safeguarded and that those guarantees must be honoured.'

This invidious distinction now sought to be made is a breach of faith with those minorities whose position has been lowered by this discrimination. From a Constitutional point of view it is an obnoxious distinction. From the point of view of total war it is bound to cause more disaffection and disloyalty in the country. It is for the British to consider whether in this attempt to win the friendship of those who have probably already decided to choose other friends they should lose those who are their real friends.

My advice to the British Government is that they should withdraw these proposals. If they cannot fight for right and justice and their plighted word they should better make peace. They can thereby at least save their honour.

CHAPTER TWENTY SEVEN

Labour Minister in the British Government of India

WHEN DR AMBEDKAR was appointed as the "Labour Member" in the Viceroy's Executive Council, in addition to the Department of Labour, he was also made in-charge of the then Central Public Works Department (CPWD) which included Power, Water and Mineral Resources. His contribution as the Cabinet Minister in the British Government of India can be seen from the thought-provoking speeches that Dr Ambedkar delivered during the four-year period.

I. AS LABOUR MINISTER

In a speech titled: "Why Indian Labour is Determined to Win the War", broadcast on All India Radio[91] (January 1943), Dr Ambedkar said,

> Labour believes that Victory for the Allied Nations is the only hope of such a New Order coming into being. If the Allies fail, sure enough there will be a New Order. But the New Order will be no other than the Nazi Order. It will be an Order in which liberty will be found to be suppressed, equality denied, and fraternity expurgated as a pernicious doctrine.

He also said,

> Only two things will, in the opinion of Labour, abolish war. One is to win the War and the other is to establish a just peace. In the view of Labour both are equally important. Labour holds that the origin of war does not lie in man's thirst for blood. The origin of war is to be found in the vile peace that victors often impose upon the vanquished. According to Labour, the duty of the pacifist is not to sulk and to refuse to fight when war is on. Labour believes that the duty of the pacifist is to be active and alert both when the war is on and also when the terms of peace are being forged.

91. For Full text, see *Ambedkar Speaks*, op cit, Vol II, pp 114-9.

The pacifist fails to do the right thing at the right time. The pacifists are active against war when war is on. They are inactive and indifferent when the war is over and peace is being made. In this way pacifists lose both war as well as peace.

On "Nationalism" and "Independence", from the Labour's perspective, Dr Ambedkar said:

> As to nationalism, Labour's attitude is quite clear; Labour is not prepared to make a fetish of nationalism. If nationalism means the worship of the ancient past—the discarding of everything that is not local in origin and colour—then Labour cannot accept nationalism as its creed. Labour cannot allow the living faith of the dead to become the dead faith of the living. Labour will not allow the ever expanding spirit of man to be strangled by the hand of the past which has no meaning for the present and no hope for the future. Nor will it allow it to be cramped in a narrow jacket of local particularism. Labour must constantly insist upon renovating the life of the people by being ever ready to borrow in order to repair, transform and recreate the body politic.
>
> Independence means nothing more than that a nation has liberty to determine its form of government and its social order without dictation from outside. The worth of independence depends upon the kind of government and the kind of society that is built up. There is not much value in independence if the form of government and order of society are to be those against which the world is fighting today. Labour thinks that more emphasis ought to have been placed on New India, and less on *'Quit India'*.

★ ★ ★

While chairing the Third Meeting of the Standing Labour Committee (May 7, 1943) Dr Ambedkar expressed desire to use the machinery of the Tripartite Conference (i.e., Labour, Employers and the Government) as an advisory body to help achieving further progress in respect of labour welfare measures.

Importantly, Dr Ambedkar favoured setting up of Employment Exchanges for skilled and semi-skilled personnel, insertion of a Fair Wage Clause in Government contracts and appointment of Labour Officers in industrial undertakings to maintain close touch with labour, hear its grievances and secure redress expeditiously.

★ ★ ★

In a speech to the Indian Federation of Labour in Mumbai (May 10, 1943), Dr Ambedkar deplored the "utter hollowness" and the 'superficiality' of the then Labour Movement, and appealed to the Labour Leaders present to sink their differences and present a united front against capitalism.

Dr Ambedkar delivered an elaborate speech on "Labour and Parliamentary Democracy" at a Study Camp of All India Trade Union Workers in New Delhi under the auspices of the Indian Federation of Labour (September 8, 1943).

According to Dr Ambedkar,

In several parts of the world, Parliamentary Democracy is vitiated because of the failure to realize that political democracy cannot succeed where there is no social and economic democracy. Some may question this proposition. To those who are disposed to question it, I will ask a counter-question. Why Parliamentary Democracy collapsed so easily in Italy, Germany and Russia? Why did it not collapse so easily in England and USA? To my mind, there is only one answer— namely, there was a greater degree of economic and social democracy in the latter countries than it existed in the former. Social and economic democracy are the tissues and the fiber of a Political Democracy. The tougher the tissue and fiber, the greater the strength of the body. Democracy is another name for equality.

Dr Ambedkar lamented:

The labouring classes have failed to acquaint itself with literature dealing with the government of mankind. Everyone from the Labouring Classes should be acquainted with Rousseau's Social contract, Marx's Communist Manifesto, Pope Leo XIII's Encyclical on the conditions of Labour and John Stuart Mill on Liberty, to mention only four of the basic programmatic documents on social and governmental organization of modern times. But the labouring Classes will not give them the attention they deserve. Instead Labour has taken delight reading false and fabulous stories of ancient kings and queens and has become addicted to it.

Dr Ambedkar exhorted the Trade Unions to broaden their perspective and ambition. He said,

I am not against Trade Unions. They serve a very useful purpose. But it would be great mistake to suppose that Trade Unions are a panacea for all the ills of labour. Trade Unions, even if they are powerful, are not strong enough to compel capitalists to run capitalism better. Trade Unions would be much more effective if they had behind them a Labour Government to rely on. Control of Government must be the target for Labour to aim at. Unless Trade Unionism aims at controlling government, trade unions will do very little good to the workers and will be a source of perpetual squabbles among Trade Union Leaders.

★ ★ ★

While addressing the First Session of the Plenary Labour Conference, New Delhi (September 6, 1943), Dr Ambedkar explained the rationale behind the Tripartite Labour Conference. [92] He said:

92. Later, while addressing the Plenary Session of Tripartite Labour Conference (November 15, 1944), Dr Ambedkar dealt with the defects in the Constitution and Procedures of the Tripartite Conference.

The motive for calling such a Conference was two-fold. For a long time the conviction had gained ground that the industrial problems and problems of Labour Welfare could not be solved unless the three parties—Government, Employers and Employees—developed a sense of responsibility towards one another, showed more respect for the views of one another and agreed to work in a spirit of give and take and that there was not much chance of such a sense of mutual respect and responsibility growing up so long as one was engaged in talking at the other. A plan to bring them together and to let them talk to each other across the table was felt to be necessary for the realization of this purpose.

Dr Ambedkar also recounted:

It was put to the Conference whether the time had not arrived for establishing a permanent and a representative body to discuss industrial problems of Labour Welfare both in their legislative and administrative aspects, and also to advise the Government of India as to the most satisfactory line of action in dealing with those problems. The representatives who were then present unanimously accepted the proposal, and resolved to constitute two bodies, one bigger to be called the Plenary Labour Conference and the other smaller to be called the Standing Labour Committee.

The Tripartite Labour Conference has its genesis in the exigencies of war. But I am happy to say that it is to last beyond the War. It is going to be an institution which will have a permanent place in the economic structure of the country.

Dr Ambedkar, in the same Conference, made two fundamental observations:

Those who are living under the capitalistic form of industrial organization and under the form of political organization called Parliamentary Democracy must recognize the contradiction of their systems. The first contradiction is between fabulous wealth and abject poverty not in its simple form but in its aggravated form in which we see it, wealth to those who do not work and poverty for those who do.

The second contradiction lies between the political and the economic system in politics, equality; in economics, inequality. One man one vote, one vote one value is our political maxim. Our maxim in economics is a negation of our political maxim. There might be differences of opinion in the matter of resolving these contrasts. But there can be no difference of opinion on the point that these contradictions do exist.

Ever since the basis of social life was changed from status to contract, insecurity of life has become a social problem and its solution has occupied the thoughts of all those who believe in the betterment of human life. There has been an enormous energy spent in enunciating the rights of man and the different sorts of freedom which must be regarded as his inalienable birth right. All this, of course, is very good, is very cheering. What I wish to say is that there will be little security unless and until… these rights are translated into terms which the common man can understand, namely, peace, a house, adequate clothing, education, good health, and, above all, the right to walk with dignity on the world's great boulevards without the fear of a fall.

We, in India, cannot fail to recognize these problems or bypass them. We must be prepared for the revaluation of values. It will not be enough to make industrial

> development of India as our goal. We shall have to agree that any such industrial development shall be maintained at a socially desirable level. It will not be enough to bend our energies for the production of more wealth in India. We shall have to agree not merely to recognize the basic right of all Indians to share in that wealth as a means for a decent and dignified existence but to devise ways and means to insure him against insecurity.

As Labour Minister, Dr Ambedkar moved several Bills in the Central Legislative Assembly. Two of these Bills are especially noteworthy:

(a) The Indian Trade Unions (Amendment) Bill (November 13, 1943) had three important features. In the first place, the Bill seeks to compel an employer to recognize a trade union. In the second place, the Bill imposes certain conditions on a trade union in order to make the trade union, if I may say so, worthy of recognition by an employer. The third feature of the Bill is to make non-recognition by an employer of a trade union, which has observed all the conditions prescribed in this measure and which has, therefore, qualified itself for recognition, an offence which is made punishable by law.
(b) The Factories Act, 1934 (April 4, 1944, November 1, 1944 and February 21, 1946) which dealt with a range of issues including powers to Government to ask for certain particulars (through Inspector of Factories) from the occupiers of a factory, making provision for making washing places obligatory on all factories, and give power to Government to prescribe the requisite number of fire escapes, compensatory holidays for the loss of compulsory holidays, issues relating to holidays with pay, reduction in the hours of work and the rate of payment of overtime.

Dr Ambedkar used the forum of the Standing Labour Committee, time and again, to discuss the issues of labour welfare. Illustratively, health insurance for industrial workers (Sixth meeting, March 17, 1945) and housing for industrial workers (Seventh meeting, December, 1945).

II. AS MINISTER FOR PUBLIC WORKS

As the Minister-in-charge of the Central Public Works Department (CPWD), Dr Ambedkar took lead in developing four mega projects:

(a) Multi-purpose Development of Damodar Valley for Bengal and Bihar (August 1945) aimed at creating (i) an aggregate controlled reservoir capacity of about 4,700,000 acre-feed; (ii) sufficient water for perennial irrigation of about 760,000 acres besides water for navigation purposes; (iii) electrical energy amounting to 300,000 kilowatts; and (iv) it would serve to promote directly the welfare of 5 million people, and indirectly of many more millions.

(b) Multi-purpose Plan for Development of Orissa's Rivers (November 1945) aimed at advancing the State's prosperity by irrigation, by navigation and by producing cheap electrical power.

(c) Post-War Electric Power Development (February 1945) based on the so-called Triple Program on the lines undertaken by the Central Electricity Board in UK. The Triple Program in the UK comprised:

- The creation of large-scale power stations located in the main industrial areas under the control of public supply undertakings;
- The construction of main transmission system (with smaller secondary lines attached to it for tapping agricultural and other outlying areas) so that the entire region to be developed by the main system can be held in a power ring or a series of power rings radiating out from the largescale power stations; and
- Standardization of frequency as far as possible within the region to be developed by the power system.

While addressing the Policy Committee on "Public Works and Electric Power", Dr Ambedkar said (February 2, 1945):

> We have felt more and more that if the services offered by electricity are to be brought to the door of producers as well as the consumers at the cheapest possible rates compatible with efficiency, we may have to follow albeit cautiously and gradually, the triple programme.
>
> This triple programme constitutes the foundation of the 'Grid' system, as we know it, to be operating in the U.K. since 1926 and it is my hope that if such a scheme of regional development is adopted in this country, we may before long bring the great boon of cheap electricity service to the door of everyone, high or low.

(d) Developing Policy Regarding Mineral Resources of India. In the Central Legislative Assembly, Dr Ambedkar made a statement on this subject (March 12, 1945) which, *inter alia,* indicated:

> To summarize the matter briefly, the mineral policy of the Government of India and the action which the Government of India propose to take in furtherance of that policy falls into two parts: in the first place, we propose to reconstitute the Geological Survey of India in order to make it a more potent instrument for the furtherance of our policy. Accordingly, a detailed scheme of expansion of the survey has been drawn up and administratively approved. The new branches of the Geological Survey which we propose to set up will deal with engineering geology, industrial utilization of minerals, central mineral development, geophysical work, oil development. It will include the establishment of a natural history museum, and a publicity section in order to keep the public informed of what is being done.
>
> The second part of our mineral policy consists of legislation, which the Government of India propose to initiate for the purpose of establishing control

> over minerals. In defining the limits of legislative control over the minerals, we propose to take into consideration the following circumstances. One, the importance of the mineral from the defence point of view on all-India mineral development; two, the technical nature of the mineral; three, the purposes for which the mineral is used; four, the value of the mineral or of the products into the making of which the mineral enters. Our legislative provisions will fall into two classes, or rather divide the minerals into two classes: those which will be subjected to general control: and under general control we propose to confine ourselves to the granting of prospecting and mining leases, the terms and conditions of such licenses and termination thereof. Then there will be other minerals, which will be selected for more detailed control. The number of such minerals which are suggested for more detailed control are about 28. I do not propose to detail them here. The detailed control will include besides the power to grant licenses, the power to control the method of mining, of processing, of grading, of standardizing, to direct improvement of mining and procuring methods, and also the power to initiate research for increased utilization and for other necessary purposes.

Dr Ambedkar's contribution as the Labour Member could be seen either in terms of the thought-provoking speeches that he delivered or in terms of specific reforms that he initiated.

The speeches Dr Ambedkar delivered as the Labour Member brought several issues pertinent to the labour movement in sharp focus. In a meeting organized by the Bombay Presidence Committee of the Indian Federation of Labour on May 10, 1943, Ambedkar observed that the Indian labour movement was hollow and superfluous on account of the unfortunate split in its ranks which had diffused its strength. In a similar vein, while delivering the Presidential address at the seventh Indian Labour Conference in November, 1945, Dr Ambedkar appealed to the labour to ask the moneyed classes,"If you do not mind paying taxes to meet the expenditure on War, why do you object to raising funds when their purpose is to raise labour standard. How many uneducated persons could have been educated, and how many sick persons could have been restored to health, if the money spent on War had been spent on public welfare."

While inaugurating a Conference of the Regional Labour Commissioners at Bombay in December, 1945, Dr Ambedkar identified three conditions necessary for preventing industrial disorder, viz., a machinery for conciliation, an amendment to the Trade Disputes Act and a minimum wage legislation. Regarding the potential for industrial peace, he observed that industrial peace on the basis of power was no longer a possibility. On the basis of law, it was possible, but uncertain. He advocted industrial peace based on social justice. Such an approach, which he argued was triangular in nature, must start with the workers who must recognize on their part the duty to work, which was same as elimination of shirking. The employer on his part must pay reasonable wages which was another name for elimination of exploitation and provide comfortable conditions of work which was another name for labour welfare. Finally, the State and the society must realize that the maintenance of proper industrial relations was a public affair and not merely a matter of a contract between the employer and the employee.

At another plane, Ambedkar devoted himself in initiating specific reforms aimed at promoting labour welfare. On May 7, 1943, presiding over the Third Meeting of the Standing Labour Committee, Dr Ambedkar deliberated on the issue of establishment of an Employment Exchange for streamlining avenues for employment. In September, 1943, while presiding over the Tripartite Labour Conference, Dr Ambedkar defined the demands of the labour for food, clothing, shelter, education, cultural amenities and health resources. At this persuasion, the Conference passed a resolution to set up a machinery to examine the issues relating to wages and earnings and to collect the material necessary for planning a policy of social security for labour. In April 1944, DrAmbedkar moved an amending Bill proposing holidays with pay for industrial workers in perennial factories. Finally, in August 1945, Dr Ambedkar presided over the deliberations of the Standing Labour Committee which discussed rules for industrial housing and employers' responsibilities.

During this period, as Member (i.e., Minister) in the Viceroy's Executive Council Dr Ambedkar's Ministry included not only the labour portfolio but also irrigation, power and other public works. On January 3, 1945, he addressed a joint meeting of representatives of the Central, Bengal and Bihar Governments in Calcutta on the issue of flood control. A disastrous flood of the Damodar River in 1945 had led to the setting up of what was to become the Damodar Valley Project. Dr Ambedkar projected his plan as modeled on the Tennessee Valley Project in the USA. He then set up the Central Waterways, Irrigation and Navigation Committee. Dr Ambedkar was also involved in the planning of the Hirakud Dam in Orissa. Notably, Dr Ambedkar projected his conception of the role of "big dams" in the development of India, which were to be multi-purpose projects that would include irrigation, electricity generation and water transport. As part of the Viceroy's Council, he was also involved in the earlier post-War planning, through secondary memberships of the Reconstruction Committee and the Subordinate Irrigation and Electricity Committees, of which he was also the Head. It was here that Dr Ambedkar could fully articulate the roles of electric power and irrigation in industrialization and thereby give thrust to the overall economic planning of Independent India.

CHAPTER TWENTY EIGHT

Confidential Memorandum to the British Government: Grievances of the Scheduled Castes

DR AMBEDKAR WAS appointed to the British Viceroy's Executive Council as a Member on July 9, 1942. While working in the British India's Cabinet as a Labour Minister, Dr Ambedkar prepared a Memorandum on "Grievances of the Scheduled Castes"[93] and submitted to the Governor-General on October 29, 1942. The Memorandum was marked "Confidential: Not for Circulation".

The Memorandum presents, with detailed facts and figures, the following grievances of the Scheduled Castes:

(1) Political Grievances

  (a) Inadequate Representation in the Central Legislature
  (b) Inadequate Representation in the Central Executive
  (c) Inadequate Representation in the Public Services
  (d) Absence of Representation in the Federal Public Services Commission

(2) Educational Grievances

  (e) Want of Aid for University and for Advanced Education
  (f) Want of Facilities for Technical Training

(3) Other Grievances

  (g) Neglect of Untouchables in Government Publicity
  (h) Closed-doors for Untouchables in Government Contracts

Here are excerpts from the Confidential Memorandum:

This Memorandum sets out the grievances of the Scheduled Castes in British India, and suggests the measures that are necessary for redressing them. In listing the

93. For the full text of the Memorandum, see BAWS, Vol.10, pp. 403-32.

grievances attention has been focussed only on those grievances which the Central Government alone can.

PART I POLITICAL GRIEVANCES

(1) Inadequate Representation in the Central Legislature

As at present constituted, the Central Assembly consists of 141 members. Of these 102 are elected and 39 nominated. Of the nominated members, 19 are non-Officials and 20 are Officials. Of this total of 141 there are two who belong to the Scheduled Castes. Consider as against this the population of the Scheduled Castes. Taking the figure of 40 millions, which is the figure given in the Census of 1940 there can be no doubt that the representation of the Scheduled Castes in the Central Legislature is ridiculously low....

It gives the total extent of the representation which different communities have secured through election as well as nomination. More striking are the figures given: the Hindus have been allowed 54.9 per cent by election. In addition, they are given 21 per cent out of the quota reserved for nomination. The Muslims have got 33.5 per cent by election. This is great deal in excess of what they are entitled to on the basis of their population. In addition, they are allowed the benefit of 37 per cent, out of the quota reserved for nomination. The same is the case with the Sikhs and the Parsis. Both of them have representation through election much beyond what their numbers would justify. Yet each is allowed to have the benefit of 10.5 per cent out of the quota for nomination. As against this, there is the naked fact that the Scheduled Castes who number 40 millions, and who form the third largest community in India have no seat by election, and only one by nomination.

Given these facts, two comments become quite in order. In the first place, the Legislature is quite an unbalanced body. It suffers from both the evils from over-representation of some communities and under-representation of other communities. The evil exists in its most aggravated form. For the over-representation is of communities which are strong and powerful, and the under-representation is of communities, which are weak and poor. The second comment relates to the wrong use of the power of nomination. The power of nomination was reserved under the Constitution to rectify the inequalities of representation. There is no principle, which seems to govern either the election or the nomination in so far as they relate to the composition of the Central Legislature. If at all there is any principle, it is to give Peter more than Paul and then to rob Paul who has almost nothing to enrich Peter who has almost everything.

There is no justification for so grave a wrong done to the Scheduled Castes in the matter of representation. In a Legislature in which the Muslims and the Hindus are waging a war against each other for rights and privileges and in which both are careful not to lose anything to a third party like the Scheduled Castes. What support can a single representative of the Scheduled Caste in a House of 141 get in his right for the rights of the Scheduled Castes? No generosity was shown by the Government of India to the Scheduled Castes in making its proposal for the composition of the Central Legislative Assembly. They gave them one seat by nomination, and it has continued to be one since 1921.

The result of this meagre representation has been quite deplorable. A single representative of the Scheduled Castes in an Assembly of 141 cannot but feel the utter helplessness of his position. He has to contend against a vast volume of anti-Scheduled Caste prejudices arising from the Hindu side of the House. He cannot depend upon the support either of the Muslim block who are fighting their battle to advance their interests. Nor can he depend upon the Official Block, which has been more careful to preserve its good relations with the major Hindu and Muslim blocks than to support the just interests of the Scheduled Castes. It is not even possible for the single and solitary representative of the Scheduled Castes in the Assembly to ventilate the grievances of the Scheduled Castes. I am informed that under the rules made by the President of the Legislative Assembly, the President gives the first chance to speak to those Hon'ble members who belong to a recognized Party. I also understand that the President does not recognize a party unless it has the minimum strength of ten members. This means that ordinarily the representative of the Scheduled Castes has no chance of speaking in the House unless he chooses to join a party. For a representative of the Scheduled Castes to be faced with this kind of situation is not a very happy tiling. To join a party means for him to subordinate the interests of the Scheduled Castes to that of a party, the principles and interests of which may be quite inconsistent with the principles and interests of the Scheduled Castes. On the other hand, not to join a party means to lose altogether the right to speak....

It is, therefore, greatly necessary that the representation of the Scheduled Castes in the Assembly should be augmented. Of course, this can be done only when vacancies occur in nominated non-official seats. When they do occur, justice requires that such vacancies should go to increase the representation of the Scheduled Castes in the Assembly.

(2) Inadequate Representation in the Central Executive

The Government of India has been very tardy in recognizing the right of the Scheduled Castes for representation in the Central Executive. This has been a very sore point with the Scheduled Castes. For they hold that whatever may have been their political status in the past, since the Round Table Conference their political status had become equal to the status of that of the Muslims, and if the Muslims have a right to representation in the Central Executive, so have the Scheduled Castes. The Scheduled Castes feel that their representation in the Cabinet is very inadequate. In a Cabinet of fifteen, there is only one Member of the Scheduled Castes, while the Muslims have three Members. The grievances arise by reason of the great contrast between the representation granted to the various communities and their needs and their numbers. If population alone was the criterion, there is no doubt that the Scheduled Castes are very near to the Muslims in the matter of population. It is, therefore, only fair to say that if the Muslims have three, the Scheduled Castes should at least have two in a Cabinet of fifteen. As it is, the communal formation of the Cabinet seems to be governed by no principle….

I am sure I am not disclosing any secrets when I say that in the course of the interview that I had with Sir Stafford Cripps when he came to India he told me that one of the principal objects of His Majesty's Government was to stabilize the position of the Scheduled Castes by their inclusion in the Central Executive which was to be formed during the interim period, so that the Constituent Assembly which under his proposals was to meet to draft the new Constitution will find their positions established beyond challenge. I request that this policy should be given effect to when the next step in the direction of the Indianization of the Executive Council takes place.

(3) Absence of Representation in the Public Services

No greater injustice has been done to the Scheduled Castes than in the matter of their employment in Public Services. Those Services with which the Central Government is particularly concerned. They fall into two classes:

(a) The ICS.
(b) The Central Services:
  (i) Those recruited on an all-India basis; and
  (ii) Those recruited locally.

Anyone who examines the communal composition of these Services can have no manner of doubt that the Scheduled Castes have been rigorously excluded from both these Services….

Out of 1,056 men in the ICS there is only I from the Scheduled Castes. Such is the state of affairs so far as the ICS is concerned. In the matter of their recruitment to the Central Services the condition of the Scheduled Castes is equally bad.

What are the reasons for the exclusion of the Scheduled Castes? As will be seen, the reasons are to be found in the difference in the principles and methods for securing communal representation which the Government of India has adopted towards the Scheduled Castes and the other minority communities in India.

It goes without saying that there is a striking contrast between the provisions made by the Government of India for securing the recruitment of the Scheduled Castes, and for the other minor communities to the Public Services. This contrast can be expressed in one sentence. The recruitment of the other communities is owing to the Resolution, (No.F.14-17-8-33 of July 4, 1934), not left to be a matter of discretion. It has been made a matter of obligation. The recruiting authority must fill in vacancy by recruiting a person, belonging to the community for which the vacancy is reserved. The recruitment of the Scheduled Castes on the other hand has been made a mere matter of discretion. The recruiting authority may fill an unreserved vacancy by appointing a person from the Scheduled Castes.

It is owing to this difference between 'must' and 'may' that the Muslims and other communities have been so well represented in the Public Services, and the Scheduled Castes so completely excluded. No better result is possible so long as the Government of India leaves the matter of recruitment of the Scheduled Castes in public services to the discretion and goodwill of the appointing officers. These officers are either Europeans, Hindus or Muslims. The European is blissfully ignorant of the Scheduled Castes, and he has never made the protection of the interests of the Scheduled Castes his special concern. So long as his general authority is maintained he is prepared to follow the advice of his Hindu or Muslim subordinates. The Muslims are naturally striving to strengthen their own position. They are concerned to see that as many vacancies as possible should go to the Muslims: at any rate all those, which are reserved, to them. The Hindus who had so far the monopoly in the Public Service and who never know how to share the good things of life with others want to keep the balance to themselves. With their self-interest combined with their age-old prejudices against the Scheduled Castes, the Hindus will never be fair to them. It is a sheer delusion to leave to the discretion of such officers the question of the recruitment of the Scheduled Castes and to hope that the Scheduled Castes will as a result of it secure a fair share of representation.

The question of entry into the Public Service is an important question for all minority communities. But to the Scheduled Castes it is a vital question, a question of life and death. There are many reasons why this must be so. In the first place, it is a question of opening up a career for young men from the Scheduled Castes. Trade and Industry, as openings for a career, are all blocked to young men of the Scheduled Castes. It is only in Government service that they can find a career.... For there is another aspect which relates to the effect which the bestowal of Government patronage has in encouraging the spread of education in a community. The case of the Hindu community is quite in point.

The rapid progress, which the Hindu community has made, is, of course, very striking. But it is very seldom realized that the reason why education has taken such deep root in the Hindu society is entirely due to the assurance that education opens up a career by entry in Government service. Such assurance of career is absolutely necessary in the case of the Scheduled Castes who are so backward in education.

There is a third argument far more weighty than the two which have been referred to above. It relates to the interest of the general population of the Scheduled Caste people as distinguished from the interests of the educated classes from the Scheduled Castes. This will be clear if it is realized how important public administration is from the point of view of public welfare. Good laws may prove of no avail if the administration is bad. Administration is, therefore, a vital question for the Scheduled Castes who are more interested in good administration than in good laws.

Is the present administration good administration? What do the Scheduled Castes think of the present-day administration? There can be no doubt that the view universally held is that the whole administration is hostile, unjust, and perverse in its attitude towards the Scheduled Castes all over India. Indeed much of the suffering and harassment of the Scheduled Caste population arises from the fact that the discretion vested in public servants is in almost all cases exercised against the interests of the Scheduled Castes and with the object of keeping them down. This is as it must be given the mentality of the Hindu and Muslim officers, towards the Scheduled Castes. This will continue to be so as long as the personnel of the administration is drawn from classes who have been opposed to the Scheduled Castes and who believe in their suppression. There cannot be a more powerful argument than that of the advantage and welfare of the general population of the Scheduled Castes to show that the entry of the Scheduled Castes in the Public Service must be regarded as a most vital consideration.

All this shows how the position of the Scheduled Castes has remained deplorable, and how Government which is striving to be considerate to other communities but not even trying to be correct towards the Scheduled Castes, is responsible for this result.

The condition of the Scheduled Castes is not only deplorable, but it is also intolerable. This is the result of the present policy of the Government of India under which the quantum of recruitment of the Scheduled Castes in the Public Services instead of fixed by rule, as is done in the case of the other minorities is left to the discretion of the appointing authorities. The appointing authorities are mostly Caste Hindus, and it is not possible to expect them to give the benefit of this discretion to the Scheduled Castes. I have no doubt that the interests of the Scheduled Castes will continue to be neglected and sacrificed to serve the interests of other communities so long as the present system continues. The Government of India should without further delay equalize the position of the Scheduled Castes and:

(a) Declare that they are a minority for the purpose of Services like the other communities.
(b) Fix 13½ per cent as the proportion of annual vacancies in the ICS and both in the Central Services that are recruited on an all India basis and that are recruited locally, as the share to which they are entitled, and which in equity and justice should be reserved for them. Unless this is done the Scheduled Castes will never get their due share in Public Services.

The difficulty lies in the Scheduled Castes not being declared a minority. It is essential that this obstacle in their way be removed. The reason is that under the resolution of July 4, 1934, it is only when a community is declared to be a minority that it becomes entitled to the benefit of reservation in the Public Services.... It is difficult to see what objection there can be to a declaration that the Scheduled Castes are a minority. The term minority is a political term and whatever may be its *de jure* definition its *de facto* definition can never be in doubt. The matter is settled by the terms of Communal Award so that any community, which is covered by the Communal Award of His Majesty's Government, must be held to be a minority. Indeed that is the basis on which the Government of India could declare that the Muslims, Sikhs, Indian Christians, and Anglo-Indians are minorities. If these communities are minorities, and they are minorities because they are covered by the Communal Award—then it is difficult to see how the claim of the Scheduled Castes to be declared a Minority be denied. For they too are covered by the same Award. Secondly, if Government is bound to declare them a minority then it follows as a natural consequence that Government is bound to define their share in the Services and make it available by the same means and methods by which the share of other communities has been secured to them. Nor can anybody oppose the quantum of share to which they are entitled as the legitimate share of the Scheduled Castes. It has been shown that their population in British India is 13.6 per cent and nothing more than a share of 13.6 per cent in the Services is claimed for them. This cannot injure the Hindus, for their population is 50 per cent and they are getting 63 per cent which is 13 per cent more than is their due.

The opposition to this claim of the Scheduled Castes comes from very strange and unexpected quarters. It should come from the Hindus. But it cannot. The mutual rights of the Scheduled Castes and the Hindus are defined by the Poona Pact, which was made in 1932. It is an agreement by which the Hindus have accepted that the Scheduled Castes are a minority, and that they are entitled to adequate share in the Public services of the Country. It is true that the term 'adequate' was not given a quantitative expression. That is because it was done in a hurry to save Mr Gandhi from the hands of death. But there can be no doubt that 'adequate' was never intended to be anything less than the population ratio. The Hindus, therefore, cannot oppose the claim of the Scheduled Castes and, as a matter of fact, they do not. The party opposing the claim of the Scheduled Castes is the Government of India and nobody else....

This is the most tragic part of the story. The Government of India has said that they were trustees for the welfare of the Scheduled Castes. As trustees, they should be more ready to safeguard the rights of the Scheduled Castes than to safeguard the rights of the other minorities. There would have been some excuse for the Government of India hesitating to allot to the Scheduled Castes their rights in the matter of recruitment to the Public Services if there was any obstacle placed in their way by the Hindus. But there is no such excuse. Would it be wrong if it was said that the enemies of the Scheduled Castes are not the Hindus and that their real enemy is the Government of India?

Besides the two remedies suggested, namely (a) declaring them a minority and (b) fixing their proportion in the annual vacancies, it will be necessary to sanction other remedies to the Scheduled Castes for securing to them their fair share in the services. They are:

(i) Raising the age bar,
(ii) Reduction in examination fees, and
(iii) Appointment of a Scheduled Caste officer to see that the provisions made in the interests of the Scheduled Castes in this behalf are carried by all Departments concerned.

PART II: EDUCATIONAL GRIEVANCES

(1) Want of Assistance for Advanced Education

Looking at the growth of Advanced Education among the Scheduled Caste boys, the following conclusions are deducible:—

(a) That education in Arts and Law is progressing satisfactorily.
(b) That education in Science and Engineering has made no progress.
(c) That Advanced Education in foreign Universities is a very far cry.

This sad situation needs to be properly appreciated....

The status and condition of the Scheduled Castes will be improved only when the representatives of the Scheduled Castes come to occupy Executive posts as distinguished from Ministerial posts. Executive posts are strategic posts, posts from which a new direction can be given to the affairs of the State. The attainment of Executive post it is obvious requires a high degree of education. Such posts will not be open except to those who have acquired advanced education.

Education in Arts and Law cannot be of much value to the Scheduled Castes either to the graduates themselves or to the people. It has not been of very high value even to Hindus. What will help the Scheduled Castes is education of an advanced type in Science and Technology. But it is obvious that education in Science and Technology is beyond the means of the Scheduled Castes and this is why so many of them send their children to take up courses in Arts and Law. Without Government assistance, the field of Advanced Education in Science and Technology will never become open to the Scheduled Castes, and it is only just and proper that the Central Government should come forward to aid them in this connection.

This problem will be solved if the following proposals are accepted by the Government of India:

(a) An annual grant of Rs 2 lakhs for scholarships for Scheduled Caste students taking Science and Technology courses tenable at the Universities or other Scientific and Technical Training Institutions in India.
(b) An annual grant of one lakh of rupees to be spent on scholarships for the education of Scheduled Caste students for Science and Technology in

> foreign Universities in England, the Dominions, in Europe and in America.

There is nothing to prevent the Government of India from undertaking this responsibility. Education, it is true, is not a Central subject for Legislative purposes. Still, Section 150(2) of the Government of India Act says that the Central Government may make grants for any purpose, notwithstanding that the purpose is not one with respect to which the Central Legislature may make laws. This power has been used by the Government of India to support Educational Institutions....

The grant made to the Universities is really grant made to the Hindu and Muslim communities for supporting higher education. That being so, there is no reason why the Central Government should not undertake to make a similar grant of 3 lakhs of rupees annually to promote higher education among the Scheduled Castes. If the Government is interested in raising the status of the Scheduled Castes, which they have often proclaimed to be their duty, it is high time that a similar provision was made for them in the education budget of the Central Government.

The scheme if it is given effect to will revolutionise the condition and status of the Scheduled Castes. The Scheduled Castes lay great store by it. They would even be prepared for the scheme being made a loan system rather than a system of grants. The Scheduled Caste boys who receive these scholarships shall be glad to take advantage of it even if they are required to refund the sums received by them when they are employed or they may be made to serve the Government for a term under a lower scale of salary. There can be no objection to Government accepting these proposals.

For the purpose of assisting Advanced Scientific and Technical Education among the Scheduled Caste students I am making two other proposals....

(2) Want of Facilities for Technical Training Technical Education

From the point of raising the economic condition, technical education for the Scheduled Castes is more important than literary education. But technical education is also very costly and it is not possible for children of the Scheduled Castes to take technical education, and without technical education their economic condition will not be improved. Owing to the social system of the Hindus, the Scheduled Castes occupy economically a very low place in the Indian economy. In times of prosperity he is last to be employed, and in times of depression he is first to be discharged. This, of course, is a result of the social prejudices of the Hindus, which operate against him. But there is also the other difficulty, which stands in his way and that he is generally an unskilled labourer with no technical knowledge.

It seems to me that the Government of India can do a great deal to improve his lot by enabling him to acquire technical skill which he does not now possess and this can be easily done by introducing a system of apprenticeship for the Scheduled Caste boys in undertakings run or controlled by the Government of India, in which the possibilities of giving such technical training do exist.

I am referring only to two:

(a) Apprenticeships in Government Printing Presses
(b) Apprenticeships in Railway Workshops

I, therefore, suggest the scheme of apprenticeship whereby annually a good number of boys from the Scheduled Castes should be given training in the printing press and the Railway Workshops. The cost of it cannot be very great.

PART III: OTHER GRIEVANCES

(1) Neglect in the Matter of Publicity

It is quite well known that the Government of India engages itself very largely in giving publicity to the saying and doings of different individuals and parties who represent the main forces operating in India. As an illustration of this I would refer to the Volume called 'India and the Aggressor' (The Trend of Indian Opinion Between 1935-40) issued by the Bureau of Public Information of the Government of India. Now the most annoying part of this volume is the complete neglect of the sayings and doings of the Scheduled Castes.

Of course, Government may say that it is not bound to do publicity work for parties and communities, and that the parties and communities may do their own publicity. But that is not the case here. The Government of India, as I have shown, does engage itself very much in this work of publicity. And when a Government does it, it is bound to treat all parties on equal footing in the matter of publicity and give a true and correct picture of the movements and forces operating in the country.

(2) Closed-door in Government Contracts

A good part of Government needs in Public Works is carried out not departmentally but by contracts. This is so in normal times. In war times the work done for Government by the contract system has expanded several hundred fold. I can speak only of the Central Public Works Department. The list of approved contractors maintained by the Central Public Works Department is 1,171. Of these, I am told, there is only one contractor belonging to the Scheduled Castes. The rest of them are Hindus, Sikhs and Muslims. It should be possible for Government to arrange things in such a manner as to make its contract system allow an open door to members of all communities to profit by it. There are many persons of the Scheduled Castes who could be trusted to carry out a Government contract. Already, many members of the Scheduled Castes are working as employees of Hindu, Muslim or Sikh contractors. The result is that the Hindu, Muslim or Sikh contractors are taking profit while the Scheduled Caste men are working on a meagre wage.

There is not much difficulty in getting a certain number of men from the Scheduled Castes put on the list of approved contractors. But what is important is to enable them to get a contract. There are two rules in the matter of Government contracts:

(a) That a contract is to be given generally to a contractor whose tender is the lowest;
(b) That Government is not bound to accept the lowest tender.

It is, therefore, a matter of discretion, which is exercised by the Officer in charge whether a contract will go to a particular contractor or not. This discretion is not likely to be exercised in favour of a Scheduled Caste contractor. His tender may be the lowest but owing to communal prejudice he may not accept it and rely on the second rule that he is not bound to accept the lowest. If his tender is higher than the lowest, he will not accept it although he is free to do so. He will rely on the first of the two rules. Either way he will have his justification for rejecting the tender of the Scheduled Caste contractors.

There is, of course, no remedy against communal basis. The only thing that strikes me that we can do is to amend the rule by saying that a tender of a Scheduled Caste contractor, if it is not higher than the lowest by 5 per cent, shall be deemed to be the lowest. This, of course, involves financial loss and the Finance Department will have to agree to it. I cannot give any idea of the approximate cost of such a concession. I am sure it will not be heavy as to break the camel's back.

PART IV: DUTY OF GOVERNMENT TOWARDS DISTRESSED PEOPLE

Some of the proposals submitted in this Memorandum on behalf of the Scheduled Castes, particularly those which are put forth to remove political grievances, do not involve any financial burden on the public treasury. They are really not proposals so much as political demands which, by reason of their logic and their justice, Government must grant. The difficulty arises only with regard to the acceptance of those proposals, which involve a financial burden upon the revenues of the Central Government. Financial burden there is. But, it will not do to reject them merely on that account. For there can be no doubt that Government has a duty towards the Scheduled Castes, and if they accept their duty in this behalf, they are bound to discharge it even if it involves a certain amount of financial burden on the public purse.

The policy of the British Government towards the Scheduled Castes has been one of complete and continuous neglect. It began from the very beginning when the British Government realised that its duty was not merely to maintain law and order, and extended to giving the people education and looking after their welfare....

In 1882 Government of India appointed the Hunter Commission to examine the Educational Policy. This Commission made a number of important proposals to spread education among Muslims. With regard to the Untouchables it did nothing. All that it did was to express an opinion that Government should accept the principle that nobody be refused admission to Government College or School merely on the ground of Caste, but qualified it by saying that the principle should be applied with due caution!

This antagonism when it passed away, its place was taken up by negligence and indifference. This negligence and indifference made its appearance not merely in the field of education. It also made its appearance in other fields, particularly in the Army. The whole Army of the East India Company consisted of the Depressed Classes. Indeed, but for the Depressed Classes Army, the British would never have been able to conquer India. The Untouchables continued to fill the Army till 1892. In 1892 their recruitment in the army was stopped all of a sudden and they were thrown in the street in utter distress with no education and no means to pursue other ways of honourable living.

Who can raise the Scheduled Castes from the distress in which they are now grovelling? It is certain they cannot do it by their own effort. Their resources are too scanty to afford them the means to raise themselves. They cannot depend upon the charity of the Hindus. The charity of the Hindus is beyond question, communal in its scope and its benefits are confined to those who belong to the community of the donor. The Hindu donors are either businessmen or high State officials. The tragedy is that they make their money out of the general public. But when it comes to a question of doing charity they forget the public and remember their own Caste and their community. The Scheduled Castes have neither of these sources available to them and they are rigorously excluded from the charity founded by both. The only source, therefore, on which they can rely is financial aid from Government. I venture to say that it is the duty of the Central Government to come to the rescue of people who are in distress by no fault of theirs as is the case with the Scheduled Castes. The Central Government is bound to take steps to assist the Scheduled Castes to concede their just claims and to compete on more equal terms with their competitors.

CHAPTER TWENTY NINE

Civil Disobedience Campaign and the "Quit-India" Movement

JUST ABOUT THE time that Dr Ambedkar took over as the Cabinet Minister in the Viceroy's Executive Council (July 1942), Mahatma Gandhi announced the Civil Disobedience Campaign.

Dr Ambedkar, on the eve of his departure to Delhi (July 27, 1942) gave an interview to the *Times of India* where he described Gandhiji's all-out open rebellion as both irresponsible and insane, a bankruptcy of statesmanship....It would be madness, he said, to weaken law and order at a time when the barbarians were at the gates of India....[94]

On August 9, 1942, Gandhiji announced the "Quit-India" movement. The Viceroy's Executive Council, of which Dr Ambedkar was now a Member, resolved that the decision of the Congress was a challenge plunging India into confusion and anarchy...[95]

The Congress leaders were arrested all over the country and placed under detention. The popular discontent, mass disturbance and subsequent arrests and the suppression of the movement by the British with an iron fist inevitably led to a massive political upheaval throughout the country.

While debating on the "Situation in India" in the Central Legislative Assembly, Dr Ambedkar blamed Gandhiji and the Congress for the 'disorder' which he felt were harming the Indians more (September 18, 1942). Dr Ambedkar said:

> I think it is very necessary that the Members (of the Executive Council) should take the burden upon themselves, and I, therefore, propose to deal with some of the points that have been made by that section of the House which thinks that the action was not justified.

94. Keer, Dhananjay, op cit, p.354.
95. Keer, Dhananjay, op cit, p.354.

Sir, the critics of Government have said that the Government were not justified in arresting the members of the Congress, and if I understand the argument correctly, the argument seems to be that Congress is a body which believes in non-violence and that if the Congress had been allowed to be free they certainly would have controlled the situation in such a manner that they would have prevented violence from emerging. It seems to me that the Members who take that line have not correctly read what has happened to the Congress and the members of the Working Committee during the last two years with regard to the principle of non-violence. Sir, as I read the proceedings of the Congress during the last two or three years, the impression that has been left upon my mind is that there has been a terrible landslide in the principle of non-violence as has been proclaimed by the Congress. The non-violence has been deeply buried—I have no hesitation on that point at all.

Let me give the House a few facts. Sir, on the 22nd of December, 1939, the Congress first gave the threat of Civil Disobedience. On the 19th March, 1940, the Congress had its Annual Session at Ramgarh. At the Annual Session Mr Gandhi was made the dictator, and given sole charge to lead the struggle. Mr. Gandhi became the Commander-in-Chief under that resolution. But on the 22nd of June, 1940, barely within three months, Mr Gandhi was deposed from his place as a Commander-in-Chief. The Working Committee refused to accept the principle of non-violence as a guiding principle for its action, and Mr Gandhi had to tender his resignation. On the 15th December, 1940, the All-India Congress Committee met in Bombay and there a resolution was passed by which Mr Gandhi was again made the Commander-in-Chief and requested to carry on the struggle. Mr Gandhi continued to be the Commander till December 1941. In December 1941, a Working Committee meeting was held in Bardoli and a resolution was passed again deposing Mr Gandhi.

The important feature of the incident that took place in December 1941 is, I think, not quite well-known to the Members of this House. There was a great schism at Bardoli between Mr Gandhi and his followers who believed in non-violence out and out, and the other members of the Working Committee who did not believe in non-violence. The matters were put to issue at Wardha at a meeting of the All-India Congress Committee. Everybody in India, certainly the members of the Working Committee, expected that Mr Gandhi would push the issue to a decision, and either have the Working Committee's resolution passed at Bardoli rescinded or, if it was not possible for him to do so, tender his resignation. One of the most astounding things that Mr Gandhi did at Wardha when the resolution came up for ratification before the All-India Congress Committee was that the apostle of non-violence instructed his followers not to carry the matter to a division. Not only that, he continued to associate himself with the Working Committee and continued to be its Commander-in-Chief. Sir, if that is not evidence that the Congress was saturated with a spirit of violence, right under the very nose of the Congress—Mr Gandhi—I do not know what better evidence one could offer on that point.

There is another point which, I think, Honourable Members are not aware of and about which I would like to make some reference. It is not only a fact that almost all members of the Congress Working Committee—at any rate a great many of them—had ceased to have any faith in non-violence, a great many of them had become indifferent to the principle, but there is enough body of evidence to indicate that inside the Congress there was an attempt being made for a planned campaign of violence....

An incident occurred at Deoli Detention Camp where Mr Jai Prakash Narain was kept. The House probably is aware that the Jail Superintendent in charge of the Camp succeeded in getting hold of some papers which Mr Jai Prakash Narain was surreptitiously trying to pass out of the Jail to his wife. That incident occurred in December 1941.... That document, if I read it correctly, reveals four or five points.

First of all—and I am using the words of Mr Jai Prakash Narain himself—the *Satyagraha* which Mr Gandhi was carrying on was held by a majority of Congressmen as a stupid farce; it had no sense, it had no meaning. Secondly, Mr Jai Prakash Narain maintained that if the Congress wanted to achieve its goal, it had better give up the task of attending to moral victories, and should try to achieve political victories. That was again a hit against Mr Gandhi.

The second fact which the document revealed was that there were in existence in India certain parties who were not only not believing in non-violence, but were pledged to violence, and the parties that are referred to in that document, I find, are these, which are said to be within the Congress: The Communist Party of India, the Revolutionary Socialist Party in Bengal, the Congress Socialist Party, the Hindustan Socialist Republican Association. It was the project of Mr Jai Prakash Narain that all these bodies, except perhaps the Communist Party, should be amalgamated into one single organization which should be a secret party, working within the Congress and working below ground, subterranean—to use the exact technical terminology. Mr Jai Prakash Narain also suggested that this secret party should not only be within the Congress, but should resort to political dacoities for the purpose of getting funds to carry on its own policy. If these two matters, to which I have made reference, do not convince reasonable people that the Congress was not to be trusted in the lip service which it rendered to the principle of non-violence, I do not know that there can be any better evidence by which a reasonable man can be convinced.

In the same speech, Dr Ambedkar also discussed the demand that was being made for a National Government. He argued that the veto, which was till then vested in the Secretary of the State for India, should have been vested in the Legislature; but since there were no fresh elections, the existing Legislatures could not be regarded as sufficiently representative. He said:

Now, Sir, it is quite true and I do not think I am saying anything derogatory to this House, that, having regard to the efflux of time, this House is almost in a deceased state. It was elected for three years, but it has been sitting for almost nine years. I do not know to what extent the present Members of this house can be said to derive a mandate from their Constituencies, which can be regarded as direct and fresh, if it has not become stale by the efflux of time. I won't say anything about it, but let us proceed further and examine the composition of the House.

Examine the Legislature from any point of view you like, examine it from the point of view of the mandate, examine it from the point of view of the composition of the Legislature, its representative character, examine it also from the point of view of the electorate which is represented, and I have no doubt about it that this House cannot be regarded as sufficiently representative to impose a veto on a National Government.

The point, therefore, is this. Either you must acknowledge the fact that this House is not representative enough to have the veto deposited in it, or you must consider whether during the period of the War, it is possible for us to enter upon re-fashioning this Legislative Assembly in such a manner that it will contain within itself a sufficient number of Hindus, a sufficient number of *Musalmans*, a sufficient number of Depressed Classes, and all the other elements which go to make up the national life of the country.

Therefore, my submission is that this demand which has been made for a National Government is certainly the result of confused thinking, is the result of the desire of the most people to avoid what I regard as the most crucial question, namely, a communal settlement, because until we get a communal settlement, it is quite impossible to re-fashion this House in a manner in which it would be regarded as fit to receive the veto powers over the Executive that may be fashioned under the new Constitution.

The "Quit-India" movement came to an end after a few weeks of disorder and mob violence. Gandhiji then started a 21-day fast on February 10, 1943. The fast rocked the whole nation, and there were cries of "Release Gandhiji" all over the country. There was a lot of pressure on the Indian Members of the Viceroy's Council to resign. Most Members did, except Dr Ambedkar (and Srivastava of Hindu *Mahasabha*). In fact, in a speech (Marathi) in Mumbai (May 9, 1943), Dr Ambedkar said, "Gandhi and Jinnah should retire."

Asserting that Mr Gandhi and the Congress High Command had displayed "utter political bankruptcy", Dr Ambedkar, pleaded that Mr Gandhi should retire from active politics. He added that Mr Jinnah, President of the All India Muslim League, "who has taken up an impossible position should also retire." He emphasized that unless both these leaders quit the stage, it was absolutely hopeless to make any move to lift Indian politics from the present quagmire. It was only then that Indian politics might be expected to move on a line that might help the country towards its progress.

Dr Ambedkar said that Mr Gandhi was by far the most fortunate politician that had ever been born. He was fortunate because he had all the necessaries for effective politics for the mere asking, while other political leaders had to spend half their lives in collecting them. Mr Gandhi had both "man-power and money-power" in abundance, while the late Mr Tilak, Mr Ranade and Mr Gokhale never had "money-power" and as for "man-power", they had to spend the whole of their lives in collecting it.

With all that, Mr Gandhi's political career had been a series of failures during the last 25 years. His politics was no doubt very exciting as compared with the placid politics of Gokhale or Ranade. But there was one thing quite certain, namely, that the politics and methods of Gokhale and Ranade would never have led the country to its present unfortunate position of having to divide the country. Mr. Gandhi's politics had resulted in that tragedy, "Instead of getting *Swaraj* and discussing that solitary question." Dr Ambedkar declared, "We at the end of the journey have been presented with totally different problems, which probably Gokhale and Ranade would never have permitted to arise."

"The people of India," continued Dr Ambedkar, "have placed blind faith in Mr Gandhi and the Congress High Command. They have completely lost critical faculty, and they have never the courage to tell Mr Gandhi where he is wrong."

PART VI

ON WAR-PATH WITH MAHATMA GANDHI

CHAPTER THIRTY

Ranade, Gandhi and Jinnah

THE DECCAN SABHA of Poona invited Dr Ambedkar to deliver an Address on the 101st birth anniversary of late Justice Mahadev Govind Ranade which fell on January 18, 1940. Initially, he was reluctant to accept the invitation. For he knew that his views on social and political problems, a discussion of which could not be avoided in a discourse on Ranade, would not be very pleasing to the audience and even perhaps to the Members of the Deccan Sabha.[96] In the end, however, he accepted their invitation, and delivered the Address in Pune on January 18, 1943. The Address was published as a book during the same year.

The Address in the printed form differs from the Address as delivered in two respects: One Section of the Address was omitted from the Address, as delivered for brevity. Another difference lies in the omission of a large portion of the Section which was devoted to a comparison of Ranade with Phule.

The publication of the Address took place under peculiar circumstances. Ordinarily reviews follow publication. In this case the situation was reversed. What is worse is that the reviews condemned the Address in scathing terms. As stated by Dr Ambedkar in the Preface:

> I am condemned because I criticized Mr Gandhi and Mr Jinnah for the mess they have made of Indian politics, and that in doing so I am alleged to have shown towards them hatred and disrespect.... As for myself, I am not in the least perturbed by the condemnation of this Address by the Press.
>
> The condemnation is by the Congress Press. I know the Congress Press well. I attach no value to its criticism. It has never refuted my arguments. It knows only to criticize, rebuke and revile me for everything I do and to misreport, misrepresent and pervert everything I say. Nothing that I do, pleases the Congress Press. This animosity of the Congress Press towards me can to my mind not unfairly be explained as a reflex of the hatred of the Hindus for the Untouchables. That their animosity has become personal is clear from the fact that the Congress Press feels offended for my having

96. Quoted from the Preface of the Book.

criticized Mr Jinnah who has been the butt and the target of the Congress for the last several years.

However strong and however filthy be the abuses which the Congress Press chooses to shower on me, I must do my duty. I am no worshipper of idols. I believe in breaking them. I insist that if I hate Mr Gandhi and Mr Jinnah—1 dislike them, I do not hate them—it is because I love India more. That is the true faith of a nationalist. I have hopes that my countrymen will some day learn that the country is greater than the men, that the worship of Mr Gandhi or Mr Jinnah and service to India are two very different things and may even be contradictory of each other.

★ ★ ★

Here are some excerpts from the book:

I. VIEWS ON CAUSES OF HISTORICAL CHANGES[97]

There are friends of Ranade, who do not hesitate to describe him as a great man, and there are others who with equal insistence deny him that place. Where does the truth lie? But this question must, I think, wait upon another, namely, is history the biography of great men? The question is both relevant as well as important. For, if great men were not the makers of history, there is no reason why we should take more notice of them than we do of cinema stars. Views differ. There are those who assert that, however great a man may be, he is a creature of Time—Time called him forth, Time did everything, he did nothing. Those who hold this view, in my judgement, wrongly interpret history.

There have been three different views on the causes of historical changes. We have had the Augustinian theory of history, according to which history is only an unfolding of a divine plan in which mankind is to continue through war and suffering until that divine plan is completed at the day of judgement. There is the view of Buckle who held that history was made by Geography and Physics. Karl Marx propounded a third view. According to him, history was the result of economic forces. None of these three would admit that history is the biography of great men. Indeed, they deny man any place in the leaking of history. No one except theologians accepts the Augustinian theory of history. As to Buckle and Marx, while there is truth in what they say, their views do not represent the whole truth. They are quite wrong in holding that impersonal forces are everything and that man is no factor in the making of history. That impersonal forces are a determining factor cannot be denied. But that the effect of impersonal forces depends on man must also be admitted. Flint may not exist everywhere. But where it does exist, it needs man to strike flint against flint to make fire. Seeds may not be found everywhere. But where they do exist, it needs man to ground it to powder and make it a delectable and

97. All sectional captions are by the author. In the Book, there are no such captions.

nutritious paste and thereby lay the foundation of agriculture. There are many areas devoid of metals. But where they do exist, it needs a man to make instruments and machines which are the basis of civilization and culture….

★ ★ ★

II. WHO CAN BE CALLED A GREAT MAN?

Who can be called a great man? If asked of military heroes such as Alexander, Attila, Caesar and Tamerlane, the question is not difficult to answer. The military men make epochs and effect vast transitions. They appeal and dazzle their contemporaries by their resounding victories. They become great without waiting to be called great. As the lion is among the deer, so they are among men. But it is equally true that their permanent effect on the history of mankind is very small. Their conquests shrink, and even so great a General as Napoleon after all his conquests left France smaller than he found it. When viewed from a distance they are seen to be only periodical, if necessary, incidents in the world's movement, leaving no permanent mark on the character of the society in which they live….

The answer becomes difficult when the question is asked about a person who is not a military general. For, it then becomes a question of tests, and different people have different tests.

Carlyle, the apostle of Hero Worship, had a test of his own. He laid it down in the following terms: "I should say sincerity, a deep, great genuine sincerity, is the first characteristic of all men in any way heroic…."

Lord Rosebery proposed another test when dealing with Napoleon—who was as great an Administrator as a General. In answering the question, "Was Napoleon Great?" Rosebery used the following language:

> If greatness stands for natural power, for predominance, for something human beyond humanity, then Napoleon was assuredly great. Besides that indefinable spark which we call genius, he represents a combination of intellect and energy which has never perhaps been equalled, never certainly surpassed.

There is a third test, suggested by the philosophers or, to be more accurate, by those who believe in divine guidance of human affairs. They have a different conception of what is a great man. To summarize the summary of their view, a great man is launched into the world, as a great natural or supernatural force, as a scourge and a scavenger boon to cleanse society and lead it on to the right path who is engaged in a vast operation, partly positive, mainly negative, but all relating to social regeneration.

Which of these is the true test? In my judgement all are partial and none is complete. Sincerity must be the test of a great man…. Nonetheless, no one can accept that sincerity is the primary or the sole test. For sincerity is not enough. A great man must have sincerity. For it is the sum of all moral qualities without which no man can be called great. But there must be something more than mere sincerity in a man to make him great. A man may be sincere and yet he may be a fool, and a fool is the very antithesis of a great man. A man is great because he finds a way to save society in its hours of crisis. But what can help him to find the way? He can do so only with the help of intellect. Intellect is the light. Nothing else can be of any avail. It is quite obvious that without the combination of sincerity and intellect no man can be great. Is this enough to constitute a great man? At this stage we must, I think, make a distinction between an eminent individual and a great man. For I am certain that a great man is something very different from an eminent individual. Sincerity and intellect are enough to mark out an individual as being eminent as compared to his fellows. But they are not enough to raise him to the dignity of a great man. A great man must have something more than what a merely eminent individual has. What must be that thing? Here comes the importance of the philosophers' definition of a great man. A great man must be motivated by the dynamics of a social purpose and must act as the scourge and the scavenger of society. These are the elements which distinguish an eminent individual from a great man and constitute his title deeds to respect and reverence.

III. WAS RANADE A GREAT MAN?

Was Ranade a great man? He was, of course, great in his person. Vast in physique.... He was a man of sanguine temperament, of genial disposition and versatile in his capacity. He had sincerity which is the sum of all moral qualities.... It was the natural sincerity, a Constitutional trait and not an assumed air. He was not only big in his physique and in his sincerity. He was also big in intellect. Nobody can question that Ranade had intellect of a high calibre. He was not merely a lawyer and a judge of the High Court, he was a first Class economist, a first Class historian, a first Class educationist and a first Class divine. He was not a politician.... Indeed it would be difficult to find in the history of India any man who could come up to Ranade in the width of his learning, the breadth of his wisdom and the length of his vision. There was no subject which he did not touch, and in which he did not acquire profundity. His reading was on the scale of the colossal and every inch he was a scholar. He was great not merely by the standard of his Time, but he was great—measured by any standard. As I have said, no claim for being a great man can rest on the foundation of sincerity and intellect either singly or in combination. Ranade could not be called great if he had these two qualities and no more. His title to being a great man must rest upon the social purposes he served and on the way he served them. On that there can be no doubt.

Ranade is known more as a social reformer than as a historian, economist or educationist. His whole life is nothing but a relentless campaign for social reform. It is on his role as a social reformer that this title to being a great man rests. Ranade had both the vision and the courage which the reformer needs, and in the circumstances in which he was born his vision was no small a virtue than his courage.

Ranade was born in 1842 some 24 years after the battle of Kirkee which brought the Maratha Empire to an end. The downfall of the Maratha Empire evoked different feelings among different people.... There can be no doubt that a large majority of the people of Maharashtra were stunned by the event. When the whole of India was enveloped by the advancing foreign horde and its people being subjugated piece by piece, here in this little corner of Maharashtra lived a sturdy race who knew what liberty was, who had fought for it inch by inch and established it over miles and miles.... What could be the natural reaction to so great a catastrophe? Can it be other than resignation, defeatism and surrender to the inevitable?

How did Ranade react? Very differently. He held out the hope that the fallen shall rise. Indeed he developed a new faith on which this hope was founded. Let me quote his own words. He said: "I profess implicit faith in two articles of my creed. This country of ours is the true land of promise. This race of ours is the chosen race."

He did not rest quiet by merely enunciating this new Mosaic Gospel of hope and confidence. He applied his mind to the question of the realization of this hope. The first requisite was, of course, a dispassionate analysis of the causes of this downfall. Ranade realized that the downfall was due to certain weaknesses in the Hindu social system and unless these weaknesses were removed the hope could not be realized. The new gospel was, therefore, followed by a call to duty. That duty was no other than the duty to reform Hindu society. Social reform became, therefore, the one dominant purpose of his life.

He developed a passion for social reform and there was nothing he did not do to promote it. His methods included meetings, missions, lectures, sermons, articles, interviews, letters—all carried on with an unrelenting zeal. He established many societies. He founded many journals. But he was not content with this. He wanted something more permanent, something more systematic for promoting the cause of social reform. So he founded the Social Conference, an All-India Organization which ran as an adjunct to the Indian National Congress. Year after year the Conference met to discuss the social ills and to find the ways of remedying them, and year after year Ranade attended its annual sessions as though it was a pilgrimage and fostered the cause of social reform.

In fostering the cause of social reform Ranade showed great courage. Many people of this generation will perhaps laugh at such a claim. Courting prison has become an act of martyrdom in India. It is regarded both as a patriotic act and also as an act of courage.... Prison life today has lost all its terrors. It has become a mere matter of detention. Political prisoners are no longer treated as criminals. They are placed in a separate class. There are no hardships to suffer, there is no reputation to lose and there is no privation to undergo. It calls for no courage. But even when prison life had, as in the time of Mr Tilak, its rigours the political prisoners could make no claim to greater courage than a social reformer. Most people do not realize that society can practise tyranny and oppression against an individual in a far greater degree than a Government can. The means and scope that are open to society for oppression are more extensive than those that are open to Government, also they are far more effective. What punishment in the penal code is comparable in its magnitude and its severity to excommunication? Who has greater courage—the social reformer who challenges society and invites upon himself excommunication or the political prisoner who challenges Government and incurs sentence of a few months or a few years' imprisonment?

There is also another difference which is often lost sight of in estimating the courage shown by the social reformer and the political patriot. When the social reformer challenges society there is nobody to hail him a martyr. There is nobody even to befriend him. He is loathed and shunned. But when the political patriot challenges Government he has whole society to support him. He is praised, admired and elevated as the saviour. Who shows more courage? The social reformer who fights alone, or the political patriot who fights under the cover of vast mass of supporters?

It would be idle to deny that Ranade showed courage in taking up the cause of social reform. Indeed, he showed a high degree of courage. For let it be remembered that he lived in times when social and religious customs, however gross and unmoral, were regarded as sacrosanct and when any doubt questioning their divine and moral basis was regarded not merely as heterodoxy but as intolerable blasphemy and sacrilege.

IV. RANADE'S PATH OF SOCIAL REFORM

His path as a reformer was not smooth. It was blocked from many sides. The sentiments of the people whom he wanted to reform were deeply rooted in the ancient past. They held the belief that their ancestors were the wisest and the noblest of men, and the social system which they had devised was of the most ideal character. What appeared to Ranade to be the shames and wrongs of the Hindu society were to them the most sacred injunctions of their religion. This was the attitude of the common man.

The intelligentsia was divided into two schools—a school which was orthodox in its belief but un-political in its outlook, and a school which was modem in its beliefs, but primarily political in its aims and objects. The former was led by Mr Chiplunkar and the latter by Mr Tilak. Both combined against Ranade and created as many difficulties for him as they could. They not only did the greatest harm to the cause of social reform, but as experience shows they have done the greatest harm to the cause of political reform in India.

The un-political or the orthodox school believed in the Hegelian view—namely, to realize the ideal and idealize the real. In this it was egregiously wrong. The Hindu religious and social system is such that you cannot go forward to give its ideal form a reality because the ideal is bad; nor can you attempt to elevate the real to the status of the ideal because the real i.e., the existing state of affairs, is worse than worse could be. This is no exaggeration.

Take the Hindu religious system or take the Hindu social system, and examine it from the point of social utility and social justice. It is said that religion is good when it is fresh from the mint. But Hindu religion has been a bad coin to start with. The Hindu ideal of society as prescribed by Hindu religion has acted as a most demoralizing and degrading influence on Hindu society.... It is a religion which is not intended to establish liberty, equality and fraternity. It is a gospel which proclaims the worship of the superman—the Brahmin by the rest of the Hindu society. It propounds that the superman and his Class alone are born to live and to rule. Others are born to serve them, and to nothing more. They have no life of their own to live, and no right to develop their own personality. This has been the gospel of the Hindu Religion.

Hindu philosophy, whether it is *Vedanta*, *Sankhya*, *Nyaya*, *Vaishashika*, has moved in its own circle without in anyway affecting the Hindu religion. It has never had the courage to challenge this gospel. That Hindu philosophy that everything is Brahma remained only a matter of intellect. It never became a social philosophy. The Hindu philosophers had both their philosophy and their Manu held apart in two hands, the right not knowing what the left had. The Hindu is never troubled by their inconsistency.

As to their social system, can things be worst? The Caste System is in itself a degenerate form of the *Chaturvarnya* which is the ideal of the Hindu. How can anybody who is not a congenital idiot accept *Chaturvarnya* as the ideal form of society? Individually and socially it is a folly and a crime. One Class and one Class alone to be entitled to education and learning! One Class and one Class alone to be entitled to arms!

One Class and one Class alone to trade! One Class and one Class alone to serve! It is not enough for a social structure to be good for a fair weather. It must be able to weather the storm. Can the Hindu Caste System stand the gale and the wind of an aggression? It is obvious that it cannot. Either for defence or for offence a society must be able to mobilize its forces. With functions and duties exclusively distributed and immutably assigned, what way is there for mobilization? Ninety per cent of the Hindus—Brahmins, *Vaishyas* and *Shudras*—could not bear arms under the Hindu social system. How can a country be defended if its army cannot be increased in the hour of its peril. It is not Buddha who, as is often alleged, weakened Hindu society by his gospel of non-violence. It is the Brahmin theory of *Chaturvarnya* that has been responsible not only for the defeat but for the decay of Hindu society....

Is there any society in the world which has unapproachables, unshadowables and useables? Is there any society which has got a population of Criminal Tribes? Is there a society in which there exists today primitive people, who live in jungles who do not know even to clothe themselves? How many do they count in numbers? Is it a matter of hundreds, is it a matter of thousands? I wish they numbered a paltry few. The tragedy is that they have to be counted in millions, millions of Untouchables, millions of Criminal Tribes, millions of Primitive Tribes!! One wonders whether the Hindu civilization is civilization or infamy? This is about the ideal.

Turn now to the state of things as it existed when Ranade came on the scene. It is impossible to realize now the state of degradation they had reached when the British came on the scene and with which the reformers like Ranade were faced. Let me begin with the condition of the intellectual Class. The rearing and guiding of a civilization must depend upon its intellectual Class—upon the lead given by the Brahmins. Under the old Hindu Law the Brahmin enjoyed the benefit of the clergy and not be hanged even if he was guilty of murder, and the East India Company allowed him the privilege till 1817.... His profession had lost all its nobility. He had become a pest. The Brahmin systematically preyed on society and profiteered in religion. The *Puranas* and the *Shastras* which lie manufactured in tons are treasure trove of sharp practices which the Brahmins employed to befool, beguile and swindle the common mass of poor, illiterate and superstitious Hindus.... The Hindu Society had its moral bonds loosened to a dangerous point.

The East India Company had in 1819 to pass a Regulation (VII of 1819) to put a stop to this moral degeneracy.... Public conscience there was none, and in the absence of conscience, it was futile to expect moral indignation against the social wrongs. Indeed the Brahmins were engaged in defending every wrong for the simple reason that they lived on them. They defended Untouchability which condemned millions to the lot of the helot. They defended Caste, they defended female child marriage, and they defended enforced widowhood—the two great props of the Caste System. They defended the burning of widows, and they defended the social system of graded inequality with its rule of hypergamy which led the Rajputs to kill in their thousands the daughters that were born to them. What shames! What wrongs! Can such a society show its face before civilized nations? Can such a society hope to survive? Such were the questions which Ranade asked. He concluded that on only one condition it could be saved—namely, rigorous social reform.

★ ★ ★

V. POLITICAL REFORMS VERSUS SOCIAL REFORMS

His greatest opponents, however, came from the political school of the intelligentsia. These politicals developed a new thesis. According to that thesis, political reform was to have precedence over social reform. The thesis was argued from platform to platform, and was defended by eminent people like Mr Justice Telang, a Judge of the Bombay High Court, with the consummate skill of an acute lawyer. The thesis caught the imagination of the people.... The grounds on which Mr Justice Telang defended the Politicians' thesis were, of course, logical. But he totally forgot that logic is not reason, and analogy is not argument. Neither did he have a correct understanding of the inter-relation between the 'social' and the 'political' which Ranade had.

Let us examine the reasons for the thesis.... The following (argument) strike me as being the most impressive. In the first place, it could be said that we want political power first because we want to protect the rights of the people. This answer proceeds from a very frugal theory of Government as was propounded by the American statesman Jefferson according to whom politics was only an affair of policing by the State so that that the rights of people were maintained without disturbance. Assume that the theory is a sound one. The question is, what is there for the State to police if there are no rights? Rights must exist before policing becomes a serious matter of substance. The thesis that political reform should precede social reform becomes on the face of it an absurd proposition unless the idea is that the Government is to protect those who have vested rights and to penalize those who have none.

The second ground that could be urged in support of the thesis is that they wanted political power because they wanted to confer on each individual certain Fundamental Rights by law, and that such conferring of the political rights could not lake place unless there was political power first obtained. This, of course, sounds very plausible. But is there any substance in it? The idea of making a gift of Fundamental Rights to every individual is no doubt very laudable. The question is how to make them effective? The prevalent view is that once rights are enacted in a law then they are safeguarded. This again is an unwarranted assumption. As experience proves, rights are protected not by law but by the social and moral conscience of society. If social conscience is such that it is prepared to recognize the rights which law chooses to enact, rights will be safe and secure. But if the Fundamental Rights are opposed by the community, no Law, no Parliament, no judiciary can guarantee them in the real sense of the word. What is the use of the Fundamental rights to the Negroes in America, to the Jews in Germany and to the Untouchables in India? As Burke said, there is no method found for punishing the multitude. Law can punish a single solitary recalcitrant criminal. It can never operate against a whole body of people who are determined to defy it. Social conscience... is the only safeguard of all rights Fundamental or non-Fundamental.

The third argument of the politicals could be based on the right to self-Government. That self-Government is better than good Government is a well-known cry. One cannot give it more value than one can give to a slogan, and all would like to be assured that self-Government would also be a good Government. There is no doubt that the politicals wanted good Government and their aim was to establish a democratic form of Government. But they never stopped to consider whether a democratic form of Government was possible. Their contention was founded on a series of fallacies. A democratic form of Government presupposes a democratic form of society. The formal framework of democracy is of no value and would indeed be a misfit if there was no social democracy. The politicals never realized that democracy was not a form of Government. It was essentially a form of society. It may not be necessary for a democratic society to be marked by unity, by community of purpose, by loyalty to public ends and by mutuality of sympathy. But it does unmistakably involve two things. The first is an attitude of mind, an attitude of respect and equality towards their fellows. The second is a social organization free from rigid social barriers. Democracy is incompatible and inconsistent with isolation and exclusiveness, resulting in the distinction between the privileged and the unprivileged. Unfortunately, the opponents of Ranade were never able to realize the truth of this fact.

One may judge it by any test and it will be found that the stand that Ranade took in this controversy and his plan of work were correct and fundamental is if they were not the pre requisites of political reform. Ranade argued that there were no rights in the Hindu society which the moral sense of man could recognize. There were privileges and disabilities, privileges for a few and disabilities for a vast majority. Ranade struggled to create rights. Ranade wanted to vitalize the conscience of the Hindu society which had become moribund as well morbid. Ranade aimed to create a real social democracy, without which there could be no sure and stable politics. The conflict was between two opposing points of view and it centered round the question which is more important for the survival of a nation, political freedom or strong moral fibre. Ranade took the view that moral stamina was more important than political freedom....

Ranade was not only wise but he was also logical. He told his opponents against playing the part of Political Radicals and Social Tories. In clear and unmistakable terms he warned them saying:

> You cannot be liberal by halves. You cannot be liberal in politics and conservative in religion. The heart and the head must go together. You cannot cultivate your intellect, enrich your mind, enlarge the sphere of your political rights and privileges, and at the same time keep your hearts closed and cramped. It is an idle dream to expect men to remain enchained and enshackled in their own superstition and social evils, while they are struggling hard to win rights and privileges from their rulers. Before long these vain dreamers will find their dreams lost.

Experience has shown that these words of Ranade have been true, even prophetic. Let those who deny this consider: Where are we today in politics and why are we where we are? It is now 50 years since the National Congress was born. Its stewardship has passed hands, I won't say from the sane to the insane, or from realists to idealists, but from moderates to radicals. Where does the country stand today at the end of 50 years of political marching? What is the cause of this deadlock? The answer is simple. The cause of deadlock is the absence of Communal settlement. Ask why is communal settlement necessary for political settlement, and you realize the fundamental importance of the stand that Ranade took. For the answer to this question is to be found in the wrong social system, which is too undemocratic, too over-weighed in favour of the classes and against the masses, too Class conscious and too communally minded. Political democracy would become a complete travesty if it were built upon its foundations.... It is the defects of social system which has given rise to the communal problem, and which has stood in the way of India getting political power.

Ranade's aim was to cleanse the old order if not to build a new one. He insisted on improving the moral tone of Hindu society. If he had been heard and followed, the system would have at least lost its rigours and its rigidity. If it could not have avoided Communal settlement it would have made it easy. For his attempts, limited as they were, would have opened the way to mutual trust. But the politicals had developed a passion for political power which had so completely blinded them that they refused to see virtue in anything else. Ranade has had his revenge. Is not the grant of political safeguard a penalty for denying the necessity of social reform?

How much did Ranade achieve in the field in which he played so dominant a part? In a certain sense the question is not very important. Achievement is never the true measure of greatness.... And yet Ranade's record of achievement was not altogether bare. The problems facing the then social reformers contained in the statement on social reform prepared by Rai Bahadur P Anandcharly were five: (a) early marriage; (b) remarriages of widows; (c) liberty for our countrymen to travel... or sojourn in foreign lands; (d) women's rights of property; and (e) education of women. Of this programme he achieved a great part. If he did not achieve all, there were the odds against him, which should never be forgotten. A clever, determined and an insincere intelligentsia came forward to defend orthodoxy and give battle to Ranade....

The decline of social reform was quite natural. The odium of social reform was too great. The appeal of political power is too alluring. The result was that social reform found fewer and fewer adherents. In course of time the platform of the Social Reform Conference was deserted and men flocked to the Indian National Congress. The politicians triumphed over the social reformers. I am sure that nobody will now allow that their triumph was a matter for pride. It is certainly a matter of sorrow. Ranade may not have been altogether on the winning side, but he was not on the wrong side and certainly never on the side of the wrong as some of his opponents were.

★ ★ ★

VI. HOW DOES RANADE COMPARE WITH OTHERS

How does Ranade compare with others? Comparisons are always odious and unpleasant.... Ranade was a social reformer, and as a social reformer he could be usefully compared with other social reformers. Particularly illuminating will be the comparison between Ranade and Jotiba Phule. Phule was born in 1827 and died in 1890. Ranade was born in 1842 and died in 1901. Thus Phule and Ranade were contemporaries, and both were foremost social reformers.... Comparisons of Ranade with social reformers and with politicians cannot but be illuminating and there is enough material for such comparisons. The question really is one of time and taste.... Left to myself I would have preferred to use my available time to compare Ranade with Phule. For I regard social reform more fundamental than political reform. Unfortunately, my taste is different from the taste of the audience.... The task I am undertaking is a very unpleasant one and if I venture upon it, it is only because it is my duty to expound fully and the desire of the public to know truly the value of Ranade's political philosophy and his place among politicians of today.

Who are the present-day politicians with whom Ranade is to be compared? Ranade was a great politician of his day. He must, therefore, be compared with the greatest of today. We have on the horizon of India two great men, so big that they could be identified without being named—Gandhi and Jinnah. What sort of a history they will make may be a matter for posterity to tell.... They hold leading strings. One leads the Hindus, the other leads the Muslims. They are the idols and heroes of the hour. I propose to compare them with Ranade.

How do they compare with Ranade? It is necessary to make some observations upon their temperaments and methods with which they have now familiarized us. I can give only my impressions of them, for what they are worth. The first thing that strikes me is that it would be difficult to find two persons who would rival them for their colossal egotism, to whom personal ascendancy is everything and the cause of the country a mere counter on the table. They have made Indian politics a matter of personal feud. Consequences have no terror for them; indeed they do not occur to them until they happen. When they do happen they either forget the cause, or if they remember it, they overlook it with a complacency which saves them from any remorse. They choose to stand on a pedestal of splendid isolation. They wall themselves off from their equals. They prefer to open themselves to their inferiors. They are very unhappy at, and impatient of, criticism, but are very happy to be fawned upon by flunkeys. Both have developed a wonderful stagecraft, and arrange things in such a way that they are always in the limelight wherever they go. Each, of course, claims to be supreme. If supremacy was their only claim, it would be a small wonder. In addition to supremacy, each claims infallibility for himself. Pius IX during whose sacred regime as Pope the issue of infallibility was raging said, "Before I was Pope, I believed in Papal infallibility, now I feel it." This is exactly the attitude of the two leaders whom Providence—may I say in his unguarded moments—has appointed to lead us....

The spirit of domination exhibited by these two great men has transgressed all limits. By their domination they have demoralized their followers and demoralized politics. By their domination they have made half their followers fools and the other half hypocrites. In establishing their supremacy, they have taken the aid of 'big business' and money magnates. For the first time in our country, money is taking the field as an organized power. The questions which President Roosevelt propounded for American Public to consider will arise here, if they have not already arisen: Who shall rule—wealth or man? Which shall lead, money or intellect? Who shall fill public stations, educated and patriotic free men or the feudal serfs of corporate Capital? For the present, Indian politics, at any rate the Hindu part of it, instead of being spiritualized has become grossly commercialized, so much so that it has become a byword for corruption. Many men of culture are refusing to concern themselves in this cesspool. Politics has become a kind of sewage system, intolerably unsavory and unsanitary. To become a politician is like going to work in the drain.

Politics in the hands of these two great men have become a competition in extravaganza. If Mr Gandhi is known as Mahatma, Mr Jinnah must be known as Qaid-i-Azim. If Gandhi has the Congress, Mr Jinnah must have the Muslim League. If the Congress has a Working Committee and the All-India Congress Committee, the Muslim League must have its Working Committee and its Council. The session of the Congress must be followed by a session of the League....

When is all this to end? When is there to be a settlement? There are no near prospects. They will not meet, except on preposterous conditions. Jinnah insists that Gandhi should admit that he is a Hindu. Gandhi insists that Jinnah should admit that he is one of the leaders of the Muslims. Never has there been such a deplorable state of bankruptcy of statesmanship as one sees in these two leaders of India. They are making long and interminable speeches, like lawyers whose trade it is to contest everything, concede nothing and talk by the hour. Suggest anything by way of solution for the deadlock to either of them, and it is met by an everlasting 'Nay'. Neither will consider a solution of the problems which is not eternal. Between them Indian politics has become 'frozen' to use a well-known banking phrase, and no political action is possible.

How does Ranade strike as compared to these two? He had not a tinge of egotism in him. His intellectual attainments could have justified any amount of pride, nay, even insolence. But he was the most modest of men. Serious youths were captivated by his learning and geniality. Many, feeling completely under his sway, responded to his ennobling influence and moulded their whole lives with the passionate reverence for their adored master. He refused to be satisfied with the praises of fools, and was never afraid of moving in the company of equals and of the give and take it involves. He never claimed to be a mystic relying on the inner voice. He was a rationalist prepared to have his views tested in the light of reason and experience. His greatness was natural. He needed no aid of the stage nor the technique of an assumed eccentricity nor the means of a subsidized press. Ranade was principally a social reformer. He was not a politician in the sense of one who trades in politics. But he has played an important part in the political advancement of India. To some of the politicians he acted as the teacher who secured such signal successes, and who dazzled their critics by their brilliance. To some he acted as the guide, but to all he acted as the philosopher.

What was the political philosophy of Ranade? It may be summed up in three propositions:

(1) We must not set up as our ideal something which is purely imaginary. An ideal must be such that it must carry the assurance that it is a practicable one.
(2) In politics, sentiment and temperament of the people are more important than intellect and theory. This is particularly so in the matter of framing a Constitution. A Constitution is as much a matter of taste as clothes are. Both must fit, both must please.
(3) In political negotiations the rule must be what is possible. That does not mean that we should be content with what is offered. No. It means that you must not refuse what is offered when you know that your sanctions are inadequate to compel your opponent to concede more.

These are the three main doctrines of Ranade's political philosophy. It would be quite easy to illustrate them by appropriate quotations from his writings and his speeches.... Who could quarrel with Ranade on these three propositions and if there be one, on which? On the first only a visionary will quarrel. We need not take any notice of him. The second proposition is so evident that we could only ignore it at our peril. The third proposition is something on which a difference of opinion is possible. Indeed it is this which divided the Liberals from the Congressmen. I am not a liberal, but I am sure the view Ranade held was the right one. There can be no compromise on principle, and there should not be. But once the principle is agreed upon, there can be no objection to realize it by instalments. Graduation in politics is inevitable, and when the principle is accepted it is not harmful and indeed it may in certain circumstances be quite advantageous. On this third proposition there was really no difference between him and Tilak, except this: Tilak would have the possible maximised by the application of sanctions; Ranade would look askance at sanctions. This is all. On the rest they were agreed. The absence of sanctions in Ranade's political philosophy need not detract much from its worth....

★ ★ ★

VII. CELEBRATING RANADE

In celebrating the birthday of Ranade we must not overlook what the critics and opponents are likely to say.... The opponents will say if I condemn idolatry when it pertains to Mr Gandhi and to Mr Jinnah how do I join in idolizing Mr Ranade? These are very pertinent questions. True hero-worship is dying. Of that there is no doubt....

But hero-worship is certainly not dead in India. India is still par excellence the land of idolatry. There is idolatry in religion, there is idolatry in politics. Heroes and hero-worship is a hard, if unfortunate, fact in India's political life. I agree that hero-worship is demoralizing for the devotee and dangerous to the country. I welcome the criticism in so far as it conveys a caution that you must know that your man is really great before you start worshipping him. This unfortunately is not an easy task.

Ranade never received the honours of apotheosis as these great men of India today are destined to receive. How could he? He did not come with a message hot from Senai. He performed no miracles.... If he was not a genius, he did not display that perverse super subtlety of intellect, and a temper of mind which is fundamentally dishonest and which has sown the seeds of distrust, and which has made settlement so difficult of achievement. There is nothing exuberant and extravagant in Ranade. He refused to reap cheap notoriety by playing the part of an extremist. He refused to mislead people by playing upon and exploiting the patriotic sentiments of the people. He refused to be a party to methods which are crude which have volume but no effect and which are neither fool-proof nor knave-proof and which break the back even of the most earnest and sincere servants of the country and disable them from further effort. In short, Ranade was like the wise Captain who knows that his duty is not to play with his ship clever and masterful tricks, just for effect and show in the midst of the ocean, but to take it safely to its appointed port.

In the second place this celebration of Ranade's birthday is not all an act of hero-worship.... In short in celebrating Ranade's birthday we are not worshipping a boss who is elected by no one, accountable to no one and removable by no one, but paying our tribute of admiration to a leader who led and did not drive people, who sought to give effect to their deliberate judgement and did not try to impose his own will upon them by trickery or by violence.

In the third place, it is not for hero-worship for which this gathering has assembled. This is an occasion to remind ourselves of the political philosophy of Ranade. To my mind, it has become necessary to remind ourselves of it from time to time. For his is a philosophy which is safe and sound, sure, if slow. Even if it does not glitter it is none the less gold....

The generation which Ranade served was wise in taking him as its political guide, friend and philosopher. His greatness lies in the fact that he can be a guide, friend and philosopher to this present, nay, even to future generations.

There is one charge against Ranade which is frequently made and which I think must be met. It is said of Ranade that he believed that the conquest of India by the British was Providential, that it was in the best interest of India, that she should remain within the British Empire and that therein lay her final destiny. In short Ranade is accused of being opposed to India's Independence.

The charge is false and without foundation. The statement of Ranade far from casting any reflection upon his self-respect testify to his wisdom and to his sagacity. What did Ranade want to convey by these statements? As I understand them, I think

Ranade wanted to convey two things. The first thing he wanted to convey was that the conquest of India by Britain has given India the time, the opportunity and the necessary shelter for rebuilding, renovating and repairing her economic and social structure, to refit herself for bearing the strain of any foreign aggression when she does become free. The second thing Ranade wanted to convey was that going out of the British Empire by India before she had satisfied and solidified herself into a single nation, unified in thought, in feeling, and charged with a sense of a common destiny, was to invite chaos and disruption in the name of independence.

CHAPTER THIRTY ONE

Mr Gandhi and the Emancipation of the Untouchables

IN RESPONSE TO an invitation from the Chairman of the Indian Section of the Institute of Pacific Relations, Dr Ambedkar wrote a paper in August 1942 titled, "The Problem of the Untouchables of India" for the Conference which was due to be held on December 1942 in Quabec, Canada.[98] The Paper was subsequently printed in the proceedings of the Conference. When Dr Ambedkar was told by the Secretary of the Pacific Relations Conference that the proceedings have been made public and there can be no objection to the publication of his Paper, then alone he published the Research Paper as a Monograph (90 pages) in September 1943.

Dr Ambedkar argued that Imperialism, Racialism and Anti-Semitism are very serious problems facing the world and observed:

> There is no doubt these are the plague glands in which nation's cruelty to nation, and man's inhumanity to man have their origin. There is no doubt that these problems must be tackled if a new and a better world is to emerge from the ashes of this terrible and devastating war. What my fear is that the problem of the Untouchables may be forgotten as it has been so far. That would indeed be a calamity. For the ills which the Untouchables are suffering, if they are not as much advertised as those of the Jews, are not less real. Nor are the means and the methods of suppression used by the Hindus against the Untouchables less effective because they are less bloody than the ways which the Nazis have adopted against the Jews. The Anti-semitism of the Nazis against the Jews is in no way different in ideology and in effect from the Sanatanism of the Hindus against the Untouchables....
>
> The world owes a duty to the Untouchables as it does to all suppressed people to break their shackles and to set them free. I accepted the invitation to write this Paper because I felt that it was the best opportunity to draw the attention of the world to this problem in comparison to which the problem of the slaves, the Negroes and the Jews is nothing. I hope the publication of this Paper will serve as a notice to the Peace

98. Dr Ambedkar had deputed his colleague N Shivraj to Canada to present the paper.

Conference that this problem will be on the Board of Causes which it will have to bear and decide and also to the Hindus that they will have to answer for it before the bar of the world....

The Decennial Census in India today is a matter of a first rate concern to everybody. This is so because politics in India has become a matter of numbers. Census in India is deliberately cooked for securing political advantages which numbers give. To what extent the cooking of the Census has taken place it is difficult to say. That being so, the Census figure regarding the total population of the Untouchables in British India cannot be accepted as giving a correct total. But one cannot be far wrong if it was said that the present number of the Untouchables to British India is round about 60 million people....

Most parts of the world have had their type of what are called the 'lowly'. The Romans had their slaves, the Spartans their helots, the British their villeins, the Americans their Negroes and the Germans their Jews. So the Hindus have their Untouchables. But none of these can be said to have been called upon to face a fate which is worse than the fate which pursues the Untouchables. Slavery, serfdom, villeinage have all vanished. But Untouchability still exists and bids fair to last as long as Hinduism will last....If there is any cause of freedom in this Indian turmoil for independence, it is the cause of the Untouchables. The cause of the Hindus and the cause of the *Musalmans* is not the cause of freedom. Theirs is a struggle for power as distinguished from freedom....

The Congress is a body of middle Class Hindus supplied by the Hindu Capitalists whose object is not to make Indians free but to be independent of British control, and to occupy places of power now occupied by the British. If the kind of Freedom which the Congress wants was achieved there is no doubt that the Hindus would do to the Untouchables exactly what they have been doing in the past....

The so-called National Scheme insists upon the territorial constituency as being both proper and sufficient for producing a representative Legislature in India. What is called the Communal Scheme denies that a territorial Constitution can produce a truly representative legislature in India in view of the peculiar social structure of the Indian Society as it exists today....National Scheme is on merits quite unsound and on motives worse than Communal.

The Hindu prefers the territorial constituency because he knows that it will enable him to collect and concentrate all political power in the hands of the Hindus, and who can deny that his calculation is incorrect? In a purely territorial constituency the contest, the Hindu knows, will be between a huge majority of Hindu voters and a small minority of Untouchable voters. Given this fact the Hindu majority—if it is a purely territorial constituency—is bound to win in all constituencies.... In the Hindu Social System, the communities are placed in an ascending scale of reverence and a descending scale of contempt. It needs no prophet to predict what effect these social attitudes will have on voting. No Caste Hindu will cast a vote in favour of an Untouchable candidate, for to him he is too contemptible a person to go to the Legislature. On the other hand, there will be found many voters among the Untouchables who would willingly cast their votes for a Hindu candidate in preference to an Untouchable candidate. That is because he is taught to revere the former more than himself or his Untouchable kinsmen....

There is still a controversy over the question of joint versus separate electorates. Here again I want to set out the pros and cons of this controversy. The objection to separate electorate raised by the Hindus is that separate electorate means the fragmentation of the nation. The reply is obvious. First of all, there is no nation of Indians in the real sense of the word. The nation does not exist, it is to be created, and I think it will be admitted that the suppression of a distinct and a separate community is not the method of creating a nation....

Separate electorate is the only mechanism by which real representation can be guaranteed to the Untouchables. The Hindu argument against separate electorate is insubstantial and unsupportable. Special electorates are devised as a means of protecting the minorities. Why not permit a minority like the Untouchables to determine what kind of electorate is necessary for its protection? If the Untouchables decide to have separate electorates why should their choice not prevail?

The real objection to separate electorates by the Hindus is different from this ostensible objection raised in the name of a nation. The real objection is that separate electorate does not permit the Hindus to capture the seats reserved for the Untouchables. On the other hand, the joint electorate does. The Hindu in opposing the so-called communal Scheme of the Untouchables with his so-called National Scheme is not fighting for a principle, nor is be fighting for the nation. He is simply fighting for his own interests. He is fighting to have in his hands the undivided control over political power. His first line of defence is not to allow any shares to be drawn up. That is why he fought for purely territorial constituencies. Failing that he takes his second line of defence. He wants that if he is made to concede power he must not lose control over it. This is secured by joint electorates and frustrated by separate electorates. That is why the Hindu objects to separate electorates and insists on joint electorates....

The Untouchables demand that a certain proportion of posts in the Public Services of the country shall be reserved for them, subject to the rule of minimum qualification. Higher education in India is the monopoly of Hindus, and particularly of high-Caste Hindus. By reason of Untouchability, the Untouchables are denied the opportunity for education. The State will not take the financial responsibility of giving them higher education—they are demanding it by their resolution, and the Hindus will not extend the benefit of their charities to the Untouchables—Hindu Charity being shamefully communal—so that to ask the Untouchables to rely upon the results of competitive examination for entry into the public services is to practise a fraud upon them....

Isn't the self-government supposed to be better than good Government? What else are the Untouchables demanding? What the Untouchables are not prepared to do is to forgo self-government for good government. Good Government based on highest qualification will be a communal Government, for the Hindus alone can claim qualifications higher than minimum qualifications. This is what they do not want. What they say is that minimum qualifications are enough for efficient government, and since it makes self-government possible, minimum qualification should be the rule for entry in Public Service. It ensures self-government as well as efficient government....It is the village system which perpetuates Untouchability, and the Untouchables, therefore, demand that it should be broken, and the Untouchables who are as a matter of fact socially separate should be made separate geographically and territorially also, and be grouped into separate villages exclusively of Untouchables in which the distinction of the high and the low, and of Touchable and Untouchable will find no place.

In framing a Constitution the social structure must always be kept in mind. The political structure must be related to the social structure. The operation of the social forces is not confined to the social field. They pervade the political field also. This is the viewpoint of the Untouchables, and I am sure this is incontrovertible. The Hindus are quite conscious of this argument and also of its strength. But what they do is to deny that the structure of the Hindu Society is in any way different from the structure of European society. They attempt to meet the argument by saying that there is no difference between the Caste System of the Hindus and the Class System in Western Society. This is, of course, palpably false and discloses a gross ignorance both of the Caste System as well as of the Class System....

The Caste System is a system which is infested with the spirit of isolation and in fact it makes isolation of one Caste from another a matter of virtue. There is isolation in the Class System but it does not make isolation a virtue nor does it prohibit social intercourse. The Class System, it is true, produces groups. But they are not akin to Caste groups. The groups in the Class System are only non-social while the Castes in the Caste System are in their mutual relations definitely and positively anti-social. What the Untouchables are asking, to put it in general terms, is a proper correlation of means to ends. End may be the same. But because the end is the same it does not follow that the means must also be the same. Indeed ends may remain the same and yet means must vary according to time and circumstances. Those who are true to their ends must admit this fact and must agree to adopt different means if they wish that the end they have in view is not stultified....

It is the Caste basis of Hindu society which requires that its political structure should be different and suited to its social structure. There are people who admit this but argue that Caste can be abolished from Hindu society. I deny that. Those who advocate such a view think that Caste is an institution like a Club or a Municipality or a County Council. This is a gross error. Caste is Religion, and religion is anything but an institution. It may be institutionalised, but it is not the same as the institution in which it is embedded. Religion is an influence or force suffused through the life of each individual moulding his character, determining his actions and reactions, his likes and dislikes. These likes and dislikes, actions and reactions are not institutions which can be lopped off. They are forces and influences which can be dealt with by controlling them or counteracting them. If the social forces are to be prevented from contaminating politics and perverting it to the aggrandisement of the few and the degradation of the many then it follows that the political structure must be so framed that it will contain mechanisms which will bottle the prejudices and nullify the injustice which the social forces are likely to cause if they were let loose....

The justification for these demands is easy and obvious. It arises from the undeniable fact that what divides the Untouchables from the Hindus is not mere matter of difference on non-essentials. It is a case of fundamental antagonism and antipathy. No evidence of this antipathy and antagonism is necessary. Given this antagonism it is simply impossible to ask the Untouchables to depend upon and trust the Hindus to do them justice when the Hindus get their freedom and independence from the British....There can be no doubt that the Hindus have all these ages despised, disregarded and disowned the Untouchables as belonging to a different and contemptible strata of Society if not to a different race. Why should the Untouchables entrust their fate to such people? How could the Untouchables be legitimately asked to leave their interest into the hands of a people who as a matter of fact are opposed to them in their motives and interests, who do not sympathise with the living forces operating among the Untouchables, who are themselves not charged with their wants, cravings and desires, who are inimical to their aspirations, who in all certainty will deny justice to them and to discriminate against them and who by reason of the sanction of their religion have not been and will not be ashamed to practise against the Untouchables any kind of inhumanity. The only safety against such people is to have the political rights which the Untouchables claim as safeguards against the tyranny of the Hindu majority defined in the Constitution. Are the Untouchables extravagant in demanding this safety?

Every Hindu is a social Tory and political Radical. Mr Gandhi is no exception to this rule. He presents himself to the world as a liberal but his liberalism is only a very thin veneer which sits very lightly on him as dust does on one's boots. You scratch him and you will find that underneath his liberalism he is a blue blooded Tory. He stands for the cursed Caste. He is a fanatic Hindu upholding the Hindu religion....

I should have thought the Hindus would be too ashamed of this stigma of Untouchability on them to appear before the world with a demand for their freedom. That they do clamour for freedom is evidence that their conscience is dead, that they feel no righteous indignation, and to them Untouchability is neither a moral sin nor a civil wrong....

Is it to prepare the Untouchables to win their freedom from their Hindu masters, to make them their social and political equals? Mr Gandhi had never had any such object before him and he never wants to do this, and I say that he cannot do this. This is the task of a democrat and a revolutionary. Mr Gandhi is neither. He is a Tory by birth as well as by faith. The work of the *Harijan Sevak Sangh* is not to raise the Untouchables. His main object, as every self-respecting Untouchable knows, is to make India safe for Hindus and Hinduism....

Mr Gandhi wants Hinduism and the Hindu Caste System to remain intact. Mr Gandhi also wants the Untouchables to remain as Hindus. But as what? Not as partners but as poor relations of the Hindus. Mr Gandhi is kind to the Untouchables. But for what? Only because he wants to kill by kindness them and their movement for separation and independence from Hindus. The *Harijan Sevak Sangh* is one of the many techniques which has enabled Mr Gandhi to be a successful humbug....

Democracy and democratic life, justice and conscience which are sustained by a belief in democratic principle are foreign to the Hindu mind. To leave democracy and freedom in such Tory hands would be the greatest mistake democrats could commit....

CHAPTER THIRTY TWO

What Congress and Gandhi have Done to Untouchables

MAHATMA GANDHI WAS released on May 6, 1944 from Aga Khan Palace where he was detained in the aftermath of the "Quit India" movement. Apparently, alarmed by Gandhiji's high blood pressure, the British decided to let him go, so as to avoid having to face any uproar in the event that something untoward happened to him during the internment. In fact, Pandit Nehru, Vallabhbhai Patel and other leaders were not released for the next 13 months. Gandhiji's request to consult them was turned down. As such, Gandhiji devoted himself to bridging the widening chasm between the Congress and the Muslim League. Gandhiji went to Panchgani, a Hill Station near Satara, from where C Rajagopalachari announced that on behalf of Gandhiji, a new offer for solution of the communal deadlock was sent to Jinnah.

Recognizing Gandhiji's overtures to Mohammed Ali Jinnah, Dr Ambedkar was tempted to hold an olive branch to Gandhiji. In a letter to Gandhiji, Dr Ambedkar observed that in addition to the settlement of the Hindu-Muslim problem, it was also necessary to settle the Hindu-Untouchable issue, if India's political goal was to be achieved. Dr Ambedkar assured Gandhiji that, on his part, he was willing to formulate points on which a settlement was needed. In response to Dr Ambedkar's letter, Gandhiji wrote on August 6, 1944 that for him, the question of the Depressed Classes was one of religious and social reform. Expressing his appreciation for Dr Ambedkar's abilities, Gandhiji added that he would love to own him as his colleague and co-worker, "I know to my cost that you and I hold different views on this very important question."[99]

Agitated by Gandhiji's stubbornness, Dr Ambedkar released his new book in June 1945, entitled: *What Congress and Gandhi Have Done to the Untouchables*. It criticized Gandhiji and the Congress severely.

99. Keer, Dhananjay, op. cit pp. 363-4.

The book records what Dr Ambedkar calls: "The deeds of the Congress and Mr Gandhi from 1917 to date, in so far as they touch the problem of the Untouchables." According to Dr Ambedkar:

> Mr Gandhi does not merely claim for himself the championship of the Untouchables. He claims similar championship for the Congress. The Congress, he says, is fully pledged to redress the wrongs done to the Untouchables and argues that any attempt to give political safeguards to the Untouchables is unnecessary and harmful. It is, therefore, a great pity that no detailed study of these claims by Mr Gandhi and the Congress has been undertaken so far.

That is precisely what Dr Ambedkar undertakes to do in this exceptionally important book, the first of its kind.

The book begins with the resolution passed by the Congress about the Depressed Classes in 1917, first time in its then existence of 32 years, which Dr Ambedkar calls a "strange event" and demonstrates that it was only a formal fulfilment of a condition, which the Depressed Classes had made for giving their support to the Congress-League Scheme of political reforms.

After the emergence of Mahatma Gandhi as a national leader, the Constructive Program of Social Amelioration (also called the Bardoli Program 1922) became an important feature of the Congress. However, Congress abandoned its Plan, which Dr Ambedkar called a "shabby show".

Then came the three Round Table Conferences (1930-32). Dr Ambedkar describes in full details the happenings at the Second Round Table Conference, especially the Gandhi-Ambedkar debate, announcement of the Communal Award by the British Government, Mahatma Gandhi's fast against it and subsequent compromise between Mahatma Gandhi and Dr Ambedkar in the form of the Poona Pact (1932). As observed by Dr Ambedkar, "At the Round Table Conference he (i.e., Gandhiji) claimed to be the sole champion of the Untouchables, and was not even prepared to share the honour with anyone else. I remember what a scene he created when his claim was contested."

After the elections to Provincial Legislatures, the Congress Party 'advertised' the election results to bolster up its claim to represent the Untouchables. The main point in the advertisement was that out of 151 seats assigned to the Scheduled Castes, the Independent Labour Party organized by Dr Ambedkar got only 12 seats, while the rest of the seats were captured by the Congress. Dr Ambedkar regarded the Congress version of the election results as an "utter perversion", and maintained that his work "proves beyond the shadow of doubt that the story that Congress captured all the seats reserved for the Scheduled Castes and that the Independent Labour Party was failure is a wicked lie."

Dr Ambedkar not only attempted to expose what he called a "false claim" but also refuted the "false charge" that Untouchables were the tools of the British. Against the backdrop, Dr Ambedkar then analysed the 'real issue'—the fundamental issue in the controversy between the Congress and Untouchables: "Are the Untouchables a separate element in the national life of India or not?"

Dr Ambedkar concludes the book with two chapters, the names of which say it all!

(a) "Beware of Mr Gandhi!"
(b) "Gandhism: The Doom of the Untouchables"

Here are some excerpts from these two concluding chapters:

BEWARE OF MR GANDHI

Congressmen never hesitate to impress upon the Untouchables that Mr Gandhi is their saviour. Not only do Congressmen all over India hold out Mr Gandhi as a real saviour but they go forth to persuade the Untouchables to accept the fact that he is their only saviour. When pressed for evidence, they tell the Untouchables that if anyone ever took a vow to go on a fast unto death for the sake of the Untouchables it was Mr Gandhi and none else. Indeed, without any compunction they tell the Untouchables that whatever political rights the Untouchables have got under the Poona Pact, they are the result of Mr Gandhi's efforts.

I do not know how many Untouchables will be found prepared to swallow such a lie. But this much I think has been proved by the Nazis that if a lie is a big lie too big for the common man's intelligence to scrutinize and if it is repeated continuously, the lie has all the chances of being accepted as truth and if not accepted as truth has all the chances of growing upon the victims of propaganda and win their acquiescence. It is, therefore, necessary for me to expose the part played by Mr Gandhi in the movement of the Untouchables and to warn the Untouchables against succumbing to this propaganda.

In making a survey of the part played by Mr Gandhi it is well to begin by ascertaining when Mr Gandhi for the first time realized that Untouchability was an evil.

It is no doubt very interesting to know that in that age of blind orthodoxy Mr Gandhi should have become aware that Untouchability was a sin and that too at so early an age as 12. What the Untouchables, however, want to know is what did Mr Gandhi do to remove the evil. I give below an extract from a biographical note about Mr Gandhi.....

From this biographical note, it is clear that Mr. Gandhi began his public life in 1894 when he founded the Natal Indian Congress. From 1894 to 1915, he was in South Africa. During this period, he never thought of the Untouchables.

Mr Gandhi returned to India in 1915. Did he then take up the cause of the Untouchables? In these five years, Mr. Gandhi was completely absorbed in transforming the Congress into a militant organization—a war machine fit to fight and shake British Imperialism. He took up the cause of the Khilafat with a view to bring the Muslims to join the Congress and did his level best to rally the Hindus for the support of the Khilafat.

What did Mr. Gandhi do for the Untouchables during this period? Congressmen will, of course, refer to the Bardoli Programme. It is true that in the Bardoli Programme the uplift of the Untouchables was an item. But what is important is to know what happened to it? To tell the story in a summary form the Bardoli Programme was not a programme for the removal of Untouchability. The programme openly recognised Untouchability and planned to do no more than provide separate wells and separate schools for the Untouchables. The Sub-Committee appointed to draw up a programme for the uplift of the Untouchables consisted of persons who had never shown any interest in the Untouchables and some of them were even hostile to them. Swami Shraddhanand, the one and only person in the Sub-Committee who can be said to be charged with the desire to do something substantial for the Untouchables, was forced to resign. A paltry sum of money was allotted for carrying on the work of the Committee. The Committee was dissolved without meeting even once. The work of the uplift of the Untouchables was declared to be a work best suited to the Hindu *Mahasabha*. Mr Gandhi took no interest in that part of the Bardoli Programme, which related to the Untouchables. On the contrary instead of siding with Swami Shraddhanand he sided with the reactionaries and opponents of Swami Shraddhanand, knowing full well that they did not want anything on a big scale done for the Untouchables.So much for what Mr. Gandhi did in 1921 in connection with the Bardoli Programme.

What did Mr. Gandhi do after 1922. On March 19, 1922, Mr Gandhi was tried for sedition and sentenced to six years' imprisonment. In 1924, Mr Gandhi on account of his illness was released from gaol before his time. When he came out, Mr Gandhi found that the Congress was divided into two warring camps on the issue of the boycott of the Legislature. The quarrel was a bitter one and both sides were engaged in slinging mud at each other. Mr Gandhi knew that if the quarrel continued the Congress would be weakened and wanted to patch it up. Neither side was prepared to give in. There were statements and counter-statements. Ultimately, Mr Gandhi made certain proposals for restoring peace between the two wings which were accepted by both sides. The proposals were intended to please both sides. To please the protagonists of Council Entry he proposed that the Congress should recognise entry in the Legislatures as legitimate part of Congress activity and the opponents of Council Entry should stop their propaganda against it. To please the opponents of Council Entry he proposed that the Congress should accept a new basis for franchise, namely: The Congress franchise instead of being 4 annas per annum should be a tender of 2,000 yards of hand-spun and self-spun yarn with the penalty clause attached to it.

Here was an opportunity for Mr Gandhi to advance his anti-Untouchability campaign. He could have proposed that if a Hindu wishes to enroll himself as a member of the Congress he should prove that he does not observe Untouchability and that the employment of an Untouchable in his household should be adduced in support of his claim in this behalf and that no other evidence would be allowed to be tendered. Such a proposal could not have been impracticable for almost every Hindu, certainly those who call themselves high Caste Hindus, keeps more than one servant in his household. If Mr Gandhi could make the Hindu accept spinning and boycott as franchises for membership of the Congress he could also make acceptable the employment of an Untouchable in a Hindu household a franchise for membership of the Congress. But Mr Gandhi did not do it.

After 1924 till 1930 there is a complete blank. Mr Gandhi does not appear to have taken any active steps for the removal of Untouchability or got himself interested in any activity beneficial to the Untouchables during this period. While Mr Gandhi was inactive the Untouchables had started a movement called the *Satyagraha* movement. The object of the movement was to establish their right to take water from public wells and entry into public temples. The *Satyagraha* at the Chowdar Tank situated in Mahad, a town in the Kolaba District of the Bombay Presidency, was organized to establish the right of the Untouchables to take water from public watering places. The *Satyagraha* at the Kala Ram Temple situated in Nasik, a town in the Nasik District of the Bombay Presidency, was organized to establish the right of the Untouchables to enter Hindu temples. There were many minor *Satyagrahas*. These were, however, the two principal ones over which the efforts of the Untouchables and their opponents, the Caste Hindus, were concentrated. The din and noise caused by them were heard all over India. Thousands of men and women from the Untouchables took part in these *Satyagrahas*. Both men and women belonging to the Untouchables were insulted and beaten by the Hindus. Many were injured and some were imprisoned by Government on the ground of causing breach of the peace. This *Satyagraha* movement went on for full six years when it was brought to a close in 1935 at a Conference held in Yeola in Nasik District in which the Untouchables as a result of the adamantine attitude of the Hindus in refusing to give them equal social rights resolved to go out of the Hindu fold.

This *Satyagraha* movement was no doubt independent of the Congress. It was organized by the Untouchables, led by the Untouchables and financed by the Untouchables. Yet, the Untouchables were not without hope of getting the moral support of Mr. Gandhi. Indeed they had very good ground for getting it. For the weapon of *Satyagraha*—the essence of which is to melt the heart of the opponent by suffering—was the weapon which was forged by Mr Gandhi, and who had led the Congress to practise it against the British Government for winning *Swaraj*. Naturally the Untouchables expected full support from Mr Gandhi to their *Satyagraha* against the Hindus the object of which was to establish their right to take water from public wells and to enter public Hindu temples. Mr Gandhi, however, did not give his support to the *Satyagraha*. Not only did he not give his support, he condemned it in strong terms.

In this connection reference may be made to two novel weapons for redressing human wrongs. Mr Gandhi claims exclusive credit for forging and perfecting them.

First is *Satyagraha*. Mr Gandhi has put into action this weapon of *Satyagraha* many a time against the British Government for the removal of political wrongs. But Mr Gandhi has never used the weapon of *Satyagraha* against Hindus to get them to throw open wells and temples to the Untouchables. Fasting is another weapon of Mr Gandhi. It is said that there have been altogether 21 fasts to the credit of Mr Gandhi. Some were for the sake of Hindu-Muslim unity and quite a number as atonements for the immoralities committed by the inmates of his Ashram. One was against the order of the Government of Bombay refusing to give the work of a scavenger in the gaol to a prisoner although he demanded it. In these 21 fasts there is not one undertaken for the removal of Untouchability. These are very significant facts.

In 1930 came the Round Table Conference. Mr Gandhi joined the deliberations of the Conferencein 1931. The Conference was concerned with a vital question of framing a Constitution for a self-governing India. It was unanimously held that if India was to be a self-governing country then the Government must be a Government of the people, by the people and for the people. Everybody agreed that only when a Government is in a real sense a Government by the people that it could be a Government of the people and for the people. The problem was how to make it a Government by the people in a country rent into communities, majorities and minorities, who are charged not merely with social cleavages but also with social antagonisms. Having regard to these circumstances it was agreed that in India there was no possibility of government by the people unless Legislature and the Executive were framed on the basis of communal representation.

The problem of the Untouchables loomed large at the Conference. It assumed a new aspect. The question was: Should the Untouchables be left as they were to the tender mercies of the Hindus, or should they be given the means to protect themselves by extending to them the principle of communal representation? The Untouchables strongly objected to be left to the pleasure of the Hindus and demanded the same protection as was given to the other minorities. The contention of the Untouchables was accepted by all. It was just and logical. They contended that the chasm between the Hindus and Muslims, between Hindus and Sikhs, between Hindus and Christians is nothing as compared with the chasm between the Hindus and the Untouchables. It is the widest and the deepest. The chasm between the Hindus and the Muslims is religious and not social. That between the Hindus and the Untouchables is both religious and social. The antagonism arising out of the chasm existing between Hindus and Muslims cannot spell political disaster to the Muslims because the relationship between the Hindus and the Muslims is not that of master and slave. It is one of mere estrangement. On the other hand, the chasm between Hindus and the Untouchables must spell political disaster for the Untouchables because the relationship between the two is that of master and slave. The Untouchables contended that the attempts to close the gap between them and the Hindus by means of social process had been tried for ages. They had all failed. There was no hope of their success. Since power is being transferred into the hands of the Hindu majority they must have political safeguards of the same sort as, if not better than, those conceded to the Muslims and other minorities.

Here was an opportunity to Mr Gandhi to show his sympathy to the Untouchables by lending his support to their demand and thereby strengthen their power of resistance against the tyranny and oppression of the Hindus. Instead of showing his sympathy, Mr Gandhi used every means in his power to defeat them. He made a pact with the Muslims with a view to isolate the Untouchables. Failing to win the *Musalmans* to his side, he went on a fast unto death to compel the British Government to withdraw their decision for giving to the Untouchables the same political rights as given to the Muslims and other minority communities. When the fast failed and Mr Gandhi was obliged to sign a pact—called the Poona Pact—which conceded the political demands of the Untouchables he took his revenge by letting the Congress employ foul electioneering tactics to make their political rights of no avail.

In 1933, Mr Gandhi took up two movements. First was the Temple entry Movement. He took personal responsibility for seeing through these two measures. One was the opening of the Guruvayur temple. The other was the passing of the Temple entry Bill sponsored by Mr Ranga Iyer in the Central Legislature.

Mr Gandhi said that he would fast unto death if the trustee of the Guruvayur temple did not throw it open to the Untouchables by a certain date. The Guruvayur temple still remains closed to the Untouchables but Mr Gandhi has not fulfilled his vow of going on fast. Surprising, as it may be, he has done nothing to get the temple declared open to the Untouchables although it is now thirteen years since he took the vow.

Mr Gandhi virtually coerced the Governor-General to give his sanction to the introduction of the Temple entry Bill. The Congress party in the Central legislature which was pledged to carry through the Bill refused to support it when the stage of referring it to a Select Committee came on the ground that the Bill gave offence to the Hindus and in the election that was pending the Hindus would seek revenge on the Congress and defeat it at the poll if the Congress supported the Bill. To the great chagrin of Mr Ranga Iyer, the Congress Party let him down, by leaving the Bill to die. Mr Gandhi did not mind this. He even went to the length of justifying the conduct of the Congress Party.

The other movement which Mr Gandhi sponsored in 1933 was the establishment of the *Harijan Sevak Sangh* with a network of branches all over India. There were three motives which lay behind the organization of the *Sangh*. First was to prove that Hindus had enough charitable spirit towards the Untouchables and that they would show it by their generous contributions towards their uplift. The second motive was to serve the Untouchables by helping them in the many difficulties with which they were faced in their daily life. The third motive was to create in the minds of the Untouchables a sense of confidence in the Hindus from whom they were estranged in matters political.

None of the three objects has been realized. In the first flush, the Hindus contributed a total of about 8 lakhs of rupees for the *Sangh* which is, of course, nothing as compared to the crores they have contributed for general political purposes. After that they have gone dry. The *Sangh* is now depending for its finances either on Government grants or on the income derived from the sale of Mr Gandhi's autographs or on the munificence of some wealthy merchant who makes a contribution to the *Sangh*, not because he loves the Untouchables but because he thinks it profitable to please Mr Gandhi. The branches of the *Sangh* are being closed every year. The *Sangh* is contracting and contracting so rapidly that very soon it will have only a centre and no circumference.

That the Hindus have lost interest in the *Sangh* is not the only regrettable aspect of this activity of Mr Gandhi. The *Sangh* has not been able to secure the goodwill and the co-operation of the Untouchables for whose benefit it is supposed to have been started. This is due to various reasons. The work of the *Sangh* is of the most inconsequential kind. It does not catch anyone's imagination. It neglects most urgent purposes for which the Untouchables need help and assistance. The *Sangh* rigorously excludes the Untouchables from its management. The Untouchables are no more than beggars mere recipients of charity. The result is that the Untouchables feel no concern for the *Sangh*. They look upon it as a foreign body set up by the Hindus with some ulterior motive.

Here was an opportunity for Mr Gandhi to make the *Sangh* a real bridge between the Hindus and the Untouchables. He could make it a virile institution by improving its programme of work and by allowing the Untouchables to participate in its working. Mr Gandhi has done nothing of the kind. He has allowed the *Sangh* to languish. It is dying peacefully and may perish even during the life-time of Mr Gandhi.

There need be no surprise if this survey of Mr Gandhi's anti-Untouchability campaign, of his sayings and his doings baffles and puzzles the reader. There need be no wonder if the reader were to pause and ask a few questions on the lines set out below to clear his own mind:

In 1921, Mr Gandhi collected one crore and thirty-five lakhs of rupees for the Tilak Swaraj Fund. Mr Gandhi insisted that there was no possibility of winning *Swaraj* unless Untouchability was removed. Why did he not protest when only a paltry sum of Rs 43,000 was given to the cause of the Untouchables?

In 1922 there was drawn up the Bardoli Programme of constructive work. Uplift of the Untouchables was an important item in it. A Committee was appointed to work out the details. The Committee never functioned and was dissolved and the uplift of the Untouchables as an item in the constructive programme was dropped. Only Rs 800 were allotted to the Committee for working expenses. Why did Mr. Gandhi not protest against this niggardly and step-motherly treatment of the Committee by the Congress Working Committee? Why did not Mr Gandhi support Swami Shradhanand who was fighting with the Congress Working Committee for large funds being assigned to the Committee? Why did not Mr Gandhi protest against the dissolution of the Committee? Why did not Mr. Gandhi appoint another Committee? Why did he allow the work for the Untouchables to drop out as though it was of no importance?

Mr Gandhi had at the very outset of his campaign for *Swaraj* insisted that there were five conditions precedent for winning *Swaraj*: (a) Hindu-Moslem Unity; (b) Removal of Untouchability; (c) Universal adoption of hand-spun and hand-woven khadi; (d) absolute non-violence; and (e) complete non-co-operation. Mr Gandhi had not only laid down these conditions but had told Indians that without the fulfilment of these conditions there could be no *Swaraj*. In 1922, he fasted for the sake of Hindu-Moslem unity. In 1924, he made production of hand-spun yarn the basis of franchise for Congress membership. Why did he not make non-observance of Untouchability the basis of Congress franchise in 1924 or at any time subsequent thereto?

Mr Gandhi has gone on fast many a time to achieve a variety of objects which are dear to him. Why has Mr Gandhi not fasted even once for the sake of the Untouchables?

Mr Gandhi has devised *Satyagraha* as a weapon to redress wrongs and to win freedom and has practised it against the British Government. Why has not Mr Gandhi started *Satyagraha* even once against the Hindus on behalf of the Untouchables for securing admission to wells, temples and other public places to which access is denied by the Hindus?

Following Mr Gandhi's lead the Untouchables started *Satyagraha* from 1929 onwards against the Hindus for admission to wells and temples. Why did Mr. Gandhi condemn their *Satyagraha*?

Mr Gandhi declared that he would fast if the Guruvayur temple was not thrown open to the Untouchables by the Zamorin. The temple has not been thrown open. Why did not Mr Gandhi go on fast?

Mr Gandhi in 1932 threatened the British Government with dire consequences if the Governor-General did not give permission to Mr Ranga Iyer to introduce his Temple entry Bill on behalf of the Congress Party in the Central Legislature. As fresh elections to the Central Legislature were announced the Congress Party withdrew its support to the Bill and Mr Ranga lyer had to drop it. If Mr Gandhi was earnest and sincere about Temple entry, why did Mr Gandhi support the action of the Congress Party? What was more important—Temple entry for the Untouchables or Electoral victory to the Congress?

Mr Gandhi knows that the difficulty of the Untouchables does not lie in their not having civic rights. Their difficulty lies in the conspiracy of the Hindus who threaten them with dire consequences if the Untouchables dare to exercise them. The real way of helping the Untouchables is to have some organization for the protection of civic rights which will undertake the duty of prosecuting Hindus who assault the Untouchables or proclaim social and economic boycott against them and thereby prevent them from exercising their civic rights. Why did not Mr Gandhi include this as one of the objects of the *Harijan Sevak Sangh*?

Before Mr Gandhi came on the scene, the Depressed Classes Mission Society was formed by the Caste Hindus for the uplift of the Untouchables. The moneys were subscribed by the Hindus. Yet, the Society's affairs were conducted by Joint Boards consisting of Hindus and Untouchables. Why has Mr Gandhi excluded the Untouchables from the management of the *Harijan Sevak Sangh*?

If Mr Gandhi is the real friend of the Untouchables, why did he not leave it to the Untouchables to decide whether political safeguards were the best means for their protection? Why did he go to the length of making a pact with the Muslims in order to isolate and defeat the Untouchables? Why did Mr Gandhi declare a fast unto death the object of which was to deprive the Untouchables of the benefit of the Communal Award by this extreme form of coercion?

After having accepted the Poona Pact, why did not Mr Gandhi keep faith with the Untouchables by telling the Congress not to despoil the politics of the Untouchables by contesting the seats reserved for the Untouchables by getting such Untouchables elected as were prepared to become the tools of the Hindus?

After having accepted the Poona Pact why did not Mr Gandhi keep up the gentleman's agreement and instruct the Congress High Command to include representatives of the Untouchables in the Congress Cabinets?

Why did Mr Gandhi disapprove of the appointment by Dr Khare of Mr Agnibhoj— a member of the Scheduled Castes—as a minister in the Congress Cabinet in the CP when Mr Agnibhoj was in every way qualified to be a Minister? Did Mr Gandhi say that he was opposed to the creation of such high ambitions among persons belonging to the Scheduled Castes?

What is the explanation that Mr Gandhi has to offer? What is the explanation that Mr Gandhi's friends have to offer? Mr Gandhi's anti-Untouchability campaign is marked by so many twists and turns, inconsistencies and contradictions, attacks and surrenders, advances and retreats that the whole campaign has become a matter of mystery. Few have a belief in its efficacy and quite a large number hold that there is not enough earnestness and sincerity behind it. Some explanation is, therefore, necessary. It is more for the sake of Mr Gandhi's reputation for earnestness and sincerity that for the sake of giving a clear understanding of Mr Gandhi's aims and methods to the reader that one would like Mr Gandhi and his friends to explain the points raised in the foregoing questions.

It would no doubt be interesting to know what Mr Gandhi and his friends may have to say in reply to these questions. Everybody interested in this question will naturally be looking forward to it. It will not, however, do for anyone else to anticipate the reply and then deal with it. They must be left to frame it in their own way and select their own time to do so. ln the meantime, one may well ask what the Untouchable have to say about Mr Gandhi and his anti-Untouchability campaign. It is not difficult to state what view the Untouchables take of Mr Gandhi's anti-Untouchability campaign.

Do the Untouchables regard Mr Gandhi as being in earnest? The answer is in the negative. They do not regard Mr Gandhi as being in earnest. How can they? How can they look upon a man being in earnest who when in 1921 the whole country was aroused to put the Bardoli programme in action remained completely indifferent to the anti-Untouchability part of it? How could they look upon a man as being in earnest who, when out of one crore and twenty-five lakhs of *Swaraj* Fund, found that only forty-three thousand rupees were allotted to the cause of the Untouchables did not raise any protest at this niggardly treatment of a long neglected cause? How can they regard a man as being in earnest who when, in 1924, he got an opportunity to impose upon the Hindus the obligation to remove Untouchability did not do so even though he had the power and the occasion to enforce it?

Such a step would have served three purposes. It would have put the nationalism of Congressmen to test. It would have helped to remove Untouchability, and it would have proved that Mr Gandhi was sincere in his talks about the evil of Untouchability and its being a sin and a stigma on Hinduism. Why did not Mr Gandhi do it? Does this not show that Mr Gandhi was more interested in the spread of spinning than in the removal of Untouchability? Does this not show that removal of Untouchability was the least part of Mr Gandhi's programme and that it was not even last? Does it not show that the statements by Mr Gandhi that Untouchability is a blot on Hinduism and that there will be no *Swaraj* without the removal of Untouchability were just empty phrases with no earnestness behind them? How could they believe in the earnestness of a person who takes a vow to fast if the Guruvayar temple is not opened to the Untouchables, but will not go on fast even when the temple remains closed?

How could they accept a man to be in earnest when he sponsors a Bill for securing Temple entry and subsequently becomes a party to dropping it? How could they accept the earnestness of a man who contents himself with saying that he will not go into a temple if it is not open to the Untouchables when what is required of him is to adopt every means to get the temples thrown open to the Untouchables? How could they believe in the earnestness of a man who is ready to fast for everything but will not fast for the Untouchables? How can they believe in the earnestness of a man who is prepared to practice *Satyagraha* for everything and against everybody but who will not practise it against the Hindus for the sake of the Untouchables? How can they believe in the earnestness of a man who does nothing more than indulge in giving sermons on the evils of Untouchability?

Do they regard Mr Gandhi as honest and sincere? The answer is that they do not regard Mr Gandhi as honest and sincere. At the outset of his campaign for *Swaraj*, Mr Gandhi told the Untouchables not to side with the British. He told them not to embrace Christianity or any other religion. He told them that they could find salvation in Hinduism. He told Hindus that they must remove Untouchability as a condition precedent to *Swaraj*. Yet in 1921 when only a paltry sum out of the Tilak Swaraj Fund was allotted to the Untouchables, when the Committee to plan the uplift of the Untouchables was unceremoniously wound up, Mr Gandhi did not raise a word of protest.

Mr Gandhi had under his command a sum of Rs One crore and twenty-five lakhs belonging to the Tilak Swaraj Fund. Why did Mr Gandhi not insist upon a substantial portion of this amount being earmarked for the uplift of the Untouchables? That Mr Gandhi showed almost complete indifference to the cause of the Untouchables is beyond dispute. What is surprising is the explanation which Mr Gandhi offered for his indifference. He said that he was busy in planning a campaign to win *Swaraj* and that he had no time to spare for the cause of the Untouchables. He not only did not blush at his explanation, but he offered a moral justification for his indifference to the cause of the Untouchables. He took the stand that there was nothing wrong in his devoting himself entirely to the political cause of India to the exclusion of the cause of the Untouchables, for in his opinion, the good of the whole includes the good of the part and that as the Hindus are slaves of the British, slaves cannot emancipate slaves.

Phrases such as "slaves of slaves" and "greater includes the less" may be admirable dialectics, though they cannot have more truth than the saying that because the country's wealth has increased, therefore, everybody's wealth has increased. But we are not considering Mr Gandhi's ability as a dialectician. We are testing his sincerity. Can we accept a man's sincerity who evades his responsibility and contents himself with an excuse? Can the Untouchables believe that Mr Gandhi is the champion of their cause?

How can they regard Mr Gandhi as honest and sincere if they consider Mr Gandhi's conduct towards them and towards the Muslims and Sikhs in the matter of Constitutional safeguards?

Mr Gandhi used to justify his discrimination between the Scheduled Castes and other Minorities in the matter of Constitutional safeguards by another plea. The plea was that there were historical reasons, which compel him to recognise the Muslims and the Sikhs. He has never explained what those reasons are. They cannot be other than those, which hold the Muslims and the Sikhs as the fragments of old ruling communities. One does not mind Mr Gandhi having succumbed to such puerile and undemocratic arguments, though he could have insisted that he would treat all minorities on equal basis and would not give any weight to such illogical and irrelevant considerations. The question is: How could the admission of such a plea have prevented Mr Gandhi from opposing the demand of the Scheduled Castes? Why did Mr Gandhi regard himself as bound by no other reasons except the historical reasons? Why did not Mr Gandhi think that if historical reasons were decisive in the case of Muslims and Sikhs, moral reasons were decisive in the case of the Untouchables? The fact is that the plea of historical reasons is a hollow plea. It was not a plea at all. It was an excuse for not conceding the demand of the Untouchables.

Mr Gandhi is never so much disgusted, as he is when he is confronted with the question of Majority versus Minority. He would like to forget it and ignore it. But circumstances will not let him do either and he is often forced to deal with the issue. The last time he dealt with it was on October 21, 1989 in the form of an Editorial in the *Harijan* under the heading "The Fiction of Majority". The article is full of venom and Mr Gandhi has not hesitated to pour all the ridicule he could on those who were constantly raising the question. In the article he vehemently denied that the Muslims are a Minority. He denied that the Sikhs are a Minority and denied that the Indian Christians are a Minority. His contention was that they were not minorities in the technical sense of Oppressed Communities, they were minorities, they were to in the numerical sense only, which meant that they were no minorities at all. What did Mr Gandhi have to say about the Scheduled Castes? Could he deny their contention that they are a Minority? Let me quote Mr. Gandhi's own words. Mr Gandhi said:

> I have endeavoured to show that there is no such things as real minorities in India whose rights can be endangered by India becoming independent. With the exception of the Depressed Classes there is no minority which is not able to take care of itself.

Here is an admission on the part of Mr Gandhi that the Scheduled Castes are a minority in the real sense of the word and that they are the only minority in India who will not be able to take care of themselves in a free India governed by a Hindu Communal Majority. Notwithstanding this inner conviction, Mr Gandhi maintained in a most vehement manner that he would not concede any political safeguards to the Untouchables. How can the Untouchables accept such a man as sincere and honest?

Mr Gandhi opposed the demands of the Untouchables for political safeguards at the Round Table Conference. He did everything to defeat the object of the Untouchables. To weaken the force behind their demand and isolate them, he tried to buy over the Muslims by offering to concede the whole of their fourteen demands. Mr Gandhi at the meeting of the Minorities Sub-Committee had said: "Who am I to oppose the demand of the Untouchables if the Committee gave it its approval." It was wrong for Mr Gandhi to have tried to defeat the verdict of the Committee by offering to give the Muslims their full demand formulated in Mr Jinnah's fourteen points in return for their agreeing to oppose the demands of the Scheduled Castes!! His was a most subtle piece of strategy. He offered the *Musalmans* a most difficult choice between having their 14 points and withdrawing their support to the demand of the Untouchables, or siding with the Untouchables and losing their 14 points. In the end Mr Gandhi's strategy failed, and neither did the *Musalmans* lose their 14 points nor did the Untouchables lose their case. But the episode remains as a witness to Mr Gandhi's perfidy. What else can be the appropriate description of the conduct of a man who offers criminal inducement to another for getting him to break his promise, who calls a person his friend and then contrives to stab him in the back? How can such a man be regarded by the Untouchables as honest and sincere?

Mr Gandhi left the decision of the communal question to the arbitration of the British Prime Minister. Notwithstanding Mr Gandhi's efforts to defeat the Untouchables His Majesty's Government conceded them their political demands. As a party to the arbitration Mr Gandhi was bound to abide by the decision. But

Mr Gandhi decided to defy it, and he did it by going on a fast unto death. Mr Gandhi shook India and the world outside by his Fast unto Death. The object of the Fast was to compel the British Government to withdraw the Constitutional Safeguards which the British Prime Minister had proposed in his Award for the protection of the Untouchables under the new Constitution. One of Mr Gandhi's disciples has described the fast as an Epic Fast. Why it should be described as an Epic Fast it is not easy to follow. There was nothing heroic about it. It was the opposite of heroic. It was an adventure. It was launched by Mr Gandhi because he believed that both the Untouchables and the British Government would quake before his threat of fast unto death, and surrender to his demand. Both were prepared to call off his bluff and as a matter of fact did call it off. All his heroism vanished the moment Mr Gandhi found that he had overdone the trick. The man who started by saying that he would fast unto death unless the safeguards to the Untouchables were completely withdrawn, and the Untouchables reduced to the condition of utter helplessness without rights and without recognition was plaintively pleading, "My life is in your hands, will you save me?" Mr Gandhi's over impatience to sign the Poona Pact—though it did not cancel the Prime Minister's Award as he had demanded but only substituted another and a different system of constituent safeguards—is the strongest evidence that the hero had lost his courage and was anxious to save his face and anyhow save his life.

There was nothing noble in the fast. It was a foul and filthy act. The fast was not for the benefit of the Untouchables. It was against them and was the worst form of coercion against a helpless people to give up the Constitutional safeguards of which they had become possessed under the Prime Minister's Award and agree to live on the mercy of the Hindus. It was a vile and wicked act. How can the Untouchables regard such a man as honest and sincere?

After having gone on a fast unto death, he signed the Poona Pact. People say that Mr Gandhi sincerely believed that political safeguards were harmful to the Untouchables. But how could a honest and sincere man who opposed the political demands of the Untouchables who was prepared to use the Muslims to defeat them, who went on a fast unto death, in the end accept the very same demands—for there is no difference between the Poona Pact and the Communal Award—when he found that there was no use opposing as opposition would not succeed? How can an honest and sincere man accept as harmless the demands of the Untouchables which once he regarded as harmful?

Do the Untouchables regard Mr Gandhi as their friend and ally? The answer is in the negative. They do not regard him as their friend. How can they? It may be that Mr Gandhi honestly believes that the problem of the Untouchables is a social problem. But how can they believe him to be their friend when he wishes to retain Caste and abolish Untouchability, it being quite clear that Untouchability is only an extended form of Caste and that, therefore, without abolition of Caste there is no hope of abolition of Untouchability?

It may be that Mr Gandhi honestly believes that the problem of Untouchables can be solved by social processes. But how can the Untouchables regard a man as their friend who develops a fanatic and frantic opposition to political processes being employed, when everyone was agreed that the use of political processes cannot mar the effect of social process, and may be depended upon to help and accelerate the solution of the problem. How could a man be regarded as the friend of the Untouchables when he does not believe the Untouchables reaching to places of power and authority in the State. In this controversy over political safeguards Mr Gandhi could have pursued any of the following courses. He could have been the champion of the Untouchables. As such, he should not only have welcomed their demand for safeguards but he should have proposed them himself without waiting for the Untouchables to do so. Not only should he have proposed them himself but he should have fought for them. For, what could give greater happiness to a genuine champion of the Untouchables than to see that provision was made to enable them to become members of the Legislature, Ministers of Executive, and occupants of high offices in the State? Surely, if Mr Gandhi is a champion of the Untouchables these are the very provisions he should have fought for. Secondly, if he did not wish to be the champion of the Untouchables, he could have been their ally. He could have helped them by giving them his moral and material support. Thirdly, if Mr Gandhi did not like to play the part of a champion and was averse to be even an ally of the Untouchables, the next thing he could have done consistent with his proclaimed and much advertised sympathies for the Untouchables, was to be their friend. Again as a friend he could have taken up the attitude of benevolent neutrality—declining to fight but ready to render all help for getting the demand for safeguards accepted. Failing benevolent neutrality he could have taken the attitude of strict neutrality and could have told the Untouchables to get the safeguards if the Round Table Conference was prepared to give them and that he would neither help nor hinder. Abandoning all these sober considerations, Mr Gandhi came out as an open enemy of the Untouchables. How can the Untouchables regard such a man as their friend and ally?

That Mr Gandhi's anti-Untouchability campaign has failed is beyond cavil. Even the Congress papers admit it. Writing on March 10, 1940 the *Harijan Bandu*, Mr Gandhi's Gujarathi paper, said:

> The Untouchability of the '*Harijans*' in the matter of entry into schools persists nowhere so much still as in Gujarat.

The Untouchables have always said that Mr Gandhi's anti-Untouchability campaign has failed. After 25 years of labour, hotels have remained closed, wells have remained closed, temples have remained closed and in very many parts of India—particularly in Gujarat—even schools have remained closed. The extracts produced from the papers form, therefore, a very welcome testimony especially because the papers are Congress papers. As they fully corroborate what the Untouchables have been saying on the point, nothing further need be said on the subject except to ask one question. Why has Mr Gandhi failed? According to me, there are three reasons which has brought about this failure.

The first reason is the Hindus to whom he makes his appeal for the removal of Untouchability do not respond. Why is this so? It is a common experience that the words a man uses and the effect they produce are not always commensurate. What he says has its momentum indefinitely multiplied, or reduced to nullity, by the impression that the hearer for good reason or bad happens to have formed of the spirit of the speaker. This gives a clue to know why Mr Gandhi's sermons on Untouchability have completely failed to move the Hindus, why people hear his after-prayer sermons for few minutes and then go to the comic opera and why there is nothing more to it. The fault is not entirely of the Hindu public. The fault is of Mr Gandhi himself. Mr Gandhi has built up his reputation of being a Mahatma on his being an harbinger of political freedom and not on his being a spiritual teacher. Whatever may be his intentions, Mr Gandhi is looked upon as an apostle of *Swaraj*. His anti-Untouchability campaign is looked upon as a fad if not a side-show. That is why the Hindus respond to his political biddings, but never to his social or religious preaching. The momentum of his anti-Untouchability campaign must, therefore, remain a nullity. That was a mistake. A politician is not the man for it. That is why the hope held out to the Untouchables that Mr Gandhi's sermons will do the trick has failed.

The second reason is that Mr Gandhi does not wish to antagonize the Hindus even if such antagonism was necessary to carry out his anti-Untouchability programme. A few instances will illustrate Mr Gandhi's mentality.

Most of Mr Gandhi's friends give credit to Mr Gandhi for sincerity and earnestness for the cause of the Untouchables, and expect the Untouchables to believe in it on the mere ground that Mr Gandhi is the one man who keeps on constantly preaching to the Hindus the necessity of removing Untouchability. They have lost sight of the old proverb that an ounce of practice is worth a ton of preaching and have never cared to ask Mr Gandhi to explain why does he not cease to preach to the Hindus the necessity of removing Untouchability and launch a campaign of *Satyagraha* or start a fast. If they would ask for such an explanation they would know why Mr. Gandhi merely contents himself with sermons on Untouchability.

The true reasons why Mr Gandhi will not go beyond sermons were revealed to the Untouchables for the first time in 1929 when the Untouchables in the Bombay Presidency opened a campaign of *Satyagraha* against the Hindus for establishing their civic rights in the matter of temple entry and taking water from public wells. They hoped to get the blessings of Mr Gandhi in as much as *Satyagraha* was Mr Gandhi's own weapon to get wrongs redressed. When appealed to for support, Mr Gandhi surprised the Untouchables by issuing a statement condemning their campaign of *Satyagraha* against the Hindus. The argument urged by Mr Gandhi was very ingenious. He stated that *Satyagraha* was to be used only against foreigners; it must not be used against one's own kindred or countrymen, and as the Hindus were the kindred and countrymen of the Untouchables by rules of *Satyagraha,* the latter were debarred from using the weapon against the former!! What a fall from the sublime to the ridiculous! By this Mr Gandhi made nonsense of *Satyagraha*. Why did Mr Gandhi do this? Only because he did not want to annoy and exasperate the Hindus.

As a second piece of evidence, I would refer to what is known as the Kavitha incident. Kavitha is a village in the Ahmedabad District in Gujarat. In 1935, the Untouchables of the village demanded from the Hindus of the village that their children should be admitted in the common school of the village along with other Hindu children. The Hindus were enraged at this outrage and took their revenge by proclaiming a complete social boycott.

> *Harijan* boys are thus practically banned from the village school with nobody to help them. This has caused despondency among the *Harijans* to such an extent that they are thinking of migration in a body to some other village.

This was a report made to Mr Gandhi. What did Mr Gandhi do? The following is the advice Mr Gandhi gave to the Untouchables of Kavitha:

> There is no help like self-help. God helps those who help themselves. If the *Harijans* concerned will carry out their reported resolve to wipe the dust of Kavitha off their feet, they will not only be happy themselves but they will pave the way for others who may be similarly treated. If people migrate in search of employment how much more should they do so in search of self-respect? I hope that well-wishers of *Harijans* will help these poor families to vacate inhospitable Kavitha.

Mr Gandhi advised the Untouchables of Kavitha to vacate. But why did he not advise Mr Thakkar to prosecute the Hindus of Kavitha and help the Untouchables to vindicate their rights? Obviously, he would like to uplift the Untouchables if he can, but not by offending the Hindus. What good can such a man do to promote the cause of the Untouchables? All this shows that Mr Gandhi is most anxious to be good to the Hindus. That is why he opposes *Satyagraha* against the Hindus. That is why he opposed the political demands of the Untouchables, as he believed that they were aimed against them. He is anxious to be so good to the Hindus that he does not care if he is thereby becoming good for nothing for the Untouchables. That is why Mr Gandhi's whole programme for the removal of Untouchability is just words, words and words and why there is no action behind it.

The third reason is that Mr Gandhi does not want the Untouchables to organize and be strong. For he fears that they might thereby become independent of the Hindus and weaken the ranks of Hindus. This is best illustrated by the activities of the "*Harijan Sevak Sangh*". The whole object of the *Sangh* is to create a slave mentality among the Untouchables towards their Hindu masters. Examine the *Sangh* from any angle one may like, and the creation of slave mentality will appear to be its dominant purpose.

The work of the *Sangh* reminds one of the mythological demoness Putana described in the *Bhagvat*—a companion to the Mahabharat. Kansa, the king of Mathura, wanted to kill Krishna, as it was predicted that Kansa will die at the hands of Krishna. Having come to know of the birth of Krishna, Kansa asked Putana to undertake the mission to kill Krishna while he was yet a baby. Putana took the form of a beautiful woman and went to Yashoda, the foster-mother of Krishna, and having applied liquid poison to her breast pleaded to be employed as a wet nurse for suckling the baby Krishna and thus have the opportunity to kill it. The rest of the story it is unnecessary to pursue. The point of the story is that the real purpose is not always the same as the ostensible purpose and a nurse can be a murderess. The *Sangh* is to the Untouchables what Putana was to Krishna. The *Sangh* under the pretence of service is out to kill the spirit of independence from among the Untouchables. The Untouchables, in the early stages of their agitation, had taken the support of some well-meaning Hindus, and had followed their leadership. By the time of the Round Table Conference, the Untouchables had become completely self-reliant and independent. They were no longer satisfied with charity from the Hindus. They demanded what they said was their right. There is no doubt that it is to kill this spirit of independence among the Untouchables that Mr Gandhi started the "*Harijan Sevak Sangh*". The "*Harijan Sevak Sangh*" by its petty services has collected a swarm of grateful Untouchables who are employed to preach that Mr Gandhi and the Hindus are the saviours of the Untouchables. Daniel O'Connel, the Irish leader, once said that no man can be grateful at the cost of his honour, no woman can be grateful at the cost of her chastity, and no country can be grateful at the cost of its liberty. The Untouchables are too simple-minded to know that the cost of the service which the "*Harijan Sevak Sangh*" offers to render is loss of independence. This is exactly what Mr Gandhi wants.

The worst part of the activities of the "*Harijan Sevak Sangh*" is the help rendered to the Untouchable students kept in the hostels maintained by the *Sangh*. These Untouchable students remind me of Bhishma and Kocha, two prominent characters which figure in the Mahabharata.

During their stay in the hostels they play the part of Bhishma by singing the praises of Mr Gandhi and the Congress. When they come out of the hostels they play the part of Kacha and denounce Mr Gandhi and the Congress. I am extremely pained to see this. Nothing worse could happen to the youth of the Untouchables than this moral degeneration. But this is the greatest disservice which his "*Harijan Sevak Sangh*" has done to the Untouchables. It has destroyed their character. It has destroyed their independence. This is what Mr Gandhi wants to happen.

Take a fourth illustration. The *Sangh* is run by the Caste Hindus. There are some Untouchables who have demanded that the institution should be handed over to the Untouchables and should be run by them. Others have demanded that the

Untouchables should have representation on the governing Board. Mr Gandhi has flatly refused to do either on two very ingenious grounds which no man with the greatest cunning could improve. Mr Gandhi's first argument is that the "*Harijan Sevak Sangh*" is an act of penance on the part of the Hindus for the sin of observing Untouchability. It is they who must do the penance. Therefore, the Untouchable can have no place in running the *Sangh*. Secondly, Mr Gandhi says the money collected by him is given by the Hindus and not by the Untouchables, and as the money is not of the Untouchables, the Untouchables have no right to be on the Governing Body. The refusal of Mr Gandhi may be tolerated but his arguments are most insulting, and a respectable Untouchable will be forgiven if he refuses to have anything to do with the *Sangh*. One should have thought that the *Harijan Sevak Sangh* was a Trust and the Untouchables its beneficiaries. Any trio in law would admit that the beneficiaries have every right to know the aims and objects of the Trust, its funds and whether the objects are properly carried out or not. The beneficiaries have even the right to have the Trustees removed for breach of trust. On that basis it would be impossible to deny the claim of the Untouchables for representation on the Managing Board. Evidently, Mr Gandhi does not wish to accept this position. A self-respecting Untouchable who has no desire to cringe and who does not believe in staking the future of the Untouchables on the philanthropy of strangers cannot have any quarrel with Mr Gandhi. He is quite prepared to say that if meanness is a virtue, then Mr Gandhi's logic is superb and Mr Gandhi is welcome to the benefit of it. Only he must not blame the Untouchables if they boycott the *Sangh*.

These, however, could not be the real reasons for not allowing the Untouchables to run the *Sangh*. The real reasons are different. In the first place, if the *Sangh* was handed over to the Untouchables, Mr Gandhi and the Congress will have no means of control over the Untouchables. The Untouchables will cease to be dependent on the Hindus. In the second place, the Untouchables having become independent will cease to be grateful to the Hindus. These consequences will be quite contrary to the aim and object, which have led Mr Gandhi to found the *Sangh*. He wants to create among the Untouchables what is known among Indian Christians as the mission compound mentality. That is why Mr Gandhi does not wish to hand over the Sangh to the control and management of the Untouchables. Is this consistent with a genuine desire for the emancipation of the Untouchables? Can Mr Gandhi be called a liberator of the Untouchables? Does this not show that Mr Gandhi is more anxious to tighten the tie which binds the Untouchables to the apron-strings of the Hindus than to free them from the thraldom of the Hindus?

These are the reasons why Mr Gandhi's anti-Untouchability campaign has failed.

The very idea of political power to the Untouchables is hateful to Mr Gandhi. Why should not the Untouchables say, "Beware of Mr Gandhi," when they know that he would not allow the use of political processes for the emancipation of the Untouchables though Mr Gandhi is fully alive to the fact that the social processes on which he laid so much store for helping them have completely failed.

GANDHISM: THE DOOM OF THE UNTOUCHABLES

Hitherto when Indians have been talking about the reconstruction of Indian social and economic life they have been talking in terms of individualism versus collectivism, Capitalism versus Socialism, conservatism versus radicalism and so on. But quite recently a new "ism" has come on the Indian horizon. It is called Gandhism. It is true that very recently Mr Gandhi had denied that there is such a thing as Gandhism. This denial is nothing more than the usual modesty which Mr Gandhi wears so well. It does not disprove the existence of Gandhism. There have been quite a number of books with the title of Gandhism without any protest from Mr Gandhi. It has already caught the imagination of some people both inside and outside India. Some have so much faith in it that they do not hesitate to offer it as an alternative to Marxism.

The followers of Gandhism may well ask: Mr Gandhi may not have done what the Untouchables expected him to do; but does not Gandhism offer any hope to the Untouchables? The followers of Gandhism may accuse me of remembering only the short, slow, intermittent steps taken by Mr Gandhi for the sake of the Untouchables and of forgetting the potential length of the principles enunciated by him. I am prepared to admit that it does sometimes happen that a person, who enunciates a long principle, takes only a short step and that he may be forgiven for the short step in the hope that some day the principle will by its native dynamics force a long step covering all who were once left out. Gandhism is in itself a very interesting subject for study.

What is Gandhism? What does it stand for? What are its teachings about economic problem? What are its teachings about social problem?

At the outset it is necessary to state that some Gandhists have conjured up a conception of Gandhism which is purely imaginary. According to this conception, Gandhism means return to the village, and making the village self-sufficient. It makes Gandhism a mere matter of regionalism. Gandhism, I am sure, is neither so simple nor so innocent as regionalism is. Gandhism has a much bigger content than regionalism. Regionalism is a small insignificant part of it. It has a social philosophy and it has an economic philosophy. To omit to take into account the economic and social philosophy of Gandhism is to present deliberately a false picture of Gandhism. The first and foremost requisite is to present a true picture of Gandhism.

To start with Mr Gandhi's teachings on social problem, Mr. Gandhi's views on the Caste System—which constitutes the main social problem in India—were fully elaborated by him in 1921-22 in a Gujarathi Journal called *Nava Jivan*. The article is written in Gujarathi. I give below an English translation of his views as near as possible in his own words. Says Mr Gandhi:

> 1. I believe that if Hindu Society has been able to stand, it is because it is founded on the Caste System.
>
> 2. The seeds of *Swaraj* are to be found in the Caste System. Different Castes are like different sections of military division. Each division is working for the good of the whole.

3. A community which can create the Caste System must be said to possess unique power of organization.

4. Caste has a ready-made means for spreading primary education. Every Caste can take the responsibility for the education of the children of the Caste. Caste has a political basis. It can work as an electorate for a representative body. Caste can perform judicial functions by electing persons to act as judges to decide disputes among members of the same Caste. With Castes it is easy to raise a defence force by requiring each Caste to raise a brigade.

5. I believe that inter-dining or inter-marriage are not necessary for promoting national unity. That dining together creates friendship, is contrary to experience. If this was true there would have been no war in Europe.... Taking food is as dirty an act, as answering the call of nature. The only difference is that after answering call of nature we get peace while after eating food we get discomfort. Just as we perform the act of answering the call of nature in seclusion, so also the act of taking food must also be done in seclusion.

6. In India, children of brothers do not inter-marry. Do they cease to love because they do not inter-marry? Among the *Vaishnavas* many women are so orthodox that they will not eat with the members of the family, nor will they drink water from a common water pot. Have they no love? The Caste System cannot be said to be bad because it does not allow inter-dining or inter-marriage between different Castes.

7. Caste is another name for control. Caste puts a limit on enjoyment. Caste does not allow a person to transgress Caste limits in pursuit of his enjoyment. That is the meaning of such Caste restrictions as inter-dining and inter-marriage.

8. To destroy Caste System and adopt Western European social system means that Hindus must give up the principle of hereditary occupation which is the soul of the Caste System. Hereditary principle is an eternal principle. To change it is to create disorder. I have no use for a Brahmin if I cannot call him a Brahmin for my life. It will be a chaos if every day a Brahmin is to be changed into a *Shudra* and a *Shudra* is to be changed into a Brahmin.

9. The Caste System is a natural order of society. In India it has been given a religious coating. Other countries not having understood the utility of the Caste System it existed only in a loose condition and consequently those countries have not derived from Caste System the same degree of advantage which India has derived.

These being my views I am opposed to all those who are out to destroy the Caste System.

In 1922, Mr Gandhi was a defender of the Caste System. Pursuing the inquiry, one comes across a somewhat critical view of the Caste System by Mr Gandhi in the year 1925. This is what Mr Gandhi said on February 3, 1925:

I gave support to Caste because it stands for restraint. But at present Caste does not mean restraint, it means limitations. Restraint is glorious and helps to achieve freedom. But limitation is like chain. It binds. There is nothing commendable in Castes as they exist today. They are contrary to the tenets of the *Shastras*. The number of Castes is infinite and there is a bar against inter-marriage. This is not a condition of elevation. It is a state of fall.

In reply to the question: "What is the way out," Mr Gandhi said:

> The best remedy is that small Castes should fuse themselves into one big Caste. There should be four such big Castes, so that we may reproduce the old system of four *Varnas*.

In short, in 1925 Mr Gandhi became an upholder of the *Varna* System.

The old *Varna* System prevalent in ancient India had society divided into four orders: (1) Brahmins, whose occupation was learning; (2) *Kshatriyas* whose occupation was warfare; (3) *Vaishyas*, whose occupation was trade; and (4) *Shudras*, whose occupation was service of the other classes. Is Mr Gandhi's *Varna* System the same as this old *Varna* System of the orthodox Hindus? Mr Gandhi explained his *Varna* System in the following terms.[100]

> 1. I believe that the divisions into *Varna* is based on birth.
>
> 2. There is nothing in the *Varna* System which stands in the way of the *Shudra* acquiring learning or studying military art of offence or defence. Contra it is open to a *Kshatriya* to serve. The *Varna* System is no bar to him. What the *Varna* System enjoins is that a *Shudra* will not make learning a way of earning a living. Nor will a *Kshatriya* adopt service as a way of earning a living. Similarly, a Brahmin may learn the art of war or trade. But he must not make them a way of earning his living. Contra a *Vaishya* may acquire learning or may cultivate the art of war. But he must not make them a way of earning his living.
>
> 3. The *Varna* System is connected with the way of earning a living. There is no harm if a person belonging to one *Varna* acquires the knowledge or science and art specialized in by persons belonging to other *Varnas*. But as far as the way of earning his living is concerned he must follow the occupation of the *Varna* to which he belongs which means he must follow the hereditary profession of his forefathers.
>
> 4. The object of the *Varna* System is to prevent competition and Class struggle and Class war. I believe in the *Varna* System because it fixes the duties and occupations of persons,
>
> 5. *Varna* means the determination of a man's occupation before he is born.
>
> 6. In the *Varna* System no man has any liberty to choose his occupation. His occupation is determined for him by heredity.

Turning to the field of economic life, Mr Gandhi stands for two ideals:

One of these is the opposition to machinery. As early as 1921 Mr Gandhi gave vent to his dislike for machinery. Writing in the *Young India* of January 19, 1921, Mr Gandhi said:

---

100. The extracts are taken from an article by Mr Gandhi on the subject and is reproduced in the *Varna Vayavastha*—a book which contains Mr Gandhi's writings in original Gujarathi.

> Do I want to put back the hand of the clock of progress? Do I want to replace the mills by hand-spinning and hand-weaving? Do I want to replace the railway by the country-cart? Do I want to destroy machinery altogether? These questions have been asked by some journalists and public men. My answer is: I would not weep over the disappearance of machinery or consider it a calamity.

His opposition to machinery is well evidenced by his idolization of *charkha* (the spinning wheel) and by insistence upon hand-spinning and hand-weaving. This opposition to machinery and his love for *charkha* is not a matter of accident. It is a matter of philosophy. This philosophy Mr Gandhi took special occasion to propound in his presidential address at the Kathiawad Political Conference held on January 8, 1925. This is what Mr Gandhi said:

> Nations are tired of the worship of lifeless machines multiplied ad infinitum. We are destroying the matchless living machines viz., our own bodies by leaving them to rust and trying to substitute lifeless machinery for them. It is a law of God that the body must be fully worked and utilized. We dare not ignore it. The spinning wheel is the auspicious symbol of Sharir Yajna—body labour. He who eats his food without offering this sacrifice steals it. By giving up this sacrifice we became traitors to the country, and banged the door in the face of the Goddess of Fortune.

Anyone who has read Mr Gandhi's booklet on Hind *Swaraj* (Indian Home Rule) will know that Mr Gandhi is against modern civilization. The book was first published in 1908. But there has been no change in his ideology. Writing in 1921 Mr Gandhi said:[101]

> The booklet is a severe condemnation of 'modern civilization'. It was written in 1908. My conviction is deeper today than ever. I feel that if India would discard 'modern civilization' she can only gain by doing so.

In Mr. Gandhi's view[102]: "Western civilization is the creation of satan."

The second ideal of Mr Gandhi is the elimination of Class-war and even Class struggle in the relationship between employers and employees and between landlords and tenants. Mr Gandhi's views on the relationship between employers and employees were set forth by him in an article on the subject which appeared in the *Nava Jivan* of June 8, 1921 from which the following is an extract:

> Two paths are open before India, either to introduce the Western principle of 'Might is right' or to uphold the Eastern principle that truth alone conquers, that truth knows no mishap, that the strong and the weak have alike a right to secure justice. The choice is to begin with the labouring Class. Should the labourers obtain an increment in their wages by violence? Even if that be possible, they cannot resort to anything like

101. *Young India,* January 26, 1921.
102. *Dharma Manthan,* p. 65.

> violence, howsoever legitimate may be their claims. To use violence for securing rights may seem an easy path, but it proves to be thorny in the long run. Those who live by sword die also by sword. The swimmer often dies by drowning. Look at Europe. No one seems to be happy there, for not one is contented. The labourer does not trust the capitalist and the capitalist has no faith in the labourer. Both have a sort of vigour and strength but even the bulls have it. They fight to the very bitter end. All motion is not progress. We have got no reason to believe that the people of Europe are progressing. Their possession of wealth does not argue the possession of any moral or spiritual qualities.

Mr Gandhi does not wish to hurt the propertied Class. He is even opposed to a campaign against them. He has no passion for economic equality. Referring to the propertied Class Mr Gandhi said quite recently that he does not wish to destroy the hen that lays the golden egg. His solution for the economic conflict between the owners and workers, between the rich and the poor, between landlords and tenants and between the employers and the employees is very simple. The owners need not deprive themselves of their property. All that they need do is to declare themselves Trustees for the poor. Of course, the Trust is to be a voluntary one carrying only a spiritual obligation.

Is there anything new in the Gandhian analysis of economic ills? Are the economics of Gandhism sound? What hope does Gandhism hold out to the common man, to the down-and-out? Does it promise him a better life, a life of joy, and culture, a life of freedom, not merely freedom from want but freedom to rise, to grow to the full stature which his capacities can reach?

There is nothing new in the Gandhian analysis of economic ills in so far as it attributes them to machinery and the civilization that is built upon it. The arguments that machinery and modern civilization help to concentrate management and control into relatively few hands, and with the aid of banking and credit facilitate the transfer into still fewer hands of all materials and factories and mills in which millions are bled white, in order to support huge industries thousands of miles away from their cottages; or that machinery and modern civilisation cause deaths, maimings and cripplings—far in excess of the corresponding injuries by war—and are responsible for disease and physical deterioration caused directly and indirectly by the development of large cities— with their smoke, dirt, noise, foul air, lack of sunshine and out-door life, slums, prostitution and unnatural living which they bring about—are all old and worn-out arguments. There is nothing new in them. Gandhism is merely repeating the views of Rousseau, Ruskin, Tolstoy and their school.

The ideas which go to make up Gandhism are just primitive. It is a return to nature, to animal life. The only merit is their simplicity. As there is always a large corps of simple people who are attracted by them, such simple ideas do not die, and there is always some simpleton to preach them. There is, however, no doubt that the practical instincts of men—which seldom go wrong—have found them unfruitful, and which society in search of progress has thought it best to reject.

The economics of Gandhism are hopelessly fallacious. The fact that machinery and modern civilization have produced many evils may be admitted. But these evils are no argument against them. For the evils are not due to machinery and modern civilization. They are due to wrong social organization which has made private property and pursuit of personal gain matters of absolute sanctity. If machinery and civilization have not benefited everybody, the remedy is not to condemn machinery and civilization but to alter the organization of society so that the benefits will not be usurped by the few but will accrue to all.

In Gandhism the common man has no hope. It treats man as an animal, and no more. It is true that man shares the Constitution and functions of animals, nutritive, reproductive, etc. But these are not distinctively human functions. The distinctively human function is reason, the purpose of which is to enable man to observe, meditate, cogitate, study and discover the beauties of the Universe and enrich his life and control the animal elements in his life. Man thus occupies the highest place in the scheme of animate existence. If this is true what is the conclusion that follows? The conclusion that follows is that while the ultimate goal of a brute's life is reached once his physical appetites are satisfied, the ultimate goal of man's existence is not reached unless and until he has fully cultivated his mind. In short, what divides the brute from man is culture. Culture is not possible for the brute, but it is essential for man. That being so, the aim of human society must be to enable every person to lead a life of culture which means the cultivation of the mind as distinguished from the satisfaction of mere physical wants. How can this happen?

Both for society as well as for the individual there is always a gulf between merely living and living worthily. In order that one may live worthily, one must first live. The time and energy spent upon mere life, upon gaining of subsistence detracts from that available for activities, of a distinctively human nature and which go to make up a life of culture. How then can a life of culture be made possible? It is not possible unless there is sufficient leisure. For it is only when there is leisure that a person is free to devote himself to a life of culture. The problem of all problems which human society has to face is how to provide leisure to every individual. What does leisure mean? Leisure means the lessening of the toil and effort necessary for satisfying the physical wants of life. How can leisure be made possible? Leisure is quite impossible unless some means are found whereby the toil required for producing goods necessary to satisfy human needs is lessened. What can lessen such toil? Only when machine takes the place of man. There is no other means of producing leisure. Machinery and modern civilization are thus indispensable for emancipating man from leading the life of a brute, and for providing him with leisure and making a life of culture possible. The man who condemns machinery and modern civilization simply does not understand their purpose and the ultimate aim which human society must strive to achieve.

Gandhism may be well suited to a society which does not accept democracy as its ideal. A society which does not believe in democracy may be indifferent to machinery and the civilisation based upon it. But a democratic society cannot. The former may well content itself with life of leisure and culture for the few and a life of toil and drudgery for the many. But a democratic society must assure a life of leisure and culture to each one of its citizens. If the above analysis is correct then the slogan of a democratic society must be machinery, and more machinery, civilisation and more civilization. Under Gandhism the common man must keep on toiling ceaselessly for a pittance and remain a brute. In short, Gandhism with its call of back to nature, means back to nakedness, back to squalor, back to poverty and back to ignorance for the vast mass of the people.

The division of life into separate functions and of society into separate classes may not be altogether obliterated. In spite of many social and economic changes, in spite of the abolition of legal serfdom, legal slavery and the spread of the notion of democracy, with the extension of science, of general education through books, newspapers, travel and general intercourse in schools and factories there remains and perhaps will remain enough cleavage in society into a learned and an ignorant Class, a leisure and a labouring Class.

But Gandhism is not satisfied with only notional Class distinctions. Gandhism insists upon Class structure. It regards the Class structure of society and also the income structure as sacrosanct with the consequent distinctions of rich and poor, high and low, owners and workers as permanent parts of social organization. From the point of view of social consequences nothing can be more pernicious. Psychologically, Class structure sets in motion influences which are harmful to both the classes. There is no common plane on which the privileged and the subject classes can meet. There is no endosmosis, no give-and-take of life's hopes and experiences. The social and moral evils of this separation to the subject Class are, of course, real and obvious. It educates them into slaves, and creates all the psychological complex which flows from a slave mentality. But those affecting the privileged Class, though less material and less perceptible, are equally real. The isolation and exclusiveness following upon the Class structure creates in the privileged classes the anti-social spirit of a gang. It feels it has interests 'of its own' which it makes its prevailing purpose to protect against everybody even against the interests of the State. It makes their culture sterile, their art showy, their wealth luminous and their manners fastidious. Practically speaking, in a Class structure there is, on the one hand, tyranny, vanity, pride, arrogance, greed, selfishness, and, on the other, insecurity, poverty, degradation, loss of liberty, self-reliance, independence, dignity and self-respect. Democratic society cannot be indifferent to such consequences. But Gandhism does not mind these consequences in the least. It is not enough to say that Gandhism is not satisfied with mere Class distinctions. It is not enough to say that Gandhism believes in a Class structure. Gandhism stands for more than that. A Class structure which is a faded, jejune, effete thing, a mere sentimentality, a mere skeleton is not what Gandhism wants. It wants Class structure to function as a living faith. In this there is nothing to be surprised at. For Class structure in Gandhism is not a mere accident. It is its official doctrine.

The idea of trusteeship which Gandhism proposes as a panacea by which the moneyed classes will hold their properties in trust for the poor is the most ridiculous part of it. All that one can say about it is that if anybody else had propounded it, the author would have been laughed at as a silly fool who had not known the hard realities of life, and was deceiving the servile classes by telling them that a little dose of moral rearmament to the propertied classes—those who by their insatiable cupidity and indomitable arrogance have made, and will always make this world a vale of tears for the toiling millions—will recondition them to such an extent that they will be able to withstand the temptation to misuse the tremendous powers which the Class structure gives them over servile classes.

The social ideal of Gandhism is either Caste or *Varna*. Though it may be difficult to say which, there can be no doubt that the social ideal of Gandhism is not democracy. For whether one takes for comparison Caste or *Varna* both are fundamentally opposed to democracy. It would have been something if the defence of Caste System, which Gandhism offers was strong and honest. But his defence of the Caste System is the most insensible piece of rhetoric one can think of. Examine Mr Gandhi's arguments in support of Caste, and it will be found that everyone of them is specious, if not puerile.

The first three arguments call for pity. That the Hindu Society has been able to stand while others have died out or disappeared is hardly a matter for congratulation. If it has survived it is not because of Caste, but because the foreigner who conquered the Hindus did not find it necessary to kill them wholesale. There is no honour in mere survival. What matters is the plane of survival. One can survive by unconditional surrender. One can survive by beating a cowardly retreat and one can survive by fighting. On what plane have the Hindus survived? If they can be said to have survived after fighting and beating their enemies the virtue ascribed to the Caste System by Mr Gandhi could be admitted. The history of the Hindus has been one of surrender—abject surrender. It is true others have surrendered to their invaders. But in their case surrender is followed by a revolt against the foreign ruler. The Hindus have not only never withstood the onslaught of the foreign invader, they have never even shown the capacity to organize a rebellion to throw off the foreign yoke. On the other hand, the Hindus have tried to make slavery comfortable. On this one may well argue the contrary, namely, that this helpless condition of the Hindus is due entirely to the Caste System.

Argument is plausible. But it cannot be said that Caste is the only machinery for discharging such functions as the spread of primary education or the judicial settlement of disputes. Caste is probably the worst instrument for the discharge of such functions. It can be easily influenced and easily corrupted. Such functions have been discharged in other countries much better than they have been in India although they have had no Caste System. As to using the Caste as basis for raising military units the idea is simply fantastic. Under the occupational theory underlying the Caste System this is unthinkable. Mr Gandhi knows that not a single Caste in his own Province of Gujarat has ever raised a military unit. It did not do it in the present World War. But it did not do so even in the last World War, when Mr Gandhi toured through Gujarat as a Recruiting Agent of British Imperialism. In fact, under the Caste System a general mobilization of the people for defence is impossible, since mobilization requires a general liquidation of the occupational theory underlying the Caste System.

Arguments contained in para 5 and 6 are as stupid as they are revolting.... It is quite true the family is an ideal unit in which every member is charged with love and affection for another member although there is no inter-marriage among members of a family. It may even be conceded that in a *Vaishnava* family members of the family do not inter-dine, and yet they are full of love and affection for one another. What does all this prove? It does not prove that inter-dining and inter-marrying are not necessary for establishing fraternity. What it proves is that where there are other means of maintaining fraternity—such as consciousness of family tie—inter-dining and inter-marriage are not necessary. But it cannot be denied that where—as in the Caste System—no binding force exists inter-marriage and inter-dining are absolutely essential. There is no analogy between family and Caste, inter-Caste dinner and inter-Caste marriage are necessary because there are no other means of binding the different Castes together while in the case of a family there exists other forces to bind them together. Those who have insisted upon the ban against inter-dining and inter-marriage have treated it as a question of relative values. They have never elevated it to the level of a question of absolute value. Mr Gandhi is the first one to do it. Inter-dining is bad and even if it was capable of producing good, it should not be resorted to and why? Because eating is a filthy act, as filthy as answering the call of nature! The Caste System has been defended by others. But this is the first time I have seen such an extraordinary, if not a shocking, argument used to support it. Even the orthodox may say, "Save us from Mr Gandhi," It shows what a deep-dyed Hindu Mr Gandhi is. He has outdone the most orthodox of orthodox Hindus. It is not enough to say that it is an argument of a cave man. It is really an argument of a mad man.

The argument in favour of the Caste System outlined in para 7 is not worth much in terms of building up moral strength. The Caste System no doubt prohibits a man from satisfying his lust for a woman who is not of his Caste. The Caste System no doubt prohibits a man from satisfying his craving for food cooked in the house of a man who is not of his Caste. If morality consists of observing restraints without regard to the sense or sensibility of restraints, then the Caste System may be admitted to be a moral system. But Mr Gandhi does not see that these easy restraints are more than balanced by vast liberties permitted by Hinduism. For Hinduism places no restraint upon a man marrying hundred women and keeping hundred prostitutes within the ambit of his Caste. Nor does it stop him from indulging in his appetite with his Castemen to any degree.

The argument in para 8 begs the whole question. The hereditary system may be good or may not be good. It may be agreeable to some. It may be disagreeable to others. Why elevate it into an official doctrine? Why make it compulsory? In Europe it is not an official doctrine and it is not compulsory. It is left to the choice of an individual most of whom do follow the profession of their ancestors and some don't.

Who can say that compulsory system has worked better than the voluntary system? If a comparison of the economic condition of the people in India and the people of Europe is any guide, there would be very few rationally-minded people who would be found to support the Caste System on this ground. As to the difficulty in changing nomenclature to keep pace with frequent changes in occupation it is only artificial, it arises out of the supposed necessity of having labels for designating persons following a particular profession. The Class labels are quite unnecessary, and could well be abolished altogether without causing difficulty. Besides what happens today in India? Men's callings and their Class labels are not in accord. A Brahmin sells shoes. Nobody is disturbed because he is not called a *Chamar*. A *Chamar* becomes an officer of the State. Nobody is disturbed because he is not called a Brahmin. The whole argument is based on a misunderstanding. What matters to society is not the label by which the individual's Class is known, but the service he offers.

The last argument set out in para 9 is one of the most astounding arguments I have heard in favour of the Caste System. It is historically false. No one who knows anything about the Manu Smriti can say that the Caste System is a natural system. What does Manu Smriti show? It shows that the Caste System is a legal system maintained at the point of a bayonet. If it has survived it is due to (1) prevention of the masses from the possession of arms; (2) denying to the masses the right to education; and (3) depriving the masses of the right to property. The Caste System far from natural is really an imposition by the ruling classes upon the servile classes.

That Mr Gandhi changed over from the Caste System to the *Varna* System does not make the slightest difference to the charge that Gandhism is opposed to democracy. In the first place, the idea of *Varna* is the parent of the idea of Caste. If the idea of Caste is a pernicious idea, it is entirely because of the viciousness of the ides of *Varna*. Both are evil ideas and it matters very little whether one believes in *Varna* or in Caste. The idea of *Varna* was most mercilessly attacked by the Buddhists who did not believe in it. Orthodox or the Sanatan Vedic Hindus had no rational defence to offer. All that they could say was that it was founded on the authority of the Vedas and that as the Vedas were infallible so was the *Varna* System. This argument was not enough to save the *Varna* System against the rationalism of the Buddhists. If the idea of the *Varna* survived it was because of the Bhagvat Gita, which gave a philosophical foundation to the *Varna* System by arguing that the *Varna* was based on the innate qualities of man. The Bhagvat Gita made use of the Sankhya philosophy to bolster and buttress the *Varna* idea which would have otherwise petered away by making sense of a thing that is absolute nonsense. Bhagvat Gita had done enough mischief by giving a fresh lease of life to the *Varna* System by basing it upon a new and plausible foundation, namely, that of innate qualities.

The *Varna* System of the Bhagvat Gita has at least two merits. It does not say that it is based on birth. Indeed it makes a special point that each man's *Varna* is fixed according to his innate qualities. It does not say that the occupation of the son shall be that of the father. It says that the profession of a person shall be according to his innate qualities, the profession of the father according to the father's innate quality and that of the son according to the son's innate qualities. But Mr Gandhi has given a new interpretation of the *Varna* System. He has changed it out of recognition. Under the old orthodox interpretation Caste connoted hereditary occupation but *Varna* did not. Mr Gandhi by his own whim has given a new connotation to the *Varna*. With Mr Gandhi *Varna* is determined by birth and the profession of a *Varna* is determined by the principle of heredity so that *Varna* is merely another name for Caste. That Mr Gandhi changed from Caste to *Varna* does not indicate the growth of any new revolutionary ideology. The genius of Mr Gandhi is selfish, always and throughout. He has all the precocity of an elf with no little of its outward guise. Like an elf he can never grow up and grow out of the Caste ideology.

Mr Gandhi sometimes speaks on social and economic subjects as though he was a blushing red. Those who will study Gandhism will not be deceived by the occasional aberrations of Mr Gandhi in favour of democracy and against capitalism. For Gandhism is in no sense a revolutionary creed. It is conservatism in excelsis. So far as India is concerned, it is a reactionary creed blazoning on its banner the call of Return to Antiquity. Gandhism aims at the resuscitation and reanimation of India's dread, dying past.

Gandhism is a paradox. It stands for freedom from foreign domination, which means the destruction of the existing political structure of the country. At the same time, it seeks to maintain intact a social structure which permits the domination of one Class by another on a hereditary basis which means a perpetual domination of one Class by another. What is the explanation of this paradox? Is it a part of a strategy by Mr Gandhi to win the whole-hearted support of the Hindus, orthodox and unorthodox, to the campaign of *Swaraj*? If it is the latter, can Gandhism be regarded as honest and sincere? Be that as it may, there are two features of Gandhism which are revealing but to which unfortunately no attention has so far been paid. Whether they will make Gandhism more acceptable than Marxism is another matter. But as they do help to distinguish Gandhism from Marxism, it may be well to refer to them.

The first special feature of Gandhism is that its philosophy helps those who have, to keep what they have and to prevent those who have not from getting what they have a right to get. No one who examines the Gandhian attitude to strikes, the Gandhian reverence for Caste and the Gandhian doctrine of Trusteeship by the rich for the benefit of the poor can deny that this is upshot of Gandhism. Whether this is the calculated result of a deliberate design or whether it is a matter of accident may be open to argument. But the fact remains that Gandhism is the philosophy of the well-so-do and the leisure Class.

The second special feature of Gandhism is to delude people into accepting their misfortunes by presenting them as best of good fortunes. One or two illustrations will suffice to bring out the truth of this statement.

The Hindu sacred law penalized the *Shudras* (Hindus of the fourth Class) from acquiring wealth. It is a law of enforced poverty unknown in any other part of the world. What does Gandhism do? It does not lift the ban. It blesses the *Shudra* for his moral courage to give up property!! It is well worth quoting Mr Gandhi's own words. Here they are[103]:

> The *Shudra* who only serves (the higher Caste) as a matter of religious duty, and who will never own any property, who indeed has not even the ambition to own anything, is deserving of thousand obeisance. The very Gods will shower down flowers on him.

Another illustration in support is the attitude of Gandhism towards the scavenger. The sacred law of the Hindus lays down that a. scavenger's progeny shall live by scavenging. Under Hinduism scavenging was not a matter of choice, it was a matter of force. What does Gandhism do? It seeks to perpetuate this system by praising scavenging as the noblest service to society!! Let me quote Mr Gandhi: As a President of a Conference of the Untouchables, Mr Gandhi said[104]:

> I do not want to attain *Moksha*. I do not want to be reborn. But if I have to be reborn, I should be born an Untouchable, so that I may share their sorrows, sufferings and the affronts levelled at them, in order that I may endeavour to free myself and them from that miserable condition. I, therefore, prayed that if I should be born again, I should do so not as a Brahmin, *Kshatriya*, *Vaishya*, or *Shudra*, but as an *Ati-Shudra*.
>
> I love scavenging. In my Ashram, an eighteen-year-old Brahmin lad is doing the scavenger's work in order to teach the Ashram scavenger cleanliness. The lad is no reformer. He was born and bred in orthodoxy. But he felt that his accomplishments were incomplete until he had become also a perfect sweeper, and that. if he wanted the Ashram sweeper to do his work well, he must do it himself and set an example.... You should realize that you are cleaning Hindu Society.

Can there be a worse example of false propaganda than this attempt of Gandhism to perpetuate evils which have been deliberately imposed by one Class over another? If Gandhism preached the rule of poverty for all and not merely for the *Shudra* the worst that could be said about it is that it is a mistaken idea. But why preach it as good for one Class only? Why appeal to the worst of human failings, namely, pride and vanity in order to make him voluntarily accept what on a rational basis he would resent as a cruel discrimination against him? What is the use of telling the scavenger that even a Brahmin is prepared to do scavenging, when it is clear that according to Hindu *Shastras* and Hindu notions, even if a Brahmin did scavenging he would never be subject to the disabilities of one who is a born scavenger? For in India, a man is not a scavenger because of his work. He is a scavenger because of

103. Quoted from *Varna Vyavastha,* p. 51.
104. *Young India,* April 27, 1921.

his birth irrespective of the question whether he does scavenging or not. If Gandhism preached that scavenging is a noble profession with the object of inducing those who refuse to engage in it, one could understand it. But why appeal to the scavenger's pride and vanity in order to induce him and him only to keep on to scavenging[105] by telling him that scavenging is a noble profession and that he need not be ashamed of it? To preach that poverty is good for the *Shudra* and for none else, to preach that scavenging is good for the Untouchables and for none else and to make them accept these onerous impositions as voluntary purposes of life, by appeal to their failings is an outrage and a cruel joke on the helpless classes which none but Mr Gandhi can perpetuate with equanimity and impunity. In this connection one is reminded of the words ofVoltaire who in repudiation of an "ism" very much like Gandhism said:"Oh! mockery to say to people that the suffering of some brings joy to others and works good to the whole.What solace is it to a dying man to know that from his decaying body a thousand worms will come into life?"

Criticism apart, this is the technique of Gandhism—to make wrongs done appear to the very victim as though they were his privileges. If there is an "ism" which has made full use of religion as an opium to lull the people into false beliefs and false security, it is Gandhism. Following Shakespeare one can well say,"Plausibility I Ingenuity! Thy name is Gandhism."

Such is Gandhism. Having known what is Gandhism, the answer to the question, "Should Gandhism become the law of the land, what would be the lot of the Untouchables under it," cannot require much scratching of the brain. How would it compare with the lot of the lowest Hindu? Enough has been said to show what would be his lot should the Gandhian social order come into being. Insofar as the lowest Hindu and the Untouchable belong to the same disinherited Class, the Untouchable's, lot cannot be better. If anything, it might easily be worse. Because in India even the lowest man among the Caste Hindus—why even the aboriginal and Hill Tribe man—though educationally and economically not very much above the Untouchables, is still superior to the Untouchables. It is not he regards himself as superior to the Untouchables.The Hindu society accepts his claim to superiority over the Untouchables. The Untouchable will, therefore, continue to suffer the worst fate as he does now, namely, in prosperity he will be the last to be employed and in depression the first to be fired.

What does Gandhism do to relieve the Untouchables from this fate? Gandhism professes to abolish Untouchability.That is hailed as the greatest virtue of Gandhism. But what does this virtue amount to in actual life? To assess the value of this anti-Untouchability which is regarded as a very big element in Gandhism, it is necessary to understand fully the scope of Mr Gandhi's programme for the removal of Untouchability. Does it mean anything more than that the Hindus will not mind

105. Some of the Provinces of India have laws which make refusal by a scavenger to do scavenging a crime for which he can be tried and punished by a criminal court.

touching the Untouchables? Does it mean the removal of the ban on the right of the Untouchables to education? It would be better to take the two questions separately.

To start with the first question, Mr Gandhi does not say that a Hindu should not take a bath after touching the Untouchables. If Mr Gandhi does not object to it as a purification of pollution then it is difficult to see how Untouchability can be said to vanish by touching the Untouchables. Untouchability centres round the idea of pollution by contact and purification by bath to remove the pollution. Does it mean social assimilation with the Hindus? Mr Gandhi has most categorically stated that removal of Untouchability does not mean inter-dining or inter-marriage between the Hindus and the Untouchables. Mr Gandhi's anti-Untouchability means that the Untouchables will be classed as *Shudras* instead of being classed as *Ati-Shudras.*[106] There is nothing more in it. Mr Gandhi has not considered the question whether the old *Shudras* will accept the new *Shudras* into their fold. If they don't then the removal of Untouchability is a senseless proposition for it will still keep the Untouchables as a separate social category. Mr Gandhi probably knows that the abolition of Untouchability will not bring about the assimilation of the Untouchables by the *Shudras*. That seems to be the reason why Mr Gandhi himself has given a new and a different name to the Untouchables. The new name registers by anticipation what is likely to be the fact. By calling the Untouchables *Harijans,* Mr Gandhi has killed two birds with one stone. He has shown that assimilation of the Untouchables by the *Shudras* is not possible. He has also by his new name counteracted assimilation and made it impossible.

Regarding the second question, it is true that Gandhism is prepared to remove the old ban placed by the Hindu *Shastras* on the right of the Untouchables to education and permit them to acquire knowledge and learning. Under Gandhism, the Untouchables may study law, they may study medicine, they may study engineering or anything else they may fancy. So far so good. But will the Untouchables be free to make use of their knowledge and learning? Will they have the right to choose their profession? Can they adopt the career of lawyer, doctor or engineer? To these questions the answer which Gandhism gives is an emphatic. The Untouchables must follow their hereditary professions. That those occupations they are unclean is no answer; That before the occupation became hereditary it was the result of force and not volition does not matter. The argument of Gandhism is that what is once settled is settled for ever even if it was wrongly settled. Under Gandhism the Untouchables are to be eternal scavengers. There is no doubt that the Untouchables would much prefer the orthodox system of Untouchability. A compulsory state of ignorance imposed upon the Untouchables by the Hindu *Shastras* made scavenging bearable. But Gandhism which compels an educated Untouchable to do scavenging is nothing short of cruelty. The grace in Gandhism

106. *Young India,* February 5, 1925.

is a curse in its worst form. The virtue of the anti-Untouchability plank in Gandhism is quite illusory. There is no substance in it.

What else is there in Gandhism which the Untouchables can accept as opening a way for their ultimate salvation? Barring this illusory campaign against Untouchability Gandhism is simply another form of Sanatanism which is the ancient name for militant orthodox Hinduism. What is there in Gandhism which is not to be found in orthodox Hinduism? There is Caste in Hinduism, there is Caste in Gandhism. Hinduism believes in the law of hereditary profession, so does Gandhism. Hinduism enjoins cow-worship. So does Gandhism. Hinduism upholds the law of *karma*, predestination of man's condition in this world, so does Gandhism. Hinduism accepts the authority of the *Shastras*. So does Gandhism. Hinduism believes in avatar or incarnation of God. So does Gandhism. Hinduism believes in idols, so does Gandhism.[107] All that Gandhism has done is to find a philosophic justification for Hinduism and its dogmas. Hinduism is bald in the sense that it is just a set of rules which bear on their face the appearance of a crude and cruel system. Gandhism supplies the philosophy which smoothens its surface and gives it the appearance of decency and respectability and so alters it and embellishes it as to make it even attractive. What philosophy does Gandhism propound to cover the nudity of Hinduism? This philosophy can be put in a nutshell. It is a philosophy which says that "All that is in Hinduism is well, all that is in Hinduism is necessary for public good." Those who are familiar with Voltaire's Candide will recognize that it is the philosophy of Master Pangiloss and recall the mockery Voltaire made of it. The Hindus are, of course, pleased with it. No doubt, it suits them and accords with their interest. Professor Radhakrishnan—whether out of genuine feeling or out of sycophancy we need not stop to inquire—has gone to the length of describing Mr.Gandhi as 'God on Earth'. What do the Untouchables understand this to mean? To them it means that: This God by name Gandhi came to console an afflicted race: He saw India and changed it not saying all is well and will be, if the Hindus will only fulfil the law of Caste. He told the afflicted race, "I have come to fulfil the law of Caste. Not a little, not a jot shall I allow to abate from it."

What hope can Gandhism offer to the Untouchables? To the Untouchables Hinduism is a veritable chamber of horrors. The sanctity and infallibility of the Vedas, *Smritis* and *Shastras*, the iron law of Caste, the heartless law of *karma* and the senseless law of status by birth are to the Untouchables veritable instruments of torture which Hinduism has forged against the Untouchables. These very instruments which have mutilated, blasted and blighted the life of the Untouchables are to be found intact and untarnished in the bossom of Gandhism. How can the Untouchables say that Gandhism is a heaven and not a chamber of horrors as Hinduism has been? The only reaction and a very natural reaction of the Untouchables would be to run away from Gandhism.

---

107. Mr Gandhi's articles of faith have been outlined by him in *Young India* of October 6, 1921.

Gandhists may say that what I have stated applies to the old type of Gandhism. There is a new Gandhism, Gandhism without Caste. This has reference to the recent statement[108] of Mr Gandhi that Caste is an anachronism. Reformers were naturally gladdened by this declaration of Mr Gandhi. And who would not be glad to see that a man like Mr Gandhi having such terrible influence over the Hindus, after having played the most mischievous part of a social reactionary, after having stood out as the protagonist of the Caste System, after having beguiled and befooled the unthinking Hindus with arguments which made no distinction between what is fair and foul should have come out with this recantation? But is this really a matter for jubilation? Does it change the nature of Gandhism? Does it make Gandhism a new and a better 'ism' than it was before. Those who are carried away by this recantation of Mr Gandhi forget two things. In the first place all that Mr Gandhi has said is that Caste is an anachronism. He does not say it is an evil. He does not say it is anathema. Mr Gandhi may be taken to be not in favour of Caste. But Mr. Gandhi does not say that he is against the *Varna* System. And what is Mr Gandhi's *Varna* System? It is simply a new name for the Caste System and retains all the worst features of the Caste System.

The declaration of Mr Gandhi cannot be taken to mean any fundamental change in Gandhism. It cannot make Gandhism acceptable to the Untouchables. The Untouchables will still have ground to say: "Good God! Is this man Gandhi our Saviour?"

★ ★ ★

Dr Ambedkar had correctly anticipated the reaction to the book. In the Preface to the First Edition, Dr Ambedkar said: "With the Hindus who have been blind devotees of Mr Gandhi, this study…will not find favour: indeed it is sure to provoke their wrath."

Referring to the title: "Beware of Mr Gandhi". Dr Ambedkar added:

> The Untouchables are not the only community in India which thinks of Mr Gandhi in these terms. The same view of Mr Gandhi is entertained by the Muslims, the Sikhs and the Indian Christians…. In my judgement, there cannot be a greater tragedy for a leader to be distrusted by everybody as Mr Gandhi is today. I am, however, certain that this is not how the Hindus will react. As usual, they will denounce the book and call me names…. but I must do my duty, no matter what my adversaries may have to say.

★ ★ ★

108. *Hindustan Times*, April 15, 1945.

PART VII

POLITICAL UPHEAVALS
(1946-47)

CHAPTER THIRTY THREE

On the Shape and Form of the Future Constitution of India

ALL-INDIA SCHEDULED Caste Federation's Third Conference was held in Mumbai on May 6, 1945. Dr Ambedkar was a Special Invitee to the Conference. At that time, Dr Ambedkar was serving as Labour Member in the Viceroy's Executive Council. He, in fact, remarked, "For the moment, the responsibility for leading the movement of the Scheduled Castes and facing its day-to-day problems does not lie on my shoulders. On account of my office, I am out of it and I have no desire to take it up."[109]

Under the circumstances, Dr Ambedkar chose to speak in the Conference not on a sectarian subject confined only to the Scheduled Castes, but on a topic, which is general and has a wider appeal. He observed that Scheduled Castes are often charged as being selfish, interested only in themselves; (and) that they have no constructive suggestions to make for the solution of the country's political problems. In order to refute this charge in a positive way by showing that the Scheduled Castes are capable of putting forth constructive proposals for the general political advancement of the country, Dr Ambedkar chose to speak in the Conference on "The shape and form of the future Constitution of India". This Speech was published in the same year as a booklet with the title: "Communal Deadlock and a Way to Solve It".

Dr Ambedkar articulated his position on the following lines:

- A Constitution, framed by the British Government and imposed upon the Indians, sufficed in the past. But in the future Constitution, imposition by the British will not do.
- The past Constitutions contained a Breakdown Clause. But the future Constitution cannot contain such a clause. In the future Constitution of India,

109. The quotes in the opening section are from the original speech, reproduced in BAWS Vol1, pp.357-9. For fuller summary, see *Ambedkar Speaks*, op cit, Vol. III, pp 295-318

it would not be possible to maintain a distinction between Constitutional Government and Government with the provision for stepping in when the Constitutional Government failed. The past Constitutions of India did not treat India as a Dominion State. The future Constitution will proceed on the assumption that India will be a Dominion.

- Dr Ambedkar stated that he was wholly opposed to the proposals of a Constituent Assembly, "It is absolutely superfluous." He regarded it as a most dangerous project, which may invoke this country in a Civil War. Dr Ambedkar provides a very illuminating comparison between the Constituent Assembly as envisioned the Cripps Mission and the one proposed by the Sapru Committee. After reviewing both sets of proposals, Dr Ambedkar concludes: "It is my considered opinion that the proposal of Constituent Assembly is more dangerous than profitable and should not be entertained."
- According to Dr Ambedkar, "The only function which could be left to a Constituent Assembly is to find a solution of the Communal Problem.... If the Communal question has become difficult of solution, it is not because it is insoluble, nor because we had not yet employed the machinery of Constituent Assembly. It has become insoluble because the approach to it is fundamentally wrong. The defect in the present approach is that it proceeds by methods, instead of by principles. The principle is that there is no principle. There is only a server of methods."
- This, according to Dr Ambedkar, has led to a policy of limitless demand followed by endless appeasement of some community. On the other hand, "There is a community economically poor, socially degraded, educationally backward and which is exploited, oppressed and tyrannized without shame and without remorse, disowned by society, unowned by Government and which has no security for protection and no guarantee for justice, fairplay and equal opportunity. Such a community is told that it can have no safeguards, not because it has no case for safeguards, but only because the bully on whom the bill of rights is presented, thinks that because the community is not politically organized to have sanctions behind its demand, he can successfully bluff."

Dr Ambedkar presented a detailed set of proposals for solving the Communal Problem, along with the governing principles, as detailed in the excerpts reproduced below:

I. RESPONSIBILITY FOR FRAMING THE CONSTITUTION

Before I set out in concrete terms the Constitutional proposals I have in mind, I wish to raise two preliminary issues. First is, who should frame a Constitution for India? It is necessary to raise this question because there are quite a lot of people in India who are hoping, if not asking, the British Government to resolve the deadlock and to frame a Constitution for India. I think there is a gross fallacy in such a view which needs to be exposed. A Constitution, framed by the British Government and imposed upon Indians, sufficed in the past. But if the nature of the future Constitution Indians are clamouring for is borne in mind, it will be clear that an imposed Constitution will not do.

The difference between the past Constitutions and the future Constitution of India is fundamental, and those who still rely on the British for framing a Constitution for India do not seem to have realized this difference. The difference lies in this, that the past Constitutions contained a Breakdown Clause. But the future Constitution of India cannot contain such a Breakdown Clause. People in India decry the Breakdown Clause—by now the notorious Section 93 of the Government of India Act, 1935. That is because they do not know the why and the how of its place in the Act.

Its importance will become apparent if two important considerations governing the political life of a community are borne in mind. First of these considerations is that Law and Order is the medicine of the body politic, and when the body politic goes sick this medicine must be administered. Indeed, so important is this consideration that failure to administer it must be deemed to be a crime against society and civilisation. The second consideration is that, though it is true that no Government has a vested right to govern, it is equally true that there must always be a Government to govern—which I mean maintain Law and Order—until it is displaced by a better Government. The breakdown clause serves these two purposes. As such, it is of the highest value for the peace and tranquillity of the people. It is the one and only means which can save the country from anarchy. For, when Constitutional Government fails, the Breakdown Clause has at least the merit of maintaining Government.

In the past this distinction between Constitutional Government and Government with the provision for Government stepping in when Constitutional Government failed was a feasible proposition. It was feasible because while the British Government gave Indians the right to a Constitutional Government, it kept to itself the right to govern, should Constitutional Government fail. In the future Constitution of India, it would not be possible to maintain this distinction.

It would not be possible for the British Government to give the Indians the right to Constitutional Government and also to keep to itself the right to govern in case there was a breakdown in the Constitutional Government. The reason is quite obvious. The past Constitutions of India did not treat India as a Dominion. The future Constitution will proceed on the assumption that India will be a Dominion. The breakdown clause or the possibility of Government stepping in, when Constitutional Government has failed, can be reconciled in the case of a country, which has no Dominion Status. But the two are irreconcilable in the case of a Dominion. In the case of a Dominion or for the matter of that in the case of any free country, there is either a Constitutional Government or a Rebellion.

What does this mean? It means that it is impossible to frame a Constitution for an Indian Dominion with a possibility of a breakdown. To put the same thing in a different language, the Constitution must be so made that it will not only command the obedience but also the respect of all; and all or if not all, at any rate, all important elements in the national life of India shall be prepared to uphold it and to give it their support. This can happen only if the Constitution is framed by Indians for Indians and with the voluntary consent of Indians.

If the Constitution is imposed by the British Government and is not accepted by one section and is opposed by another, there will arise in the country an element, hostile to the Constitution, and which will devote its energies not to working the Constitution but to breaking it. The anti-Constitution party may look upon destroying the Constitution as its only duty and may engage itself in "pronouncing" against a party working the Constitution in the real Latin American fashion.

It is useless for the British to frame a Constitution for India which they will not remain to enforce. The same result will ensure if the Constitution is imposed by one powerful section or a combination of such sections on other sections. I am, therefore, firmly of opinion that if Indians want Dominion Status, they cannot escape the responsibility of framing their own Constitution. The position is thus inescapable.

II. CONSTITUENT ASSEMBLY

The second question that I wish to raise is that should there be a Constituent Assembly, charged with the function of making a Constitution? Constituent Assembly is on the lips of everybody. The Congress Party, in their resolutions passed before the Congress Ministries resigned, demanded that the Constitution for India should be made by a Constituent Assembly composed of Indians. A Constituent Assembly was included in the Cripps proposals. The Sapru Committee has followed suit.

I must state that I am wholly opposed to the proposals of a Constituent Assembly. It is absolutely superfluous. I regard it as a most dangerous project, which may involve this country in a Civil War. In the first place, I do not see why a Constituent Assembly is at all necessary. Indians are not in the same position as the Fathers of the American Constitution were, when they framed the Constitution of the United States. They had to evolve ideas, suitable for the Constitution for a free people. They had no Constitutional patterns before them to draw upon. This cannot, however, be the case for Indians as Constitutional ideas and Constitutional forms are ready at hand. Again, room for variety is very small. There are not more than two or three Constitutional patterns to choose from. Thirdly, there are hardly any big and purely Constitutional questions about which there can be said to be much dispute among Indians. It is agreed that the future Indian Constitution should be Federal. It is also more or less settled what subjects should go to the Centre and what to the Provinces. There is no quarrel over the division of revenues between the Centre and the Provinces, none on franchise, and none on the relation of the Judiciary to the Legislature and the Executive. The only point of dispute, which is outstanding, centers round the question of the residuary powers—whether they should be with the Centre or with the Provinces. But that is hardly a matter worth bothering about. Indeed, the provision contained in the present Government of India Act could be adopted as the best compromise.

Having regard to this, I cannot see why a Constituent Assembly is necessary to incubate a Constitution. So much of the Constitution of India has already been written out in the Government of India Act, 1935, that it seems to be an act of supererogation to appoint a Constituent Assembly to do the thing over again. All that is necessary is to delete those sections of the Government of India Act, 1935, which are inconsistent with Dominion Status.

The only function which could be left to a Constituent Assembly is to find a solution of the Communal Problem. I am quite positive that whatever be the terms of reference of the Constituent Assembly, the Communal Question should not form a part of them. Consider the composition of the Constituent Assembly as suggested by the Sapru Committee. The total membership is fixed at 160. The election is by joint electorates by Members of the Provincial Legislative Assemblies under a system of proportional representation, and the decision is to be by three-fourths of the Members present and voting. Can a minority accept this Constituent Assembly as a safe body, in the impartiality of which it can place implicit confidence?

The answer to this question must depend upon what answers one can give to two other questions; firstly, does it guarantee that the representatives of a minority elected to the Assembly will be its true representatives? Secondly, does it guarantee that the decision of the Assembly with regard to the claims of any particular minority will not in fact be an imposition on the minority? On neither of these two questions can I confidently say that a minority need have no cause for fear.

Before taking up these questions, let me point out what differences there are between the Cripps Constituent Assembly and the Sapru Constituent Assembly. They may be stated as follows:

(1) The total number for the Constituent Assembly fixed by the Sapru Committee is 160. Sir Stafford Cripps had not fixed any number. But the provision contained in his proposal that the Constituent Assembly shall consist of 10 per cent of the total number of Members of the Provincial Legislatures, virtually fixed the number to about 158—a difference of only 2.

(2) The method of election to the Constituent Assembly by the Sapru Committee is by joint electorate under the system of proportional representation. In this there is no difference between the Cripps plan and the Sapru plan for the composition of the Constituent Assembly.

(3) Under the Cripps plan, there was no communal reservation. The Sapru plan departs from the Cripps plan in this respect, in as much as it reserves seats for particular communities in prescribed propositions. This difference is only normal. For, though the Cripps plan did not in terms fix the number, the scheme of proportional representation would have in fact resulted in such reservation. The difference in the quota of representation under the two schemes will be seen from the following table:

Communities and Interests			Quota of seats in the Constituent Assembly Under Cripps'	Under Sapru's
Hindus	..	..	77	51
Muslims	..	..	50	51
Scheduled Castes	..	..	15	20
Sikhs	..	..	3	8
Indian Christians	..	..	2	7
Anglo-Indians	..	..	1	2
Europeans	..	..	6	1
Aboriginal Tribes	..	..	2	3
Special Interests	..	..	..	16
Other	..	..	2	1
			158	160

The Sapru Committee has not only fixed the numbers for each Community in the composition of the Constituent Assembly but it has offered the Muslims equality with the Hindus. For this departure the Committee's plea is that in consideration for this offer it has demanded joint electorate as a basis for election to the Constituent Assembly. In this, the Committee must be said to have entirely misunderstood the Cripps proposals. Joint-Electorates were already provided for in the Cripps proposals, one Clause of which reads, "The members of the Lower Houses of the Provincial Legislatures are to form a single Electoral College." This is simply another way of saying that the election shall be by joint-electorate. It has given something for nothing to one element and thereby put the other Communities in a hazard.

(4) Under the Cripps proposal, the decision of the Assembly was to be by majority of those present and voting. Under the Sapru proposal the decision is to be by a majority of 3/4th of those present and voting.

Now to revert to the two questions, how does the position stand with regard to the first question? To give one's opinion on it, it is first necessary to know the communal distribution of the membership of the Provincial Legislative Assemblies. The following table sums up the position:

DISTRIBUTION OF SEATS BY COMMUNITIES IN THE PROVINCIAL LEGISLATIVE ASSEMBLES*

Communities	General	Women	University	Trade Unions	Com-merce	Land-lords	Total
1	2	3	4	5	6	7	8
1. Hindus ..	651	26	7	33	31	22	770
2. Muslims ..	482	10	1	5	6	13	517
3. Scheduled Castes ..	151	..	..	..	..	..	151

4. Indian Christians ..	20	1	..	..	..	..	21
5. Anglo-Indians	11	1	..	..	..	..	12
6. Sikhs ..	34	1	..	..	..	1	36
7. Europeans ..	26	..	..	..	19	1	46
8. Aboriginals ..	24	..	..	..	..	..	24
Total ..	1,399	39	8	38	56	37	1,577

* The distribution of seats for (1) Universities; (2) Trade Unions; (3) Commerce; and (4) Landlords among the communities does not stand for an exact figure. It is based on guess as to how they may be divided among the communities having regard to the relative position.

Has the communal reservation made by the Sapru proposal, and which is not to be found in the Cripps proposal, any value? That depends upon how far one community will be able to influence the election of the Members of the other communities? What are the prospects in this regard? Let me give another table:

VOTING STRENGTH IN RELATION TO SEATS

Communities	*Voters for Constituent Assembly*	*Quota of seats in the Constituent Assembly*	*Number of votes required for electing the quota*	*(+) Excess of voters over (-) Deficiency of voters below requirement*
1. Hindus	778	51	561	+217
2. Muslims	561	51	517	+44
3. Scheduled Castes	151	20	220	- 69
4. Indian Christians	21	7	77	-56
5. Sikhs	36	8	88	-52
6. Europeans	46	1	11	+35

From this table the following conclusions emerge:

(1) Taking the total votes to be 1577, and the total number to be elected 160 the quota under the proportional system of representation would roughly come to 10 + 1 = 11.

(2) Taking 11 as the quota, the Hindus will have 217, the Muslims 44 and the European 35 votes to spare, while the Scheduled Castes will be short by 69, the Indian Christians by 56 and the Sikhs by 52 votes.

To put the same thing in a different way:

(1) The Hindus with their excess of 217 votes can elect 20 non-Hindus who would be dependent upon them; the Muslims with their excess of 44 votes can elect 4 non-Muslims, who would be dependent upon them and the Europeans with their excess of 35 votes would be able to elect 3 non-Europeans who would be dependent upon them.

(2) The Scheduled Castes with a shortage of 69 votes will be able to elect only 13 members on the stock of their own votes and for 7 seats they will have to depend upon Hindu, Muslim or European voters. The Indian Christians with a shortage of 56 votes will be able to elect only 2 seats on the stock of their own voters. For the rest of the 5 seats they will have to depend upon Hindu, Muslim or European voters. Similarly, the Sikhs with a shortage of 52 will be able to elect only 3 seats on the stock of their own voters. For the rest of the 5 seats they will have to depend upon Hindu, Muslim or European voters.

Such is the position. It is evident that the excess representation granted to the smaller minorities is only an eye-wash. Their representation is made so dependent that in no sense can it be called a real representation.

Let me now take the second question. Is the rule of decision adopted by the Sapru Committee for the Constituent Assembly a safe rule? The Cripps proposal had adopted the rule of bare majority. This was an absurd proposition which no sensible man could have proposed. I know of no case where questions relating to the Constitution were left to be decided by a simple majority.

The Cripps proposals sought to excuse the adoption of the majority rule on the ground that there was to be a further provision for safeguarding the interest of the minorities. The provision was to take the form of a Treaty between the British Crown and the Indian Constituent Assembly, before Parliament was to relinquish its sovereignty and make India free.

The proposal of a Treaty would have had some sense if the Treaty was to override the Constitution. But the proposal was impossible as under the Cripps scheme India was free to become a Dominion or an Independent country as she pleased. For once India became a Dominion it would *ipso facto* acquire all the legal power necessary to pass an enactment declaring that the Treaty shall not override the Constitution. In that case, the Treaty would have been no better than a calendar which members of the minorities might, if they wished, hang on the walls of their houses. This was exactly what happened to the Irish Treaty. The Irish Treaty continued to override the Irish Constitution so long as Ireland was not a Dominion. By the moment Ireland became a Dominion the over-riding power of the Treaty was taken away by a short and simple enactment of the Parliament of the Irish Free State and the British Parliament did nothing, for it knew that Ireland was a Dominion and, therefore, it could do nothing. How so absurd a provision came to be put forth by so eminent a person to assure the minorities, I am unable to understand.

The provisions contained in the Sapru proposals appear to be an improvement. But are they really an improvement? I am sure they are not. A three-fourths majority of 160 means that a view to prevail must have the support of 120 members. Before accepting this as an improvement, one has to have some idea as to how this group of 120 is likely to be formed. If the Hindus and the Muslims combine, they will together make up 102, and will need only 18 more to make up 120. Most of the special seats and a few more from others may easily fall into the hands of this combine. If this happens the decision of the Assembly will obviously be an imposition upon the Scheduled Castes, the Sikhs, the Indian Christians etc. Similarly, if the Muslims are isolated the decision will not be a joint decision but an imposition upon the Muslims by non-Muslims. These possibilities of permutation and combination for the purpose of check mating or out manoeuvring of some communities by others, I am sorry to say, have not been taken into consideration by the Sapru Committee. There would have been some safety, if the Sapru Committee had provided that the three-fourths majority shall at least include 50 per cent of each element.

Following upon the procedure adopted in the making of the Constitution of the United States, the Sapru Committee could have added a further provision for the ratification at any rate of the communal part of the decision of the Assembly by the representatives of the minorities outside the Assembly. None of these provisions finds a place in the plan of the Constituent Assembly as designed by the Sapru Committee. Consequently the Constituent Assembly has become a snare.

There are many other arguments against the plan of a Constituent Assembly, I may mention one, which I confess has influenced me greatly. When I read the history of the Union between Scotland and England, I was shocked at the corruption and bribery that was practised to win the consent of the Scottish Parliament. The whole of the Scottish Parliament was bought. The chances of corruption and bribery being used in the Indian Constituent Assembly to buy over Members to support decisions desired by interested groups are very real. Their effects, I am sure, cannot be overlooked. If this happens, it will not only make mockery of the Constituent Assembly but I feel quite certain that any attempt made to enforce its decision will result in a civil war. It is my considered opinion that the proposal of Constituent Assembly is more dangerous than profitable and should not be entertained.

II. NECESSITY OF A NEW APPROACH

I shall be asked that if the Constituent Assembly is not the correct approach. What is the alternative? I know I shall be confronted with such a question. But I am confident in my view that if the Communal Question has become difficult of solution, it is not because it is insoluble, nor because we had not yet employed the machinery of Constituent Assembly. It has become insoluble because the approach to it is fundamentally wrong. The defect in the present approach is that it proceeds by methods, instead of by principles. The principle is that there is no principle. There is only a series of methods. If one method fails another is tried. It is this swing from one method to another which has made the Communal Problem a jigsaw puzzle. There being no principle, there is no guide to tell why a particular method has failed. There being no principle, there is no assurance that the new method will succeed.

The attempts at the solution of the Communal Problem are either in the nature of coward's plan to cow-tow to the bully or of bully's plan to dictate to the weak. Whenever a community grows powerful and demands certain political advantages, concessions are made to it to win its goodwill. There is no judicial examination of its claim; no judgment on merits. The result is that there are no limits to demands and there are no limits to concessions.

A start is made with a demand for separate electorate for a minority. It is granted. It is followed by a demand for a separate electorate for a community irrespective of the fact whether it is a minority or majority. That is granted. A demand is made for separate representation on a population basis. That is conceded. Next, a claim is made for weightage in representation. That is granted. It is followed by a demand for statutory majority over other minorities with the right for the majority to retain separate electorates. This is granted. This is followed by a demand that the majority rule of another community is intolerable, and, therefore, without prejudice to its rights to maintain majority rule over other minorities, the majority of the offending community should be reduced to equality. Nothing can be made absurd that this policy of eternal appeasement. It is a policy of limitless demand followed by endless appeasement.

Frankly, I don't blame the community that indulges in this strategy. It indulges in it because it has found that it pays. It pursues it because there are no principles to fix the limits and it believes that more could be legitimately asked and would be easily given. On the other hand, there is a community—economically poor, socially degraded, educationally backward and which is exploited, oppressed and tyrannized without shame and without remorse, disowned by society, unowned by Government and which has no security for protection and no guarantee for justice, fairplay and equal opportunity. Such a community is told that it can have no safeguards, not because it has no case for safeguards, but only because the bully on whom the bill of rights is presented thinks that because the community is not politically organized to have sanctions behind its demand he can successfully bluff.

All this differential treatment is due to the fact that there are no principles, which are accepted as authoritative and binding on those who are parties to the Communal question. The absence of principles has another deleterious effect. It has made impossible for public opinion to play its part. The public only knows methods, and notes that one method has failed, another is being suggested. It does not know why one method has failed and why another is said to be likely to succeed. The result is that the public, instead of being mobilized to force obstinate and recalcitrant parties to see sense and reason, are only witnessing the discussions of Communal Questions whenever they take place as mere shows.

IV. PROPOSALS FOR SOLUTION OF THE COMMUNAL PROBLEM

The Communal Problem raises three questions:

(1) The question of representation in the Legislature;
(2) The question of representation in the Executive; and
(3) The question of representation in the Services.

(1) Representation in Public Services

To take the last question first. This can hardly be said to be a subject of controversy. The principle that all communities should be represented in the Public Services in a prescribed proportion and no single community should be allowed to have a monopoly has been accepted by the Government of India. This principle has been embodied in the Government of India Resolutions of 1934 and 1943 and rules to carry it out have been laid down. It has even prescribed that any appointment made contrary to the rules shall be deemed to be null and void.

All that is necessary is to convert administrative practice into statutory obligation. This can be done by adding a Schedule to the Government of India Act, which will include the provisions contained in these Resolutions and similar provisions for the different Provinces and make the Schedule a part of the Law of the Constitution.

(2) Representation in the Executive

This question raises three points:

(A) The quantum of representation in the Executive;
(B) The nature of the Executive;
(C) The method of filling the places in the Executive.

(A) Quantum of Representation

For the solution of this question, the principle which should be adopted is that the representation of the Hindus, the Muslims and the Scheduled Castes should be equal to the quantum of their representation in the Legislature.

With regard to the other minorities such as the Sikhs, Indian Christians and Anglo-Indians, it is difficult to give them representation in the Executive in strict proportion to their representation in the Legislature. This difficulty arises largely from the smallness of their numbers. If they are to get representation in the Executive in exact proportion to their numbers, the Executive would have to be enlarged to a fantastic degree. All that can be done, therefore, is to reserve a seat or two for them in the Cabinet for their representation and to establish a convention that they will get a fair portion of representation in the corps of Parliamentary Secretaries that will have to be raised, when the new Constitution comes into existence.

(B) Nature of the Executive

In the Constitution of the Executive, I would propose the adoption of following principles:

(i) It must be recognized that in a country like India, where there is a perpetual antipathy between the majority and the minorities, and on which account the danger of communal discrimination by majority against minorities forms an ever-present menace to the minorities, the executive power assumes far greater importance than the legislative power.

(ii) In view of (i) above, the system under which a party which has secured a majority at the poll is deemed entitled to form a Government on the presumption that it has the confidence of the majority is untenable in Indian conditions. The majority in India is a communal majority and not a political majority. That being the difference, the presumption that arises in England cannot be regarded as a valid presumption in the conditions of India.

(iii) The Executive should cease to be a Committee of the majority party in the Legislature. It should be so constituted that it will have its mandate not only from the majority but also from the minorities in the Legislature.

(iv) The Executive should be non-Parliamentary in the sense that it shall not be removable before the term of the Legislature.

(v) The Executive should be Parliamentary in the sense that the members of the Executive shall be chosen from the members of the Legislature and shall have the right to sit in the House, speak, vote and answer questions.

(C) Method of Filling Places

In this connection, I would propose the adoption of the following principles:-

(i) The Prime Minister as the Executive Head of the Government should have the confidence of the whole House.

(ii) The person representing a particular minority in the Cabinet should have the confidence of the members of his community in the Legislature.

(iii) A member of the Cabinet shall not be liable to be removed except on impeachment by the House on the ground of corruption or treason.

Following these principles, my proposal is that the Prime Minister and the members of the Cabinet from the majority community should be elected by the whole House by a single transferable vote and that the representatives of the different Minorities in the Cabinet should be elected by a single transferable vote of the members of each minority community in the Legislature.

(3) REPRESENTATION IN THE LEGISLATURE

This is the most difficult question. All other questions depend upon the solution of this question. It raises two points:

(A) The quantum of representation; and

(B) The nature of the electorate.

(A) Quantum of Representation

I would first put forth my proposals and then explain the principles on which they are based...

V. PRINCIPLES UNDERLYING THE PROPOSALS

I may now proceed to state the principles on which this distribution has been made. They are:

(1) Majority Rule is untenable in theory and unjustifiable in practice. A majority community may be conceded a relative majority of representation but it can never claim an absolute majority.
(2) The relative majority of representation given to a majority community in the legislature should not be so large as to enable the majority to establish its rule with the help of the smallest minorities.
(3) The distribution of seats should be so made that a combination of the majority and one of the major minorities should not give the combine such a majority as to make them impervious to the interest of the minorities.
(4) The distribution should be so made that if all the minorities combine they could, without depending on the majority, form a Government of their own.
(5) The weightage taken from the majority should be distributed among the minorities in inverse proportion to their social standing, economic position and educational condition so that a minority which is large and which has a better social, educational and economic standing gets a lesser amount of weightage than a minority whose numbers are less and whose educational, economic and social position is inferior to that of the others.

If I may say so, the representation is a balanced representation. No one community is placed in a position to dominate others by reason of its numbers. The Muslim objection to the Hindu majority and the Hindu and Sikh objections to the Muslim majority are completely eliminated, both in the Central as well as in the Provinces.

NATURE OF THE ELECTORATE

With regard to the question of electorates the following propositions should be accepted:

(1) Joint-electorate or separate electorate is a matter of machinery for achieving a given purpose. It is not a matter of principle.
(2) The purpose is to enable a minority to select candidates to the Legislature who will be real and not nominal representatives of the minority.

(3) While separate electorate gives an absolute guarantee to the minority, that its representatives will be no other except those who enjoy its confidence, a system of joint-electorates which will give equal protection to the minorities should not be overlooked.

(4) A four-member constituency, with a right to the minorities to have a double vote and requiring a minimum percentage of minority votes, may be considered as a possible substitute.

MATTERS NOT COVERED

(1) Questions of Special Safeguards

There are other demands made on behalf of particular minorities such as:-

(a) Provision of a Statutory Officer to report on the condition of minorities.
(b) Statutory provision of State aid for education, and
(c) Statutory provision for land settlement. But they are not of a communal character. I do not, therefore, wish to enlarge upon them here.

(2) Aboriginal Tribes

It will be obvious that my proposals do not cover the Aboriginal Tribes, although they are larger in number than the Sikhs, Anglo-Indians, Indian Christians and Parsees. I may state the reasons why I have omitted them from my scheme. The Aboriginal Tribes have not as yet developed any political sense to make the best use of their political opportunities and they may easily become mere instruments in the hands either of a majority or a minority and thereby disturb the balance without doing any good to themselves. In the present stage of their development, it seems to me that the proper thing to do for these backward communities is to establish a Statutory Commission to administer what are now called the "Excluded Areas" on the same basis as was done in the case of the South African Constitution. Every Province in which these "Excluded Areas" are situated should be compelled to make an annual contribution of a prescribed amount for the administration of these areas.

(3) Indian States

It will also be noticed that my proposals do not include the Indian States. I am not opposed to the Indian States provided the terms and conditions of inclusion are such that:

(a) The dichotomy of divided sovereignty between British India and Indian States is completely done away with;

(b) The judicial and political boundaries which separate British India from Indian States will disappear, that there will be no such entities as British or Indian States and in their place there will be only one entity, namely, India; and
(c) The terms and conditions of inclusion do not prevent India from having full and plenary powers of a Dominion. I have worked out a scheme for the fusion of the Indian States and British India, which will permit the realization of these objects. I do not wish to overburden this address with the details of the plan. For the moment, it is better if British India marches to her goal without complicating its progress by an entanglement with the Indian States.

PAKISTAN IN THE LIGHT OF PROPOSALS

My proposals are for an United India. They are made in the hope that the Muslims will accept them in preference to Pakistan as providing better security than Pakistan does. I am not against Pakistan. I believe it is founded on principle of self-determination, which it is now too late to question. I am prepared to give them the benefit of the principle, on condition that the Muslims do not deny the benefit of the principles to the non-Muslim residents of the area. But I believe I am entitled to draw the attention of the Muslims to another and a better plan of security. I claim that my plan is better than the plan of Pakistan. Let me state the points which tell in favour of my plan. They are:-

(1) Under my proposal the danger of a communal majority which is the basis of Pakistan is removed.
(2) Under my proposal the weightage at present enjoyed by the Muslims is not disturbed.
(3) The position of Muslims in the non-Pakistan Provinces is greatly strengthened by an increase in their representation, which they may not get if Pakistan comes, and which will leave them in a more helpless condition than they are in at present.

A WORD TO HINDUS

Much of the difficulty over the Communal Question is due to the insistence of the Hindus that the rule of majority is sacrosanct and that it must be maintained at all costs. The Hindu does not seem to be aware of the fact that there is another rule, which is also operative in fields where important disputes between individual and nations arise and that rule is a rule of unanimity. If he will take the trouble to examine the position he will realize that such a rule is not a fiction, but it does exist. Let him take the Jury system. In the jury trial, the principle is unanimity. The decision is binding upon the judge only if the verdict of the jury is unanimous. Let him take another illustration that of the League of Nations. What was the rule for decisions in the League of Nations? The rule was a rule of unanimity. It is obvious that if the principle of unanimity was accepted by the Hindus as a rule of decision in the Legislature and in the Executive there would be no such thing as a Communal Problem in India.

One may well ask the Hindu that if he is not prepared to concede Constitutional safeguards to the minorities, is he prepared to agree to the rule of unanimity. Unfortunately, he is not prepared to accept either.

About the rule of majority, the Hindu is not prepared to admit any limitations. The majority he wants is an absolute majority. He will not be satisfied with relative majority. He should consider whether his insistence on absolute majority is fair proposition, which political philosophers can accept. He is not aware that even the Constitution of the United States does not lend support to the absolutistic rule of majority rule on which the Hindu has been insisting upon.

Let me illustrate the point from the Constitution of the United States. Take the clause embodying Fundamental Rights. What does that clause mean? It means that matters included in Fundamental Rights are of such supreme concern that a mere majority rule is not enough to interfere with them. Take another illustration also from the Constitution of the United States. The Constitution says that no part of the Constitution shall be altered unless the proposition is carried by three-fourths majority and ratified by the States. What does this show? It shows that the United States Constitution recognizes for certain purposes mere majority rule is not competent.

All these cases are, of course, familiar to many a Hindu. The pity of it is he does not read from them the correct lesson. If he did, he would realize that the rule of the majority rule is not as sacrosanct a principle as he thinks it is. The majority rule is not accepted as a principle but is tolerated as a rule. I might also state why it is tolerated. It is tolerated for two reasons; one because the majority is always a political majority, and second, because the decision of a political majority accepts and absorbs so much of the point of view of the minority that the minority does not care to rebel against the decision.

In India, the majority is not a political majority. In India the majority is born; it is not made. That is the difference between a communal majority and a political majority. A political majority is not a fixed or a permanent majority. It is a majority which is always made, unmade and remade. A communal majority is a permanent majority fixed in its attitude. One can destroy it, but one cannot transform it. If there is so much objection to a political majority, how very fatal must be the objection to a communal majority?

It may be open to the Hindus to ask Mr Jinnah why in 1930 when he formulated his fourteen points he insisted upon the principle of majority rule to such an extent that one of the fourteen points stipulated that in granting weightage, limits should be placed whereby a majority shall be reduced to a minority or equality. It may be open to the Hindus to ask Mr Jinnah, if he is in favour of a Muslim majority in

Muslim Provinces, why he is opposed to a Hindu Majority in the Centre? The Hindu must, however, realize that these posers may lead to the conclusion that Mr Jinnah's position is inconsistent. They cannot lead to the affirmation of the principle of majority rule.

The abandonment of the principle of majority rule in politics cannot affect the Hindus very much in other walks of life. As an element in social life they will remain a majority. They will have the monopoly of trade and business which they enjoy. They will have the monopoly of the property which they have. My proposals do not ask the Hindus to accept the principle of unanimity. My proposals do not ask the Hindus to abandon the principle of majority rule. All I am asking them is to be satisfied with a relative majority. Is it too much for them to concede this.

Without making any such sacrifice, the Hindu majority is not justified in representing to the outside world that the minorities are holding up India's freedom. This false propaganda will not pay. For, the minorities are doing nothing of the kind. They are prepared to accept freedom and the dangers in which they likely to be involved; provided they granted satisfactory safeguards. This gesture of the minorities is not to be treated as a matter for which Hindus need not be grateful. It may well be contrasted with what happened in Ireland. Mr Redmond, the leader of the Irish Nationalist, once told Carson, the leader of Ulster, "Consent to United Ireland. Ask for any safeguard and they shall be granted to you." He is reported to have turned round and said, "Damn your safeguards; we don't want to be ruled by you." The minorities in India have not said that. They are ready to be satisfied with safeguards. I ask the Hindus, "Is this not worth a mass? I am sure it is."

VI. CONCLUSION

These are some of the proposals I have had in mind for the solution of the Communal Problem. They do not commit the All-India Scheduled Castes Federation. They do not even commit me. In putting them forth, I am doing nothing more than exploring a new way. My emphasis is more on the principle I have enunciated than on the actual proposals. If the principles are accepted then I am sure the solution of the Communal Question will not be as baffling as it has been in the past.

The problem of solving the Indian deadlock is not easy. I remember reading a historian describing the condition of Germany before the Confederation of 1867 as one of 'Divinely Ordained Confusion'. Whether that was true of Germany or not, it seems to me that they form a very accurate description of the present conditions of India. Germany did get out of this confusion, if not at one stroke, at least by successive stages until just before the war she became a unified people, unified in mind, unified in outlook and unified by belief in a common destiny.

India has not so far succeeded in evolving order out of her confusion. It is not that she had no opportunities to do so. In fact, there have been quite a number. The first opportunity came in 1927 when Lord Birkenhead gave a challenge to Indians asking them to produce a Constitution for India. That challenge was taken up. A committee was formed to frame a Constitution. A Constitution was produced and was known as 'The Nehru Constitution'. It was, however, not accepted by Indians and was buried without remorse. A second opportunity presented itself to Indians in 1930 when they assembled at the Round Table Conference. There again, Indians failed to play their part and write out their own Constitution. A third attempt is the one recently made by the Sapru Committee. The proposals of this Committee too have fallen flat.

There is neither enthusiasm nor optimism left to indulge in another attempt. One is pursued by a sense of fatality, which suggests that as every attempt is doomed to failure, none need be made. At the same time, I feel that no Indian ought to be so down-hearted or so callous as to let the deadlock stink, as thought it was a dead dog, and say that he is prepared to do nothing more than be a mere witness to the political dog-fight that is going on in this country.

The failures of the past need not daunt anybody. They do not daunt me. For, I have a feeling that though it is true that all attempts to reach an agreement on the communal question have failed, the failure have been due not so much to any inherent fault of the Indians as they have been due to a wrong approach. I feel confident that my proposals, if considered dispassionately, should be found acceptable. They constitute a new approach and as such I commend them to my countrymen.

Before I conclude, I must, however, warn my critics that they may be able to amend my proposals in some respect; but it will not be easy to reject them. If they do reject them, the first thing they shall have to do is to controvert the principles on which they are based.

CHAPTER THIRTY FOUR

Provincial Elections 1945-46

IN JUNE 1945, the Viceroy Lord Wavell announced (what came to be called later) the Wavell Plan, according to which other prominent leaders like Nehru, Patel and others were finally released from jails, and a Conference at Simla was convened in the last week of June, 1945.

In the Simla Conference, the Caste Hindus were represented by the then Congress President Maulana Azad while the Muslims were represented by Jinnah. Being a Member of Viceroy's Executive Council, Dr Ambedkar could not represent the Scheduled Castes, which was done by N Shivraj. Through his colleague N Shivraj, Dr Ambedkar demanded three seats in the Central Executive of the Interim Ministry to be formed. This was deemed to be justified on the basis of population and in view of the fact that Muslims were going to get five seats. The Conference could not arrive at any decision, apparently because the Congress insisted on Muslim nominees of its own.[110]

★ ★ ★

In July 1945, general elections were held in Britain and the Labour Party dislodged the Tories and came to power with Clement Attlee as the Prime Minister. In August 1945, Lord Wavell went to London for consultation, returned to India in mid-September 1945 and announced general elections in India.

★ ★ ★

The elections of 1945-46 were meant to serve two purposes: (a) renewal of the Provincial Assemblies, first time since the elections of 1937; and (b) endowing the Country with a Constituent Assembly. It was also going to be the first election

110. Keer, Dhananjay, op cit, pp 372.

which Dr Ambedkar's Scheduled Caste Federation (SCF) was fighting as a party of Depressed Classes on an all-India basis.

The election campaigns started gathering momentum in October, 1945. The Congress Party entered the electoral arena with the slogan: "Quit India" whereas the Muslim League came up with the slogan: "Pakistan or Perish". Both parties had big-time funding and electorate machinery. The Scheduled Caste Federation (SCF) led by Dr Ambedkar had neither the electioneering machinery nor adequate funding.

★ ★ ★

Dr Ambedkar inaugurated his election campaign in Pune (October 2-4, 1945). In his inaugural speech, Dr Ambedkar emphasized that the Scheduled Castes must get their share in the political power and that the then forthcoming election was the question of life and death for the Scheduled Castes. This extremely important speech exemplifies Dr Ambedkar's election strategy.[111] Here are some excerpts from the speech:

> The system of elections has begun since 1892. Gradually, Hindus, Muslims and Christians participated according to their capacity. Surprisingly, the Untouchables did not have right to vote till 1935. That means up to 1935, the Untouchables did not know anything about the elections. In 1937, the Untouchables won 15 out of 15 seats in Bombay Assembly. Congress won two of our seats. We also defeated two of their candidates and won their two seats, equating the tally. Congress had to be satisfied with a gain of big zero. The community which did not know anything about politics had won the elections in the very first opportunity in 1937. This is not a simple achievement....
>
> Congress is in politics for last about 50-60 years. It should introspect what it has achieved during all those years.... Congress had made several lofty promises; how many of them have they fulfilled? Because Congress has now remained the party of Hindus only; Muslims have left Congress. Christians have left, Parsis also have separated and we are already separate!
>
> I will take a short review of the performance of Congress just to enlighten the Hindus. If somebody asks me to tell in one or two words what is the achievement of Congress, then I would say, 'Defeat at every step'. Whenever Congress roared like a lion, every time it had to duck itself. Initially, Mr Gandhi was very fierce. His people would disobey the law, destroy civic life and would go to jails. This was the politics of Mr Gandhi. Mr Gandhi sort of gave a burning torch in the hands of his followers. And in 1921, they burnt one police *chowki*. Mr Gandhi got frightened and he abandoned those methods. He went to the Round Table Conference in 1931. After his return he was jailed.... He felt so much harassed in the jail that desperate Mr Gandhi wrote a letter to the Viceroy Willingdon for his release. But the Viceroy did not budge despite several letters from Mr Gandhi. Lastly, Mr Gandhi requested his old friend General

---

111. Marathi Speech. For English Summary, see *Ambedkar Speaks*, op cit, Vol.III, pp.326-30.

Stamstus to intervene. Then, General Stamstus wrote a letter to the Viceroy Willingdon. Thus, after lots of pleading, Mr Gandhi got himself released from the jail.

Lokmanya Tilak would fight for his demands and whatever is achieved he would accept and continue his struggle for the remaining demands. Mr Gandhi's principle was 'Emperor's difficulty is our opportunity'. Congress adopted this objective. The World War started in 1939. For three years from 1939 to 1941, Congress did nothing. For half of 1942, Congress sat quiet and in August 1942, they passed a resolution 'Quit India (*Chale Jao*)'. This slogan was written on each and every house. Now, by just writing a slogan '(*Chale Jao*)' on the door, if the tenant vacates the house then nobody will be required to go to the court. This resolution was passed at 10 o'clock on August 8, 1942 and by 11o' clock all the Congress leaders were put into jail. And those who were not in jail, they went on rampage throughout the country. They burnt courts, buildings, shops, looted the markets and did all those things. Whose property they have damaged? Was there any loss to the British Government? Was there any loss to the Englishman? Now, this entire loss was of poor public of India....

Now, what happened at Simla Conference in 1945? It was a rule in the Assembly that whenever the Viceroy would read any proposal all of us should stand up. But leaders of the Congress would not follow that. They used to say that we do not recognize the Viceroy and, therefore, we will not stand up in front of him. But what happened in Simla Conference? The moment the Viceroy declared (June 1945), all the Congress leaders unashamedly ran to Simla by whatever mode they could. They made a big crowd in Simla. The same Congressmen who used to say that they do not recognize the Viceroy went to his house in Simla.

Such is Mr Gandhi's style of politics. This is politics of the defeated. The Congress people are the failed kids of politics. Congress has such a huge amount of money that they can do whatever they like. But, how has it been utilized? What has been the use of so much sacrifices made by the Hindus? What has been the use of so much sacrifices made at the instances of Mr Gandhi? The fellow who could not achieve anything despite all the support of people and all the favorable conditions in my opinion is not fit for leadership....

When the Congress was established, its founders had understood well the importance of unity of all. Therefore, you will observe initially there were people from all the religions—Hindu, Muslims, Christians, Parsis, etc. and also of all the Castes. Therefore, everybody was kind about Congress.

Mr Gandhi took over the Congress in 1920. Since then barring Maulana Azad all the leaders of Congress are Hindus. There are only two Muslims on its Working Committee. This country has now come to such a difficult passé that the differences of Castes have assumed political importance. So, the differences between the Caste have now got company of political differences....

I have been repeatedly telling you that unless we get political power, there cannot be our social and religious emancipation. We must become partners in the power that is to be received by this country if we want social equality and independence; if we want to live with dignity, and if we want to progress. Political power is very effective weapon. We should worship this weapon like a God. It is possible to obtain this weapon in the next elections. Therefore, the forthcoming election is the question of life and death for us. In this war of life and death, we must win. We should make serious preparation to win this war. And we should start these preparations right now.

Presently there are 15 Ministers to look after the affairs of our country. I am one of those 15 Ministers.... I am there only for the last two years, and what I have achieved for you during those two years? I could convince the Government to grant Rs 3 lakh for the education of Untouchables, with which at least 300 students will get education every year. This time 30 students are being sent to foreign countries for higher education. And every year thereafter, 15 students will be sent.... The batch of 30 students this year include one *Bhangi*, one *Mang* and so many *Chamars*. What I am trying to tell you is that every Caste amongst the Untouchables is going to get benefit of this scheme of higher education to the Scheduled Castes.

The Muslims have got reservation of 25 per cent in Provincial services as well as in Central services. Similarly, a certain percentage of posts is reserved for the Christians, Sikhs and Anglo-Indians. But nobody has thought about the Scheduled Castes. What arrangement had been made for us? We were not given even a small portion of the share of reservation, but now I have got it done. Now, the Scheduled Castes will have reservation of 8.33 per cent. After I joined the Government many of our people have reached to higher positions....

I am not telling this for self-aggrandizement or to boast about myself. I am telling this just to show you what we can do if we get the political power. Had there been one more Minister, we would have done much more. It will not be possible to achieve anything without political power and, therefore, we must strive to get it. Politics should be the life-blood of the Scheduled Castes. We have been living rotten life for thousands of years and we have lost everything only because we had no political power. We must achieve this power. Political presence and power is a wonderful weapon. We must use it against our enemies.

We have constituted one Parliamentary Board for the forthcoming elections. There will be five members on this Board who will select candidates for the election. There will be certain rules based on which the Board will select the candidates. We must give our votes to elect such candidates only. If anybody thinks that he alone can do something in the Assembly it will be his sheer ignorance. Only organized parties can make a difference in the Assembly....

You should take a pledge to elect only those candidates which are selected by our Parliamentary Board.

I strongly believed earlier that students should not participate in the politics because if they participate in the politics they will neglect their studies and spoil their life. But this time I want to make an exception to this rule. The students should go and explain to our people who are mostly illiterate to enroll themselves in the voting list. They should also explain to them about the importance of this election.

This election is going to be memorable in the history of India, because the new Constitution is going to be drafted after the elections. Whatever Constitutional Provisions are made by the Constituent Assembly set up after this election will be long lasting. We should have our eyes on those provisions in the future Constitution. We have declared our objectives through various resolutions we have so far passed. If we are not vigilant at this time, we will lose everything. This '*Swaraj*' what is being demanded will be a '*brutal raj*' for us.

I have done my duty of showing you right path at the right time. Now, I will have to see to what extent you stand up to the call of your duty. I believe that you will do your duty, very well.

★ ★ ★

Dr Ambedkar travelled all over the country and made forceful speeches with passionate appeals. His election speeches in today's Maharashtra (Mumbai, Pune, Nashik, Manmad, Ahmednagar, Khandesh, Nagpur, Solapur, Satara), Ahmedabad and Madras received a lot of enthusiastic response.

The election results (March 1946), however, were most disappointing for Dr Ambedkar. The election results revealed a stark division along religious lines. The Congress swept the general constituencies, while the Muslim League captured nearly all the Muslim seats. The Scheduled Caste Federation (SCF) fared badly, gaining only two seats in the Provincial Assemblies—one in Bengal and the other in the Central Provinces and Berar. This was a major setback to Dr Ambedkar.[112]

---

112. According to Jaffrelot, "This setback partly reflected the voting system. In the primaries in which only Untouchables voted, the SCF gained more votes than the Congress in the Presidencies of Madras and Bombay and in the Central Provinces. But these good results could not translate into a commensurate number of seats because of the electoral system. The situation in the United Provinces was especially revealing of the distortions inherent in the electoral system. There twenty seats were reserved for Scheduled Castes, including four urban constituencies, which were the only ones the SCF contested. In the primaries, nine of the party's candidates were successful as against four for Congress, but in the second round the latter won all the seats, thanks to the support of non-Dalit votes. The most dramatic result occurred in Agra, where four SCF candidates polled 46.39 per cent of valid votes as against to 27.1 per cent for four Congress candidates."

CHAPTER THIRTY FIVE

Cabinet Mission

BY EARLY 1946, the British Government realized that it was no longer possible for them to keep India in bondage. This became clear when on March 15, 1946 the then Prime Minister Clement Attlee explicitly acknowledged India's right to attain full Independence within or even without the British Commonwealth. The British Prime Minister also said that he would not allow a minority to place their veto on the advance of the majority.

Following this historic announcement, a British Cabinet Mission arrived in India on March 24, 1946. The Cabinet Mission held discussions with a wide range of Indian leaders including Dr Ambedkar.

The British Cabinet Mission toIndia aimed to discuss and plan for the transfer of power from the British Government to Indian leadership, providing India with Independence. Formulated at the initiative of Clement Attlee, the Prime Minister of Britain, the Mission consisted of three British Cabinet Ministers; Lord Pethick Lawrence, the Secretary of State for India, Sir Stafford Cripps, and AV Alexander. Lord Wavell, the Viceroy of India, did not participate.

The Mission's objectives were:

(1) Hold preparatory discussions with elected representatives of British India and the Indian States in order to secure agreement as to the method of framing the Constitution;
(2) Set up a Constituent Assembly; and
(3) Set up an Executive Council with the support of the main Indian parties.

Dr Ambedkar met the Cabinet Mission on April 5, 1946 and presented the case for the Depressed Classes, strongly repudiating the accusation that they were putting a veto on India's political advancement. Dr Ambedkar, in fact, submitted a detailed Memorandum to the Cabinet Mission demanding the inclusion of several safeguards in the new Constitution including separate electorates, adequate representation in the Central and Provincial Legislatures and in the Central and Provincial Executives, in the Public Services and on the Public Service Commissions, besides providing earmarked sums for the Scheduled Castes.

The Minutes of the Meeting (April 5, 1946) between Dr Ambedkar and the Cabinet Mission are summarized as under:

> Dr Ambedkar said that he had little to add to the memorandum of which copies had been supplied to the delegation, giving the text of the resolution passed by the Working Committee of the All-India Scheduled Castes Federation at its meeting on April 2nd. Paragraph 5 of this memorandum contained a list of safeguards, which were largely designed to secure to the Scheduled Castes adequate representation in Government and the Public Services. The Federation would never accept any Constitution in which these were not included.

On the question of Pakistan, Dr Ambedkar doubted whether Muslims as a whole would really be benefited by the new State. So many of them would have to remain in Hindustan and would be unwilling or unable to migrate. He wondered whether Pakistan was a permanent or a passing mood on the part of the Muslims. Quite probably it would pass. But it was impossible to wait and see and the Muslim demand had grown so strong that it had become necessary to meet it somehow.

In reply to an inquiry on the method of representation of the Scheduled Castes in the Constituent Assembly, Dr Ambedkar said that he did not want a Constituent Assembly at all. It would be dominated by the Caste Hindus, and the Scheduled Caste members would be no more than a small minority, which would always be outvoted even if a three-quarters or a two-thirds majority were required for the Assembly's decisions. All the assurances of protection, which His Majesty's Government had given to the minorities, would go by the board. Moreover, there would be an immense amount of corruption in the Assembly—members would be bought over to vote against the interests of their communities.

His own proposal was that the tasks envisaged for the Constituent Assembly should be divided into two classes, viz:

(a) Constitutional questions properly so-called, e.g. the relations between the Legislature and the Executive and their respective composition and functions. There was no great controversy about these matters, which did not excite the emotions. To deal with them was beyond the mental capacity of the type of man whom Provincial Assemblies might be expected to send up, and was a job for experts.
(b) Communal questions.

Questions under the first of these headings should be referred to a commission presided over by an eminent constitutional lawyer from Great Britain or the USA. The other members should be two Indian experts and one representative each of the Hindu and Muslim communities. The terms of reference of the Commission should be the Government of India Act of 1935 and they should be required to recommend what changes should be made in the Act as it stood.

Questions under (b) should be referred to a conference of the leaders of the different communities. If the conference failed to arrive at an agreed solution, His Majesty's Government would have to make an award. This would no doubt be accepted if it were reasonable.

Dr Ambedkar then described the position of the Scheduled Castes today. It was estimated that they numbered sixty million, though this figure was probably inaccurate; firstly, because there were no reliable statistics for the States and, secondly, because the census had become mixed up with politics. All these people were subject to very serious disabilities. In the villages they were without land and were virtually the slaves of the Caste Hindus. As an instance of the power of the latter, he said that when some Untouchables had escaped from their villages to take up well-paid work under the Military authorities, the Caste Hindus had managed to force them back to work for them. Owing to the preponderance of Caste Hindus in the Subordinate Police and Revenue Services the Government was already, from the point of view of the Untouchables, not a British but a Hindu one. An example had been the recent arrest of 100 of their boys in Bombay for throwing stones at Mr Gandhi, when the police had also taken the opportunity to do considerable damage in the Scheduled Caste area of the city.

Politically, although the Scheduled Castes like the other communities had been granted separate electorates in 1932, they had virtually been deprived of them by the Poona Pact. Instead, they had got the system of double elections which meant that in the second election, in which all the Hindus voted, the Caste Hindus could nullify the result of the first election in which Untouchables were the only voters. He referred to the figures appended to the Working Committee's resolution of April 2 which showed, firstly, that in many cases the Congress Scheduled Caste candidates, though outvoted by the Federation candidates in the primary elections, had beaten them in the final elections; and, secondly, how small was the number of Scheduled Caste voters in comparison with the total of general voters. Even so, Congress had resorted to loot and arson to ensure the success of their candidates—he produced a volume of photographs to show what they had done.

The Central Legislature had been in existence since 1919, yet no questions were ever asked, resolutions moved or anything else done with the object of helping the Scheduled Castes.

In the Indian States the position of the Scheduled Castes was especially bad. There were even certain foods, which they were not allowed to eat. In the representative institutions, which were now being established in certain States, no community had been given separate representation except the Muslims. The Political Department should have taken greater interest in these constitutional experiments, and should have seen to it that the Scheduled Castes were given separate electorates. The Delegation should see the President of the All-India Scheduled Castes States Conference.

The Scheduled Castes had been the earliest source of manpower for the East India Company's army, and so it was with their help that the British had conquered India. They had been the friends of the British ever since. Yet the British had never consciously and deliberately helped them, though since 1892 they had given enormous help to the Muslims.

He thought that if India became independent it would be one of the greatest disasters that could happen. Before they left, the British must ensure that the new constitution guaranteed to the Scheduled Castes the elementary human rights of life, liberty and the pursuit of happiness, and that it restored their separate electorates and gave them the other safeguards which they demanded. At present disillusionment was driving his followers towards terrorism and communism. He was on trial with them for the efficacy of constitutional methods.

Lord Pethick-Lawrence said that up to now Indian politics had been dominated by two issues, the question of winning independence from British rule and the Hindu-Muslim problem. Once these were out of the way party divisions would probably be on economic issues. Surely, the Scheduled Castes would have a better chance of getting their rights by allying themselves with the left wing rather than by relying on the British who were about to hand over power. In reply Dr Ambedkar reiterated that so long as there were joint electorates, Scheduled Caste voters would be so few that Hindu candidates could safely ignore their wishes. Caste Hindus would never support Scheduled Caste candidates. Admittedly under the present system they had to vote for Untouchables in the final elections; but their object in doing so was never to favour their own candidate but merely to outvote the candidate put up by his own Federation. Separate electorates were fundamental, since without them the Scheduled Castes would never have their own representatives.

The Mission held talks with the representatives of the Indian National Congress and the All-India Muslim League, the two largest political parties in the Constituent Assembly of India. The two parties planned to determine a power-sharing arrangement between Hindus and Muslims to prevent a communal dispute, and to determine whether British India would be better-off unified or divided. The Congress party under Gandhiji and Pandit Nehru wanted a strong Central government with more powers compared to the State governments. The All-India Muslim League under Jinnah wanted to keep India united but with political safeguards provided to Muslims such as 'guarantee' of 'parity' in the Legislatures.

On May 14, 1946, Dr Ambedkar wrote a letter to Mr AV Alexander, Member, Cabinet Mission, as a desperate follow-up on behalf of the Scheduled Castes. The letter says:

> It is a pity that your efforts to bring about a settlement between the Congress and the League should have failed. I know you deserve every sympathy, and every gratitude. At the same time, I cannot help saying that the Mission's effort to settle reminds me of an old *Baniya* who being without a son to inherit his wealth married a young girl with

the hope of begetting a heir. The bride conceived but the bridegroom was stricken with a fell-disease. He, however, refused to die without having a look at the baby and would not wait for delivery, which was far off. He was so impatient that he called the doctor, asked him to open the stomach of his wife and let him see whether it was a boy or a girl. The result of the operation was that both the baby and the mother died. If I may say so, the Mission wanted to do very much what the *Baniya* did. You may not be aware but there are many who, like me, feel that the Mission was engaged in bringing about a forced delivery earlier than the natural period of gestation.

To my mind, it is only right to say that the Hindus and the Muslims are today mentally incompetent to decide upon the destiny of this country. Both Hindus and Muslims are just crowds. It must be within your experience that a crowd is less moved by material profit than by a passion collectively shared. It is easier to persuade a mass of men to sacrifice itself collectively than to act upon a cool assessment of advantages. A crowd easily loses all sense of profit and loss. It is moved by motives which may be high or low, genial or barbarous, compassionate or cruel, but is always above or below reason. The common sense of each is lost in the emotion of all. It is easier to persuade a crowd to commit suicide than to accept a legacy. It is not for me to advise you how you should proceed. The Mission has found greater wisdom and higher inspiration in the *Bhangi Basti* and in 10, Aurangazeb Road. I would be the last person to say anything in depreciation of such wisdom and inspiration. But I do think that if the Mission were not to exhibit the 'pathetic spectacle of an old man in a hurry', a phrase used by Chamberlain to describe Gladstone...they will find that they have an easier situation to deal with.

That is a matter for the Mission, for the major parties and those who have put their faith in the major parties. I am concerned in knowing how you propose to deal with the problem of the Untouchables and their demand for constitutional safeguards. In the official statement issued by the Mission on the last day of the Simla talks, it is said that the Mission will announce the next step it proposes to take within a few days after they return to Delhi. Obviously, the eyes of all the Scheduled Castes are turned towards this announcement. What the Mission will do will ultimately decide their fate. The decision of the Mission will either open to the Untouchables the path of life, liberty and pursuit of happiness or it will drive a nail in their coffin. The question being one of life and death, it would not be wrong if I were to engage your attention for a few minutes with the problem of the Untouchables.

The problem of the Untouchables is a formidable one for the Untouchables to face. But fortunately it is simple to understand if only the following facts are borne in mind. The Untouchables are surrounded by a vast mass of Hindu population which is hostile to them and which is not ashamed of committing any inequity or atrocity against them. For a redress of these wrongs which are matters of daily occurrence, the Untouchables have to call in the aid of the administration. What is the character and composition of this administration? To be brief, the administration in India is completely in the hands of the Hindus. It is their monopoly. From top to bottom it is controlled by them. There is no Department which is not dominated by them. They dominate the Police, the Magistracy and the Revenue Services, indeed any and every branch of the administration. The next point to remember is that the Hindus in the administration are not merely non-social, they are positively anti-social and inimical to the Untouchables. Their one aim is to discriminate against the Untouchables and to deny and deprive them not only of the benefits of law, but also of the protection of the law against tyranny and oppression. The result is that the Untouchables are placed between the Hindu population and the Hindu-ridden administration, the one committing wrongs against them and the other protecting the wrong-door instead of the victims.

Against this background, what can *Swaraj* of the Congress variety mean to the Untouchables? It only means one thing, namely, that while today it is only the administration that is in the hands of the Hindus, under *Swaraj* the Legislature and Executive will also be filled with Hindus. It goes without saying that *Swaraj* would aggravate the sufferings of the Untouchables. For, in addition to their having to face an hostile administration, the Untouchables will have to face an hostile or indifferent Legislature, a callous Executive and an administration uncontrolled and unbridled in venom and in harshness in its iniquitous attitude towards the Untouchables. To put it differently, under *Swaraj* of the Congress variety, the Untouchables will have no way of escape from the destiny of degradation which the Hindus and Hinduism have fixed for them.

I hope this will give you some idea as to why the Untouchables have been insisting that the only way by which the Untouchables can prevent this *Swaraj* from becoming a calamity to them is to have their representatives in the Legislature so that they may keep on protesting against wrongs and injustices done to them by the Hindus, to have their representatives in the Executive so that they may make plans for their betterment and to have representatives in the services so that the administration may not be wholly hostile to them. If you accept the justice of the demand of the Untouchables for constitutional safeguards, you will have no difficulty in understanding why the Untouchables want separate electorates. The Untouchables will be a minority in the Legislature. They are destined to remain a minority. They cannot overcome the majority which being communal in its making is, so to say, fixed and pre-ordained. All they can do is to place themselves in a position to be able to determine the terms on which they will be prepared to work with the majority and not be compelled to accept the terms prescribed by the majority, and, secondly, if the majority refuses to work with them and declines to redress their wrongs, they would at least be free to utter their protest against the majority on the floor of the Legislature. How are the Untouchables to maintain their freedom to protest? Only if their representatives in the Legislatures do not owe their election to the votes of the majority. This is the basis of their demand for separate electorates.

No safeguard are going to be of any value to the Untouchables unless the Untouchables get a separate electorate. Separate electorate is the crux of the matter. I have before me a copy of the representation submitted to the Cabinet Mission by three Congress *Harijans* who were interviewed by the Mission on the April 9, 1946. They were no better than the three tailors of Tooly Street who had the audacity to present an address to the Parliament saying: "We the people of England." Apart from this, it is instructive to note that there is no difference between the demands put forth by me on behalf of the Scheduled Castes Federation and the demands put forth by these Congress *Harijans*. The only difference that exists relates to the question of electorates. I do not know how you interpret the demands of the Congress Harijans. They are not really demands. They represent what the Congress is prepared to give to the Untouchables by way of political safeguards. This is not merely my understanding. It is my knowledge. For I have been informed by persons who know the mind of the Congress that if I was prepared to accept joint electorates, the Congress on its part would be quite prepared to concede all other demands of mine. You must be wondering why should the Congress be prepared to concede all the demands of the Scheduled Castes and object only to one, namely, separate electorates. There will be no wonder if you know what game the Congress is playing. It is a very deep game. Realizing that there is no escape from giving the Untouchables some safeguards, the Congress wants to find out some way by which it can make them of no effect. It is in the system of joint electorates that the Congress sees an instrument of making the safeguards of no effect. That is why the Congress is insisting upon joint electorates. For joint electorates means giving the Untouchables office without power. What the Untouchables want is office with power. This, they can only get through separate electorates and that is why they are insisting upon it.

I believe the case in favour of separate electorates for the Scheduled Castes is a cast-iron case. Every other party except the Congress accepts it. The arguments in favour of separate electorates have been set out by me in my letter of May 3, 1946 addressed to Lord Wavell which he must have shown to you and it is, therefore, unnecessary to repeat them here. The question is: What the Mission is going to do with this demand of the Scheduled Castes. Are they going to make the Untouchables free from political yoke of the Hindus? Or, are they going to throw them to the wolves by favouring the system of joint electorates in order to make friends with the Congress and the Hindu majority whom it represents? The Scheduled Castes are entitled to ask His Majesty's Government that before the British abdicate, His Majesty's Government shall make sure that *Swaraj* does not become a strangle hold for the Untouchables.

Allow me to say that the British have a moral responsibility towards the Scheduled Castes. They may have moral responsibilities towards all minorities. But it can never transcend the moral responsibility which rests on them in respect of the Untouchables. It is a pity how few Britishers are aware of it and how fewer are prepared to discharge it. British Rule in India owes its very existence to the help rendered by the Untouchables. Many Britishers think that India was conquered by the Clives, Hastings, Cootes and so on. Nothing can be a greater mistake. India was conquered by an army of Indians and the Indians who formed the army were all Untouchables. British Rule in India would have been impossible if the Untouchables had not helped the British to conquer India. Take the Battle of Plassey which laid the beginning of British Rule or the battle of Kirkee which completed the conquest of India. In both these fateful battles the soldiers who fought for the British were all Untouchables.

What have the British done to these Untouchables who fought for them? It is a shameful story. The first thing they did was to stop their recruitment in the army. A more unkind, more ungrateful and more cruel act can hardly be found in history. In shutting out the Untouchables from the Army, the British took no note that the Untouchables had helped them to establish their rule and had defended it when it was menaced by a powerful combination of native forces in the Mutiny of 1857. Without any consideration as to its effects upon the Untouchables the British by one stroke of the pen deprived them of their source of livelihood and let them fall to their original depth of degradation. Did the British help them in any way to overcome their social disabilities? The answer again must be in the negative. The schools, wells and public places were closed to the Untouchables. It was the duty of the British to see the Untouchables, as citizens, were entitled to be admitted to all institutions maintained out of public funds. But the British did nothing of the kind and what is worst, they justified their inaction by saying that Untouchability was not their creation. It may be that Untouchability was not the creation of the British. But as Government of the day, surely the removal of Untouchability was their responsibility. No Government with any sense of the functions and duties of a Government could have avoided it. What did the British Government do? They refused to touch any question which involved any kind of reform of Hindu society. So far as social reform was concerned, the Untouchables found themselves under a Government distinguished in no vital respect from those native Governments under which they had toiled and suffered, lived and died, through all their weary and forgotten history. From a political standpoint, the change was nominal. The despotism of the Hindus continued as ever before. Far from being curbed by the British High Command, it was pampered. From a social point of view, the British accepted the arrangements as they found them and preserved them faithfully in the manner of the Chinese tailor who, when given an old coat as a pattern, produced with pride an exact replica, rents and patches and all. And what is the result? The result is that though 200 years have elapsed since the establishment of the British Rule in India the Untouchables have remained Untouchables, their wrongs remained unredressed and their progress hampered at every stage. Indeed, if the British Rule has achieved anything in India it is to strengthen and reinvigorate Brahmanism which is the inveterate enemy of the Untouchables and which is the parent of all the ills from which the Untouchables have been suffering for ages.

You have come here to announce that the British are abdicating. It cannot be wrong for an Untouchable to ask, 'To whom are you leaving this legacy of authority and power?' To the protagonist of Brahmanism, which means to the tyrants and oppressors of the Untouchables. Such a method of liquidating the British Empire in India need not raise any qualms of conscience among members of other parties. But what about the British Labour Party? The Labour Party claims to stand for the unprivileged and the down-trodden. If it is true to its salt, I have no doubt that it will stand by the sixty millions of the Untouchables of India and do everything necessary to safeguard their position, and not allow power to pass into the hands of those who by their religion and their philosophy of life are unfit to govern and are in fact the enemies of the Untouchables. It will be no more than bare act of atonement on the part of the British for the neglect of the Scheduled Castes whose trustees they always claimed to be.

What has led me to unburden myself at such length is the anxiety caused by the apparent silence of the Mission over the question of constitutional safeguards raised by the Untouchables. This anxiety has been deepened by the attitude taken by the Mission towards the pledges given to the Untouchables and to the minorities by His Majesty's Government. The attitude of the Mission in regard to these pledges reminds one of Lord Palmerston who said, 'We have no permanent enemies; we have no permanent friends; we have only permanent interest.' You can well imagine what a terrifying prospect it would present to the Untouchables if the impression was created that the Mission was adopting this Palmerston maxim as its guide. You came from the under-

> privileged classes of Great Britain and I have full faith that you will do your best to prevent a possible betrayal of the 60 millions of India's under-privileged. That is why I have thought of placing their case before you. If you will allow me to say the Untouchables have got a feeling that they have no greater friend in the Mission than yourself.

After initial dialogue, the Mission proposed its plan over the composition of the new government on May 16, 1946. Promulgated on May 16 1946, the Plan to create a United Dominion of India as a loose confederation of Provinces came to be known as the Plan of May 16. The Plan proposals were as follows:

(1) A United Dominion of India would be given the independence.
(2) Muslim-majority Provinces would be grouped—Baluchistan, Sind, Punjab and North-West Frontier Province would form one group, and Bengal and Assam would form another.
(3) Hindu-majority Provinces in Central and Southern India would form another group.
(4) The Central government would be empowered to run foreign affairs, defence and communications, while the rest of powers and responsibility would belong to the Provinces, coordinated by groups.

The Plan of May 16, 1946 had thus envisaged a United India in line with Congress and Muslim League aspirations. But that was where the consensus between the two parties ended since Congress abhorred the idea of having groupings of Muslim majority Provinces and that of Hindu majority Provinces with the intention of "balancing" each other at the Central Legislature. The Muslim League could not accept any changes to this Plan since the same "balance" or "parity" that Congress was loath to accept formed the basis of Muslim demands of "political safeguards" built into post-British Indian laws so as to prevent absolute rule of Hindus over Muslims.

Reaching an impasse, the British proposed a second alternative: Plan of June 16, 1946. This Plan sought to arrange for India to be divided into Hindu-majority India and a Muslim-majority India that would later be renamed Pakistan, since Congress had vehemently rejected "parity" at the Centre. A list of Princely States of India that would be permitted to accede to either Dominion or attain independence was also drawn up.

* * *

On June 29, 1946, a caretaker Government was announced and the Cabinet Mission left for London leaving it to the Viceroy to work out the necessary details. This meant disbanding of the Viceroy's Executive Council of which Dr Ambedkar was a Minister-Member. Dr Ambedkar, like other Members of the Executive Council, bade good bye to the Viceroy, and returned to Mumbai in the third week of June 1946.

★ ★ ★

While these political developments were unfolding, Dr Ambedkar undertook a major initiative for education of the Depressed Classes. He had long envisaged a college oriented to Scheduled Castes; the original idea for the Sikh Khalsa College in Mumbai had been part of this Scheme. In 1945 Dr Ambedkar drew up proposals for the People's Education Society, and got a promise of Rs 6 lakh from the Government. Consequently, the People's Education Society was established in July 1945, and in April 1946, Siddharth College of Arts was founded in Mumbai. Milind College was established later in Aurangabad.

★ ★ ★

In the meantime, Dr Ambedkar vigorously kept pursuing the matter with the Cabinet Mission as well as other British authorities.

On May 22, 1946, Dr Ambedkar wrote a letter to Lord Pethick-Lawrence seeking clarifications on the following:

(1) Whether the term 'minorities' in paragraph 20 of the statement includes the Scheduled Castes?
(2) Paragraph 20 lays down that the Advisory Committee on the rights of citizens, minorities and tribal and excluded areas should contain full representation of the interests affected. Who is to see whether the Advisory Committee does in fact contain full representation of the interests affected?
(3) Whether, in order to see that there is full representation of the interests affected, HMG propose to reserve to themselves the right to add to the Committee by nomination of persons from outside the Constituent Assembly representing such interests? The necessity for nomination from outside seems to be essential, for otherwise there is no other method for securing representation of tribal and excluded areas from within the Constituent Assembly. If the necessity for nomination is admitted, will the principle of nomination of members of the Scheduled Castes from outside the Constituent Assembly be extended to secure full representation of the Scheduled Castes on the Advisory Committee?
(4) In paragraph 22 of the Statement, there is a provision for a treaty between the Union Constituent Assembly and the United Kingdom providing for certain matters arising out of the transfer of power. Will this proposed treaty include a provision for the protection of the minorities as was stipulated in the Cripps proposals? If the Treaty is not to have such a provision, how does HMG propose to make the decisions of the Advisory Committee binding on the Constituent Assembly?

Lord Pethick-Lawrence responded to Dr Ambedkar on May 28, 1946. Here's what he said in the letter:

> You will appreciate that the object of the Delegation is to set up machinery whereby Indians can frame their own Constitution for an independent India. The object of our Statement is to provide a basis on which the parties can come together for that purpose and we hope that it will be accepted and worked by all concerned. We have limited our Statement to the minimum which seemed to us necessary for that purpose. Other matters which arise will fall to be decided by the Constituent Assembly.
>
> It is certainly our intention that the term 'minorities' in paragraph 20 of the Statement includes the Scheduled Castes. On the other hand, it will be for the Constituent Assembly itself to set up the Advisory Committee and we assume that it will desire that it should be fully representative.
>
> It is not our intention to interfere with the Constituent Assembly. The personnel of the Advisory Committee is not, however, limited by our Statement to persons who are members of the Constituent Assembly.

★ ★ ★

On June 17, 1946, Dr Ambedkar sent a telegram to Mr Attlee, the Prime Minister of Britain. The telegram read:

> At time of last year's Simla Conference, Viceroy on my protest and with consent of Home Government promised increased Scheduled Castes representation in Interim Government to two seats in Council of 14. I had demanded three. Compromise I accepted two. New proposals Interim Government announced yesterday give Scheduled Castes only one seat. This is gross breach of solemn promise given after due deliberation. One seat most unfair. Mission is treating sixty million Untouchables as being equal to four millions Sikhs, three million Christians in matter of representation. Scheduled Caste nominee does not represent Scheduled Castes, is elected entirely by Hindu votes and is creature of Congress. Representation to Scheduled Castes Congressman is no representation to Scheduled Castes. It is representation to Congress. Cabinet Mission heaping upon Scheduled Castes one wrong after another, bent on sacrificing them with view to appease Congress and destroying their independent position in public life in country. Please intervene and redress wrong by directing Mission to give Scheduled Castes two seats to be filled by nominees of Federation which Mission knows alone represents Scheduled Castes. Scheduled Castes insist on two seats or none. To avoid misunderstanding of my motive, I like to state that I have no desire to be in Interim Government and will stand out. Am fighting for rights of Scheduled Castes. Hope there is some sense of justice left in British Government—Ambedkar.

The telegram was followed up by a lengthy letter dated July 1 enclosing (possible) a Memorandum titled: "A Critique of the Proposals of Cabinet Mission for Indian Constitutional Changes in so far as they affect the Scheduled Castes (Untouchables)". The Memorandum argued:

The Cabinet Mission sent out to India by the Labour Government early this year to resolve the political deadlock in India set out a Scheme for the framing of the Constitution by a Constituent Assembly. This Constituent Assembly is to be composed of representatives chosen by the members of the Provincial Legislatures by a single transferable vote. For the purposes of the composition of the Constituent Assembly the Cabinet Mission's Scheme has divided the members of the Provincial Legislatures into three categories (1) Muslims, (2) Sikhs, and (3) General, each with a fixed quota of seats. Each category has a separate electorate whereby the Muslim representatives of the Constituent Assembly will be elected by the Muslim members of the Provincial Legislature, the Sikhs by the Sikh members and the General by all the rest. The 'General' includes (1) Hindus, (2) Scheduled Castes, (3) Indian Christians, and (4) Anglo-Indians.

The Scheduled Castes of India were greatly surprised to find that they were lumped together with the Hindus. It has been declared time and again by His Majesty's Government that His Majesty's Government recognizes that the Scheduled Castes are separate element in the national life of India and that His Majesty's Government will not impose any Constitution to which the Scheduled Castes are not a willing party. The question is asked why the Cabinet Mission recognized the Muslims and the Sikhs as separate elements and why they refused to give the Scheduled Castes the same status?

Prime Minister Attlee responded to Dr Ambedkar on August 1, 1946 as follows:

I am afraid that I cannot accept the view that the Cabinet Mission and the Viceroy were unjust to the Scheduled Castes. The reason why they have revised the policy followed at the Simla Conference of 1945 is, as you suggest, the result of the elections to the Provincial Legislatures, which were held last spring. The Mission made a careful study of the voting figures and I have examined them myself. We appreciate that there are grounds for the view that the present electoral system does not do justice to those Scheduled Caste candidates who are opposed to Congress. On the other hand, I do not find that the figures substantiate what you say about the achievements of candidates belonging to your Federation at the primary elections.[113] While I do not propose to go into the matter in detail here the facts are that primary elections were held in only 43 of the 151 seats reserved for the Scheduled Castes. Of these 43 primary elections, the Scheduled Castes Federation contested 22 and topped the poll in only 13.

In your letter you make three specific requests.[114] As regards the first, His Majesty's Government are anxious that the Constituent Assembly should have the fullest possible

113. In his letter of July 1 Dr Ambedkar wrote: "That results of the Primary Elections—wherever they took place in India—provided that the candidates put up by the Federation came to the top and those put up by the Congress went down to the bottom."

114. These were: To state openly that his Majesty's Government holds that the Scheduled Castes are a minority within the meaning of paragraph 20 of the Cabinet Mission's Statement. That His Majesty's Government will see that satisfactory safeguards which will enable them to live from the fear of the Majority are provided for the Scheduled

freedom of action consistent with the terms of the Cabinet Mission's Statements of May 16 and May 25. We ourselves, of course, consider the Scheduled Castes to be an important minority which should be represented on the Minority Advisory Committee. But the declaration for which you ask could not be confined to the Scheduled Castes and would have to be a statement of all the elements who we consider should be included as Minorities in the Advisory Committee. Even though it would be only an expression of opinion on the part of His Majesty's Government, it would inevitably be interpreted as an attempt to interfere with the Assembly's freedom and as such would be likely to cause serious resentment. In these circumstances I cannot believe that such a declaration would be of value to the cause of the Scheduled Castes.

Turning to your second request, I do not find that my speech in the House of Commons on March 15 last contained the words which you attribute to me.[115] What I said was, "We are very mindful of the rights of minorities and minorities should be able to live free from fear." This remains the view of His Majesty's Government, which found expression in paragraph 4 of the Cabinet Mission's Statement of May 25. I do not consider that His Majesty's Government would be wise to make at this stage any further pronouncement elaborating what was said in that paragraph.

Your final request is that in the Interim Government the Scheduled Castes should have at least two representatives who should be nominees of the Scheduled Castes Federation. I regret that I cannot hold out any hope of this being possible.

I was very glad to see that you had been elected to the Constituent Assembly.

★ ★ ★

Castes before it agree to sign the Treaty for cessation of sovereignty. That in the Interim Government the Scheduled Castes should have at least two representatives which should be the nominees of the Scheduled Castes Federation.

115. Dr Ambedkar had noted that the Cabinet Mission had already made the point that there must be adequate provision for the protection of the minorities. His second request would be met if there were added to this statement the words: "Safeguards which will enable the Scheduled Castes to live from the fear of the Majority." These were words, Dr Ambedkar claimed, which Mr. Attlee himself had used in his speech on March 15.

CHAPTER THIRTY SIX

Into the Constituent Assembly

GIVEN THE INDIFFERENCE of the British[116] and the ridicule of the Congress Party, the defeated, distressed and desperate Dr Ambedkar decided to turn his back on the British and in the broader interests of the Untouchables, decided to offer his services to the Congress Party. The rapprochement of Dr Ambedkar took place in the new elected Constituent Assembly.

According to the Cabinet Mission's Plan, the British Government had envisaged the election of a Constituent Assembly without giving Untouchables any guarantee of representation. When members were being elected to the Constituent Assembly by Provincial Assemblies, with his Scheduled Caste Federation (SCF) unable to make up the required numbers, Dr Ambedkar stood hardly any chance. Fortunately, Jogendra Nath Mandal,[117] a SCF leader in Bengal, came forward. He had entered into an alliance with the Muslim League. With their help, he commandeered the

116. Dr Ambedkar made a last minute effort to connect with the British by making a trip to Britain in October, 1946.

Dr MR Jayakar objected to the timing of the resolution moved by Pandit Jawaharlal Nehru. He moved an amendment, seeking postponement of the passing of the resolution, as he wanted the Muslim League to join the task of laying down the Fundamentals of the Constitution. This resolution created a tense atmosphere in the House. Amidst this tense situation Dr Ambedkar was invited by the President of the Constituent Assembly Dr Rajendra Prasad unexpectedly to have his say on December 17, 1946. When Dr Ambedkar started, the House was all attention. Dr Dhananjay Keer writes,

"Everybody thought that Dr Ambedkar by playing such dangerous role would go under with the mover of the amendment. To rise against the will and the objections of the Congress bosses, who were the nation's most powerful leaders, was to meet one's Waterloo. The Congress Members were ready with their hands raised to cripple their avowed enemy and throw him down."

117. After the Partition, Mandal went to Pakistan and became temporary Chairman of Pakistan's Constituent Assembly and later as Pakistan's first Minister of Law and Labour.

numbers to get Dr Ambedkar elected to the Consituent Assembly from the Bengal Province (July 19, 1946).

In spite of the boycott by the Muslim League, the Constituent Assembly met for the first time on December 9, 1946 and elected Dr Rajendra Prasad as its President. On December 13, Pandit Nehru laid the foundation of the Constituent Assembly's work by moving a Resolution on the Declaration of Objectives. In a memorable speech, Pandit Nehru declared an Independent Sovereign Republic as India's objective. During the discussion on Nehruji's Resolution, Dr MR Jayakar moved an amendment seeking postponement of the passing of the Resolution until the Muslim League members joined the Constituent Assembly.

The amendment moved by Dr MR Jayakar was in good faith, but several Members (including some from the Congress), were unhappy as they found it "obstructionist" and resorted to heckling Dr Jayakar. In that state of consternation, Dr Rajendra Prasad, as the President of the Constituent Assembly, unexpectedly called upon Dr Ambedkar to express his views. Dr Ambedkar grabbed the opportunity and rose to the occasion literally, in more ways than one. He said:

> Mr Chairman, the Resolution in the light of the discussion that has gone on since yesterday, obviously divides itself into two parts, one part which is controversial and another part which is non-controversial. The part which is non-controversial is the part which comprises paragraphs (5) to (7) of this Resolution. These paragraphs set out the objectives of the future Constitution of this country. I must confess that, coming as the Resolution does from Pandit Jawaharlal Nehru who is reputed to be a Socialist, this Resolution, although non-controversial, is to my mind very disappointing. I should have expected him to go much further than he has done in the part of the Resolution. As a student of history, I should have preferred this part of the Resolution not being embodied in it at all.
>
> When one reads that part of Resolution, it reminds one of the Declaration of the Rights of Man which was pronounced by the French Constituent Assembly. I think I am right in suggesting that, after the lapse of practically 450 years, the Declaration of the Rights of Man and the principles which are embodied in it has become part and parcel of our mental makeup. I say they have become not only the part and parcel of the mental make-up of modern man in every civilized part of the world, but also in our own country which is so orthodox, so archaic in its thought and its social structure, hardly anyone can be found to deny its validity. To repeat it now as the Resolution does is, to say the least, pure pedantry. These principles have become the silent immaculate premise of our outlook. It is, therefore, unnecessary to proclaim as forming a part of our creed.
>
> The Resolution suffers from certain other lacunae. I find that this part of the Resolution, although it enunciates certain rights, does not speak of remedies. All of us are aware of the fact that rights are nothing unless remedies are provided whereby people can seek to obtain redress when rights are invaded. I find a complete absence of remedies. Even the usual formula that no man's life, liberty and property shall be taken without the due process of law, finds no place in the Resolution. These Fundamental Rights set out are made subject to law and morality. Obviously what is

law, what is morality will be determined by the Executive of the day and when the Executive may take one view another Executive may take another view and we do not know what exactly would be the position with regard to Fundamental Rights if this matter is left to the Executive of the day.

Sir, these are here certain provisions which speak of justice, economical, social and political. If this Resolution has a reality behind it and a sincerity, of which I have not the least doubt, coming as it does from the Mover of the Resolution, I should have expected some provision whereby it would have been possible for the State to make economic, social and political justice a reality and I should have, from that point of view, expected the Resolution to state in most explicit terms that in order that there may be social and economic justice in the country, that there would be nationalization of industry and nationalization of land, I do not understand how it could be possible for any future Government which believes in doing justice socially, economically and politically, unless its economy is a socialistic economy. Therefore, personally, although I have no objection to the enunciation of these propositions, the Resolution is, to my mind, somewhat disappointing, I am, however, prepared to leave this subject where it is with the observations I have made.

Now I come to the first part of the Resolution, which includes the first four paragraphs. As I said from the debate that has gone on in the House, this has become a matter of controversy. The controversy seems to be centred on the use of that word 'Republic'. It is centred on the sentence occurring in Paragraph 4 "sovereignty is derived from the people." Thereby it arises from the point made by my friend Dr Jayakar yesterday that in the absence of the Muslim League it would not be proper for this Assembly to proceed to deal with Resolution.

Now, Sir, I have got not the slightest doubt in my mind as to the future evolution and the ultimate shape of the social, political and economic structure of this great country. I know today we are divided politically, socially and economically. We are a group of warring camps, and I may go even to the extent of confessing that I am probably one of the leaders of such a camp. But, Sir, with all this, I am quite convinced that given time and circumstances nothing in the world will prevent this country from becoming one *(Applause)*.

With all our castes and creeds, I have not the slightest hesitation that we shall in some form be a united people (*Cheers*). I have no hesitation in saying that notwithstanding the agitation of the Muslim League for the partition of India, some day enough light would dawn upon the Muslims themselves and they too will begin to think that a United India is better even for them (*Loud cheers and applause).*

So far as the ultimate goal is concerned, I think none of us need have any apprehensions. None of us need have any doubt. Our difficulty is not about the ultimate future. Our difficulty is how to make the heterogeneous mass that we have today take a decision in common and march on the way which leads us to unity. Our difficulty is not with regard to the ultimate, our difficulty is with regard to the beginning. Mr Chairman, therefore, I should have thought that in order to make us willing friends, in order to induce every party, every section in this country to take on to road it would be an act of greatest statesmanship for the majority Party even to make a concession to the prejudices of people who are not prepared to march together and it is for that that I propose to make this appeal.

Let us leave aside slogans, let us leave aside words which frighten people. Let us even make a concession to the prejudices of our opponents, bring them in, so that they may willingly join with us on marching upon that road, which as I said, if we walk long enough, must necessarily lead us to unity. If I, therefore, from this place support Dr Jayakar's amendment, it is because I want all of us to realize that whether we are right or wrong, whether the position that we take is in consonance with our legal rights, whether that agrees with the Statement of May the 16th or December 6th, leave all that aside. This is too big a question to be treated as a matter of legal rights. It is not a legal question at all. We should leave aside all legal considerations and make some attempt, whereby those who are not prepared to come will come. Let us make it possible for them to come that is my appeal.

In the course of the debate that took place, there were two questions which were raised, which struck me so well that I took the trouble of taking them down on a piece of paper. The one question was, I think, by my friend, the Prime Minister of Bihar who spoke yesterday in this Assembly. He said, how can this Resolution prevent the League from coming into the Constituent Assembly? Today my friend, Dr Shyama Prasad Mookerjee, asked another question. Is this Resolution inconsistent with the Cabinet Mission's Proposal?

Sir, I think they are very important questions and they ought to be answered and answered categorically. I do maintain that this Resolution whether it is intended to bring about the result or not, whether it is a result of cold calculation or whether it is a mere matter of accident, is bound to have the result of keeping the Muslim League out.

In this connection I should like to invite your attention to paragraph 3 of the Resolution, which I think is very significant and very important. Paragraph 3 envisages the future Constitution of India. I do not know what is the intention of the mover of the Resolution. But I take it that after this Resolution is passed, it will act as a sort of a directive to the Constituent Assembly to frame a Constitution in terms of para 3 of the Resolution. What does paragraph 3 say? Paragraph 3 says that in this country there shall be two different sets of polity, one at the bottom, autonomous Provinces or the States or such other areas as care to join a United India. These autonomous units will have full power. They will have also residuary powers. At the top, over the Provincial units, there will be a Union Government, having certain subjects for legislation, for execution and for administration. As I read this part of the Resolution, I do not find any reference to the idea of grouping an intermediate structure between the Union on the one hand and the Provinces on the other. Reading this para in the light of the Cabinet Mission's Statement, or reading it even in the light of the Resolution passed by the Congress at its Wardha session, I must confess that I am a great deal surprised at the absence of any reference to the idea of grouping of the Provinces. So far as I am personally concerned, I do not like the idea of grouping (*hear, hear*) I like a strong united Centre (*hear, hear*) much stronger than the Centre we had created under the Government of India Act of 1935.

But, Sir, these opinions, these wishes have no bearing on the situation at all. We have travelled a long road. The Congress Party, for reasons best known to itself consented, if I may use that expression, to the dismantling of a strong Centre which had been created in this country as a result of 150 years of administration and which, I must say, was to me a matter of great admiration and respect and refuge. But having given up that position, having said that we do not want a strong Centre, and having accepted that there must be or should be an intermediate polity, a sub-federation between the Union Government and the Provinces I would like to know why there is no reference in para 3 to the idea of grouping.

I quite understand that the Congress Party, the Muslim League and His Majesty's Government are not *ad idem* on the interpretation of the Clause relating to grouping. But I always thought that—I am prepared to stand corrected if it is shown that I am wrong—at least it was agreed by the Congress Party that if the Provinces which are placed within different groups consent to form a Union or Sub-federation, the Congress would have no objection to that proposal. I believe I am correct in interpreting the mind of the Congress Party.

The question I ask is this. Why did not the Mover of this Resolution make reference to the idea of a Union of Provinces or grouping of Provinces on the terms on which he and his party was prepared to accept it? Why is the idea of Union completely effaced from this Resolution? I find no answer, none whatever. I, therefore, say in answer to the two questions which have been posed here in this Assembly by the Prime Minister of Bihar and Dr Shyama Prasad Mookerjee, as to how this Resolution is inconsistent with the Statement of May 16th or how this Resolution is going to prevent the Muslim League from entering this Constituent Assembly, that here is para 3 which the Muslim League is bound to take advantage of and justify its continued absentation.

Sir, my friend Dr Jaykar, yesterday, in arguing his case for postponing a decision on this issue, put his case, if I may say so, without offence to him, somewhat in a legalistic manner. The basis of his argument was, have you right to do so? He read out certain portions from the statement of the Cabinet Mission which related to the procedural part of the Constituent Assembly and his contention was that the procedure that this Constituent Assembly was adopting in deciding upon this Resolution straightaway was inconsistent with the procedure that was laid down in that Paper.

Sir, I like to put the matter in a somewhat different way. The way I like to put it is this, I am not asking you to consider whether you have the right to pass this Resolution straightaway or not. It may be that you have the right to do so. The question I am asking is this. Is it prudent for you to do so? Is it wise for you to do so? Power is one thing; wisdom is quite a different thing and I want this House to consider this matter from the point of view, namely, whether it would be wise, whether it would be statesman like, whether it would be prudent to do so at this stage. The answer that I give is that it would not be prudent, it would not be wise.

I suggest that another attempt may be made to bring about a solution of the dispute between the Congress and the Muslim League. This subject is so vital, so important that I am sure it could never be decided on the mere basis of dignity of one party or the dignity of another party. When deciding the destinies of nations, dignities of people, dignities of leaders and dignities of parties ought to count for nothing. The destiny of the country ought to count for everything. It is because I feel that it would in the interest not only of this Constituent Assembly so that it my function as one whole, so that it may have the reaction of the Muslim League before it proceeds to decision that I support Dr Jayakar's amendment—we must also consider what is going to happen with regard to the future, if we act precipitately.

I do not know what plans the Congress Party, which holds this House in its possession, has in its mind? I have no power of divination to know about what they are thinking about. What are their tactics, what is their strategy, I do not know. But applying my mind as an outsider to the issue that has arisen, it seems to me there are only three ways by which the future will be decided. Either there shall have to be surrender by the one party to the wishes of the other—that is one way. The other way would be what I call a negotiated peace and the third way would be open war.

Sir, I have been hearing from certain Members of the Constituent Assembly that they are prepared to go to war. I must confess that I am appalled at the idea that anybody in this country should think of solving the political problems of this country by the method of war. I do not know how many people in this country support that idea. A good many perhaps do and the reason why I think they do, is because most of them, at any rate a great many of them believe that the war that they are thinking of would be a war on the British.

Well, Sir, if the war that is contemplated, that is in the minds of people, can be localized, circumscribed, so that it will not be more than a war on the British, I probably may not have much objection to that sort of strategy. But will it be a war on the British only? I have no hesitation and I do want to place before this House in the clearest terms possible that if war comes in this country, and if that war has any relation to the issue with which we are confronted today, it will not be a war on the British. It will be a war on the Muslims. It will be a war on the Muslims or which is probably worse, it will be a war on a combination of the British and the Muslims. I cannot see how this contemplated war be of the sort different from what I fear it will be.

Sir, I like to read to the House a passage from Burke's great speech on Conciliation with America. I believe this may have some effect upon the temper of this House. The British people, as you know, were trying to conquer the rebellious colonies of the United States, and bring them under their subjection contrary to their wishes. In repelling this idea of conquering the colonies this is what Burke said:

'First, Sir permit me to observe that the use of force alone is but temporary. It may subdue for a moment; but it does not remove the necessity of subduing again; and a nation is not governed which is perpetually to be conquered. My next objection is its uncertainty. Terror is not always the effect of force and an armament is not a victory. If you do not succeed, you are without resource for, conciliation failing, force remains; but, force failing no further hope of reconciliation is left. Power and authority are sometimes bought by kindness; but they can never be begged as alms by an impoverished and defeated violence....A further objection to force is that you impair the object by your very endeavours to preserve it. The thing you fought for is not the thing which you recover; but depreciated, sunk, wasted and consumed in the contest.'

These are weighty words which it would be perilous to ignore. If there is anybody who has in his mind the project of solving the Hindu-Muslim problem by force, which is another name of solving it by war, in order that the Muslims may be subjugated and made to surrender to the Constitution that might be prepared without their consent, this country would be involved in perpetually conquering them.

The conquest would not be once and for ever. I do not wish to take more time than I have taken and I will conclude by again referring to Burke. Burke has said somewhere that it is easy to give power, it is difficult to give wisdom. Let us prove by our conduct that if this Assembly has arrogated to itself sovereign powers, it is prepared to exercise them with wisdom. That is the only way by which we can carry with us all sections of the country. There is no other way that can lead us to unity. Let us have no doubt on that point.

★ ★ ★

This speech helped change the attitude of Congress leaders like Pandit Nehru towards Dr Ambedkar. Dr Ambedkar was opposing partition, and speaking in favour of a United government, with a strong Centre. This historic speech changed the course of Dr Ambedkar's political career. The speech drew the longest and the most vociferous applause. As Mr NV Gadgil, an eye-witness to this, even observed, "His speech was so statesmanlike, so devoid of bitterness and so earnestly challenging that the whole of Assembly listened to it in rapt silence. The speech was greeted with tremendous ovation and he was smothered with congratulations in the lobby." The speech had its ultimate effect, and the Constituent assembly postponed the consideration of the objective resolution till the next session.

While working on the Constituent Assembly, in March 1947, Dr Ambedkar prepared a Memorandum on the Safeguards for the Scheduled Castes and submitted to the Constituent Assembly on behalf of the All-India Scheduled Caste Federation. This was subsequently published in the same year for the general public, with the title: 'States and Minorities'.

STATES AND MINORITIES

The Memorandum has been couched in the form of Articles of the Constitution of the United States of India for the sake of "giving point and precision" and presented along with a lot of Explanatory Notes and Statistical Material.

- According to Dr Ambedkar, the Constituent Assembly faced two most difficult issues: (a) the problem of the Minorities; and (b) the problem of Indian States.
- The Memorandum defines Fundamental Rights, Minority Rights and Safeguards for the Scheduled Castes. Dr Ambedkar contested the new dispensation from the "High and Mighty Hindu Majority" that the Scheduled Castes are not a minority. He emphasized that the Scheduled Castes are more than a minority and that any protection given to the citizens and to the minorities will not be adequate for the Scheduled Castes. Their social, economic and educational condition is so much worse than that of the citizens

and other minorities that in addition to protection they would get as citizens, and as minorities the Scheduled Castes would require special safeguards against the tyranny and discrimination of the majority. Dr Ambedkar proposed a formula that would disable the communal majority from claiming a political majority. According to the formula minorities would get representation positively disproportionate to their ratio in population while for the majority community it would be capped so that minorities are not overwhelmed by the majority.

- Dr Ambedkar held very definite and distinct views about the problem of the Indian States. Dr Ambedkar insisted that every Princely State to be admitted into the Union must have the capacity to bear the burden of modern administration to maintain peace within its own borders and he warned the Constitent Assembly that they should not in their eagerness to bring the Princely States into the Union compromise on the basic principles of democracy.

CHAPTER THIRTY SEVEN

In the Run-up to Independence

THE CABINET MISSION left India by end-June 1946, after announcing a Caretaker Government in the place of Viceroy's Executive Council. The details to be settled were left with the Viceroy. Political turmoil started gathering momentum immediately thereafter.

★ ★ ★

On July 10, 1946, Jawaharlal Nehru, held a press conference in Bombay declaring that the Congress had agreed only to participate in the Constituent Assembly and "regards itself free to change or modify the Cabinet Mission Plan as it thought best". The Congress ruled out the June 16 Plan, seeing it as the division of India into small States.

Dr Ambedkar and his political party: Scheduled Caste Federation (SCF) launched a *Satyagraha* in Pune (July 1946), Nagpur (September 1946) and in few other places demanding an explanation from the Congress leaders regarding their rights and representation in the soon-to-be-free India. But with the routing of the SCF in the elections, the British started ignoring, indeed marginalizing Dr Ambedkar. Shri BG Kher, the Chief Minister of the Bombay Province, reacted sarcastically, indeed, saying:

> One does not know whether their (i.e. Scheduled Castes) grievance is against the Cabinet Mission's failure to give them what they want, or against the defeat of Dr Ambedkar and his party in the recent election, or whether it is due to a general sense of frustration[118]

118. As quoted in Keer, Dhananjay, op cit. p. 382.

In the same vein, even Mahatma Gandhi referred to Dr Ambedkar's agitation as a "parody of *Satyagraha* in the show staged by Ambedkar" and remarked that even if its means were non-violent, the cause was certainly vague.[119]

In the meantime, the Viceroy began organizing the transfer of power to a Congress-League coalition. But League President Muhammad Ali Jinnah denounced the hesitant and conditional approval of the Congress and rescinded League approval of both plans. Thus Congress leaders entered the newly styled Viceroy's Executive Council: Jawaharlal Nehru became the head—Vice-President in title, but possessing the executive authority. Vallabhbhai Patel became the Home member—responsible for internal security and government agencies. Congress-led governments were formed in most Provinces—including in the NWFP, in Punjab. The League led governments in Bengal and Sind. The Constituent Assembly was instructed to begin work to write a new Constitution for India.

Jinnah and the League condemned the new government, and vowed to agitate for Pakistan by any means possible. Disorder arose in Punjab and Bengal, including the cities of Delhi, Bombay and Calcutta. On the League-organized Direct Action Day, over 5,000 people were killed across India, and Hindu, Sikh and Muslim mobs began clashing. Viceroy Wavell stalled the Central government's efforts to stop the disorder, and the Provinces were instructed to leave this to the Governors, who did not undertake any major action. To end the disorder and rising bloodshed, Wavell encouraged Nehru to ask the League to enter the government. While Patel and most Congress leaders were opposed to conceding to a party that was organizing disorder, Nehru conceded in hope of preserving communal peace.

League leaders entered the Executive Council under the leadership of Liaquat Ali Khan, the future first Prime Minister of Pakistan who became the Finance Minister. But the Council did not function in harmony—separate meetings were not held by League ministers, and both parties vetoed the major initiatives proposed by the other, highlighting their ideological differences and political antagonism.

At the arrival of the new (and proclaimed as the last) viceroy, Lord Mountbatten of Burma in early 1947, Congress leaders expressed the view that the coalition was unworkable. This led to the eventual proposal, and acceptance of the partition of India.

On June 3, 1947, the new Viceroy, Lord Mountbatten, announced the British Government's Plan for India's future. The Plan envisaged a partition of the country; there would now be two Central Governments (i.e., Divided India and Pakistan) and accordingly, two Constituent Assemblies. Gandhiji who had earlier considered Pakistan a sin, a patent untruth and had solemnly asked the protagonists of partition to "vivisect me before you vivisect India" finally changed his mind, and "instructed" Pandit Nehru (who had gone to Noakhali (East Bengal) to consult Gandhiji) to sign "an accord with Jinnah" giving him "a universally acceptable and inoffensive

119. *Harijan*, August 9, 1946.

formula for his Pakistan". The following week, Pandit Nehru moved a Resolution in the All-India Congress Committee which was passed by a vote of 99-52.[120]

The British Parliament passed the Act of Indian Independence on July 15 and accordingly the Constituent Assembly became a sovereign body. Since Bengal was partitioned, several Members including Dr Ambedkar lost their seats in the Constituent Assembly. However, with the changed attitude of Congress leaders such as Pandit Nehru towards Dr Ambedkar, when Barrister MRJayakar[121] resigned his position in the Constituent Assembly from the Bombay Province, Nehru and Sardar Patel suggested Dr Ambedkar's name to fill the vacancy in July 1947. Thus, Dr Ambedkar returned to the Constituent Assembly, this time with the support of the Congress Party.

On August 15, 1947, India became a free nation and Dr Ambedkar was inducted into the new Cabinet of free India. Prime Minister Nehru appointed Dr Ambedkar as the Union Minister of Law, apparently under pressure from Gandhiji. Seemingly, Nehru and Patel were lukewarm about allocating the Ministerial berth to Dr Ambedkar, but Gandhiji insisted on his inclusion in the project of national construction.[122] This conjecture is further supported by a conversation between Gandhiji and two visiting foreigners, when Gandhiji had reportedly expressed the wish that Dr Ambedkar should become a part of the first government of Independent India.[123]

Dr Ambedkar was made a Member of the Drafting Committee of the Indian Constitution (August 29, 1947). Subsequently, he was chosen as the Chairman of the Drafting Committee. As the first Union Minister of Law of Independent India and as the Chairman of the Drafting Committee for the proposed Indian Constitution, Dr Ambedkar was now at the zenith of his political career. His new responsibilities gave him an indelible place in the foundation of modern India.

---

120. Lelyweld, Joseph (2011), op cit, p. 310.
121. Barrister MR Jayakar then became the founder Vice Chancellor of Pune University
122. Gaikwad, SM "Ambedkar and Indian Nationalism", *Economic and Political Weekly*, March 7, 1998.
123. Gore, MS, *The Social Context of an Ideology*, p.180

PART VIII

NATION BUILDING POST-INDEPENDENCE

CHAPTER THIRTY EIGHT

Drafting the Constitution of India

THE CONSTITUENT ASSEMBLY appointed the Drafting Committee for preparing a Draft Constitution of India (August 29, 1947). The seven-Member Drafting Committee included Dr Ambedkar. The very next day, in the first meeting of the Drafting Committee, Dr Ambedkar was unanimously elected as its Chairman.

Dr Ambedkar devoted himself wholeheartedly to the formidable task of drafting the Constitution of India. He worked tirelessly despite his failing health and completed the Draft Constitution of India within six months. The Draft Constitution was submitted to Dr Rajendra Prasad, Chairman, Constituent Assembly, on February 14, 1948, barely a fortnight after the brutal assassination of Mahatma Gandhi.

The Draft Constitution was placed in the public domain for eight months and thereafter, came up for discussion in the Constituent Assembly. Dr Ambedkar introduced the Draft Constitution (315 Articles and 8 Schedules) in the Constituent Assembly on November 4, 1948. Dr Ambedkar's brilliant exposition of the salient and special features of the Draft Constitution of India has been reproduced here in full. Here's what Dr Ambedkar said:

> I introduce the Draft Constitution as settled by the Drafting Committee and move that it be taken into consideration.
>
> The Drafting Committee was appointed by the Constituent Assembly on August 29, 1947. The Drafting Committee was in effect charged with the duty of preparing a Constitution in accordance with the decisions of the Constituent Assembly on the reports made by the various Committees appointed by it, such as the Union Powers Committee, the Union Constitution Committee, the Provincial Constitution Committee and the Advisory Committee on Fundamental Rights, Minorities, Tribal Areas, etc. The Constituent Assembly had also directed that in certain matters the provisions contained in the Government of India Act, 1935, should be followed. Except on points which are referred to in my letter of the February 21, 1948 in which I have referred to the departures made and alternatives suggested by the Drafting Committee, I hope the Drafting Committee will be found to have faithfully carried out the directions given to it.

The Draft Constitution as it has emerged from the Drafting Committee is a formidable document. It contains 315 Articles and 8 Schedules. It must be admitted that the Constitution of no country could be found to be so bulky as the Draft Constitution. It would be difficult for those who have not been through it realize its salient and special features.

The Draft Constitution has been before the public for eight months. During this long time friends, critics and adversaries have had more than sufficient time to express their reactions to the provisions contained in it. I dare say that some of them are based on misunderstanding and inadequate understanding of the Articles. But there the criticisms are and they have to be answered.

For both these reasons it is necessary that on a motion for consideration I should draw your attention to the special features of the Constitution and also meet the criticism that has been levelled against it.

Before I proceed to do so I would like to place on the table of the House Reports of three Committees appointed by the Constituent Assembly: (1) Report of the Committee on Chief Commissioners of Provinces; (2) Report of the Expert Committee on Financial Relations between the Union and the States; and (3) Report of the Advisory Committee on Tribal Areas, which came too late to be considered by that Assembly though copies of them have been circulated to Members of the Assembly. As these reports and the recommendations made therein have been considered by the Drafting Committee, it is only proper that the House should formally be placed in possession of them.

Turning to the main question. A student of Constitutional Law, if a copy of a Constitution is placed in his hands, is sure to ask two questions. Firstly, what is the form of Government that is envisaged in the Constitution and, secondly, what is the form of the Constitution? For these are the two crucial matters which every Constitution has to deal with. I will begin with the first of the two questions.

In the Draft Constitution there is placed at the Head of the Indian Union a functionary who is called the 'President of the Union'. The title of this functionary reminds one of the President of the United States. But beyond identity of names there is nothing in common between the form of Government prevalent in America and the form of Government proposed under the Draft Constitution. The American form of Government is called the Presidential system of Government. What the Draft Constitution proposes is the Parliamentary system. The two are fundamentally different.

Under the Presidential system of America, the President is the Chief Head of the Executive. The administration is vested in him. Under the Draft Constitution, the President occupies the same position as the King under the English Constitution. He is the Head of the State but not of the Executive. He represents the Nation but does not rule the Nation. He is the symbol of the nation. His place in the administration is that of a ceremonial device on a seal by which the nation's decisions are made known. Under the American Constitution the President has under him Secretaries in charge of different Departments. In like manner the President of the Indian Union will have under him Ministers in charge of different Departments of administration. Here again there is a fundamental difference between the two. The President of the United States is not bound to accept any advice tendered to him by any of his Secretaries. The

President of the Indian Union will be generally bound by the advice of his Ministers. He can do nothing contrary to their advice nor can he do anything without their advice. The President of the United States can dismiss any Secretary at any time. The President of the Indian Union has no power to do that so long as his Ministers command a majority in Parliament.

The Presidential system of America is based upon the separation of the Executive and the Legislature so that the President and his Secretaries cannot be Members of the Congress. The Draft Constitution does not recognize this doctrine. The Ministers under the Indian Union are Members of Parliament. Only Members of Parliament can become Ministers. Ministers have the same rights as other Members of Parliament, namely, that they can sit in Parliament, take part in debate and vote in its proceedings.

Both systems of Government are, of course, democratic and the choice between the two is not very easy. A democratic Executive must satisfy two conditions: (1) It must be stable Executive; and (2) it must be a responsible Executive. Unfortunately, it has not been possible so far to devise a system which can ensure both in equal degree. You can have a system which can give you more stability but less responsibility or you can have a system which can give you more responsibility but less stability. The American and the Swiss Systems give more stability. The British system, on the other hand, gives you more responsibility but less stability. The reason for this is obvious. The American Executive is a non-Parliamentary Executive which means that it is not dependent upon a majority in Parliament. Being a non-Parliamentary Executive, the Congress of the United States cannot dismiss the Executive. A Parliamentary Government must resign the moment it loses the confidence of a majority of the Members of Parliament.

Looking at it from the point of view of responsibility, a non-Parliamentary Executive being independent of Parliament tends to be less responsible to the Legislature, while a Parliamentary Executive being more dependent upon a majority in Parliament becomes more responsible. The Parliamentary system differs from a non-Parliamentary system in as much as the former is more responsible than the latter but they also differ so as to the time and agency for assessment of their responsibility. Under the non-Parliamentary system such as the one that exists in the USA the assessment of responsibility of the Executive is periodic. It takes place once in two years. It is done by the electorate. In England, where the Parliamentary system prevails, the assessment of responsibility of the Executive is both daily and periodic. The daily assessment is done by Members of Parliament, through questions, Resolutions, No-confidence motions, Adjournment motions and Debates on Addresses. Periodic assessment is done by the Electorate at the time of the election which may take place every five years or earlier. The daily assessment of responsibility which is not available under the American system is, it is felt, far more effective than the periodic assessment and far more necessary in a country like India. The Draft Constitution in recommending the Parliamentary system of Executive has preferred more responsibility to more stability.

So far I have explained the form of Government under the draft Constitution. I will now turn to the other question, namely, the form of the Constitution.

Two principal forms of the Constitution are known to history—one is called Unitary and the other Federal. The two essential characteristics of a Unitary Constitution are:

(1) the supremacy of the Federal Polity, and
(2) the absence of subsidiary Sovereign polities.
Contrary-wise, a Federal Constitution is marked: by the existence of a Central Polity and subsidiary polities side by side, and
(3) by each being sovereign in the field assigned to it.

In other words, Federation means the establishment of a Dual Polity. The Draft Constitution is Federal Constitution in as much as it establishes what may be called a Dual Polity. This Dual Polity under the proposed Constitution will consist of the Union at the Centre and the States at the periphery, each endowed with sovereign powers to be exercised in the field assigned to them respectively by the Constitution. This Dual Polity resembles the American Constitution. The American Polity is also a Dual Polity; one of it is known as the Federal government and the other States which correspond respectively to the Union Government and the State Governments of the Draft Constitution.

Under the American Constitution, the Federal Government is not a mere league of the States nor are the States administrative units or agencies of the Federal Government. In the same way, the Indian Constitution proposed in the Draft Constitution is not a league of States, nor are the States administrative units or agencies of the Union Government. Here, however, the similarities between the Indian and the American Constitution come to an end. The differences that distinguish them are more fundamental and glaring than the similarities between the two.

The points of difference between the American Federation and the Indian Federation are mainly two. In the USA there is a citizenship of the U.S.A. But there is also a citizenship of the State. No doubt, the rigours of this double citizenship are much assuaged by the fourteenth amendment to the Constitution of the United States which prohibits the States from taking away the rights, privileges and immunities of the citizens of the United States. At the same time, as pointed out by Mr William Anderson, in certain political matters, including the right to vote and to hold public office, States may and do discriminate in favour of their own citizens. This favouritism goes even further in many cases. Thus to obtain employment in the service of States or local Government one is in most places required to be a local resident or citizen. Similarly, in the licensing of persons for the practice of such public professions as law and medicine residence or citizenship in the State is frequently required: and in business where the public regulation must necessarily be strict, as in the sale of liquor, and of stocks and bonds, similar requirements have been upheld.

Each State has also certain rights in its own domain that it holds for the special advantage of its own citizens. Thus wild game and fish in a sense belong to the State. It is customary for the States to charge higher hunting and fishing license fees to non-residents than to its own citizens. The States also charge non-residents higher tuition in State Colleges and Universities, and permit only residents to be admitted to their hospitals and asylums except in emergencies.

In short, there are a number of rights that a State can grant to its own citizens or residents that it may and does legally deny to non-residents, or grant to non-residents only on more difficult terms than those imposed on residents. The advantages, given to the citizens in his own State, constitute the special rights of State citizenship. Taken all together they amount to a considerable difference in rights between citizens and non-citizens of the States. The transient and the temporary sojourner is everywhere under some special handicaps.

The proposed Indian Constitution is a Dual Polity with a single citizenship. There is only one citizenship for the whole of India. It is Indian Citizenship. There is no State citizenship. Every Indian has the same rights of citizenship no matter in what State he resides.

The Dual Polity of the proposed Indian Constitution differs from the Dual Polity of the USA in another respect. In the USA the Constitutions of the Federal and the State Governments are loosely connected. In describing the relationship between the Federal and State Governments in the USA. Bryce has said:

'The Central or National Government and the State Governments may be compared to a large building and a set of smaller buildings standing on the same ground, yet distinct from each other.'

Distinct they are, but how distinct are the State Governments in the USA from the Federal Government? Some idea of this distinctness may be obtained from the following facts:

(1) Subject to the maintenance of the Republican form of Government, each State in America is free to make its own Constitution.

(2) The people of a State retain forever in their hands, altogether independent of the National Government, the power of altering their Constitution.

To put it again in the words of Bryce:

'A State (in America) exists as a Commonwealth by virtue of its own Constitution, and all State Authorities, legislative, executive and judicial are the creatures of, and subject to, the Constitution.'

This is not true of the proposed Indian Constitution. No State (at any rate those in Part I) has a right to frame its own Constitution. The Constitution of the Union and of the States is a single frame from which neither can get out and within which they must work.

So far I have drawn attention to the differences between the American Federation and the proposed Indian Federation. But there are some other special features of the proposed Indian Federation which mark it off not only from the American Federation but from all other Federations. All Federal Systems including the American are placed in a tight mould of Federalism. No matter what the circumstances, it cannot change its form and shape. It can never be Unitary. On the other hand, the draft Constitution can be both Unitary as well as Federal according to the requirements of time and circumstances. In normal times, it is framed to work as a Federal System. But in times of war it is so designed as to make it work as though it was a Unitary System. Once the President issues a Proclamation which he is authorized to do under the provisions of Article 275,[124] the whole scene can become transformed, and the State becomes a Unitary State. The Union under the Proclamation can claim, if it wants: (1) the power to legislate upon any subject even though it may be in the State List; (2) the power to give directions to the States as to how they should exercise their executive authority in matters which are within their charge; (3) the power to vest authority for any purpose in any officer; and (4) the power to suspend the financial provisions of the

124. Article 352

Constitution. Such a power of converting itself into a Unitary State no Federation possesses. This is one point of difference between the Federation proposed in the Draft Constitution, and all other Federations we know of.

This is not the only difference between the proposed Indian Federation and other Federations. Federalism is described as a weak, if not an effete, form of Government. There are two weaknesses from which Federation is alleged to suffer. One is rigidity and the other is legalism. That these faults are inherent in Federalism, there can be no dispute. A Federal Constitution cannot but be a written Constitution, and a written Constitution must necessarily be a rigid Constitution. A Federal Constitution means division of Sovereignty by no less a sanction than that of the law of the Constitution between the Federal Government and the States, with two necessary consequences: (1) that any invasion by the Federal Government in the field assigned to the States and vice versa is a breach of the Constitution; and (2) such breach is a justifiable matter to be determined by the Judiciary only. This being the nature of Federalism the Federal Constitution cannot escape the charge of legalism. The faults of a Federal Constitution have been found in a pronounced form in the Constitution of the United States of America.

Countries which have adopted Federalism at a later date have attempted to reduce the disadvantages following from the rigidity and legalism which are inherent therein. The example of Australia may well be referred to in this matter. The Australian Constitution has adopted the following means to make its Federation less rigid:

(1) By conferring upon the Parliament of the Commonwealth large powers of Concurrent Legislation and few powers of exclusive Legislation.

(2) By making some of the Articles of the Constitution of a temporary duration to remain in force only until Parliament otherwise provides.

It is obvious that under the Australian Constitution, the Australian Parliament can do many things, which are not within the competence of the American Congress and for doing which the American Government will have to resort to the Supreme Court and depend upon its ability, ingenuity and willingness to invent a doctrine to justify it in the exercise of authority.

In assuaging the rigour of rigidity and legalism, the Draft Constitution follows the Australian plan on a far more extensive scale than has been done in Australia. Like the Australian Constitution, it has a long list of subjects for concurrent powers of legislation. Under the Australian Constitution, Concurrent subjects are 39. Under the Draft Constitution they are 37. Following the Australian Constitution, there are as many as six Articles in the Draft Constitution, where the provisions are of a temporary duration, and which could be replaced by Parliament at any time by provision suitable for the occasion. The biggest advance made by the Draft Constitution over the Australian Constitution is in the matter of exclusive powers of legislation vested in Parliament. While the exclusive authority of the Australian Parliament to legislate extends only to about three matters, the authority of the Indian Parliament as proposed in the Draft Constitution will extend to ninety-one matters. In this way the Draft Constitution has secured the greatest possible elasticity in its Federalism which is supposed to be rigid by nature.

It is not enough to say that the Draft Constitution follows the Australian Constitution or follows it on a more extensive scale. What is to be noted is that it has added new ways of overcoming the rigidity and legalism inherent in Federalism which are special to it and which are not to be found elsewhere.

First is the power given to Parliament to legislate on exclusively Provincial subjects in normal times. I refer to Articles 226,[125] 227[126] and 229.[127] Under Article 226 Parliament can legislate when a subject becomes a matter of national concern as distinguished from purely Provincial concern though the subject is in the State list, provided a resolution is passed by the Upper Chamber by $^{2}/3^{rd}$ majority in favour of such exercise of the power by the Centre. Article 227 gives a similar power to Parliament in a national emergency. Under Article 229, Parliament can exercise the same power if Provinces consent to such exercise. Though the last provision also exists in the Australian Constitution, the first two are a special feature of the Draft Constitution.

The second means adopted to avoid rigidity and legalism is the provision for facility with which the Constitution could be amended. The provisions of the Constitution relating to the amendment of the Constitution divide the Articles of the Constitution into two groups. In the one group are placed Articles relating to (a) the distribution of legislative powers between the Centre and the State; (b) the representation of the States in Parliament; and (c) the powers of the Courts. All other Articles are placed in another group. Articles placed in the second group cover a very large part of the Constitution, and can be amended by Parliament by a double majority, a majority of not less that two-thirds of the Members of each House present and voting, and by majority of the total Membership of each House. The amendment of these Articles does not require ratification by the States. It is only in these Articles which are placed in group one that an additional safeguard of ratification by the States is introduced. One can, therefore safely say that the Indian Federation will not suffer from the faults or rigidity or legalism. Its distinguishing feature is that it is a flexible Federation.

There is another special feature of the proposed Indian Federation which distinguishes it from other Federations. A Federation being a Dual Polity based on divided authority with separate legislative, executive and judicial power for each of the two polities is bound to produce diversity in laws, in administration and in judicial protection. Upto a certain extent this diversity does not matter. It may be welcomed as being an attempt to accommodate the powers of Government to local needs and local circumstances. But this very diversity when it goes beyond a certain point is capable of producing chaos and has produced chaos in many Federal States. One has only to imagine twenty different laws—if we have twenty States in the Union—of marriage, of divorce, of inheritance of property, family relations, contracts, torts, crimes, weights and measures, of bills and cheques, banking and commerce, of procedures for obtaining justice and in the standards and methods of administration. Such a state of affairs not only weakens the States, but also becomes intolerant to the citizen who moves from State to State only to find that what is lawful in one State is not lawful in another.

The Draft Constitution has sought to forge means and methods whereby India will have Federation, and at the same time will have uniformity in all basic matters which

125. Article 249
126. Article 227
127. Article 229

are essential to maintain the unity of the country. The means adopted by the Draft Constitution are three.

(1) A single judiciary;

(2) Uniformity in Fundamental laws, Civil and Criminal; and

(3) A common all-India Civil Service to man important posts.

A dual judiciary, a duality of legal codes and a duality of Civil Services, as I said, are the logical consequences of a Dual Polity which is inherent in a Federation. In the USA the Federal Judiciary and the State Judiciary are separate and independent of each other. The Indian Federation though a Dual Polity has no Dual Judiciary at all. The High Courts and the Supreme Court form one single integrated judiciary having jurisdiction and providing remedies in all cases arising under the Constitutional law, the civil law or the criminal law. This is done to eliminate all diversity in all remedial procedures. Canada is the only country which furnishes a close parallel. The Australian system is only an approximation.

Care is taken to eliminate all diversity from laws which are at the basis of civic and corporate life. The great Codes of Civil and Criminal laws, such as the Civil Procedure Code, Penal Code, the Criminal Procedure Code, the Evidence Act, Transfer of Property Act, Laws of Marriage, Divorce and Inheritance are placed in the Concurrent List so that the necessary uniformity can always be preserved without impairing the Federal system.

The Dual Polity which is inherent in a Federal system, as I said, is followed in all federations by a dual service. In all Federations there is a Federal Civil Service and State Civil Service. The Indian Federation though a Dual Polity will have a Dual Service but with one exception. It is recognized that in every country there are certain posts in its administrative set-up which might be called strategic from the point of view of maintaining the standard of administration. It may not be easy to spot such posts in a large and complicated machinery of administration. But there can be no doubt that the standard of administration depends upon the calibre of the Civil servants who are appointed to these strategic posts. Fortunately for us, we have inherited from the past a system of administration which is common to the whole of the country, and we know what are these strategic posts. The Constitution provides that without depriving the States of their right to form their own Civil Service there shall be an All-India Service recruited on an all-India basis with common qualifications, with uniform scale of pay, and the Members of which alone could be appointed to these strategic posts throughout the Union.

Such are the special features of the proposed Federation. I will now turn to what the critics have had to say about it.

It is said that there is nothing new in the Draft Constitution, that about half of it has been copied from the Government of India Act of 1935, and that the rest of it has been borrowed from the Constitutions of other countries. Very little of it can claim originality.

One likes to ask whether there can be anything new in a Constitution framed at this hour in the history of the world. More than hundred years have rolled over when the first written Constitution was drafted. It has been followed by many countries reducing their Constitutions to writing. What the scope of a Constitution should be has long been settled. Similarly, what are the fundamentals of Constitution—are recognized all over the world. Given these facts, all Constitutions in their main provisions must look similar. The only new things, if there can be any, in a Constitution framed so late in the day are the variations made to remove the faults, and to accommodate it to the needs of the country. The Charge of producing a blind copy of the Constitutions of other countries is based, I am sure, on an inadequate study of the Constitution. I have shown what is new in the Draft Constitution, and I am sure that those who have studied other Constitutions and who are prepared to consider the matter dispassionately will agree that the Drafting Committee in performing its duty has not been guilty of such blind and slavish imitation as it is represented to be.

As to the accusation that the Draft Constitution has produced a good part of the provisions of the Government of India Act. 1935, I make no apologies. There is nothing to be ashamed of in borrowing. It involves no plagiarism. Nobody holds any patent rights in the fundamental ideas of a Constitution. What I am sorry about is that the provisions taken from the Government of India Act 1935, relate mostly to the details of administration. I agree administrative details should have no place in the Constitution. I wish very much that the Drafting Committee could see its way to avoid their inclusion in the Constitution. But this is to be said on the necessity which justifies their inclusion. Grote, the historian of Greece, has said that:

'The diffusion of Constitutional morality, not merely among the majority of any community but throughout the whole, is the indispensable condition of a government at once free and peaceable; since even any powerful and obstinate minority may render the working of a free institution impracticable, without being strong enough to conquer ascendency for themselves.'

By Constitutional morality Grote means:

'A paramount reverence for the forms of the Constitution enforcing obedience to authority acting under and within these forms, yet combined with the habit of open speech of action subject only to defined legal control, and unrestrained censure of those very authorities as to all their public acts combined too with a perfect confidence in the bosom of every citizen amidst the bitterness of party contest that the forms of the Constitution will not be less sacred in the eyes of his opponents that in his own.'

While everybody recognizes the necessity of the diffusion of Constitutional morality for the peaceful working of a democratic Constitution, there are two things interconnected with it which are not, unfortunately, generally recognized. One is that the form of administration has close connection with the form of the Constitution. The form of the administration must be appropriate to, and in the same sense as, the form of the Constitution. The other is that it is perfectly possible to pervert the Constitution, without changing its form by merely changing the form of the administration and to make it inconsistent and opposed to the spirit of the Constitution. It follows that it is only where people are saturated with Constitutional morality; such as the people who are described by Grote, the historian, that one can take the risk of omitting from the Constitution details of administration, and leaving it for the Legislature to prescribe them. The question is, can we presume such a diffusion of Constitutional morality? Constitutional morality is not a natural sentiment. It has to be cultivated. We must realize that out people have yet to learn it. Democracy in India is only a top-dressing on an Indian soil, which is essentially undemocratic.

In these circumstances it is wiser not to trust the Legislature to prescribe forms of administration. This is the justification for incorporating them in the Constitution.

Another criticism against the Draft Constitution is that no part of it represents the ancient Polity of India. It is said that the new Constitution should have been drafted on the ancient Hindu model of a State and that instead of incorporating Western theories the new Constitution should have been raised and built upon Village Panchayats and District Panchayats. There are others who have taken a more extreme view. They do not want any Central and Provincial Governments. They just want India to contain so many village Governments. The love of the intellectual Indians for the village community is, of course, infinite if not pathetic (laughter). It is largely due to the fulsome praise bestowed upon it by Metcalfe who described them as little republics having nearly everything that they want within themselves, and almost independent of any foreign relations. The existence of these village communities, each one forming a separate little State in itself has according to Metcalf, contributed more than any other cause to the preservation of the people of India, through all the revolutions and changes which they have suffered, and is in a high degree conducive to their happiness, and to the enjoyment of a great potion of the freedom and independence. No doubt the village communities have lasted where nothing else lasts. But those who take pride in the village communities do not care to consider what little part they have played in the affairs and the destiny of the country, which has been well described by Metcalfe himself who says:

'Dynasty after dynasty tumbles down, revolution succeeds to revolution. Hindoo, Pathan, Mogul, Maharatha, Sikh, English, are all masters in turn, but the village communities remain the same. In times of trouble they arm and fortify themselves. A hostile army passes through the country. The village communities collect their little cattle within their walls, and let the enemy pass unprovoked.'

Such is the part the village communities have played in the history of their country. Knowing this, what pride can one feel in them? That they have survived through all vicissitudes may be a fact. But mere survival has no value. The question is on what plane they have survived. Surely on a low, on a selfish level. I hold that these village republics have been the ruination of India. I am, therefore, surprised that those who condemn Provincialism and Communalism should come forward as champions of the village. What is the village but a sink of localism, a den of ignorance, narrow-mindedness and communalism? I am glad that the Draft Constitution has discarded the village and adopted the individual as its unit.

The Draft Constitution is also criticized because of the safeguards if provides for minorities. In this, the Drafting Committee has no responsibility. It follows the decisions of the Constituent Assembly. Speaking for myself, I have no doubt that the Constituent Assembly has done wisely in providing such safeguards for minorities as it has done. In this country both the minorities and the majorities have followed a wrong path. It is wrong for the majority to deny the existence of minorities. It is equally wrong for the minorities to perpetuate themselves. A solution must be found which will serve a double purpose. It must recognize the existence of the minorities to start with. It must also be such that it will enable majorities and minorities to merge some day into one. The solution proposed by the Constituent Assembly is to be welcomed because it is a solution which serves this two-fold purpose.

To diehards who have developed a kind of fanaticism against minority protection I would like to say two things. One is that minorities are explosive force which, if it erupts, can blow up the whole fabric of the State. The history of Europe bears ample and appalling testimony to this fact. The other is that the minorities in India have agreed to place their existence in the hands of the majority. In the history of negotiations for preventing the partition of Ireland, Redmond said to Carson, 'Ask for any safeguards you like for the Protestants minority but let us have a United Ireland,' Carson's reply was, 'Damn your safeguards. We don't want to be ruled by you.' No minority in India has taken this stand. They have loyally accepted the rule of the majority which is basically a communal majority and not a political majority. It is for the majority to realize its duty not to discriminate against minorities. Whether the minorities will continue or will vanish must depend upon this habit of the majority. The moment the majority loses the habit of discriminating against the minority, the minorities can have no ground to exist. They will vanish.

The most criticized part of the Draft Constitution is that which relates to the Fundamental Rights. It is said that Article 13[128] which defines Fundamental Rights is riddled with so many exceptions that the exceptions have eaten up the Rights altogether. It is condemned as a kind of deception. In the opinion of the critics Fundamental Rights are not Fundamental Rights unless they are also absolute rights. The critics rely on the Constitution of the United States and to the Bill of Rights embodied in the first ten Amendments to that Constitution in support of their contention. It is said that the Fundamental Rights in the American Bill of Rights are not real because they are not subjected to limitations or exceptions.

I am sorry to say that the whole of the criticism about Fundamental Rights is based upon a misconception. In the first place, the criticism in so far as it seeks to distinguish Fundamental Rights from non-Fundamental Rights is not sound. It is incorrect to say that Fundamental Rights are absolute, while non-Fundamental Rights are not absolute. The real distinction between the two is that non-Fundamental Rights are created by agreement between parties while Fundamental Rights are the gift of the law. Because Fundamental Rights are the gift of the State, it does not follow that the State does not qualify them. In the second place, it is wrong to say that Fundamental Rights in America are absolute. The difference between the position under the American Constitution and the Draft Constitution is one of form and not of substance. That the Fundamental Rights in America are not absolute rights is beyond dispute. In support of every exception to the Fundamental Right set out in the Draft Constitution, one can refer to at least one judgment of the United State Supreme Court in justification of the limitation on the right of free speech contained in Article 13[129] of the Draft Constitution. In *Gitlow Vs New York* in which the issue was the Constitutionality of a New York 'criminal anarchy' law which purported to punish utterance calculated to bring about violent change, the Supreme Court said:

'It is a fundamental principle, long established, that the freedom of speech and of the press which, secured by the Constitution, does not confer an absolute right to speak or publish, without responsibility, whatever one may choose or an unrestricted and unbridled license that gives immunity for every possible use of language and prevents the punishments of those who abuse this freedom.'

128. Article 19
129. Article 19

It is, therefore, wrong to say that the Fundamental Rights in America are absolute while those in the Draft Constitution are not.

It is argued that if any Fundamental Rights require qualification, it is for the Constitution itself to qualify them as is done in the Constitution of the United States and where it does not do so, it should be left to be determined by the Judiciary upon a consideration of all the relevant considerations. All this, I am sorry to say, is a complete misrepresentation if not a misunderstanding of the American Constitution. The American Constitution does nothing of the kind. Except in one matter, namely, the right of Assembly, the American Constitution does not itself impose any limitations upon the Fundamental Right guaranteed to the American citizens. Nor is it correct to say that the American Constitution leaves it to the judiciary to impose limitations on Fundamental Rights. The right to impose limitation belongs to the Congress. The real position is different from what is assumed by the critics. In America, the Fundamental Rights as enacted by the Constitution were no doubt absolute. Congress, however, soon found that it was absolutely essential to qualify these Fundamental Rights by limitations. When the question arose as to the Constitutionality of these limitations before the Supreme Court, it was contended that the Constitution gave no power to the United States Congress to impose such limitation. The Supreme Court invented the doctrine of police power and refuted the advocates of absolute fundamental rights by the argument that every State has inherent in it police power which is not required to be conferred on it expressly by the Constitution. To use the language of the Supreme Court in the case I have already referred to. It said:

'That a State in the exercise of its police power may punish those who abuse this freedom by utterances inimical to the public welfare tending to corrupt public morals, incite to crime or disturb the public peace is not open to question….'

What the Draft Constitution has done is that instead of formulating Fundamental Right in absolute terms and depending upon our Supreme Court to come to the rescue of Parliament by inventing the doctrine of Police power, it permits the State directly to impose limitations upon the Fundamental Rights. There is really no difference in the result. What one does directly the other does indirectly. In both cases, the Fundamental Rights are not absolute.

In the Draft Constitution the Fundamental Rights are followed by what are called 'Directive Principles'. It is a novel feature in a Constitution framed for Parliamentary Democracy. The only other Constitution framed for Parliamentary Democracy which embodies such principles is that of Irish Free State. These Directive Principles have also come up for criticism. It is said that they are only pious declarations. They have no binding force. The criticism is, of course, superfluous. The Constitution itself says so in so many words.

If it is said that the Directive Principles have no legal force behind them, I am prepared to admit it. But I am not prepared to admit that they have no sort of binding force at all. Nor am I prepared to concede that they are useless because they have no binding force in law.

The Directive Principles are like the instrument of instructions which were issued to the Governor-General and to the Governors of the Colonies and to those of India British Government under the 1935 Act. Under the Draft Constitution it is proposed to issue such instruments to the President and to the Governors. The texts of these instruments of instructions will be found in Schedule IV of the Constitution. What are called Directive Principles is merely another name for Instrument of Instructions. The only difference is that they are instructions to the Legislature and the Executive. Such a thing is, to my mind, to be welcomed. Whenever, there is a grant of power in general terms for peace, order and good Government, it is necessary that it should be accompanied by instructions regulating its exercise.

The inclusion of such instructions in Constitution such as is proposed in the Draft becomes justifiable for another reason. The Draft Constitution as framed only provides a machinery for the government of the country. It is not a contrivance to install any particular Party in power as has been done in some countries. Who should be in power is left to be determined by the people, as it must be, if the system is to satisfy the test of democracy. But whoever captures power will not be free to do what he likes with it. In the exercise of it, he will have to respect these Instruments of Instructions which are called Directive Principles. He cannot ignore them. He may not have to answer for their breach in a court of law. But he will certainly have to answer for them before the electorate at election time. What great value these Directive Principles possess will be realized better when the forces of right contrive to capture power.

That it has no binding force is no argument against their inclusion in the Constitution. There may be a difference of opinion as to the exact place they should be given in the Constitution. I agree that it is somewhat odd that provisions which do not carry positive obligations should be placed in the midst of provisions which do carry positive obligations. In my judgment their proper place is in Schedule III A& IV which contain instrument of Instructions to the President and the Governors. For, as I have said, they are really Instruments of Instructions to the Executive and the Legislatures as to how they should exercise their powers. But that is only a matter of arrangement.

Some critics have said that the Centre is too strong. Others have said that it must be made stronger. The Draft Constitution has struck a balance. However much you may deny powers to the Centre, it is difficult to prevent the Centre from becoming strong. Conditions in modern world are such that centralization of powers is inevitable. One has only to consider the growth of the Federal Government in the USA which, notwithstanding the very limited powers given to it by the Constitution, has outgrown its former self and has overshadowed and eclipse the State Governments. This is due to modern conditions. The same conditions are sure to operate on the Government of India, and nothing that one can do will help to prevent it from being strong. On the other hand, we must resist the tendency to make it stronger. It cannot chew more that it can digest. Its strength must be commensurate with its weight. It would be a folly to make it so strong that it may fall by its own weight.

The Draft Constitution is criticized for having one sort of Constitutional relations between the Centre and Provinces and another sort of Constitutional relations between the Centre and the Indian States. The Indian States are not bound to accept the whole list of subjects included in the Union List but only those which come under Defence, Foreign Affairs and Communications. They are not bound to accept the State List contained in the Draft Constitution. They are free to create their own Constituent Assembly and to frame their own Constitutions. All this, of course, is very unfortunate and, I submit, quite indefensible. This disparity may even prove dangerous to the efficiency of the State. So long as the disparity exists, the Centre's authority over all-India matters may lose its efficacy. For, power is no power if it cannot be exercised in all cases and in all places. In a situation such as may be created by war, such limitations on the exercise of vital power in some areas may bring the whole life of the State in complete jeopardy. What is worse is that the Indian States under the Draft Constitution are permitted to maintain their own armies. I regard this as a most retrograde and harmful provision which may lead to the break-up of the unity of India and the overthrow of the Central Government. The Drafting Committee, if I am not misrepresenting its mind, was not at all happy over this matter. They wished very much that there was uniformity between the Provinces and the Indian States in their Constitutional relationship with the Centre. Unfortunately, they could do nothing to improve matters. They were bound by the decisions of the Constituent Assembly and the Constituent Assembly in its turn was bound by the agreement arrived at between the two negotiating Committees.

But we may take courage from what happened in Germany. The German Empire as founded by Bismark in 1870 was a composite State, consisting of 25 units. Of these 25 units, 22 were Monarchical States and 3 were Republican-City States. This distinction, as we all know, disappeared in the course of time and Germany became one land with one people living under one Constitution. The process of the amalgamation of the Indian States is going to be much quicker than it has been in Germany. On the August 15, 1947 we had 600 Indian States in existence. Today by the integration of the Indian States with Indian Provinces or merger among themselves, or by the Centre having taken them as Centrally Administered Areas there have remained some 20/30 States as viable States. This is a very rapid process and progress. I appeal to those States that remain to fall in line with the Indian Provinces and to become full units of the Indian Union on the same terms as the Indian Provinces. They will thereby give the Indian Union the strength it needs. They will save themselves the bother of starting their own Constituent Assemblies, and drafting their own separate Constitutions and they will lose nothing that is of value to them. I feel hopeful that my appeal will not go in vain and that before the Constitution is passed, we will be able to wipe off the differences between the Provinces and the Indian States.

Some critics have taken objection to the description of India in Article 1 of the Draft Constitution as a Union of States. It is said that the correct phraseology should be a Federation of States; it is true that South Africa which is a Unitary State is described as a Union. But Canada which is a Federation is also called a Union. Thus the description of India as a Union, though its Constitution is Federal, does no violence to usage but what is important is that the use of the word Union is deliberate. I do not know why the word 'Union' was used in the Canadian Constitution. But I can tell you why the Drafting Committee has used it. The Drafting Committee wanted to make it clear that though India was to be a Federation, the Federation was not the result of an agreement by the States to join in a Federation, and that the Federation not being the result of an agreement, no State has the right to secede from it. The Federation is a Union because it is indestructible. Though the country and the people may be divided into different States for convenience of administration the country is one integral whole, its people a single people living under single '*imperium*' derived from a single source. The Americans had to wage a civil war to establish that the States have no right to secession and that their Federation was indestructible. The Drafting Committee thought that it was better to make it clear at the outset rather than to leave it to speculation or to dispute.

The provisions relating to amendment of the Constitution have come in for a virulent attack at the hands of the critics of the Draft Constitution. It is said that the provisions contained in the Draft make amendment difficult. It is proposed that the Constitution should be amendable by a simple majority at least for some years. The argument is subtle and ingenious. It is said that this Constituent Assembly is not elected on adult suffrage while the future Parliament will be elected on adult suffrage and yet the former has been given the right to pass the Constitution by a simple majority while the latter has been denied the same right. It is paraded as one of the absurdities of the Draft Constitution. I must repudiate the charge because it is without foundation. To know how simple are the provisions of the Draft Constitution in respect of the amending Constitution one has only to study the provisions for amendment contained in the American and Australian Constitutions. Compared to them those contained in the Draft Constitution will be found to be the simplest. The Draft Constitution has eliminated the elaborate and difficult procedure such as a decision by a Convention or a Referendum. The powers of amendment are left with the Legislature, Central and Provincial. It is only for amendments of specific-matters—and they are only few—that the ratification of the State Legislatures is required. All other Articles of the Constitution are left to be amended by Parliament. The only limitation is that it shall be done by a majority of not less than two-thirds of the Members of each house present and voting and majority of the total Membership of each House. It is difficult to conceive a simple method of amending the Constitution.

What is said to be the absurdity of the amending provisions is founded upon a misconception of the position of the Constituent Assembly and of the future Parliament elected under the Constitution. The Constituent Assembly in making a Constitution has no partisan motive. Beyond securing a good and workable Constitution it has no axe to grind. In considering the Articles of the Constitution it has no eye on getting through a particular measure. The future Parliament if it met as a Constituent Assembly, its Members will be acting as partisans seeking to carry amendments to the Constitution to facilitate the passing of Party measures which they have failed to get through Parliament by reason of some Article of the Constitution which has acted as an obstacle in their way. Parliament will have an axe to grind while the Constituent Assembly has none. That is the difference between the Constituent Assembly and the future Parliament. That explains why the Constituent Assembly though elected on limited franchise can be trusted to pass the Constitution by simple majority and why the Parliament though elected on adult suffrage cannot be trusted with the same power to amend it.

I believe I have dealt with all the adverse criticisms that have been levelled against the Draft Constitution as settled by the Drafting Committee. I don't think that I have left out any important comment or criticism that has been made during the last eight months during which the Constitution has been before the public. It is for the Constituent Assembly to decide whether they will accept the Constitution as settled by the Drafting Committee or whether they shall alter it before passing it.

But this I would like to say. The Constitution has been discussed in some of the Provincial Assemblies of India. It was discussed in Bombay, Central Provinces, West Bengal, Bihar, Madras and East Punjab. It is true that in some Provincial Assemblies serious objections were taken to the financial provisions of the Constitution and in Madras to Article 226.[130] But excepting this, in no Provincial Assembly was any serious objection taken to the Articles of the Constitution. No Constitution is perfect and the Drafting committee itself is suggesting certain amendments to improve the Draft Constitution. But the debates in the Provincial Assemblies give me courage to say that the Constitution as settled by the Drafting Committee is good enough to make in this country to start with.

I feel that it is workable, it is flexible and it is strong enough to hold the country together both in peace time and in war time. Indeed, if I may say so, if things go wrong under the new Constitution, the reason will not be that we had a bad Constitution. What we will have to say is that Man was vile, Sir I move.

★ ★ ★

Over the next 13 months or so, the Constituent Assembly went through three readings of the Draft Constitution, discussing and adopting the Articles of the Constitution, one by one.

While replying to the debate during the third (and final) reading of the Constitution on November 25, 1949, Dr Ambedkar made an eloquent and spell-binding speech which is timeless. He said:

Looking back on the work of the Constituent Assembly it will now be two years, eleven months and seventeen days since it first met on December 9, 1946. During this period the Constituent Assembly has altogether held eleven sessions. Out of these eleven sessions, the first six were spent in passing the Objectives Resolution and the consideration of the Reports of Committees on Fundamental Rights, on Union Constitution, on Union Powers, on Provincial Constitution, on Minorities and on the Scheduled Areas and Schedules Tribes. The seventh, eighth, ninth, tenth and the eleventh sessions were devoted to the consideration of the Draft Constitution. These eleven sessions of the Constituent Assembly have consumed 165 days. Out of these, the Assembly spent 114 days for the consideration of the Draft Constitution.

Coming to the Drafting Committee, it was elected by the Constituent Assembly on August 29, 1947. It held its first meeting on August 30. Since August 30 it sat for 141 days during which it was engaged in the preparation of the Draft Constitution. The Draft Constitution, as prepared by the Constitutional Adviser as a text for the Drafting Committee to work upon, consisted of 243 Articles and 13 Schedules. The first Draft Constitution as presented by the Drafting Committee to the Constituent Assembly contained 315 Articles and 8 Schedules. At the end of the consideration stage, the number of Articles in the Draft Constitution increased to 386. In its final form, the Draft Constitution contains 395 Articles and 8 Schedules. The total number of

130. Article 249

amendments to the Draft Constitution tabled was approximately 7,635. Of them, the total number of amendments actually moved in the House were 2,473.

I mention these facts because at one stage it was being said that the Assembly had taken too long a time to finish its work, that it was going on leisurely and wasting public money. It was said to be a case of Nero fiddling while Rome was burning. Is there any justification for this complaint?

Let us note the time consumed by Constituent Assemblies in other countries appointed for framing their Constitutions. To take a few illustrations, the American Convention met on May 25 1787 and completed its work on September 17, 1787 i.e., within four months. The Constitutional Convention of Canada met on October 10, 1864 and the Constitution was passed into law in March 1867 involving a period of two years and five months. The Australian Constitutional Convention assembled in March 1891 and the Constitution became law on July 9, 1900, consuming a period of nine years. The South African Convention met in October 1908 and the Constitution became law on September 20, 1909 involving one year's labour.

It is true that we have taken more time than what the American or South African Conventions did. But we have not taken more time than the Canadian Convention and much less than the Australian Convention. In making comparisons on the basis of time consumed, two things must be remembered. One is that the Constitutions of America, Canada, South Africa and Australia are much smaller than ours. Our Constitution, as I said, contains 395 Articles while the American has just seven Articles, the first four of which are divided into sections which total up to 21, the Canadian has 147, Australian 128 and South African 153 sections. The second thing to be remembered is that the makers of the Constitutions of America, Canada, Australia and South Africa did not have to face the problem of amendments. They were passed as moved. On the other hand, this Constituent Assembly had to deal with as many as 2,473 amendments. Having regard to these facts, the charge of dilatoriness seems to me quite unfounded and this Assembly may well congratulate itself for having accomplished so formidable a task in so short a time....

Examining the criticism levelled, Dr Ambedkar said:

The condemnation of the Constitution largely comes from two quarters, the Communist Party and the Socialist Party. Why do they condemn the Constitution? Is it because it is really a bad Constitution? I venture to say 'No'. The Communist Party wants a Constitution based upon the principle of the Dictatorship of the Proletariat. They condemn the Constitution because it is based upon Parliamentary Democracy. The Socialists want two things. The first thing they want is that if they come in power, the Constitution must give them the freedom to nationalize or socialize all private property without payment of compensation. The second thing that the Socialists want is that the Fundamental Rights mentioned in the Constitution must be absolute and without any limitations so that if their Party fails to come into power, they would have the unfettered freedom not merely to criticize, but also to overthrow the State.

These are the main grounds on which the Constitution is being condemned. I do not say that the principle of Parliamentary Democracy is the only ideal form of political democracy. I do not say that the principle of no acquisition of private property without compensation is so sacrosanct that there can be no departure from it. I do not say that Fundamental Rights can never be absolute and the limitations set upon them can never be lifted. What I do say is that the principles embodied in the Constitution are the views of the present generation or if you think this to be an over-statement, I say they are the views of the Members of the Constituent Assembly. Why blame the Drafting Committee for embodying them in the Constitution? I say why blame even the Members of the Constituent Assembly? Jefferson, the great American statesman who played so great a part in the making of the American Constitution, has expressed some very weighty views which makers of Constitution can never afford to ignore. In one place, he has said:

'We may consider each generation as a distinct nation, with a right, by the will of the majority, to bind themselves, but none to bind the succeeding generation, more than the inhabitants of another country.'

In another place, he has said:

'The idea that institutions established for the use of the nation cannot be touched or modified, even to make them answer their end, because of rights gratuitously supposed in those employed to manage them in the trust for the public, may perhaps be a salutary provision against the abuses of a monarch, but is most absurd against the nation itself. Yet our lawyers and priests generally inculcate this doctrine, and suppose that preceding generations held the earth more freely than we do, had a right to impose laws on us, unalterable by ourselves, and that we, in the like manner, can make laws and impose burdens on future generations, which they will have no right to alter, in fine, that the earth belongs to the dead and not the living.'

I admit that what Jefferson has said is not merely true, but is absolutely true. There can be no question about it. Had the Constituent Assembly departed from this principle laid down by Jefferson it would certainly be liable to blame, even to condemnation. But I ask, has it? Quite the contrary.

One has only to examine the provision relating to the amendment of the Constitution. The Assembly has not only refrained from putting a seal of finality and infallibility upon this Constitution by denying to the people the right to amend the Constitution as in Canada or by making the amendment of the Constitution subject to the fulfilment of extraordinary terms and conditions as in America or Australia, but has provided a most facile procedure for amending the Constitution. I challenge any of the critics of the Constitution to prove that any Constituent Assembly anywhere in the world has, in the circumstances in which this country finds itself, provided such a facile procedure for the amendment of the Constitution. If those who are dissatisfied with the Constitution have only to obtain a two-third majority and if they cannot obtain even a two-third majority in the Parliament elected on adult franchise in their favour, their dissatisfaction with the Constitution cannot be deemed to be shared by the general public.

There is only one point of Constitutional import to which I propose to make a reference. A serious complaint is made on the ground that there is too much of centralization and that the States have been reduced to Municipalities. It is clear that this view is not only an exaggeration, but is also founded on a misunderstanding of what exactly the Constitution contrives to do.

As to the relations between the Centre and the States, it is necessary to bear in mind the fundamental principle on which it rests. The basic principle of Federalism is that the Legislative and Executive authority is partitioned between the Centre and the States not by any law to be made by the Centre but by the Constitution itself. This is what Constitution does. The States under our Constitution are in no way dependent upon the Centre for their legislative or executive authority. The Centre and the States are co-equal in this matter. It is difficult to see how such a Constitution can be called centralism. It may be that the Constitution assigns to the Centre too large a field for the operation of its legislative and executive authority than is to be found in any other Federal Constitution. It may be that the residuary powers are given to the Centre too large a field for the operation of its legislative and executive authority than is to be found in any other Federal Constitution. It may be that the residuary powers are given to the Centre and not to the States. But these features do not form the essence of Federalism. The chief mark of Federalism as I said lies in the partition of the legislative and executive authority between the Centre and the Units by the Constitution. This is the principle embodied in our Constitution. There can be no mistake about it. It is, therefore, wrong to say that the States have been placed under the Centre. Centre cannot, by its own will, alter the boundary of that partition, nor can the Judiciary. For as has been well said:

'Courts may modify, they cannot replace. They can revise earlier interpretations as new arguments, new points of view are presented. They can shift the dividing line in marginal cases, but there are barriers they cannot pass, definite assignments of power they cannot reallocate. They can give a broadening construction of existing powers, but they cannot assign to one authority powers explicitly granted to another.'

The first charge of centralization defeating Federalism must, therefore, fall.

The second charge is that the Centre has been given the power to override the States. This charge must be admitted. But before condemning the Constitution for containing such overriding powers, certain considerations must be borne in mind. The first is that these overriding powers do not form the normal feature of the Constitution. Their use and operation are expressly confined to emergencies only. The second consideration is: Could we avoid giving overriding powers to the Centre when an emergency has arisen? Those who do not admit the justification for such overriding powers to the Centre even in an emergency do not seem to have a clear idea of the problem which lies at the root of the matter. The problem is so clearly set out by a writer in that well-known magazine *The Round Table* in its issue of December 1935 that I offer no apology for quoting the following extract from it. Says the writer:

'Political Systems are a complex of rights and duties resting ultimately on the question, to whom, or to what authority does the citizen owe allegiance. In normal affairs the question is not present, for the law works smoothly, and a man goes about his business obeying one authority in this set of matters and another authority in that. But in a moment of crisis, a conflict of claims may arise, and it is then apparent that ultimate allegiance cannot be divided. The issue of allegiance cannot be determined in the last resort by a juristic interpretation of Statutes. The law must conform to the facts or so much the worse for the law. When all formalism is stripped away, the bare question is: What authority commands the residual loyalty of the citizen. Is it the Centre or the Constituent State?'

The solution of this problem depends upon one's answer to this question which is the crux of the problem. There can be no doubt that in the opinion of the vast majority of the people, the residual loyalty of the citizen in an emergency must be to the Centre and not to be Constituent States. For it is only the Centre which can work for a common end and for the general interests of the country as a whole. Herein lies the justification for giving to the Centre certain overriding powers to be used in an emergency. And after all what is the obligation imposed upon the constituent States by these emergency powers? No more than this—that in an emergency, they should take into consideration alongside their own local interests, the opinions and interests of the nation as a whole. Only those who have not understood the problem, can complain against it....

Dr Ambedkar also reflected about the future. He said:

On January 26, 1950, India will be an independent country *(Cheers)*. What would happen to her Independence? Will she maintain her Independence or will she lose it again? This is the first thought that comes to my mind. It is not that India was never an independent country. The point is that she once lost the independence she had. Will she lose it a second time? It is this thought which makes me most anxious for the future. What perturbs me greatly is the fact that not only India has once before lost her independence, but she lost it by the infidelity and treachery of some of her own people. In the invasion of Sind by Mahommed-Bin-Kasim, the military commanders of King Dahar accepted bribes from the agents of Mahommed-Bin-Kasim and refused to fight on the side of their King. It was Jaichand who invited Mahommed Ghori to invade India and fight against Prithvi Raj and promised him the help of himself and the Solanki kings. When Shivaji was fighting for the liberation of Hindus, the other Maratha noblemen and the Rajput Kings were fighting the battle on the side of Moghul Emperors. When the British were trying to destroy the Sikh Rulers, Gulab Singh, their principal commander, sat silent and did not help to save the Sikh kingdom. In 1857, when a large part of India had declared a War of Independence against the British, the Sikhs stood and watched the event as silent spectators.

Will history repeat itself? It is the thought which fills me with anxiety. This anxiety is deepened by the realization of the fact that in addition to our enemies in the form of Castes and Creeds we are going to have many political Parties with diverse and opposing Political Creeds. Will Indians place the country above their Creed or will they place Creed above country? I do not know. But this much is certain that if the Parties place Creed above country, our Independence will be put in jeopardy a second time and probably be lost forever. This eventuality we must all resolutely guard against. We must be determined to defend our Independence with the last drop of our blood *(Cheers)*.

On January 26, 1950, India would be a democratic country in the sense that India from that day would have a government of the people, by the people and for the people. The same thought comes to my mind. What would happen to her democratic Constitution? Will she be able to maintain it or will she lose it again. This is the second thought that comes to my mind and makes me as anxious as the first.

It is not that India did not know what Democracy is. There was a time when India was studded with republics, and even where there were monarchies, they were either elected or limited. They were never absolute. It is not that India did not know

Parliaments or Parliamentary Procedure. A study of the Buddhist Bhikshu *Sanghas* discloses that not only there were Parliaments—for the *Sanghas* were nothing but Parliaments—but the *Sanghas* knew and observed all the rules of Parliamentary Procedure known to modern times. They had rules regarding seating arrangements, rules regarding Motions, Resolutions, Quorum, Whip, Counting of Votes, Voting by Ballot, Censure Motion, Regularization, *Res Judicata,* etc. Although, these rules of Parliamentary Procedure were applied by the Buddha to the meetings of the *Sanghas*, he must have borrowed them from the rules of the Political Assemblies functioning in the country in his time.

This democratic system India lost. Will she lose it a second time? I do not know, but it is quite possible in a country like India—where democracy from its long disuse must be regarded as something quite new—there is danger of democracy giving place to dictatorship. It is quite possible for this new-born democracy to retain its form but give place to dictatorship in fact. If there is a landslide, the danger of the second possibility becoming actuality is much greater.

If we wish to maintain democracy not merely in form, but also in fact, what must we do? The first thing in my judgement we must do is to hold fast to Constitutional methods of achieving our social and economic objectives. It means we must abandon the bloody methods of revolution. It means that we must abandon the method of civil disobedience, non-cooperation and *Satyagraha*. When there was no way left for Constitutional methods for achieving economic and social objectives, there was a great deal of justification for unconstitutional methods. But where Constitutional methods are open, there can be no justification for these unconstitutional methods. These methods are nothing but the Grammar of Anarchy and the sooner they are abandoned, the better for us.

The second thing we must do is to observe the caution which John Stuart Mill has given to all who are interested in the maintenance of democracy, namely, not to lay their liberties at the feet of even a great man, or to trust him with powers which enable him to subvert their institutions. There is nothing wrong in being grateful to great men who have rendered life-long services to the country. But there are limits to gratefulness. As has been well said by the Irish Patriot Daniel O' Connel, 'no man can be grateful at the cost of his honour, no woman can be grateful at the cost of her chastity and no nation can be grateful at the cost of its liberty.' This caution is far more necessary in the case of India than in the case of any other country. For in India, *Bhakti* or what may be called the path of devotion or hero-worship, plays a part in its politics unequalled in magnitude by the part it plays in the politics of any other country in the world. *Bhakti* in religion may be a road to the salvation of the soul. But in politics, *Bhakti* or hero-worship is a sure road to degradation and to eventful dictatorship.

The third thing we must do is not to be content with mere political democracy. We must make our political democracy a social democracy as well. Political democracy cannot last unless there lies at the base of it social democracy. What does social democracy mean? It means a way of life which recognizes liberty, equality and fraternity as the principles of life. These principles of liberty, equality and fraternity are not to be treated as separate items in a trinity. They form a union of trinity in the sense that to divorce one from the other is to defeat the very purpose of democracy. Liberty cannot be divorced from equality, equality cannot be divorced from liberty. Nor can liberty and equality be divorced from fraternity. Without equality, liberty would produce the supremacy of the few over the many. Equality without liberty would kill individual initiative. Without fraternity, liberty and equality could not become a natural course of things. It would require a constable to enforce them.

We must begin by acknowledging the fact that there is complete absence of two things in Indian Society. One of these is equality. On the social plane, we have in India a society based on the principle of graded inequality which means elevation for some and degradation for others. On the economic plane, we have a society in which there are some who have immense wealth as against many who live in abject poverty. On the 26th of January 1950, we are going to enter into a life of contradictions. In politics we will have equality and in social and economic life we will have inequality. In Politics we will be recognizing the principle of one man one vote and one vote one value. In our social and economic life, we shall, by reason of our social and economic structure, continue to deny the principle of one man one value. How long shall we continue to live this life of contradictions? How long shall we continue to deny equality in our social and economic life? If we continue to deny it for long, we will do so only by putting our political democracy in peril. We must remove this contradiction at the earliest possible moment or else those who suffer from inequality will blow up the structure of political democracy which this Assembly has so laboriously built up.

The second thing we are wanting in is recognition of the principle of fraternity. What does fraternity mean? Fraternity means a sense of common brotherhood of all Indians—if Indians being one people. It is the principle which gives unity and solidarity to social life. It is a difficult thing to achieve. How difficult it is can be realized from the story related by James Bryee in his volume on American Commonwealth about the United States of America.

The story is—I propose to recount it in the words of Bryee himself that:

'Some years ago the American Protestant Episcopal Church was occupied at its triennial convention in revising its liturgy. It was thought desirable to introduce among the short sentence prayers, a prayer for the whole people, and an eminent New England divine proposed the words 'O Lord, bless our nation'. Accepted one afternoon on the spur of the moment, the sentence was brought up next day for reconsideration, when so many objections were raised by the laity to the word 'nation' as importing too definite a recognition of national unity, that it was dropped, and instead there were adopted the words 'O Lord, bless these United States'.'

There was so little solidarity in the USA at the time when this incident occurred that the people of America did not think that they were a nation. If the people of the United States could not feel that they were a nation, how difficult it is for Indians to think that they are a nation.

I remember the days when politically-minded Indians resented the expression 'The people of India'. They preferred the expression, 'The Indian nation'. I am of opinion that in believing that we are a nation, we are cherishing a great delusion. How can people divided into several thousands of Castes be a nation? The sooner we realize that we are not as yet a nation in the social and psychological sense of the word, the better for us. For then only we shall realize the necessity of becoming a nation and seriously think of ways and means of realizing the goal.

The realization of this goal is going to be very difficult—far more difficult than it has been in the United States. The United States has no Caste problem. In India there are Castes. The Castes are anti-national. In the first place because they bring about separation in social life. They are anti-national also because they generate jealousy and antipathy between Caste and Caste. But we must overcome all these difficulties if we wish to become a nation in reality. For fraternity can be a fact only when there is a nation. Without fraternity, equality and liberty will be no deeper than coats of paint.

These are my reflections about the tasks that lie ahead of us. They may not be very pleasant to some. But there can be no gainsaying that political power in this country has too long been the monopoly of a few and the many are not only beasts of burden, but also beasts of prey. This monopoly has not merely deprived them of their chance of betterment, it has sapped them of what may be called the significance of life. These down-trodden Classes are tired of being governed, they are impatient to govern themselves. This urge for self-realization in the down-trodden classes must not be allowed to develop into a Class struggle or Class war. It would lead to a division of the House. That would indeed be a day of disaster. For, as has been well said by Abraham Lincoln, a house divided against itself cannot stand very long. Therefore, the sooner room is made for the realization of their aspiration, the better for the few, the better for the country, the better for the maintenance for its independence and the better for the continuance of its democratic structure. This can only be done by the establishment of equality and fraternity in all spheres of life. That is why I have laid so much stress on them.

I do not wish to weary the House any further. Independence is no doubt a matter of joy. But let us not forget that this Independence has thrown on us great responsibilities. By Independence, we have lost the excuse of blaming the British for anything going wrong. If hereafter things go wrong, we will have nobody to blame except ourselves. There is great danger of things going wrong. Times are fast changing. People including our own are being moved by new ideologies. They are getting tired of government of the people. They are prepared to have Government for the people and are indifferent whether it is Government of the people and by the people. If we wish to preserve the Constitution in which we have sought to enshrine the principle of Government of the people, for the people and by the people, let us resolve not to be tardy in the recognition of the evils that lie across our path and which induce people to prefer Government for the people to Government by the people, nor to be weak in our initiative to remove them. That is the only way to serve the country. I know of no better.

★ ★ ★

While many credit Dr Ambedkar as the father of the Indian Constitution, even hailing him as the modern Manu after the legendary author of the Laws of Manu (i.e. *Manusmriti*), which ironically was put to fire by him in 1927, more recently, in a serious indictment of Dr Ambedkar, Arun Shouri labelled him as "the False Manu". Shourie's criticism of Dr Ambedkar rests on three points: First, since the Drafting Committee was responsible only for shaping the articles drafted by the specialized Sub-Committees, whose suggestions were later discussed in the Plenary Sessions, Dr Ambedkar couldn't have been in any position to influence the text of the Constitution; secondly, the guidelines for each article were decided by the Congress Party to which Dr Ambedkar was not privy. Thirdly, Dr Ambedkar found himself in a minority on numerous occasions in the sub-committees, the Drafting Committee and during the Plenary Sessions.

Arun Shourie's criticism of Dr Ambedkar is blatantly false, besides being grossly unfair. In addition to being the Chairman of the Drafting Committee, Dr Ambedkar was a Member of two Committees: the Advisory Committee and the Union of the Powers Committee; in the former case, in fact, he was a Member of two important Sub-Committees i.e., the one on Fundamental Rights and also the one on rights of the minorities. Moreover, even where Dr Ambedkar was not responsible for drafting the primary texts (i.e. preparing the first drafts), as the Chairman of the Drafting Committee, he was responsible for reformulating them in the form of articles for the consideration of the Constituent Assembly. Furthermore, the Constituent Assembly discussed several drafts (there were three readings of the Draft), and each time, unmistakably, it was Dr Ambedkar who as the Chairman of the Drafting Committee, took the lead in directing the discussion and firming up the formulations. It was Dr Ambedkar who received all the proposals of the various Committees, and, therefore, it was his responsibility to reformulate these articles. Even those editorial tasks were willy-nilly entrusted to Dr Ambedkar on account of the chronic absenteeism that the Drafting Committee was subjected to. As one of the Members of the Drafting Committee, TT Krishnamachari (who subsequently became the Finance Minister of India), admitted later:

> So it happened ultimately that the burden of drafting this Constitution fell on Dr Ambedkar and I have no doubt that we are grateful to him for having achieved this task in a manner that is undoubtedly commendable.[131]

In this regard, the comment by Dr Rajendra Prasad, the Chairman of the Constituent Assembly, is perhaps most illuminating, when he said:

> Sitting in the Chair, and watching the proceedings from day to day, I have realized, as nobody else could have, with what zeal and devotion the (available) members of the

---

131. Constituent Assembly Debates, Volume 7, p. 231. In fact, TT Krishnamachari explained: "Of the seven members nominated (to the Drafting Committee), one had resigned from the House and was replaced. One died and was not replaced. One was away in America and his place was not filled up and another person was engaged in State Affairs and there was a void to that extent. One or two people were far away from Delhi and perhaps for their health did not permit them to attend."

> Drafting Committee, and especially its Chairman Dr Ambedkar, in spite of his indifferent health have worked. We could never make a decision, which was or could be ever as right as when we put him on the Drafting Committee, and made him its Chairman. He has not only justified his selection but has added lustre to the work which he has done.

It is, thus, abundantly clear that Arun Shourie's criticism is entirely invalid, emanating as it does from "extraneous" reasons. There is not an iota of doubt that Dr Ambedkar played a decisive and determining role in the shaping of India's Constitution. Not only did Dr Ambedkar re-draft the Committee's proposals, he followed them through the Drafting Committee and the Constituent Assembly to their logical end. Indeed, the most balanced view about Dr Ambedkar's contribution came from Michael Brecher (Pandit Nehru's biographer), who described Dr Ambedkar as the Chief Architect of the Indian Constitution and as the Field General of the campaign for a new Constitution.

CHAPTER THIRTY NINE

First Law Minister of Independent India

ON AUGUST 3, 1947, the names of the Council of Ministers for the Central Government were announced. Prime Minister Pandit Jawaharlal Nehru's Cabinet included Dr Ambedkar as the Law Minister of India.

One of the early responsibilities of Dr Ambedkar as the Law Minister was to streamline the working of the Constituent Assembly, which was already functioning (since December 9, 1946), and of which Dr Ambedkar was a Member. On August 29, 1947, Dr Ambedkar moved the Constituent Assembly, thus:

> I beg to move that this Assembly do proceed to take into consideration the Report on the Functions of the Constituent Assembly under the Indian Independence Act, 1947, submitted by the Committee appointed by the President in pursuance of the decisions of the Assembly on August 20, 1947.
>
> Altogether, the Committee has made five recommendations. Its first recommendation is (1) that it is open to the Constituent Assembly to function as Legislature and that it should function as such; (2) that while functioning as Legislature it should adopt the rules of the Legislative Assembly as far as possible with necessary amendments; (3) the necessary amendments should be made under the orders of the President of the Constituent Assembly; (4) the work of the Constituent Assembly as a Constitution-making body and as an ordinary Legislature should be separated and should be conducted in separate sessions to be held on separate days; (5) the power of prorogation should vest in the President and not in the Governor-General as found in the Adaptation of the Government of India Act. After having made these recommendations, the Committee considered whether there were any difficulties which would stand in the way of giving effect to their recommendations and found three which they had to resolve in order to give effect to their recommendations.
>
> The first was whether one and the same person should preside over both the bodies, the Constituent Assembly and the Legislature.
>
> The second difficulty which the Committee came across was with regard to the representatives of the States. The question, therefore, that arises is this, whether a body of people, who are Members of the Constituent Assembly and who are bound by the Instrument of Accession and have responsibility for a shorter number of items, should

be permitted to take part in motions and in debates relating to certain other subjects which were not included in the list contained in the Instrument of Accession.

The third question which the Committee felt they had to deal with was the position of the Ministers. As the House knows, there are certain Ministers who are at present not Members of the Constituent Assembly. They are five in all who fall in that category. The question, therefore, arises for consideration whether the Ministers who are members of the Constituent Assembly should take part in the proceeding of the Constituent Assembly and also in the Legislature.

Sir, there are two other matters about which the Committee has made no recommendation, and it is necessary that I should refer to them. The first matter is the question of double membership. As the House knows there are certain Members of the Constituent Assembly who are also Members of the Provincial Legislature. So far there is no anomaly, because the Constituent Assembly is not a Legislature. But when the Constituent Assembly begins to function as a Legislative Body, this conflict due to double membership will undoubtedly arise.

Second question about which the Committee has made no recommendation is relating to the administrative organization of the Assembly. As the administrative organization in the Assembly is a single unified organization, it is under the exclusive control of the President of the Constituent Assembly. So long as the Constituent Assembly had only this single and solitary function to perform, namely, to prepare the Constitution, there was no difficulty in this matter. But when the Constituent Assembly will function in its double capacity, once as the Constitution-making body and another time as the law-making body with another person at the head of it, namely, the Speaker or the Deputy Speaker, questions with regard to the adjustment of the staff may arise.

Dr Ambedkar, as the Law Minister, skillfully resolved all these issues to the satisfaction of the Members of the Constituent Assembly.

★ ★ ★

As the first Law Minister of Independent India, Dr Ambedkar actively participated in the deliberations of the Central Legislative Assembly, not only when the subject matter pertained to the Law Ministry, but also on several other occasions given his wide-ranging experience. Dr Ambedkar's interventions are far too many to cover in their entirety, but an illustrative one, consider the following:

A Resolution was moved in the Central Legislative Assembly (November 15, 1950) to the effect that a minimum standard of education should be prescribed in order that the candidate may become lawfully entitled to stand for elections. In his response, Dr Ambedkar said:

I must confess that when I got the text of the Resolution moved by Professor Shah I was considerably puzzled, because I felt that in a Resolution of this sort there should not merely be words indicating to Government that there exists in the Constitution a certain article which permitted them to legislate on it but should have also included in it specific suggestions as to what the Government should do in a legislation of this sort. As I said, I was considerably puzzled and therefore it was very difficult for me to come to any definite conclusion as to the attitude I should adopt with regard to this Resolution.

I now see that the object of Professor Shah in framing the Resolution in the terms in which he has framed it was really deliberate. He wanted the House to give him some idea as to what should be incorporated in a legislation under sub-clause (c) of the relevant Article in the Constitution. Well, I have no objection to a procedure of this sort but I should have thought that if Professor Shah was so keen as he appeared to be for a legislation of this sort, he should not have had an empty mind without any kind of a suggestion of his own. However, I suppose those who have supported his resolution have correctly interpreted his mind and taking into account the various speeches that have been made in support of Professor Shah's Resolution, it appears that many Members who are keen about adding some qualification other than those mentioned in the Constitution have in their mind some kind of an educational qualification. But none of them has been very precise: none of them has given me any idea as to what is the standard of education that they would like to prescribe in order that the candidate may become lawfully entitled to stand.

As a standard, are you not making the membership of this House to be a monopoly of the few? I fear that will be the consequence, supposing you lower down your standard, say, for instance, to the fourth standard, in order that no community may be excluded from the opportunity of sending its members to this House. Is that qualification any good? It is of no value at all.

Therefore, my submission is this, that it is a good thing. I am not going to outcry the feeling that there ought to be some education in Members who come to represent their various constituencies in this House. But I just cannot see how you can give legal effect to it. Therefore, my suggestion is that this is a matter which had better be left to the people themselves, or to the political parties who will run the Government. I have no doubt about it that if the political parties, for their own particular purposes, do not attend to this matter, people themselves in course of time will attend to it. People are not going to allow persons who cannot discharge their functions properly in this House to be continued and returned for ever. They want results. They want their welfare to be attended to, and I am sure about it that they will realize that the only instrumentality through which they can achieve this purpose is to send good men to this House. Therefore, I think the proper course is to leave the matter to the people.

Inside the Central Legislative Assembly and outside, Dr Ambedkar always insisted to strictly follow the Constitutional Principles. In a lecture delivered in the Legislative Chamber, Trivandram (Kerala) (June 10, 1950) Dr Ambedkar said:

For public conscience, to behave in accordance with the Constitutional Provisions, is more important than the Constitution itself. Both the Constituents i.e. the Government and the people should observe the principles and directives as stipulated in the Constitution if the Parliamentary Democracy is to succeed in this country. These principles of democracy for the people.

To respect the system of formation of government, observance of laws, habit of independent thinking, and observation of laws of the majority.

But the Government also should follow certain principles. If it appears that the majority of the people of the country has lost faith in the Government then following the best Constitutional traditions, the Government should step down. The Government should respect the sentiments of minorities. And most importantly, the Government should function without any discrimination against any segment of the society.

Most of the Constitutions have failed because those were prepared without taking into account the customs and intellectual/economic conditions of the various segments of society. The persons occupying the position of power should always remember that the power to make the Constitution, Laws and Governance are granted upon certain conditions by the People of the country. The People grant those powers on the condition and with the hope that the government in-charge will do the governance efficiently. Those who cannot fulfil these aspirations of the People should step down.

The Government should offer appropriate opportunity for those sections of the society which are in minority to express their opinion and aspirations. The Government should respect their opinion and take appropriate steps to fulfil their aspirations. This is the basic foundation of the Parliamentary Democracy.

The second basic principle is governance without discrimination. You will be aware that the British people assess the competence of their political parties on the basis of their performance in the Governance. Therefore, in Britain there is no practice of pleasing the powers that be. In India, however, the conditions are deplorable. The Party in power tries to oblige certain sections of the society whereas it discriminates against the others.

The People should ensure that the orthodox tendencies of meanness, and Untouchability and Casteism do not revive in the country. They should ensure that the Dictatorship or Mobacracy does not take roots in the country. It will be extremely harmful. People should be cautious about this and behave accordingly.

I hope the people and the Government follow the best Constitutional traditions and set the nation on the path of progress.

★ ★ ★

SECOND MARRIAGE

On April 15, 1948, at the age of 57, Dr Ambedkar married Dr Sharada Kabir, whose name was changed to Smt Savita Ambedkar. Dr Sharada Kabir was a Saraswat Brahmin lady who worked as an assistant to Dr Madhav Malvankar, who was treating Dr Ambedkar for diabetes and high blood pressure. In Smt. Savita, Dr Ambedkar found a much-needed companion and "a home nurse" in his wife? Among Dr Ambedkar's followers, however, the marriage remained controversial. Many disliked her and even blamed her later for Dr Ambedkar's death. For most Ambedkarites, *Rama Mata* continues to hold the position of the beloved wife of Dr Ambedkar.

★ ★ ★

The reason for Dr Ambedkar joining the Congress Government in Independent India was certainly pragmatic rather than opportunistic. However, even as he was working vigorously on the Draft Constitution and moderating the discussions in the Constituent Assembly and forging a consensus, Dr Ambedkar was getting increasingly uncomfortable with the Congress Party.

A crisis situation emerged in April 1948 when while addressing the United Provincial Scheduled Castes Conference, Dr Ambedkar reportedly said that he had joined the Central Government and not the Congress Party. The Congress Party was a burning house; and he would not be surprised if it was completely ruined in a couple of years. To be sure, there was a furore over the speech. In a letter to one of his trusted colleagues, Dr Ambedkar wrote that there was a heated debate between Pandit Nehru, Sardar Patel and him, and that he had offered to resign if they felt embarrassed. The issue was, however, settled soon thereafter when Dr Ambedkar issued a statement clarifying that his speech was extempore and was misreported. In the statement, Dr Ambedkar reiterated that he had joined the Cabinet because the cause of Scheduled Castes would be better served by joining the cabinet; furthermore, he hated the principle of opposition for opposition's sake.

In his public speeches around the time, Dr Ambedkar continued to emphasize that political power was the key to all social progress, and that the Scheduled Castes could achieve their salvation if they captured power by organizing themselves into a third party and held the balance of power between the ruling political parties, the Congress and the Socialists. While the Congress Party tried to co-opt him—and hence possibly defuse his capacity to mobilize against the social *status quo*, Dr Ambedkar chose to remain a free man and continued to advocate social reform.

With Dr Ambedkar studiously maintaining a separate identity of his own and his political base within the Scheduled Castes, the levels of discomfort between him and the Congress Party continued to grow leading to a major crisis in their relationship—indeed, a head-on collusion, which came in the form of the controversy over the Hindu Code Bill.

CONTROVERSY OVER THE HINDU CODE BILL

The most controversial of Dr Ambedkar's activities in the turmoil of the early post-Independence years was his effort to get the Hindu Code Bill passed. This piece of legislation was, in many ways, the culmination of a century of legislative efforts to reform the traditions of Hindu society, from the Abolition of *Sati* (1829) to the Hindu Women's Right to Property Act (1937). Dr Ambedkar had hoped that it would emerge as one of the cornerstones of modern India.

During the debates in the Constituent Assembly, Dr Ambedkar had demonstrated his firm resolve to reform Indian society by recommending the adoption of a Common Civil Code, vehemently opposing Members, especially Muslim representatives, who were strongly in favour of maintaining personal laws. However, Dr Ambedkar could get nothing more than an Article in the Directive Principles stipulating that: "The State shall endeavour to secure for the citizens a Uniform Civil Code throughout the territory of India." This recommendation had remained only on paper, especially in view of the hard line by the Muslims and conservative Hindus.

In fact, the British Government had decided to consolidate the Hindu personal laws in one code and had accordingly appointed a Hindu Law Committee in 1941 under the chairmanship of BN Rau, which published a draft Hindu Code in August 1944. The Code was introduced in the Legislature in April 1947 but in the face of political turmoil, especially the Independence and partition, it could not be taken up for discussion.

In 1948, Prime Minister Nehru entrusted the drafting of the new Hindu Code to a sub-committee of the Constituent Assembly and nominated Dr Ambedkar as the Chairman of the Committee.

The original Draft Hindu Code had the following main provisions: daughters, as well as sons, to be given a share of the inheritance upon the deaths of their parents, widows to be granted absolute estate, monogamy as the rule of law, and divorce to be allowed under certain circumstances. In the revised Draft Hindu Code, Dr Ambedkar incorporated as essential principles equality between men and women as regards property and adoption, legal status only to monogamous marriages and elimination of the "Caste bar in civil marriages" as also of the need for a concrete justification for a petition for divorce.

The Hindu Code Bill, indeed, was an effort at unprecedented comprehensive social reform that was championed by Dr Ambedkar in the Parliament for nearly four years. What is presented here is a synoptic view of the Hindu Code Bill through a number of submissions and presentations made by Dr Ambedkar in the Parliament as the Union Law Minister.

- This Bill, the aim of which is to codify the rules of Hindu Law which are scattered in innumerable decisions of the High Courts and of the Privy Council, which form a bewildering motley to the common man and give rise to constant litigation. The Bill seeks to codify the law relating to seven different matters. Firstly, it seeks to codify the law relating to the rights of property of a deceased Hindu who has died intestate without making a will, both female and male. Secondly, it prescribes a somewhat altered form of the order of succession among the different heirs to the property of a deceased dying intestate. The next topic it deals with is the law of maintenance, marriage, divorce, adoption, minority and guardianship.
- To begin with the question of inheritance. Under this head the Bill enacts a new principle, at least for certain parts of British India. So far as inheritance is concerned, the Hindus are governed by two different systems of law. One system I know as *Mitakshara* and the other is known as *Dayabhag*. The two

systems have a fundamental difference. According to *Mitakshara*, the property of a Hindu is not his individual property.

- The Hindu Code contained in this Bill adopts the *Dayabhag* rule, under which the property is held by the heir as his personal property with an absolute right to dispose it of either by gift or by will or any other manner that he chooses.
- In other words, it universalizes the law of inheritance by extending the *Dayabhag* rule to the territory in which the rule of the *Mitakshara* now operates.
- Coming to the question of the order of succession among the heirs there is also fundamental difference of a general character between the rule of the *Mitakshara* and the rule of the *Dayabhag*. Under the *Mitakshara* rule the agnates of a deceased are preferred to his cognates; under the *Dayabhag* rule the basis of heirship is blood relationship to the deceased and not the relationship based on cognatic or agnatic relationship. That is one change that the Bill makes; in other words, here also it adopts the rule of the *Dayabhag* in preference to the rule of the *Mitakshara*.
- In the order of succession to a deceased Hindu, the Bill also seeks to make four changes. One change is that the widow, the daughter, the widow of a pre-deceased son, all are given the same rank as the son in the matter of inheritance. In addition to that, the daughter also is given a share in her father's property; her share is prescribed as half of that of the son. The second change which the Bill makes so far as the female heirs are concerned is that the number of female heirs recognized now is much larger than under either the *Mitakshara* or the *Dayabhag*. The third change made by the Bill is this that under the old law, whether the *Mitakshara* or *Dayabhag*, a discrimination was made among female heirs, as to whether a particular female was rich or poor in circumstances at the death of the testator, whether she was married or unmarried, or whether she was with issue or without issue. All these considerations which led to discrimination in the female heirs are now abolished by this Bill. A woman who has a right to inherit gets it by reason of the fact that she is declared to be an heir irrespective of any other considerations. The last change that is made relates to the rule of inheritance in the *Dayabhag*. Under the *Dayabhag* the father succeeds before in preference to the mother, under the present Bill the position is altered so that the mother comes before father. So much for the order of succession of heirs to a deceased male Hindu.
- So far as *stridhan* is concerned, the present bill makes two changes. The one change it makes is that it consolidates the different categories of *stridhan* into one single category of property and lays down a uniform rule of succession; there is no variety of heirs to the *stridhan* in accordance with the different categories of the *stridhan*—all *stridhan* is one and there is one rule of succession. The second change which the Bill seeks to make with regard to their heirs is that the son also is now given a right to inherit the *stridhan*, and he is given half the share which the daughter takes.

- In formulating this Bill and making changes in rules of succession, it is provided that while the daughter is getting half the share in the father's property, the son is also getting half the share in the mother's property so that in a certain sense the Bill seeks to maintain an equality of position between the son and the daughter.
- Coming to the question of the woman's estate… under the Hindu Law where a woman inherits property she gets only what is called a "life estate". She can enjoy the income of the property, but she cannot deal with the corpus of the property, except for legal necessity. The Bill, here again, introduces two changes. It converts this limited estate into an absolute estate just as the male when he inherits gets an absolute estate in the property that he inherits and, secondly, it abolishes the right of the reversioners to claim the property after the widow.
- The Bill provides in one of the most salutary provisions, namely, that this property which is given as *dowry* to a girl on the occasion of her marriage shall be treated as a trust property, the use of which will ensure to the woman and she is entitled to claim that property when she comes to the age of 18, so that neither her husband nor the relations of her husband will have any interest in that property, nor will they have any opportunity to waste that property and make her helpless for the rest of her life.
- There is another part of the Bill which is important and it relates to the rights of a wife to claim separate maintenance when she lives separately from her husband. Generally, under the provisions of the Hindu law, a wife is not entitled to claim maintenance from her husband if she does not live with him in his house. The Bill, however, recognizes that there are undoubtedly circumstances where if the wife has lived away from the husband, it must be for causes beyond her control it would be wrong not to recognize the causes and not to give her separate maintenance. Consequently, the Bill provides that a wife shall be entitled to claim separate maintenance from her husband if he is (1) suffering from a loathsome disease; (2) if he keeps a concubine; (3) if he is guilty of cruelty; (4) if he has abandoned her for two years; (5) if he has converted to another religion; and (6) any other cause justifying her living separately.
- The Code recognizes two forms of marriages. One is called "sacramental" marriage and the other is called "civil" marriage. As Members will know, this is a departure from the existing law. The existing Hindu law recognizes only what is called "sacramental" marriage, but it does not recognize what we call a "civil" marriage. Comparing the rules of marriage contained in the Bill and the existing law, it may be noticed that there are three differences which the Bill makes. One is this, that while the existing law requires identity of Caste and sub-Caste for a valid sacramental marriage, the Bill dispenses with this condition. Marriage under the Bill will be valid irrespective of the Caste or sub-Caste of the parties entering into the marriage.
- The second provision in this Bill is that identity of *gotrapravara* is not a bar to a marriage while it is under the existing law. The third distinctive feature is this,

that under the old law, polygamy was permissible. Under the new law it is monogamy which is prescribed. The sacramental marriage was a marriage which was indissoluble. There could be no divorce. The present Bill makes a new departure by introducing into the law provisions for the dissolution of marriage. Any party which marries under the new Code has three remedies to get out of the contract of marriage. One is to have the marriage declared null and void, secondly, to have the marriage declared invalid; and thirdly, to have it dissolved.

- Then coming to the question of divorce, there are seven grounds on which divorce could be obtained. (1) desertion; (2) conversion to another religion; (3) keeping a concubine or becoming a concubine; (4) incurably unsound mind; (5) virulent and incurable form of leprosy; (6) venereal diseases in communicable form; and (7) cruelty.
- Coming to the question of adoption, there again, most of the rules embodied in the Bill are in no way different from the rules obtaining under the present law. There are two new provisions in this part dealing with adoption. Firstly, under the Code, it will be necessary for the husband if he wants to make an adoption to obtain the consent of his wife and if there are more than one, at least the consent of one of them. Secondly, it also lays down that if the widow wants to adopt, she can only adopt if there are positive instructions left by the husband authorizing her to adopt and in order to prevent litigation as to whether the husband has, as a matter of fact, left instructions to his wife.
- The Code also provides that the adoption may also be evidenced by registration. The Code makes a salutary provision that there may be registration of adoption by a Hindu.
- The points which arise out of this Bill for consideration and which are new are these: First the abolition of birth-right and not to take property by survivorship. The Second point that arises for consideration is the giving of half-share to the daughter. Thirdly, the conversion of the women's limited estate into an absolute estate. Fourthly, the abolition of Caste in the matter of marriage and adoption. Fifthly, the principle of monogamy, and sixthly the principle of divorce.

Dr Ambedkar submitted the revised Hindu Code Bill to the Constituent Assembly in October 1948. It was going to have a difficult history. The Bill gave rise to a widespread and bitter controversy. The questioning of customs governing the private lives of Hindus led to a hue and cry in the name of protection of religious beliefs. This continued for nearly three years, while the Bill remained pending under contentious debate, with the orthodox attacking it by proclaiming the sacred nature of Hindu marriage. Marriage and the family were declared as the true foundations of Hindu society, and the proponents of this belief argued that dissolving a marriage would ruin a society that had endured for millennia.

In October 1950, Dr Ambedkar circulated amongst the Members of Parliament, a 39-page booklet containing the nature and scope of the changes in the Hindu Code Bill revised in the light of representations received from various Hindu organizations throughout the country. He also delivered speeches in various fora in different parts of the country, which aimed at building a consensus. But there were no signs of the controversy dying out. President Dr Rajendra Prasad in his letter to Sardar Patel had expressed strong reservations against the Hindu Code Bill, pointing out that the "new concepts and new ideas are not only foreign to the Hindu law but are susceptible to dividing every family".[132] Dr Prasad privately campaigned against the Bill on the grounds that Members of the provisional Parliament did not have the mandate to address critical issues. Congress Party President Pattabhi Sitaramayya also opposed the Bill on the grounds that it would alienate the Party's support base on the eve of the general elections of 1951-52.

On the other hand, Prime Minister Nehru fully supported the Hindu Code Bill and had even declared that his Government would resign if the Hindu Code Bill were not passed by Parliament. This was despite the fact that Sardar Patel had declared his stern opposition to the Bill and had even announced that the Bill would not be taken up by Parliament at all.

On August 10, 1951, Dr Ambedkar wrote to Prime Minister Nehru that his health was causing him anxiety, and that he was keen that the Bill be taken up in Parliament on priority. In response, the Prime Minister stated that there was opposition to the Bill both inside the Government as well as outside and that it would be taken up in Parliament at the beginning of September 1951. In order to diffuse the opposition, Prime Minister Nehru strategically even split the Code into four sub-sets. It was decided that the Marriage and Divorce part of the Hindu Code Bill would be treated as a separate bill and would be taken up in Parliament on September 17, 1951.

The truncated Hindu Code in the form of Marriage and Divorce Bill was hotly debated in the Parliament. The debate demonstrated the hostility that had built up amongst most traditionalist Congressmen. After four days of discussions, Dr Ambedkar made an impassioned speech on September 20,1951

Responding to the criticisms, Dr Ambedkar asserted that the arguments about the unchanged nature of Hindu society and its survival meant nothing. Rather, he pointed out, the question was of the quality of what had survived. The new marriage system proposed was not, he argued, an imitation of the West but was based on the values of liberty, equality and fraternity enshrined in the Constitution. In contrast, he reasoned, the "sacramental marriage of the traditionalists is polygamy for the man and perpetual slavery for the woman". He made a reference to the story of Rama and Sita as an indication of the degraded condition of womenfolk in Hinduism, thus creating a further uproar in the House, which alienated him even further.

---

132. Quoted in Jaffrelot Christophe, op cit. p.116.

The Bill failed finally. Pandit Nehru, who had vowed to support it, never issued a whip and was clearly unable and unwilling to bring the traditionally minded members of the Congress into line. A little later, Dr Ambedkar attributed Pandit Nehru's back-tracking to pressure from the Congress Party. He said in a statement:

"I have never seen a case of chief whip so disloyal to the Prime Minister and the Prime Minister so loyal to a disloyal whip."[133]

There is a view that Pandit Nehru feared that Congress MPs would reject the Bill en masse and/or the President Dr Rajendra Prasad would indeed carry out his threat not to promulgate it as a law.[134]

Dr Ambedkar, ailing and disgusted, resigned from his seat in the Cabinet on September 27, 1951. In his resignation letter to the Prime Minister, he stated:

> For a long time I have been thinking of resigning my seat from the Cabinet. The only thing that had held me back from giving effect to my intention was the hope that it would be possible to give effect to the Hindu Code Bill before the life of the present Parliament comes to an end. I even agreed to break up the Bill and restricted it to Marriage and Divorce in the fond hope that at least this much of our labour may bear fruit. But even that part of the Bill has been killed. I see no purpose in my continuing to be a Member of your Cabinet.

As a matter of civility to the Prime Minister and to the Cabinet, Dr Ambedkar expressed his willingness to continue till motions standing in his name were finished. Pandit Nehru agreed to accept his resignation from the last date of the ongoing session, after appreciating his hard labour, and indicated that the fates and the Rules of Procedure were against the Hindu Code Bill.

In a surprise move, Pandit Nehru asked for a copy of Dr Ambedkar's parting speech in advance. In response, Dr Ambedkar informed the Prime Minister on October 4, 1951 that if he prepared a speech he would give an advance copy to the Prime Minister and that he had obtained permission of the Deputy Speaker to make his statement on October 11, 1951.

When the Parliament began its session on October 11, at some point Dr Ambedkar rose to speak. Surprisingly, the Deputy Speaker ruled that he would have been allowed to speak at that juncture only if he had submitted a copy of his statement to the Chair earlier. When some MPs wondered aloud whether the behaviour of the Deputy Speaker did not amount to pre-censorship, in a departure from democratic and Parliamentarian traditions, the (Deputy) Speaker said that as the custodian of the rights and privileges of Parliament, it was necessary for him to see that the statement contained nothing irrelevant or libellous. Turning to Dr Ambedkar, the Deputy Speaker continued: "Hon'ble Minister ...." Before he could proceed further, Dr Ambedkar cut him off, retorting that he was no longer a

133. Quoted in Som R, "Jawaharlal Nehru and the Hindu Code", *Modern Asian Studies*, 1994, p.185-7.

134. Jaffrelot, Christophe, op cit, p.117.

Minister and that he did not intend to submit to that kind of dictate. He collected his papers and stormed out of the House.

RESIGNATION FROM THE CABINET

After the walk-out, Dr Ambedkar distributed copies of his statement to newspaper reporters. His statement cited five points on which he differed from the Union Cabinet:

(1) Pandit Nehru had left him out of every Cabinet Committee, even though as Prime Minister, he had promised him the Planning Department, while indicting him into the Cabinet;
(2) The apathy of the Congress Government towards the uplift of the Scheduled Castes;
(3) The unwillingness of the Government to bring about the right solution for the Kashmir issue;
(4) The wrong foreign policy of India which increased enemies rather than friends; and,
(5) Pandit Nehru's lukewarm policy towards the Hindu Code Bill. Dr Ambedkar categorically stated that it was his impression that Prime Minister Nehru, though sincere, had lacked the earnestness and determination required to get the Hindu Code Bill through.

Beyond all these stated reasons for resignation, there was probably an unstated one too: independent India's first general elections were approaching and Dr Ambedkar wanted to fight them from his own party's platform[135]. Nevertheless, it is highly significant that Dr Ambedkar chose to leave the Union Cabinet of the Congress Government over the issue of the Hindu Code Bill. This goes to show that Dr Ambedkar believed in the top down political path of social reform based on concrete implementation of measures that would inevitably alter time-honoured social customs. The failure of the Hindu Code Bill perhaps made Dr Ambedkar realize that although the Congress Party had approved the Constitutional framework of Parliamentary democracy, most Congressmen were not prepared to support concrete advances that called the social *status quo* into question. Clearly, it must have demonstrated to him that the economic radicalism shown by the emergence of a planned, state-directed and substantially State-owned economy was not matched by social radicalism, as yet.

Dr Ambedkar concluded his statement by saying that:

> The Hindu Code Bill was the greatest social reform measure ever undertaken by the Legislature in this country. No law in the past or the future can be compared to it in its significance. To leave inequality between Class and Class, between sex and sex,

135. Jaffrelot, Christophe, op. cit, p.117

> which is the soul of Hindu society untouched, and to go on passing legislation relating to economic problems is to make a farce of our Constitution and to build a palace on a dung heap.[136]

* * *

Although Dr Ambedkar resigned from the Union Cabinet of Ministers on the issue of gender equality which he had sought to achieve through the Hindu Code Bill, hardly anybody in India gives him any credit as the champion of gender equality. He was only a leader of Untouchables, after all. On the contrary, the orthodox Hindu leaders, in fact, derided him as a Modern Manu because he dared to dispute the laws of Manu.[137]

136. As explained by Omvedt (2004), the word "Class" here refers to Caste, as was done frequently at the time.
137. Incidentally, as noted by Raja Sekhar Vundru, one of Dr Ambedkar's objectives in 1951 i.e., making women coparceners was finally realized in 2005. See, *Outlook* (August 20, 2012).

CHAPTER FORTY

Defeat in the First General Elections (1952)

WHEN DR AMBEDKAR resigned from the Union Cabinet his health had deteriorated considerably. He suffered from diabetes, rheumatism and high blood pressure, besides frequent and severe leg pain. But Dr Ambedkar was back into opposition politics and he set out immediately to gear up for the first general elections scheduled for January, 1952.

GENERAL ELECTIONS (1952)

Dr Ambedkar convened a meeting of the Executive Body of the Scheduled Castes Federation in New Delhi (early October 1951) to finalize the Election Manifesto, which he himself had drafted.

The Election Manifesto of the SCF marked an important turning point away from State socialism, and towards democratic universalism. Dr Ambedkar viewed economic policy on the basis of no "ism"—only rationalism and pragmatism. The election manifesto, in fact, clearly stated:

> The policy of the party is not tied to any particular dogma or ideology such as Communism, Socialism, Gandhism. The Party will be ready to adopt any plan of social and economic betterment of the people irrespective of its origin and provided it is consistent with its principles. Its outlook on life would be purely rational and modern.[138]

There is a view that this Election Manifesto represents "a clear retreat from his earlier argument for an economic pattern of State socialism. He was still concerned about State action, as was evidenced by his interest in the Planning Commission, but his reiteration that there would be no dogma, no pre-conceived pattern

138. Khairmode C, (2000).

indicated a conscious break with Marxist economics. He was, in other words, becoming a social democrat."[139]

Dr Ambedkar's democratic universalism was evident, on the one hand, from his emphasis on the parliamentary form of government which was described as 'the best form of government, both in the interest of the public and in the interest of the individual', and, on the other hand, from his twin strategy of "Caste" identity (broadened to appeal to Scheduled Tribes and OBCs in addition to SCs) and 'Class' identity (appealing to "labouring classes")

In the context of economic policy, in respect of poverty, the stress was on economic growth: poverty could only be reduced by increasing production or "controlling the excessive growth of population". In agriculture, the Manifesto supported mechanization, with equipment to be provided by the state, and the establishment of large-scale farms on a collective or cooperative basis. For landless labourers, the Manifesto recommended development of irrigation and making waste lands available for cultivation. In respect of industry, the Manifesto insisted the policy would "not be bound by any dogma or pattern". Whether or not to "nationalize" an enterprise would depend on what was possible and essential; there would be no preconceived patterns. There was a call only for the nationalization of insurance. Accordingly, very few state-owned industries were envisaged.

The Manifesto also announced that (for general elections of 1952) no alliance would be made with the Congress, with "communal parties" or with the communists. During the election campaign, the Scheduled Castes Federation allied itself with the Socialist Party for electoral purposes.

The first-ever parliamentary elections of independent India took place in January 1952. The election results were most discouraging for Dr Ambedkar. Both the SCF and the Socialists fared badly while the Congress party carried the day. The SCF won only 2.3 per cent of the valid votes and only two seats in the Lok Sabha (one in Bombay Presidency and one in Hyderabad). In the Bombay Presidency Shri PN Rajbhoj was elected to Parliament, while Shri BC Kamble was elected to the Bombay Legislative Assembly.

Dr Ambedkar himself contested from Bombay City North, a double-member Lok Sabha Constituency that was supposed to elect both a general and a reserved category candidate. He lost the Lok Sabha election in his stronghold of Mumbai to Congress candidate Narayan Kajrolkar by little more than 14,000 votes. He blamed his defeat on the Communists, especially on SA Dange, who had allegedly wasted more than 78,000 votes. (In the electoral system at that time, reserved constituencies were lumped with general constituencies, and each voter had two votes, one for each seat.) Dr Ambedkar alleged that the Communists had propagated against him telling the voters to cast both their votes for one candidate, which was illegal. Dr Ambedkar even moved the Court charging electoral fraud against the Communists, headed by SA Dange. Dr Ambedkar lost the case, adding to his frustration.

139. Omvedt, Gail, op cit, p.138.

Although defeated at the Lok Sabha polls, Dr Ambedkar had not lost hope of going back to Parliament. He asked his trusted colleagues (esp. Kamalakant Chitre) to sound relevant persons and political parties about his interest in the Rajya Sabha. Accordingly, things were "arranged" [140] and Dr Ambedkar was elected as a Member of Rajya Sabha in March 1952.

Dr Ambedkar remained keen on joining the Lok Sabha so that he might give the people the other point of view from the opposition. He did contest another Lok Sabha election in May 1954 (i.e. By-election in Bhandara, Maharashtra jointly with Ashok Mehta of the Socialist Party). However, electoral success continued to elude Dr Ambedkar—he lost the Lok Sabha by-election by only around 8400 votes to a 'seventh class pass' unknown Congressman Bhaurao Borkar.[141] Consequently, Dr Ambedkar continued as Rajya-Sabha Member until his *Nirvana* in December, 1956.

With Dr Ambedkar moving towards broader identity formations on all fronts, it was natural that he should propose to broaden and transform his political party too. The heritage he decided to associate with was the democratic one rather than the socialist one, another confirmation of the change in the direction of his political and economic thinking. The new party would, he said, be founded on the principles of liberty, equality and fraternity, but it would no longer have the militant working Class identity that the earlier ILP, with its red flag, had claimed. Instead, Dr Ambedkar chose a name for the party that symbolized, for him, the end of slavery in the United States—the Republican Party, the party of Lincoln. The Republican Party of India (RPI) would be one with a broadly social democratic programme, but one directed against forms of Caste enslavement that still existed in India. While in terms of cadre it was and would remain an incarnation of the old SCF, a party almost entirely of Dalits, its broader aspirations were now clearly identified with all oppressed sections of society. The RPI was formally established only after Dr Ambedkar's death, but its basis was the outline that he had provided.

As Independent India moved into the future, claiming to implement a socialist pattern of society without decisively resolving the issues of its Caste-ridden, patriarchal society, Dr Ambedkar was increasingly moving towards Buddhism, the religion he saw as a liberating force.

---

140. Keer, Dhananjay, op. cit, p. 441. It is not clear what those "arrangements" were; was the Congress' support involved? Most likely, but not clear from the available records.

141. According to S. Anand, in spite of "reserved seats" "the first-past-the-post (FPTP) method ensures that those elected are inevitably pliable candidates propped up by parties with majoritarian interests". See *Outlook,* August 20, 2012.

PART IX

SEARCH FOR IDENTITY

CHAPTER FORTY ONE

"Who Were the *Shudras*"

DR AMBEDKAR WROTE this provocatively original treatise (200+pages) with the title: "Who Were the *Shudras*: How They Came to be the Fourth *Varna* in the Indo-Aryan Society" after studying the religious history of India over 15 years. The book was first published in October 1946. His motivation in writing this classic has been clarified in the Preface to the book, which includes the following:

(1) Excluding the Untouchables, the *Shudras* form about 75 to 80 per cent of the Hindu population. A treatise dealing with so vast a population cannot be considered to be dealing with a trivial problem.

(2) The present-day *Shudras* are a collection of Castes drawn from heterogeneous stocks and are racially different from the original *Shudras* of the Indo-Aryan Society. Unfortunately, the Code (i.e., the legal system of pains and penalties) is applied to the present-day *Shudras* in the same rigorous manner in which it was applied to the original *Shudras*. Accordingy, "How such a Code came into being cannot, therefore, be regarded as of mere antiquarian interest to the *Shudras* of today."

(3) Dr Ambedkar was surprised at how the meek and non-violent looking Hindu can be violent when anybody attacks his Sacred Books. He became aware of it as never before when the year before he received a shower of letters from angry Hindus after his speech in Madras, which were full of filthy abuse, unmentionable and unprintable, and full of dire threats to (his) life. Against this background, Dr Ambedkar's determination not to be deterred from catching a thief by the menaces of a ruffian prompted him to write this book.

(4) Dr Ambedkar believed that the book contains an exposure of the real character of the conspiracy against the *Shudras*, which no Brahmin scholar could have had the courage to present. At the same time, Dr Ambedkar was aware that the non-Brahmin scholar may find it difficult to remain true to the spirit of the historian. He was careful in adding, therefore, that in writing

> about the *Shudras* I have had present in my mind no other consideration except that of pure history.... I have not made this book a preface to non-Brahmin politics.

Interestingly, this book has been "Inscribed to the Memory of Mahatma Jotiba Fule (1827-1890)" whom he describes as:

> The Greatest *Shudra* of Modern India who made the lower classes of Hindus conscious of their slavery to the higher classes and who preached the gospel that for India social democracy was more vital than independence from foreign rule.

★ ★ ★

This classic treatise can be summarised in Dr Ambedkar's own words (as far as possible) as under:

I. THE RIDDLE OF THE *SHUDRAS*

- Any attempt to discover who the *Shudras* were and how they came to be the fourth *Varna* must begin with the origin of the *Chaturvarnya* in the Indo-Aryan society. A study of the *Chaturvarnya* must in its turn start with a study of *Purusha Sukta*. The *Purusha Sukta* is a theory of the origin of the Universe.
- Verses 11 and 12 of the *Purusha Sukta* explain how the four classes, namely; (1) Brahmins or priests; (2) *Kshatriyas* or soldiers; (3) *Vaishyas* or traders; and (4) *Shudras* or menials; arose from the body of the Creator. These verses contain a divine injunction prescribing a particular form of the constitution of society. This ideal of *Chaturvarnya* was the mould in which the life of the Indo-Aryan community in its early or liquid state was cast. The *Purusha Sukta* would really have been unique if it had preached a classless society as an ideal form of society. But preaches instead a Class-composed society as its ideal.
- The scheme of the *Purusha Sukta* is unique, in as much as it fixes a permanent warrant of precedence among the different classes, which neither time nor circumstances can alter. The warrant of precedence is based on the principle of graded inequality among the four classes, whereby it recognises the Brahmin to be above all, the *Kshatriya* below the Brahmin but above the *Vaishya* and the *Shudra*, the *Vaishya* below the *Kshatriya* but above the *Shudra* and the *Shudra* below all.
- The *Purusha Sukta* appears to make the explaining of the four Classes of the Aryan society to be its primary concern. In doing this, the *Purusha Sukta* stands in complete contrast not only with other theologies but with the other parts of the Rig Veda as well. In (Rig Veda) there is no reference at all to the separate creation of Classes. The *Rig Veda* ignores the Classes and refers to the creation of men only. The *Purusha Sukta* goes beyond. It follows up the notion of division of labour and converts the scheme of division of work into a scheme of division

of workers into fixed and permanent occupational categories. Why does the *Purush Sukta* commit itself to such a perversity? Why did it recognise the communal divisions within the tribes? These are some of the riddles of the *Purush Sukta.*

- In propounding the doctrine of *Chaturvarnya,* the *Purush Sukta* plays a double game. It proceeds first to raise the real, namely, the existence of the four classes in the Indo-Aryan Society, to the status of an ideal. This is a deception because the ideal is in no way different from facts as they exist. After raising the real to the status of the ideal, it proceeds to make a show of giving effect to what it regards as an ideal. This again is a deception because the ideal already exists in fact. This attempt of the *Purusha Sukta* to idealise the real and to realise the ideal, is a kind of political jugglery. To idealize the real, which more often than not is full of inequities, is a very selfish thing to do. The principle underlying the *Purush Sukta* is, therefore, criminal in intent and anti-social in its results. For, it aims to perpetuate an illegal gain obtained by one Class and an unjust wrong inflicted upon another.
- A sociological scrutiny of the *Purusha Sukta,* one relating to the position of the *Shudra, reveals an* astonishing plan of equating different classes to different parts of the body of the Creator. The equation of the different classes to different parts of the body is not a matter of accident. It is deliberate. The idea behind this plan seems to be to discover a formula which will solve two problems, one of fixing the functions of the four classes and the other of fixing the gradation of the four classes after a pre-conceived plan.
- The later developments of *Chaturvarnya* are mainly two. First is the creation of the fifth Class next below the *Shudras.* The second is the separation of the *Shudras* from the first three *Varnas.* These changes have become so integrated with the original scheme of the *Purusha Sukta* that they have given rise to peculiar terms, such as *Savarnas, Avarnas, Dvijas, non-Dvijas,* and *Traivarnikas.* The *Brahmins, Kshatriyas, Vaishyas and Shudras* are *Savarnas.* The Untouchables or *Ati-Shudras* are called *Avarnas.* Logically, the *Brahmins, Kshatriyas, Vaishyas* and *Shudras* are within the *Chaturvarnya.* The Untouchables or the *Ati-Shudras* are outside the *Chaturvarnya.* The *Brahmins, Kshatriyas* and *Vaishyas* have the right to wear the sacred thread. Logically, they are *Dvijas.* The *Shudras* and the *Ati-Shudras* have no right to wear the sacred thread. Logically, they are both *non-Dvijas.*
- The *Brahmins, Kshatriyas, Vaishyas* and *Shudras* are all within the four corners of the *Chaturvarnya.* They are all *Savarnas.* Why then is the *Shudra* denied the right of the *Traivarnikas*? Can there be a greater riddle than the riddle of the *Shudras*?

II. THE BRAHMANIC THEORY OF THE ORIGIN OF THE *SHUDRAS*

- The ancient Brahmins were evidently conscious of the fact that the origin of the four classes was an unusual and uncommon social phenomenon and that the place of the *Shudra* in it was very unnatural and that this called for some explanation. Otherwise, it would be impossible to account for the innumerable attempts to explain the origin of the *Chaturvarnya* and of the *Shudra*.

- But what is one to say of these explanations? The variety of them is simply bewildering. Some allege that *Purusha* was the origin of the four *Varnas,* and some attribute their origin to Brahma, some to Prajapati and some to Vratya. The same source gives differing explanations. Some explanations such as those in terms of Prajapati, or Brahma are theological. Others in terms of Manu or Kasyapa are in humanistic terms. It is imagination running riot. There is in them neither history nor sense. All these speculations are really the twaddles of idiots and ravings of madmen.

III. THE BRAHMANIC THEORY OF THE STATUS OF THE *SHUDRAS*

- Turning to the Brahmanic view of the civil status of the *Shudra*, what strikes one is the long list of disabilities, accompanied by a most dire system of pains and penalties to which the *Shudra* is subjected by the Brahmaiac law-givers. The disabilities and penalties of the *Shudra* found in the *Samhitas* and the *Brahmanas* are so deadening that it would be impossible to believe them unless one sees them in cold print.
- One is also struck by the consideration that *Shudra* alone has been selected by the Brahmanic law-givers as a victim for their law-making authority. The question is: why was the *Vaishya* let off, and why the fury directed towards the *Shudras*? Also striking is the close connection of the disabilities of the *Shudra* with the privileges of the Brahmin. The *Kshatriyas* and *Vaishyas* have no rights worth speaking of against the *Shudras*. The only *Traivarnika* who has special rights and privileges is the Brahmin.
- These disabilities have no parallel anywhere in the world. A survey of rights and disabilities of the Roman Law may well give comfort to Hindus that the Brahmanic Law was not the only law which was guilty of putting certain classes under disabilities, although the disabilities imposed by the Roman Law have nothing of the cruelty which characterises the disabilities imposed by the Brahmanic Law. Notably, the basis of rights and disabilities in Roman Law was the same for all. They did not differ from community to community. The Roman Law of rights and disabilities was not communal while the Brahmanic Law was. In matters of criminal law it made no distinction between one citizen and another. The same offence the same punishment, no matter who the complainant and who the accused was. The *Dharma Sutras* and the *Smritis* follow an entirely different principle. For the same offence the punishment varies according to the community of the accused and the community of the complainant. If the complainant is a *Shudra* and the accused belonged to any one of the three classes the punishment is less than what it would be if the relations were reversed. Yet another barbarity which distinguishes the Brahmanic

Law from the Roman Law is that the Brahmanic Law not only seeks to impose disabilities but it endeavours to make them permanent. It will be a crime for a *Shudra* to study the Vedas or hear it being pronounced and if he does commit such a crime his tongue should be cut or molten lead should be poured into his ear. Can anything be more barbarous than preventing a man to grow out of his disability? The disabilities of the *Shudra* have no relation to his personal conduct. It is not the result of infamy. The *Shudra* is punished just because he was a *Shudra*.

IV. *SHUDRAS* VERSUS ARYANS

- The Brahmanic writers do not give us any clue as to who the *Shudras* were and how they came to be the fourth *Varna*. It is, therefore, necessary to turn to the Western writers. According to the Western scholars:
  (1) The people who created the Vedic literature belonged to the Aryan race.
  (2) This Aryan race came from outside India and invaded India.
  (3) The natives of India were known as *Dasas* and *Dasyus* who were racially different from the Aryans.
  (4) The Aryans were a white race. The *Dasas* and *Dasyus* were a dark race.
  (5) The Aryans conquered the *Dasas* and *Dasyus*.
  (6) The *Dasas* and *Dasyus* after they were conquered and enslaved were called *Shudras*.
  (7) The Aryans cherished colour prejudice and, therefore, formed the *Chaturvarnya* whereby they separated the white race from the black race such as the *Dasas* and the *Dasyus*.
- Let us examine the question of Aryan race. According to one view, the Aryan race existed in a physiological sense with typical hereditary traits. According to Professor Max Muller, the Aryan race existed only in a philological sense, as a people speaking a common language. What is the testimony of the Vedic literature? As examination of the Vedic literature shows that there occur two words in the *Rig Veda*—one is Arya with a short 'a' and the other is Arya with a long 'a'. The word Arya with a short 'a' is used in the Rig Veda in 88 places. The word Arya with a long 'a' is used in the Rig Veda in 31 places. But in none of these is the word used in the sense of race. The terms 'Arya' and 'Arya' which occur in the Vedas have not been used in the racial sense at all.
- On the question of locating the original home of the Aryan race, there is a bewildering variety of views and options. Benfey places the cradle of the Aryans in the region to the North of the Black Sea, but Geiger places it more to the North-West, in Central and Western Germany. Another school holds that the original home of the Aryan race was in Caucasia. On the other hand, Bal Gangadhar Tilak concludes that the Vedic poets i.e., the Vedic Aryans must have had the Arctic region as their home. Question is: was the horse to be found in the Arctic region? If the answer is in the negative, the Arctic home theory becomes very precarious.

- What evidence is there of the invasion of India by the Aryan race and the subjugation by it of the native tribes? So far as the *Rig Veda* is concerned, there is not a particle of evidence suggesting the invasion of India by the Aryans from outside India. As to the question of conquest and subjugation, references can undoubtedly be found in the *Rig Veda* where *Dasas* and *Dasyus* are described as enemies of the Aryas. But before drawing any conclusion from it in favour of conquest and subjugation by the Aryans, the following points must be taken into consideration. First is the paucity of references in the *Rig Veda* to wars between the Aryans, on the one hand, and the *Dasas* or *Dasyus,* on the other. Evidence may show the occurrence of sporadic riots between the two. It is certainly not evidence of a conquest or subjugation. The second point about the *Dasas* is that whatever conflict there was between them and the Aryans, the two seem to have arrived at a mutual settlement, based on peace with honour. The third point to note is that whatever the degree of conflict, it was not a conflict of race. It was a conflict which had arisen on account of difference of religions. In the face of these statements from the *Rig Veda,* there is obviously no room for a theory of a military conquest by the Aryan race of the non-Aryan races of *Dasas* and *Dasyus*.
- It might be useful to discuss it from the side of the *Dasas* and the *Dasyus*. In what sense are the names *Dasa* and *Dasyu* used? Are they used in a racial sense? The evidence indicates that the distinction between the Aryans, on the one hand, and the *Dasas* and *Dasyus,* on the other, was not a racial distinction of colour or physiognomy. That is why a *Dasa* or *Dasyu* could become an Arya.
- That the theory of the Aryan race set up by Western writers falls to the ground at every point goes without saying. In the first place, the Western theory is based on nothing but pleasing assumptions and inferences based on such assumptions. In the second place, the theory is a perversion of scientific investigation. It is not allowed to evolve out of facts. On the contrary, the theory is preconceived and facts are selected to prove it. The theory of the Aryan race is just an assumption and no more.
- The theory of invasion is an invention. This invention is necessary because of a gratuitous assumption which underlies the Western theory. The assumption is that the Indo-Germanic people are the purest of the modern representatives of the original Aryan race. Its first home is assumed to have been somewhere in Europe. These assumptions raise a question: How could the Aryan speech have come to India? This question can be answered only by the supposition that the Aryans must have come into India from outside. Hence, the necessity for inventing the theory of invasion. Yet another assumption is that the Aryans were a superior race. Knowing that nothing can prove the superiority of the Aryan race better than invasion and conquest of native races, the Western writers have proceeded to invent the story of the invasion of India by the Aryans and the conquest by them of the *Dasas* and *Dasyus*.

- It is also assumed that the European races were white and had a colour prejudice against the dark races. The theory proceeds to find evidence for colour prejudice in the Aryans who came into India. This it finds in the *Chaturvarnya*—an institution by the established Indo-Aryans after they came to India and which, according to these scholars, is based upon *Varna* which is taken by them to mean colour.
- Not one of these assumptions is borne out by facts. The theory of the Aryan race is based on the premise of a common language and it is supposed to be common because it has a structural affinity. The assertion that the Aryans came from outside and invaded India is not proved and the premise that the *Dasas* and *Dasyus* are aboriginal tribes[142] of India is demonstrably false. Again to say that the institution of *Chaturvarnya* is a reflection of the innate colour prejudice of the Aryans is really to assert too much. If colour is the origin of Class distinction, there must be four different colours to account for the different classes which comprise *Chaturvarnya*.
- The Aryan race theory is so absurd that it ought to have been dead long ago. But far from being dead, the theory has a considerable hold upon the people. There are two explanations which account for this phenomenon. The first explanation is to be found in the support which the theory receives from Brahmin scholars. The reasons are obvious. The Brahmin believes in the two-nation theory. He claims to be the representative of the Aryan race and he regards the rest of the Hindus as descendants of the non-Aryans. The theory helps him to establish his kinship with the European races and share their arrogance and their superiority. He likes particularly that part of the theory which makes the Aryan an invader and a conqueror of the non-Aryan native races. For it helps him to maintain and justify his overlordship over the non-Brahmins. The second explanation why the Aryan race theory is not dead is because of the general insistence by European scholars that the word *Varna* means *colour* and the acceptance of that view by a majority of the Brahmin scholars. Indeed, this is the mainstay of the Aryan theory. In this regard, the evidence in the *Rig Veda* is quite inconclusive. However, the evidence from the Indo-Iranian Literature, especially Zenda Avesta, leaves no doubt that the word *Varna* originally meant a Class holding a particular faith and it had nothing to do with colour or complexion.
- The conclusions that follow from the examination of the Western theory may now be summarized. They are:

  (1) The Vedas do not know any such race as the Aryan race.

142. For a discussion whether in their origin the European races were white or dark, see the observations of Professor Ripley, *infra,* p. 76.

(2) There is no evidence in the Vedas of any invasion of India by the Aryan race and its having conquered the *Dasas* and *Dasyus* supposed to be natives of India.
(3) There is no evidence to show that the distinction between Aryans, *Dasas* and *Dasyus* was a racial distinction.
(4) The Vedas do not support the contention that the Aryas were different in colour from the *Dasas* and *Dasyus*.

V. ARYANS AGAINST ARYANS

- Those who uphold the theory of an Aryan race invading India and conquering the *Dasas* and *Dasyus* fail to take note of certain verses in the Rig Veda. These verses convey that there were two different communities of Aryas who were not only different but oppose and inimical to each other. The existence of two Aryas is not a mere matter of conjecture or interpretation.
- The first piece of evidence is the discrimination which existed for a long time in the matter of the recognition of the sacred character of the different Vedas. Why was the Rig Veda regarded as sacred? Why was the Atharva Veda treated as vulgar? The answer is that the two belonged to two different races of Aryans and it is only when they had become one that the Atharva Veda came to be regarded on a par with the Rig Veda.
- Secondly, compare two ideologies of creation scattered through the entire Brahamic literature. The result of comparison may be set down in the following propositions: (1) one refers to a human being Manu as the progenitor, the other refers to God Brahma or Prajapati as the originator; (2) one is historical in its drift, the other is supernatural; (3) one speaks of the deluge, the other is completely silent about it; (4) one aims at explaining the four *Varnas,* the other aims at explaining the origin of society only. These differences are many. Particularly fundamental seems to be the difference in regard to *Chaturvarnya.* It is true that an attempt is made to combine the two. All that has happened is that instead of one we have two explanations of *Chaturvarnya,* supernatural *Chaturvarnya* produced by *Purusha,* and natural *Chaturvarnya* as developed among Manu's sons. What is the significance of the existence of two such ideologies fundamentally different and irreconcilable? To me, it seems that they are the ideologies of two different Aryan races—one believing in *Chaturvarnya* and the other not believing in *Chaturvarnya*—who at a later stage became merged into one.
- The third and the most unimpeachable evidence in support of my view comes from the anthropometrical survey of the Indian people. It can be seen that there is a solid foundation in anthropometry and history that there were in India two Aryan races and not one.
- The Western theory, it is clear, is only a hurried conclusion drawn from insufficient examination of facts. It is extraordinary that a theory with such a

slender and insecure foundation in fact should have been propounded by Western scholars should have held the field for such a long time.

VI. *SHUDRAS* AND *DASAS*

- Who are the *Shudras*? One view is that 'the *Dasus* and the *Dasyus* were either savages or non-Vedic Aryan Tribes. Those of them that were captured in war were probably made slaves and formed the *Shudra* Caste. Accordingly, to another Vedic scholar and upholder of the Western theory the *Shudras* are the same as *Dasas* and *Dasyus* and further the *Shudras* were the non-Aryan original inhabitants of India and were in a primitive and a savage state of civilisation. The first proposition is not one proposition but is really two propositions rolled in one. One is that the *Dasas* and *Dasyus* are one and the same people. The other is that they and the *Shudras* are one and the same people.
- The first proposition that the *Dasas* and *Dasyus* are one and the same people is a proposition of doubtful validity. Such references to them as are to be found in the Rig Veda are not decisive.
- About the second proposition that the *Shudras* are the same as the *Dasas* and *Dasyus*, one can definitely say that it is without any foundation whatsoever. To make out a case that the *Shudras* are the same as the *Dasas* and *Dasyus*, an attempt is made to treat the word *Shudra* as a derivative word. To say that *Shudra* is not a proper name but is a derivative word is too silly for words. We have direct evidence in support of the proposition that *Shudra* is a proper name of a tribe or a clan and is not a derivative word as is sought to be made out. Various pieces of evidence can be adduced in favour of this proposition.
- Let us now turn to the other proposition and examine the various elements of which it is composed. There are two elements in the proposition. First is: Are the words *Dasyus* and *Dasas* used in the racial sense indicative of their being non-Aryan tribes? The second element is that assuming they were: is there anything to indicate that they were the native tribes of India? Unless and until these two questions are answered in the affirmative, there is no possibility of identifying the *Dasyus* and *Dasas* with the *Shudras*.
- About the *Dasyus*, there is no evidence to show that the term is used in a racial sense indicative of a non-Aryan people. On the other hand, there is positive evidence in support of the conclusion that it was used to denote persons who did not observe the Aryan form of religion. Regarding the *Dasas*, the question is whether there is any connection between them and the Azhi-Dahaka of the Zend Avesta. If the suggestion that the *Dasa* in the Rig Veda is the same as Dahaka in the Avesta, is accepted, then obviously the *Dasas* were not native tribes aboriginal to India. Were they savages? The *Dasas* and *Dasyus* were not a primitive people. They were as civilized as the Aryans and, in fact, more powerful than the Aryans. Such is the testimony of the Rig Veda.

- That the *Dasas* and *Dasyus* were the same as the *Shudras* is a pure figment of imagination. It is only a wild guess. It is tolerated because persons who make it are respectable scholars. So far as evidence is concerned, there is no particle of it, which can be cited in support of it.
- Another fact which is to be noted is that the names *Dasas* and *Dasyus* completely disappear from the later Vedic literature. It means they were completely absorbed by the Vedic Aryans. But it is quite different with the *Shudras*. The early Vedic literature is very silent about them. But the later Vedic literature is full of them. This shows that the *Shudras* were different from the *Dasas* and *Dasyus*.
- According to the evidence of the Rig Veda, there are two categories of Aryans, the Vedic and the non-Vedic. Given this fact, it would be quite easy for an Arya of one Class to speak of an Arya of another Class, as though the two were separate and opposed. Interpreted in this way, the statements in which *Shudras* are set against the Aryans, do not mean that they were not Aryas. They were Aryas of a different Sect or Class.
- That the *Dharma Sutras* call the *Shudra* Anarya does not mean anything. There are two arguments against accepting the testimony of the *Dharma Sutra*. In the first place, the *Dharma Sutras* and other treatises are books written by the enemies of the *Shudra*. As such, they have no evidentiary value. There is another reason why the evidence of the *Dharma Sutras* that the *Shudras* are non-Aryans should not be accepted. It is contrary to the view taken by Manu. According to him, "in the seventh generation[143] a *Shudra* under certain circumstances could become a Brahmin." Such a conception would have been impossible if the *Shudra* was not an Aryan. That the *Shudra* is non-Aryan also contrary to the view taken by the school of Arthashastra. Kautilya calls the *Shudra* an Aryan in the most emphatic and express terms possible.
- Coming to the question of *Shudras* having been made slaves, it is nonsense, if not mendacious. It is founded on two assumptions. First is that the *Dasas* are described as slaves in the Rig Veda. The second is that the *Dasas* are the same as *Shudras*. It is true that the word *Dasa* is used in the Rig Veda in the sense of slave or servant. But the word in this sense occurs in only 5 places and no more. But even if it did occur more than five times, would it prove that the *Shudras* were made slaves? Unless and until it is proved that the two were the same people, the suggestion is absurd. It is contrary to known facts.
- *Shudras* participated in the coronation of kings. That the *Shudras* were invited to be present at the coronation of the king along with Brahmins is evidenced by the description of the coronation of Yudhishthira, the eldest brother of the Pandavas, which is given in the Mahabharata.

---

143. The rule which requires that for establishing his nobility a man must be able to trace his six uninterrupted degrees of unsullied lineage of not merely free-born, but full-born, appears to be a universal rule in ancient times.—See W. E. Hearn, *The Aryan Household*, Chapter VIII.

- *Shudras* were members of the two political assemblies of ancient times, namely, the Janapada and Paura and as a member of these the *Shudra* was entitled to special respect even from a Brahmin. Otherwise, there is no meaning in Manu saying that a Brahmin should not live in a country where the king is a *Shudra*. That means *Shudras* were kings. This proves that the *Shudras* were ministers and that they were almost equal to the Brahmins in number. The *Shudras* were not poor and lowly. They were rich.
- What significance can there be to the enslavement of the *Shudras*, assuming it was a fact? Why should the Aryans particularly want to make slaves of the *Shudras*? What is more important is why should they make different laws for the *Shudra* slaves? The Western theory does not help us to answer our questions.

VII. WHO WERE THE *SHUDRAS*?

- The *Shudras* were Aryans. The primary piece of evidence on which this thesis rests is a passage. The important statements contained in this passage are three: (1) that Paijavana was a *Shudra*; (2) that this *Shudra* Paijavana performed sacrifices; and (3) the Brahmins performed sacrifices for him and accepted *Dakshina* from him. The Paijavana of the Mahabharata is no other than Sudas of the Rig Veda. From the Rig Veda, we know that his real name was Sudas, that he was a *Kshatriya*. He was more than a *Kshatriya*. He was a king and a mighty king. To this, the Mahabharata adds a fresh and a new detail, namely, that he was a *Shudra*. A *Shudra* to be an Aryan, a *Shudra* to be a *Kshatriya* and a *Shudra* to be a king!! Can there be a greater revelation?
- There is no doubt that Sudas belonged to the Bharatas. The next question is: who were these Bharatas and whether they are the people after whom India got the name Bharata Bhumi or the land of the Bharatas. There are two Bharatas quite distinct from each other. One tribe of the Bharatas are the Bharatas of the Rig Veda. What is more important is that if India has been named *Bharata Bhumi* it is after the Bharatas of the Rig Veda. This shows to what illustrious line of kings this *Shudra* Sudas belonged. The Bharatas were, of course, Aryans and, therefore, Sudas must have been an Aryan. It is, therefore, indisputable that Sudas, whether taken as a Bharata or as a Tritsu, was an Aryan.
- And now to the last question: What does *Shudra* signify? In the light of this new discovery that Sudas was a *Shudra*, the word now stands in a totally different light. We have, however, no information to determine which of these corresponds to the clan, which to the phratry and which to the tribe. That being so, it is difficult to say whether *Shudra* was the name of a clan, a phratry or a tribe. Professor Weber is inclined to the view of those who regard the *Shudras* as an Aryan tribe which immigrated into India before the others. His conclusion that the *Shudras* were Aryans hits the nail squarely on the head. The only point of doubt is whether the *Shudras* were a tribe. That they were Aryans and *Kshatriyas* is beyond doubt.

VIII. THE NUMBER OF *VARNAS*, THREE OR FOUR?

- That there were from the very beginning four *Varnas* in the Indo-Aryan society is a view which is universally accepted by all classes of Hindus, and also by European scholars. If the thesis that the *Shudras* were *Kshatriyas* is accepted, then it follows that this theory is wrong and that there was a time when there were only three *Varnas* in the Indo-Aryan society, viz.. Brahmins, *Kshatriyas* and *Vaishyas*.
- There is strong and cogent evidence to show that there were originally only three *Varnas* among the Indo-Aryans. The first piece of evidence is that of the Rig Veda itself. The Rig Veda does not mention *Shudra* as a separate *Varna*. The true conclusion to be drawn from the Rig Veda is that there were only three *Varnas* and that *Shudras* were not regarded as a fourth and a separate *Varna*. Two Brahmanas, the *Satapatha* and the *Taittiriya*, both speak of the creation of three *Varnas* only. They do not speak of the creation of the *Shudras* as a separate *Varna*. On the other side, there is, of course, the evidence contained in the *Purusha Sukta* of the Rig Veda, which maintains that there were four *Varnas* from the very beginning. The question now is: which of the two should be accepted as the correct? How is this question to be decided?
- The main question is whether the *Purusha Sukta* is a later composition added to the original Rig Veda. The question has been dealt with on the basis of the language of the Sukta as compared with the language of the rest of the Rig Veda. The point is that if the *Purusha Sukta* had been an old, hoary text, sanctified by ancient tradition, could the other Vedas have taken such a liberty with it? Could they have changed it and chopped it as they have done? The two verses, which explain the origin of the four *Varnas*, are in the form of question and answer. The point is: Why should these verses be introduced in a question form breaking the narrative form? The only explanation is that the writer wanted to introduce a new matter and in a pointed manner. This means that not only the *Purusha Sukta* is a later addition to the Rig Veda, but these particular verses are much later than even the *Purusha Sukta*.
- Some critics have gone to the length of saying that the *Purusha Sukta* is a forgery by the Brahmins to bolster up their claim to superiority. There is, therefore, nothing surprising if the Brahmins did forge the *Purusha Sukta*, if not the whole, at least the two versus 11 and 12, at some later stage, long after the fourth *Varna* had come into being, with a view to give the system of *Chaturvarnya* the sanction of the Veda.
- There is only one conclusion, that the *Sukta* is an addition to the Rig Veda made at a later stage and is, therefore, no argument that there were four *Varnas* from the very beginning of the Aryan Society. I, therefore, see no difficulty in concluding that there was a time when the Aryan Society had only three *Varnas* and the *Shudras* belonged to the second or the *Kshatriya Varna*.

IX. BRAHMINS VERSUS *SHUDRAS*

- The thesis that the *Shudras* were *Kshatriyas* and that if they became the fourth *Varna* it was because they were degraded to that position does not wholly solve the problem. It only raises another problem. This problem is why were the *Shudras* degraded? My answer is that the degradation of the *Shudras* is the result of a violent conflict between the *Shudras* and the Brahmins. Fortunately, there is abundant evidence of it.
- There is direct evidence of a violent conflict between the *Shudra* king, Sudas and Vasishtha, the Brahmin Rishi. Vasishtha and Vishvamitra were enemies and were enemies first and enemies last. There was no incident to which one of them was a party in which the other did not know himself as an opponent
- The enmity between Vasishtha and Vishvamitra was not an enmity between two priests. It was an enmity between a Brahmin priest and a *Kshatriya* priest. Vasishtha was a Brahmin. Vishvamitra was a *Kshatriya*. The dispute was going on between Brahmins and *Kshatriyas* on the following points:
(i) The right to receive gifts; (ii) The right to teach the Vedas (The *Khastriya* had only the right to study the Vedas. He had no right to teach the Vedas); and (iii) The right to officiate at a sacrifice (*Kshatriya* had the right to perform sacrifices, but he had no right to officiate as a priest at a sacrifice).
- In this dispute between Vasishtha and Vishvamitra, Sudas seems to have played an important part. Vasishtha was the family priest of Sudas. It was Vasishtha who helped him to win the battle against the ten kings. Notwithstanding this, Sudas removed Vasishtha from office. In his place he appointed Vishvamitra as his purohita[144] who performed *yajna* for Sudas. This is the first deed of Sudas which created enmity between Sudas and Vasishtha. There was another deed which Sudas committed which widened and intensified the enmity. He threw into fire Shakti, the son of Vasishtha, and burned him alive. The story is reported in the Satyayana Brahmana. Understood as a history of conflict between Brahmins and *Shudras*, it helps one to understand how the *Shudras* came to be degraded from the second to the fourth *Varna*.

X. THE DEGRADATION OF THE *SHUDRAS*

- The technique employed by the Brahmins for this purpose was to refuse to perform the *Upanayana* of the *Shudras*. It is by this technique that the Brahmins accomplished their end and thereby wreaked their vengeance upon the *Shudras*.

---

144. There is no direct evidence for this. Tradition accepts this as correct which seems to have been based upon Rig Veda, III. 53.9. This is confirmed by Yaska in his Nirukta (II. 24) where he says, "They then relate a story. The *Rishi* Vishvamitra was the purohita of Sudas, the son of Paijavana."

- From the description of the *Upanayana* ceremony two things are clear. First is that the purpose of *Upanayana* was to initiate a person in the study of the Vedas which commenced with the teaching of Gayatri *Mantra* by the Acharya to the Brahmachari. The second thing that is clear is that certain articles were regarded as very essential for the *Upanayana* ceremony. They are: (1) two garments one for the lower part of the body technically called *Vasa* and the other for the upper part of the body called *Uttariya;* (2) *Danda* or wooden staff; (3) *Mekhala* or a girdle of grass tied across the waist. Anyone who compares this description of *Upanayana* as it was performed in ancient times with the details of the ceremony as performed in later days is bound to be surprised at the absence of any mention of thread called *Yajnopavita* to be worn as a part of his *Upanayana.* The centre of the modern ceremony of *Upanayana* is the wearing of this thread and the whole purpose of the *Upanayana* has come to be the wearing of this *Yajnopavita.*
- The thread ceremony and the *Upanayana* ceremony had different purposes to serve. At some later date the two merged into one. The reason for this merger appears to be very natural. The *Upanayana* without the thread ceremony involved the danger of the Acharya taking the boy in his *gotra.* It was to avoid the danger that the father of the boy performed the thread ceremony before handing him over to the Acharya. This is the probable reason why the two ceremonies came to be performed simultaneously.
- *Upanayana* means the teaching of the Veda by the Vedic Brahmin. (1) Is absence of *Upanayana* the test of Shudradom? (2) Did the *Shudra* ever have the right to *Upanayana?* (3) How can the loss of *Upanayana* result in the general degradation of *Shudras*? (4) What power did the Brahmins have to deny *Upanayana* to the *Shudras*?
- To begin with the first. The best way to deal with this question is to refer to the judicial decisions in order to find out what the Courts in India have regarded as the surest criterion for determining who is a *Shudra.* Unfortunately, it is a most confusing medley of opinion which settles little and unsettles much. The Courts have not made any distinction between the *de facto* position of the community and its position *de jure* in regard to *Upanayana,* and have proceeded on the assumption that what is true *de facto* must also be true *de jure.* It is this fault in the application of the criterion of *Upanayana* which has produced anomalies and absurdities, such as one community having one status in one area and quite a different status in a different area. The real criterion is not the wearing of the sacred thread but the right to wear the sacred thread. Understood in its proper sense, it may be said without fear of contradiction that the right to *Upanayana* is the real and the only test of judging the status of a person whether he is a *Shudra* or a *Kshatriya.*
- The second objection is quite untenable. To assume, as the objection does, that from the very beginning the Aryan Society treated its different classes differently in the matter of *Upanayana* is, to my mind, a very unnatural supposition. For

there is ample evidence both circumstantial as well as direct to show that both *Shudras* as well as women had at one time the right to wear the sacred thread and did have it performed.

- The explanation that there was no *Upanayana* of the *Shudra* because he was a non-Aryan is a modern invention which has been shown to be completely baseless. Either there was once an *Upanayana* and it was stopped or the *Upanayana* was from the very beginning withheld. Either may be true. Since there is no reason why the benefit of the *Upanayana* was withheld from the *Shudra* from the beginning, the presumption must be in favour of my thesis which states that they had the right to *Upanayana*, that they were deprived of it at some stage.
- *Upanayana* was one of the *Samskaras* and like other *Samskaras*, its significance was just spiritual. The denial of the *Upanayana* to the *Shudras* necessarily brought about a change in its significance. In addition to its spiritual significance it acquired a social significance which it did not have before. When *Upanayana* was open to everyone, Aryan or non-Aryan, it was not a matter of social significance. It was a common right of all. It was not a privilege of the few. Once it was denied to the *Shudras*, its possession became a matter of honour and its denial a badge of servility. The denial of *Upanayana* to the *Shudras* introduced a new factor in the Indo-Aryan society. It made the *Shudras* look up to the higher classes as their superiors and enabled the three higher classes to look down upon the *Shudras* as their inferiors. This is one way in which the loss of *Upanayana* brought about the degradation of the *Shudras*. Without *Upanayana*, a person was doomed to social degradation, to ignorance and to poverty. The stoppage of *Upanayana* was a most deadly weapon discovered by the Brahmins to avenge themselves against the *Shudras*. It had the effect of an atomic bomb. It did make the *Shudra*, to use the language of the Brahmins, a graveyard.
- From a very early time the function of performing *Upanayana* had been assigned to a guru or a teacher called the Acharya and the boy went and stayed in the Acharya's house. The Acharya must be a man learned in the Vedas. But the first and foremost qualification of an Acharya is that he must be a Brahmana. It was only in times of difficulty (i.e., when a Brahmana is not available) that a person was allowed to have a *Kshatriya* or a *Vaishya* teacher. This exception was permitted only during the period when the distinction between the right to learn the Vedas and the right to teach the Vedas had not been made. But when that distinction came to be made—and it was made in very early times—in fact the conflict between Vasishtha and Vishvamitra was just on this very point—the Brahmin alone came to possess the right to be an Acharya fit to officiate at an *Upanayana*. None but a Brahmin could perform the *Upanayana* ceremony. *Upanayana* performed by anybody else is not a valid *Upanayana*. The other operative part of the Indo-Aryan religious system is the obligation imposed upon the Brahmin not to do any unauthorized act of a religious character.

- Consider the combined effect of these two facts: (1) the Brahmin's exclusive right to officiate at an *Upanayana;* and (2) the penalties to which he is made liable for performing an unauthorized *Upanayana.* The combined effect of these two factors was to vest in the Brahmin the power of performing as well as of denying *Upanayana.*
- That the Brahmins were conscious of the possession of this power to deny *Upanayana* is also beyond doubt. So far as the records go, there are 16 reported cases in which they have threatened various communities by putting it into operation against them. Given the powers and the motive, there is nothing strange if they used it against the *Shudras.* As to whether there was enough provocation, the matter is hardly open to question. On the side of the Brahmins, it is evident that their pretensions to social superiority and their claim for special privileges had become outrageous in character and unbearable in extent. On the side of the *Kshatriya* kings they could not be supposed to be willing to take things lying low. How could they? It must not be forgotten that most of the *Kshatriya* kings who came into conflict with the Brahmins belonged to the solar line.[145] They differed from the *Kshatriyas* of the lunar line in learning, in pride and in martial spirit. The former challenged the Brahmins. The latter succumbed to them and became their slaves. The *Kshatriyas* belonging to the solar line were not merely the equals of Brahmins in the matter of learning, they were their superiors. Several of them were the authors of the Vedic hymns and were known as *Rajarishis.* This was particularly true of those who came into conflict with the Brahmins.
- In the list of the authors of the Vedic hymns there are not only names of many *Kshatriyas,* there are names of many of the *Kshatriyas* who had come into conflict with the Brahmins. The *Kshatriyas* were the leaders among the Vedic hymn makers. The most famous Vedic hymn, namely, the *Gayatri mantra* is the production of Vishvamitra who was a *Kshatriya.* It was impossible for the *Kshatriyas* of this calibre not to take up this challenge of the Brahmins. Their pride which was born out of their prowess and their learning must have been so greatly wounded by the pretensions of the Brahmins that when they did take up the challenge of the Brahmins they did it in a ruthless spirit. They hit the Brahmins hip and thigh.
- On the point of possible reconciliation between the Brahmins and the *Shudras,* there is no doubt some evidence on which some people might rely. The evidence consists of stories of reconciliation which are scattered throughout the

---

145. Only Pururavas and Nahusha belong to the Lunar line of *Kshatriyas* as may be seen from the following genealogical tree:
Soma = Tara----Budha = ila --- pururavs = Urvashi---Ayus---Nahusha
If it is borne in mind that ila the mother of Pururavas was the daughter of Manu Vaivasvata, it will be seen that they too were the kith and kin of the solar *Kshatriyas* who came into conflict with the Brahmins.

Mahabharata and the Puranas. In my opinion, far from accepting it, one should beware of such evidence.The stories are all doctored with a view to glorify the Brahmins and humiliate the *Kshatriyas*. Who can take such dirty, filthy, abominable and vainglorious stories of reconciliation as true historical facts? Only a supporter of Brahminism can do so. All this leaves no doubt that there was no reconciliation between the Brahmins and the *Shudras*.

- It does appear rather strange that the *Shudras* should have suffered silently the perpetration of such an act as the denial of the *Upanayana*. In the times of the Rig Veda, Brahmins were a Class by themselves, had developed Class-consciousness and were keen on maintaining Class interests. In that event it would have been difficult for the *Shudras* to break up the conspiracy of the Brahmins. In the first place did the *Shudras* realise what the effect of the loss of *Upanayana* was going to be on their future status? I am sure they did not. Secondly, were the *Kshatriyas* a united body of people? I doubt if they were. Thirdly, had the other *Kshatriya* kings any sympathy for the *Shudras*? There was not much love lost between the *Shudras* and the other non-*ShudraKshatriyas*. Taking all these circumstances into consideration, there is nothing strange if the *Shudras* suffered the denial of the *Upanayana* by the Brahmins to be a fact.

XI. THE THEORY IN THE CRUCIBLE

Dr Ambedkar finally summarizes his thesis as under:

(1) The *Shudras* were one of the Aryan communities of the Solar race.
(2) The *Shudras* ranked as the *Kshatriya Varna* in the Indo-Aryan Society.
(3) There was a time when the Aryan Society recognized only three *Varnas,* namely. Brahmins, *Kshatriyas* and *Vaishyas.* The *Shudras* were not a separate *Varna* but a part of the *Kshatriya Varna.*
(4) There was a continuous feud between the *Shudra* kings and the Brahmins in which the Brahmins were subjected to many tyrannies and indignities.
(5) As a result of the hatred towards the *Shudras* due to their tyrannies and oppressions, the Brahmins refused to invest the *Shudras* with the sacred thread.
(6) Owing to the loss of the sacred thread, the *Shudras* became socially degraded, fell below the rank of the *Vaishyas* and came to form the fourth *Varna.*

- It now remains to assess the validity of this thesis. It is really wrong to suppose that my theory is based on the solitary passage in the Mahabharata or on the identification of Paijavana with Sudas. The case is supported by several parallel chains. The description of Paijavana as *Shudra* and the identification of Paijavana with Sudas of the Rig Veda is not the only chain which supports the thesis. There are other chains. One of these is the admission in the Satapatha and Taittiriya Brahmanas that there were only three *Varna*s and the *Shudras* did not form a separate *Varna.* The second consists of evidence that *Shudras* were kings and ministers of State. The third consists of evidence that the *Shudras* were at one time entitled to *Upanayana*.

- With regard to my thesis it will be seen that it can explain everyone of the riddles. The thesis explains how the *Shudras* could be kings and ministers and why the *rishis* should praise them and desire to be in their good books. The thesis also explains why there was a controversy over the *Upanayana* of the *Shudra* and also why the law not only denied the right to the *Shudra* but imposed penalties upon a Brahmin, helping to make it effective. Indeed there is no riddle which the thesis does not solve. The thesis, if I may say so, is a close and a perfect fit. Few theses can, therefore, have a better title deed than this.

CHAPTER FORTY TWO

"The Untouchables: Who Were they and Why they Became Untouchables"

THIS IS ANOTHER provocatively original treatise (pages 140+) with the title : "The Untouchables: Who Were They and Why They Became Untouchables", first published in October 1948, as a worthy sequel to Dr Ambedkar's earlier book: "Who Were the *Shudras*?" This book has been "Inscribed to the Memory of Nandnar, Ravidas and Chokhamela, three renowned saints who were born among the Untouchables and who by their piety and virtue won the esteem of all".

The motivation for writing this treatise, as explained by Dr Ambedkar in the Preface to the book, is as follows:

(1) Besides the *Shudras*, the Hindu Civilisation has produced three Social Classes whose existence has not received the attention it deserves. The three classes are: (a) The Criminal Tribes who number about 20 millions or so; (b) The Aboriginal Tribes who number about 15 millions; and (c) The Untouchables who number about 50 millions. The existence of these Classes is an abomination. The Hindu Civilisation, gauged in the light of these social products, could hardly be called civilisation. It is a diabolical contrivance to suppress and enslave humanity. Its proper name would be infamy. What else can be said of a civilization which has produced a mass of people who are taught to accept crime as an approved means of earning their livelihood, another mass of people who are left to live in full bloom of their primitive barbarism in the midst of civilization and a third mass of people who are treated as an entity beyond human intercourse and whose mere touch is enough to cause pollution?

(2) In any other country the existence of these Classes would have led to searching of the heart and to investigation of their origin. But neither of these has occurred to the mind of the Hindu. The reason is simple. The Hindu does not regard the existence of these Classes as a matter of apology or shame and feels no responsibility either to atone for it or to inquire into its origin and

growth. On the other hand, every Hindu is taught to believe that his civilisation is not only the most ancient but that it is also in many respects altogether unique. No Hindu ever feels tired of repeating these claims....That the existence of such Classes is a unique phenomenon, no Hindu need repeat, for nobody can deny the fact. One only wishes that the Hindu realized that it was a matter for which there was more cause for shame than pride.

(3) The inculcation of these false beliefs in the sanity, superiority and sanctity of Hindu Civilisation is due entirely to the peculiar social psychology of Hindu scholars. Today all scholarship is confined to the Brahmins. But unfortunately no Brahmin scholar has so far come forward to play the part of a Voltaire who had the intellectual honesty to rise against the doctrines of the Catholic Church in which he was brought up.... It is a grave reflection on the scholarship of the Brahmins that they should not have produced a Voltaire. Every Brahmin is interested in the maintenance of Brahmanic supremacy be he orthodox or unorthodox, be he a priest or a *grahastha*, be he a scholar or not. How can the Brahmins afford to be Voltaires? A Voltaire among the Brahmins would be a positive danger to the maintenance of a civilisation which is contrived to maintain Brahmanic supremacy... But what annoys one is the intolerance of the Brahmin scholar towards any attempt to expose the Brahmanic literature. He himself would not play the part of an iconoclast even where it is necessary. And he would not allow such non-Brahmins as have the capacity to do so to play it. If any non-Brahmin were to make such an attempt the Brahmin scholars would engage in a conspiracy of silence, take no notice of him, condemn him outright on some flimsy grounds or dub his work useless. As a writer engaged in the exposition of the Brahmanic literature, I have been a victim of such mean tricks.

(4) Notwithstanding the attitude of the Brahmin scholars, I must *pursue* the task I have undertaken. For the origin of these Classes is a subject which still awaits investigation. The Untouchables are the most numerous of the three. Their existence is also the most unnatural. And yet there has so far been no investigation into their origin. That the Hindus should not have undertaken such an investigation is perfectly understandable. The old orthodox Hindu does not think that there is anything wrong in the observance of Untouchability. To him it is a normal and natural thing. As such it neither calls for expiation nor explanation. The new modern Hindu realises the wrong. But he is ashamed to discuss it in public for fear of letting the foreigner know that Hindu Civilisation can be guilty of such a vicious and infamous system or social code as evidenced by Untouchability. But what is strange is that Untouchability should have failed to attract the attention of the European student of social institutions. It is difficult to understand why. The fact, however, is there.

(5) This book may, therefore, be taken as a pioneer attempt in the exploration of a field so completely neglected by everybody. The book deals not only with

> the origin of Untouchability, but it also deals with almost all questions connected with it. It will be found that the book points to a new way of looking at old things.

While presenting his conclusions emanating from historical research, Dr Ambedkar warns:

> A thesis would not be unsound merely because in some parts it is based on guess. My critics should remember that we are dealing with an institution the origin of which is lost in antiquity. The present attempt to explain the origin of Untouchability is not the same as writing history from texts which speak with certainty. It is a case of reconstructing history where there are no texts, and if there are, they have no direct bearing on the question. The origin of Untouchability lies buried in a dead past which nobody knows. To make it alive is like an attempt to reclaim to history a city which has been dead since ages past, and present it as it was in its original condition. It cannot but be that imagination and hypothesis should pay a large part in such a work. But that in itself cannot be a ground for the condemnation of the thesis. For without trained imagination no scientific inquiry can be fruitful and hypothesis is the very soul of science.
>
> It is, therefore, unnecessary for me to apologize for having resorted to constructing links where they were missing. Nor can my thesis be said to be vitiated on that account for nowhere is the construction of links based on pure conjecture. The thesis in great part is based on facts and inferences from facts. And where it is not based on facts or inferences from facts, it is based on circumstantial evidence of presumptive character resting on considerable degree of probability. There is nothing that I have urged in support of my thesis which I have asked my readers to accept on trust. I have at least shown that there exists a preponderance of probability in favour of what I have asserted. It would be nothing but pedantry to say that a preponderance of probability is not a sufficient basis for a valid decision. I do not want anything more from my critics than a fair and unbiased appraisal.

The Classic may be summarized as follows:

A. UNTOUCHABILITY: A COMPARATIVE SURVEY

- Untouchability is the notion of defilement, pollution, contamination and the ways and means of getting rid of that defilement. The pattern of pollution and purification in Primitive and Ancient Society is the same. We can safely conclude that there are no people Primitive or Ancient who did not entertain the notion of pollution.
- In the matter of pollution there is nothing to distinguish the Hindus from the Primitive or Ancient peoples. Manu's statement that the Brahmin was 'ever pure' must be understood in its usual sense of exalting the Brahmin above everything. Manu also prescribes the period of defilement. It varies. At the end of the period there must be performed a purificatory ceremony appropriate to the occasion.

Besides the individual pollution the Hindus believe also in territorial and communal pollution and purification e.g. every village has an annual *jatra*.

- There is another form of Untouchability observed by the Hindus. It is the hereditary Untouchability of certain communities. Such a list of communities was prepared by the Government of India in 1935. This terrifying list includes 429 communities. It means that today there exist in India 50-60 millions of people whose mere touch causes pollution to the Hindus. Surely, the phenomenon of Untouchability among Primitive and Ancient society pales into insignificance before this phenomenon of hereditary Untouchability. This type of Untouchability among Hindus stands in a Class by itself. The impurity of the Untouchables of India is permanent. They are born impure; they are impure while they live; they die the death of the impure; and they give birth to children who are born with the stigma of Untouchability affixed to them. It is a case of permanent, hereditary stain which nothing can cleanse. Moreover, the Hindu society insists on segregation of the Untouchables. This is a fundamental feature of Untouchability as it is practised by the Hindus. It is not a case of social separation, a mere stoppage of social intercourse for a temporary period. It is a case of territorial segregation and putting the impure people inside a barbed wire into a sort of a cage.
- Untouchability among Hindus is thus a unique phenomenon, unknown to humanity in other parts of the world. Nothing like it is to be found in any other society—Primitive, Ancient or Modern.

B. PROBLEM OF HABITAT

- How did the Untouchables come to live outside the village? The *Shastras* say that the *Antyajas* should live and have their abode outside the village. What made them or forced them to do so?
- How did Primitive Society become a settled community? Primitive Society was no doubt nomadic. It was migratory because its wealth, namely, the cattle, was migratory. When Primitive Society learnt the art of farming and of cultivating land, wealth changed its form from cattle to land. With this change Primitive Society became settled at the same place.
- The problems which faced Primitive Society in its transition from Nomadic life to Settled life were mainly two. One confronted the Settled Community. The other confronted the Broken men. All tribes did not take to settled life at one and the same time. Some became settled and some remained nomadic. Also the tribes were never at peace with one another. They were always at war.
- The Nomadic tribes had come to realize that the Settled tribes were doubly wealthy. Like the Nomadic tribes, they had cattle. But in addition to cattle, they had corn which the Nomadic tribes did not and which they greatly coveted. The Nomadic tribes systematically organized raids on the Settled tribes with the object of stealing the wealth belonging to the Settled tribes. Being engaged

in agriculture, the Settled tribes could not always convert their ploughs into swords. This explains how and why during the transition period the Settled tribes were faced with the problem of their defence.

- Continuous tribal warfare was the normal life of the Primitive tribes. In a tribal war it often happened that a tribe instead of being completely annihilated was defeated and routed. In many cases a defeated tribe became broken into bits. As a consequence of this there always existed in Primitive times a floating population consisting of groups of Broken tribesmen roaming in all directions.
- That Primitive Society was fundamentally tribal meant two things. Firstly, every individual in Primitive Society belonged to a tribe.... Outside the tribe no individual had any existence. Secondly, tribal organization being based on common blood and common kinship, an individual born in one tribe could not join another tribe and become a member of it. The Broken Men had, therefore, to live as stray individuals. They did not know who would attack them and to whom they could go for protection. That is why shelter and protection became the problem of the Broken Men.
- We can say that the two struck a bargain whereby the Broken Men agreed to do the work of watch and ward for the Settled tribes and the Settled tribes agreed to give them food and shelter.
- Where were the Broken Men to live? In the midst of the settled community or outside the Settled community? In deciding this question two considerations must have played a decisive part. One consideration is that of blood relationship. The second consideration is that of strategy. Both these considerations were decisive in favour of placing their quarters outside the village. The Untouchables were originally only Broken Men. It is because they were Broken Men that they lived outside the village.
- The Hindu theory of priority in creation does not and cannot apply to the Untouchable. In my view, the word *Antya* means not end of creation but end of the village. It tells us that there was a time when some people lived inside the village and some lived outside the village and that those who lived outside the village, i.e. on the *Antya* of the village were called *Antyaja*[146] e.g., the Mahars caste of Maharashtra
- What is said to have occurred in India also occurred elsewhere e.g. Ireland and Wales. In those regions it was the substitution of common territory for common blood as the bond of union that led to the disappearance of the separate quarters of the Broken Men. Should not such a thing have happened in India? The

146. According to Manash Bhattacharjee, Dr Ambedkar tried to interpret what the texts "conceal or suggest" risking uncertainties about the "truth". The risk allowed Ambedkar to traverse with acumen between the textual and the social...In that masterstroke (about *Antyaja*), Ambedkar linked the language of "othering" with the practice of "ostracising", See *Outlook* (August 20, 2012).

answer is that the notion of Untouchability perpetuated difference between kindred and non-kindred, tribesmen and non-tribesmen in another form; namely; between Touchables and Untouchables. Untouchability is the new factor which prevented the amalgamation from taking place in the way in which it took place in Ireland and Wales, with the result that the system of separate quarters has become a perpetual and a permanent feature of the Indian village.

C. OLD THEORIES OF THE ORIGIN OF UNTOUCHABILITY

- Let's examine the theory of racial difference as the origin of Untouchability. The racial theory of Mr Rice contains two elements:
  (1) That the Untouchables are non-Aryan, non-Dravidian aboriginals; and
  (2) That they were conquered and subjugated by the Dravidians.
- According to Mr Rice, there have been two invasions of India. First is the invasion of India by the Dravidians. They conquered the non-Dravidian aborigines, the ancestors of the Untouchables, and made them Untouchables. The second invasion is the invasion of India by the Aryans. The Aryans conquered the Dravidians and made them *Shudras*. The theory is too mechanical, a mere speculation and too simple to explain a complicated set of facts relating to the origin of the *Shudras* and the Untouchables.
- In ancient Indian history we do often come across four names: the Aryans, Dravidians, *Dasas* and Nagas. Are these the names of different races or are they merely different names for a people of the same race? The general assumption is that they are different races.
- Starting with the Aryans it is beyond dispute that they were not a single homogeneous people. It is also beyond dispute that they were divided into two sections and the two had different cultures. One of them may be called Rig Vedic Aryans and the other the Atharva Vedic Aryans. Their literary developments also lay along different paths. The Rig Vedic Aryans produced Brahmanas, Sutras and Aranyakas. The Atharva Vedic Aryans produced the Upanishads. Whether these two sections of Aryans were two different races we do not know. We also do not know whether the word Aryan is a term indicative of race. Historians have made a mistake in proceeding on the assumption that the Aryans were a separate race.
- A greater mistake lies in differentiating the *Dasas* from the Nagas. The *Dasas* are the same as Nagas. *Dasa* is a sanskritized form of the Indo-Iranian word *Dahaka*, who was the king of the Nagas. Consequently, the Aryans called the Nagas after the name of their king *Dahaka*, which in its Sanskrit form became *Dasa*, a generic name applied to all the Nagas.
- Who were the Nagas? Undoubtedly, they were non-Aryans. The mention of the Nagas in the Rig Veda shows that the Nagas were a very ancient people. It

must also be remembered that the Nagas were in no way an aboriginal or uncivilised people. History shows a very close association by inter marriage between the Naga people with the Royal families of India. Not only did the Naga people occupy a high cultural level but history shows that they ruled a good part of India.

- Who are the Dravidians? Are they different from the Nagas? Or are they two different names for a people of the same race? The popular view is that the Dravidians and Nagas are names of two different races. Nonetheless, it is a fact that the term Dravidians and Nagas are merely two different names for the same people. It is natural to ask why the term Dravidian has come to be restricted to the people of South India if they are really Nagas. The Dravidians of the South India were of the same stock as the *Asuras* or Nagas of the North. The word 'Dravida' is the Sanskritized form of the word "Tamil". It is the name of the language of the people and does not denote the race of the people. Tamil or Dravida was not merely the language of South India but it was the language of the whole of India. In fact, it was the language of the Nagas throughout India. The Nagas in North India gave up Tamil which was their mother tongue and adopted Sanskrit in its place. The Nagas in South India retained Tamil as their mother tongue and did not adopt Sanskrit the language of the Aryans. This is the real reason why the people of South India have come to be called Dravidians. The special application of the use of the word Dravida for the people of South India must not, therefore, obscure the fact that the Nagas and Dravidas are the one and the same people. They are only two different names for the same people. Nagas was a racial or cultural name and Dravida was their linguistic name.
- Thus the *Dasas* are the same as the Nagas and the Nagas are the same as the Dravidians. In other words, what we can say about the races of India is that there have been at the most only two races in the field, the Aryans and the Nagas.
- Suppose there was indeed a third aboriginal race living in India before the advent of the Dravidians, can it be said that those pre-Dravidian aboriginals were the ancestors of the present-day Untouchables of India? There are two tests we can apply to find the truth. One is the anthropometric test and the other is the ethnological. Application of anthropometry to the various strata of Hindu society disproves that the Untouchables belong to a race different from the Aryans and the Dravidians. For the ethnological test it should be remembered that the people of India were once organized on tribal basis. Each tribe was divided into clans and the clans were composed of groups of families. Each group of families had a totem which was some object, animate or inanimate. Those who had a common totem formed an exogamous group popularly known as *Gotra* or *Kul*. An examination of the distribution of the totems among the different Castes and communities should serve as a good test for determining race. *Kul* and *Gotra* are Hindu equivalents of the totem of the Primitive Society. If the same *Kul* and *Gotra* were found to exist in different Castes and

communities it would be possible to say that the Castes though socially different were racially one. Two such studies have been made, one in Maharashtra by Risley and another in the Punjab by Mr Rose and the result flatly contradict the theory that the Untouchables are racially different from the Aryans or the Dravidians. The racial theory of the origin of Untouchability must, therefore, be abandoned.

- Another theory of the origin of Untouchability is based on the unclean and filthy occupations of the Untouchables. Evidence about the Aryans shows that the Aryans were like other people and their notions of purity and impurity did not fundamentally differ from those of other ancient people. For example, Narada *Smriti* shows that the Aryans did not at all mind engaging themselves in filthy occupations. If scavenging was not loathsome to an Aryan how can it be said that engaging in filthy occupations was the cause of Untouchability. The theory of filthy occupation as an explanation of Untouchability is, therefore, not tenable.

D. NEW THEORIES OF THE ORIGIN OF UNTOUCHABILITY

- The Census Report for the year 1910 marked a new departure from the prevailing practice. Among other things, it shows that (1) the Untouchables do not receive the Mantra from a Brahmin; (2) that the Untouchables are not served by good Brahmins as family priests at all; (3) that Untouchables have their own priests reared from themselves; and (4) that Untouchables eat beef and do no reverence to the cow.
- We must ask why the Brahmins refused to officiate at the religious ceremonies of the Broken Men? Is it the case that the Brahmins refused to officiate? Or is it that the Broken Men refused to invite them? Why did the Brahmin regard Broken Men as impure? Why did the Broken Men regard the Brahmins as impure? What is the basis of this antipathy? This antipathy can be explained on one hypothesis. It is that the Broken Men were Buddhists. As such they did not revere the Brahmins, did not employ them as their priests and regarded them as impure. The Brahmin, on the other hand, disliked the Broken Men because they were Buddhists and preached against them contempt and hatred with the result that the Broken Men came to be regarded as Untouchables. On this reasoning it is possible to conclude that one of the roots of Untouchability lies in the hatred and contempt which the Brahmins created against those who were Buddhist.
- Can the hatred between Buddhism and Brahmanism be taken to be the sole cause why Broken Men became Untouchables? Obviously, it cannot be. The hatred and contempt preached by the Brahmins was directed against Buddhists in general and not against the Broken Men in particular. Since Untouchability stuck to Broken Men only, it is obvious that there was some additional

circumstance which has played its part in fastening Untouchability upon the Broken Men.

- Can we say that the Broken Men came to be treated as Untouchables because they ate beef? The correlation between Untouchability and the use of the dead cow is great. Moreover, if there is anything that separates the Untouchables from the Hindus, it is beef-eating. In this context it is not far-fetched to suggest that those who have a nausea against beef-eating should treat those who eat beef as Untouchables. This new theory receives support from the Hindu *Shastras*. We may, therefore, conclude that while the Broken Men were exposed to scorn and contempt on the ground that they were Buddhists, the main cause of their Untouchability was beef-eating.

E. THE NEW THEORIES AND SOME HARD QUESTIONS

- The theory of beef-eating as the cause of Untouchability also gives rise to many questions.
  (1) Did the Hindus never eat beef? (2) What led the Hindus to give up beef-eating? (3) What led the Brahmins to become vegetarians? (4) Why did beef-eating give rise to Untouchability? and (5) When was Untouchability born?
- When the learned Brahmins argue that the Hindus not only never ate beef but they always held the cow to be sacred and were always opposed to the killing of the cow, it is impossible to accept their view. There is clear and ample evidence in Rig Veda as well as Brahmanas and *Dharma Sutras* that the Hindus at one time did kill cows and eat beef. Why did the non-Brahmins give up beef-eating? It was due to their desire to imitate the Brahmins that the non-Brahmins gave up beef-eating. Why did the Brahmins give up beef-eating? If the non-Brahmins underwent one revolution, the Brahmins had undergone two. They gave up beef-eating which was one revolution. To have given up meat-eating altogether and become vegetarians was another revolution. For generations the Brahmins had been eating beef. In a period overridden by ritualism, there was hardly a day on which there was no cow sacrifice to which the Brahmin was not invited by some non-Brahmin. For the Brahmin every day was a beef-steak day. The Brahmins were, therefore, the greatest beef-eaters. The *Yajna* of the Brahmins was nothing but the killing of innocent animals carried on in the name of religion with pomp and ceremony with an attempt to enshroud it in mystery with a view to conceal their appetite for beef. The Brahmins were not merely beef-eaters but they were also butchers.
- Why did the Brahmins give up beef-eating? This was not done as a result of the preachings of Manu, the Divine Law-maker. The revolution took place in spite of Manu and contrary to his directions. What made the Brahmins take this step? Was philosophy responsible for it? Or was it dictated by strategy?
- It was strategy which made the Brahmins give up beef-eating and start worshipping the cow. The clue to the worship of the cow is to be found in the

struggle between Buddhism and Brahmanism and the means adopted by Brahmanism to establish its supremacy over Buddhism. The strife between Buddhism and Brahmanism is a crucial fact in Indian history. That their struggle, which extended for 400 years, has left some indelible marks on religion, society and politics of India.

- Buddhism was at one time the religion of the majority of the people of India. It continued to be the religion of the masses for hundreds of years. It attacked Brahmanism on all sides as no religion had done before. As a result of the spread of Buddhism, the Brahmins had lost all power and prestige at the Royal Court and among the people. They were smarting under the defeat they had suffered at the hands of Buddhism and were making all possible efforts to regain their power and prestige. Buddhism had made so deep an impression on the minds of the masses and had taken such a hold of them that it was absolutely impossible for the Brahmins to fight the Buddhists except by accepting their ways and means and practising the Buddhist creed in its extreme form. After the death of Buddha his followers started setting up the images of the Buddha and building stupas. The Brahmins followed it. They, in their turn, built temples and installed in them images of Shiva, Vishnu and Ram and Krishna etc., all with the object of drawing away the crowd that was attracted by the image worship of Buddha.
- The Buddhists had rejected the Brahmanic religion which consisted of *Yajna* and animal sacrifice, particularly of the cow. The objection to the sacrifice of the cow had taken a strong hold of the minds of the masses especially as they were an agricultural population and the cow was a very useful animal. The Brahmins in all probability had come to be hated as the killer of cows. That being the case, the Brahmins could do nothing to improve their position against the Buddhists except by giving up the *Yajna* as a form of worship and the sacrifice of the cow.
- Why did the Brahmins become vegetarian? The answer is that without becoming vegetarian the Brahmins could not have recovered the ground they had lost to their rival, namely, Buddhism.
- The strategy was to go one better than the Buddhist Bhikshus not only by giving up meat-eating but to become vegetarians. The Buddhist Bhikshus were not vegetarians. Why then did the Brahmins give up meat-eating and become vegetarians? It was because they did not want to put themselves merely on the same footing in the eyes of the public as the Buddhist Bhikshus. They wanted to oust the Buddhists from the place of honour and respect which they had acquired in the minds of the masses by their opposition to the killing of the cow for sacrificial purposes.
- What is more astonishing is the fact that cow-killing was made a *Mahapataka*, a mortal sin or a capital offence by the Gupta Kings who were champions of Hinduism. Why should a Hindu king have come forward to make a law against

cow-killing granted by the Laws of Manu? The answer is that the Brahmins had to suspend or abrogate a requirement of their Vedic religion in order to overcome the supremacy of the Buddhist Bhikshus.

- Beef-eating, instead of being treated as a purely secular matter, was made a matter of religion. This happened because the Brahmins made the cow a sacred animal. This made beef-eating a sacrilege. The Broken Men became guilty of sacrilege. Once the cow became sacred and the Broken Men continued to eat beef, there was no other fate left for the Broken Men except to be treated unfit for association, i.e., as Untouchables.
- Why did the Broken Men not stop eating beef? Even during the period when beef-eating was common to both, the Settled Tribesmen and the Broken Men, a system had grown up whereby the Settled Community ate fresh beef, while the Broken Men ate the flesh of the dead cow. The dead cow had become an exclusive possession and perquisite of the Broken Men.
- As to why they did not imitate, imitation was too costly. They could not afford it. The flesh of the dead cow was their principal sustenance. Without it they would starve. In the second place, carrying the dead cow had become an obligation though originally it was a privilege. As they could not escape carrying the dead cow they did not mind using the flesh as food in the manner in which they were doing previously.

F. UNTOUCHABILITY AND THE DATE OF ITS BIRTH

- The orthodox Hindus insist that Untouchability is very ancient in its origin. In support of their contention, reliance is placed on the fact that the observance of Untouchability is enjoined not merely by the *Smritis* which are of a later date but it is also enjoined by the *Dharma Sutras* which are much earlier and which, according to certain authors, date some centuries before BC. The *Dharma Sutras* do speak of a Class whom they call *Asprashya*. There is also no doubt that the term *Asprashya* does mean Untouchables. Neither the *Dharma Sutras* nor the *Smritis,* however, help us to ascertain who were included in the category of *Asprashya*.
- It is possible to completely disprove the theory that the communities mentioned in the *Dharma Sutras* were Untouchables. The maximum number of communities mentioned in the *Smritis* is only 12, while the number of communities mentioned in the Order-in-Council comes to 429. There are communities mentioned in the *Smritis* which do not find a place in the Order-in-Council at all. If the two lists refer to one and the same class of people, why do they differ and differ so widely? The two lists are different because the list contained in the *Shastras* is a list of the Impure and the list contained in the Order-in-Council is a list of the Untouchables. The reason why some of those in the list of the

Impure appear in the list of the Untouchables is that the Impure at one time became Untouchables e.g. *Chamar*. It proves that the *Chamar* who was at one time an Impure subsequently became an Untouchable and had, therefore, to be included in both the lists. What has made the difference between the *Chamar* and the other impure communities is the fact of beef-eating. It is only those among the Impure who were eating beef that became Untouchables, when the cow became sacred and beef-eating became a sin.

- There was a time when the village in India consisted of a Settled Community and Broken Men and that though both lived apart, the former inside the village and the latter outside it, there was no bar to social intercourse between the members of the Settled Community and the Broken Men. When the cow became sacred and beef-eating became taboo, society became divided into two—the Settled Community became a Touchable community, and Broken Men became an Untouchable community.

G. DETERMINATION OF DATES OF UNTOUCHABILITY

- There are obvious difficulties in the way of fixing a precise date for the birth of Untouchability. Nobody can venture to fix a precise date to a phenomenon which probably began as a cloud no bigger than man's hand and grew till it took its final all-pervading shape as we know it today. When could the seed of Untouchability be said to have been sown? It is possible to give an approximate date. For this the first thing to do is to begin by fixing the upper time-limit at which Untouchability did not exist and the lower time-limit at which it had come into operation.
- In Vedic times there was no Untouchability. As to the period of the Dharma Sutras, we have seen that there was Impurity but there was no Untouchability. Was there Untouchability in the time of Manu? This question cannot be answered offhand. There is a passage in which he says that there are only four *Varnas* and that there is no fifth *Varna*. If the text does refer to the Untouchables then it follows that Untouchability did exist in the time of Manu. I am sure this interpretation is wrong.
- In support of my conclusion I rely on two circumstances. In the first place, there was no Untouchability in the time of Manu; there was only Impurity. In the second place, there is evidence to support the view that this passage has reference to slaves and not to Untouchables. The Narada *Smriti* speaks of the slaves as the fifth Class. I see no reason why the expression fifth Class in Manu Smriti should not be taken as a reference to slaves. If this reasoning is correct, it cuts at the very root of the contention that Untouchability existed in the time of Manu and that Manu was not prepared to include them as part of the *Varna* System. There is, therefore, no reason to conclude that there was Untouchability in the time of Manu. We can definitely say that Manu Smriti did not enjoin Untouchability.

- What is the date of Manu Smriti? There is no unanimity among savants. Some regard it as very ancient and some regard it as very recent. After taking all facts into consideration Professor Buhler has argued that Manu Smriti in the shape in which it exists now came into existence in the Second Century AD. According to Mr Daphtary, Manu Smriti came into being after the year 185 BC and not before. According to him, Manu Smriti has a close connection with the murder of the Buddhist Emperor Brihadratha of the Maurya dynasty by his Brahmin Commander-in-Chief Pushyamitra Sunga and as that event took place in 185 BC, he concludes that Manu Smriti must have been written after 185 BC. It was an epoch-making event. Its significance cannot be measured by treating it simply as a change of dynasty. It was a political revolution as great as the French Revolution, if not greater. It was a bloody revolution-engineered by the Brahmins to overthrow the rule of the Buddhist Kings. .
- Triumphant Brahmanism was needed to make *Chaturvarnya* the law of the land whose validity was denied by the Buddhists. It needed to make animal sacrifice, which was abolished by the Buddhists, legal. Triumphant Brahmanism wanted a sacred text, infallible in its authority, to justify their transgressions. A striking feature of the Manu Smriti is that it not only makes *Chaturvarnya* the law of the land; not only it makes animal sacrifice legal but it goes to state when a Brahmin could justifiably resort to arms and when he could justifiably kill the King. In this the Manu Smriti has done what no prior Smriti has done. It is a complete departure. It is a new thesis. Why should the Manu Smriti do this? The only answer is, it had to strengthen the revolutionary deeds committed by Pushyamitra by propounding philosophic justification.
- Having got the date of the Manu Smriti we can say that in the Second Century AD, there was no Untouchability. Now to turn to the possibility of determining the lower limit to the birth of Untouchability. For this we must go to the Chinese travellers who are known to have visited India and placed on record what they saw of the modes and manners of the Indian people. Certain parts of description of the treatment given to the *Chandalas* do seem to lend support to the conclusion, that is, a case of Untouchability.
- When Fa-Hian came to India it was the reign of the Gupta Kings. The Gupta Kings were patrons of Brahmanism. It was a period of the triumph and revival of Brahmanism. It is quite possible that what Fa-Hian describes is not Untouchability but an extremity to which the Brahmins were prepared to carry the ceremonial impurity which had become attached to some community, particularly to the *Chandalas*. The description given by Yuan Chwang applies to communities other than the *Chandalas*. It is, therefore, just possible that when Yuan Chwang came to India, Untouchability had emerged.
- We can conclude that while Untouchability did not exist in 200 AD, it had emerged by 600 AD. We know that Manu did not prohibit the eating of beef nor did he make cow-killing an offence. When did it become an offence? As has been shown by Dr D R Bhandarkar, cow killing was made a capital offence

by the Gupta kings sometime in the 4^{th}Century AD. We can, therefore, say with some confidence that Untouchability was born some time about 400 AD. It is born out of the struggle for supremacy between Buddhism and Brahmanism which has so completely moulded the history of India and the study of which is so woefully neglected by students of Indian history.

PART X

NATION-BUILDING
FROM THE OPPOSITION SIDE

CHAPTER FORTY THREE

Constructive Criticism in Upper House Debates

DR AMBEDKAR, EVEN in the Opposition, always and consistently offered constructive criticism and sage advice on a wide range of issues.

(1) ON CONSTITUTIONAL AMENDMENTS

While speaking on the Constitution (Third Amendment) Bill, 1954 (September 15, 1954) Dr Ambedkar said:

> Now what is the basic principle underlying this provision relating to the amendment of the Constitution? It seems to me that a student who scrutinizes these two Articles relating to the amendment of the Constitution in Australia and America will find that there are two principles which underlie any action relating to the amendment of the Constitution. The first is this that there must be notice to the people. The people must know that the Government is going to undertake the amendment of the Constitution. The second principle is that there must be consent of the voters either directly as in America or indirectly by the States by ratifying resolution.
>
> Now, Sir, is our Government observing these fundamental rules? It is quite true that our Constitution is a very fluid one. It is not as rigid, not half as rigid as the American Constitution or the Australian Constitution, and those who were in charge of framing the Constitution were fully conscious of the fact that the situation must be left fluid because it may be that circumstances would arise which would require amendment of the Constitution, and you cannot allow the Constitution to hold up the solution of social problems which are emergent. It was because of that it was proposed that the provisions contained in Article 368 should suffice.
>
> Simply because they have obtained a majority they assume that they have not only the power to make any law whatsoever relating to any of the entries which give them the power to make laws but they have also got the power, merely by being elected, even without notifying their intention to the people as such, to even amend the Constitution. Is the Constitution not different in any sense from an ordinary law? Is it merely a scrap of paper to be amended at the whim of anybody? There is a saying in Marathi – I do not know whether I can translate it into English properly – and that

saying is a very good one and very appropriate. We say, if the old woman dies it really does not matter very much but what we are afraid of is that *Yama* gets habituated to coming often and often and what we want to prevent is the *Yama's* invasion. It does not matter if the old woman is dead or snatched away.

This is exactly what has been happening and I have been noticing the great contempt or the low regard or respect which the Government has for the Constitution. You may amend the Constitution; nobody has any objection to amending it but certainly you ought to treat the Constitution on a somewhat different footing, a better footing, a special footing. Tell the people what you are intending to do and then you may do it. Otherwise, it might become necessary even to amend Article 368 in a manner so as to prevent this facile invasion of the Constitutional provisions.

★ ★ ★

While speaking on the Constitution (Fourth Amendment) Bill, 1954 (March 19, 1955), when a Member of Parliament raised a question: "Last time when you spoke, you said you would burn the Constitution."

Dr Ambedkar retorted:

Do you want a reply to that? I would give it to you right here. My friend says that the last time when I spoke, I said that I wanted to burn the Constitution. Well, in a hurry I did not explain the reason. Now that my friend has given me the opportunity, I think I shall give the reason. The reason is this. We built a temple for a God to come in and reside but before the God could be installed in it the devil had taken possession of it. What else could we do except to destroy the temple? We do not intend that it should be occupied by the *Asuras*. That is the reason why I said I would rather like to burn it.

(Another Member): Destroy the devil rather than the temple.

Dr Ambedkar:

You cannot do it. We have not got the strength. If you will read *Sathpath* Brahmin, you will see that the Gods have always been defeated by the '*Asuras*' and that the '*Asuras*' had the '*Amrit*' with them which the Gods had to take away in order to survive in the battle.

(2) ON SOCIO-ECONOMIC ISSUES

While discussing the "Report of Commissioner for Scheduled Castes and Tribes for 1953" (September 6, 1954), Dr Ambedkar said:

I think there is one criticism that one can legitimately make against the Commissioner himself in the matter of drafting and presenting his Report. I was referring to his chapter dealing with complaints, because I thought that would be one of the most interesting and instructive chapters in that book. We are all aware of the fact that the Scheduled Castes in particular are subjected to all sorts of tyrannies, oppressions and maltreatment at the hands of the villagers in the midst of whom they live....

And it would undoubtedly be a matter of great interest to know what are the tyrannies, maltreatments and oppressions to which they are being subjected almost every day. I have no doubt that the Commissioner's report would be the proper place where such complaints would be recorded, but I find the Commissioner absolutely silent over this matter of the gravest importance for the Scheduled Castes.

Then providing details of a number of cases of Caste-based oppression, Dr Ambedkar said:

Now, Sir, I come to the question of the economic emancipation of the Scheduled Castes. This, I think along with education and services is the most important thing for the raising of the status of the Scheduled Castes. Now what are the means of raising the economic status of the Scheduled Castes? Obviously the economic emancipation of the Scheduled Castes will depend upon the opportunity that they get for what might be called entry into gainful occupation. Unless and until doors are open to them where they can find gainful occupation, their economic emancipation is not going to take place. They are going to remain slaves, if not slaves, serfs of the land-owning classes in the villages. There can be no doubt on that point at all. Now, Sir, out of these gainful occupations I personally feel no doubt that the most important thing on which Government ought to concentrate is the giving of land to the Scheduled Castes....

They must be settled on land so that they might obtain independent means of livelihood, cease to be afraid of anybody, walk with their heads erect and live fearlessly and courageously. I think this is a thing which all the Ministers are agreed upon. I take it that the one thing that Government ought to do is to provide land for the Scheduled Castes. Let us take that question. Firstly, is there land available to be given to the Scheduled Castes? Has Government any power to sequester land from those who are owning land now, take it away and give it to the Scheduled Castes? Is it possible for the Scheduled Castes to be financed by the Government in the matter of purchasing lands if land was to be sought? These are the three ways by which land could be given to the Scheduled Castes. Government should by law limit the holding of those who hold land and take away the excess and hand it over to the Scheduled Castes. Secondly, the Government may finance the purchase of land if any is to be sold....

Sir, it is clear to everybody that land-holding in India is not merely a matter of economic livelihood. It is a matter of social status. A person holding land has a higher status than a person not holding land. Now it is quite clear that in the villages this matter of economic status is of the utmost importance to everybody. And no Hindu wishes that an Untouchable should possess a piece of land so that he may reach a higher status than his community is entitled to under the social system. Sir, the question of a Scheduled Caste man getting a bit of land in the village seems to me to be utterly impossible. I do not know to what extent the Government will be able to make a law limiting the holdings. There might easily be a revolution. If the Government had, in passing land legislation, instead of giving the title of the property to the peasant, kept the title to themselves as paramount owners of land, they might have been able to pass a law that as the land belonged to the Government nobody would be allowed to hold more than a certain number of acres....

But the Government has committed one of the greatest acts of folly in creating these peasant proprietors. Sir, once Talleyrand told Napoleon, 'Why do you want all this bother with Europe? Why do you want to create all this enmity? Why should you not be content with becoming the King of France with me as your Prime Minister?' There were a certain number of soldiers standing outside the palace of Napoleon holding their guns with bayonets shining in the light of the sun. Napolean was a very abusive person. He told Talleyrand: 'You were so much done in a silk stocking. Do you see my battalions?' He said, 'Yes, I see them.' Then Napolean asked, 'Why should I not be an Emperor?' To that Talleyrand replied and my friends will remember that reply: 'You can do anything with these bayonets except sit on them....'

Now, you have created these peasant proprietors. You can't sit on them: they will sit on you. You have bungled and bungled most wrongly notwithstanding the advice of many people not to do it. But just to win political elections, you did it and you are bearing the fruits of it now. However, this limitation of holdings, therefore, is an impossible thing....

I happened to study the report of the United Provinces Tenancy Committee appointed by my friend Mr Govind Vallabh Pant. I know every line of it and I wonder whether the people who raised the cry that holdings ought to be limited know anything about the facts of it. What is the average holding in Uttar Pradesh? The lowest is about 1 acre and the highest is about four or five acres. That is all that there is and the further fact is that every inch of land in the U. P. has been under cultivation and in occupation. You can do nothing there and that, I am sure, is the case in most of the other States....

Therefore, my submission to the Honourable Home Minister is this that unless you want to go on fooling the Scheduled Castes by telling them, 'Oh, keep quiet, we are going to give you a piece of land. Either we will have a ceiling or we will finance your purchase.' We will do this or do that, unless you want to go on fooling them like this, you ought to think of some other method of doing that. This is a problem which you must solve and if you do not solve it, you know what consequences there might be – most evil consequences. The fire is burning outside; it may easily come in and the Scheduled Castes may carry the banner and you and your Constitution will go under. Nothing will remain....

Now, Sir, I am going to make one suggestion to my honourable friend and it is this: I find from the Planning Commission's Report that a very large amount of what might be called cultivable waste is to be found in this country. According to the Planning Commission it is 98 million acres. Now, my suggestion to my friends is this: The Government is going, I understand, to amend the Constitution. They are fond of amending the Constitution. Why have a Constitution at all, I do not understand, if you are amending it every Saturday? However, as you are amending it, I suggest that you amend it and put the cultivation of waste land in List No. 1 so that it will come within the purview of the Central Government. The State Governments have not got the means of developing that land. They are living like dog in the manger, neither developing it themselves nor allowing anybody else to do it. Therefore, there can be nothing wrong in taking over the waste land by amending the Constitution in List No. 1....

The second thing which I am going to suggest is one which many people may not find pleasant but I think there is no harm in suggesting. It is this: you again levy the salt tax. The salt tax was the lightest tax that we had in our country. At the time it was abolished, the revenue was about Rs 10 crores and it might easily go up to Rs 20 crores now. No doubt, the abolition of salt tax was done in the memory of Mr Gandhi. I respect him and I suggest to you that you levy the tax and create a Trust Fund in the name of Mr Gandhi – Gandhi Trust Fund for the development or settlement of the Untouchables. After all, the Untouchables, according to all of us, were the nearest and dearest to him and there is no reason why Mr Gandhi may not bless this project from Heaven, namely, levying the tax and using it for the development of waste land and settling the Scheduled Castes on this waste land....

There is promise but a scope for performance. You know in the game of poker there is a difference between promise and performance. I give you a scheme where there is not only promise but there is also performance. I do not understand why the people of this country should not contribute through the means of the salt tax for the elevation of the Scheduled Castes. You may keep it quite outside the Budget just as a sort of a Gandhi Welfare Scheme which will perpetuate the name of Mr Gandhi and which will give relief to the people whom he wanted to protect and whom he wanted to elevate. This is my suggestion to the Honourable Home Minister and I hope he will give this matter his most serious consideration....

Sir, I have done and I do not want to say anything more. The only thing that I would like to say is this that in all this effort which is being made by the Government, by the various social workers and the social agencies, there is one thing which gives me a very sad thought and it is this that our Prime Minister has taken no interest in this matter at all. In fact, he seems to be not only apathetic but anti-Untouchable. I happen to have read his biography and I find that he castigated Mr Gandhi because Mr Gandhi was prepared to die for the purpose of doing away with separate electorates which was given to the Scheduled Castes. He had said in his biography, 'Why on earth Mr Gandhi is bothering with this trifling problem?' Sir, I was shocked and surprised to hear the Prime Minister—rather Mr Nehru then in 1934—uttering these words. I thought that since the responsibility of Government had fallen on his shoulder he may have changed his view and thought that he must now take the responsibility which Mr Gandhi was prepared to take on his shoulder, but I do not find any kind of a change in his mind....

Sir, in the year 1952, a conference was held at Nagpur under the Presidentship of my Honourable friend Babu Jagjivan Ram. I understood that there was a very big *shamiana*. Two silver chairs were placed on the dais, one for Mr Jagjivan Ram and one for Pandit Jawaharlal Nehru. There was an audience of two hundred to three hundred and one thousand police. Pandit Jawaharlal Nehru was supposed to inaugurate that conference. I have got his speech here, but I do not wish to trouble the House by reading it, but this is the gist of it. He was, I am told, in great anger against Babu Jagjivan Ram for having organized the conference. He said loudly 'I do not recognize that there is such a problem as that of the Untouchables. There is a general problem of the economically poor and the problem of the Untouchables is a part of that problem. It will take its place and receive its attention along with the other problems. There is no occasion, no purpose in bestowing any special thought upon it....'

Sir, if the Prime Minister is prepared to throw such cold water—not cold, water from the refrigerator, so to say—what enthusiasm can we expect from the rest of the workers who have taken upon themselves the duty or the responsibility or the interest in carrying on with this particular problem: I do not think that Untouchability will vanish. They believe, 'yes'. I think 'no' as I said, because it has a mental twist. It will take years and years. At the same time, there is no reason why we should not strongly agitate for seeing, whether Untouchability goes or not, that the social, economic, political and Constitutional Rights of the Scheduled Castes are fully protected. To that extent efforts must necessarily be directed....

Sir, there is one other word I should like to say. People might say that I have taken most of the time with the Scheduled Castes. I have not said anything with regard to the tribes and I am not going to say anything, because there are many friends who are more qualified to speak about them than I am. I shall, therefore, not venture to enter that field, but there is one thing which, I think, one can say and should say, because I find there is a good deal of confusion in the minds of the people as regards the relative position of the Scheduled Castes, the Tribal Castes and the Criminal Tribes....

Now, Sir, with regard to the Scheduled Castes, the position is this: they are prepared – in fact, not prepared – but they are already within the pale of civilization. They are not outside. Their struggle is to achieve equality of opportunity and equality of status. That is their problem. With regard to the Tribal people, their problem is totally different. They are outside the Hindu civilization. And the question that has to be considered with regard to these Tribal people is this: do they want to come within the Hindu civilization and be assimilated and then acquire equality of status and equality of opportunity? I was talking to many leaders of the Tribal communities – many men and women of the Tribal community – they seem to be most reluctant to come within the pale of Hindu civilization....

They prefer to live outside, they do not want to come in....

With regard to the Criminal Tribes, theirs is a purely economic problem: how well can you give them the opportunity to earn a decent living? If they can get the opportunity to earn a decent living, they will cease to be criminals....

Now, Sir, one question asked is this. It seems to me a matter of great regret that the Hindu civilization which is so many years old, some say six thousand years old – many people will not be satisfied with that period probably they want to take it back – never mind about it, let it be six thousand years old – has produced five crores of Untouchables, some two crores of Tribal People; and some fifty thousand Criminal Tribes people. What can one say of this civilization?

With a civilization which has produced these results, there must be something very fundamentally wrong, and I think it is time the Hindus looked at it from this point of view - whether they can be proud of the civilization which has produced these communities like the Untouchables, the Criminal Tribes and the Tribal People. I think they ought to think twice – not twice a hundred times – they are conventionally called civilized – whether they could be called civilized with this kind of results produced by their civilization....

(3) ON UNTOUCHABILITY

While participating in the debate on "Untouchability Offences Bill, 1954," (September 16, 1954), Dr Ambedkar said:

> Now, Sir, I find there are certain very grave omissions in the Bill and it is to these omissions that I propose to draw the attention of the House. There is really, as a matter of fact, no provision for the removal of any bar against the exercise of civil and Constitutional rights. No doubt, the ultimate result of the Bill would be freedom to exercise civil and Constitutional rights but I personally think that it would have been much better if my friend had expressly stated that the Bill was intended to remove any kind of a bar against the exercise of any civil and Constitutional rights....
>
> I would just like to read to him a provision from the Civil Rights Bill as they call it in the United States. This is how the provision reads. Don't read the title page of the book—it will hurt you. It is the United States Constitution Amendment XIV taken from Government of Ireland Act, 1920 and also Professor Keith's Command Paper. This is how that provision reads. I have, of course, converted it to make it applicable to the Untouchables but the original is taken from the text of the Civil Rights Bill:
>
> All subjects of the State are equal before the law and possess equal civil rights. Any existing enactment, regulation, order, Customs or interpretation of law by which any penalty, disadvantage, disability is imposed upon or any discrimination is made against any subject of the State on account of Untouchability, shall, as from the day on which this Constitution comes into operation, cease to have any effect.
>
> I think such a positive statement was necessary. It is no doubt contained in Article 13 but there can be no harm in repeating the whole of that Article 13 with such amendments as are necessary in this Bill. I don't know why the Bill is silent. The Bill seems to give the appearance that it is a Bill of a very minor character, just a *dhobi* not washing the cloth, just a barber not shaving or just a *mithaiwala* not selling *laddus* and things of that sort....
>
> People would think that these are trifles and piffles and why has Parliament bothered and wasted its time in dealing with *dhobis* and barbers and *ladduwalas*. It is not a Bill of that sort. It is a Bill which is intended to give protection with regard to civil and fundamental rights and, therefore, a positive Clause, I submit, ought to have been introduced in this Bill, which the Bill does not have now in its present form. That is one omission which I think requires to be made good....
>
> The other omission, which I find, is of a very grave character, is that there is no provision against social boycott. Now I feel from my experience that one of the greatest and the heinous means which the village community applies in order to prevent the Scheduled Castes from exercising these rights is social boycott. They boycott them completely. It is a kind of non-cooperation. This is not merely my opinion but it is the opinion of a Committee that was appointed by the Bombay Government in order to investigate into the conditions of the Scheduled Castes and also of the Depressed Classes and Aboriginal Tribes. I might mention to the House that the late Thakkar Bapa was a member of this Committee and he had signed this report....

I will just read only one para from the report of that Committee which relates to the question of social boycott. It is paragraph 102. This is what the Committee said:

'Although we have recommended various remedies to secure to the depressed classes their rights to all public utilities, we fear that there will be difficulties in the way of their exercising them for a long time to come. The first difficulty is the fear of open violence against them by the orthodox classes. It must be noted that the Scheduled Castes form a small minority in every village opposed to which is a great majority of the orthodox who are bent on protecting their interests and dignity from any supposed invasion of the depressed classes at any cost. The danger of prosecution by the police has put a limitation upon the use of violence by the orthodox classes and consequently such cases are rare. The second difficulty arises from the economic position in which the depressed classes are found today. The depressed classes have no economic independence in most parts of the presidency. Some cultivate the land of the orthodox classes as their tenants at will. Others live on their earnings as farm labourers employed by the orthodox classes, and the rest subsist on the food or grain given to them by the orthodox classes in lieu of service rendered to them as village servants. We have heard of numerous instances where the orthodox classes have used their economic power as a weapon against those depressed classes in the villages when the latter have dared to exercise these rights and have evicted them from their land and stopped their employment and discontinued their remuneration as village servants. This boycott is often planned on such an extensive scale as to include the prevention of the depressed classes from using the commonly used paths and the stoppage of the sale of the necessities of life by the village *bania*. According to the evidence, sometimes small causes suffice for the proclamation of a social boycott against the depressed classes. Frequently it follows on the exercise by the depressed classes of their right to the use of the common well; but cases have been by no means rare where stringent boycott has been proclaimed simply because a Depressed Class man has put on the sacred thread, has bought a piece of land, has put on good clothes or ornaments, or has carried a marriage procession with the bridegroom on the horse through the public street. We do not know of any weapon more effective than this social boycott which could have been invented for suppression of the Depressed Classes. The method of open violence pales away before it, for it has the most far-reaching and deadening effect. It is more dangerous because it passes as a lawful method consistent with the theory of freedom of contract. We agree that this tyranny of the majority must be put down with a firm hand if we are to guarantee the depressed classes the freedom of speech and action necessary for their uplift.'

This is the conclusion of a committee which was specially appointed to consider the condition of the Scheduled Castes. I do not find any provision to deal with this point of social boycott….

The third omission—I do not know whether it is an omission or not, I speak subject to correction. I wish the Law Minister was here because it is purely a legal matter. But there is no doubt about it that our Home Minister was a Law Minister in the beginning and certainly has been a practicing lawyer and he could not be unfamiliar with what I am saying….

Now the question that I ask myself is, are these offences mentioned in this Bill compoundable or non-compoundable? The Bill says nothing about it. It is completely silent. The other day when we were discussing the Report of the Commissioner for the Scheduled Castes and Scheduled Tribes, Honourable Members will recall that the Commissioner drew pointed attention to the fact that the Untouchables were not able to prosecute the persecutors because of want of economic and financial means and consequently they were ever ready to compromise with the offenders whenever the offenders wanted that the offence should be compromised....

The fact was that the law remained a dead letter and those in whose favour it was enacted are unable to put it in action and those against whom it is to be put in action are able to silence the victim. That has been the conclusion of the Commissioner for Scheduled Castes and Scheduled Tribes. Such a situation is not to be tolerated....

The offences must not be made compoundable if the offence is to be brought home to the guilty Party. If the guilty Parties by compounding the offence either by payment of a small sum or something like that are able to get away they can continue their career of harassment of the Untouchables until the moon and the sun are there and Untouchability would never end....

Now, Sir, I come to the question of certain defective provisions. I have said about omissions and I want to say something about the defective provisions. The first such provision to which I shall refer is the Clause relating to punishment, which is Clause 8. The punishment prescribed in the Bill is six months' imprisonment or fine which may extend to Rs 500 or both....

My Honourable friend was very eloquent on the question of punishment. He said that the punishment ought to be very-very light and I was wondering whether he was pleading for a lighter punishment because he himself wanted to commit these offences. He said, 'Let the punishment be very light so that no grievance shall be left in the heart of the offender.'

I suppose his primary premise is that the offenders who offend the Untouchables are really very kindly people, overwhelming with love and kindness and that this is merely an errant act which really ought to be forgiven. It is a matter of great solace to me that he has not prescribed the punishment of being warned and then discharged. That, I think, would be the best Section 561 of the Criminal Procedure Code....

Yes, that would be the best; if our object is to make the offender a loving person; well, let him be warned and discharged. He will continue to love and no soreness will remain in his heart. Why should he have that? Unfortunately, my Honourable friend has thought that, that could not be and, therefore, he has suggested this punishment.

Now, Sir, having had a little practice in criminal law, I think the rules on which punishment is based are two mainly. One is to deter the offender from repeating his offence. That, I think, is the primary rule of criminal jurisprudence. Punishment is necessary; otherwise the offender may go on repeating his offence. It is to prevent him that there must be a punishment. The second object of punishment is to prevent a man from adopting a criminal career. If a man once begins a criminal career then he may continue to do so unless there is some deterrent punishment to prevent him from adopting that career.

Now, Sir, if you accept these two principles, is the punishment proposed by my Honourable friend adequate for the purpose of the Bill? In the first place the six months' imprisonment is really the maximum and a Magistrate may only inflict one day's imprisonment and let the man be off. There is no minimum fixed that the imprisonment shall not be less than six months or three months or whatever it is. The whole matter is left in the hands of the Magistrate. What sort of a Magistrate he may be, it may be quite possible and I can quite imagine that he may be Pandit from Kashi sitting in judgment in the Magistrate's chair. What conscience would he have in the matter of administering this law?

Now, as I said, in this case if you want to see that the law is observed, there ought to have been a minimum punishment below which the Magistrate could not go. Secondly, the punishment is alternative, imprisonment or fine. The Magistrate may very well inflict the alternative punishment of fine and there might be an offender who might be prepared even to pay the five hundred rupees in order to escape the clutches of the law. What good can such punishment do?

The Indian Penal Code prescribes a variety of punishments, a variety of them in Section 53: death, transportation, imprisonment, forfeiture of property, fine, whipping, detention in reformatory. There are seven offences for which the Penal Code fixes death penalty; for 50 offences the punishment is transportation; for 21 offences—simple imprisonment; for 12 offences – fine. In all other cases the imprisonment is rigorous.

Why my friend has thought so little for this Bill as not to prescribe adequate punishment, it is very difficult for me to understand. I mean, the least that one can expect from him is to prescribe a minimum, maybe three months, it does not matter, a minimum of three months' imprisonment and fine if he wants to fix fine – I am not for inflicting a fine because that only benefits the treasury, but if you say that the fine will go to the victim, I am for fine also. Otherwise, I do not want fine.

Shri BB Sharma(Uttar Pradesh): Why Not the Maximum Penalty of Death?

Well, if you like it, have it—I am not so cruel as that and I do not think you are sincere in suggesting it, and, as I said, there are not cases in the Indian Penal Code where minimum punishment has not been prescribed or rigorous imprisonment has not been prescribed. There are three Sections here which prescribe rigorous imprisonment, Sections 194, 226 and 449. Then the Penal Code has prescribed the minimum period of imprisonment in Sections 397 and 398. I do not see why, when there is the precedent, the precedent should not be....

Dr KN Katju: What is 397?

Dacoity. That is worse than dacoity. I think, to starve a man and not to allow him to take water, I think, it is almost causing death. That is, I think, one drawback in the Bill.

Then, Sir, the second drawback in the Bill is that there is no provision for taking security for good behavior. The Criminal Procedure Code has got four Sections, Sections 107, 108, 109 and 110, and they all enable the magistrate to demand security for good behaviour. I don't understand why this Bill should not contain a provision to that effect. When for instance we find in Rajputana and other States the Caste Hindus are agitating to harass the Untouchables because they exercise civil and constitutional rights, why should you not take security for good behaviour?

Shri JS Bisht (Uttar Pradesh): These are all the Provisions in the Criminal Procedure Code.)

That is what exactly I am saying, that there is a precedent in the Criminal Procedure Code for taking security from persons who do not keep peace, for good behaviour, from persons disseminating seditious matter, from vagrants and from habitual offenders, for good behaviour. I am not certain that these provisions could be invoked for the purpose of taking security from persons offending against this law. It may be that specific provision dealing with the cases dealt with in this Bill has to be made, and that can only be made by a specific provision in this Bill….

Then, Sir, there is another provision which finds a place in the Indian Police Act. Section 15 of the Act, under which when some people in the village or the villagers as a whole disturb the peace, the Government can quarter upon them additional police and recover the cost of the additional police from the inhabitants of that village. That is a general provision….

I am not sure again whether that provision could be invoked by the Government for the purpose of enforcing this Act. That Act is a general Act, disturbance of peace and so on and so forth. This is quite a different case and we should have thought that a specific Clause on the lines of Section 15 of the Police Act should have found a place in this Bill if outlawing of Untouchability is intended to be an effective thing. But that again is not there….

Now, Sir, I come to another question about which I certainly feel a certain amount of doubt. Who is to administer this law, the Centre or the States? And if the Centre is to administer the law, is it not better that this Bill should contain a Clause to that effect, that it shall be administered by the Central Government? I make this suggestion because I feel that the States might raise an objection that this is a concurrent piece of legislation and being a concurrent piece of legislation the States have the right ordinarily to administer these Acts. I do not think that this is a concurrent piece of legislation in which the States can claim to have a right to administer….

I claim that this is a Central law although it does not fall in List I of the Seventh Schedule. The provisions contained in Article 35 are quite clear. It has been stated in Article 35 that any law to be made for inflicting punishment for any infringement of a law made in pursuance of Article 17 shall be by Parliament and not by the State. Those are the very express words….

Therefore, there can be no doubt in my mind that this law will have to be by virtue of the Constitution administered by the Centre and not by the States. I say this because my Honourable friend might be saying that since we have made the offences under this Act cognizable, it does not matter if he law is administered by the States but that argument cannot stand at all in virtue of Article 35 and I would suggest to him that he should introduce an express provision in the Bill that the Law shall be administered by the Centre….

If my friend's contention or the contention of the States is that this is also a concurrent piece of legislation, I would like to draw his attention to the proviso to Article 73 which is a very important one and which relates to the administration of laws in the concurrent field. My Honourable friend will remember that in the scheme of things in the Government of India Act of 1935 we had the same kind of classification of subjects—List I—Central subject, List II—State subject, and List III—Concurrent subject, but the Government of India Act contained an express provision that the power of the Centre to make law in the concurrent field was confined merely to law making. It could not encroach upon the field of administration....

The reasons why such a provision was made in the Government of India Act, 1935, are quite irrelevant to the times in which we find ourselves now, but when we made the Constitution we refused to accept such a provision. We said that although generally the Centre may leave a law in this concurrent field for administration to the States the choice must be given to the Centre to determine whether any particular law in the concurrent field made by it shall be administered by it and not by the States. The intention has been carried out in the proviso in the Article 73. We said that if the Centre so determines that the law made in the concurrent field shall be administered by the Centre then the States cannot interfere in the matter at all. Therefore, I am strongly of the opinion that this contention is invalid....

(4) ON CENTRE-STATE RELATIONS

While discussing the relationship between the Centre (Congress-ruled) and non-Congress State Governments (September 14, 1953), Dr Ambedkar severely criticized the 'intolerant' attitude of the former towards the latter. Dr Ambedkar said:

I am sorry to say that to resort to Article 356 in a situation of this sort besmirches the name of the Government that they are using this Article 356 for Party purposes. It is a wrong thing which ought not to be done. This is always being done and the people have got a very legitimate ground for suspicion that the Government is manipulating the Articles in the Constitution for the purpose of maintaining their own Party in office in all parts of India. Sir, as I was looking up here yesterday, somebody made a reference on this side that we must maintain the unity of India. Yes, we must maintain the unity of India. What is the way of maintaining the unity of India? My Honourable friend thinks that the way to maintain the unity of India is to have a Government of the same complexion, a Government of the same Party from Cape Comorin to East Punjab....

Whatever it is, unless and until they see that all through out India there is one type of Government subject to one High Command carrying out the behests of that Command—whether it is good or bad—they are not satisfied; they do not think that the unity of India has been achieved....

Sir, there are many people who feel sorry that the Congress is in power. I am not sorry for that. They have won the power by legitimate means. We have decided that the people shall make the choice. Rightly or wrongly, by fair means or foul means, the choice has been made and I am perfectly prepared to abide it. I have no sense of grievances at all. If my turn is over it is over. If my turn is to come, it may come. I do not know when, but I am not going to do anything unfair by the Constitution....

Now, the other point I was going to place before the House is this: As I said, my Honourable friends on the Treasury Benches are just obsessed by the fact that they must have Congress Governments in every State. Well, Sir, the other day I was looking into a book issued by the Brooklyn Institute in Washington about the relationship between the State Government and the Central Government in the United States. I was considerably surprised to find that there were several elections – I am sorry I did not take out the figure I did not know that this debate was coming, otherwise I might have been given the House some interesting figures about it....

Innumerable elections have taken place in which the Republican Party has been returned at the Centre and the Democratic Party has been returned to the State Governments or the Democrats have held the Central Government and the Republicans have held the Provincial Governments. If the American people and the Republican Party and the Democratic Party can tolerate a Central Government consisting of people who do not belong to their group, why is it that our friends are so intolerant about other people having their chance in running the Government of their State?

It may be that some of them might administer the State in such a way that our Congress friends might have something to learn from them. Why be so dogmatic? Why be so tyrannical and why manipulate the Constitution in this way? You are going to bring the Constitution into complete disrepute if you are going to create the impression that all the provisions in the Constitution which we introduced for the purpose of safety are going to be used for the purpose of Party politics. I warn you very severely and as, I have said, I have no axe to grind. I am not going to approach anybody for any office. Nothing of that kind. I shall not do it. That is not my way of doing it....

Therefore, I am giving you an independent piece of advice that you should use the Constitution for the legitimate purpose for which it had been created. Thereby you will not only create respect for yourself but will also create respect for the democratic way of life which is so completely absent in this country. Sir, I have done....

(5) ON FOREIGN POLICY

While speaking on the international situation, Dr Ambedkar argued that India's foreign policy was flawed. On August 24, 1954, Dr Ambedkar said in the Upper House:

I am glad that it cannot be said of our Prime Minister. He has certain principles on which he is proceeding. It is for the House to decide whether the principles on which he is proceeding are principles which can furnish us a safe guide and whether they are valid principles on which the destiny on this country could be staked. That is the only question that we can discuss and it is to these principles that I am going to confine myself.

The principles on which the Prime Minister is proceeding—and he has said so himself – are mainly three. One is peace, the second is co-existence between communism and free democracy, and the third is opposition to SEATO. These are the three main props on which his Foreign Policy is based. Now, Sir, in order that one may be able to assess the validity and the adequacy of these principles, I think, it is necessary to have some knowledge of the background of the present-day problems with which we are concerned and for which these principles are enunciated.

Now, the background to my mind, is nothing else but the expansion of communism in the world. It is quite impossible to follow the principle or to understand the validity and the nature of the principle unless one bears in mind the problem that the world has to face today – that part of the world which believes in Parliamentary and free democracy, viz, the expansion of communism in the world. I propose to give some figures to the House which I have collected in this matter. I am not going back into the long past but I am going to start from May 1945 when the War came to an end. By May 1945, Russia had consumed ten European States.(Interruption)

Now, Sir, I was saying that if we take stock of the situation from May 1945, and find out what has happened, this is the situation. Russia has consumed, as I said, ten European States: one is Finland; two, Estonia; three, Latvia; four, Lithuania; five, Poland; six, Czechoslovakia; seven; Hungary; eight, Rumania; nine, Bulgaria; and ten, Albania.

Well, Sir, this is the background, I say against which the adequacy of the principles on which the foreign policy of this Government is based, must be considered. I will take first the principle of peace. We want peace; nobody wants war. The only question is, what the price of this peace is going to be. At what price are we purchasing this peace? Now, it is quite obvious that peace is being purchased by what might be called partitioning and dismembering of countries. I can quite understand the dismemberment of Austria – Hungary where different nationalities with different languages, different sovereign autocracy of the Austrian Empire. The first World War brought about the end of the Austrian Empire on the well-known principle of self-determination. But here what you are doing is this. There are countries which are culturally one, which are socially homogeneous, which have one language, one race, one destiny, desiring to live together. You go there, cut them up and divide the carcass, and hand over a part of the carcass to what? To countries who are interested in spreading communism. From the figures which I have given there can be no doubt about it that communist countries today are as big as giant – nobody has seen a giant – I have not seen anyhow.... (Interruption).

Here you have a vast country endlessly occupied in destroying other people, absorbing them within its fold on the theory that it is liberating them. The Russian liberation, so far as I can understand, is liberation followed by servitude; it is not liberation followed by freedom. But the point is this – and it worries me considerably. You are, by this kind of a peace, doing nothing more but feeding the giant every time the giant opens his jaw and wants something to eat. When you are feeding the giant regularly and constantly, the question that I should ask myself is this: Is it not conceivable that this giant may one day turn to us and say: 'I have now consumed everything that there was to be consumed: you are the only person that remains, and I want to consume you.

Shri HP Saksena: Then we will Consume the Giants

Let us not boost ourselves too much. We have not been tried as yet in an international bout and when we are tried in an international bout I think it will be found out whether we can face the situation ourselves. But the point that I was making is this: This principle of feeding the giant seems to me a most obnoxious principle and how, for instance as I said, can we expect to be relieved? Will the Russians show any gratitude because the Indian Prime Minister and the Indian Parliament have supported the partition of Indo-China or supported the partition of Korea, and will they not turn to us? I think this is a question which the Indians should bear in mind and not forget or overlook....

Now the other question, namely, co-existence. This co-existence to my mind is an astounding principle unless it is very strictly limited. The question is: Can Communism and free democracy work together? Can they live together? Is it possible to hope that there will not be a conflict between them? The theory, at any rate, seems to me utterly absurd, for communism is like a forest fire; it goes on burning and consuming anything and everything that comes in its way. It is quite possible that countries which are far distant from the centre of communism may feel safe that the forest fire may be extinguished before it reaches them or it may be that the fire may never reach them. But what about the countries which are living in the vicinity of this forest fire? Can you expect that human habitation and this forest fire can long live together? I have seen comments from Canadian statesmen and from European statesmen congratulating the policy of co-existence. Their praises and their encomiums do not move me in the least. I attach no value to their view and to their opinion. The statesmen of Canada can very easily say that co-existence is possible because Canada is separated from China and Russia by thousands and thousands of miles. Similarly, England after having pulled itself out from the great conflagration, now thinks that she is too exhausted to do anything and, therefore, likes to enunciate and support the principle of co-existence. But there again it is a matter of distance.

One must not forget that in the foreign policy of a country the geographical factor is one of the most important factors. Each Country's foreign policy must vary with its geographical location in relation to the factor with which it is dealing. What is good for Canada may not be good for us. What is good for England may not be good for us. Therefore, this co-existence seems to me a principle which has been adopted without much thought on the part of the Prime Minister.

Then, Sir, I will say a few words with regard to the SEATO. I was very carefully listening to the Prime Minister's observations with regard to the SEATO, and I was glad to find that he had not made up his mind about the SEATO. If I heard him correctly, he said that in view of the fact that this county has accepted the chairmanship of some Commission in accordance with the Geneva decisions it may not be compatible for him and for this country to join the SEATO at the same time. The two things would undoubtedly be incompatible. But apart from that I think the merits of the SEATO must be considered.

The repugnance to SEATO appears to me to arise from two sources. I think I am not letting out any secret nor am I accusing the Prime Minister of anything of which he does not know, that the Prime Minister had a certain amount of hostility, or if he does not like that word, estrangement between himself and the United States. Somehow, he and the USA do not see eye to eye together. That is one reason why I think he always had a certain amount of repugnance to anything that comes from the United States.

Shri B Gupta: Are you Speaking for Match-making?

Mr Chairman: The Prime Minister is quiet and you are talking.

And secondly from the fear of what Russia will think if India joins the SEATO. Here again, I think, it is necessary to give the House some background against which the merits of the SEATO may be assessed. Now, Sir, what is the background of all this? The background is this:

I have given a list of countries which have gone under the Russian regime. I think it is well known that this happened largely because, if I may say so, of the foolishness of the Americans during the last Great War. The Russians got possession of these territories with the consent of Mr Roosevelt and with the reluctant willingness of Mr Churchill. Mr Churchill expressed, when the War ended, that they had done a great mistake, and a great wrong, in sacrificing the liberty of so many nations for the sake of winning victory against Hitler. And the same feeling, I think, is expressed by him in his last volume which he called 'Triumph and Tragedy.' It is because of this that he named his last volume 'Triumph and Tragedy.'

Now, Sir, what the Americans are doing if I understand their policy correctly, is this: Their point of view is that Russia should be satisfied with what she has got during the War, the ten countries. As a matter of fact, I should have thought that it should have been the duty of the Americans and the Britishers to extricate these countries, to liberate them, to make them free. But neither country has the will nor the moral stamina nor the desire to engage itself in such a stupendous task. They are, therefore, following, what maybe called a second line of defence, and that second line of defence is that Russia should not be allowed, or China should not be allowed to occupy any further part of the free world. I think that is the principle to which all freedom-loving people would agree. There could be no objection to it.

And it is to prevent Russia from making further aggression that they are planning the SEATO. The SEATO is not an organization for committing aggression on any country. The SEATO is an organization for the purpose of preventing aggression on free countries. I wonder whether the Prime Minister will not be prepared to accept this principle, that at any rate, such part of the free world as has, by accident, remained free should be allowed to remain free and not to be subjugated. Is India not exposed to aggression? I have no time. Otherwise, I was going to point the House how this country has been completely encircled on one side by Pakistan and the other Muslim countries. I do not know what is going to happen, but now that the barrier between Egypt and England has been removed by the handing over of the Suez Canal, I think there may be very little difficulty in the Muslim countries joining with Pakistan and forming a bloc on that side. On this side by allowing the Chinese to take possession of Lhasa, the Prime Minister has practically helped the Chinese to bring their border down to the Indian border. Looking at all these things, it seems to me that it would be an act of levity not to believe that India, if it is not exposed to aggression right now, is exposed to aggression and that aggression might well be committed by people who always are in the habit of committing aggression....

Now, I come to the other question. What will Russia say if we join SEATO? And the question that I like to ask is this: What is the key-note of Russian foreign policy? What is it? The key-note of our foreign policy is to solve the problems of the other countries, and not to solve the problems of our own. We have here the problem of Kashmir. We have never succeeded in solving it. Everybody seems to have forgotten that it is a problem. But I suppose, some day we may wake up and find that the ghost is there. And I find that the Prime Minister has launched upon the project of digging a tunnel connecting Kashmir to India. Sir, I think, it is one of the most dangerous things that a Prime Minister could do. We have been hearing of a tunnel under the English Channel to connect France with England. We have been hearing it for 50 years, I think someone has been proposing, and yet the English have never done anything to carry out the project, because it is a double-edged weapon. The enemy, if he conquers France, can use the tunnel and rush troops into England and conquer England. That might also happen. The Prime Minister, in digging the tunnel, thinks that he alone would be able to use it. He does not realise that it can always be a two-way traffic, and that a conqueror who comes to the other side and captures Kashmir, can come away straight to Pathankot, and probably come into the Prime Minister's House—I do not know....

The Prime Minister has been depending upon what may be called the *Panchsheel* taken by Mr Mao and recorded in the Tibet Treaty of non-aggression. Well, I am somewhat surprised that the Prime Minister should take this *Panchsheel* seriously. The *Panchsheel,* as you, Sir, know it well, is the essential part of the Buddhist religion, and if Mr Mao had any faith in the *Panchsheel*, he certainly would treat the Buddhists in his own country in a very different way. There is no room for *Panchsheel* in politics and, secondly, not in the politics of a Communist country. The Communist countries have two well-known principles on which they always act. One is that morality is always in a flux. There is no morality. Today's morality is not tomorrow's morality. You can keep your word in accordance with the morality of today and you can break your word with equal justification tomorrow because tomorrow's morality will be different....

The second thing is that when the Russian Communist State is dealing with the other States, each transaction is a unit by itself. When we deal with somebody, we begin with goodwill and end with gratitude. When the Russians deal with somebody, they do not begin with goodwill, nor do they end with any gratitude. Each transaction begins and ends by itself, and that is what I am sure the Prime Minister will find at the end when the situation ripens. The Prime Minister has always been saying that there is such a thing as the principle, 'Asia for Asiatics.' Yes, in so far as colonialism is concerned, that principle is perfectly true. Asia must be for Asiatics, but we are dealing with a situation like this? Asia is divided now, it is a divided House now. More than half of Asia is Communist. It has adopted a different principle of Government. The rest of Asia follows a different life and a different principle of Government. What unity can there be among Asiatics? What is the use of talking about Asia for Asiatics? There can be no such thing at all. Asia is already becoming the cockpit of war and strife among Asians themselves. Therefore, it is better to align ourselves with what we call free nations if we believe in freedom.

CHAPTER FORTY FOUR

Public Pronouncements of a Social Democrat

AFTER RESIGNING FROM the Union Cabinet Dr Ambedkar continued to participate in public meetings and share his deep insights for successful working of democracy in India. There are three very significant speeches that Dr Ambedkar delivered, extracts of which are presented here:

I. WHAT IS PARLIAMENTARY DEMOCRACY

During the discussion in the Constituent Assembly there was a variety of opinion as regards the nature of the Constitution that we should have. Some preferred British system; some American system. There were others who did not want either of these two types of Government. But after a long discussion, a large majority of members came to a conclusion that the system of the Parliamentary Government as it is in Britain is best suited to our country….

There are some Sections of people who do not like Parliamentary Government. Communists want the Russian type of Government. The Socialists are also against the present Constitution of India. They are agitating against it. They have declared that if they come to power, they will modify it. Personally speaking, I am very greatly attached to the Parliamentary System of Government. We must understand what it means and we must preserve it in the Constitution…

What is meant by Parliamentary Government? There is a book on English Constitution by Walter Bagehot. It is, indeed, a classic treatise. It was later expanded by other authorities on Constitutional Government like Laski and others. He has put the conception of the Parliamentary Government in one sentence. He says Parliamentary Government means Government by discussion and not by fisticuffs. You will always find in British system of Government that they hardly ever resort to fisticuffs while taking any decision. You will find in British system of Government that they hardly ever resort to justify while taking any decision. The decision is always taken after discussion. Nobody introduces element of disturbance in British Parliament….

Look at the French Politics. Decisions are arrived at more often than by knocking knock-out blows. You will find that this system is hardly adequate to those not born in that system. It is an alien institution to them. We must learn, understand and make it a success….

Parliamentary Democracy is unknown to us at present. But India, at one time, had Parliamentary Institutions. India was far more advanced in ancient times. If you go through the *'Suktas'* of *Mahaparinibbana,* you will find ample evidence in support of my point. In these '*Suktas*' it is stated that while Bhagwan Buddha was dying at Kusinara (Kusinagara), a message to the effect was sent to the *Mallas* who were sitting in session at that time. They were devoted to Parliamentary Institutions. When they received the message about Buddha, they decided that they shall not close the session but would carry on with their work and will go to Kusinagara after finishing of the business of the Parliament. There are innumerable references in our literature to prove that Parliamentary System of Government was not unknown to us....

There are many rules about Parliamentary Procedure. May's Parliamentary Practice is generally followed. One rule that is invariably followed everywhere is that there can be no discussion without a motion. That is why there is no discussion on a question. This rule was also practiced in our land in ancient times. The system of secret ballot now in vogue is also not new to us....

It was followed in Buddhist *Sanghas.* They had the ballot papers which they called, '*Salapatraka Grahakas*'. Unfortunately, we have lost all this past heritage that was good. Historians of India must tackle this question as to why these Parliamentary institutions disappeared from our land. But I find that they cannot or do not want to find out the reasons for it. Ancient India was the master of the World. There was such intellectual freedom in ancient India as was nowhere else to be found...

Then why this ancient civilization went to dogs? Why was India subjected to autocratic monarchies? We were familiar with Parliamentary institutions. We know about votes, voting, committees and other things related to Parliamentary institutions. Today, Parliamentary System of Government is alien to us. If we go to village, we will find that the villagers do not understand what is vote, what is party. They find it something strange, something alien. It is, therefore, a great problem as to how to preserve this institution. We will have to educate public, we will have to tell them the benefits of Parliamentary Democracy and of Parliamentary System of Government....

We know what Bagehot means by Parliamentary Government. But today his definition is of no use, it is utterly inadequate. There are three main things inherent in the Parliamentary System of Government.

Parliamentary Government means negation of hereditary rule. No person can claim to be hereditary ruler. Whoever wants to rule must be elected by the people from time to time. He must obtain the approval of the people. Hereditary rule has no sanction in the Parliamentary System of Government....

Secondly, any law, any measure applicable to the public life of the people must be based on the advice of the people chosen by the people. No single individual can presume the authority that he knows everything, that he can make the laws and carry the Government. The laws are to be made by the representatives of the people in the Parliament. They are the people who can advise the men in whose name the law is proclaimed. That is the difference between the monarchical system of Government and the Democratic System of Government....

In monarchy, the affairs of the people are carried on in the name of a monarch and under the authority of a monarch. In democracy, the affairs of the public are carried on in the name of the head of the State, but the laws and the executive measures are the authority on which the Government is carried on. The head of the State is the titular head; he is merely a symbol. He is a consecrated *'Murti'*. He can be worshipped but he is not allowed to carry out the Government of the country. The Government of the country is carried out, though in his name, by the elected representatives of the people...

Thirdly and lastly, Parliamentary System of the Government means that at a stated period those who want to advise the Head of the State must have the confidence of the people in themselves renewed. In Britain, formerly, the elections to the Parliament were every seven years. The Chartists agitated against this. They wanted annual elections. The motive behind this agitation was very praiseworthy, indeed. It would have been best in the interests of the people if annual election were held, had it been possible, of course. But, Parliamentary elections are very costly affairs. So some sort of compromise was arrived at and five years period was supposed to be a responsible period at which the Legislators and the Ministers were to go back to the People and obtain the fresh renewal of their confidence....

This is also not enough. Parliamentary System of Government is much more than Government by discussion. There are two pillars on which the Parliamentary system of Government rests. These are the fulcrums on which the mechanism works. Those two pillars are *(i)* an Opposition and *(ii)* free and fair elections...

For the last 20 or 30 years, we acclimatized to one single political Party. We have nearly forgotten the necessity and importance of 'Opposition' for the fair working of Parliamentary Democracy. We are continuously told that Opposition is an evil. Here again we are forgetting what the past history has to teach us. You know that there were *'Nibandhkaras'* to interpret the *Vedas* and *Smrities.* They used to begin their comments on *'Slokas'* and *'Sutras'* by stating firstly the *'Purva Paksha'* the one side of the question. They used to follow up by giving the *'Uttar Paksha'*—other side....

By this they wanted to show us that the question raised was not an easy question: it is a question where there is dispute, discussion and doubt. Then they used to give what they termed as *'Adhikaram'* where they used to criticize both the '*Pakshas*'. Finally, they gave the *'Siddhant'* their own decisions. Here from we can find that all our ancient teachers believed in two-Party system of Government....

One important thing in the Parliamentary Democracy is that people should know the other side, if there are two sides to a question. Hence, a functional Opposition is required. Opposition is the key to a free political life. No democracy can do without it. Britain and Canada, the two exponents of Parliamentary Systems of Governments recognize this important fact and in both countries the Leader of Opposition is paid salary by the Government....

They regard the Opposition as an essential thing. People of these countries believe that the Opposition should be as much alive as the Government. The Government may suppress the facts, the Government may have only one-sided propaganda. The people have provision against this eventuality in these two countries....

Now the question arises as to whether there is any desire on the part of the Party in power to permit any Opposition to be created. Congress does not want any Opposition. Congress is attempting to gather people of sundry views under one canopy. I ask you whether this is a desirable trend in the political life of this country?

Free and fair elections are the other pillar on which Parliamentary Democracy rests. Free and fair elections are necessary for the transfer of power from one section of the community to the other in a peaceful manner and without any bloodshed. In olden times, if a king died, there was at least one murder in the palace. Revolution used to take place in palace resulting in murders before the new king used to take the reins of his country into his authority. This has been the history of India. Elections must be completely free and fair. People must be left to themselves to choose those whom they want to send to the Legislatures....

What about free and fair elections? We must not lose sight of the fact that 'Big Business' is trying to play a great part in political life of this country. The amount that is being contributed to Congress on behalf of the 'Big Business' is very dangerous thing. If moneyed people try to influence the elections by contributing to the election fund of any political party, what will be the result? If the part to which they have supported financially come into power, they will naturally try to extract concessions for themselves either by modifying the present legislation or by influencing the party in power to legislate in such a manner as would be beneficial to their interests....

Today the same thing is happening. Congress is accepting the financial help of the *Banias*, Marwaries and other multi-millionaires. Congress is eating their food and it follows; therefore, naturally that congress will have to take the side of these 'Big Business' at all crucial times....

We also find that the Government servants are influencing the elections in favour of the party which is feeding them and their dependants. No less a personality than Dr Shyama Prasad Mookerjee, at the inaugural session of the Bhartiya Jan Sangh at Delhi recently, openly charged the government servants of helping the Congress and thereby nullifying the elections from being free and fair. Under these circumstances, do you, gentlemen, think that there is any hope for the Parliamentary Democracy to succeed?

If Parliamentary Democracy fails in this country and it is bound to fail for the reasons mentioned by me, the only result will be rebellion, anarchy and Communism. If the people in power do not realize that people will not tolerate hereditary authority, then this country is doomed, either Communism will come, Russia having the sovereignty over our country, destroying individual liberty and our independence or the Section of the people who are disgruntled for the failure of the party in power will start rebellion and anarchy will prevail....

Gentlemen, I want you to take note of these eventual certainties and if you wish that Parliamentary System of Government and Parliamentary Democracy prevail in this country, if you are satisfied that we will be assured of our liberty of thought, speech and action, if we should preserve our Independence, if we cherish the inherent right of individual liberty, then it is your duty as students, as intelligent community of our country, to strive your utmost to cherish this Parliamentary System of Government in its true spirit and work for it.

★ ★ ★

A year later, Dr Ambedkar gave an address on the "Conditions Precedent for the Successful Working of Modern Democracy" at the Poon District Law Library, Pune (December 22, 1958). He said:

The subject which I am going to speak to you this evening is according to my wording of the subject: 'Conditions Precedent for the Successful Working of Democracy'. What are the conditions precedent which must exist in order that the democratic form of Government may continue to work without any kind of hindrance. That is the subject on which I propose to make a few observations....

SETTING FOR THE SUBJECT

Now, before I actually deal with the subject-matter I propose to make a few preliminary observations in order to provide, what I call, a setting for the subject....

The first preliminary observation I propose to make is this that democracy is always changing its form. We speak of democracy, but democracy is not always the same. The Greeks spoke of Athenian Democracy. But as everyone knows, the Athenian Democracy was as different from our modern democracy as chalk is from cheese. The Athenian Democracy consisted of people 50 per cent of whom were slaves. Only 50 per cent were free. The 50 per cent who formed slaves had no place in the Government at all. Surely our democracy is quite different from the Athenian Democracy.

The second thing to which I would like to draw your attention by a preliminary observation is that even in the same country democracy is not always the same. You take the history of England. Nobody can say that the English Democracy before the English Revolution of 1688 was the same as the English Democracy which came after the revolution of 1688. Nor can anyone say that the English Democracy as existed between 1688 and 1832 when the first Reform Bill was passed, is the same as the democracy that developed after the passing of the Act of 1832. Democracy keeps on changing its form....

The third thing that I would like to draw your attention is that democracy not only undergoes changes in form; democracy always undergoes changes in purposes. You take the ancient English Democracy. What was the purpose of that democracy? It was to curb the King, to prevent the King from exercising what we now in law call his prerogative rights. The King even went to the extent of saying that although Parliament may be there, as an enactment-making body, 'I as a King have got the prerogative to make the law and my law shall prevail.' It was this kind of autocracy of the King which made democracy to come into being....

Today what is the purpose of the democracy? *The purpose of modern democracy is not so much to put a curb on an autocratic King but to bring about the welfare of the people.* That is a distinct change in the purpose of democracy. You will, therefore, see that in the title which I have given to my subject, I have deliberately used the words 'conditions precedent for the success of modern democracy'.

Democracy Defined

Again what do we mean by democracy? Let us have a clear understanding before I proceed to my subject. Democracy has been defined, as you know, by various people, writers of political science and philosophers, sociologists and so on. I take only two for the purpose of illustrating my point. I do not know whether any of you is acquainted with that famous book by Walter Bagehot on the English Constitution, the first modern attempt to give a clear picture of democracy. If you refer to that book of Walter Bagehot, his definition of democracy is 'government by discussion'. That is how he defined democracy....

Take another illustration that is of Abraham Lincoln. In his famous Getisburg speech which he made after the conquest of the Southern States, he defined democracy as 'A government of the people, by the people, and for the people'. Well, many other definitions could be added in order to give an idea what people mean by democracy. Personally for myself, I define democracy in a different way, in a much more concrete way I think....

My definition of democracy is '*a form and a method of government whereby revolutionary changes in the economic and social life of the people are brought about without bloodshed.*' That is my definition of democracy....

If democracy can enable those who are running it to bring about fundamental changes in the social and economic life of the people and the people accept those changes without resorting to bloodshed, then I say that there is democracy. That is the real test. It is perhaps the severest test....

But when you are judging the quality of a material, you must put it to the severest test. And this is how I propose to define democracy at any rate so far as today's address is concerned. Now, how can such a democracy be successful? This is the main subject, matter of my address....

Now, unfortunately there are no dogmas laid down by any of the authors who have written about this subject of democracy which can give us any idea in concrete, as to what are the conditions precedent according to their judgment to make democracy a success. One has to read history and as a result of reading history to find out the break-down period in democracy's life in the different parts of the world where it had functioned and come to one's own conclusion....

Condition No. 1

The first condition which I think is a condition precedent for the successful working of the democracy is that there must be no glaring inequalities in the society. There must not be an oppressed Class. There must not be a suppressed Class. There must not be a Class which has got all the privileges and a Class which has got all the burdens to carry. Such a thing, such a division, such an organization of a society has within itself the germs of a bloody revolution, and perhaps it would be impossible for the democracy to cure them....

Lincoln once said, although people have not understood his meaning, in the same Gattisberg's speech that 'a House divided against itself cannot stand.' He was, of course, referring to the conflict between the Southern States and the Northern States. He said, 'If you of the Southern States and we of the Northern States are divided, we shall not be able to stand together when a foreign enemy comes.' That was probably the meaning that he wanted to convey when he said that the House divided cannot stand....

But I think that phrase of his or sentence of his, is pregnant with much deeper meaning and it means, as I understand it, that the deep cleavages between Class and Class are going to be one of the greatest hindrances in the success of democracy. Because in democracy what happens? In democracy, everybody, even the oppressed, the suppressed, those who are deprived of their rights and those who carry the burden, they have the right to vote in the same way as those who have all the privileges, and probably those who are privileged are fewer than those who are unprivileged and since we adopt a majority rule as the rule of decision, it is quite possible that if the privileged few will not willingly and voluntarily surrender their privileges, then the distance between them and the lower orders will destroy democracy and bring into existence something quite different....

There is, therefore, no doubt in my mind that if you examine the history of democracy in various parts of the world, you will find that one of the causes for the breakdown of democracy is the existence of these social cleavages.

Condition No. 2

The second thing which a successful working of democracy requires is the existence of Opposition. Now, I have seen many people not only in this country but in England condemning the Party system. I was just recently reading, just before I came, a small little book published by the Hansard Society on the Party system in England and here is one whole chapter devoted to this question whether the Party system is a good system and should be tolerated. There is a variety of views...

Now, it seems to me that all those who are against Party system and who must be taken also on that very account to be against Opposition, seem completely to misunderstand what democracy means. What does democracy mean? I am not defining it. I am asking a functional question. It seems to me that democracy means a veto of power. Democracy is a contradiction of hereditary authority or autocratic authority. Democracy means that at some stage somewhere there must be a veto on the authority of those who are ruling the country. In autocracy there is no veto. The king once elected is there with his inherent or divine right to rule. He does not have to go before his subjects at the end of every five years to ask them, 'Do you think I am a good man? Do you think I have done well during the last five years? If so, will you re-elect me?' There is no veto on the part of anybody on the power of the King...

But in democracy we have provided that at every five years those who are in authority must go to the people and ask whether in the opinion of the people they are well qualified to be entrusted with power and authority to look after their interests, to mould their destiny, to defend them. That is what I call veto. Now, a democracy is not satisfied with a quinquennial veto that the Government should go at the end of five years only to the people and in the meantime there should be nobody to question the authority of the Government....

Democracy requires that not only that the Government should be subject to the veto, long-term veto of five years, at the hands of the people, but there must be an immediate veto. There must be people in the Parliament immediately ready there and then to challenge the Government. No, if you understand what I am saying, democracy means that nobody has any perpetual authority to rule, but that rule is subject to sanction by the people and can be challenged in the House itself....

You will see how important it is to have an Opposition. Opposition means that the Government is always on the anvil. The Government must justify every act that it does to those of the people who do not belong to its Party. Unfortunately, in our country all our newspapers, for one reason or other, I believe, it is the revenue from advertisements, have given far more publicity to the Government than to the Opposition, because you cannot get any revenue from the Opposition. They get revenue from the Government and you find columns after columns of speeches reeled out by members of the ruling Party in the daily newspapers and the speeches made by the Opposition are probably put somewhere on the last page in the last column. I am not criticizing what is democracy. I am saying what is the condition precedent for a democracy. *The Opposition is a condition precedent for democracy.* But do you know that in England not only is the Opposition recognised, but the leader of the Opposition is paid a salary by the Government in order to run the Opposition. He gets a Secretary, he gets a small staff of stenographers and writers, he has a room in the House of Commons where he does his business. In the same way, you will find that in Canada the leader of the Opposition gets a salary in the way as a Prime Minister does, because in both these countries democracy feels that there must be someone to show whether the Government is going wrong. And this must be done incessantly and perpetually and that is why they do not mind spending money on the leader of the Opposition....

Condition No. 3

I think there is a third condition which may also be called a condition precedent for the success of democracy and that is equality in law and administration. One need not at this stage delite too much on equality before the law, although there might be cases here and there when there is no equality before the law. But what is important is equality of treatment in administration. It is quite possible for good many of you to imagine or to recall cases where a Party Government is carrying on the administration for the benefit of the members of the Party. At any rate, I can recall a great many instances of this sort. Suppose there is a law which says that nobody shall deal in a particular commodity without a licence. Nobody can quarrel with that law because it is universal. There is no discrimination in that particular piece of legislation....

But let us go further and see what happens when a man goes to a particular officer or to the Minister with an application for licence in trading in a particular commodity. I do not know, it is quite possible again that probably the Minister may first look at his hat. What sort of a coloured hat he is wearing? If he is wearing a hat which appeals to him and it assures him that he is a Party man and another man goes with another sort of dress or belonging to another Party and in making his decision the licence is given to the first and refused to the second, although both of them on merits are equally qualified to have that licence, then obviously this is a discrimination in administration and there is no equity....

Of course, the question of licence, i.e. the granting of this privilege and that privilege is perhaps small thing and affects only a very small Class of people. But let us go further and see what would happen if this kind of discrimination enters administration. Supposing a member of a certain Party is being prosecuted for a certain offence for which there is abundant evidence, and suppose the head of the Party in that particular area goes to the District Magistrate and tells him that it is not right for him to prosecute this man because he belongs to his Party and says, 'well, if you don't do it, I shall refer the matter to the Minister and get you transferred from this place to some other place.'

You can just imagine what chaos and injustice would result in administration. The sort of a thing which used to happen in the United States which is called a Spoil System, that is to say, when one Party came in office, it removed all the employees that were employed by their predecessor including even the clerks and the peons and they filled their vacancies by those gentlemen who helped the new Party to go in power. The United States, as a matter of fact, had no administration worth speaking of for a number of years. Subsequently, they themselves realized that this was not helpful to democracy. They abolished this Spoil System....

In England, in order that administration should remain pure, impartial, away from politics and policy, they have made a distinction between what is called political offices and civil offices. The civil service is permanent. It serves all the Parties whichever is in office and carries out the administration without any kind of interference from the Minister. Such a thing at one time did exist in our country when the British were here....

For any officer to say something which is contrary to the wishes of the Minister is, to my mind, utterly impossible. But in those days it was quite possible, because we too in India like Great Britain had made that wise decision that administration must not be interfered with by the Government, and that the function of the Government was to lay down policy but not to interfere and to make any discrimination....

This is very fundamental and I am afraid we had already departed from that and may completely abnegate and abolish the thing we have had so far....

Condition No. 4

The fourth condition precedent, in my judgement, for the successful working of democracy is the observance of Constitutional morality. Many people seem to be very enthusiastic about the Constitution. Well, I am afraid, I am not. I am quite prepared to join that body of people who want to abolish the Constitution, at any rate to redraft it. But what we forget is that we have a Constitution which contains legal provisions, only a skeleton....

The flesh of that skeleton is to be found in what we call Constitutional morality. However, in England it is called the conventions of the Constitution and people must be ready to observe the rules of the game. Let me give you one or two illustrations which come to my mind at this moment....

You remember when the 13 American colonies rebelled, their leader was Washington. It is really a very inadequate way of defining his position in the American life of that day merely to say that he was a leader. To the American people Washington was God. If you read his life and history, he was made the first President of the United States after the Constitution was drafted. After his term was over, what happened? He refused to stand for the second time. I have not the least doubt in my mind that if Washington had stood ten times one after the other for the Presidentship, he would have been elected unanimously without a rival. But he stepped down the second time....

When he was asked why, he said, 'My dear people, you have forgotten the purpose for which we made this Constitution. We made this Constitution because we did not want a hereditary monarchy and we did not want a hereditary ruler or a dictator. If after abandoning and swerving away from the allegiance of the English King, you come to this country and stick to worship me year after year and term after term what happens to your principles? Can you say that you have rightly rebelled against the authority of the English King when you are substituting me in his place.' He said, 'Even if your royalty and fidelity to me compels you to plead that I should stand a second time, I as one who enunciated that principle that we should not have hereditary authority, must not fall a prey to your emotion.' Ultimately, they prevailed upon him to stand at least a second time. And he did. And the third time when they approached him, he spurned them away....

Let me give you another illustration. You know Windsor Edward the VIII whose serial story has now been published in the *Times of India*. I had gone to the Round Table Conference and there was a great controversy going on there as to whether the King should be allowed to marry the woman whom he wanted to marry, especially when he was prepared to marry her in a morganatic marriage, so that she may not be a Queen or whether the British people should deny him even that personal right and force him to abdicate. Mr Baldwin, was of course, against the King's marriage. He would not allow him, and said, 'If you do not listen to me, you will have to go....'

Our friend Mr Churchill was the friend of Edward the VIII and was encouraging him. At that time the Labour Party was in the Opposition. They had no majority and I remember very well the Labour Party people considered whether they could not make capital out of this issue and defeat Mr. Baldwin; because there was a large number of conservatives who in their loyalty wanted to support the King; and I remember the late Professor Laski writing a series of Articles in the *Herald* condemning any such move on the part of the Labour Party....

He said, 'By our convention we have always agreed that the King must accept the advice of the Prime Minister and if he does not accept the advice of the Prime Minister, the Prime Minister shall force his ejection.' That being our convention, it would be wrong on our part to defeat Mr Baldwin, on an issue which increases the authority of the King....

And the Labour Party listened to his advice and did nothing of the kind. They said, they must observe the rules of the game. If you read English history, you will find many such illustrations where the Party leaders have had before them many temptations to do wrong to their opponents in office or in Opposition by clutching at an issue which gave them temporary power, but which they refused to fall a prey to, because they knew that they would damage the Constitution and damage democracy....

There is one other thing which I think is very necessary in the working of democracy and it is this that in the name of democracy there must be no tyranny of the majority over the minority. The minority must always feel safe that although the majority is carrying on the Government, the minority is not being hurt, or the minority is not being hit below the belt. This is a thing which is very greatly respected in the House of Commons. Good many of you must be remembering the results of elections in England in 1931 when Mr Ramsay MacDonald left the Labour Party and formed the National Government. When the election came, the Labour Party which I think numbered somewhere about 150 or so, had only 50 members out of 650 with Mr Baldwin as the Prime Minister. I was then there. But I have never heard of a single instance of this small minority of 50 members belonging to the Labour Party under the huge majority of the Conservatives ever complaining that they were denied their due rights of speech, or Opposition or making motions of any kind as you probably know....

You take our own Parliament. I am not justifying what the Members of the Opposition are doing by constantly bringing in motions of Censure or Adjournment motions. It is not a very happy thing to work in Parliament to be constantly dunning these adjournment motions. All the same, you must have noticed that there is hardly any motion, whether of Adjournment or Censure which has been admitted for the debate. It surprises me considerably. In my reading of the English Parliamentary debates I have very seldom come across a case where a demand for adjournment has been refused either by the Speaker, provided, of course, it is an order by the Government....

When I was a Member of the Bombay Legislative Assembly, there were a few of our friends Mr Morarji, Mr Munshi and Mr Kher and others who were in office. They never allowed a single motion of adjournment to be discussed. Either our friend Mr Mavlankar who was then the Speaker helped them by ruling it out or as he admitted, the Minister objected to it. You know what happens when a Minister objects?

When a Minister objects, the man who proposes the adjournment motion has to produce 30 to 40 people, whatever the quota is. It may be that if Government were constantly to oppose adjournment motions of the small community which is represented in the House by a group of few members such as 4, 5 or 6, such small minorities can never get a chance to ventilate their grievances....

What happens is that these minorities develop a contempt for Parliamentary people and develop a revolutionary spirit something unconstitutional. It is, therefore, necessary that when democracy is working, the majority on which it is based must not act in a tyrannical manner.

One other point I will refer and then close. I think that democracy does require the functioning of moral order in society.Somehow, our political scientists have never considered this aspect of democracy. Ethics is something separate from politics. You may learn politics and you may know nothing about ethics as though politics can work without ethics....

To my mind it is an astounding proposition. After all, in democracy what happens? Democracy is spoken of as a free Government. And what do we mean by free Government? Free Government means that in vast aspects of social life people are left free to carry on without interference of law, or if law has to be made, then the law-maker expects that society will have enough morality in it to make the law a success. The only person who, I think, has referred to this aspect of democracy is Laski. In one of his books he has very categorically stated that the moral order is always taken for granted in democracy. If there is no moral order, democracy will go to pieces as it is going now probably in our own country....

The last thing that I refer to is that democracy requires 'public conscience'. There is no doubt about it that although there is injustice in every country, the injustice is not equally spread. There are some where the impact of injustice is very small. There are some against whom the impact is very great. And there are some who are absolutely crushed under the burden of injustice....

One might very easily cite the case of Jews in England. They were the people who suffered certain injustice which the Christians never did. What happened was that the Jews alone had to struggle in order to get this injustice removed. But the English Christians never helped them. In fact, they liked it....

The only man who helped the Jews in England was the King. This may be extraordinary. But the reason also is extraordinary and the reason is this: Under the old Christian law the children of the Jews could not inherit the property of the father for no other reason except that he was a Jew and not a Christian, and the King being the residuary legatee of the State received the property of a dead Jew. Now the King liked that sort of thing. He was very happy. When the children of the dead Jew went to the King in application the King handed over to them a little bit of the property of their dead father and kept the rest for himself. But as I said, no Englishman ever helped the Jews, and the Jews continued to struggle for their liberation....

This is the result of what is called 'public conscience'. Public conscience means conscience which becomes agitated at every wrong, no matter who is the sufferer and it means that everybody whether he suffers that particular wrong or not, is prepared to join him in order to get him relieved...

You take South Africa, the most recent example. Well, the people who are suffering there are the Indians. Are not they? The white people are not suffering yet you find this Reverend Scott who is a white man doing his level best and in order to get this injustice removed. Recently, I have been reading that a large number of young boys and girls belonging to the white race are also joining the struggle of the Indians in South Africa. That is called 'public conscience'. I do not want to shock you, but sometimes I feel how forgetful we are....

We are talking about South Africa. I have been wondering within myself whether we who are talking so much against segregation and so on do not have South Africa in every village. There is; we have only to go and see. There is South Africa everywhere in the village and yet I have very seldom found anybody not belonging to the Scheduled Class taking up the cause of the Scheduled Class and fighting, and why?

Because there is no 'public conscience'. Myself and my India is the only world within which I am bound. If this sort of thing happens, the minority which is suffering from injustice gets no help from others for the purpose of getting rid of this injustice. It again develops a revolutionary mentality which puts democracy in danger....

Now, as I said, what I have said is not a series of dogmas which have been worked out by any political scientists, but the result of what is impressed upon me as a result of reading the political histories of various countries, and I believe that these are the most essential conditions for the purpose of preserving democracy....

I have no doubt about it that the subject about which I have spoken this evening, to my mind, is a subject of the greatest importance to this nation. We have somehow developed the idea that we have got Independence. The Britishers have gone. We have got a Constitution which provides for democracy. Well, what more do we want?"

We cannot rest as we say on our ears, and do nothing more. Let me warn you against this kind of smug feeling that with the making of the Constitution our task is done. It is not done. It has only begun...

You must remember that democracy is not a plant which grows everywhere. It has grown in America. It has grown in England. To some extent, it has grown in France. Yes, these are examples by which we can take a certain amount of courage to ourselves to see what has happened elsewhere. You must be remembering that as a result of the first European War and the break-up of the Austria-Hungarian empire, Wilson created, on the basis of self-determination, small nationalities independent of Austria. They all began with democratic Constitution, democratic Government and they had also Fundamental Rights provided in their Constitution which was made obligatory for them to have the Peace Treaty of Versailes. My friends, what has happened to that democracy? Do you see any trace of it there now? It has all gone. It has all vanished. They are probably under the dominance or surveillance of other countries. There is no democracy left....

Take some of the most recent examples. Syria had got a democratic government. After a few years there was a military rebellion and the Commander-in-Chief of Syria became the ruler of Syria and democracy vanished in air. Take another example. What happened in Egypt? There too, they had been a democratic government beginning right from 1922 for 30 years. In one night Faruk had to leave and Nagib became the dictator of Egypt and he abolished the Constitution....

With all these examples before us, I think we ought to be very cautious and very considerate regarding our own future. You ought to consider whether we ought not to take some very positive steps in order to remove some of the stones and the boulders which are lying in our path in order to make our democracy safe....

On yet another occasion, Dr Ambedkar spoke on democracy. He said:

The subject assigned to me is: 'What are the prospects of democracy in India?' Most Indians speak with great pride as though their country was already a democracy. The foreigners also, when they sit at a dinner table to do diplomatic honour to India, speak of the Great Indian Prime Minister and the Great Indian Democracy....

From this, it is held without waiting to argue that where there is a Republic, there must be democracy. It is also supposed that where there is Parliament which is elected by the people on adult sufferage and the laws are made by the People's Representatives in Parliament elected after every few years, there is democracy. In other words, democracy is understood to be a political instrument and where this political instrument exists, there is democracy....

Is there democracy in India or is there no democracy in India? What is the truth? No positive answer can be given unless the confusion caused by equating democracy with Republic and by equating democracy with Parliamentary Government is removed....

Democracy is quite different from a Republic as well as from Parliamentary Government. The roots of Democracy lie not in the form of Government, Parliamentary or otherwise. A Democracy is more than a form of Government. It is primarily a mode of associated living. The roots of Democracy are to be searched in the social relationship, in the terms of associated life between the people who form a society.

What does the word 'Society' connote? To put it briefly when we speak of 'Society', we conceive of it as one by its very nature. The qualities which accompany this unity are praiseworthy community of purpose and desire for welfare, loyalty to public ends and mutuality of sympathy and co-operation....

Are these ideals to be found in Indian society? The Indian Society does not consist of individuals. It consists of an innumerable collection of cases which are exclusive in their life and have no common experience to share and have no bond of sympathy. Given this fact it is not necessary to argue the point. The existence of the Caste System is a standing denial of the existence of those deals of society and therefore of democracy....

Indian Society is so imbedded in the Caste System that everything is organized on the basis of Caste. Enter Indian Society and you can see Caste in its glaring form. An Indian cannot eat or marry with an Indian simply because he or she does not belong to his or her Caste. An Indian cannot touch an Indian because he or she does not belong to his or her Caste. Go and enter politics and you can see Caste reflected therein. How does an Indian vote in an election? He votes for a candidate who belongs to his own Caste and no other. Even the Indian Congress exploits the Caste System for election purpose as no other political Party in India does. Examine the lists of its candidates in relation to the social composition of the constituencies and it will be found that the candidate belongs to the Caste which is the largest one in that constituency. The Congress, as a matter of fact, is upholding the Caste System against which it is outwordly raising a outcry against the existence of Caste....

Go into the field of industry. What will you find? You will find that all the topmost men drawing the highest salary belong to the Caste of the particular industrialist who owns the industry. The rest hang on for life on the lowest rungs of the ladder on a pittance. Go into the field of commerce and you will see the same picture. The whole commercial House is one camp of one Caste, with 'NO ENTRY' board on the door for others....

Go into the field of charity. With one or two exceptions all charity in India is communal. If a Parsi dies, he leaves his money for Parsis. If a Jain dies, he leaves his money for Jains. If a Marwadi dies, he leaves his money for Marwadis. If a Brahmin dies, he leaves his money for Brahmins. Thus, there is no room for the downtrodden and the outcastes in politics, in industry, in commerce, and in education....

There are other special features of the Caste System which have their evil effects and which militate against Democracy. One such special feature of the Caste System lies in its being accompanied by what is called 'Graded Inequality'. Castes are not equal in their status. They are standing one above another. They are Jealous of one another. It is an ascending scale of hatred and descending scale of contempt. This feature of the Caste System has most pernicious consequences. It destroys willing and helpful co-operation....

Caste and Class differ in the fact that in the Class System there is no complete isolation as there is in the Caste System. This is the second evil effect in the Caste System accompanied by inequality. This manifests itself in the fact that the stimulus and response between two Castes is only one-sided. The higher Caste act in one recognized way and the lower Caste must respond in one established way. It means that when there is no equitable opportunity to receive the stimulus from and to return the response from different Caste, the result is that the influences which educate some into masters, educate others into slaves. The experience of each Party loses its meaning when the free interchange of varying modes of life experience is arrested. It results into a separation of society, into a privileged and a subject Class. Such a separation prevents social endosmosis....

There is a third characteristic of the Caste System which depicts the evils thereof which cuts at the very roots of democracy. It is that one Caste is bound to one occupation. Society is no doubt stably organized when each individual is doing that for which he has aptitude by nature in such a way as to be useful to others; and that it is the business of society to discover these aptitudes and progressively to train them for social use. But there is in a man an indefinite pluralities of capacities and activities which may characterize an individual. A society to be democratic should open a way to use all the capacities of the individual. Stratification is stunting of the growth of the individual and deliberate stunting is a deliberate denial of democracy....

How to put an end to the Caste System? The first obstacle lies in the system of graded inequality which is the soul of the Caste System. Where people are divided into two classes, higher and lower, it is easier for the lower to combine to fight the higher, for there is no single lower Class. The Class consists of lower and lowerer. The lower cannot combine with the lowerer. For the lower is afraid that if he succeeds in raising the lowerer, he may well himself lose the high position given to him and his Caste....

The second obstacle is that the Indian Society is disabled by unity in action by not being able to know what is its common good. Plato has said that the organization of society depends ultimately upon knowledge of the end of existence. If we do not know its end, if we do not know its good, we shall be at the mercy of accident and caprice. Unless we know the good of the end, we have no criterion for rationally deciding what the possibilities are which we should promote. Question is, can the Indian Society in its Caste-bound state achieve what is the ultimate question? We come upon the most insuperable obstacle that such knowledge is not possible save in a just and harmonious social order. Can there be a harmonious Social Order under the Caste System? Everywhere the mind of the Indians is distracted and misled by false valuations and false perspectives. A disorganized and factional society sets up number of different models and standards. Under such conditions it is impossible for individual Indian to reach consistency of mind on the question of Caste....

Can education destroy Caste? The answer is 'Yes' as well as 'No'. If education is given as it is today, education will have no effect on Caste. It will remain as it will be. The glaring example of it is the Brahmin Caste cent percent of it is educated, nay, majority of it is highly educated. Yet, not one Brahmin has shown himself to be against Caste. In fact, an educated person belonging to the higher Caste is more interested after his education to retain the Caste System than when he was not educated. For education gives him an additional interest in the retention of the Caste System, namely, by opening additional opportunity of getting a bigger job....

From this point of view, education is not helpful as means to dissolve Caste. So far is the negative side of education. But education may be solvent if it is applied to the lower strata of the Indian Society. It would raise their spirit of rebellion. In their present state of ignorance they are the supporters of the Caste System. Once their eyes are opened they will be ready to fight the Caste System....

The fault of the present policy is that though education is being given on a larger scale, it is not given on the right strata of Indian Society. If you give education to that strata of Indian Society which has a vested interest in maintaining the Caste System for the advantages it gives them, then the Caste System will be strengthened. On the other hand, if you give education to the lowest strata of Indian Society which is interested in blowing up the Caste System, the Caste System will be blown up. At the moment the indiscriminate help given to education by the Indian Government and American Foundation is going to strengthen the Caste System. To make rich richer and poor poorer is not the way to abolish poverty. The same is true of using education as a means to end the Caste System. To give education to those who want to keep up the Caste System is not to improve the prospect of Democracy in India but to put our Democracy in India in greater jeopardy.

CHAPTER FORTY FIVE

Linguistic Reorganization of States

IMMEDIATELY AFTER THE Independence, there were political movements for creation of new, linguistic-based Provinces. At that time, six Linguistic Provinces already existed, viz., East Punjab, United Provinces, Bihar, West Bengal, Assam and Orissa. Three more Provinces, viz., Bombay, Madras and Central Provinces were clamouring for being reconstituted on linguistic basis. In response, the Linguistic Provinces Commission was constituted. Dr Ambedkar prepared a Statement for the Commission which was submitted and also published as a book titled: *Maharashtra as a Linguistic Province,* first published in 1948.

Dr Ambedkar first takes up the question of the merits of the proposal for Linguistic Provinces: He said:

> The generality of those who advocate the creation of Linguistic Provinces do so because they believe that the Provinces have different languages and cultures. They should, therefore, have the fullest scope to develop their languages and their cultures. In other words, the Provinces have all the elements of a distinct nationality and they should be allowed the freedom to grow to their fullest in nationhood.

According to Dr Ambedkar,

> Among the many effects that may be envisaged, the following are obvious:
>
> (1) Linguistic Provinces will result in creating as many nations as there are groups with pride in their race, language and literature. The Central Legislature will be a League of Nations and the Central Executive may become a meeting of separate and solidified nations filled with the consciousness of their being separate in culture and, therefore, in interests. They may develop the mentality of political insubordination, i.e., refusal to obey the majority or of staging walk-outs. The development of such a mentality is not to be altogether discounted. If such a mentality grows it may easily make the working of the Central Government impossible.
>
> (2) The creation of Linguistic Provinces would be fatal to the maintenance of the necessary administrative relations between the Centre and the Provinces. If each Province adopts its own language as its official language the Central Government will have to correspond in as many official languages as there are Linguistic Provinces. This must be accepted as an impossible task....

No one can contemplate such a situation with equanimity. It may lead to a break-up of India. Instead of remaining united, India may end in becoming Europe—faced with the prospect of chaos and disorder.

On the other hand, there are several advantages. Dr Ambedkar argued:

There can be no doubt that the reconstruction of Provinces on linguistic basis has certain definite political advantages. The main advantage of the scheme of Linguistic Provinces which appeals to me quite strongly is that Linguistic Provinces would make democracy work better than it would in mixed Provinces. A Linguistic Province produces what democracy needs, namely, social homogeneity. Now the homogeneity of a people depends upon their having a belief in a common origin, in the possession of a common language and literature, in their pride in a common historic tradition and community of social customs.... The absence of a social homogeneity in a State creates a dangerous situation especially where such a State is raised on a democratic structure. History shows that democracy cannot work in a State where the population is not homogeneous. In a heterogeneous population divided into groups which are hostile and anti-social towards one another the working of democracy is bound to give rise to cases of discrimination, neglect, partiality, suppression of the interests of one group at the hands of another group which happens to capture political power. The reason why in an heterogeneous society, democracy cannot succeed is because power instead of being used impartially and on merits and for the benefit of all, is used for the aggrandizement of one group and to the detriment of another. On the other hand, a state which is homogeneous in its population can work for the true ends of democracy, for there are no artificial barriers or social antipathies which lead to the misuse of political power.

It follows that if democracy is to function properly, the subjects of the State must be so distributed as to form a single homogeneous group. The Constitution for the Provinces of India which is on the anvil is designed for a democratic form of Government. It follows that each Province must be homogeneous in its population if democracy in the Province is to be successful. This is simply another way of saying that each Province must be a linguistic unit if it is to be fitted to work a democratic Constitution. Herein lies the justification for Linguistic Provinces.

Can the solution of this problem be postponed? In this connection, Dr Ambedkar said: "The situation in the non-Linguistic Provinces has become exasperating if not dangerous...."

According to Dr Ambedkar the solution for the linguistic problems should be sought on the following lines:

The Solution of the Difficulties

The solution must satisfy two conditions. While accepting the principle of Linguistic Provinces it must provide against the break-up of India's unity. My solution of the problem, therefore, is that, while accepting the demand for the re-constitution of Provinces on linguistic basis, the Constitution should provide that the official language of every Province shall be the same as the official language of the Central Government.

It is only on that footing that I am prepared to accept the demand for Linguistic Provinces."

Dr Ambedkar then makes out a strong case for an unilingual Maharashtra as a Province with a single Legislature and single Executive by merging with it all the contiguous Marathi-speaking districts of the Central Province and Berar with the City of Bombay as its capital. He demonstrates that Maharashtra would be a fully viable Province. He said:

> Coming to the specific question of Maharashtra Province it is necessary to be satisfied that it will be a viable Province. For being declared a viable Province, a Province must satisfy certain tests. It must be of a certain size, it must have a certain volume of population and a commensurate amount of revenue. A Province must not only be self-supporting—which any Province can be, by choosing to live on a lower plane—but it must have sufficient revenue to provide for a minimum standard of administration required by efficiency and the needs of social welfare.

Dr Ambedkar demonstrates that it does. In fact, he said:

> Some comparisons are necessary to get an idea if a Province of this size, with this population and with so much revenue will be viable.... It is obvious that Maharashtra whether one takes its abridged edition or the unabridged edition of it will be several times bigger than Delaware which is the smallest State in USA in point of area and also several times bigger than New York which is the biggest state in USA in point of population.
>
> There is no controversy regarding the unification of Maharashtra into one Province. The controversy relates to the way it should be brought about. One view is that the new Maharashtra Province should be a unitary Province, with a single Legislature and a single Executive. The other view is that Maharashtra should be a Federation of two sub-Provinces, one sub-Province to consist of the Marathi-speaking districts of the Bombay Presidency and the other of the Marathi-speaking districts of the present Province of the Central Provinces and Berar.... When it is decided to create a Linguistic Province, I am definitely of opinion that all areas which are contiguous and which speak the same language should be forced to come into it. There should be no room for choice nor for self-determination. Every attempt must be made to create larger provincial units. Smaller provincial units will be a perpetual burden in normal times and a source of weakness in an emergency. Such a situation must be avoided. That is why I insist that all parts of Maharashtra should be merged together in a single Province.

CONTROVERSY OVER BOMBAY

Dr Ambedkar said

> Should the City of Bombay be included in Maharashtra or not is another point over which there has been a controversy.... My memorandum would be woefully incomplete if I omitted to deal with the *pros* and *cons* of this controversy....

On the contentious issue whether the city of Bombay should be included in Maharashtra or not Dr Ambedkar refutes each and every argument advanced by then leading University Professors (e.g., *Vakil, Dantwala* and *Gheewala*) in support of the separation of Bombay from Maharashtra and its constitution into a separate Province. Dr Ambedkar strongly maintains that Bombay and Maharashtra are not merely inter-dependant but they are really one and integral.

GROUND FOR THE EXCLUSION OF BOMBAY FROM MAHARASHTRA

Dr Ambedkar further deals with the points put forth in favour of separating Bombay from Maharashtra:

> The arguments urged in favour of separating Bombay from Maharashtra are set out below:
>
> (1) Bombay was never a part of Maharashtra
> (2) Bombay was never a part of the Maratha Empire.
> (3) The Marathi-speaking people do not form a majority of the population of the City of Bombay.
> (4) Gujarathis have been old residents of Bombay.
> (5) Bombay is a trade centre for vast areas outside Maharashtra. Therefore, Bombay cannot be claimed by Maharashtra. It belongs to the whole of India.
> (6) It is the Gujarathi-speaking people of Bombay who have built up the trade and industry of Bombay. The Maharashtrians have been only clerks and coolies. It would be wrong to place the owners of trade and industry under the political dominance of the working classes who form the bulk of Maharashtrians.
> (7) Maharashtra wants Bombay to be included in Maharashtra because it wants to live on the surplus of Bombay
> (8) A multi-lingual State is better. It is not so fatal to the liberty of smaller people.
> (9) Regrouping of Provinces should be on rational lines and not on national lines.
>
> On an examination of these points it is obvious that points (1) and (2) are preliminary in the sense that they help us to decide on whom rests the burden of proof. If it is proved that Bombay is part of Maharashtra, then the burden of proof for separating it from Maharashtra must fall upon those who urge that it should be separated and not upon those who claim that it should remain part of Maharashtra. I will, therefore, deal with these two points first.

VERDICT OF HISTORY AND GEOGRAPHY

These points can be considered both in the light of history as well as of geography. I am, however, convinced that history cannot help us to decide the issue.... It is definitely against assimilation. The*Musalmans* conquered Hindus.But the *Musalmans* remained *Musalmans* and the Hindus remained Hindus. The Gujarathis were conquered by Maharashtrians and were ruled by them for some years. What effect has it produced upon the Gujarathis? Nothing. Gujarathis have remained Gujarathis and Maharashtrians have remained Maharashtrians.... This being the case, what help can Indian History give in the decision of the issue?

Let us now turn to geography and ask for its verdict. It seems to be a better witness than history. For this purpose one must consider the location of Bombay in relation to the Province of Maharashtra. The Province of Maharashtra once it is created will be triangular in shape. One side of this triangle is formed by the Western Coast Line of India between Daman in the North and Karwar in the South. The City of Bombay lies in between Daman and Karwar. The Province of Gujarat starts from Daman and spreads northwards. The Kanada Province starts from Karwar and spreads southwards.... If the unbroken territory between Daman and Karwar is geographically part of Maharashtra, how could Bombay be held not to be a part of Maharashtra? This is an incontrovertible fact of nature. Geography has made Bombay part of Maharashtra. Let those who want to challenge the fact of nature do so. To an unbiased mind it is conclusive proof that Bombay belongs to Maharashtra.

BOMBAY AND THE MARATHA EMPIRE

That the Marathas did not care to make it a part of their Empire does in no way affect the validity of the conclusion drawn from geography. That the Marathas did not care to conquer it does not prove that Bombay is not a part of Maharashtra. It only means that the Maratha power was a land power and did not, therefore, care to spend its energy in the conquest of a seaport....

MARATHI-SPEAKING POPULATION—MAJORITY OR MINORITY

There is no unanimity on this question....What conclusion can be drawn from it? Does it defeat the claim of Maharashtra to include Bombay? Ever since the British became the masters of India, India has been one country with a right to free movement from place to place. If people from all parts of India were allowed to come to Bombay and settle there, why should the Maharashtrians suffer? It is not their fault. The present state of the population cannot, therefore, be a ground for excluding Bombay from Maharashtra....

ARE GUJARATHIS NATIVES OF BOMBAY?

Are the Gujarathis natives of Bombay? If they are not, how did they come to Bombay?... No Gujarathi would claim that the Gujarathis are the natives of Bombay, How did they come to Bombay?...The Gujarathis did not come to Bombay voluntarily. They were brought to Bombay by the officers of the East India Company to serve as commercial *Adatias* or go-betweens. They were brought because the East India Company's officers who had their first factory in Surat had got used to Surti Banias as their go-betweens in carrying on their trade. This explains the entry of Gujarathis in Bombay. Secondly, the Gujarathis did not come to Bombay to trade on the basis of free and equal competition with other traders. They came as privileged persons with certain trading rights given to them exclusively by the East India Company....

BOMBAY—AN EMPORIUM OF INDIA

That Bombay is an emporium for the whole of India may be admitted. But it is difficult to understand how it can be said that because of this, Maharashtra cannot claim Bombay. Every port serves a much larger area than the country to which it belongs. No one, on that account, can say the country in which the port is situated cannot claim it as a part of its territory....Why then should Maharashtrians be denied the right to claim Bombay merely because it serves as a port for Provinces other than Maharashtra? It would be different if the Province of Maharashtra were to get a right to close the Port to non-Maharashtrians. Under the Constitution, it will not have that right. Consequently, the inclusion of Bombay in Maharashtra will not affect the right of non-Maharashtrians to use the port as before....

GUJARATHIS—OWNERS OF TRADE AND INDUSTRY OF BOMBAY

It may be granted that the Gujarathis have a monopoly of trade. But, as it has already been pointed out, this monopoly, they have been able to establish because of the profits they were able to make, which were the result of the privileges given to them by the East India Company on their settlement in Bombay. Who built up the trade and industry of Bombay is a matter for which no very great research is necessary. There is no foundation in fact for the statement that the trade and industry of Bombay was built up by Gujarathis.... It was built up by Europeans and not by Gujarathis. The Gujarathis have been just merchants which is quite a different thing from being industrialists.

Once it is established that Bombay belonged to Maharashtra, the claim of Maharashtra to include Bombay cannot be defeated by the argument that the trade and industry of Bombay is owned by the Gujarathis. The claim of mortgagor to his land cannot be defeated by the mortgagee on the ground that the mortgagee has built up permanent structures on the land. The Gujarathis assuming they have built up the trade and industry of Bombay are in no better position than a mortgagee is.

But who have built up the trade and industry of Bombay seems to me quite irrelevant to the decision of the issue whether Bombay should or should not be included in Maharashtra. This argument based on monopoly of trade and industry is really a political argument. It means that the owners may rule the workers but the workers must not be allowed to rule the owners. Those who use this argument do not seem to know what they are up against. The one thing they are up against is whether this argument is to be confined only to the City of Bombay or whether it is to have a general application....

There is no reason why it should not have a general application. For just as in Bombay City, society is divided into owners and workers or into capitalists and wage-earners, such also is the case of society in Gujarat or for the matter of that in every province of India. If the owners and capitalists of Bombay are to be protected by the exclusion of Bombay from Maharashtra because Maharashtrians belong to the working classes, what is the method they suggest for protecting the capitalists of Gujarat from the working classes of Gujarat? Those Gujarathi Professors like Vakils and Dantwalas who are searching their brains to supply arguments to the Gujarathi capitalists of

Bombay have not thought of finding ways and means for protecting the Gujarathi capitalists of Gujarat against the working classes of Gujarat. The only remedy they can suggest is the abandonment of adult suffrage. That is the only way by which they can protect the capitalists if they are out to protect capitalists in general and not the Gujarathi capitalists of Bombay in particular....

There is, however, one argument which the Professors could urge. It is that the Maharashtrians being in a majority would discriminate against the Gujarathi capitalists of Bombay if Bombay was included in Maharashtra....

One could appreciate such an argument. But those who like to use this argument must remember two things:

(a) That Maharashtra is not the only place in which such a situation can arise. It may arise in any province. I like to refer to Bihar. In Bihar the land in which coal is found belongs to the people of Bihar. But the coal-owners are Gujarathis, Kathiawaris or Europeans. Is there no possibility of Biharis making a discrimination against Gujarathi and Kathiawari coal-owners? Are the coalfields of Bihar to be excluded from the Province of Bihar and constituted into a separate Province in the interest of Kathiawari and Gujarathi coal-owners?

(b) The Constitution of India has noted the possibility of discrimination being made against a minority and has made more than ample provision for preventing it. There the fundamental rights. There are the provisions against discrimination; there are the provisions of payment of compensation, and there are the High Courts with the inherent rights to issue high prerogative writs both against individuals and Governments to stop any harm, injustice or harassment being done to any citizen. What more protection do the Gujarathi traders and industrialists of Bombay want against the possibility of discrimination?

Maharashtra's Eye on Bombay's surplus

Before accusing Maharashtrians of having an eye on the surplus of Bombay it must be proved that Bombay has a surplus. What appears as surplus is due really to bad accounting.... It is a fallacy to charge all such expenditure to Maharashtra and exempt Bombay from it and then argue that Bombay has a surplus....

The statement that the Maharashtrians want Bombay because they want to live on the surplus revenue of Bombay, besides being wrong in fact raises a question of motive. I do not know if the Maharashtrians are actuated by any such motive. They are not a commercial community. Unlike other communities, the Maharashtrians have no nose for money, and I am one of these who believe that it is one of their greatest virtues. Money has never been their God. It is no part of their culture. That is why they have allowed all other communities coming from outside Maharashtra to monopolize the trade and industry of Maharashtra....

But supposing such a motive in the minds of the Maharashtrians, what is wrong in it? It is quite open to Maharashtrians to contend that they have a greater claim on Bombay's surplus because they have played and they will continue to play a greater part in supplying labour for the building up of the trade and industry of Bombay more than the people from other Provinces have done or likely to do. It would be difficult for any economist with any reputation to say who could deny that labour has as much claim on the wealth produced as capital if not more....

Secondly, the surplus from Bombay is not consumed by Maharashtra alone but is consumed by the whole of India. The proceeds of the Income-tax, Super-tax, etc. which Bombay pays to the Central Government are all spent by the Central Government for all-India purposes and is shared by all other Provinces. To Professor Vakil it does not matter if the surplus of Bombay is eaten up by United Provinces, Bihar, Assam, Orissa, West Bengal, East Punjab and Madras. What he objects to is Maharashtra getting any part of it. This is not an argument. It is only an exhibition of his hatred for Maharashtrians....

Granting that Bombay was made into a separate Province, what I don't understand is how Professor Vakil is going to prevent Maharashtra from getting share of Bombay surplus revenue. Even if Bombay is made separate Province, Bombay will have to pay income-tax, super-tax, etc. and surely Maharashtra will get a part of the revenue paid by Bombay to the Centre either directly or indirectly. As I have said the argument has in it more malice than substance....

General Arguments Against the Inclusion of Bombay in Maharashtra

I will now turn to the Points (8) and (9) which have been urged by Professors Dantwala and Gheewala. Their arguments strike at the very root of the principle of Linguistic Provinces....

The sum total of the arguments of the two Professors is that Linguistic Provinces are bad. This cry against Linguistic Provinces is too late. Since when the two Professors having been holding these views is not known. Are they opposed to Gujarat being reconstituted on Linguistic Provinces also has not been made clear by them. Or, is it that they believed in the principle of Linguistic Provinces but hurried to disavow it when they realized that the admission of the principle involves the surrender of Bombay to Maharashtra. It is perhaps one of these cases where a person not finding argument limited to his purpose is forced to resort to an argument which proves more than he is anxious to allow. I am, however, prepared to examine the substance of their argument....

In the first place, in a country like India in which society is throughout communally organized it is obvious that in whatever way it is divided into areas for administrative purposes, in every area there will always be one community which by its numbers happens to be a dominant community. As a dominant community it becomes a sole heir to all political power, which the area gets. If Marathi-speaking people in a unified Maharashtra with Bombay thrown into it will become dominant over the Gujarathi-speaking people, will this prospect be confined to Maharashtra only? Will such a phenomena not occur within the Marathi-speaking people? Will it not be found in Gujarat if Gujarat became a separate Province? I am quite certain that within the Marathi-speaking people who are sharply divided between the Marathas and the non-Marathas, the Marathas being a dominant Class will reduce both Gujarathi-speaking and the non-Marathas to a subject condition. In the same way in Gujarat in some parts the Anavil Brahmins form a dominant Class. In other parts it is the Patidars who form a dominant Class. It is quite likely that the Anavils and the Patidars will reduce the condition of the other communities to subjection. The problem, therefore, is not a problem peculiar to Maharashtra. It is a general problem....

What is the remedy for this problem? Professor Gheewala believes that the remedy lies in having a mixed State.... The real remedy is not a mixed State but an absolute State with no power to the people which is generally captured by a communal majority and exercised in the name of the people. Is Professor Gheewala prepared for this remedy? One need have no doubt to what his answer would be....

In the second place, Professor Gheewala has confounded nationality in the social sense of the term with nationality in its legal and political sense. People often speak of nationality in speaking about Linguistic Provinces. Such use of the term can be only in the non-legal and non-political sense of the term. In my scheme there is no room even for the growth of separate provincial nationality. My proposal nips it in the bud. But even if the commonly suggested pattern of Linguistic Provinces with the language of the Province as the official language were adopted. Provinces cannot have that attribute of sovereignty which independent nations have....

It is very difficult to understand what exactly Professor Gheewala wants. Broadly he wants two things: He wants a mixed State and he also wants that a dominant section should not be in a position to reduce the smaller sections to subjection. I cannot see how Linguistic Provinces can come in the way of achieving it. For even after Provinces have been re-constituted on linguistic basis.

(a) Provinces will continue to be a conglomeration of communities which will give Professor Gheewala the mixed State that he wants;

(b) If Professor Gheewala wants a more pronounced form of a mixed State to protect smaller communities or nationalities, he will certainly have it at the Centre.

As I have said, I do not think a mixed State is either a good State or stable State. But if Professor Gheewala prefers it, he will have it in one form or another, both in the Provinces as well as at the Centre, in the former in the form of different communities and in the latter in the form of the representatives of different Provinces....

With regard to his second objective, there will be double protection. In the first place, the citizen will have such protection as a mixed State he thinks can give. Secondly, citizenship will be common throughout India....

There is no provincial citizenship. A Gujarathi in Maharashtra will have the same rights of citizenship in Maharashtra as Maharashtrian will have....

Given these facts, I fail to understand what objection Professor Gheewala can have to Linguistic Provinces?

Professor Gheewala has made two other recommendations. He says,(1) if Provinces have to be reconstituted, constitute them on rational basis rather than on linguistic basis; and (2) make nationality a personal thing.

To reconstitute Provinces on economic basis—which is what is meant by rational basis—appears more scientific than reconstituting them on linguistic basis. However, unscientific linguistic reorganization of Provinces I cannot see how they can come in the way of rational utilization of economic resources of India. Provincial boundaries are only administrative boundaries. They do not raise economic barriers for the proper utilization of economic resources. If the position was that the resources contained within a Linguistic Province must only be explained by the people of the Province and no other than it could no doubt be said that the scheme of Linguistic Provinces was mischievous. But such is not the case. So long as Linguistic Provinces are not allowed to put a ban on the exploitation of the resources of the people by anybody capable of wishing to exploit them a Linguistic Province will yield all the advantages of a rationally planned Province….

The proposal of making nationality as a personal thing and put it on the same footing as religion may be dismissed as being too Utopian. It would raise many administrative problems. It will come when the world is one and all nationals are its citizens. Nationality will automatically vanish as being quite useless….

So far I have dealt with the arguments advanced by those who are opposed to the inclusion of Bombay in Maharashtra. I have taken pains to do so not because I felt that they were very weighty. I did so because I felt it desirable to prevent the common man from being misled. The possibility of this happening was there and for two reasons. In the first place, those who have come forward with these arguments are not ordinary men. They are University Professors. Secondly, these Professors came out with their arguments after Professor Gadgil had put forth the case for the inclusion of Bombay in Maharashtra. Unfortunately, no attempt has so far been made to refute the arguments of the adversaries of Professor Gadgil. The result has been the creation of an impression that Professor Gadgil's adversaries have carried the day. It was absolutely essential to remove this impression….

THE OTHER SIDE

There are, however, arguments which the adversaries of Professor Gadgil have not thought of but which may be advanced with justice as well as force in favour of the claim of Maharashtrians for the inclusion of Bombay in Maharashtra. It is quite possible that these arguments may suggest themselves to the Commission. But I don't like to leave it to chance. I, therefore, propose to set them out below even though the Commission might think that it was unnecessary.

CALCUTTA AND BOMBAY

In deciding upon the issue of exclusion of Bombay from Maharashtra the Commission will have to take into account the position of Calcutta. Like Bombay it is the chief emporium of the whole of eastern part of India. Like the Maharashtrians in Bombay the Bengalis in Calcutta are in a minority. Like the Maharashtrians in Bombay, the Bengalis do not own the trade and industry of Calcutta. The position of the Bengalis vis-à-vis Calcutta is worse than the position of the Maharashtrians vis-à-vis Bombay. For, the Maharashtrians can at least claim that they have supplied labour if not capital for the trade and industry of Bombay. The Bengalis cannot even say this. If the Commission can accept the arguments urged for the separation of Bombay from Maharashtra, it must be equally prepared to recommend the separation of Calcutta from West Bengal. For it is a very pertinent question to ask that if for the reasons given Bombay can be separated from Maharashtra why when the same reasons exist Calcutta be not separated from West Bengal.

Is Bombay Viable?

Before Bombay can be separated it must be proved that financially Bombay is a viable Province. As I have already said if proper accounting of revenue and expenditure was made, Bombay on the basis of present level of taxation may not be a self-sufficient Province. If that be so, the proposal for creating Bombay as a separate Province must fall to the ground. It is no use comparing Bombay with Provinces like Orissa and Assam. The standard of administration, the standard of living and consequently the level of wages in Bombay are all so high that I doubt that even with a crushing rate of taxation Bombay will be able to raise the necessary amount of revenue to meet the expenditure.

The Aim Behind Greater Bombay

This doubt regarding viability of Bombay Province is heightened by the indecent haste shown by the Government of Bombay in creating Greater Bombay by including within the limits of Bombay the adjoining parts of Maharashtra. It seems that the object of including such area cannot but be to make Bombay viable. What else can it be? So long as Bombay remained part of Maharashtra it did not matter to Maharashtrians in which administrative area a portion of Maharashtra was included. But when Bombay is to be a separate Province it will take a long time to make Maharashtrians part with their territory to make Bombay greater and viable. What is more important is the scheme of greater Bombay casts responsibility upon the Linguistic Provinces Commission to decide whether they could, with justice, force Maharashtrians not only to submit to the demand of the Gujarathis to give up Bombay but also to submit to their further demand to hand over a part of territory of Maharashtra to make Bombay a viable Province. The Commission cannot escape this responsibility....

Maharashtra and Bombay are not merely inter-dependent, they are really one and integral. Severance between the two would be fatal to both. The sources of water and electricity for Bombay lie in Maharashtra. The intelligentsia of Maharashtra lives in Bombay. To sever Bombay from Maharashtra would be to make the economic life of Bombay precarious and to dissociate the masses of Maharashtra from its intelligentsia without whose lead the masses of Maharashtra will be nowhere....

Arbitration as a Solution

I have seen a suggestion made in some quarters that the problem of Bombay should be settled by arbitration. I have never heard of a more absurd suggestion than this. It is as absurd as the suggestion to refer matrimonial cause to arbitration. The matrimonial tie is too personal, to be severed by a third party. Bombay and Maharashtra are tied together by God to use a Biblical phrase. No arbitrator can put them asunder. The only agency which is authorized to do so is the Commission. Let it decide....

★ ★ ★

In the context of political movements for creation of new, linguistic based Provinces, and creation of the new State of Andhra in 1953 (by bringing together 16 northern

Telugu-speaking districts of Madras Province), the then Prime Minister Pandit Nehru appointed in December 1953, the States Reorganization Commission (Chairman: Fazal Ali) which submitted its Report in 1955....

On account of his failing health, Dr Ambedkar could not participate in the debate on the subject inside the Parliament and outside in the campaign carried out by partisans in favour of their views. Dr Ambedkar felt that, "Creation of Linguistic States was a burning issue of the day....The question is too important for me to sleep over in silence."

According to Dr Ambedkar, "The formation of Linguistic States, although essential, cannot be decided by any sort of hooliganism. Nor must it be solved in a manner that will serve party interest. It must be solved by cold-blooded reasoning." That is precisely what Dr Ambedkar attempted to do in this book, which was published in December, 1955 with the title: Thoughts on Linguistic States.

In doing so, Dr Ambedkar was aware of inconsistencies in his views as expressed in this Monograph and his own public statements made earlier. Anticipating criticism on that count, Dr Ambedkar stated in the Preface of the Book:

> Readers may find certain inconsistencies in my views as expressed in this brochure and as expressed formerly in certain public statements. Such changes in my view are, I am sure, very few. The former statements were made on the basis of fragmentary data. The whole picture was then not present to the mind. For the first time it met my eye when the report of the States Reorganization Commission came out. This is sufficient justification for any change in my views which a critic may find....
>
> To a critic who is a hostile and malicious person and who wants to make capital out of my inconsistencies my reply is straight. Emerson has said that consistency is the virtue of an ass and I don't wish to make an ass of myself. No thinking human being can be tied down to a view once expressed in the name of consistency. More important than consistency is responsibility. A responsible person must learn to unlearn what he has learned. A responsible person must have the courage to rethink and change his thoughts. Of course, there must be good and sufficient reasons for unlearning what he has learned and for recasting his thoughts. There can be no finality in thinking.

According to Dr Ambedkar what the Commission has created is not a mere disparity between the States by leaving UP and Bihar as they are, but by adding to them a new and bigger Madhya Pradesh and Rajasthan. It creates a new political problem of the consolidated Hindi-speaking North versus the balkanized South.

Considering the vast cultural differences between the two sectors and the apprehensions of dominance of the North articulated by a conflict between the two in course of time, Dr Ambedkar observes that the Commission should have followed the principle of "One State one language" and not "one language one State."

Dr Ambedkar favours formation of unilingual States as against multi-lingual States for the reasons that the former fosters the fellow-feeling which is the foundation of a stable and democratic State, while the latter with its enforced juxtaposition of two different linguistic groups leads to faction fights for leadership and discrimation in administration—factors which are incompatible with democracy. His support for unlingual States is, however, qualified by the condition that its official language shall be Hindi and until India becomes fit for this purpose, English shall continue. He foresees the danger of a unligual State developing an independent nationality if its regional language is raised to the status of official language.

To remove the disparity between the large States of the North and the small States of the South which has been accentuated by the absence of the provision for equal representation of the States in the Central Legislature irrespective of their areas and populations, Dr Ambedkar's remedy is to divide the large States into units with a population not exceeding two crores.

He suggests tentatively division of Bihar and Madhya Pradesh into two States each and of United Provinces into three States.[147] Each of these States being unilingual the division will not affect the concept of a linguistic States.

His proposal for Maharashtra is to divide it, as in ancient times, into three States of Western, Central and Eastern Maharashtra with Bombay City as a separate city State of Maharashtra.Such smaller States, in his opinion, will meet the requirements of efficient administration and the special needs of different areas. It will also satisfy their sentiments.In a smaller State the proportion of majority to minority which in India is not political but communal and unchangeable, decreases and the danger of the majority practicing tyranny over the minority is also minimized.

To give further protection to minorities against such tyranny, Dr Ambedkar suggests amendment of the Constitution that will provide a system of plural-member constituencies (two or three) with cumulative voting. Dr Ambedkar also advocates the creation of a second capital for India and locating it in the South preferably in the city of Hyderabad to ease the tension and political polarization of the North and the South.

---

147. Splitting Bihar and Madhya Pradesh into two has become a reality in the year 2000.

PART XI

EMBRACING BUDDHISM AND NIRVANA

CHAPTER FORTY SIX

Gravitating Towards Buddhism

ON OCTOBER 14, 1956, Dr Ambedkar formally embraced Buddhism and converted around five lakh of his followers from Hinduism to Buddhism. This momentous decision was the culmination of a long process, spread over nearly five decades.

As noted before, Dr Ambedkar's interest in Buddhism dates back to his school days when a teacher named Krishnaji Arjun Keluskar gave him in 1908 a copy of the biography of Lord Buddha titled, *Life of the Buddha* written by him which had a profound influence on his young mind.

The first time Dr Ambedkar made a reference to conversion to another religion was in 1927, when during the Mahad Chavdar Lake *Satyagraha*, he said:

> We want equal rights in society. We will achieve them as far as possible while remaining within the Hindu fold, or, if necessary, by kicking away the worthless Hindu identity.

Initially, Dr Ambedkar made an all-out effort to bring about reforms in the Hindu society. He wanted to remove the Untouchability, while remaining within the Hindu religion. His Mahad *Satyagraha* (1927) and Nashik Kalaram Temple *Satyagraha* (1930) are clear examples of his sustained efforts to reform the Hindu society from within.

Finally, however, Dr Ambedkar realized, painfully, that it is impossible to change the attitude of Caste Hindus and, therefore, he decided to abandon the Hindu religion.

The turning point came in October 1935 when Dr Ambedkar made the shocking announcement: "I was born a Hindu Untouchable ...but ... I will not die a Hindu."

In 1936, Dr Ambedkar laid out the option to convert, as a choice between the following three religions: Islam, Christianity and Sikhism, each of which had apparently different advantages. Of the three choices, Dr Ambedkar felt that conversion to Islam or Christianity would denationalize the Depressed Classes and, therefore, diffuse the freedom struggle, whereas embracing Sikhism would "not only not harm the destiny of the country, but...will (actually) help the destiny of the country." In fact, in May 1936, Dr Ambedkar deputed his son Yashwant and his nephew (and sometime later 13 more followers) to the Golden Temple in Amritsar to study Sikhism. Dr Ambedkar indicated his inclination towards Sikhism in August 1936 because he preferred to have some responsibility for the future of Hindu Culture and civilization.[148] Within a short time, however, Dr Ambedkar dropped the idea mainly because he saw no hope of emancipation when Sikh Untouchables told him of the atrocities they had suffered at the hands of the Jats. Dr Ambedkar's early consideration to abandon Hinduism thus proved short-lived and he turned his attention to the political struggle instead.

While addressing a public gathering of Untouchables in Mumbai (August 28, 1937), Dr Ambedkar appealed to his followers to give up observing all the religious festivals under the Hindu religion. He assured them that conversion is sure to take place. But the matter needs thorough examination. "The new religion to be adopted must be adopted only after a close searching examination."

In the meantime, through painstaking research on history of Indian society, Dr Ambedkar arrived at the conclusion that Buddhism prevailed in India for more than 1200 years, during which time, the entire Indian society was cohesive, united and free from any discrimination based on the accident of birth (and the caste).

In a path-breaking address to Madras Rational Society, Madras (September 24, 1944) Dr Ambedkar argued: Indian history is nothing but struggle between Buddhism and Brahminism. There was in ancient India a great struggle between Buddhism and Brahminism. The Buddhists were revolutionaries, and Brahmins were counter-revolutionaries. In the course of the same Address, Dr Ambedkar pointed out: "Buddha was the first person to preach the message of liberty, equality and fraternity in the history of the world."

Throughout this period, however, his affinity for Buddhism seems to have been growing in his mind. In 1934, when he built a house in Mumbai, he named it 'Rajgriha' after the capital of the ancient Buddhist kings. In the mid-1940s, when Dr Ambedkar established a number of educational institutions, they were all named 'Siddharth' or 'Milind'—both in the Buddhist tradition. In fact, even while in the Constituent Assembly, he was actively involved in adopting many Buddhist symbols for the Indian Republic e.g., the Chakra (i.e., the wheel of Dharma) on the Indian National Flag, the lions of Ashoka—the Buddhist emperor of ancient India—as the national emblem, and also the inscription of a Buddhist maxim on the pediment of the Rashtrapati Bhavan. Dr Ambedkar also lobbied for Buddha Jayanti, the birth anniversary of Lord Buddha, to feature in India's calendar of official holidays.

Dr Ambedkar had already begun to write articles in *Janata* elaborating on the meaning and significance of Buddhism. In 1948, Dr Ambedkar re-published Laxmi Narasu's famous book: 'The Essence of Buddhism', which had offered a modernist

148. Quoted in Bhagwan Das (ed.) *Thus Spoke Ambedkar* p. 307.

interpretation of Buddhism, denying *karma* as rebirth. In the same year, Dr Ambedkar published his book 'Untouchables', which presented Untouchables as the descendants of those Buddhists who were marginalized. In 1950, Dr Ambedkar published an article titled, 'The Buddha and the Future of His Religion' in the Journal of the Mahabodhi Society which argued that Buddhism was a religion for the whole world: "if the new world [which be it] realized is very different from the old, must have a religion and the new world needs a religion far more than the old world did then it can only be the religion of the Buddha."

In 1950, Dr Ambedkar began advocating rationality in the choice of religion. In the same year, participating in Conference of the World Fellowship of Buddhists in Candy, Sri Lanka (May 26, 1950), Dr Ambedkar began advocating the Eighth Fold Path of Buddhism. In the same Conference at Colombo (June 6, 1950), Dr Ambedkar argued out that Buddhism paved the way for democracy and socialistic pattern of society. He pointed out : "(unlike Brahminism) equality is the main feature of Buddhism. The religion of the Buddha gives freedom of thought and freedom of self-development to all…the rise of Buddhism in India was as significant as the French Revolution".

While addressing a public gathering at a Buddha Vihar in Mumbai (September 29, 1950), Dr Ambedkar said:

> As long as there is no purity of mind, wrong-doing and utter disregard of morals would continue in everyday life; and as long as man does not know how to behave with man, and creates barriers between man and man, India can never be prosperous. To end all these troubles, India must embrace Buddhism. Buddhism is the only religion based on ethical principles and teaches how to work for the good and well-being of the common man.

Dr Ambedkar then declared that he would devote the rest of his life to the revival and spread of Buddhism in India.

In July 1951, he formed the Bharatiya Bauddha Janasangh which became the Bharatiya Bauddha *Mahasabha* in May 1955.

During an All India Radio (AIR) broadcast on October 3, 1954, Dr Ambedkar said:

> Positively my Social Philosophy may be said to be enshrined in three words: liberty, equality and fraternity. Let no one, however, say that I borrowed my philosophy from the French Revolution. I have not. My philosophy has roots in religion and not in Political Science. I have derived them from the teachings of my master, the Buddha…. My philosophy has a mission. I have to do the work of conversion (to Buddhism).

In 1956 Dr Ambedkar addressed the World Buddhist Conference in Kathmandu on 'Marxism versus Buddhism.' This talk was based on an unpublished essay entitled 'Buddha or Karl Marx.' In it Dr Ambedkar outlined the propositions of Marxism, including Class conflict, exploitation, and nationalization or abolition of private property as a solution to human ills or *dukkha*. He noted that many of the propositions had been demolished by logic and experience. According to Dr Ambedkar:

> The French Revolution was welcomed because it aimed to produce equality. We welcome the Russian Revolution because it aimed at producing equality. But it cannot be too much emphasized that in producing equality, society cannot afford to sacrifice fraternity or liberty.... It seems that the three can coexist only if one follows the way of the Buddha.

In 1955, Dr Ambedkar started writing a book titled *Buddha and His Dhamma* intended as a simple, eloquent and rationalistic Buddhist gospel, which was published in 1957, a year after his *Nirvana*.

CHAPTER FORTY SEVEN

Buddha and his *Dhamma*

BUDDHA AND HIS *Dhamma* is Dr Ambedkar's mnemonic opus. Professor Christopher Queen of Harvard University calls it "a daring interpretation of traditional teachings" which "tells the story of earthly Buddha and summarises his teachings"[149].

I. THE BUDDHA AND HIS PREDECESSORS

(A) THE BUDDHA AND THE SANKHYA PHILOSOPHY

Among the ancient philosophers of India the most pre-eminent was Kapila. His philosophical approach was unique, and the philosopher stood in a Class by himself. His philosophy was known as the *Sankhya* Philosophy.

Of all the philosophers, the Buddha was greatly impressed by the doctrines of Kapila and his *Sankhya* philosophy. He was the only philosopher whose teachings appeared to the Buddha to be based on logic and facts. But he did not accept everything which Kapila taught. Only three things did the Buddha accept from Kapila's philosophy: He accepted that reality must rest on proof. Thinking must be based on rationalism. He accepted that there was no logical or factual basis for the presumption that God exists or that he created the Universe. He accepted that there was *Dukha* (suffering) in the world.

(B) THE BRAHMANIC PHILOSOPHY

Next to the *Vedas* are the religious books known as the *Brahmanas*. Both were held as sacred books. Indeed the *Brahmanas* are a part of the *Vedas*. The two went together and were called by a common name *Sruti*.

There were four thesis on which the *Brahmanic* Philosophy rested:

149. "Lit again Paths", *Outlook* (August 20, 2012)

(i) The first thesis was that the *Vedas* are not only sacred but that they are infallible and they are not to be questioned.

(ii) The second thesis of the *Brahmanic* Philosophy was that salvation of the soul—that is escape from transmigration—can be had only by the due performance of *Vedic* sacrifices and observances of religious rites and ceremonies and the offering of gifts to Brahmins.

(iii) As the third thesis of the Brahmani Philosophy, the *Brahmanas* not only had a theory of an ideal religion as contained in the *Vedas* but they also had a theory for an ideal society. The pattern of this ideal society was named *Chaturvarna*. It is imbedded in the *Vedas* and as the *Vedas* are infallible and as their authority cannot be questioned so also *Chaturvarna* as a pattern of society was binding and unquestionable.

This pattern of society was based upon certain rules:

The first rule was that society should be divided into four classes: (1) Brahmins; (2) *Kshatriyas*; (3) *Vaishyas*; and (4) *Shudras*.

The second rule was that there cannot be social equality among these four classes. They must be bound together by the rule of graded inequality. The Brahmins to be at the top, the *Kshatriyas* to be kept below the Brahmins but above the *Vaishyas*, the *Vaishyas* to be below the *Kshatriyas* but above the *Shudras* and the *Shudras* to be the lowest of all. These four classes were not to be equal to one another in the matter of rights and privileges. The rule of graded inequality governed the question of rights and privileges. The Brahmin had all the rights and privileges which he wished to claim. But a *Kshatriya* could not claim the rights and privileges which a Brahmin could. He had more rights and privileges than a *Vaishya* could claim. The *Vaishya* had more rights and privileges than a *Shudra*. But he could not claim the rights and privileges which a *Kshatriya* could. And the *Shudra* was not entitled to any right, much less any privilege. His privilege was to subsist without offending the three superior classes.

The third rule of *Chaturvarna*is related to the division of occupations. The occupation of the Brahmin was learning and teaching and the performance of religious observances. The occupation of the *Kshatriya* was fighting. Trade was assigned to the *Vaishyas*. The occupation of the *Shudras* was service of the three superior classes. These occupations assigned to different classes were exclusive. One Class could not trespass upon the occupation of the other.

The fourth rule of *Chaturvarna* related to the right to education. The pattern of *Chaturvarna* gave the right to education to the first three classes, the Brahmins, *Kshatriyas* and *Vaishyas*. The *Shudras* were denied the right to education. This rule of *Chaturvarna* did not deny the right to education to the *Shudra* only. It denied the right to education to all women including those belonging to the classes of Brahmins, *Kshatriyas* and *Vaishyas*.

There was a fifth rule. According to it, man's life was divided into four stages. The first stage was called *Brahmacharya;* the second stage was called *Grahastashram;* the third stage was called *Vanaprastha* and the fourth stage was called *Sannyasa.* The object of the first stage was study and education. The object of the second stage was to live a married life. The object of the third stage was to familiarize a man with the life of a hermit i.e., severing family ties, but without deserting his home. The object of the fourth stage was to enable a man to go in search of God and seek union with him. The benefits of these stages were open only to the male members of the three superior classes. The first stage was not open to the *Shudras* and women. Equally the last stage was not open to the *Shudras* and women. Such was the divine pattern of an 'ideal society' called *Chaturvarna.* The Brahmins had idealized the rule and had realized the ideal without leaving any cracks or loopholes.

(iv) The fourth thesis of Brahmanic Philosophy was the doctrine of *Karma.* It was part of the thesis of transmigration of the soul. The *Karma* of the Brahmins was an answer to the question: 'Where did the soul land on transmigration with his new body on new birth?' The answer of the Brahmanic Philosophy was that it depended on a man's deeds in his past life. In other words, it depended on his *Karma.*

(C) Buddha's Opposition to the Brahmanic Philosophy

The Buddha was strongly opposed to the first tenet of Brahmanism. He repudiated their thesis that the *Vedas* are infallible and their authority could never be questioned. In his opinion, nothing was infallible and nothing could be final. Everything must be open to re-examination and reconsideration whenever grounds for re-examination and reconsideration arise. Man must know the truth and real truth. To him freedom of thought was the most essential thing. And he was sure that freedom of thought was the only way to the discovery of truth. Infallibility of the Vedas meant complete denial of freedom of thought. For these reasons this thesis of the *Brahmanic* Philosophy was most obnoxious to him.

The Buddha was equally an opponent of the second thesis of the *Brahmanic* Philosophy. The Buddha did admit that there was virtue in a sacrifice. But he made a distinction between true sacrifice and false sacrifice. Sacrifice in the sense of self-denial for the good of others was considered true sacrifice by the Buddha. Sacrifice in the sense of killing an animal as an offering to God for personal benefit was regarded as a false sacrifice.

The *Brahmanic* sacrifices were mostly sacrifices of animals to please their Gods. He condemned them as false sacrifices. He would not allow them even when these sacrifices were to be performed with the object of getting salvation for the soul. The opponents of sacrifices used to ridicule the Brahmins by saying: "If one can go to heaven by sacrificing an animal why should not one sacrifice one's own father. That would be a quicker way of going to heaven." The Buddha wholeheartedly agreed with this view.

The theory of *Chaturvarna* was as repugnant to the Buddha as the theory of sacrifices was repulsive to him. The organization of society set up by Brahmanism in the name of *Chaturvarna* did not appear to him a natural organization. Its Class composition was compulsory and arbitrary. It was a society made to order. He preferred an open society and a free society.

The *Chaturvarna* of the Brahmins was a fixed order never to be changed. Once a Brahmin always a Brahmin, once a *Kshatriya* always a *Kshatriya*, once a *Vaishya* always a *Vaishya* and once a *Shudra* always a *Shudra*. Society was based on status conferred upon an individual by the accident of his birth. Vice, however heinous, was no ground for degrading a man from his status, and virtue, however great, had no value to raise him above it. There was no room for worth nor for growth.

Inequality exists in every society but it was different with Brahmanism. The inequality preached by Brahmins was its official doctrine, It was not merely a passing trend. Brahmanism did not believe in equality. In fact, it was opposed to equality. Brahmanism was not content with (mere) inequality. The soul of Brahmanism lay in graded inequality. Far from producing harmony, graded inequality, the Buddha thought, might produce in society an ascending scale of hatred and a descending scale of contempt, and might be a source of perpetual conflict. The occupations of the four classes were also fixed. There was no freedom of choice. Besides, they were fixed not in accordance with skill but in accordance with birth.

On a careful review of the rules of *Chaturvarna* the Buddha had no difficulty in coming to the conclusion that the philosophic foundations on which the social order was reared by Brahmanism were wrong, if not selfish. It was clear to him that it did not serve the interests of all, much less did it advance the welfare of all. Indeed, it was deliberately designed to make many serve the interests of the few. In it man was made to serve a Class of self-styled supermen. It was a calculated strategy to suppress and exploit the weak and to keep them in a state of complete subjugation.

The law of *Karma* as formulated by the Brahmins, thought the Buddha, was calculated to sap the spirit of revolt completely. No one was responsible for the suffering of man except he himself. Revolt could not alter the state of suffering; for suffering was fixed by his past *Karma* as his lot in this life.

The *Shudras* and women—the two classes whose humanity was most mutilated by Brahmanism, had no power to rebel against the system. They were denied the right to knowledge with the result that by reason of their enforced ignorance they could not realize what had made their condition so degraded. They could not know that Brahmanism had robbed them completely of the significance of their life. Instead of rebelling against Brahmanism they had become the devotees and upholders of Brahmanism. The right to bear arms is the ultimate means of achieving freedom which a human being has. But the *Shudras* were denied the right to bear arms. Under Brahmanism the *Shudras* were left as helpless victims of a conspiracy of selfish Brahmanism, powerful and deadly *Kshatriyas* and wealthy *Vaishyas*.

Could it be amended? Knowing that it was a divinely ordained social order, the Buddha knew that it could not be. It could only be ended.

For these reasons the Buddha rejected Brahmanism as being opposed to the true way of life.

II. THE BUDDHA'S VISION

This survey of the philosophical and religious thoughts shows that at the time when the Buddha formulated his *Sasana*, certain ideas had a firm grip on the minds of the people. They were:

- Belief in the infallibility of the *Vedas*;
- Belief in *Moksha* or Salvation of the soul i.e., cessation of the cycle of birth and death;
- Belief in the efficacy of rites, ceremonies and sacrifices as means of obtaining *Moksha*;
- Belief in *Chaturvarna* as the ideal for social organization;
- Belief in *Iswara* as the creator of the universe and in Brahmaas the principle underlying the universe.
- Belief in *Atmana,* or the soul.
- Belief in *Sansara,* (rebirth), i.e., transmigration of the soul.
- Belief in *Karma*, i.e., the determination of man's position in present life by deeds done by him in his past life.

(1) What the Buddha Rejected

In formulating the principles of his *Sasana* the Buddha dealt with this old stock of ideas in his own way. Following are the ideas which he rejected:

- He condemned indulging in speculation as to the whence, whither and what am I?
- He discarded heresies about the soul and refrained from identifying it with either the body, sensations, volitions or the consciousness.
- He discarded all the Nihilistic views which were promulgated by certain religious teachers.
- He condemned such views as were held by heretics.
- He discarded the theory that the cosmic progress had a known beginning.
- He repudiated the theory that a God created man or that he came out of the body of some Brahma.
- The existence of the soul he either ignored or denied.

(2) What the Buddha Modified

- He accepted the great grand law of cause and effect with its corollaries.
- He repudiated the fatalistic view of life and other equally foolish view that a God predestined as to what should happen for man and the world.
- He discarded the theory that all deeds committed in some former birth have the potency to produce suffering, making present activity impotent. He denied the fatalistic view of *Karma*. He replaced the view of *Karma* by a much more scientific view of *Karma*.
- Transmigration *(sansara)* replaced the doctrine of re-birth.
- He replaced the doctrine of *moksha* or salvation of the soul by the doctrine of *Nibbana*.

(3) What the Buddha Accepted

The first distinguishing feature of the Buddha's teachings lay in the recognition of the mind as the centre of everything. Mind precedes things, dominates them, creates them. If mind is comprehended all things are comprehended. Mind is the leader of all its faculties. The very mind is made up of those faculties. The first thing to attend to is the culture of the mind. The second distinguishing feature of the Buddha's teachings is that mind is the fount of all the good and evil that arises within and befalls us from without. Whatsoever, there is of evil, connected with evil, belonging to evil—that issues from the mind. Whatsoever there is of good, connected with good, belonging to good – all issues from mind.

If one speaks or acts with a pounded mind then affliction follows him as the wheels of the cart follow the feet of the bullocks who pulls the cart. The cleaning of the mind is, therefore, the essence of religion.

The third distinguishing feature of his teachings is the avoidance of all sinful acts.

The fourth distinguishing feature of his teachings is that real religion lies not in the books of religion but in the observance of the tenets of the religion.

(4) What the Buddha Taught

The Buddha claimed no place for Himself in His own *Dhamma*.

The Buddha did not promise to give salvation. He said He was *Marga Data* (Way Finder) and not *Moksha Data* (Giver of Salvation).

The Buddha did not claim any Divinity for himself or for His *Dhamma*. It was discovered by man for man. It was not a Revelation.

Most religions are described as revelations. But the Buddha's religion is not a Revelation. A revealed religion is so called because it is a message of God to His creatures to worship their maker (i.e., God) and to save their souls. Often the message is sent through a chosen individual who is called a Prophet to whom the message is revealed and who reveals it to the people is then called a religion. The obligation of the Prophet is to ensure salvation to the faithful. Salvation of the faithful means the saving of their souls, from being sent to hell provided they obey God's commands and recognize the Prophet as his messenger.

The Buddha never claimed that he was a Prophet or a messenger of God. He repudiated any such description. A more important point than this is that his religion is a discovery. As such it must be sharply distinguished from a religion which is called Revelation. His religion is a discovery in the sense that it is the result of inquiry and investigation into the conditions of human life on earth and understanding of the working of human instinct with which man is born. It is also about the moulding of a human's instincts and dispositions which man has formed as a result of history and tradition, which are working to his detriment.

All Prophets have promised salvation. The Buddha is the one teacher who did not make any such promise. He made a sharp distinction between a *moksha data* and a *marga data,* one who gives salvation and one who only shows the way. He was only a *marga data*. Salvation must be sought by each for himself through his own effort.

Besides what is salvation?

With Mohammad and Jesus salvation means saving the soul from being sent to hell by the intercession of the Prophet. With Buddha salvation means *Nibbana* and *Nibbana* means control of passions. What promise of salvation can there be in such a *Dhamma?*

Every founder of religion has either claimed divinity for himself or for his teachings. Moses, although he did not claim for himself any divine origin, did claim divine origin for his teachings. He told his followers that if they wished to reach the land of milk and honey they must accept the teachings because they were the teachings of Jehovah the God. Jesus claimed divinity for himself. He claimed that he was the Son of God. Naturally, His teachings acquired a divine origin. Krishna said that he was God himself and the Gita was his own word.

The Buddha made no such claim either for himself or his *Sasana*. He claimed that he was one of the many human beings and his message to the people was the message of man to man. He never claimed infallibility for his message. The only claim he made was that his message was the only true way to salvation as he understood it. It was based on universal human experience of the life in the world. He said that it was open to anyone to question it, test it and find what truth it contained.

III. RELIGION AND DHAMMA

A. What is Religion?

The word 'religion' is an indefinite word with no fixed meaning. It has varied from time to time. Most of the phenomena such as lightning, rain and floods, the occurrence of which the primitive man could not explain, any weird performance done to control these phenomena was called magic. Religion, therefore, came to be identified with magic.

Then came the second stage in the evolution of religion. In this stage religion came to be identified with beliefs, rituals, ceremonies, prayers and sacrifices. But this conception of religion is derivative. The pivotal point in religion starts with the belief that there exists some power which causes these phenomena which primitive man did not know and could not understand. Magic lost its place at this stage. This power was originally malevolent. But later it was felt that it could also be benevolent. Beliefs, rites, ceremonies and sacrifices were necessary both to propitiate a benevolent power and also to conciliate an angry power. Later that power was called God or the Creator.

Then came the third stage that it is this God who created this world and also man. This was followed by the belief that man has a soul and the soul is eternal and is answerable to God for man's actions in the world.

This is, in short, the evolution of the concept of Religion.

This is what Religion has come to be and this is what it connotes—belief in God, belief in soul, worship of God, curing of the erring soul, propitiating God through prayers, ceremonies, sacrifices, etc.

B. How Dhamma Differs From Religion?

What the Buddha calls *Dhamma* differs fundamentally from what is called Religion. Religion, it is said, is personal and one must keep to oneself. One must not let it play its part in public life. Contrary to this, *Dhamma* is social. It is fundamentally and essentially so. *Dhamma* is righteousness, which means right relations between man and man in all spheres of life. In other words, Society cannot do without *Dhamma.*

Now what is *Dhamma*? And why is *Dhamma* necessary?

According to the Buddha, Dhamma consists of *Prajna* and *Karuna.*

What is *Prajna*? And why *Prajna*? *Prajna* is understanding. The Buddha made *Prajna* one of two corner-stones of His *Dhamma* because he did not wish to leave any room for superstition. What is *Karuna*? And why *Karuna*? *Karuna* is love. Because, without *Karuna* Society can neither live nor grow, that is why the Buddha made it the second corner-stone of His *Dhamma.*

Such is the definition of the Buddha's *Dhamma.*

How different is this definition of *Dhamma* from that of Religion. So ancient, yet so modern is the definition of *Dhamma* given by the Buddha. So aboriginal yet so original. Not borrowed from anyone, yet so true. A unique amalgam of *Pradnya* and *Karuna* is the *Dhamma* of the Buddha. Such is the difference between Religion and *Dhamma.*

C. Morality, Religion and Dhamma

What is the place of morality in Religion?

As a matter of truth morality has no place in religion. The content of religion consists of God, soul, prayers, worship, rituals, ceremonies and sacrifices. Morality comes in only wherein man comes in relation to man. Morality comes into religion as a side wind to maintain peace and order. Religion is a triangular piece. Be good to your neighbour because you are both children of God. That is the argument of religion.

Every religion preaches morality but morality is not the root of religion. It is a wagon attached to it. It is attached and detached as the occasion requires. The action of morality in the functioning of religion is, therefore, casual and occasional. Morality in religion is, therefore, not effective.

What is the place of morality in *Dhamma*?

The simple answer is morality is *Dhamma* and *Dhamma* is moralitiy. In other words, in *Dhamma* morality takes the place of God although there is no God in *Dhamma*. In *Dhamma* there is no place for prayers, pilgrimages, rituals, ceremonies or sacrifices. Morality is the essence of *Dhamma*. Without morality there is no *Dhamma*. Morality in Dhamma arises from the direct necessity for man to love man. It does not require the sanction of God. It is not to please God that man has to be moral. It is for his own good that man has to love man.

IV. BUDDHA'S FIRST SERMON

The Buddha began by saying that his path which is his *Dhamma* (religion) had nothing to do with God and soul. His *Dhamma* had nothing to do with life after death. Nor has his *Dhamma* any concern with rituals and ceremonies. The centre of his *Dhamma* is man and the relation of man to man in his life on earth. This, he said, was his first postulate.

His second postulate was that men are living in sorrow, in misery and poverty. The world is full of suffering and that how to remove this suffering from the world is the only purpose of *Dhamma*.... The recognition of the existence of suffering and to show the way to remove suffering is the foundation and basis of the Buddha's *Dhamma*.

1. The Path of Purity

The Path of Purity teaches that a person who wishes to be good must recognize some principles as principles of life. According to my Path of Purity the principles of life recognized by it are: Not to injure or kill, not to steal or appropriate to oneself anything which belongs to another, not to speak untruth, not to indulge in lust, not to indulge in intoxicating drinks. The recognition of these principles, I say, is most essential for every man.

2. The Path of Righteousness (Ashtanga Marga)

The Buddha said that there are eight constituents in the *Ashtangamarga*.

(a) He began his discourse with the exposition of '*Samma Ditti*' (Right Views), the first and foremost element in the *Ashtangmarga*. '*Samma Ditti*' requires giving up of belief in the efficacy of rites and ceremonies, to have disbelief in the sanctity of the *Shastras*. '*Samma Ditti*' requires the abandonment of superstition and supernaturalism. '*Samma Ditti*' requires the abandonment of all doctrines which are mere speculations without any basis in fact or experience. *Samma Ditti* requires free mind and free thought.

(b) Every man has aims, aspirations and ambitions. '*Samma Sankappo' (Right Aims)* teaches that such aims, aspirations and ambitions shall be noble and praiseworthy and not ignoble and unworthy.

(c) '*Samma Vacca*' (Right Speech) teaches: (i) that one should speak only that which is true; (ii) that one should not speak what is false; (iii) that one should not speak evil of others; (iv) that one should refrain from slander; (v) that one should not use angry and abusive language towards any fellow man; (vi) that one should speak kindly and courteously to all; (vii) that one should not indulge in pointless, foolish talk, but let his speech be sensible and to the purpose.

(d) '*Samma Kamanto*' (Right Livelihood) teaches right behavior. It teaches that every action should be founded on respect for the feelings and rights of others. The norm is that course of conduct, which is most in harmony with the fundamental laws of existence. When a man's actions are in harmony with these laws they may be taken to be in accord with '*Samma Kamanto*'.

(e) Every individual has to earn his livelihood. But there are ways and ways of earning one's livelihood. Some are bad; some are good. Bad ways are those which cause injury or injustice to others. Good ways are those by which the individual earns his livelihood without causing injury or injustice to others. This is '*Samma Ajivo*'. (Right Means).

(f) '*Samma Vyayamo*' (Right Endeavour) is primary endeavor to remove *Avijja* (Nescience). Right endeavor has four purposes:

(g) One is to prevent states of mind which are in conflict with the *Ashtangamarga*.

(h) Second is to suppress such states of mind which may already have arisen.

(i) Third is to bring into existence states of mind which will help a man to fulfil the requirements of the *Ashtangamarga*.

(j) Fourth is to promote the further growth and increase of such states of mind as already may have arisen.

(k) '*Samma Satti*' calls for mindfulness and thoughtfulness. It means constant wakefulness of the mind. Watch and ward by the mind over the evil passions is another name for '*Samma Satti*'.

(l) There are five fetters or hindrances which come in the way of a person trying to achieve *Samma Ditti*, *Samma Sankappo*, *Samma Vacca*, *Samma Kamanto*, *Samma Ajeevo*, *Samma Vyayamo* and *Samma Satti*. These five hindrances are covetousness, ill-will, sloth and torpor, doubt and indecision. It is, therefore, necessary to overcome these hindrances and the means to overcome them is through *Samadhi*, *Samma Samadhi* is not the same as *Samadhi*. It is quite different. *Samadhi* is mere concentration. No doubt it leads to *Dhyanic* states which are self-induced, holding the five hindrances in suspense. But these *Dhyana* states are temporary. Consequently, the suspension of the hindrances is also temporary. What is necessary is a permanent turn to the mind. Such a permanent turn can be achieved only by *Samma Samadhi.*

3. The Path of Virtue

The Buddha said that the path of virtue meant the observance of the virtues called: (1) *Sila*; (2) *Dana;* (3) *Uppekha;* (4) *Nekkhama;* (5) *Virya;* (6) *Khanti;* (7) *Succa;* (8) *Adhithana;* (9) *Karuna;* and (10) *Maitri*.

Sila is moral temperament, the disposition not to do evil and the disposition to do good; to be ashamed of doing wrong. To avoid evil for fear of punishment is *Sila*. *Sila* means fear of doing wrong.

Nekkhama is renunciation of the pleasures of the world.

Dana means the giving of one's possessions, blood and limbs and even one's life, for the good of others without expecting anything in return.

Virya is right endeavor. It is doing with all your might whatever you have undertaken to do with never a thought of turning back.

Khanti is forbearance. Not to meet hatred by hatred is the essence of it. For hatred is not appeased by hatred. It is appeased only by forbearance.

Succa is truth. A person must never tell a lie. His speech must be truth and nothing but truth.

Adhithana is resolute determination to reach the goal.

Karuna is loving kindness to human beings.

Maitri is extending fellow feeling to all beings, not only to one who is a friend but also to one who is a foe and also not only to man but to all living beings.

Upekka is detachment as distinguished from indifference. It is a state of mind where there is neither like nor dislike. Remaining unmoved by the result and yet engaged in the pursuit of it.

These virtues one must practice to his utmost capacity. That is why they are called *Paramitas* (States of Perfection).

★ ★ ★

The Buddha said:

> You are likely to call my *Dhamma* pessimistic because it calls the attention of mankind to the existence of suffering. I tell you such a view of my *Dhamma* would be wrong. No doubt, my *Dhamma* recognizes the existence of suffering but forget not that it also lays equal stress on the removal of suffering. My *Dhamma* has in it both hope and purpose. Its purpose is to remove *Avijja,* by which I mean ignorance of the existence of suffering. There is hope in it because it shows the way to put an end to human suffering.

★ ★ ★

Dr Ambedkar who sought refuge in the sacred morality of Buddhism did not live to see a printed version of this monumental book. He completed writing this book around March 1956—about 9 months before his *Nirvana* and wrote a letter to then Prime Minister Nehru requesting financial assistance for publishing the same, which unfortunately was turned down. As a result, the mnemonic opus could see the light of the day only in 1957—several months after his *Nirvana*.

The essential message of the book remains timeless. As Gail Omvedt puts it:

> Dr Ambedkar's arguments in support of Buddhism as an appropriate religion centred on its morality and rationality. The 'new world', as he noted, needed religion-as-moral light of which Buddhism was a supreme example. It was a world in turmoil, one with tremendous potential for economic development, but with increasingly visible poverty and backwardness haunting those who could see this poverty posed against the prosperity and power of an elite world—a world facing massive physiological and spiritual concerns brought about by the processes of change, social movements, wars, fascism, the Holocaust and nuclear destruction. The promises of economic development themselves were so enveloped in commercialism and technological 'fixes' that the need for moral grounding was clear. It was the morality represented by Buddhism rather than socialism that Dr Ambedkar was looking to for a solution.[150]

---

150. Omvedt, Gail, Op. Cit, p. 148.

CHAPTER FORTY EIGHT

Leading Mass Conversion to Buddhism

DR AMBEDKAR ANNOUNCED on May 24, 1956 that he would convert to Buddhism in October of the same year and declared that the conversion ceremony would take place on October 14, the day of the Hindu festival of Dassera, in Nagpur. The head of the Buddhist monks of India, the Burmese Bhikku Mahasthaveer Chandramani, was invited to carry out the ceremony.

The final ceremony was a magnificent one and it demonstrated not only Dr Ambedkar's hold over his followers, but also a massive emotional commitment to entering into a new faith. People poured into the grounds from villages and towns all over Maharashtra, dressed in their finest white clothes. As the scheduled week for the ceremony approached, five hundred thousand men, women and children who had formerly been considered Untouchables, virtually took over the city. Before the huge crowd, Dr Ambedkar took *diksha.*

Dr Ambedkar and his second wife, Savita, were the first ones to take *diksha,* which they did in the presence of the huge crowd. The Bhikku gave them the *Trisarana* i.e. the oath of allegiance to Buddha, to *Dhamma* (i.e. the Buddha's doctrine of righteousness) and to *Sangha* (i.e. the community of monks). The Bhikku then asked them to avow their allegiance to *Panchsheel* (i.e. the five principles, which include the refusal to kill, to steal, to lie, to have illegitimate sexual relations and to drink). After citing the *Trisarana* and the *Panchsheel*, both Dr Ambedkar and his wife bowed three times before the statue of Buddha and the *diksha* ceremony was completed.

Dr Ambedkar then pronounced:

> "By discarding my ancient religion which stood for inequality and oppression, today I am reborn. I have no faith in the philosophy of incarnation and it is wrong and mischievous to say that Buddha was an incarnation ofVishnu. I am no more a devotee of any Hindu God or Goddess. I will not perform *shraddha* (i.e. Hindu funeral rite). I will strictly follow the eight-fold path of Buddha. Buddhism is a true religion and I will lead a life guided by the three principles of knowledge, right path and compassion."

Dr Ambedkar then turned around, and in an unprecedented gesture, himself administered the vows to the half-million of his followers. He added an additional twenty-two vows that involved renunciation of all aspects of Brahmanic Hinduism.

(1) I shall not recognize Brahma, Vishnu and Mahesh as Gods, nor shall I worship them.
(2) I shall not recognize Ram and Krishna as Gods, nor shall I worship them.
(3) I shall not recognize Gauri and Ganapati as Gods nor shall I worship them.
(4) I do not believe in the theory of incarnation of God.
(5) I do not consider Buddha as the incarnation ofVishnu.
(6) I shall not perform *Shraddha* [a Hindu rite that one carries out for the safety of the deceased's soul] nor shall I give offerings to God.
(7) I shall not do anything, which is detrimental to Buddhism.
(8) I shall not perform any religious rites through the agency of a Brahmin.
(9) I believe that all human beings are equal.
(10) I shall endeavour to establish equality.
(11) I shall follow the eight-fold path of the Buddha.
(12) I shall observe the ten [*Paramita*] (observances) of the Buddha [the virtues in which a follower of the Buddha has to restrain himself].
(13) I shall be compassionate to all living beings and I shall nurture them with care.
(14) I shall not steal.
(15) I shall not lie.
(16) I shall not commit adultery.
(17) I shall not drink liquor.
(18) I shall lead my life striving to cultivate a harmonious blend of the three basic principles of Buddhism [Enlightenment, Precepts and Compassion].
(19) I thereby reject my old religion, Hinduism, which is detrimental to the prosperity of humankind and which discriminates between man and man and which treats me as inferior.
(20) I fully believe that Buddhism is *Saddhamma.*
(21) By my embracing Buddhism I am being reborn.
(22) I hereby pledge to conduct myself hereafter in accordance with the teachings of the Buddha.

Following Dr Ambedkar's guidance, the massive crowd renounced the worship of Brahma, Vishnu, Shiva, Ram and Krishna, and vowed not to follow the *shraddha* ceremony, but obey instead the precepts of Buddhism. Lakhs of Ambedkarites, through a collective oath, dedicated themselves to a new life, taking refuge in the Buddha, in *Dhamma* and in the *Sangha* from the hierarchies and atrocities they had experienced under Hinduism for generations. It was the culmination of a long-drawn struggle under the leadership of Dr Ambedkar by one of the most oppressed populations of the world, the Untouchables of India.

CHAPTER FORTY NINE

Self-Portrait and Own Assessment

DR AMBEDKAR ONCE wrote:

> "I am a difficult man. Ordinarily, I am as quite as water and humble as grass. But when I get into a temper I am ungovernable and unmanageable"[151]

> Dr Ambedkar, however, also said:

> Although I am said to possess a vitriolic temperament and have on many occasions crossed the floors and came into conflict with those in the authority, I have not even on a single occasion been a traitor to the country. I have always had the interest of the country at heart.

Just a couple of years ahead of his *Nirvana,* Dr Ambedkar, while delivering a speech on All India Radio elucidated his philosophy of life. He said: "We should be India first and Indian last!"

Dr Ambedkar's life-long passion was to create Casteless and classless society, which comes through clearly in several of his speeches.

* * *

Just a couple of years ahead of his *Nirvana,* Dr Ambedkar, while delivering a speech on All India Radio elucidated his philosophy of life. He said:

> Every man should have a philosophy of life, for everyone must have a standard by which to measure his conduct. And philosophy is nothing but a standard by which to measure....

---

151. Quoted in Lelyweld, Joseph(2011), p.212

> Negatively, I reject the Hindu Social Philosophy propounded in the Bhagvat Geeta based as it is, on the *Triguna* of the Sankhya philosophy which is in my judgment a cruel perversion of the philosophy of Kapila, and which had made the Caste System and the System of Graded Inequality the law of Hindu Social Life....
>
> Positively, my Social philosophy, may be said to be enshrined in three words: Liberty, Equality and Fraternity. Let no one, however, say that I have borrowed my philosophy from the French-Revolution. I have not. My philosophy has roots in religion and not in political science. I have derived them from the teachings of my Master, the Buddha. In his philosophy, liberty and equality had a place; but he added that unlimited liberty destroyed equality, and absolute equality left no room for liberty. In His Philosophy, law had a place only as a safeguard against the breaches of liberty and equality; but He did not believe that law can be a guarantee for breaches of liberty or equality. He gave the highest place to fraternity as the only real safeguard against the denial of liberty or equality of fraternity which was another name for brotherhood or humanity, which was again another name for religion....

★ ★ ★

On completion of sixty years of age, in a massive rally in Mumbai (October 28, 1954), a Purse (Rs 1,18,000) was given to Dr Ambedkar (which he promptly donated to Building Construction Fund for the Scheduled Castes). In an emotionally charged atmosphere, Dr Ambedkar went down the memory lane. According to a report:[152]

> He further said that it was wrong to presume that he was a brilliant student from the beginning. He was an ordinary boy like other boys in his community. He said that his father did not care to maintain the record of his birth date and his exact date of birth was not known. He might be above sixty or below sixty. He said that it was true that he was born at about 12 midnight, and his mother had great pains at the time of his birth. When he was born, the stars were bad and it was told by the astrologer that his mother would die soon. He was, therefore, hated by his brothers and sisters. He said that after the death of his mother he was brought up by his aunt.

He said that he had gone through religious books like *Mahabharat*, *Bhagwat Gita* in his young days but when he came across the book about Gautam Buddha, it had great impression on him and since that time he became the follower of *Buddha*. He said that the Hindus also would have to embrace *Buddha* Religion for their good. He further said that he was a devotee of *Gautam Buddha*, *Kabir* and Mahatma *Phule* and worshipper of learning, self-respect and character. He had none of the bad habits but he was fond of reading. He said that learning was essential for every individual if he wished to make progress in life.

---

152. Marathi Speech, Mumbai (May 31, 1952)

"People build houses for living. I have built Rajgriha for safe-keeping of my book collection." Dr Ambedkar would fondly recount in one of his interviews.[153]

★ ★ ★

Interestingly, from time to time, Dr Ambedkar reviewed the progress of the mass movement led by him. There are at least three such strategic reviews made public through three speeches:

The first review was (on May 3, 1936) after spending ten years in social life, in which he said:

> We have done so much good work during the past ten years. This could not have been achieved if we had waited even for hundreds of years. This divine work could not have happened without our struggle for self-respect and self-reliance. We do not have huge funds like the Congress. We also do not have manpower or other support for our social work. In spite of all the difficulties and deprivations we have covered a wide spectrum by our movement for justice. All this was possible only because of your love and enthusiasm!
>
> This divine achievement of the past 10 years because of which all the people including a mighty party like the Congress is scared of you could be possible only because of your unity. Barring few exceptions, there is unity amongst us which has increased our esteem and political importance in the eyes of all people. And ever since we declared our intention of conversion to another religion, the Muslims, Christians and Sikhs, all are after us begging to join their religion. We should retain this unity so that we could reach to our goal of leaving the Hinduism for elevation in our social status....
>
> Recently, horrible atrocities have been committed on the Untouchables by the Touchable Hindus in Jodhpur and Gujarat. This atrocious slavery will come to an end only if we leave this religion; there is no other way. If Hindus are not ready to remain under the British rule despite a Dominion Status that is being offered then why should we remain under the rule of Hindus?
>
> Another tree does not grow under any tree. It needs independent sun rays for its growth. Likewise, there cannot be our growth under this decaying tree of Hinduism. We must, therefore, change our religion....

★ ★ ★

153. Dr Ambedkar was almost obsessed with possession of books. His insatiable thirst for knowledge was translated into an exceptionally large collection of books. In fact, while in London and New York, he spent his leisure time in browsing through the second-hand book stores. From his every trip abroad, he would bring back hundreds of old and new books. Over time, Dr Ambedkar had a personal collection of books which was almost certainly unrivalled.

The second review was on attaining 50 years of age (April 26, 1942) in which Dr Ambedkar spoke like a loving father to his children, telling stories of yore and the happenings during the last 23 years. He was in a reminiscent mood, narrated the episode of the first public meeting he addressed at Kolhapur, the opposition he had to face from his own people who considered loathsome practices as a precious heritage, oppression as a birth-right. He said:

> Today you have been purified of all those evils. Like white snow of an early morning you stand now before the superstition ridden men and women of the higher Castes; the Marathas and the Bhandaris, who from the viewpoint of social and cultural outlook are miles behind you.
>
> When I started on my public career and long thereafter I considered that for good or for evil we were part of the Hindu society. I thought for long that we could rid the Hindu society of its evils and get the Depressed Classes incorporated into it on terms of equality. That motive inspired the *Mahad Chavdar Lake Satyagraha and the Nasik Temple Entry Satyagraha.* With that object we burned the *Manu Smiriti* and performed mass thread ceremonies. Experience has taught me better. I stand today absolutely convinced that for the Depressed Classes there can be no equality among the Hindus because on inequality rest the foundations of Hinduism.
>
> We no longer want to be part to the Hindu society. What then are we to do? We shall decide that at a suitable time. For the moment I only want to make it clear that we cannot be part of the Hindu society in any circumstances. We want to be partners in running the Government of this country. We want partition of political rights. Our political rights must be recognized distinctly from those of the Hindus separately....
>
> If the Hindus are prepared to recognize those rights I am ever-ready to join them in the common struggle for the freedom of the country....

Dr Ambedkar was no hero-worshipper, did not want his followers to do it either, for he was deeply conscious of the evils of hero-worship and the havoc it has caused in this country down the centuries.

Calmly, but emphatically, said Dr Ambedkar: "You have been celebrating my birthday for some 15 years past. I have never attended them. I have always been opposed to them. You have celebrated my golden jubilee now; let that be enough. Let there be no more celebrations."

The reason: "Over-regard for leaders saps self-confidence of the masses, leaves them helpless when left leaderless in hour of trial or when led by unscrupulous leaders."

"One great reason for the downfall of the Hindu society and the perpetuation of its degraded position", said Dr Ambedkar

> is the injuction of *Krishna* that whenever in difficulties they should look out for his *avatar* (incarnation) to redeem them from the slouch of despondency. That has made the Hindu community helpless in face of calamity.
>
> I don't want you to follow such a ruinous teaching. I don't want you to be dependent on any single personality for your salvation. Your salvation must lie in your own hands, through your own efforts.

The final review (March 24, 1956) was barely ten months before his Nirvana, in which he said:

> When I started my public life 25 years ago I had three objectives of my life. Firstly, spread education to each and every house of the Untouchables. I can say that this objective has been successful to a great extent. The Untouchables may not be ahead of others now, but they will definitely make progress in the future….Secondly, it was my objective to ensure that Untouchables get broader representation in the government jobs. You are all witness to the success that we have achieved in this regard.
>
> I can say that I was successful in two out of the three objectives of my public life. But, my third objective of improving the condition of innumerable Untouchables living in villages has not been successful upto my expectations. Therefore, I have decided to exclusively devote all my energy for the rest of my life for the welfare of the Untouchables living in villages…
>
> There will not be much improvement in their living conditions unless they leave the villages and settle down in the cities. But our Untouchable brethren are reluctant to come out of their attachment to the paternal villages. They feel that their livelihood is in the village; they get their food in the village. But I feel that the dignity is more important than food. What is the use of such livelihood where you are insulted at every step; where you are treated worse than a dog; and you have no dignity whatsoever? What is the use of such paternal village? The Untouchables should leave the villages and wherever they find fallow land they should capture it and start farming. If anybody tries to stop them they should resist and claim their ownership by paying appropriate land revenue to the Government. This way they should live with dignity in their own new society. This way they can create a new dignified equitable society. They can do all that is required for collective village life like running the shops and other businesses. Nobody will insult them in their village. I am going to launch a movement for capturing fallow lands for the Untouchables as soon as I recover from my sickness….
>
> It is the prime duty of all the educated people to serve their poor and ignorant brethren. It is unfortunate that once the educated person reaches some powerful position he forgets his own society. The reason for this is that they do not have attachment to their society, belonging to their brethren and they are least concerned about their own poor illiterate people. The other reason is lack of spiritual attitude amongst them. If the educated people from the Untouchable society do not take proper care and do not dedicate themselves to the welfare of their society, then the society will not prosper. It will decline further….
>
> The religion of Buddha is excellent amongst all the religions of the world. I wish that you all should join me to convert to Buddhism this year. I am not compelling you for this. It entirely depends upon your will and conscience. It has been decided that I am going to adopt Buddhism after which I will not be an Untouchable. The provision of reservation in government jobs is going to remain even after you convert to Buddhism. Even, otherwise, you should not forget that the provision for reserved seats in the State Legislatures and Parliament is only for 10 years. This is going to end soon. The reservations are not going to last forever. After all, we will have to rely on our own strength and competence. We should stand on our own feet as soon as possible. We will not be able to make much progress if we depend on the crutches of reservations for ever….

After my conversion to Buddhism I will not be able to lead you either, I will be able to remain in the Federation. I desire that somebody out of you people should come forward to assume the leadership in my place; otherwise, our Federation will collapse like a tent on a single pole. Of course, I won't be leaving the politics even after conversion to Buddhism. Only thing I will not be able to do is to contest on the ticket of the Scheduled Castes Federation. I will contest elections on my own strength. I don't care whether I win or lose....

Secondly, it was my objective to ensure that Untouchables get broader representation in the government jobs. You are all witness to the success that we have achieved in this regards....

I can say that I was successful in two out of the three objectives of my public life. But, my third objective of improving the condition of innumerable Untouchables living in villages has not been successful upto my expectations. Therefore, I have decided to exclusively devote all my energy for the rest of my life for the welfare of the Untouchables living in villages....

There will not be much improvement in their living conditions unless they leave the villages and settle down in the cities. But our Untouchable brethren are reluctant to come out of their attachment to the paternal villages. They feel that their livelihood is in the village; they get their food in the village. But I feel that the dignity is more important than food. What is the use of such livelihood where you are insulted at every step; where you are treated worst than a dog; and you have no dignity whatsoever? What is the use of such paternal village? The Untouchables should leave the villages and wherever they find fallow land they should capture it and start farming. If anybody tries to stop them they should resist and claim their ownership by paying appropriate land revenue to the Government. This way they should live with dignity in their own new society. This way they can create a new dignified equitable society. They can do all that is required for collective village life like running the shops and other businesses. Nobody will insult them in their village. I am going to launch a movement for capturing fallow lands for the Untouchables as soon as I recover from my sickness....

It is the prime duty of all the educated people to serve their poor and ignorant brethren. It is unfortunate that once the educated person reaches some powerful position he forgets his own society. The reason for this is that they do not have attachment to their society, belonging to their brethren and they are least concerned about their own poor illiterate people. The other reason is lack of spiritual attitude amongst them. If the educated people from the Untouchable society do not take proper care and do not dedicate themselves to the welfare of their society, then the society will not prosper. It will decline further....

The religion of Buddha is excellent amongst all the religions of the world. I wish that you all should join me to convert to Buddhism this year. I am not compelling you for this. It entirely depends upon your will and conscience. It has been decided that I am going to adopt Buddhism after which I will not be an Untouchable. The provision of reservation in government jobs is going to remain even after you convert to Buddhism. Even, otherwise, you should not forget that the provision for reserved seats in the State Legislatures and Parliament is only for 10 years. This is going to end soon. The reservations are not going to last forever. After all, we will have to rely on our own strength and competence. We should stand on our own feet as soon as possible. We will not be able to make much progress if we depend on the crutches of reservations for ever....

After my conversion to Buddhism I will not be able to lead you either, I will be able to remain in the Federation. I desire that somebody out of you people should come forward to assume the leadership in my place; otherwise our Federation will collapse like a tent on a single pole. Of course, I won't be leaving the politics even after conversion to Buddhism. Only thing I will not be able to do is to contest on the ticket of the Scheduled Castes Federation. I will contest elections on my own strength. I don't care whether I win or lose....

CHAPTER FIFTY

Mahaparinirvana

LESS THAN TWO months after the great conversion ceremony, Dr Babasaheb Ambedkar passed away on the morning of December 6, 1956. Millions of his followers throughout India, but especially in Maharashtra, wept as if it were their own father who had died, and people from all over the world sent their tributes.

The roads leading to Dr Ambedkar's house, Rajgriha, in Mumbai were overflowing. People from all over Maharashtra had rushed to Mumbai. They came by train, truck, bike, boat or whatever other means of transportation they could find. They all hoped to be his pallbearers. They looked lost, wordless, eager to catch a glimpse of his body. In Mumbai, everyone had to walk, since the roads were so full of people that there was no free space for any vehicle to pass. Volunteers were directing the crowds. It was announced that the cortege would move in a procession through major parts of the city.

Eventually, the two-mile-long procession arrived at Rajgriha, carrying Dr Ambedkar's body covered with flowers and wreaths. The smell of jasmine and lilies pervaded the atmosphere. Near the head of the body stood a statuette of Lord Buddha. Garlands and flowers had to be constantly cleared to enable people to catch a glimpse of him. Tearful monks chanted Buddhist prayers. People perched on treetops and on the balconies of buildings. Everyone was craning to get a better glimpse, but it was too crowded.

As the procession moved forward again, people choked and let out mournful cries. The strong man that they had always known Babasaheb to be, with shoulders broad enough to bear the woes of his people, lay quiet and unmoving. The one who had lived for them and in doing so had overworked himself had now died for them.

A great swell of people continued to walk behind the cortege chanting slogans, and the air filled with their cries: "Babasaheb *Amar Rahe*–May Babasaheb remain immortal." After about seven hours, the procession reached the cremation ground. Hundreds of policemen, along with top-ranking army officials, guided the procession, helping in maintaining order. A radio broadcast later estimated that more than half a million people had attended the funeral, the biggest ever in history.

Just before his pyre was lit at the crematorium, more than a hundred thousand people took the oath for embracing Buddhism to honour Babasaheb's last wish. His son, Yashawant, lit the pyre amid loud Buddhist chants.

The Legend Lives On

On December 6 every year, on the death anniversary of Dr Babasaheb Ambedkar, people from all over the country and abroad come to the Chaitya Bhoomi near Shivaji Park, Mumbai. About 15 to 20 lakh people assemble there to pay their respects to Dr Ambedkar and it is through their collective memory and spirit that the legend of Dr Babasaheb Ambedkar lives on....

Epilogue

A Measure of The Man

IN 2011–12, THE first ever poll was conducted in India "to determine the Greatest Indian After Mahatma Gandhi" by *Outlook* magazine in collaboration with CNN-IBN, History 18 Channels and British Broadcasting Corporation (BBC).

India was not the first country where such a poll was conducted. Similar polls had been conducted earlier in 21 countries including Great Britain and South Africa where Winston Churchill was voted as the greatest Briton while Nelson Mandela emerged as the greatest South African. Notwithstanding this prior experience and the methodology refined with it, the hunt for the "Greatest Indian After Mahatma Gandhi" was extremely difficult in India, given the vast expanse, acute heterogeneity and tremendous complexity. It was an extraordinary challenge. The greatest Indian would have to be one who had affected the lives of the "maximum number of Indians for the better, since the Independence. Leadership, genius and compassion were to be parameters."[154]

The organizers of the "Greatest Indian After Gandhi Poll", opted for a three-way voting process:

- Jury (comprising 28 eminent Indians, for shortlisting 50 nominees from a list of 100),
- Popular Votes (online or through a missed call for the favourite; 4.3 million votes were deemed valid)
- Survey (on ground conducted by ACNielsen in 15 cities, with sample size 1, 027 in each of the two phases).

Each of the three constituents were given a one-third weightage to arrive at the final cumulative ranking.

Most Indians, especially the middle class and the elite found the results of the "Greatest Indian After Gandhi Poll" rather surprising. In cumulative ranking, it was Dr B.R. Ambedkar who turned out to be the Greatest Indian After Gandhi. The

154. *Outlook* (Independence Day Special : August 20, 2012)

top five voted as "Greatest Indians After Gandhi" were Dr Ambedkar, Dr A.P.J. Abdul Kalam, Vallabhbhai Patel, Jawaharlal Nehru and Mother Teresa, in that order. In the popular valid votes (4.3 million), Dr Ambedkar received as many as 1.99 million or 46.3 per cent of the total votes. In fact, in the popular vote segment, Dr Ambedkar led from the beginning of the second phase, polling more votes than the sum total of all the remaining nine potential winners put together!

What is surprising is that Dr Ambedkar was elected as the "Greatest Indian After Gandhi" in spite of being largely kept away from mainstream media, the private sector and the Indian education system. In fact, some skeptics believed that "Dr. Ambedkar and his intellectual legacy have been lying buried, sedimented beneath the layers of indifference, hatred and contempt."[155]

Traditionally, the textbooks in India are replete with stories of the life and times of Mahatma Gandhi and Jawaharlal Nehru. Pedagogy portrays and rightly so, Gandhiji and Pandit Nehru as leaders of national stature in prose and poem, skit and song. Regrettably, Dr Ambedkar appears only briefly, if at all. And when he does appear, unmistakably he is referred to as the leader of Untouchables. Dr Ambedkar's representation in pedagogy has always been marginal or parenthetical—as a leader of a subset, a Caste leader or a leader of the subalterns.

In fact, it is grossly unfair to characterize Dr Ambedkar simply as a leader of Dalits or the downtrodden. Dr Ambedkar made outstanding contributions as an economist, sociologist, anthropologist, educationist, journalist, as an authority on Comparative Religion, as a policy-maker and administrator and as a parliamentarian, besides being a jurist who became the Principal Architect of the Indian Constitution. Above all, Dr Ambedkar was a great social reformer, a valiant champion of human rights and an emancipator of the downtrodden masses of India.

With his intellectual stature and monumental contribution—making equality and social justice the cornerstone of the world's most populous democracy, one would have expected an exalted position, a distinctive place carved out for Dr Ambedkar in the Indian pantheon.

Why has this not happened until recently? Why has Dr Ambedkar been traditionally marginalized and diminished in stature? Why has he been relegated until recently only as a Dalit leader and at best, as the Principal Architect of the Indian Constitution, and that too, rather reluctantly?

A possible explanation for this exclusion lies in the dominant inclination, if not the innate inability of the Indian psyche to disentangle every Indian from his or her caste-identity. In India, Untouchability was officially abolished by the Indian Constitution. Mercifully, today the Untouchables are no longer required to place clay pots around their necks to prevent their spit from polluting the ground. They are no longer required to attach brooms to their rumps to clean up their footprints as they walk. It must be remembered, however, that while Caste-based discrimination has changed form, it has not disappeared. Consciously or sub-consciously, Indians

---

155. S. Anand, "A Case for Bhim Rajya", *Outlook,* op cit.

still generally tend to make judgements based on caste. At one time, didn't Gandhiji himself think that Dr Ambedkar could not have been an Untouchable but a benevolent Brahmin who took a deep interest in Dalits? This misassumption provides a historic clue to the misconception about Dalits in the national consciousness. Regrettably, over the years, this mindset has not changed perceptibly. Indeed the Caste System has taken on sophisticated dimensions; it has become subtler, though no less pernicious. There tendencies explain, at least in part the neglect of Dr Ambedkar and his contribution in the national consciousness.

The question that arises then is why is this phenomenon occurring now? Is Dr Ambedkar being re-discovered posthumously, being resurrected and is being born again?

Not quite. Dr Ambedkar has always had an everyday presence in the lives of the 160-million strong Dalit communities throughout the country. His ideas and legacy have consistently been inspiring the disadvantaged and the downtrodden to challenge the dominant strands of political articulations in the country.

According to Raja Sekhar Vundru who calls Dr Ambedkar "The Other Father", Dr Ambedkar

> gave millions of Untouchables an identity of their own...(He) is now regarded as a great Indian, a person relevant for all times to come. This is not because his followers are unwavering in their devotion, or that they happen to be numerically higher than supporters of any other person (dead or living) in India, and certainly not because he probably has been represented in the highest number of statues erected for any man in history. It is because his following has transcended generations. His relevance - political, social, ideological, religious, economic - will persist as long as the clamour and struggle for justice and equal rights exists[156]

On December 6, which marks Dr Ambedkar's death anniversary, huge crowds throng every year to Chaitya Bhoomi, Mumbai to pay homage to his memory. Over the years, the numbers have been swelling—now reaching upto two million every year! Large crowds also assemble on October 14 every year now at Nagpur to observe the anniversary of Dr Ambedkar's conversion to Buddhism.

Until recently when the life-story of Dr Ambedkar and the Dalit movement were pushed to the fringes in textbooks, these annual gatherings have kept alive Dr Ambedkar's life story and contribution. As Professor Sharmila Rege[157] points out these annual gatherings spawn hundreds of stalls selling a wide range of items: from Jai Bhim caps, statues, posters, calendars, images of Dr Ambedkar, statues of Buddha to books and booklets introducing readers to the Dalit movement, life struggle of Dr Ambedkar and Ambedkarite perspective on a contemporary issues. Moreover, the *gayan* parties (singing troupes or *kalapathaks*) constitute an important segment

---

156. Raja Sekhar Vundru, "The Other Father" *Outlook*, op.cit.
157. "Songsters from the Mud house", *Outlook*, op.cit.

of these annual gatherings. Ever since the 1930s, several generations of *shahirs* (composers) have dedicated a lifetime to spreading the ideas of Dr Ambedkar.

As Rege puts it succinctly:

> Many intellectuals, barring a few, see these gatherings of the Dalit public as a process of the 'deification' of Ambedkar or the 'manipulation' of the masses by the Dalit leadership. It is common to see Ambedkar's 'rationalism' contrasted with the 'irrationality' of these gatherings, suggesting that Dalits are not carrying forward Ambedkar's true legacy... When conclusions about the emotive iconization of Ambedkar are drawn, the dynamic gatherings around the Ambedkar almanac tell another story... The invaluable labour of 'mud house cultural activists' has for long remained unsung. The mud house print and music cultures and their popularity have made an immense contribution to sustaining the memory of Ambedkar's life and works.

Dalits in India have been mounting a slow but steady rebellion. Dr Ambedkar's message to Dalits to 'educate, organize and agitate' has been reaching far and wide. Dalits, once rendered untouchable, are finding their voice and are struggling to carve out a place for themselves in the national mainstream. Their struggle goes on. Indeed, a silent revolution is currently underway. A strong Dalit middle class is emerging. Past exclusion and discrimination has impacted Dalit access to capital assets and employment opportunities. This has meant a great incidence of poverty and deprivation among Dalits. But they are catching up, aided no doubt by the Affirmative Action policies of the Government. Interestingly, as an unprecedented development, the "Dalit Indian Chamber of Commerce and Industry (DICCI)" has emerged which is forging "Dalit capitalism".

As S. Anand observes:

> this 'victory' of Ambedkar is most likely a result of the presence of a burgeoning internet savvy, mobile wielding, dedicated Dalit middle class that is almost invisibly making its presence felt. Still largely kept away from mainstream media and the private sector, the Dalits, in India and abroad, have fashioned their own websites, mailing lists and blogs besides a You Tube channel called Dalit Camera and scores of Facebook groups... It is on the worldwide web that new ways of negotiating citizenship are being forged.[158]

* * *

The "Greatest Indian After Mahatma Gandhi Poll" has not gone unchallenged. Interestingly, it was not challenged on methodological grounds, but was questioned on conceptual grounds. Although similar polls were successfully undertaken in 21 different countries, it was argued that those countries were smaller, more homogenous

---

158. S.Anand, "A Case for Bhim Rajya", *Outlook*, op cit.

and generally far less complex than India. India is a vast country with great many contributions from extraordinary men and women. To single out just one of them and anoint him or her as the greatest, it was argued, would certainly amount to belittling the contributions of the rest. There were specific issues raised especially in relation to Jawaharlal Nehru and even Mahatma Gandhi.

It has been argued: "There is no comparison between Ambedkar and Nehru in terms of shaping the Indian nation. Nehru made us what we are as a nation."[159] No doubt, we must recognize the enormity and complexity of the task history had bequeathed to Jawaharlal Nehru and, therefore, "guilt-tripping on Ambedkar cannot undermine Nehru's achievements." At the other extreme, some Ambedkarites have expressed irritation over the poll that was designed to elect the Great Indian *after* Gandhi. That way it presumes Gandhiji's "victory" over Dr Ambedkar. Some Ambedkarites even saw it as "fresh salt on an old unhealed wound."[160]

Both arguments are entirely valid and they point essentially to the limitations of the poll singling out only one individual in a complex and heterogenous country like India. These conflicting arguments, however, can be reconciled if we relax the constraint of "electing" only one Indian as the greatest and, instead, seek to identify a Trinity of Makers of Modern India.

The first constituent of this Trinity of Makers of Modern India is, of course, Mahatma Gandhi. Gandhiji was the Supreme Commander of India's freedom struggle. Between the 1920s through the 1940s, it was Mahatma Gandhi who forged a popular countrywide movement against the British Colonial Rule. Gandhiji was a "timeless inspirer". With the Seven Sins enunciated, namely, Wealth without Work, Pleasure without Conscience, Science without Humanity, Knowledge without Character, Politics without Principle, Commerce without Morality and Worship without Sacrifice, Mahatma Gandhi has been uniquely placed as modern India's moralist ideal.

The second constituent of the Trinity of Makers of Modern India is Jawaharlal Nehru. As India's first Prime Minister from 1947 to 1964, it was Pandit Nehru who oversaw India's transition from a British Colony to a Sovereign democracy. As a rational internationalist, and a democrat by instinct as well as intellectual conviction, it was Pandit Nehru who made India the nation as it prevails today. Indeed, Jawaharlal Nehru has a uniquely distinctive place in the Indian pantheon as the architect of the modern Indian nation-state.

The third in this Trinity is Dr Ambedkar, who as the philosopher of the under-privileged championed in their cause in the broadest possible terms, working relentlessly as a liberal democrat with a mission to convert the fledgling democracy into a Democratic Republic. Dr Ambedkar's brand of nationalism was not merely confined to securing freedom for India from the British Colonial Rule and to the transfer of political power to the Indians. He certainly believed in the adage:

159. Saba Naqvi, "The Higher Statesman", *Outlook*, op cit.
160. S. Anand, *Outlook,* op. cit.

"Democracy must be something beyond two wolves and a sheep voting on what to have for dinner". According to Dr Ambedkar, social change and social justice are indeed critical to the egalitarianism that any democracy must aspire to. As a social democrat, Dr Ambedkar focused on a much broader notion of sustainable national reconstruction that is, fostering inclusive growth and cultural integration in the age-old Caste-ridden, inherently unjust and discriminating society. As the principal architect of the Indian Constitution, Dr Ambedkar built the safeguards of Affirmative Action for establishing a more equitable society that is capable of delivering social justice to millions of downtrodden, thus heralding in India a new age of social equality and rationalism. In this process, Dr Ambedkar emerges not only as a valiant upholder of the Indian Democratic Republic, but also captures the uniquely distinctive place in the Indian pantheon as a rare intellectual mass-leader who awakened the social conscience of modern India.

Annexure I
Dr Ambedkar's Writings

I. Books and Monographs

A. Completed Works

1. **Administration and Finance of the East India Company**
   (Unpublished Thesis for M.A. Degree, May, 1915)
   [BAWS Vol. 6, 41 pages]
2. **The Evolution of Provincial Finance in British India**
   (Ph.D. Dissertation completed in 1917, first published in 1925)
   [BAWS Vol. 6, 249 pages]
3. **The Problem of the Rupee: Its Origin and Its Solution**
   (D.Sc. Dissertation, first published in 1923)
   [BAWS Vol. 6, 279 pages]
4. **Annihilation of Caste**
   (Book, first published in May 1936)
   [BAWS Vol. 1, 53 pages]
5. **Which Way to Emancipation?**
   (Speech–Monograph, first published in May 1936)
   [BAWS Vol. 18, 43 pages]
6. **Federation *versus* Freedom**
   (Book based on a Public Address on January 29, 1939, published in 1939)
   [BAWS Vol. 1, 72 pages]
7. **Pakistan or the Partition of India**
   (Book first published in December 1940)
   [BAWS Vol. 8, 478 pages]

8. **Ranade, Gandhi and Jinnah**
   (Book based on a Public Address on January 18, 1943, pubished 1943)
   [BAWS Vol. 1, 33 pages]

9. **Mr. Gandhi and the Emancipation of the Untouchables**
   (Monograph based on Research Paper, first published in September 1943)
   [BAWS Vol. 9, 90 pages]

10. **What Congress and Gandhi Have Done to the Untouchables**
    (Book, a Comprehensive Treatise first published in June 1945)
    [BAWS Vol. 9, 383 pages]

11. **Communal Deadlock and a Way to Solve It**
    (Monograph based on a Public Address, May 1946, published in 1945)
    [BAWS Vol. 1, 22 pages]

12. **Who Were the *Shudras?***
    How They Came to be the Fourth *Varna* in the Indo-Aryan Society
    (Book, first published in October 1946)
    [BAWS Vol. 7, 195 pages]

13. **A Critique of The Proposals of Cabinet Mission for Indian Constitutional Changes in so far as they affect the Scheduled Castes (Untouchables)**
    (Monograph, released in 1946)

14. **The Cabinet Mission and the Untouchables**
    (Monograph, published in 1946)

15. **States and Minorities**
    (Monograph based on submitted to the Constituent Assembly, March 1947)
    [BAWS Vol. 1, 66 pages]

16. **Maharashtra as a Linguistic Province**
    (Monograph based on Statement submitted to the Linguistic Provinces Commission, 1948)
    [BAWS Vol. 1, 37 pages]

17. **The Untouchables: Who Were They and Why They Became Untouchables**
    (Book, first published in October 1948)
    [BAWS Vol. 7,130 pages]

18. **Thoughts on Linguistic States : A Critique of the Report of the States Reorganization Commission,**
    (Book, first published in 1955)

19. Buddha and His *Dhamma*

(Book completed in March 1956, but published in 1957)
[BAWS Vol. 11, 599 pages]

20. Riddles in Hinduism

(Book, published posthumously in 1987)
[BAWS Vol. 4, 339 pages]

21. Dictionary of the Pali Language (Pali-English)

(Published posthumously in 1998)
[BAWS Vol. 16, 435 pages]

22. The Pali Grammar

(Published posthumously in 1998)
[BAWS Vol. 16, 88 pages]

B. Incomplete Works

1. Waiting for Visa (Autobiographical)
2. A People at Bay
3. Untouchables or the Children of India's Ghetto
4. Can I be a Hindu?
5. What the Brahmins Have Done to the Hindus
6. Essays on Bhagwat Gita
7. India and Communism
8. Revolution and Counter-revolution in Ancient India
9. Buddha and Karl Marx
10. Constitution and Constitutionalism

II. Memoranda, Evidence and Statements

1. On Franchise and Framing Constituencies

(Evidence before the Southborough Committee, 1919)
[BAWS, Vol. 1]

2. Statement of Evidence to the Royal Commission on Indian Currency

(Statement of Evidence, 1926)
[BAWS Vol. 6]

3. Protection of the Interests of the Depressed Classes

(Statement to the Simon Commission, May 29, 1928)
[BAWS Vol. 2]

4. **State of Education of the Depressed Classes in the Bombay Presidency**

   (Statement to the Simon Commission on behalf of Bahishkrita Hitakarini Sabha, May 29, 1928)
   [BAWS Vol. 2]

5. **Constitution of the Government of Bombay Presidency**

   (A Report of Dissent, May 17, 1929)
   [BAWS Vol. 2]

6. **A Scheme of Political Safeguards for the Protection of the Depressed Classes in the Future Constitution of a Self-governing India**

   (Memorandum to the Round Table Conference, 1930)
   [BAWS Vol. 2]

7. **The Claims of the Depressed Classes for Special Representation**

   (Supplementary Memorandum to the Round Table Conference, 1931)
   [BAWS Vol. 2]

8. **Franchise and Tests of Untouchability**

   (Submission to the Indian Franchise Committee–Lothian Committee, May 1, 1932)
   [BAWS Vol. 2]

9. **The Cripps Proposals on Constitutional Advancement**

   (Statement to the Press, July 18, 1942)
   [BAWS Vol. 10]

10. **Grievances of the Scheduled Castes**

    (Confidential Memorandum to the Governor–General, October 29, 1942)
    [BAWS Vol. 10]

III RESEARCH PAPERS, ARTICLES AND BOOK REVIEWS

1. **Castes in India: Their Genesis, Mechanism and Development**

   (Research Paper, first published in Indian Antiquary, *1918)*
   [BAWS Vol. 1, 15 pages]

2. **Mr. Russell and the Reconstruction of Society**

   (Book Review, published in the
   Journal of the Indian Economic Society, 1918)
   [BAWS Vol. 1]

3. **Small Holdings in India and Their Remedies**

   (Research Paper, first published in the

Journal of the Indian Economic Society, 1918)
[BAWS Vol. 1, 24 pages]

4. **Currency and Exchanges**

   (Book Review, published in The Servant of India, *1925*)
   [BAWS Vol. 6, 5 pages]

5. **The Present Problem of Indian Currency 2 Shillings versus 1s.4d. Ratio**

   (Research Paper in 2 Parts, first published in April 1925)
   [BAWS Vol. 6, 12 pages]

6. **Report of Taxation Enquiry Committee**

   (Review of the Report, first published in The Servant of India, *April 1926*)
   [BAWS Vol. 6, 3 pages]

7. **Thoughts on the Reform of Legal Education in the Bombay Presidency**

   (Article, published in Government Law College Magazine,*1936)*
   [BAWS Vol. 17(2), 14 pages]

8. **The Rise and Fall of Hindu Women**

   (Article, first published in 1950)
   [Not reproduced in BAWS]

9. **Need for Checks and Balances**

   (Article, Times of India, *April 23, 1953)*
   [BAWS Vol. 1, 5 pages]

10. **Buddha Pooja Path (Marathi)**

    (Article published in November, 1956)
    [BAWS Vol. 16, 12 pages]

IV Preface and Forewords

1. **Foreword to *Untouchable Workers of Bombay City***

   By Dr. G.R. Pradhan, February 1938
   [BAWS Vol. 17(2), 2 pages]

2. **Foreword to *Commodity Exchange***

   By P.G. Salvi, 1947
   [BAWS Vol. 6, 1 page]

3. **Preface to the *Essence of Buddhism* (3rd Edition)**

   By Professor P. Laxmi Narasu, March 1948
   [BAWS Vol. 17(2), 3 pages]

4. **Foreword to *Social Insurance and India***

   By M.R. Idgunji, 1948
   [BAWS Vol. 6, 2 pages]

5. **Preface to *Rashtra Raksha Vaidik Sadhan***

   By Swami Vedananda Teerth, 1948
   [BAWS Vol. 17(2), 1 page]

Annexure II
Life and Times of Dr Ambedkar

THE INCREDIBLE SAGA of Dr Ambedkar's life can be divided into eight different phases:

PHASE I: FROM JULY 1917 TO SEPTEMBER 1920

For administrative reasons, there was a discontinuity in higher studies that Dr Ambedkar was pursuing in London and he had to return to India in July 1917. He resumed his studies three years thereafter, in September 1920. During this interregnum, Dr Ambedkar made an brief appearance in public life. Notable developments during this phase included:

- Testimony before Southborough Committee (1917)
- Launching his first Marathi bi-weekly, *Mooknayak* (1920)
- Participation in Depressed Classes Conference in Bombay Province (1920)

PHASE II: FROM APRIL 1923 TO NOVEMBER 1930

This was the foundation phase for Dr Ambedkar's public life. It was during this period that Dr Ambedkar laid the foundation of his social movement. Major events during this phase included:

- Establishment of Dr Ambedkar's first social organization called *Bahishkrut Hitakarini Sabha* (1924),
- Testimony before the Hilton Young Commission (1925) (which later, in 1935, led to the establishment of the Reserve Bank of India),
- Nomination as a Member of Bombay Province Legislative Council (1927)
- Beginning of a Mass Movement—the Mahad *Satyagrapha* (1927)
- Public Burning of *Manusmriti* (1927)
- Launch of a new Marathi bi-weekly, *Bahishkrut Bharat (*1927)
- Launch of a Marathi bi-weekly, *Janata (*1930)
- All-India Depressed Classes Conference, Nagpur (1930)

During this phase, Dr Ambedkar made an undelible mark on the social movement in the country at the Provincial level. So significant was the impact of his contribution that he was selected by the British Government to participate in the Round Table Conference to be held in London. Dr Ambedkar was one of the only two delegates chosen from entire British India to represent the Untouchables in the country. This paved the way for Dr Ambedkar to emerge on the national stage.

Phase III: November 1930 to August 1936

This phase begins with Dr Ambedkar's participation in the First Round Table Conference and ends with him formally taking a plunge into politics by launching his own political party called the Independent Labour Party. The salient features of this phase include:

- First Round Table Conference (November 1930 to January 1931)
- First Meeting of Dr Ambedkar and Mahatma Gandhi (August 1931)
- Second Round Table Conference (Sepember–December 1931),
- Gandhi–Ambedkar conflict, Gandhiji's fast against Dr Ambedkar conflict-resolution in terms of the Poona Pact (September 1932)
- Third Round Table Conference (November–December 1932)
- Election as President, Bombay Municipal Employees Union (April 1934)
- Announcement of the intention to leave the Hindu religion, which sent shockwaves throughout the country (October 1935)
- Launch of his own political party—Independent Labour Party (ILP) and making a formal entry into politics

Phase IV: 1937 to July 1942

This phase is marked by the emergence of Dr Ambedkar as a political leader in Bombay Province, besides being a frontline labour leader. Significant events during this phase include:

- Notable success to Independent Labour Party (ILP) in elections to Bombay Province Legislature Assembly (1937)
- Mass Movement against the *Khoti system*(1937)
- Mass struggle against the *Mahar Vatan* (1937)
- Opposition to Trade Disputes Bill, 1938 and widespread recognition as a Labour Leader.

Dr Ambedkar's significant contribution during this phase led to his nomination to Viceroy's Executive Council as Labour Member (that is, as a Minister).

Phase V: July 1942 to May 1946

This is a distinctive phase in Dr Ambedkar's career wherein he served as a Minister in the British Government in India. As a Member of the Viceroy's Executive Council, Dr Ambedkar handled a very important portfolio including Labour and Employment, Energy, Minerals and Water Management. Besides serving in the Ministerial position with distinction, the phase witnessed two important developments:

- Launching a new broad-based political party called Scheduled Castes Federation (SCF) (July 1942)
- Founding an educational institution, titled, People's Education Society (PES) (July 1945)

Phase VI: May 1946 to July 1946

This short phase was marked by extreme uncertainty and restlessness for Dr Ambedkar. Following the dissolution of the Viceroy's Executive Council, when a Caretaker Government was formed at the Center on June 19, 1946, Dr Ambedkar was not included in the Cabinet (Shri Jagjeevan Ram was included instead). The uncertainty continued till July 1946 when Dr Ambedkar was elected to the Contituent Assembly from Bengal Province. Noteworthy developments during this phase include the following:

- Formation of Care-taker Government at the Center
- Protest movement organized by Dr Ambedkar against the Plan announced by the Three-Ministers' Cabinet Mission of the British Government. The protests covered Bombay Province, Kanpur, Lucknow, etc.

Phase VII: July 1946 to September 1951

This momentous phase begins with Dr Ambedkar being elected as a Member of the Constituent Assembly and ends when he resigned from the Union Cabinet as the Law Minister in September, 1951. During this phase, Dr Ambedkar dedicated himself to re-building the newly Independent India. Signifcant, indeed historic events, during the period include:

- Election to Constituent Assembly from Bengal (July 1946)
- Re-election to Constituent Assembly from Bombay (July 1947)
- Appointment as the First Law Minister of India (August 1947)
- Appointment as the Chairman of the Drafting Committee for the Constitution of India (August 1947)
- Approval to the Constitution of India (November 1950)

This phase is characterized by phenomenal and path-breaking work by Dr Ambedkar as the Principal Architect of the Indian Constitution. In addition, Dr Ambedkar made his distinct mark as the first Law Minister of Independent India and laid the foundation of the legal framework in modern India. Dr Ambedkar resigned from the Union Cabinet on September 8, 1951, mainly on account of his differences with the then Prime Minister, Jawaharlal Nehru regarding the Hindu Code Bill.

Phase VIII: September 1951 to 6 December 1956

The final phase in the incredible saga of Dr Ambedkar's life witnessed him withdrawing from active politics and gravitating towards Buddhism. Important events during this phase include the following :

- General Elections (1952)
- Contesting Lok Sabha election and defeat (1952)
- Joining Rajya Sabha (1952)
- Launch of periodical titled, *Prabuddh Bharat* (February, 1956)
- Leading a historic conversion to Buddhism with five lakh followers (October, 1956)
- *Mahapari Nirvana* (6 December 1956).

References

Ambedkar, Dr Babasaheb, 1979–2012, *Writings and Speeches (BAWS): Vol.1–22*, Mumbai: Government of Maharashtra.

Das, Bhagawan (ed.), 1969–79, *Thus Spoke Ambedkar: Vol.1–3*, Lucknow: Dalit Today Prakashan, New Delhi: Samyak Prakashan.

Gaikwad, S.M., 1998, "Ambedkar and Indian Nationalism", *Economic and Political Weekly*, XXXIII(10), 7 March.

Gore, M.S., 1993, *The Social Context of an Ideology: Ambedkar's Political and Social Thought,* New Delhi: Sage Publications.

Jadhav, Narendra (ed.), 2013a, *Ambedkar Speaks,* Vol.1–3, New Delhi: Konark Publishers.

———, 2013b, *Ambedkar Writes,* Vol.1–2, New Delhi: Konark Publishers.

Jaffrelot Christophe, 2000, *Dr Ambedkar and Untouchability Analyzing and Fighting Caste,* London: Hurst and Company.

Kamble B.C., Samagra, 1984–2008, *Ambedkar Charitra: Vol 1–24 (Marathi)*, Pune: Sugawa Prakashan, Reprint.

Khairmode C.B., 1984–2008, *Dr Bhimrao Ramji Ambedkar Charutra Granth: Vol 1–12 (Marathi)*, Pune: Sugawa Prakashan, Reprint.

Keer, Dhananjay, 1954, *Dr Ambedkar: Life and Mission,* Mumbai: Popular Prakashan.

Lelyveld, Joseph, 2011, *Great Soul Mahatma Gandhi and His Struggle with India,* New Delhi: Harper Collins and the India Today Group.

Mahatma Gandhi, 1936a, "Dr Ambedkar's Indictment", *Harijan*, 18 July.

———, 1936b, "Varna Versus Caste", *Harijan*, 15 August.

Omvedt, Gail, 2004, *Ambedkar,* New Delhi: Penguin.

Rodrigues, Valerian (ed.), 2002, *The Essential Writings of B.R. Ambedkar,* New Delhi: Oxford University Press.

Roy, B. (ed.), 1996, *Gandhi's Campaign Against Untouchability, 1933–34—An Account from the Raj's Secret Official Reports*, New Delhi: Gandhi Peace Foundation.

Shourie, A., 1997, *Worshipping False Goods: Ambedkar and the Facts that have been Erased*, New Delhi: ASA.

Som, R., 1994, "Jawaharlal Nehru and the Hindu Code: A Symbol Over Substance", *Modern Asian Studies*, 28(1), pp. 165-194.

Verma, Vidhu, 1999, "Colonialism and Liberation: Ambedkar's Quest for Distributive Justice", *Economic and Political Weekly*, 25 September.

Zellist, Eleanor, 1992, *From Untouchable to Dalit: Essays on the Ambedkar Movement*, New Delhi: Manohar.

1946–1950, *Constituent Assembly Debates: Vol. 1–12*, New Delhi: Government of India.

2012, *Outlook* (Weekly), Various Articles, Independence Day Special, 20 August.

Index

Acknowledgements

SHRI SOMNATH CHATTERJEE, Shri Montek Singh Ahluwalia, Dr Vijay Kelkar, Dr Raghunath Mashelkar, Shri Dileep Padgaonkar, Shri H.K. Dua, Shri Muchkund Dubey and Dr Pratap Bhanu Mehta, Shri Prithviraj Chavan, Chief Minister, Maharashtra.

Editorial Assistance	:	Priyanka Sarkar, Rina Tripathi, Apoorva Jadhav, Suhasini Sinha.
Technical Assistance	:	Sudha Rajagopalan, Neelam Khanduri, KavitaVaid, Padma Kalra and Prabhakar Gaikwad.
Special Assistance	:	Dinesh Jadhav, Dr Vinod Shaha, Nitin Phatangare, Ashok Kamble, Dr Manohar Jadhav, Dr Milind Bhoi and Dr Anil Hirekhan.
Cooperation	:	B. Muthuraman and Ajay Kumar (Tata group), Nayaz Qazi (UK), Dr P.D. Patil, Dr Shivajirao Kadam, Prakash Bhonde (all Pune), Dr Gangadhar Panatavane, Nandkishor Kagliwal, Dr Champalal Desarada (all Aurangabad), Jai Prakash Dagade, Bapurao Rathod, Dr Suryavanshi, Dr Suresh Waghmare (all Latur).
Family Support	:	Vasundhara, Tanmoy, Kejal, Agastya and the entire Jadhav family.
Photographs	:	Vijay Surwade (Dr Ambedkar's photographs) Subhojit Paul (Author's Photograph) Anandjog (Buddha's Picture).

* *This edition has been sponsored in part by Tata group under their Affirmative Action Programme. For details of Tata Affirmative Action Programme, please refer to page 643 of this volume.*

Tata Group and Affirmative Action

At the very heart of the US$ 97 billion Tata group is the commitment to improve the quality of life of the communities its companies serve. Two-thirds of the equity of Tata Sons, the Tata promoter holding company, is held by philanthropic trusts which have created national institutions like the Indian Institute of Science, TIFR and Tata Institute of Social Sciences, and provide development assistance to NGOs working in education, healthcare and livelihoods.

Tata companies have been actively engaged with the community, particularly disadvantaged communities, including Scheduled Castes(SCs) and Scheduled Tribes(STs), through a wide range of CSR initiatives.

THE TATA AFFIRMATIVE ACTION PROGRAMME (TAAP)

Tata Steel's tribal welfare programmes and projects among the marginalized sections supported by the trusts predate the group's affirmative action programmes of recent years.

Under TAAP, some 50 Tata companies are committed to practising positive discrimination towards the SC/ST communities—without sacrificing merit, cost or quality—in programmes under the four Es: Employment, Employability, Entrepreneurship and Education.

In Employment, close to 15% of the employees in Tata companies who declare their caste status are from the SC/ST communities. Companies are encouraged to continually grow this number by exercising positive discrimination not only for employees on their rolls but also in their eco-system: the entities they outsource many of their functions to and, going forward, their vendors and distributors. Some Tata companies have even embedded recruiting SC/ST youth in their business growth strategy, leveraging the fact that these youth are more loyal while being no less capable.

Under Employability, TAAP seeks to tie Affirmative Action with the national need to impart vocational skills to hundreds of millions of youth. Further, Tata companies are urged not to limit their involvement with their SC/ST trainees to training them, but also to help them find jobs not necessarily in their own companies.

Under Entrepreneurship, Tata companies strive to include disadvantaged communities as part of value chain, based on a belief of empowerment and value creation. These efforts include consciously selecting vendors from Scheduled Caste and Tribe communities for products and services, using SC/ST karigars, developing SC/ST youth as franchisees, and entrepreneurship development programmes.

Finally, under Education, TAAP encourages Tata companies to not just give scholarships, but to seek a deeper engagement with children so as to change their lives, in recognition of the twin facts that while education is indeed, the biggest leveller in society, its impact is visible only over time.

The Tata group's support for this volume on the intellectual biography of Dr B.R. Ambedkar, is in the spirit of the Tata Affirmative Action Programme.